EVIDENCE *for* AUTHORSHIP

Essays on Problems of Attribution

EVIDENCE *for* AUTHORSHIP

Essays on Problems of Attribution

WITH AN ANNOTATED BIBLIOGRAPHY
OF SELECTED READINGS

EDITED BY

DAVID V. ERDMAN
The New York Public Library

AND

EPHIM G. FOGEL
Cornell University

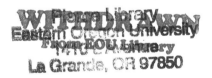

Cornell University Press
Ithaca, New York

CORNELL UNIVERSITY PRESS

First published 1966

Library of Congress Catalog Card Number: 65-24698

PRINTED IN THE UNITED STATES OF AMERICA
BY THE MAPLE PRESS COMPANY

To Charlotte and Virginia

Contents

Contents

Contents

Preface

THE essays here collected, and the items listed in the Annotated Bibliography, are concerned with the authorship of works written in English. The supply of writings on this subject has grown in recent years; so has the awareness of how complicated and exacting such investigations are when they must rely to any large extent on "internal" and "internal-external" evidence. This volume should therefore be of interest to those confronted, as scholars often (and at times unexpectedly) are, with problems of attribution. And because it focuses attention on an important yet manageably limited area of investigation, it should also prove useful to graduate students, teachers, and researchers who give serious thought to the principles and practice of literary scholarship.

The present editors were encouraged to undertake their task by the wide response to the forerunners of this collection—a series of articles in the *Bulletin of The New York Public Library* (somewhat imprecisely called "The Case for Internal Evidence") and papers added to the series from an English Institute Symposium in 1958. David Erdman chaired that symposium and edited the series. Ephim Fogel took part in the symposium discussion from the floor and published an expansion of his remarks in the *Bulletin*. Both of us then joined forces to compile a representative anthology and bibliography. Concerning decisions about his own essays or controversies in which he was involved, each of us of course yielded editorial authority to the other.

We have tried to keep editing to a minimum throughout the collection. In the *Bulletin* series especially, the writers have restrained themselves from removing an error (though a postscript may call attention to its existence), strengthening a point, or polishing a phrase. To have done otherwise would have been to secure correctness at the cost of blurring the original shape of an argument and to substitute a specious blandness for the sharp flavor of combat. One can only misrepresent the evolution of a controversy if one imposes the wisdom of hindsight on the confusion of battle. And furthermore, to the alert onlooker, a miss may be no less instructive than a bull's-eye.

Preface

The volume begins with the symposium papers, which concentrate on proposed additions to the accepted works of Marvell, Johnson, Smart, and Coleridge. Grouped with these are the comments and rebuttals they provoked, including one previously unpublished reply, followed by a brief comment. Other papers in the *Bulletin* series—except for some concerned with sources or dating rather than authorship—are included in Parts II-IV, which run chronologically through English and American literature. The sampling from journals and prefaces in these sections is perforce uneven—partly because the distribution of studies by historical periods has been uneven, partly because the sheer bulk of several valuable single studies or controversial exchanges has made their inclusion impracticable.

We have sometimes had to abridge the papers selected, but we have relied mainly on self-contained essays of relatively brief compass. These we have chosen because they seem either instructive in the analysis of assumptions about the use of evidence or lucid in the examination of particulars. Essays that excel in both these respects seem to be rare. Perhaps because many canonical scholars are acting as such quite temporarily, perhaps because many others feel (with a good deal of justice) that each problem of attribution is a special case, few have given sustained attention to general principles. Accordingly, the initial symposium brings the assumptions and responsibilities of methodical canonical investigation into the foreground of debate. Additional general discussion will be found in the Editorial Note to each part. And the "Index of Subjects" calls attention to passages which treat of "method" and "principles" or define the kinds and laws of "evidence" or enumerate various "tests" and "caveats." We recognize, nevertheless, that the plums to be relished in this sort of pudding are the particular examples of attributions demonstrated, or demolished, or pronounced "not proven." These we believe the reader will find without more guidance than Contents and "Index of Names and Titles."

We heartily agree with William Blake that "Unless You Consult Particulars You Cannot even Know or See . . . any Thing"—and that the man who generalizes may be misled by his own cunning into great follies of application. A fine essay, "How Not to Play the Game of Parallels," was written, it may be recalled, by one of the game's most adroit—and wrongheaded—practitioners. But attribution, as a more responsible scholar has observed, is not a game and not a form of exhibitionism. It is not a science either, as still another has noted, but a "scientific pursuit," depending much upon individual judgment, experience, and intuition. Individual judgment may be tempered considerably by observing the experience of others, especially the thoroughness with which they have tested, or failed to test, their intuitions.

Most of the essays in this collection place emphasis on the use of internal, or internal-external, evidence. Again and again a scholar challenges a conclusion or reopens a question not by dismissing the value of internal evidence as such but by offering countervailing internal evidence. But the important question, surely, is not whether evidence is external or internal; it is whether the data cited constitute evidence of any kind. When that question is answered, others may remain, for admissible evidence does not necessarily settle a problem that has perplexed many scholars. Even an extensive and careful investigation of vocabulary, style, ideas, and historical data may not resolve for all time and for all reasonable men such questions as the authorship of *Henry VIII* (see the entries in the "Annotated Bibliography of Selected Readings"). Uncertainties, as well as general and individual limitations of knowledge and understanding, are ineluctable features of scholarly and scientific endeavor. To admit as much is not to undermine endeavor but rather to encourage the enlargement of knowledge through the improvement of method. "Life is short, the art long, opportunity fleeting, experience deceptive, and judgment difficult." When the greatest of ancient physicians placed this truth at the head of his *Aphorisms*, his words were intended not as a counsel of despair but as a spur to the pursuit of excellence.

The inclusion of an essay in this volume, or of a title in the Annotated Bibliography, does not necessarily signify that the editors endorse it fully. It is one thing to evaluate an argument in its own terms. It is obviously another to judge it within the whole context which must ultimately determine its validity, for that judgment requires not only a specialist's knowledge of canon, genre, and period, but also the additional research that may be called for by the new hypothesis. Neither does the exclusion of an essay mean that we disapprove of its method or its particular arguments. Happily, the interesting solutions to canonical problems exceed the space at our disposal. And some solutions, such as those in recent important articles by professional statisticians, are too technical for literary scholars who, like ourselves, are ignorant of higher mathematics. (Nevertheless, because some enlightening remarks are in nontechnical language, these statistical essays should be consulted even by the untutored: see "Statistical Studies and Computer Applications" in the Annotated Bibliography.)

The Annotated Bibliography we regard as an important part of this volume. It is particularly full on major authors before 1660, especially Shakespeare, and for *Henry VIII* it presents a conspectus of canonical studies during the last hundred and fifty years. Altogether, the bibliography is such, we trust, as to provide the prospective canonical scholar with a wide range of approaches and to foster in him the humility and confidence appropriate to his vocation.*

It is a pleasure to acknowledge our gratitude to the following scholars for their courteous response to our requests for advice and assistance: Douglass Adair, Richard D. Altick, F. W. Bateson, Walter E. Bezanson, Morton W. Bloomfield, Fredson Bowers, R. S. Crane, E. Talbot Donaldson, Robert H. Elias, Sumner J. Ferris, David C. Fowler, Walter H. French, Paul Fussell, Jr., Morris Golden, Arthur Hudd, Robert E. Kaske, William R. Keast, Louis A. Landa, Frederick Mosteller, Fraser Neiman, James M. Osborn, Arthur H. Scouten, R. H. Super, Francis Lee Utley, and Don M. Wolfe. We are grateful to authors and publishers for permission to reprint (and where necessary, to abridge) the articles chosen. And we must thank those who lent offprints of articles we wished to consider but could not finally find room for. Needless to say, we alone are responsible for the final selections and for any errors of commission or omission.

We are indebted to the Secretary and Supervising Committee of the English Institute for agreeing to the inclusion of Institute essays in this volume. Special thanks are due to Cornell University for a Faculty Research Grant and to the Department of English for a Grant-in-Aid which facilitated research for essays No. 4 and No. 17 of the present collection and for much of the Annotated Bibliography. For assistance in various ways and at many stages, we are grateful to the librarians of Olin Library at Cornell University, the University College Library in London, the British Museum, the Firestone Library at Princeton University, and The New York Public Library. And finally, we want to thank Charlotte Fogel for typing large portions of the Bibliography.

D. V. E. E. G. F.

New York and Ithaca
February 1966

* In the bibliography and in the footnotes abbreviations of names of periodicals generally follow those used in the annual bibliographies in *PMLA* (*Publications of the Modern Language Association*).

I

THE CASE FOR
INTERNAL EVIDENCE:
A SYMPOSIUM HELD AT
THE ENGLISH INSTITUTE

Editorial Note to Part I

THE essays of this first part grew out of the program of the English Institute at Columbia University in September 1958. Arthur Sherbo's challenging essay on the uses and abuses of internal evidence, which opened the symposium, drew fire and counterfire throughout the discussion periods of the three-day meeting. After defining terms, it raises the question whether sufficient precision is possible in canonical studies to make them persuasive. Confident that it is, Sherbo disputes the deeply entrenched objection to reliance on literary and biographical parallels and urges the probative value of a series of "coincidences." In his earlier paper (No. 21) as well as here Sherbo selects cases of almost complete lack of external evidence—in the one attributing a *Mother Midnight* pamphlet to Christopher Smart, and in the other attributing an "Essay on Elegies" to Dr. Johnson (text given after the article). Nor does he rest his argument on stylistic grounds. Stressing the difficulty of firmly distinguishing even the famous Johnsonian style when supplied in small samples, he attends more to what is said than to how it is said.

At the English Institute, Sherbo ended, as he does here, with a call for public and impartial discussion of the general value of attribution by internal evidence—and for a show of hands. Others were quick to take up this challenge, including both Ephim Fogel, whose remarks from the floor were subsequently extended to a double essay (No. 4) and S. Schoenbaum, in a paper delivered at a later Institute session (see No. 13).

George Lord's paper (No. 2) is a complex argument concerning the "many bits of evidence of different kinds" that bear on the authorship of two satiric poems of 1667—especially concerning their similarity to another poem in the "painter" convention, most probably by Andrew Marvell. Lord points in the two poems to both ideas and style which he believes may be identified as distinctively Marvell's. The first kind of evidence calls for an evaluation of historical minutiae, and Lord's extensive citation is calculated to support his claim that he knows the details of "the mass of verse satire which the 1660's produced." As stylistic evidence (his Section III) he urges similarities

3

in structure, imagery, wit, tone, diction, and use of sources. He makes much of the striking nonce meaning of "halcyon"; he rests his case, however, on what he considers the "good grounds" of "a complex of probabilities."

Coleridge's distinction between direct and indirect kinds of evidence is cited in David Erdman's paper (No. 3) "The Signature of Style." Erdman takes exception to the claim that unrelated parallelisms (Sherbo's series of "coincidences") can have cumulative force, and he maintains that "the test of style is always crucial, at least in the negative sense." He then illustrates the danger of trusting to strong but indirect external evidence in the absence of positive stylistic evidence; he dismisses quantitative tests briefly but places considerable emphasis on the validity of positive stylistic evidence when combined with the evidence of parallels of idea or detail. Defining Coleridge's prose style, Erdman turns to the attribution of unsigned essays in the *Morning Post*—the indirect external evidence being (in part) Coleridge's known contribution of other essays during the period.

"Caveats" (No. 4) by Ephim Fogel spells out certain general propositions. Accepting the assumption that internal evidence can be used probatively, Fogel objects to the pitting of internal against external evidence and insists on stringent critical analysis of all attributions. His discussion of principles ranges widely, but he deals most fully with the attributions, made in essays No. 1, 2, and 21, to Marvell, Johnson, and Smart. He disputes the *Mother Midnight* attribution, charges both Sherbo and Lord with practicing the arbitrary excision of parallels, and attempts to refine definition further by distinguishing three main methods of arriving at probable attributions: (1) internal-external analysis, (2) literary analysis, (3) statistical analysis—the three almost always occurring in combination. Throughout, Fogel emphasizes the importance of considering the total pattern of evidence. In Sections II, III, IV he insists on the need to determine the relation of particular evidence offered to total patterns of historical or literary or statistical evidence. In evaluations of style he focuses on "configurations of thought and patterns of style" rather than on isolated details.

In "Comments on the Canonical Caveat" (No. 5), George Lord defends his attribution by adding to some of his arguments and by charging Fogel with "a misrepresentation of [his] method." One issue in the dispute is the style of the poems in question, both the subtle matter of tone or attitude and the specific detail of the percentage

4

of multiple rhymes. The statistics cited by Lord and Fogel do not agree—but, as is noted below, the discrepancy is cleared up in two previously unpublished papers.

Sherbo's "Reply" (No. 6) returns to the question of cumulative effect,[1] emphasizes the necessity of evaluating relative idiosyncrasy against a thorough knowledge of comparable writings of the period, and restates the nature of his particular use, in one instance, of the admittedly extreme appeal from the unknown to the probable.

In the final two papers (Nos. 7 and 8), Fogel and Lord take up the matter of multiple rhymes. Fogel challenges Lord's statistics on the grounds that Lord has called "two different classes of rhyme by the same name and [has counted] them as members of a single class." Lord regrets "any confusion [he] may have unwittingly added to an already complicated question." He agrees that there is a higher percentage of multiple (feminine and triple) rhyme in "The Second Advice" than in "Last Instructions" or in "the 1,500 lines of Marvell's undisputed pentameter couplets," but he believes that the evidence still permits the conclusion that the second and third "Advices" are "probably Marvell's."

---

[1] The question persists, and not only in English studies. In *The Authenticity of the Rhesus of Euripides* (Cambridge, Eng., 1964), p. viii, William Ritchie writes: "It must be stressed that the evidence is to be judged by its cumulative weight. For the sake of completeness I have sometimes recorded even quite trivial findings, if it seemed that they might contribute something to the total impression."

The Uses and Abuses
of Internal Evidence*

By Arthur Sherbo

IN 1903 Professor D. Nichol Smith recalled to the attention of Johnsonians a long-forgotten piece of Johnson's prose. It was a single sentence, added to the famous Preface to Shakespeare in 1778: "What
he [Shakespeare] does best, he soon ceases to do." There are nine
words, only one of them not a monosyllable, in this simple statement.
To my knowledge, no one has doubted for a moment that the sentence
is Johnson's. Nor do I. But I accept it, not as many others have, because, stylistically, it could only be Johnson's, but because, among
other reasons, I do not think Johnson would have allowed his fellow
editor George Steevens or anybody else to tamper with the Preface
in this fashion. In other words, the evidence of style here, unallied
with external evidence, is insufficient in my estimation. There is too
little to go on. While I am an advocate and user of the methods of
attribution by internal evidence—a more dangerous admission than
I had realized—I like to think that these methods can be used with
greater precision than in the example I have cited. I would not only
have canonical scholars right, I would have them right for the right
reasons. I assume that no responsible scholar doubts the importance
of canonical studies, even when the quarry is but a single sentence
or, indeed, a solitary phrase. For example, Johnson is said to have
added the words "and pollute his canvas with deformity" to the end
of *The Idler*, 82, written by Sir Joshua Reynolds. But quite recently
a well-known Johnsonian suggested to me that one does not "pollute"
a "canvas" with "deformity"; that the figure is a poor one. Should

* Read at the English Institute at Columbia University, Sept. 3, 1958, in
a symposium "Attribution by Internal Evidence"; reprinted from the *Bulletin
of The New York Public Library*, LXIII (1959), 5–22, with the author's permission.

we re-examine the evidence for Johnson's authorship of those few words? Or should we admit that Johnson is capable of infelicities?

I wonder, to come to definitions, how many would quarrel with the statement that internal evidence deals with essentials while external evidence deals with accidentals. When expressed thus baldly it seems almost unnecessary to go on to say that, short of an unequivocal acknowledgment by the author himself, the value of internal evidence outweighs any other. Yet most of the friends with whom I have pleaded the case for internal evidence have denied me this basic premise, directly or by unmistakable implication. Attribution of a piece to an author by a contemporary or near contemporary, anonymous or otherwise; the presence of a piece in a periodical during the time the author is known to have been contributing to it; the appearance of a piece cheek by jowl with, or sandwiched between, other canonical pieces in a collection or series; the very date of publication; a pseudonym or distinguishing signature which is associated with canonical pieces—almost any one, or a combination of these, is of greater importance to the skeptically minded than the evidence of style and ideas. Yet, after all, Boswell himself is no authority on the Johnson canon; not all the pieces remotely suggestive of Johnson in the *Gentleman's Magazine* for the period of his virtual editorship of it can be claimed for him; and the two asterisks appended to certain essays in the *Universal Visiter* are not infallible guides to his hand. I do not, be it understood, deny the importance of external evidence; I merely assert its ancillary nature.

Internal evidence divides nicely into two parts, style and ideas. Stylistic considerations include such matters as length and structure of sentences (structure includes antithesis, balance, parallelism, repetition, inversion, etc.), verbal and phrasal likes and dislikes, kind of vocabulary (i.e. Latinate or not, polysyllabic or not, frequency of certain parts of speech, etc.), characteristic imagery, peculiarity of spelling and punctuation (where one feels relatively sure a compositor is not responsible), range and density of learning and allusions, and parallels of various kinds with known works by the particular writer in question (especially those written close in time to the piece under analysis). For poetry there would be other considerations as well, but here again I must limit myself; what can be accomplished, for example, by statistical analysis of the frequency of feminine endings in an Elizabethan play of doubtful authorship or of the shifting position of the caesura in eighteenth-century couplets are matters upon which I am unprepared to speak. There is no need, of course, to break down the second division of internal evidence—ideas. It is obvious that the ideas expressed in a given piece must be consonant with those of the putative author, unless a very convincing explanation for the absence, or seeming absence, of such consonance can be advanced. Sometimes, we all realize, the ideas expressed are in direct and deliberate conflict with the known views of the author in question; we generally call this irony. Unluckily, facetiousness and irony are not always recognized when seen, and canonical studies suffer thereby.

Ideas are more easily recognized and analyzed than individual prose styles, and the scholar often has the evidence of an author's letters, diaries, recorded conversations, comments by contemporaries, etc., as further checks on that author's ideas. I hasten to add, however, that I am not suggesting that the recognition of an author's ideas is necessarily a simple business, only that it seems to me less complex and less dependent on varying opinions than recognition of style. And I do recognize that a man's ideas change more, and more often, than his literary style. Determination of individual prose styles—this is Johnson's, this is Goldsmith's, and this is Hawkesworth imitating Johnson—is often virtually impossible without the evidence of ideas. While there is the danger of mistaking for a uniquely held idea what is really almost a commonplace in the thought of the period, there is the infinitely greater danger of seeing stylistic peculiarities in what is after all the fairly common usage of a particular class or profession at a certain time. What is more, a writer often has, or deliberately employs, a dozen or more different styles: there is a style for *PMLA,* another for *College English,* a third for papers read to women's clubs, and so on. And there is one style for the criticism of poetry, a second for considerations on corn laws, a third for introducing a new periodical to the public, a fourth for reviewing books, a fifth for assuming the identity of a female correspondent to the *Rambler,* and a sixth, seventh, and eighth for what you will. These are not really different styles; they are essentially the same style being adapted to different purposes. Thus, if Professor Jones is notoriously stiff, humorless, and economical of words in his published work, it by no means follows that he may not unbend on occasion. No one, I trust, would be so misguided as to disclaim as Professor Jones's an address prepared for the English Institute solely on the grounds that it contained contractions and colloquialisms, attempts at humor, and frequent conversationally parenthetical expressions.

1: The Uses and Abuses of Evidence

Style is, then, a rather nebulous concept. What is the precise and analyzable difference between Dr. Johnson's style and that of one of his most successful imitators? Given an anonymous piece for consideration in the Johnson canon, how many sentences that a majority of Johnsonians would declare his must predominate over non-Johnsonian sentences or parts of sentences before the whole would be accepted? Does a new idea in a context unmistakably Johnsonian require that considerations of style give way to the one discordant note? What did the eighteenth century mean by a "nervous" style, and was the term used of other writers whose prose is easily distinguishable from Johnson's? (Johnson's own definition is simply "strong, vigorous," and Dr. Erdman tells me that an early reviewer used the term to describe Coleridge's style.) What exactly is meant by the "rhythms" or "cadences" of Johnson's prose, and whose ear is so attuned to them that he will not come a cropper often on the minor pieces? Is there an early and a late Johnsonian style? How much credence can one give to authorities? Who *is* an authority on Johnson's prose style? Can we, or indeed should we, rely ultimately on our ear? Or can canonical studies, calling in the statistician, become a greatly more precise discipline? We can, I hope, arrive at answers to some of these questions; others must be condemned to a state of suspension.

The very questions do, however, make one thing increasingly clear: there is a great need for concordances of the works, both prose and poetry, of a number of writers. While there is no minimizing the difficulties in the compilation of a concordance of a large body of prose, canonical studies will suffer until such concordances are prepared. As the use and value of concordances has been demonstrated in Dr. Erdman's published work, I content myself with one example. My work on Christopher Smart has convinced me that a number of his poems lie hidden in various eighteenth-century periodicals, but I know that some of these, where there is no external evidence to support my conviction, will probably never be accepted as his. The only evidence I have at my disposal is that of imagery and parallel passages, fondness for particular words and collocations of words, and, possibly, stanzaic preferences. Since most of these anonymous (or pseudonymous) poems are humorous, the ideas in them are usually few and conventional, and hence there is no help from that quarter. Now, the Smart canon, both of poetry and prose, is easily double or treble the bulk of the two-volume collection of his poetry edited by Norman Callan for the Muse's Library. The advantages to me of

9

a concordance of the complete works of Christopher Smart are obvious and enormous. No man's memory is as good as a concordance, and the question, to shift authors for the moment, whether Dr. Johnson observed a nice distinction between "less" and "fewer," recently asked me, half in jest and half in earnest, is one that is best left temporarily unanswered.

Internal evidence is very seldom encountered unaccompanied by external evidence. The anonymous poem or essay is usually allied to a bookseller or, at least, to some periodical with whom or with which the author in question has been connected. Although this sort of evidence is, by itself, very tenuous, it is still legitimately to be invoked. Hence very rarely (speaking always of printed materials) does one come upon a "pure" specimen, a piece or collection of pieces which afford no external evidence of possible authorship. It has been my extreme good fortune, however, to come upon two such collector's items within the past two or three years. One of these, the earlier found, was described in the *Bulletin of The New York Public Library* for August 1957 and there attributed to Christopher Smart. It is a fairly rare, sixty-four-page pamphlet entitled *Mother Midnight's Comical Pocket-Book*, which contains a number of parallels to, and echoes of, the poetry and prose Smart was writing at that time.[1] The chief argument against the attribution, raised by a good friend, was that each of my parallels could be explained away individually and that the clear echoes of Smart's poetry could be coincidence or clever imitation. This is, I submit, to advance the implausible in the face of the eminently plausible.

The most frequently invoked criticism of attribution by the accumulation of bits of internal evidence is, then, that a series of weak or minor arguments detracts from, rather than adds to, the validity and strength of the whole argument. Thus, when the attributor has one, two, or three fairly strong arguments, the skeptic will say he only weakens his case when he goes on to add further, much weaker arguments. What is overlooked is the fact that each of these minor points gains strength and importance by its very appearance in juxtaposition with the stronger points and, I would stress, with the other minor points also. I am insufficient mathematician to state this as a formula, although I think a few minutes with paper and pencil or chalk and blackboard would be equipment enough for me to convince the most doubting. In any event, the analogy of the easily broken separate

[1] Sherbo's essay on the *Pocket-Book* is reprinted as No. 21, below.—Eds.

twigs and the much greater resistance of a number of these twigs bound together is legitimately to be suggested. Finally, I should further suggest that a series of commonplaces (to substitute a more specific term than minor agreements) when it arrives to a sufficiently great number becomes, in its totality, something other than the mere sum of those commonplaces. Or, what may make things clearer, substitute "coincidences" for "commonplaces" and it should be obvious that a series of coincidences results in something more startling and rare than any one coincidence, however extreme it may be and however weak the individual coincidences may be. I suppose that a mathematician would explain this in terms of the laws of probability, for it is, of course, precisely that that I am discussing.

In the rest of this essay I wish to accomplish three specific things, at the same time restating, and in a few places answering, some of the questions proposed earlier. I wish, then, to reinstate a long-neglected piece to the Johnson canon; to suggest, for the first time, that another be considered for the canon; and to show, once and for all, that a third is not by Johnson, considering, at the same time, and more importantly, the matter of Johnson's hand in another's work. In order to do this and because I am fascinated by the problem, I raise the question of the Johnsonian's ability to spot Johnson's style. I once wrote that a certain piece of anonymous prose was either Johnson's or the devil's, and everybody who later discussed it with me agreed.[2] I do not recall any such unanimity either before or after that and I rather pessimistically doubt its recurrence. In any event, it is necessary to remember that the Johnson canon as it exists today is largely a tissue of conjecture based mainly on internal evidence (good, bad, and indifferent) adduced by Johnsonians from the time of Boswell to the present moment. In the passages that follow, then, I shall not expect any wide agreement, nor need anybody be chagrined if he fails to recognize the excerpts from the accepted canon of Johnson's works. The question I ask is, simply, Which are by Johnson, which not?

1. [It will be found] that the law prescribed by the alterer to himself, of sparing the tragic part, has been rather too carefully observed: many lines are retained which severe criticism would have expunged; but he that errs on the side of modesty will easily be forgiven.

2. The poems of Tyrtaeus are, it is true, *called* elegies, but with

[2] "Two Additions to the Johnson Canon," *Journal of English and Germanic Philology*, LII (1953), 543–548.

much the same propriety as if we were to call the piscatory eclogues of Sannazarius, pastorals; they walk, indeed, in the measure of elegy, but breathe all the spirit of the ode.

3. The speeches inserted in other papers have been long known to be fictitious, and produced sometimes by men who never heard the debate, nor had any authentic information. We have no design to impose thus grossly on our readers, and shall, therefore, give the naked arguments used in the discussion of every question, and add, when they can be obtained, the names of the speakers.

4. The hopes, fears, and anxieties, with all the tumults of passion which distract the lover's breast, will not give him time to think of the mode of expression, or to fetch his allusions from books; nature is contented to deliver herself with perspicuity, and where the sentiment is natural, the phrase cannot be too simple.

5. Books and pamphlets, printed originally in small numbers, being thus neglected, were soon destroyed; and though the capital authors were preserved, they were preserved to languish without regard.

6. Upon no subject whatever have so many prettinesses and absurd conceits been invented as love; yet surely where the head has been so painfully laborious, we may safely pronounce the heart to have been perfectly at ease.

7. It is observed, that, among the natives of England, is to be found a greater variety of humour, than in any other country; and, doubtless, where every man has a full liberty to propagate his conceptions, variety of humour must produce variety of writers; and, where the number of authors is so great, there cannot but be some worthy of distinction.

8. I cannot help thinking the ill success many poets have met with in paraphrasing those divine writers [of the Bible], has been principally owing to their weakening the sublimity of the poetry, by idle description, and clogging the simplicity of the sentiment with the affected frippery of epithetical ornament.

9. Shakespeare is too great for Pomp, too knowing for Books, too learned in human Nature to require the assistance, and too exhalted in his Ideas to dread the Criticism, either of an Enemy or an Editor. From [X's] hands something was expected more satisfying than what had fallen from the pen of Rowe; more characteristical of Shakespeare than Pope had produced: the learning of Warburton without his temerity; Hanmer's sagacity without his singularities; and the application of Theobald without his grovelings. That these expectations have been disappointed, I believe is in general allowed. . . .

10. Instead of elegant simplicity, we find in every part a rustic coarseness; instead of a neat and clear conciseness, a redundance of impure expression; instead of an assemblage of kindred images, allusions remote

and forced; and, in the place of a full, majestic, and continued harmony, sounds that fatigue and wound the ear, periods broken and transversed.

Number 1 is from the forgotten piece, Johnson's review of Hawkesworth's adaptation of Thomas Southerne's *Oroonoko;* it appeared in the *Critical Review,* VIII (Dec. 1759), 480–486. Numbers 2, 4, 6, and 8 are from an anonymous "Essay on Elegies," published, or possibly reprinted, in *The Universal Museum and Complete Magazine,* III (1767), 142–143; I think it is by Johnson.[3] Number 10 is from the Preface to James Hampton's translation of Polybius (1756), claimed for Johnson by Dr. Parr and discussed in Professor Allen Hazen's *Samuel Johnson's Prefaces and Dedications.* It is in these passages that I am interested. Number 3, by Johnson, is from the Preface to the *Literary Magazine;* number 5 is from George Steevens' "Advertisement" to the 1773 *Shakespeare;* number 7 is from Johnson's *Essay on the Origin and Importance of Small Tracts and Fugitive Pieces;* and number 9 is a manuscript note on the flyleaf of the first volume of Johnson's *Shakespeare* (first edition, 1765, Columbia University Library copy). The writer was a J. Atwood, possibly the James Atwood, lawyer, who died in 1780, listed in Musgrave's *Obituaries.* The two passages from the acknowledged canon were selected pretty much at random from Volume V of the 1825 Oxford *Works* because they contain, in my estimation, nothing unmistakably Johnsonian. Quotation of J. Atwood's marginalia was simply for the purpose of providing an example of the educated, nonliterary man's everyday written prose. Certain resemblances to Johnson's style are obvious. I think of these as characteristic of much of eighteenth-century nonfictional prose and deprecate ignorance of their existence. One should expect to find inversion, antithesis, parallelism, and the like in much of the prose of the period; the differences between a J. Atwood and a Dr. Johnson, speaking only of style, not of ideas, are of degree of facility and strength and polish of expression, not of kind of expression. Kind and extent of vocabulary must also be taken into account, of course. Atwood speaks of "the application of Theobald without his grovelings"; Johnson, of "a man [Theobald] of narrow and intrinsick splendour of genius, with little of the artificial light of learning, but zealous for minute accuracy, and not negligent in pursuing it." It strikes me, finally, that some allowance must be made for the difference between public and private prose. The style of Johnson's

---

[3] The full text is reprinted below, at the end of this essay.

letters, I think it is agreed, is only rarely the style of his published prose.

The pieces that are not of the acknowledged canon, are, however, of immediate concern. The review of Hawkesworth's adaptation of Southerne is attributed to Johnson in the *Biographia Dramatica* (1811); it is quoted by John W. Dodds in his study of Southerne (1933); and, in the last-named work, Professor Chauncey B. Tinker's acceptance of the piece as Johnson's is recorded in a footnote. I have no doubt the piece is Johnson's, on grounds of style alone. Since the *Critical Review* is not difficult of access, I shall quote one more sentence and then go on; actually most of the review is given over to quotation from the play. Johnson prefaces these quotations with the following: "As the writer has not amused himself with picking flowers of language, or of sentiment, and the beauty of his scenes consists principally in vigour of dialogue, and tendency to the main design, few passages can be selected as specimens, since that grace, which is derived from connection, is destroyed by separation."

Although I do not expect much argument against the inclusion of the *Critical Review* piece in the Johnson canon, I anticipate fairly violent objections to any similar honor for the anonymous essay on elegies. For one thing, the former has the blessing of a near-contemporary attribution plus the acquiescence of a distinguished Johnsonian; the latter has, to my knowledge, only one champion—and he is of this century. And yet I feel that the essay on elegies is equally entitled to a place in the canon: it is not only Johnsonian prose but better Johnsonian prose, possibly, than the review of Hawkesworth. In what follows, however, the emphasis will be on *what* is said in the essay, not on *how* it is said. Four excerpts have been quoted; the whole essay is reprinted below for those who wish to study it further.

There are six paragraphs in the essay, and a number of authors, ancient and modern, are quoted or referred to. The essay is a learned one, but the learning is worn lightly; it does not obtrude itself. With one exception, the Greek poet Tyrtaeus, all the writers and works quoted or cited were known by Johnson. Tyrtaeus might have been represented in one of the collections of Greek authors Johnson owned, but this is a minor point. Proceeding, then, more or less in order of appearance, one is struck by a reference to the "piscatory eclogues of Sannazarius," which the anonymous writer is unwilling to call pastorals. Johnson's *Rambler*, 36, comes immediately to mind, for there, too, Sannazarius' efforts are called piscatory eclogues and denied the status of true pastoral. I should point out, however, that this was pretty much a critical commonplace by this time. Anonymous and Johnson, the latter in *Rambler*, 37, both mention, what was commonly known, it is true, that some of Virgil's eclogues have been struck from the list of pastorals by the critics. Anonymous writes that Tibullus, "as he always speaks from his own heart, makes a forcible impression upon ours"; Johnson quotes a line from the Latin poet's first elegy (Book I) to Bennet Langton in his last illness, a line he had quoted and translated in *Adventurer*, 58, where the Roman poet's *"Te teneam moriens deficiente manu"* is rendered as "Held weakly by my fainting trembling hand." Anonymous writes that the "hopes, fears, and anxieties, with all the tumults of passion which distract the lover's breast, will not give him time to think of the mode of expression, or to fetch his allusions from books. . . . When we are truly affected, we have no leisure to think of art." Again the Johnsonian is struck: "Passion," writes Johnson of *Lycidas*, "runs not after remote allusions and obscure opinions," and, in the same paragraph, "Where there is leisure for fiction, there is little grief." Or, in the *Life of Hammond*, "Where there is fiction, there is no passion." And in that same third paragraph of the anonymous essay, in the discussion of "ingenious" love poetry, the writer refers to "the affected Italians, and ridiculous French poets of the last century, not to mention our own Cowley, [who] have brought their judgment in question, by an exuberant display of false wit." Discussing Cowley's love poetry in the *Lives*, Johnson cites Addison's *Spectator*, 62, in which Cowley's love conceits are called "mixed wit, that is," Johnson explains, "wit which consists of thoughts true in one sense of the expression, and false in the other," adding that there were precedents for this sort of thing in "modern Italy." Again, of course, this was no novel statement. In the second paragraph of the essay occur the words "amorous ditties," which describe the harmonious expirations of the lover wounded by his mistress's eyes; the same words occur in the *Life of Cowley*. Somewhat reminiscent of the famous pronouncement on the metaphysical poets, "To write on their plan it was, at least, necessary to read and think," is Anonymous's remark (paragraph 6) about "poets who have never read, and are determined to write." Again in the *Life of Cowley*, we find Johnson quoting, or misquoting, the *Essay on Man* to characterize the group of poems, *The Mistress*, which "plays round the head, but comes not at the heart." The line should actually read "comes not *to* the heart." Observe, then, the writer on elegies, as he criticizes some of William Mason's poems, which "play round the head, but come not near the heart." Both authors, Johnson and Anonymous, have trouble with that preposition, let alone that they elect to quote the same line in similar contexts. One will recall, too, the many times that Johnson has trouble quoting accurately, in the *Lives* and elsewhere.

When Anonymous turns to the question of alternate rhyme which many had "ridiculously imagined to be a new measure adapted to plaintive subjects," introduced by Gray in his *Elegy*, he properly points out that it is nothing but "heroic verse, and to be met with in Dryden's Annus Mirabilis; and all through the long and tedious poem of Davenant's Gondibert." When Johnson comes to Dryden's *Annus Mirabilis* in the *Lives* he mentions the "heroic stanzas of four lines . . . which he [Dryden] had learned from the *Gondibert* of Davenant." And when Johnson examines Hammond's use of alternate rhyme in his elegies he is similarly reminded of Dryden's *Annus Mirabilis*. Consonant too with Johnson's other views is the dislike for alliteration which Anonymous cleverly introduces by way of parody: Mason's lines "*a*mble *a*long by the *a*rtful *a*id of *a*lliteration." And lest the reader should miss the point, the initial *a*'s are italicized. Incidentally, unlike many of their contemporaries, neither Johnson nor Anonymous had much good to say of Mason's poetry. But they were agreed in liking Shenstone's ballads and both stress the "easiness" of that poet's lines. Indeed, Johnson says of Shenstone's elegies that the "lines are sometimes such as elegy requires, smooth and easy," which is, of course, the point that Anonymous makes over and over again of elegy in general. And it is Anonymous who speaks of "the natural, easy Shenstone."

Anonymous, and this is the last point in this series of parallels of thought and expression, devotes the last sentence of his third paragraph to the Bible, praising it for the many "instances of true and sublime simplicity." Compare Johnson on Cowley's *Davideis* where he speaks of "the nakedness and simplicity" of Sacred History. Anonymous further states that in the Bible "there are less epithets to be met with than in any authors whatever"; Johnson, still on the *Davideis*, writes that the "miracle of Creation, however it may teem with images, is best described with little diffusion of language," speaking, a few paragraphs later, of the subject as "thus originally indisposed to the reception of poetical embellishments." Anonymous censures the poets who paraphrase "those divine writers" unsuccessfully because of "their weakening the sublimity of the poetry, by idle description, and clogging the simplicity of the sentiment with the affected frippery of epithetical ornament." Johnson, in the *Life of Watts,* says that "the sanctity of the matter [of devotional poetry] rejects the ornaments of figurative diction." And, harping on the same theme in his *Life of Waller,* he writes these two sentences: "Of sentiments purely religious; it will be found that the most simple expression is the sublime" and "The ideas of Christian Theology are too simple for eloquence, too sacred for fiction, and too majestic for ornament; to recommend them by tropes and figures is to magnify by a concave mirror the sidereal hemisphere."

The practice of listing the pros and cons of any problem before arriving at a decision is often valuable. Confronted with a bare list, one is frequently able to take an undisturbed look at the problem. Let me state, in anticipation of possible objection, that all the arguments adduced are not of equal weight. Indeed, they break down into three categories: uncommon agreements (6 in number), commonplaces of criticism (8), and a doubtful category in between the others (3). The total number of agreements is seventeen; I have found *no* disagreements with Johnson's views in the essay. Since I have discussed the essay on elegies with only two or three friends, only those objections which occurred to them immediately are listed; others doubtless abound. In any event, I would include the following in the "pro" column, after noting that the anonymous author of the "Essay on Elegies" is a writer whose best sentences recall Johnson at his most characteristic and whose other sentences—and they are not many—have as much right to be looked upon as Johnson's as do so many less distinguished sentences in the acknowledged canon:

1. *Uncommon Agreements*
   a. Passion vs. fiction (with verbal similarities).
   b. Alternate rhyme vs. heroic couplet for elegy.
   c. Devotional poetry (verbal similarities).
   d. Dislike for William Mason's poetry.
   e. Misquotation of same word in same line (in same context).
   f. Use of "amorous ditties."
2. *Minor Agreements*
   a. The forcible impression made by Tibullus.
   b. Poets must read in order to write.
   c. Fondness for Shenstone's ballads (or substitute *f.* below).
3. *Commonplaces*
   a. Sannazarius not a writer of pastorals.
   b. Some of Virgil's eclogues are not thought pastorals by critics.

    c. Reference to the conceits and false wit of Italian Poets.

    d. Dislike of alliteration.

    e. Agreement on easiness of Shenstone's lines.

    f. Davenant and Dryden and "heroic verse "

    g. Praise of Gray's *Elegy.*

    h. On the attitudinizing of love poets.

The "contra" column would include:

    1. Lack of external evidence.

    2. The ideas expressed are commonplaces of criticism.

    3. Not all the sentences are characteristically Johnsonian.

    4. The style, as a whole, does not exhibit the "nervousness" one expects of Johnson's prose.

    5. The questions: Does Johnson distinguish between "less" and "fewer"? Does Johnson ever have sentence fragments? (Anonymous says "less epithets" and he has a sentence fragment in his fourth paragraph.) Would Johnson use the sentimentally patriotic "our own Cowley"?

I shall attempt answers to the questions asked and then leave the decision on the "Essay on Elegies" to the individual reader. In order, then: Johnson distinguishes between "fewer" and "less" in his *Dictionary;* I don't know whether he does elsewhere. Johnson sometimes has sentence fragments, usually in a series, where each depends on one initial statement. The possible literary chauvinism of "our own Cowley" is paralleled, if less pronouncedly, in the Preface to Shakespeare where Johnson speaks of "English Bentley."

The third specific task I set myself was to examine the question of Johnson's hand in another work. Professor Allen Hazen, in his discussion of the Preface to James Hampton's translation of Polybius (1756), states that "Dr. [Samuel] Parr considered" it "to be certainly and unmistakably by Johnson" (*Samuel Johnson's Prefaces and Dedications* [New Haven, 1937], 247), but he rejects it even though the style is good and reminiscent of Johnson. The Preface, by the way, is a long one, running to eighteen quarto pages. What Parr, who was able to recognize as Johnson's the Dedication of Bishop Pearce's *Four Evangelists,* actually wrote, however, was that "the Preface was certainly revised and improved by Johnson" (*Bibliotheca Parriana,* 226). Can Johnson's revisions and improvements, if Parr's bare assertion is accepted, be isolated? Can the scholar say: Here Johnson touched up a sentence; here added a phrase or sentence; here expressed views peculiarly his own? And, most importantly, how does one distinguish Hampton's prose style from Johnson's? The answers lie,

1: The Uses and Abuses of Evidence

I believe, in the fact that Johnson probably had nothing whatsoever to do with the Preface. Here are my reasons:

1. The Preface contains the words "the former" and "the latter"; both Boswell (ed. Hill-Powell, IV. 190) and the Reverend Thomas Twining (IV, 190, n. 2) record Johnson's detestation of these phrases. I pause to remark, what is pertinent to my suspicion of external evidence, that the offending words appear in the Preface to the Reverend Dr. James Fordyce's *Sermons to Young Women* (1766), which William Shaw attributed to Johnson. Professor Hazen is inclined on the whole to ascribe the Preface to Johnson on the authority of Shaw's statement, even though there are sentences in it that hardly sound Johnsonian (p. 34). I find it necessary, after all, to quote Boswell and Twining. The first writes that "Johnson never used the phrase *the former* and *the latter*, having observed, that they often occasioned obscurity; he therefore contrived to construct his sentences so as not to have occasion for them, and would even rather repeat the same words, in order to avoid them." The second records Johnson's advice to Dr. Burney: "As long as you have the use of your tongue and your pen, never, sir, be reduced to that shift." It can be objected that Boswell's knowledge of the entire corpus of Johnson's work was superficial, and that Twining's note is dated 1779 and may hence reflect a late opinion of Johnson's. But I have not found the phrases in Johnson and I have been on the alert for them for about five years. And neither Malone, nor any other Johnsonian, early or late, has questioned Boswell's statement. Only a concordance will possibly reveal the usage in a known Johnsonian piece.

2. The Preface is full of "the cant transmitted from age to age, in praise of the ancient Romans,"[4] another of Johnson's strong dislikes. Professor Hazen quotes Boswell (II, 2), "In writing Dedications for others, Johnson considered himself as by no means speaking his own sentiments," and argues that "Dedications" be extended to include "Prefaces," since there has been much confusion of the terms by Johnsonians. Boswell, however, was speaking of the flattering style of dedications, strongly disliked by Johnson, and had already said, in the same paragraph, that the "loftiness" of Johnson's mind "prevented him from ever dedicating in his own person." What is more, with the probable exception of the few necessary complimentary remarks to the Earl of Orrery, Johnson's Dedication for Mrs. Lennox's *Shakespear Illustrated* decidedly expresses his own "sentiments."

3. The Preface speaks of the Romans' wounds which, "though deep and bleeding, instead of draining from their members all their vital strength, serve only to call forth new streams of vigor from the heart." The same

---

[4] Boswell's words about Johnson's review of the *Memoirs of the Court of Augustus* in the *Life* (Oxford, 1934–50), I, 311.

number of the *Literary Magazine* which carried Johnson's review of Hampton also contained the first part of his review of Thomas Blackwell's *Memoirs of the Court of Augustus*. One of Blackwell's faults, according to Johnson, was his predilection for the gory, and one finds Johnson quoting Blackwell and italicizing *"bleeding Rome"* and *"bloody proscription"* in a context which leaves no doubt as to his supreme dislike for this gratuitous gore. In a continuation of this review, seven months later, Johnson lists "bleeding Rome" as one of Blackwell's "epithets of the gaudy or hyperbolical kind." This was evidently cant compounded with cant for Johnson.

4. The Preface declares that the translator has not "scrupled to en-deavor through the whole, as well by changing sometimes the expression, as by breaking the order likewise of the sentences, to soften what appeared too harsh, and to give a modest polish to all that was found too rough." While Johnson did not favor a slavishly literal translation, he could state that "rugged magnificence is not to be softened; hyperbolical ostentation is not to be repressed, nor sententious affectation to have its point blunted. A translator is to be like his author: it is not his business to excell him."[5] Yet, in his review of Hampton, he writes: "The great difficulty of a translator is to preserve the native form of his language, and the unconstrained manner of an original writer. This Mr. Hampton seems to have attained, in a degree of which there are few examples. His book has the dignity of antiquity, and the easy flow of a modern composition." I find this contradictory and puzzling, although a passage in the *Preface to the English Dictionary* does deplore the introduction of "native idiom" from a book translated "from one language into another."[6]

5. The Preface contains an apology for the absence of notes in the translation; Johnson complains of the lack of notes in his review of the book.

6. Johnson did not review any book for which he wrote the dedication or preface. Boswell (I, 309) attributed a review of Sully's *Memoirs* in the *Literary Magazine* to Johnson; Professor Hazen (112n, 110–116) thinks it "probably" written by Johnson and also attributes the dedication for these *Memoirs* to Johnson. R. W. Chapman rejects the attribution, and I find nothing inevitably Johnsonian about the dedication. Johnson did review his own edition of Sir Thomas Browne's *Christian Morals*, however, as well as Goldsmith's *The Traveller*, to which he had contributed some lines.

7. The writer of the Preface uses "Afric" and "Annibal" throughout; except in an early poem, where "Afric" appears,[7] Johnson neither truncates

[5] *Works* (Oxford, 1825), VII, 310.
[6] *Works*, v, 49.
[7] *Poems* (Oxford, 1941), ed. Smith and MacAdam, 66.

the first nor decapitates the second. The writer of the Preface uses "unsuspected" in a sense not found in Johnson's *Dictionary*. I should also point to the Preface's "corrupted text" as opposed to Johnson's "a text corrupt" and "to correct what is corrupt" in the *Proposals* to Shakespeare, published in the same year as Hampton's work. There are a mixed metaphor; some incomplete, appositive sentences; a number of verbal infelicities (one example is a sentence beginning "And this is that which"); and a bewildering use of the historical present in the Preface. All of these strike me as definitely un-Johnsonian. Indeed, there is no mention of the historical present in Johnson's Grammar prefixed to his *Dictionary*. I might add the presence of the compound "half-policied" in the Preface; Johnson's dislike of word coining and words "arbitrarily compounded" is well known.

8. Stylistic analysis of other works by Hampton, as well as the *translation* of Polybius, clearly points to him as the writer of the Preface. I will not trouble to present this evidence, although it is available, if any should be curious.

All the above makes it quite clear, I trust, that Johnson did not write the Preface to Hampton's *Polybius*. Parr seems to have wavered between attributing the whole composition of the Preface to Johnson[8] and conjecturing that he only revised and improved it. Indication is that he favored the latter view. William Beloe (1752–1827), who studied and taught under Dr. Parr, found in the Preface "a profoundness of thinking, an energy of expression, a regularity of cadence, very dissimilar from the structure of the sentences in the *Translation*, and very similar to the best peculiarities of Johnson's phraseology" (*Parriana*, I, 492–493). The Preface, attracting Parr and Beloe (the latter possibly influenced by his one-time teacher), also had the power to attract Professor Hazen, who found it "good, with many felicitous phrases and with much of the balance that is regularly found in Johnsonian prose" (p. 248). I agree wholeheartedly. But not all good prose, whatever its affinities with Johnson's style, must be credited to him. There are some peculiarities of thought and style which can be isolated and held up as Johnson's or not his, and the specific question which I have been begging for the moment is: Given the persistence of so much that was abhorrent or foreign to Johnson in the Preface to *Polybius*, what labors of revision, improvement, and polishing could he possibly have put into that piece of prose? One has only, really, to read the Preface and Johnson's review of Blackwell's

---

[8] E. H. Barker, *Parriana* (London, 1828–1829), I, 488 and 494.

Memoirs of the Court of Augustus, published immediately after the review of Hampton in the same number of the *Literary Magazine,* to realize that he could not, for example, have endured that cant in the first which he so contemptuously criticized in the second.

I hope, in conclusion, that my purpose, albeit possibly now and then obscured by a partisan enthusiasm, has been made clear. A number of questions have been proposed, and some answers have been suggested. I am more interested in the questions, for they, to adopt a Johnsonian distinction, are of *general* value, while answers to the specific questions are only of *particular* importance. I am less interested in gaining acceptance into the Johnson canon for the anonymous essay on elegies than I am in having the method of attribution by internal evidence thoroughly and impartially discussed. The same holds true for the even trickier problem of distinguishing Johnson's hand in another's work. And, I must confess finally, I am chiefly interested in taking the discussion of attribution by internal evidence out of the private into the public forum. Let us, once and for all, stand up and be counted. If there are legitimate objections to the use of internal evidence, or to my presentation, let them be stated and examined, but let there be a truce to such arguments as "I am not convinced," or "You *must* have some external evidence," or "This is all right as far as it goes, but it does not go far enough." "Why," I ask you, "are you not convinced? Why *must* there be external evidence? And how far, in the name of certainty, must one go?"

AN ESSAY ON ELEGIES

From *The Universal Museum and Complete Magazine,* III (1767), 142–143

(Here attributed to Samuel Johnson)

The critics have been very laborious in settling the boundaries of pastoral writings; and in the delicacy of their judgment, have struck many compositions both of Theocritus and Virgil out of the list, of which it may be said, as Pope handsomely says of his own, if they are not pastorals, they are something better. It were to be wished that they had used also the same judicial severity in ascertaining the nature of elegy; tho by that means, many a putter together of long and short verse in Latin, and many an alternate rhymist in English, had been at a loss to know what species of poetry he writ in. The poems of Tyrtaeus are, it is true, called elegies, but with much the same propriety, as if we were to call the piscatory eclogues of Sannazarius, pastorals; they walk, indeed, in the measure of elegy, but breathe all the spirit of the ode.

The elegiac muse seems to be the natural companion of distress, and the immediate feelings of the heart, the object of all her expression. Hence she is generally called in to the assistance of despairing lovers, who, having received their death's wound from their mistress's eyes, breathe out their amorous ditties, and like the dying swan, expire in harmony. What the elegies of Callimachus were, the learned can only conjecture; but they must have been better than those of his professed imitator Propertius, or antiquity had never been so lavish in their commendation. In Propertius, we see the versifying scholar, who perhaps never loved any woman at all: in Ovid, the poet, and the man of gallantry, who would intrigue with every woman he met; while the elegant Tibullus, one of love's devoted slaves, as he always speaks from his own heart, makes a forcible impression upon ours.

The hopes, fears, and anxieties, with all the tumults of passion which distract the lover's breast, will not give him time to think of the mode of expression, or to fetch his allusions from books; nature is contented to deliver herself with perspicuity, and where the sentiment is natural, the phrase cannot be too simple. Upon no subject whatever have so many prettinesses and absurd conceits been invented as love; yet surely where the head has been so painfully laborious, we may safely pronounce the heart to have been perfectly at ease.——Love is not ingenious; though the affected Italians, and ridiculous French poets of the last century, not to mention our own Cowley, have brought their judgment in question, by an exuberant display of false wit. The plaintive muse is generally represented to us as "passis elegia capillis," "as one that discards all shew and appears in dishevelled locks;" but the politer moderns are for putting her hair into papers; and whether the complaint turns upon the death of a friend, or the loss of a mistress, the passion must stand still, till the expression is got ready to introduce it. When we are truly affected, we have no leisure to think of art: "Simplex et ingenua est moeroris vox; flebilis; intermissa, fracta, concisa oratio." (Lowth's *Prelect.*) Then our language is unadorned, and unembarrassed with epithets, and perhaps, in that book, in which there are more instances of true and sublime simplicity, than all the ancients together, there are less epithets to be met with than in any authors whatever: and I cannot help thinking the ill success many poets have met with in paraphrasing those divine writers, has been principally owing to their weakening the sublimity of the poetry, by idle description, and clogging the simplicity of the sentiment with the affected frippery of epithetical ornament.

Elegy, it must be confessed, has often extended her province, and the

23

moral contemplations of the poet have sometimes worn her melancholy garb. As in the celebrated poem of Mr. Gray, written in a church-yard. For though she is generally the selfish mourner of domestic distress, whether it be upon the loss of a friend, or disappointment in love; she sometime enlarges her reflections upon universal calamities, and with a becoming dignity, as in the inspired writers, pathetically weeps over the fall of nations.

In short, whatever the subject is, the language of this species of poetry should be simple and unaffected, the thoughts natural and pathetic, and the numbers flowing and harmonious. Mr. Mason has written elegies, with some success: but whoever examines them, in expectation of meeting these requisites, will be disappointed; he will be sometimes pleased indeed; but seldom satisfied. For in his moral essays, or epistles, or any thing but elegies, the sentiments, which are but thinly scattered, though they glitter with the glare of expression, and amble along by the artful aid of alliteration: "Play round the head, but come not near the heart." Yet, even though we can see the labour the poet has been at, in culling his words, and pairing his epithet with his substantive, his success has not been always equal to his labours. There is, indeed, too apparently in his poems, the *curiositas verborum;* but not always the *curiosa felicitas.*

I cannot take leave of this subject, without indulging myself in one remark, which may perhaps be of use to those poets who have never read, and are determined to write. The elegy, ever since Mr. Gray's excellent one in the church-yard, has been in alternate rhime, which is by many ridiculously imagined to be a new measure adapted to plaintive subjects, introduced by that ingenious author, whereas it is heroic verse, and to be met with in Dryden's Annus Mirabilis; and all through the long and tedious poem of Davenant's Gondibert. The couplet is equally proper for this kind of poetry, as the alternate rhime; and though Gray and Hammond have excelled in the last, Pope's elegy on the death of an unfortunate young lady, will prove those numbers equally expressive and harmonious; nor shall I doubt to place our English ballads, such as have been written by Rowe, Gay, and the natural, easy Shenstone, in the rank of Elegy; as they partake more of the simple pathetic, and display the real feelings of the heart, with less parade, than those affected compositions of classical labour.

2

Two New Poems by Marvell?*

By *George de Forest Lord*

THE two poems which I would add to the Marvell canon are *The Second and Third Advice to a Painter,* published under the name of Sir John Denham in 1667 and subsequently republished in various editions of *Poems on Affairs of State.*[1] These are extended accounts of public affairs in England between the spring of 1665, when England made war on Holland, and September 1666, when the Great Fire broke out in London. "The Second Advice" is mainly concerned with the naval campaign of 1665 and "The Third Advice" with that of 1666.

* Read at the English Institute at Columbia University, Sept. 4, 1958, in a symposium "Attribution by Internal Evidence"; reprinted from the *Bulletin of The New York Public Library,* LXII (1958), 551–570, with the author's permission.

[1] The editions referred to are as follows:

(1) THE | Second Advice | *TO A* | PAINTER, | For Drawing the | HISTORY | Of our *NAVALL* Business; | *In Imitation of* Mr. WALLER. | — | Being the last Work of Sir JOHN DENHAM. | — | Printed in the Year, 1667. |

(2) THE | Second, and Third Advice | *TO A* | PAINTER, | For Drawing the | HISTORY | Of our | *NAVALL* Actions, | The two last Years, 1665. And 1666. | *In Answer to* Mr. Waller. | — | *[4 lines Horace]* | — | A. Breda, 1667. |

(3) *[Within a single line border]* DIRECTIONS | TO A | PAINTER. | FOR | Describing our Naval Business: | In Imitation of Mr. *Waller.* | — | BEING | The Last Works | OF | Sir IOHN DENHAM. | — | Whereunto is annexed, | *CLARINDONS* House-Warming. | By an Unknown AUTHOR. | — | Printed in the Year 1667. |

Directions to a Painter (item 3) contains two sequels to the second and third "Advices," the third and fourth "Advices" (actually the fourth and fifth, if Waller's *Instructions to a Painter,* 1665, is reckoned as the first). These deal quite briefly with the period covered by Marvell's "Last Instructions," but are markedly different in political point of view, in structure, and in style. There is no reason for attributing them to the author of the second and third "Advices." For a summary of the evidence against ascribing them to Marvell, see Margoliouth's notes on "Last Instructions."

Evidence for Authorship

The sequel to these poems, Marvell's "Last Instructions to a Painter," begins with a reference to the two earlier poems:

> After two sittings, now, our Lady State,
> To end her picture, doth a third time wait.

It describes at length the stormy parliamentary session of September 1666, concentrates on the humiliating Dutch invasion of the Thames in June 1667, and ends with Charles's decision to remove Clarendon in the fall of 1667.

I

My belief that Marvell wrote the second and third "Advices" as well as "Last Instructions" depends on many bits of evidence of different kinds.[2] While these bits, examined separately, may not be very impressive, they amount to a strong probability when examined together. The signature of style is not as distinct here, to be sure, as one would expect it to be in nonpolitical poems, but even among those satires always attributed to Marvell we do not find idiosyncrasies of language or imagery or tempo distinctly Marvellian. This may seem surprising in view of Marvell's highly individualized lyric style, but the circumstances under which the satires were produced inevitably led to the cultivation of anonymity. Had the satirist identified himself by stylistic earmarks or other signs he would have faced the usual penalties of maiming, stocking, or even death, for uttering seditious libels. Government agents, as the record shows, searched diligently for the author of these two satires, and "Elephant" Smith, that reckless publisher of seditious books, was brought before Lord Arlington and questioned about them. He confessed that the poems "reflected on the lord chancellor, Duchess of Albemarle, and others of the court," but, unfortunately, there is no record of the disposition of this case. Under the circumstances we cannot, then, expect to find unequivocal internal marks of authorship.

The attribution of the second and third "Advices" to Sir John Denham has long been suspect. For one thing, Denham suffered an attack of insanity in 1666 in the course of which he visited Charles II and proclaimed that he was the Holy Ghost. As Margoliouth says, Denham would have been mad indeed to publish such poems under his own name. In the second place it does not seem likely that he

---

[2] For a summary of the evidence for attributing "Last Instructions" to Marvell, see Margoliouth's edition, in which he says that "of all the satires attributed to Marvell there is none of which one can feel less doubt."

would have published in both these poems the unfaithfulness of his wife with the Duke of York. His name seems, therefore, to have been used simply as a convenient and facetious blind. The suspicion is reinforced by the fact that "Clarendon's Housewarming," a satire generally attributed to Marvell and included in a 1667 collection of "painter" poems, is there ascribed to "an unknown author."

Considerable contemporary evidence ascribes the "Denham" poems in this volume to Marvell. Anthony à Wood attributes them to him and Aubrey says that "the verses called *The Advice to the Painter* were of his making." Marvell's eighteenth-century editor, Captain Thompson, received a manuscript of Marvell's poems compiled by William Popple, the poet's nephew and close friend, containing "those two excellent satires published in the State Poems, Vol. I, p. 24," i.e., the second and third "Advices." When Thompson saw this manuscript his three volumes were already in the press, and so he omitted two poems which he felt, on this evidence, to be Marvell's. Moreover, Denham's latest editor, Theodore Banks, marshals a great deal of evidence against Denham's authorship of these two "Advices," while Margoliouth concedes that they might be attributed to Marvell "without violating the probabilities." In my opinion it would violate the probabilities to exclude them any longer from the Marvell canon.

II

The internal evidence to be considered involves both ideas and style. The first kind of evidence requires a fairly full examination of the attitudes of the three poems under discussion toward public affairs and public figures. The task of comparing them is facilitated by the appearance in Marvell's "Last Instructions" of almost all the major characters in the casts of the second and third "Advices": Edward Hyde, Earl of Clarendon, the chancellor; the Duke and Duchess of York; Sir William Coventry, the Secretary of the Navy; Henry Bennet, Lord Arlington, Secretary of State; Thomas Clifford, of the Exchequer; and Edward Montagu, Earl of Sandwich, a naval commander. Toward these prominent figures the three poems are consistently hostile or disparaging, while all three make a point of paying their humble duty to King Charles II and draw a clear line between him and his evil ministers. All three arraign the administration and its parliamentary supporters for mishandling and misappropriating public funds, for a corrupt and inefficient administration of the navy, and for foisting on the country a war with the Dutch contrary to the national interest, and they are all critical of the Clarendon Code under which the nonconformists were prosecuted. On more specific issues they are unanimously opposed to standing armies, the sale of Dunkirk to France, and the importation of Irish cattle; they blame Clarendon for arranging Charles's marriage to the barren Catherine of Portugal and accuse him of marrying his daughter Ann to the Duke of York to advance his own dynastic ambitions.

Almost as significant as the extensive agreement of the poems on these main figures and issues is their nearly total silence where certain other great figures in the administration are concerned. None of them mentions the immensely powerful and dishonest Duke of Lauderdale or the equally powerful Ashley, the future whig Earl of Shaftesbury. Where the Duke of Buckingham is mentioned he is praised as the opponent of Clarendon, who with the Earl of Bristol led an abortive attempt to destroy the chancellor in 1663. All three of these great politicians had been associated with nonconformist and parliamentary positions in the interregnum and they opposed Clarendon in various ways, factors which might have influenced Marvell in their favor.

In considering the treatment of major figures in the second and third "Advices," on the one hand, and in "Last Instructions," on the other, I would like to draw attention to general resemblances and to resemblances in specific details. Let us first consider, then, the bête noire of these three satires, Edward Hyde, Earl of Clarendon. A traveler who saw him in Rouen after his flight from England, in 1668, calls him "a fair, ruddy, fat, middle-statured man," but in all three poems he is depicted as fat to the point of grossness, and his figure is made an emblem of greed. In "The Second Advice" he is a "burden of the earth" (line 116) "whose transcendant paunch so swells of late | He seems the tympany of law and state" (117–118).

In "The Third Advice," Lady Albemarle calls him "the fat scriv'ner" (250). In "Last Instructions," Marvell describes Hyde's daughter as having the "chanc'llor's belly" (63) and Hyde himself as having a gross body and a grosser mind (179). Both "The Third Advice" and "Last Instructions" couple his name with that of an M.P. named Paston who moved a very large appropriation for the Dutch war in Parliament. In "The Second Advice" the navy is described as

> The ocean's burden and the kingdom's both,
> Whose very bulk might represent its birth
> From Hyde and Paston, [114–116]

while "Last Instructions" represents the cabal demanding of Parliament a sum

> Should Goodrick silence and strike Paston dumb,
> Hyde's avarice, Bennet's luxury should suffice. [126, 129]

From here it is only a small step to allegations that the chancellor took bribes. "The Third Advice" accuses Hyde of starting the Dutch war to avoid domestic quarrels and to line his purse:

> But a Dutch war shall all these rumors still,
> Bleed out these humors, and our purses fill. [265–266]

In "Last Instructions" he farms the taxes

> to them bid least,
> (Greater the bribe), and that's at interest [499–500]

and prepares a nest egg for himself overseas in case things should go wrong at home.

Beside these rather general allegations of cupidity, the chancellor is attacked for his insatiable ambition, particularly in plotting a barren marriage for the king in order that his daughter or her child might inherit the crown. In "The Second Advice" he is accused not only of fomenting the Dutch war to stifle domestic opposition (146–147) but of hoping

> that he yet may see, ere he goes down,
> His dear Clarinda circled in a crown [153–154]

while "The Third Advice" reveals him plotting "to mix the royal blood with ink" (250). In both poems he is accused of selling Dunkirk and the forts which Cromwell built to hold Scotland to gain money for the war ("The Second Advice," 149–150; "The Third Advice," 261). "The Third Advice" further charges him with raising his daughter's dowry from revenues earmarked for the war (255–258) and says of Queen Catherine that

> sweeter creature never saw the sun,
> If we the king wish monk, or queen a nun. [263–264]

In "Last Instructions" the chancellor's regal ambitions are stressed—

> See how he reigns in his new palace culminant,
> And sits in state divine, like Jove the fulminant! [355–356]

—and, a little later, he is represented as despising the Spanish match for Charles, which would have been preferable for diplomatic and dynastic reasons:

> So Spain could not escape his laughter's spleen,
> None but himself must choose the king a queen. [467–468]

The gravamen of the charges leveled against Clarendon by all three satires, nevertheless, is that he started the war against Holland. This is contrary to what we now know about him, just as there are good grounds for discrediting the charge that he fostered the king's marriage and helped to contrive his daughter's marriage with York. But, whatever the truth may be, the poems agree in blaming Clarendon for what they hold to be a disastrous and unnecessary war. "The Second Advice" concludes with the wish that, Icarus-like, the chancellor may,

> falling, leave his hated name
> Unto those seas his wars have set on flame. [Envoy, 15–16]

The Duchess of Albemarle, in "The Third Advice," with equal fervor, curses

> the man that first begat this war,
> In an ill hour, under a blazing star. [423–424]

"Last Instructions" summarizes all the miscarriages of the war in a series of questions which mock the administration's attempt to make a scapegoat of a minor functionary named Peter Pett. His name becomes a whipping post for the intended culprits, who agree that

> All our miscarriages on Pett must fall.
> His name alone seems fit to answer all.
> Whose counsel first did this mad war beget?
> Who all commands sold through the navy? *Pett.* [767–770]

There is no question that this poem, like the others, holds Clarendon responsible for starting the war, and it may also be worth noting that not only do the three satires unite in holding him to be the arch villain of the piece, but that out of all possible expressions of the charge "The Third Advice" and "Last Instructions" agree that he *begat* it.

All three satires agree, furthermore, in laying the blame for the miscarriages of Clarendon's policy on the same officials. Chief of these is Sir William Coventry, Secretary of the Navy. Like Clarendon, he is depicted as insatiably greedy and venal. As "The Second Advice" puts it,

> Of him the captain buys his leave to die,
> And barters it for wounds or infamy. . . .
> To pay him fees the silver trumpet spends,
> And boatswain's whistle on his place depends.
> Pilots in vain repeat the compass o'er,
> Unless they learn of him this one point more:
> The magnet constant to the pole doth hold,
> Steel to the magnet, Coventry to gold. [27–28, 31–36]

Underlings may make a good thing out of selling naval stores, but Coventry "sells the whole fleet away" (40). Coventry's purse, like Clarendon's paunch, is an emblem of his avarice:

> Now let the navy stretch her canvas wings,
> Swoll'n like his purse, with tackling like its strings,
> By slow degrees of the increasing gale,
> First under sale, and after under sail. [41–44]

In "The Third Advice" the charge is advanced that Coventry hoped to destroy George Monck, Duke of Albemarle, co-commander with Prince Rupert of the fleet, by exposing him against overwhelming odds to a Dutch attack. To encompass this end he delays the dispatch of orders to Rupert to come to Monck's assistance:

> And then, presuming of his certain wrack,
> To help him late, they send for Rupert back.
> Officious Will seem'd fittest, as afraid
> Lest George should look too far into his trade.
> At the first draught they pause with statesmen's care,
> They write it foul, then copy it as fair,
> And then compare them, when at last it's sign'd:
> Will soon his purse strings, but no seal could find.
> At night he sends it by the common post,
> To save the king of an express the cost. [303–312]

"Last Instructions" also refers to Coventry by his nickname, and shows him with his brother marshaling the court members of Parliament:

> All the two Coventrys their generals chose,
> For one had much, the other naught to lose.
> Nor better choice all accidents could hit,
> While Hector Harry steers by Will the Wit.

> They both accept the charge with merry glee,
> To fight a battle from all gun-shot free. [225–230]

The last line is a reflection upon Sir William's courage which reminds one of the account in "The Second Advice" of the Duchess of York asking the Duke's shipmates, Brouncker, Penn, and Sir William Coventry, to keep him out of danger:

> She therefore the Duke's person recommends
> To Brouncker, Penn, and Coventry as friends:
> Penn much, more Brouncker, most to Coventry,
> For they, alas! were more afraid than she. [79–82]

The narrative of "Last Instructions" concludes with a scene in which the king, having resolved on Clarendon's disgrace, finds that the Countess of Castlemaine, Arlington, and Sir William Coventry propose the same action:

> Through their feign'd speech their secret hearts he knew:
> To her own husband Castlemaine untrue,
> False to his master Bristol, Arlington,
> And Coventry, falser than anyone,
> Who to the brother, brother would betray;
> Nor therefore trusts himself to such as they. [931–936]

If we add to the sketch of Coventry in "Last Instructions" the allegation that he sold all commands in the navy (770), the figure that appears there is in all essentials like that which appears in the other two poems, a greedy and dishonest official who puts his own interests before those of his country, a coward, and a man incapable of loyalty. This is the same person whom Bishop Burnet described in 1665 as "a man of great actions and eminent virtues, the best speaker of the house, and capable of braving the chief ministry," one of whom Pepys, his intimate associate, notes: "I am still in love more and more with him for his real worth." That the three satires should represent as cheat, coward, and ruthless egotist a statesman and executive whose integrity, efficiency, and ability are witnessed by two such authorities increases the likelihood that the caricatures issued from one hand.

Next to Coventry, the official who receives the largest share of blame throughout the series of poems for national miscarriages in 1665–1667 is Henry Bennet, Lord Arlington. As Secretary of State he was ultimately responsible for the collection and interpretation of intelligence about the movements of the enemy, and he is chiefly blamed for the unlucky division of the English fleet in 1666, and for wrong information about the whereabouts of the Dutch fleet in 1667. In "The Second Advice" he appears only briefly, first as a rapacious commissioner of prizes and then as "pimp Arlington," who married an illegitimate daughter of the house of Orange. "The Third Advice" charges him with disseminating false intelligence, with plotting to destroy Albemarle, one of the co-commanders of the navy, by dividing the fleet, and with having treasonable communication with the enemy through his Dutch wife.

> But fearing that our navy, George to break,
> Might not be yet sufficiently weak,
> The Secretary, that had never yet
> Intelligence but from his own *Gazette,*
> Discovers a great secret, fit to sell,
> And pays himself for't, ere he would it tell:
> Beaufort is in the Channel! Hixy here!
> Doxy Toulon! Beaufort is ev'rywhere!
> Herewith assembles the supreme Divan,
> Where enters none but Devil, Ned, and Nan,
> And upon this pretence they straight design'd
> The fleet to separate and the world to blind.
>   .   .   .   .   .
> To write the order Bristol's clerk is chose
> (One slit in's pen, the other in his nose)
> For he first brought the news, it is his place.
> He'll see the fleet divided like his face,
> And through the cranny in his gristly part
> To the Dutch chink intell'gence may impart.
>   [281–292, 295–300]

Arlington was proud of a wounded nose which he suffered in the royal cause at Andover, and, years after, he still made much of this honorable scar with sticking plaster. The satirist makes of it an emblem of duplicity, a theme which Marvell picks up in "Last Instructions," when he shows this minister liquidating his investments at rumors of the enemy's approach (411–418). The most striking point of resemblance between these two poems, however, is the fact that they both concentrate on Arlington's failure as chief of the intelligence service and hold him to blame for the navy's ignorance of the enemy's whereabouts. Just as the administration has decided on a treaty with the Dutch, in "Last Instructions,"

a fresh news the great designment nips,
Off at the Isle of Candy, Dutch and ships.
Bab May and Arlington did wisely scoff,
And thought all safe if they were so far off.
Modern geographers, 'twas there they thought,
Where Venice twenty years the Turk had fought:
While the first year our navy is but shown,
The next divided, and the third we've none. [397–404]

May and Arlington are here accused of confusing the Isle of Candy off the coast of Essex with the one in the eastern Mediterranean.[3] This piece of sarcasm, incidentally, is exactly in the key of the comment on wrong intelligence in "The Third Advice":

Deep providence of state that could so soon
Fight Beaufort here ere he had quit Toulon! [27–28]

and the reference in the last line to the division of the fleet in the preceding year suggests that Marvell had the earlier passage in mind.

Thomas Clifford, who was soon to become, with Arlington, a chief supporter of the royal prerogative in the cabal which ruled England after Clarendon's fall, was still climbing to power in 1665. He saw much active service in the battles of that summer, but he is mentioned in "The Second Advice" only briefly as an officious errand boy of Arlington,

Wearing a signet, ready to clap on
And seize all [prizes] for his master Arlington. [255–256]

Marvell and he had been enemies at least since 1662, when they quarreled in the house, and he comes in for a fuller share of satirical contempt in the beginning of "Last Instructions," when his newly won importance as Controller of the Household made him a worthier object of scorn. There he is compared to an insect in one of Hooke's recent microscopic studies—as "a tall louse brandishing the white staff" of his office.

The Duke of York plays a large part in "The Second Advice," not only because that satire covers the same activities as Waller's panegyric, but because he was Lord High Admiral in 1665 and withdrew from active duty at the end of the summer. There he is represented

[3] The point of the joke depends in part on an allusion to the poem on which Waller modeled his panegyric, a "painter" poem by Francesco Busenello celebrating the Venetians' defeat of the Turkish fleet off Candy (now Crete) in 1656.

as more fool than knave, surrounding himself with cowardly and lubberly cronies, and failing to press a decisive victory over the Dutch after Lowestoft more through negligence than cowardice:

> Now all conspire unto the Dutchmen's loss:
> The wind, the fire, we, they themselves do cross.
> Now a sweet slumber 'gins the Duke to drown,
> And with soft diadems his temples crown.
> But first he orders all beside to watch,
> That they the foe (whilst he a nap) might catch. [231–236]

The poem goes on to tell how, while the Duke was napping, his favorite, Henry Brouncker, broke off the pursuit. This *cause célèbre*, which brought a parliamentary investigation, is alluded to in "Last Instructions:"

> Who would not follow when the Dutch were bet? [771]

York's retirement from active duty explains the shift of focus from his public to his private life in the later satires. "The Third Advice" opens with a reference to his love affair with the young wife of Sir John Denham, which marks the shift of focus:

> Sandwich in Spain, now, and the Duke in love,
> Let's, with new gen'rals, a new painter prove. [1–2]

This reference was anticipated in "The Second Advice" by the poet's promise to draw "Madame l'Édificatress" in his next. (Denham was Surveyor-General, the Royal Architect.) In "Last Instructions" the Duke's private life is treated more fully in conjunction with his Duchess', while poor old Denham is distinguished as chief of the cuckolds (154). Ann Hyde is represented as plotting her rival's death in an agony of jealousy, a jealousy aggravated by the fact that the Duke, suspicious of her relations with Henry Sidney, his groom of the bedchamber, had discharged him.

> Not unprovok'd, she tries forbidden arts,
> But in her soft breast love's hid cancer smarts.
> While she revolves at once Sidney's disgrace
> And her self scorn'd for emulous Denham's face;
> And nightly hears the hated guards away
> Galloping with the Duke to other prey. [73–78]

It was widely but falsely rumored that Lady Denham's death in January 1667 was caused by poisoned cocoa, but Ann was not among

35

the suspects. It is all the more interesting, then, that she and her father should have been charged with political assassination in "The Third Advice," where a punning line accuses them of murdering a royalist courtier and two royal heirs:

> Then Colepepper, Gloucester, and the Princess di'd:
> Nothing can live that interrupts an Hyde. [245–246]

The same pun occurs, by the way, in another satire printed as Marvell's, "Clarendon's Housewarming."

The close resemblance between the treatments of Ann Hyde in "The Third Advice" and in "Last Instructions" becomes even closer when we consider the allegations both poems make about her promiscuity. When it became known that the Duke of York was on the point of making an honest woman of his paramour, Ann then being some months pregnant, Lord Berkeley and other friends testified that they had enjoyed her favors, but they later withdrew these charges. Both poems accept the scandalous report as true, and both play with the idea of a remarkable restoration of virginity to a woman who has lost her maidenhead. "The Third Advice" tells how

> Berkeley, who swore as oft as he had toes,
> Does kneeling now her chastity depose;
> Just as the first French card'nal could restore
> Maidenhead to his widow, niece, and whore. [251–254]

It is not necessary to go into the tantalizing details about Cardinal Mazarin, except to note that he facilitated the marriage by interceding for the young lovers with the Queen Mother. "Last Instructions" makes the same kind of joke about renewed chastity, this time not in terms of miracle but in terms of the abstruse endeavors of the Royal Society:

> She perfected that engine, oft assay'd,
> How, after childbirth, to renew a maid,
> And found how royal heirs might be matur'd
> In fewer months than mothers once endur'd. [53–56]

Finally we come to an important figure about whom "The Third Advice" and "Last Instructions" are both rather equivocal, the Duke of Albemarle, who played a key part in bringing about the Restoration of Charles II. The seamstress who had been his mistress and became his Duchess is the chief character in "The Third Advice," and she arraigns the administration in blunt terms for abusing her husband, and chiefly for wearing him out in the service of the state. She finds it ironic that an Anglican government should depend so on a nonconformist officer:

> and even Presbyters [are] now call'd out for aid.
> They wish e'en George divided to command,
> One half of him at sea, th'other on land. [353–355]

With a mixture of pride and irritation she notes that

> Thou still must help 'em out when in the mire,
> Gen'ral at land, at sea, at plague, at fire. [431–432]

A similar allusion to Monck in "Last Instructions" seems to show Marvell claiming the "The Third Advice" as his own creation:

> The state affairs thus marshall'd, for the rest,
> Monck in his skirt against the Dutch is press'd.
> Often, dear Painter, have I sate and mus'd
> Why he should still b'on all adventures us'd—
> If they for nothing ill, like ashen wood,
> Or think him, like herb John, for nothing good.
> Whether his valor they so much admire,
> Or that for cowardice they all retire.
> As Heav'n in storms, they call, in gusts of state,
> On Monck and Parliament, yet both do hate.
> All causes sure concur, but most they think
> Under Herculean labors he may sink. [509–520]

In concluding this part of my argument for Marvell's authorship of these three poems, let me admit that some of the details discussed may have been commonplaces of antigovernment satire. Many of the features of Clarendon as sketched in the three poems are to be found in other lampoons written at this time. But the details of the other figures are almost all, to the best of my knowledge, peculiar to these three poems, and though some bits and pieces may appear in contemporary sources other than political verse, there is scarcely a trace of them in the mass of verse satire which the 1660's produced.

III

The rest of my discussion centers on stylistic resemblances between the second and third "Advices" and Marvell's "Last Instructions." These include similarities in structure, in imagery, in wit, in tone, and in diction.

Evidence for Authorship

Of the more than two dozen "painter" poems produced in the Restoration period, the three under discussion are the only ones which effectively use the convention and integrate the painter device with the subject matter. "The Second Advice" scores Waller's unimaginative treatment of the battle:

> Nay, Painter, if thou dare, design that fight,
> Which Waller courage only had to write,
> If thy bold hand can, without shaking, draw
> What e'en the actors trembled when they saw:
> Enough to make thy colors change like theirs,
> And all thy pencils bristle like their hairs. [1–6]

"The Third Advice" relates the painter to the situation in the same way:

> Sandwich in Spain, now, and the Duke in love,
> Let's, with new gen'rals, a new painter prove.
> Lely's a Dutchman, danger's in his art;
> His pencils may intelligence impart.
> Thou Gibson, that among the navy small
> Of muscle-shells commandest admiral,
> (Thyself so slender that thou show'st no more
> Than barnacle new-hatch'd of them before),
> Come, mix thy water-colors, and express,
> Drawing in little, what we do in less. [1–10]

Gibson was doubly qualified for such a task, being a dwarf who painted miniatures. Marvell begins "Last Instructions" in the same manner by establishing the appropriate relationship between the painter and the situation he is to paint:

> After two sittings, now, our Lady State,
> To end her picture does the third time wait.
> But ere thou fall'st to work, first, Painter, see
> If't ben't too slight grown or too hard for thee.
> Canst thou paint without colors? Then, 'tis right,
> For so we too without a fleet can fight. [1–6]

Then he goes on to suggest that a dauber of inn signs and ale-house ceilings would be the right artist for "this race of drunkards, pimps, and fools," and that he might need a microscope to discern England's glory, a point which seems to elaborate the Gibson allusion of the preceding poem.

2: Two New Poems by Marvell?

The satires all parody the solemn similes with which Waller sprinkled his narrative, such as:

So hungry wolves, though greedy of their prey,
Stop when they see a lion in their way.
His winged vessel like an eagle shows,
When through the clouds to truss a swan she goes.

The satirical similes are conspicuously unheroic and inappropriate. Commenting on the Duchess of York's pompous visit to her Duke at Harwich, "The Second Advice" remarks:

Thus the land crabs, at Nature's kindly call,
Down to the ocean to engender crawl.

"The Third Advice" compares the defiant Duke of Albemarle to "an old bustard, maim'd yet loth to yield, | Duelling the fowler in Newmarket field" (91–92). In the same key, "Last Instructions" tells the painter:

With Hooke, then, through the microscope take aim,
Where, like the new Controller, all men laugh
To see a tall louse brandish the white staff.

In their imagery all three poems draw heavily on classical myths, and the source they draw on almost exclusively is the *Metamorphoses*. "The Second Advice" compares Ann Hyde's appearance in the fleet to the birth of Venus, Prince Rupert in his lion skin to Hercules, the Earl of Sandwich ignoring a nearby fleet of enemy prizes to Ulysses passing the Sirens, the co-commanders, Rupert and Albemarle, to Castor and Pollux, Charles II to Minos of Crete, and Clarendon to Daedalus. "The Third Advice" is less learned, since so much of it is devoted to the illiterate Duchess' speech, but still we find her comparing herself to Cassandra and England to Troy, and the poet compares Rupert rescuing Albemarle to Perseus saving Andromeda. In the envoy the Duchess is incongruously, but in her capacity as a seamstress, fittingly, compared to Philomel. "Last Instructions" employs the same sort of mock-heroic images. After he has prorogued the dreaded Parliament, Clarendon is rejuvenated like "decrepit Aeson," who

hash'd and stew'd
With magic herbs, rose from the pot renew'd. [337–338]

The members of a parliamentary committee are compared to Sisyphus, Clarendon's henchmen to Cyclopes, forging weapons for him, and the standing army to Myrmidons.

In addition to these incidental mythical allusions sprinkled through the poems, there is one myth that is central to "The Second Advice" and "Last Instructions," the story of Minos, Pasiphaë, and the bull in *Metamorphoses*, VIII. At the end of his poem, Waller compared Great Britain to Crete:

> Had the old Greeks discover'd your abode,
> Crete had not been the cradle of their god:
> On that small island they had look'd with scorn,
> And in Great Britain thought the Thund'rer born.
> [Envoy, 23–26]

The envoy to "The Second Advice" pursues Waller's comparison with relish and explores its unflattering possibilities:

> Thou, like Jove's Minos, rul'st a greater Crete,
> And for its hundred cities count'st thy fleet.
> Why wilt thou that state-Daedalus allow,
> Who builds thee but a lab'rinth and a cow?
> If thou'rt a Minos, be a judge severe
> And in's own maze confine the engineer;
> Or if our sun (since he so near presumes)
> Melt the soft wax wherewith he imps his plumes,
> And let him, falling, leave his hated name
> Unto those seas his wars have set on flame.
> [Envoy, 7–16]

The satirist adapts the myth freely to comment on Clarendon's sinister influence and the marriage of Charles to Catherine de Braganza. In just the same way Marvell adapts the same myth to the situation of Roger Palmer, Earl of Castlemaine, whose countess had become Charles II's mistress in 1660. Having quarreled with his lady, Palmer left England in 1662 and visited Crete as the guest of a Venetian admiral. The purpose of the visit, according to Marvell, was

> With the bull's horn to measure his own head
> And on Pasiphaë's tomb to drop a bead. [407–408]

As Margoliouth remarks, "Palmer weeps on the tomb of the only woman who would have loved such a horned animal as he is." This allusion, however, like the one in "The Second Advice," is remarkably extensive, for it compares implicitly the great naval victory of the Venetians at Crete, celebrated in the poem Waller took as his model, with Charles's conquest of the Countess of Castlemaine and the shameful defeat of his fleet by the Dutch.[4] Furthermore, the association of Palmer with the bull's horn—like Minos he was cuckolded and like Pasiphaë's bull, deceived—shows just the same kind of complex adaptation of the myth that we found in the identification of Charles II with both Minos and the bull in "The Second Advice."

There is no question that Marvell knew Waller's panegyric and the two satirical "Advices" intimately when he wrote "Last Instructions," but the extensive use in all three satires of the *Metamorphoses* as a source for mock-heroic allusions and the similar adaptations of the myth of Pasiphaë in my opinion greatly heighten the probability that he wrote all three poems.

I should like to examine the corresponding use in all three poems of Biblical stories, but I will limit myself to brief mention of some bizarre saints' legends in "The Third Advice" and "Last Instructions." According to tradition, the fields and woods of Fontainebleau are haunted by the passionate huntsman St. Hubert, who pursues game invisible to human eyes. "The Third Advice" applies this legend to Prince Rupert's search for the French fleet under the Duc de Beaufort, which was believed to be in the Channel when it was, in fact, still in the Mediterranean:

> Rupert to Beaufort: Halloo! Ah there, Rupert!
> Like the fantastic hunting of St. Hubert
> When he, with airy hounds and horns of air,
> Pursues by Fontainebleau the witchy hare. [23–26]

"Last Instructions" employs another strange legend of a French saint to describe the grotesque physical appearance of a Member of Parliament named Wood, who suffered from a further disability, the pox:

> Headless St. Dennis so himself does bear,
> And both of them alike French martyrs were. [167–168]

An equally saucy allusion relates a parliamentary member of the opposition to the pious blacksmith who pulled Satan's nose with his tongs:

> The martial standard, Sandys displaying, shows
> St. Dunstan in it, tweaking Satan's nose. [301–302]

[4] See preceding footnote.

Enough for the mocking use of myth and legend in these satires. I would like now to give a few examples of their characteristic wit. A device which they all conspicuously employ is the naïve endorsement of some absurd action. The war began with a sneak attack, equally piratical and disastrous, on a fleet of Dutch merchantmen off the Mediterranean coast of Spain. Several ships of a squadron commanded by Sir Thomas Allen ran aground, and two had to be abandoned. The painter of "The Second Advice" is, accordingly, ordered to

> feign
> Brave Allen tilting at the coast of Spain:
> Heroic act, and never heard till now:
> Stemming th'Herculean Pillars with his prow! [7–10]

The disastrous division of the fleet comes in for the same kind of mocking approval in "The Third Advice:"

> Deep providence of state that could so soon
> Fight Beaufort here ere he had quit Toulon! [27–28]

The panicky and indiscriminate scuttling of ships in the Thames during the Dutch invasion of 1667 receives the same sort of pseudonaïve endorsement in "Last Instructions":

> Our merchantmen, lest they should burn, we drown. [712]

In the same poem an inept English embassy to seek peace with the Dutch is

> order'd, if they won't recall
> Their fleet, to threaten we will give them all. [461–462]

There is a more special likeness among the three poems in their use of puns and witty turns. "The Second Advice" describes Coventry's navy homonymously as

> First under sale and after under sail. [44]

When the skull of York's favorite, Falmouth, is smashed by a cannonball at Lowestoft, it "gives the first, last proof that it had brains" (188), and a little later, while the English pursue the beaten Dutch, the Duke retires to his cabin to rest, but first orders "all beside to watch, | That they the foe (whilst he a nap) might catch" (235–236).

In "The Third Advice" the Duchess of Albermarle complains of the readmission of bishops to the House of Lords:

The Lords' House drains the houses of the Lord,
For bishops' voices silencing the Word, [241–242]

and in the same monologue the erstwhile seamstress comments resignedly on her long separation from the Duke:

'Tis true, I want so long my nuptial gift,
But, as I oft have done, I'll make a shift. [321–322]

Marvell puts wordplay to the same use in "Last Instructions." Ann, Duchess of York, is there pretended to be an ingenious natural philosopher, who perfected, as we have seen, "that engine, oft-assay'd, | How after childbirth to renew a maid." Her ingenuity and ambition are scored when she is compared with advantage to Archimedes "for her experiment upon the crown" (52). The aging lecher, Henry Jermyn, Earl of St. Albans, was chiefly responsible for England's feeble diplomacy in France. Marvell touches on both his private and professional characters in four adroit lines:

Well he the title of St. Albans bore,
For never Bacon studi'd Nature more.
But age, allaying now his youthful heat,
Fits him in France to play at cards and treat. [35–38]

St. Albans' quite specialized interest in Nature is wittily contrasted with that of the great philosopher, just as his social successes and diplomatic failures are brought together in the one word "treat."

In the matter of diction I would like to confine myself to one rather important detail. In doing so I should say that there are many resemblances in the language of the three poems, but that space prevents the submission of the large number of examples necessary to this kind of demonstration. In his bibliography of Marvell's writings, Pierre Legouis lists as possibly Marvell's a pamphlet published in 1678, named *Flagellum Parliamentarium,* which gives brief sarcastic sketches of some two hundred members of the court party in the House of Commons. It says of Sir Richard Edgcumbe that he was "cullied to marry the halcyon, bulk-breaking Sandwich's daughter." The Earl of Sandwich commanded the fleet in 1665 and was cashiered for "breaking bulk," that is, for illegally sharing with some of his high officers a rich Dutch prize. Marvell mentions this scandal in a letter to the mayor of Hull, and in "Last Instructions" holds Sandwich to blame for "treating out the time at Bergen," in negotiating with the Danes a treacherous attack on Dutch merchantmen in that neutral harbor, instead of striking at once. "Halcyon" was rarely used in the particular sense of timorous and peace-loving—the sense in which *Flagellum Parliamentarium* applies it to Sandwich. In fact the only other instance I have ever found occurs in "Second Advice" in a passage about Sandwich, Bergen, and the anticipation of capturing prizes:

> The halcyon Sandwich does command alone.
> To Bergen now with better maw we haste,
> And the sweet prey in hope already taste. [250–252]

Although attributions from internal evidence generally fall short of positive proof, I believe that a complex of probabilities such as I have attempted to present is good grounds for accepting an attribution. Here are three satirical poems, carefully articulated with each other, making the same use of a quite special poetical convention, exhibiting the same interaction of wit and high patriotic seriousness, excoriating the same great figures of public life, drawing heavily on one source for mythological allusions; and here is a great poet and patriot, critical of the government's political and ecclesiastical position, known to be an enemy of most of the people satirized, intimately acquainted with state affairs, and—as citizen of a major port and fellow of Trinity House—equally familiar with ships and naval business. One of the poems is undoubtedly his. Is it not probable that he also wrote the others?

3

The Signature of Style*

By David V. Erdman

"ANY work," wrote Coleridge, "which claims to be held authentic, must have had witnesses, and competent witnesses; this is external evidence. Or it may be its own competent witness; this is called internal evidence." He then made a further and useful distinction—between direct and indirect kinds of evidence. "Or [the work's] authenticity may be deduced from indirect testimony, such as the absence of all contradiction; or from the absurdity of supposing it to be a forgery, as in the case of the works of Virgil, Cicero, &c. which the Jesuit Hardouin contended to have been forged by Monks, in the dark ages."[1]

"Why *must* there be external evidence?" asks Professor Sherbo, in his paper "The Uses and Abuses of Internal Evidence" (No. 1). I take him to mean "Why must there be *direct* external evidence?" For of course we must always have at least the *indirect* testimony that the work was not published before our author was born, and so on. Within the frame of reference of our present discussion—which I take to be the assessment of printed documents of such provenience as to suggest possible attribution to an author of established canon who continues to be reread for his own sake—if we agree that there need not always be direct external evidence, we may be tempted to ask, in return, whether there always *must* be internal evidence. But the answer is that there must.

We are talking of course about *good* evidence. Our actual working limits keep us to debatable instances, in every one of which there is presumably some internal and some external (if only indirect) evidence. The debate is over what constitutes evidence sufficiently good

---

* Read at the English Institute at Columbia University, Sept. 5, 1958, in a symposium "Attribution by Internal Evidence"; reprinted from the *Bulletin of The New York Public Library*, LXIII (1959), 88–109, with an author's correction in note 27.

[1] "Intercepted Correspondence," *Morning Post*, Feb. 3, 1800.

45

to persuade us that an admittedly probable attribution can be accepted as certain.

I agree with Professor Sherbo in holding that internal evidence *can* be sufficient—provided the indirect testimony is not seriously inclement. For example I have no hesitation in accepting Professor Ronald Crane's attribution to Goldsmith of "A Neglected Mid-Eighteenth-Century Plea for Originality,"[2] which appeared in the *Critical Review* in 1760 at a time when Goldsmith was among the *Review's* circle of contributors. Professor Crane adduces no direct external evidence but demonstrates a half dozen substantial parallelisms of detail, in idea and anecdote and use of sources, which amount to strong coincidence in a "particular association of doctrines" and in "the radical temper with which [these are] expressed." Crane does not dwell on his stylistic point, the temper of the expression, though its presence is reassuring. But he makes a case with parallels that are not simply added up but are grasped together as constituting a general coincidence. Unconvincing demonstrations of parallelism are those that rely on the illusion of "safety in the number of parallels used"[3] and neglect to examine their quality and the question of whether their "particular association" may be significant.

On similar grounds I am inclined to accept the attribution of the second and third "Advices to a Painter" to Marvell (*if* Marvell indeed is "undoubtedly" the author of "Last Instructions to a Painter")[4] and of the "Essay on Elegies" to Johnson (with some lingering uneasiness about the somewhat elusive question of its style).[5] But I am much more hesitant about the attribution to Christopher Smart of *Mother Midnight's Comical Pocket-Book* [in essay No. 21, reprinted below]—not because we *have* to have direct external evidence in every case, but because we are shown here neither that, nor characteristic style, nor any impressively particular association of ideas. When the parallelisms are rather diffusely scattered than closely associated,

[2] *Philological Quarterly,* xiii (1934), 21–29; reprinted below, No. 20.

[3] Inga-Stina Ekeblad, "Webster's Constructional Rhythm," *ELH, A Journal of English Literary History,* xxiv (1957), 166.

[4] George de F. Lord, above, No. 2.

[5] Arthur Sherbo, above, No. 1. The objection which Sherbo lists that "not all the sentences are characteristically Johnsonian" is not so strong as would be the more significant objection that no especially Johnsonian sentences are cited. Not an expert or frequent reader of Johnson myself, I cannot tell whether this objection is met by the sentences included in the list of scrambled Johnsonian and non-Johnsonian passages, though the immediate point of the list is rather to demonstrate the difficulty of such citation.

it is of course necessary to resort to numbers. But in that case the eligibility of each suffrage requires close scrutiny. Have unrelated commonplaces any cumulative force? Can "Taffy" (a common nickname but said to be uncommon in poetry) and a poet's fascination with female breasts have differentiative power?[6] If we must put question marks beside several of the parallelisms, how can a column of 1? + 1? + 1? be calculated?

Professor Sherbo has reminded us that the concept of "a characteristic style" is fraught with nebulosity—and that even the inimitable character of Johnsonian style does not infallibly manifest itself. It is quite true that the inimitable component is not always easily distinguishable from the imitable ones. It was not just any verse of Wordsworth's that Coleridge felt he could recognize in the deserts of Arabia. Nevertheless, granted that a writer's style is sometimes silent, it must be recognized that the test of style is always crucial, at least in the negative sense. There are styles that would rule out Marvell as author; others that would rule out Smart; others Johnson: no matter how impressive the external evidence. It should also be recognized that the test of style *can* be decisive in a positive sense.

Certainly any real neglect of this test can be perilous. Let me illustrate with a horrible example from my own work in progress. In the autumn of 1802 Coleridge sent to the London *Morning Post* several kinds of contributions from Keswick—poetry old and new, essays on the Affairs of France and on Jacobinism, and a piece of local society news from Buttermere entitled "Romantic Marriage" (published October 11):

On the 2d instant a Gentleman, calling himself Alexander Augustus Hope, Member [of Parliament] for Linlithgowshire, and brother to the Earl of Hopetown, was married . . . near Keswick, to a young woman, celebrated by the tourists under the name of *The Beauty of Buttermere*. . . . she is rather gap-toothed, and somewhat pock-fretten. But her face is very expressive, and . . . her figure and movements are graceful to a miracle. She ought indeed to have been called the Grace of Buttermere, rather than the Beauty.

There had been some doubt of this Mr. Hope's intentions, since he seemed to be courting two women at once, but his marriage "with a poor girl without money, family, or expectations, [had] weakened the suspicions entertained to his disadvantage [by] the good people

---

[6] See Sherbo's paper, No. 21, below.

of Keswick. . . ." Within a few days the newspaper was informed that the real Alexander Hope was in Vienna. Coleridge with sad alacrity investigated the true "particulars of the novel of real life . . . among our mountains," and his reports (still sent anonymously from Keswick), first still headed "Romantic Marriage" but then "The Fraudulent Marriage," were published October 22 and November 5. The real name of the bigamist imposter was John Hatfield, who fled but was captured in Wales and taken to London in December amid reports that "poor Mary of Buttermere is with child" and that another wife was visiting Hatfield in gaol.

Coleridge's authorship of the three Keswick reports is witnessed by their style and by much testimony of a circumstantial kind, plus the statements of his daughter and of Thomas De Quincey. I was on perfectly firm ground when I decided to add to the canon "A Detailed Account of the Keswick Imposter," published November 20 and December 31 in the same newspaper. The major evidence was the fact that these essays, in the first person, were avowedly contributed by the same correspondent who had sent in the first reports.[7] The test of style was passed modestly but fairly. Their prose is easily Coleridgean, yet so busily narrative that the characteristic touches are quiet; in the first essay there is only one landing place where the author takes time to pause and exhibit the signature of inimitable Coleridgean metaphor: "It seems to have been a maxim with him [our adventurer] to leave as few white interspaces as possible in the crowded map of his villainy."

That is authentic Coleridge, though it is not my present purpose to demonstrate the attribution of these 1802 accounts. Their discovery and their unobtrusive style are what tempted me to my folly concerning an essay of 1803. Further temptation lay in the opportunity to overthrow the tradition that Coleridge had ceased writing for the *Morning Post* in 1802. First I found a political editorial of January 6, 1803, that appears unmistakably his. Then I followed the directions in a letter of June 1803—"You may expect certain Explosions in the Morning Post, Coleridge versus Fox—in about a week"—a letter that continues to bear editorial annotation to the effect that no work of his after 1802 has been identified—and I found the promised ex-

---

[7] Strong external evidence is the fact that this "Detailed Account" is the source (as the earlier and briefer reports cannot be) of Thomas De Quincey's statement (*Literary Reminiscences,* ch. vii) that "Coleridge made the public merry" with insults to "the Liverpool merchant" (Crump) in the *Morning Post.*

plosions in a pair of "Essays on The Men and The Times" in the *Morning Post* of July 18 and August 20, 1803. Here was proof that Coleridge *was* still writing for Stuart: proof, because the explosions are Coleridgean in style, in matter, in allusion; because the letter announcing them is direct external evidence of his intention to write them; and because—as readers may be comforted to learn after having so much unsworn testimony waved before their eyes—these two essays of explosion bear the familiar signature of Coleridge's initials, in Greek, "ΕΣΤΗΣΕ."

When I found another report on the fraudulent Hatfield in the paper of August 19, 1803, in date just between the two signed essays, I plunged. This attribution seemed supported by abundant external evidence. In Coleridge's letters and notebooks the thought of Hatfield—and Iago—keeps popping up. His frauds remained the sensation of the year; he was tried for forgery and condemned to death at the assizes in mid-August at Carlisle; and the Wordsworths and Coleridge made a point of being in Carlisle for the trial and for an interview with the condemned imposter, as we know from Dorothy Wordsworth's Journal. We know also that the walk to Scotland they had begun was financed by a loan from Daniel Stuart, editor of the *Morning Post*. Who but Coleridge could have sent Stuart the letter from Carlisle which he published on the 19th? Though brief and lacking any striking idiosyncrasies, the report of Hatfield's trial has a lively literary tone, quoting Polly Peachum apropos of the ladies' interest in Hatfield's "blue vivid eyes, &c.," and concluding that, as "a doubt does not remain that he will be executed, [he] may now sing, with *Macheath*, 'And this way at once I please all my wives.'" I was sure Coleridge could have written this report, and I was overwhelmed by the external evidence, circumstantial though it all was (for Coleridge nowhere says "I reported the trial").

Further evidence came with Professor Coburn's publication of the Coleridge *Notebooks*. Entries there[8] confirmed the impression (obscured by a distortion of De Quincey's) that Coleridge *did* interview Hatfield in gaol: "Then visited Hatfield, impelled by Miss Wordsworth—*vain*, a hypocrite/It is not by mere Thought, I can understand this man"; they added details: "At Carlisle I alarmed the whole Court . . . by hallooing to Wordsworth who was . . . on the other side of the Hall—*Dinner!*" and also precise dates.

[8] *The Notebooks of Samuel Taylor Coleridge*, ed. Kathleen Coburn (New York, 1957), I, 1432.

What the precision of dating effected, however, was not the confirmation of my attribution but its overthrow. Coleridge's authorship of the letter to Stuart turned out, indeed, to have been impossible. For that report covers the first day of the trial, August 15, and was posted before sentence had been pronounced. Notebook entries show that Coleridge and his friends did not arrive until August 16, when they attended the sentencing, after which they dined and then visited the gaol.[9]

That was a narrow escape, for which I have to thank Miss Coburn. For the external evidence which lured me into accepting this report—oh of course I can see *now* that Coleridge would have compared Hatfield to Iago not Macheath—might never have emerged into the light of day in such clarity of detail as to compel me to reverse my judgment. It had been greased with the very best butter of external indirect evidence—which one should realize can never be good enough. Yes, we do have to have good *internal* evidence. In this instance the lack of distinctly characteristic marks of style, coupled with the lack of any direct external evidence such as the unambiguous back reference found in the new Hatfield articles of 1802 ("In the former accounts, with which I first introduced our hero . . . I have already described 'the beauty of Buttermere'"),[10] should have caused a stay of judgment in the first place.

The very brevity of some pieces of writing intensifies the problem. If the Hatfield obituary (to call it that) had been two or three thousand words long, with still no peculiarly Coleridgean turn of thought or expression, I think I should have been more skeptical. Yet brevity is not crucial as long as we rely on the quality rather than the quantity of evidence—and if we resign ourselves to the proposition that short paragraphs or essays by Coleridge in which he fails to rise above or veer aside from the fairly standard prose of other laborers in the same vineyard *ought to* escape our detection.

If on the other hand quantitative tests are applied, units of prose (or verse) much longer than newspaper articles (or sonnets) or eighteenth-century reviews (in the *Critical*)—all the material on my own work table—are required. The analyses of G. Udny Yule call for thousands of occurrences, in each unit, of the parts of speech

[9] I, 1427, 1429, 1432. Details of the trial are from W. M. Medland and Charles Weobly, *A Collection of Remarkable and Interesting Criminal Trials* (London, 1803), I, 294–295.
[10] Nov. 20, 1802.

counted.[11] (I do not know how these minimal quantities can be safely reduced.) Even supposing we had essays long enough to contain over a thousand verbs each, so that we could get the ratio of verbs to adjectives; and supposing we acquired statistics of the practice of his contemporaries for comparison, how could we be sure the ratio in any single example was significant? In a spot check of the longest essays I could find, by Coleridge and certainly not by him, I found no meaningful distributions emerging. But it must be noted that Yule and other statistical measurers of vocabulary do not themselves claim to have found tests sufficiently delicate to detect authorship.[12]

With qualitative (or should we call it "depth") analysis even a sonnet does not seem necessarily too small. Last year I published a rather tedious demonstration of a "concordance test" applied to several newspaper sonnets possibly written by Coleridge. The sonnets that failed the test were more probably not his than too short. In one instance, a *Morning Chronicle* sonnet "To Mrs. Siddons," I was successful (judging from the response of readers, including myself) in detecting the pattern of a special cluster of associated words and phrases that matched the associational clusters of known Coleridge verse closely enough to imply common authorship.[13] The Coleridge *Concordance* has not proved of much help with the prose, but the

[11] *The Statistical Study of Literary Vocabulary* (Cambridge, Eng., 1944).

[12] Paul E. Bennett, "The Statistical Measurement of a Stylistic Trait in *Julius Caesar* and *As You Like It*," *Shakespeare Quarterly*, viii (Winter 1957), 33–50, is frequently referred to as demonstrating an authorship test, but Bennett's own disclaimers should be heeded. He applies Yule's measure of "the characteristic," i.e. of the repetitiveness of the vocabulary of a given work, to two plays and finds that in regard to this aspect of style "Shakespeare is very similar to himself." So Yule had found Macaulay and Bunyan to be. And the three writers' degrees of repetitiveness fall in different bands of the spectrum. Yet Bennett wishes not to suggest that "the characteristic" will provide "an infallible test of authorship, for it may well turn out that some of Shakespeare's plays will have the same characteristic as some, say, of Jonson's plays, whereas other of his plays might yield the same characteristic as, perhaps, one of Marlowe's." The mechanized research of the future may assemble vast frequency counts—as like as not filling the whole spectrum and erasing the present appearance of possibly significant differences. Bennett adds, "The real desideratum is to develop objective measures of several different significant aspects of style; authorship might then confidently be ascribed when two or three or four of these measures were in substantial agreement."

F. W. Bateson makes the suggestion that the present qualitative weighing of Coleridge's style which takes the metaphorical passages as most distinctive might be followed by statistical pursuit of such promising matters as the metaphor-simile ratio or the ratio of main to dependent verbs.

[13] An excerpt from this article is given below, No. 27—Eds.

usefulness of a sort of homemade collection of the metaphorical language in his known prose suggests that a systematic prose concordance would be desirable. (See, however, notes 27 and 28.)

The shortest bits of prose I have attempted to identify with any success are reviews in the *Critical Review*. Here the indirect external evidence has to be quite strong: indications that Coleridge was writing for the *Critical Review* for the months in question and interested in the books in question. And the internal evidence has to be a strong combination of the appearance of Coleridgean quality (in thought and style) with impressive parallels between the reviews and Coleridge's immediately contemporary letters and verse.

Even when we are dealing with the much larger blocks of prose which Coleridge and other editorial writers contributed to the *Morning Post*, we are not on very safe ground unless we have both these kinds of internal evidence: the look of his style and the link of parallels with his known work. The severest test of our powers of recognition—and of our good judgment—comes when we are driven to rely upon the look alone. When Coleridge, in a letter of 1796, tries to define what it is that "peculiarizes my style of Writing . . . sometimes a beauty, and sometimes a fault," he can only generalize the cause, not the effect: "I feel strongly, and I think strongly; but I seldom feel without thinking, or think without feeling."[14] This is hardly a touchstone, but it indicates what must, nevertheless, be taken somehow into account—the characteristic working of our author's mind. "Links" that violate its contours are usually specious.

Consider the problem of multiple authorship as exemplified in the apparently successful effort, protracted over many years, to assign different parts of *A Cure for a Cuckold* to three different playwrights. The various scholars doing this have relied chiefly on the method of parallel passages, and in a recent issue of *ELH* Professor Inga-Stina Ekeblad, without exactly reopening the question, argues that "as long as discussions of authorship exclusively centre on 'parallels' of scattered words and phrases, so long is one liable not to see the wood for the trees."[15] Meaningful discussion must concern itself with "the very structure of an author's dramatic verse." Citing the parallels used to ascribe part of the play to Webster, she insists that "the parallelism, to mean much, should be supported by the observation [which she

[14] *Collected Letters of Samuel Taylor Coleridge*, ed. E. L. Griggs (Oxford 1956), I, 279.
[15] "Webster's Constructional Rhythm," 166.

then makes with some impressiveness] that here, as repeatedly in Webster's tragedies, one character is using a very concrete metaphor to describe to another character his emotional impact on her," and that one can observe "what we might call the 'constructional rhythm' of Webster's dramatic poetry," a characteristic [and presumably unique] movement from swift, foreboding dialogue to slow analytic speeches yielding a "pattern of simple (and yet intricate) lucidity." Miss Ekeblad does not press this demonstration; she finds herself in agreement with F. L. Lucas' distribution of scenes to various authors; she only questions the exclusive use of parallels to reach such conclusions. Yet without the parallels would she venture, I wonder, to vouch for "intricate lucidity" here and only complicated "flatness" there?

Parallels can be illusory or coincidental; recognition of the author's signature in characteristic constructional rhythms or in modes of metaphor and metaphysics can be precarious. It is the combination of the two that constitutes the most satisfactory internal evidence. The strong parallels give objective and independent support to the reader's *impression* that he recognizes unique marks of style; the recognition of such marks lifts the parallelism out of the realm of pure coincidence. Both of these are double-edged tools; properly sharpened and employed together, they are the best we have.

The extensive Coleridgean territory where these tools need to be used is that of unsigned prose contributions to the newspapers—to the *Morning Post* within the possible span of six years through August 1803 and to the *Courier* from possibly 1804 to the 1820's. Direct external testimony, confirmed by the evidence of style, has established his authorship of a great number of essays, chiefly in the political editorial department. Yet over a third of the *Morning Post* essays collected by his daughter Sara Coleridge in her edition of his *Essays on His Own Times* (1850) were presented on the contents page (or in notes) as "Contributions . . . judged, chiefly from internal evidence, to be probably Mr. Coleridge's." Sara's judgment has been accepted by all Coleridgeans of the ensuing century, I believe, and further evidence has turned up that strengthens most of her "internal" attributions. She lacked access to anything like a full run of the newspaper. Searching the file of the *Morning Post* at Peele's Coffee House, she found that Time had been "especially *edacious* of my Father's compositions, as if he anticipated an attempt to rescue them from his maw for ever." And she could not easily consult all her father's manuscripts. What I have been doing, in the last half dozen years (with the assistance of Mrs. David Glickfield, for a time),[16] is to complete and buttress Sara's work, by means of the modern availability of nearly complete newspaper files and of extant Coleridge manuscripts.

I feel confident that Sara Coleridge, if she had seen them, would have accepted virtually all of the new attributions[17]—a total of some 25,000 to 30,000 words of new essays, many confirmed by direct external evidence, the rest supported, like most of Sara's attributions now, by the combination of the two kinds of internal evidence I have been talking about: idiosyncratic style—and parallels with known writings, including jottings in the newly published *Notebooks*.

Out of Sara's "probable" attributions, I find only one of the *Morning Post* essays that I would reject, more out of caution than from any firm conviction that it is *not* by Coleridge. When she wrote that "there are few that do not contain sentences or phrases to be found elsewhere in his writings, *or* some other special marks of his style,"[18] I take her to have been very uncertain about such things as the one essay I refer to. As she went to press she herself put queries upon the two that she called the "most dubious of the *conjecturals*"[19] in the *Courier* (1811). These did not pass the test of *style*, and in questioning them she put her finger on a special problem of conjecturing the authorship of pieces of journalism: "They contain my Father's opinions, but, I now think, may not have been from his pen."

By and large it is my own impression that, for the whole period of his writing for the *Morning Post*, the opinions of Coleridge are the opinions of the newspaper—and vice versa. These opinions vary and even threaten at times to separate. In his first attack on Fox in 1802 we can see Coleridge's opinions forging ahead of those of his editor. When Coleridge in the autumn of 1800, with matter supplied by Thomas Poole, justifies the ways of monopolists in grain, we can

[16] For a preliminary list see Charlotte Woods Glickfield, "Coleridge's Prose Contributions to the *Morning Post*," *PMLA*, LXIX (1954), 681–685. (Weakest in that list, for lack of the positive evidence of style, is "Theatrical Dispute," Jan. 4, 1800.)

[17] So I wrote and spoke. But subsequent examination of her working notes, now in the Victoria College Library, Toronto (and cited with that Library's kind permission), reveals that she did see—and reject—three of my attributions: Mar. 22, Nov. 20, Dec. 31, 1802 (all discussed below). (VCL: MS 19 v. 2; S MS F10.3, F10.6.)

[18] *Essays on His Own Times* (London, 1850), I, lxxv; my italics.

[19] Sara Coleridge's italics.

see Stuart covering himself by opening his columns to some opinion on the other side of the question. But in any debatable case of attribution, the opinions expressed prove worthless as a test of authorship.

Far otherwise is the *manner* of their expression. Sara was confident that, in her father's case at least,

> there is a *countenance* in an author's mode of expression; not that a man's whole being will look forth from his writings . . . but that enough of his intellectual character and temperament will appear in his compositions . . . to render the author clearly recognizable by those well acquainted with his mental idiosyncrasy. . . .
>
> An author may shift his style as a man wears a different habit on different occasions . . . yet the writer's personal identity will shine through it.

She concedes that there are authors "who can assume different persons as well as different costumes," but puts her father in a class with Spenser, Shakespeare, Milton, Dante as far as original genius and strongly individualized products are concerned.

> My Father's genius was never hidden in the different forms it assumed or modes in which it was manfested. The identity was more impressive than the diversity in all that proceeded from his mind. In his prose writings the union of ardour with precision is one of the most general characteristics of his manner; and another is the combination of learning with imaginativeness. He was wont to illustrate a subject by images borrowed from the realm of Faëry [i.e. romance; she might have added necromancy, medicine, chemistry, meteorology, navigation] . . . and the deep treasury of Scripture. . . . His prose was that of a poet, yet possessed the appropriate prosaic rhythm; and this is the most general mark, whereby it is distinguished from the elegant or forcible writings of his distinguished contemporaries and immediate successors. Perhaps there are few *good* styles, such as are not encrusted with icy mannerisms, but pure and free and flowing, like a mountain stream in April, which are so recognizable as my Father's. . . .

Sara nevertheless declares the possibility of having been mistaken "in some of my few conjectural attributions"—a wording which, again, indicates that she considered only a fraction of her "probable" attributions really "conjectural."[20]

---

[20] Under the heading "Conjectured" in her notebook in Victoria College Library (MS 19 v. 1), beginning fol. 12 recto and continuing 12 verso and 11 verso, Sara lists 25 articles in the *Morning Post*. Of these she accepts only 6 (including Apr. 21, 1800). I accept 5 of these and 4 others on her list, including

Coleridge himself defended the validity, when dealing with original genius, of resting the case for authenticity on the combination of internal evidence with sufficiently limiting external. In the *Confessions of an Inquiring Spirit* (Letter III) he put the hypothetical case of the trustworthiness of quotations attributed to More and Bacon in competent biographies of these men, to which "no test *ab extra* could be applied." The far larger part of the material in question would, he presumed, when compared to canonical writings of these men, bear "witness in itself of the same spirit and origin." Not only "its characteristic features, but . . . its surpassing excellence" would render "the chances of its having had any other author than the giant-mind, to whom the biographer ascribes it, small indeed!"

When we have gathered from the pages of the *Morning Post* dozens of editorial essays and leading paragraphs that seem to bear witness in themselves of the same spirit and origin as other essays and paragraphs signed by Coleridge—signed either in print or in his own handwriting in the bundle of clippings that Sara inherited and that provided the basis of her edition—what are the chances of the unsigned essays' having had any other author than Coleridge?

How many contributors to the *Morning Post* were there in these years, and how gigantic were their minds, and what was their writing like? Let us consider first the limiting factors. Editorial paragraphs appearing under the masthead (leaders or leading paragraphs, without titles) spoke directly for the newspaper and were presumably written by the editor or by someone (such as Coleridge) hired by him; consultation often, perhaps always, preceded their composition. Twelve of the twenty-five new essays are in this category (I include a letter signed "The Editor"). The other thirteen are what we may call feature articles, placed separately under independent headlines such as "Ireland and La Vendee," "Our Future Prospects," "The Keswick Imposter," "Advice to the Friends of Freedom." Theoretically anyone might contribute such essays, with or without invitation; sometimes they were reprinted or translated from another journal, with or without acknowledgment. On the other hand, some were obviously

---

the 2 on the Keswick Imposter. It is interesting to note that she too staked much on metaphors. "Midas" is her only note on "March 15 [1800]" and "alto relievo" on "Feb 12 [1800]"; both point to central metaphorical passages, and she accepts both essays. She rejects "Feb 24 [1800]," however, though her note is *"coquetry* of Paul's"; I accept it, partly because of the coquetry passage. Her notes seem to indicate that these metaphors were felt to be main clues.

mere overflows from the leading paragraph area. Of the thirteen such essays now added to the canon, two are quite independent and signed by the contributor in a period when he was no longer writing leaders; two are signed by place, "Keswick," narrowing the identity to Coleridge and his neighbors; but the rest are written in an editorial "we" by someone who identifies himself with and speaks for the newspaper and its policies. Three of these are in a series, on "Reported Changes" in the British cabinet, that wanders in and out of the leader position. Another, on "General Washington's Will," is a sequel to an obituary written as a leading paragraph. The remaining five are also, in tone and statement, rather editorial pronouncements than contributions received from outside the family.

How large was the editorial family of the *Morning Post?* We know that Stuart wrote many of his own editorials and that he was assisted by his handyman George Lane, who was good at gossip and epigrams and news stories but had no mind for the political department. There is enough of a canon of Stuart's political writing (especially in the series signed "X. Y. Z." in the *Courier*) to familiarize us with his workmanlike but essentially unsoaring style. Over the years there are occasional runs of editorial matter different in style from the usual Lane-Stuart variety, some by a user of clichés in French whom I suspect to be T. G. Street, editor of Stuart's evening paper the *Courier,* whose own style seems usually easy to distinguish. And then there is the legend, evidently correct but imprecisely dated, that Stuart was assisted at times by his brother-in-law James Mackintosh—for whom Coleridge developed an especial loathing not wholly unrelated to the rivalry in their relation to Stuart. (If Sam was dilatory, Jem could write with more speed than the printer could follow.) Fortunately the style of James Mackintosh, the mechanics of his mind and rhetoric, cannot easily be mistaken for the style of Coleridge—as Coleridge himself was rather intensely aware. As early as 1796, in *The Watchman,* we find Coleridge inveighing, with Mackintosh in mind, against the style of "low-minded sophisters" as contrasted with the style of Edmund Burke, to which he recognized his own style was affinitive: "It seems characteristic of true eloquence, to reason *in* metaphors; of declamation, to argue *by* metaphors," he asserted in this connection.[21]

Mackintosh left a considerable canon of prose, and there are many

[21] *Essays,* I, 108. It is Professor Lewis Patton's observation that the passage alludes to Mackintosh.

essays in the *Morning Post* of comparable declamatory quality, whether by this or another sophister, all clearly distinguishable from the spirit and power of Coleridgean eloquence. Mackintosh often falls into mechanically parallel series, with frequent pairs of epithets or of any short members and a concluding triplet of short phrases or clauses. Unlike Coleridge's mountain stream his flow meanders or, more abruptly, causes the reader to be continually looking to right and to left like a spectator at a tennis match. (The Mackintoshian form of this would be: "like a judge or a spectator at a match or contest of the amiable sport of lawn tennis.") Mackintosh drifts carelessly from one metaphor to another, to the distress of anyone with an active imagination. Here is an example: "Desirous that my own leisure should not be *consumed in sloth,* I anxiously looked about for some way of *filling it up.* . . ."[22]

The main practical problem thus reduces itself to the differentiation of Coleridgean from Mackintoshian rhetoric and metaphor and from Stuartian horizontality of intellectual power. In practice the surest quick test, to be supported by whatever else affords, is the special quality of Coleridgean metaphor. That Burke was not alive and his writings were not of the right political orientation to have entered the pages of Stuart's paper in Coleridge's day simplifies the problem. If the differentiation from Burke's eloquence had to be attempted, the decisions would be immensely more subtle and difficult. And of course there remains the possible freak of fate that just in the period of Coleridge there was at Stuart's command a secret, unknown Anticoleridge who wrote with the same eloquence as Coleridge to baffle our research. But much of our internal evidence links phrases and images and especially whole metaphors with matter in the Coleridge correspondence and notebooks—to which we would then have to suppose our Anticoleridge to have had mysterious access. We may allow the argument from absurdity to eliminate this *Doppelgänger.*

The main thing is that Coleridge is a writer who can seldom proceed any distance incognito without being provoked into some ironic comment, some gesticulation of metaphor, or some metaphysical outcry that gives him away. Sometimes it is a single word: "sequaciousness," "weather-wisdom," "fugacious" ("a temporising, fugacious

---

[22] *Discourse on the Law of Nature and Nations* (London, 1799), first paragraph; my italics. See Coleridge's description of Mackintosh's style, *Notebooks,* I, 609.

policy"), "unadding" ("with as obstinate and *unadding* a fidelity" as a parrot,) "humanness" (a word he uses in 1806 in a letter as a conscious coinage, which is cited in the *OED* from a letter of his of 1802, and which appears in italics in one of the newly discovered essays of 1800 on Washington).[23] It may be a phrase: "the impolite obstinacy of events"; "the panic of property" (a favorite, used all his life); "the labyrinthine and improgressive steps of [Bonaparte's] tiresome figure-dance"; "enthusiasm and imagination, mutually feeding each other"; "the chasmy and incoherent accounts" of the French Constitution.

To reason *in* metaphors is to analyze their implications and employ them purposefully. An example: "assumed opinions . . . become real ones; the *suspension* of a tenet is a fainting-fit, that precedes its death." Another: efforts at free thought in France may be "as transient and void of immediate effect, as bubbles. . . . Yet still they prove the existence of a vital principle; they are the bubbles of a fountain, not such as rise seldom and silent on the muddy and stagnant pools of despotism." Here we have got into the large class of variants of his favorite "Medea's cauldron" image. Another is the "feculence, which has boiled up on the surface of the revolutionary cauldron" to be scummed off: this is found in a new essay of December 1799 and is, alone, almost enough for the identification—a clincher being the title, "Advice to the Friends of Freedom," which Coleridge repeats in a current letter in a list of contributions he says he is writing.

Two unmistakable "signatures" identify a paragraph of January 22, 1800, written as the answer of "The Editor" to a letter praising and criticising a number of editorials (which happen all to have been by Coleridge). We might guess that Stuart would ask Coleridge to write his own answer. But the matter is put beyond doubt by, especially, two characteristic flourishes of metaphor. In a reference to Ireland, the "parricidal faction" is exclaimed against "which has contrived, as it were, to mock a miracle of God, and make a Goshen of darkness in a land surrounded by dawning or noon-day light." The concept reappears in the *Biographia Literaria* (I, 168), where Coleridge speaks of "a land of darkness, a perfect Anti-Goshen."

Incidentally, the uninverted if not hackneyed use of this allusion may be cited from William Pitt. Switzerland, said Pitt, "had been exempted from the sound of war, and marked out as a land of *Goshen,*

---

[23] See "Coleridge on George Washington: Newly Discovered Essays of 1800," reprinted below, No. 24.

safe and untouched in the midst of surrounding calamities."[24] (It is curious that Pitt said this in Parliament just twelve days after the Coleridgean apologia in the newspaper. Coleridge sometimes remarked that the orators were drawing upon his newspaper eloquence. Did the freshening of the image only remind Pitt to use it in the old way? If so, it can be seen that Pitt effectually erased the signature.)

The other metaphorical flourish in this piece is the variant of another comparison used later in the *Biographia*, a special form of Coleridge's favorite play upon ventriloquism. The writer speaks of "Truth" as of "divine and spiritual" essence, and he "would personify Reason as a ventriloquist" who may throw her voice into any "uncouth Vessel." In the *Biographia* it is again Truth who is a divine ventriloquist; elsewhere it is Conscience who is a ventriloquist best heard when she throws her voice into the pocket (this first in the *Conciones* of 1795, last in the *Confessions of an Inquiring Spirit*). One may conjecture that this Answer got lost out of Coleridge's clipping file when he was writing the *Biographia*.

In illustration of Coleridge's use of metaphor as a precision instrument, let me cite three simple examples from physics, occurring three months and over two years apart.[25] The first, of political adaptability: "What a rare fluidity must a man's Principles possess, that can be emptied so rapidly from one mould into another, and assume, with such equal facility, the shape of each!" The second, of Pitt: "parental ambition [was] his mould—he was cast, rather than grew." The third, of the French Constitution: it was absurd to think "that a constitution could receive its final and faultless shape at one cast; that the passions of . . . the French, should run at once into the mould, like melted ores, and harden in a few hours into perfection." The third and second examples are from known works; the first is from a new discovery. The reasoning in each seems of the same fluidity and mould.

Coleridge himself was acutely sensitive to the difference in kind between good writing, in which "every phrase, every metaphor, every personification, should have it's justifying cause," and writing "vicious in the figures and contexture of its style." When Jeffrey deleted and replaced some paragraphs in an article Coleridge had submitted to the

[24] John Debrett's *Parliamentary Register* (London, 1800), x, 321: Feb. 3, 1800. A full-length (shorthand) report is Debrett's source on this occasion; usually he has only the very condensed newspaper reports of the debates to go on.

[25] *Morning Post*, Dec. 12, 1799, Mar. 19, 1800, Nov. 4, 1802.

Edinburgh Review, he cried out at the mutilation of his work by the insertion of paragraphs "in a vulgar style of rancid commonplace metaphors."[26]

Consider the rancid metaphor of cheese parings and candle ends for the spoils of office. Working back from the cheese to the creature it nourishes, Coleridge achieves this dramatic image of the effect of one's brother's elevation to prime minister on an insignificant creature like Hely Addington:

Mr Hely Addington is a true Bat! In the gentle owl-light of preferment, when it was neither light nor dark with the family, he soared aloft, as a bird; but now that the family greatness has risen, like the morning sun, he resigns the privilege of wings, becomes a true snug mouse, and feeds upon the cheese-parings and candle-ends.

This and other passages of the same power (though most of them lack close parallels in the canon)[27] seem to me effectually to establish

---

[26] *Collected Letters*, II, 812; *Biographia Literaria*, ed J. Shawcross (1907), II, 68; letter to Street, Sept. 19, 1809.

[27] The concordance does help now and then. If we look into "bat," "owl," "wings," "snug," and "mouse," we find a lament of 1796 about the "Statesman" and "Cit" and "Priest" who are secure in their preferment: "The Priest, and Hedgehog, in their robes are snug!" (the Bard, in contrast, being poor, naked, and luckless). In verses of about 1799 we find the true Statesman (William Tell) whose "soul found wings, and soared aloft." Finally, in a song of 1801, we find the New Philosophers, who are "but owls" and their trade "but *mousing*." All these might be mere coincidences. But years later (E. H. Coleridge guesses 1824 in *Poetical Works*, I, 451–453) Coleridge returned to and expanded the contrast between himself as Bard and the Cit and (this time) the comfortable true Bat. Like a true bird grown up among bats or rats, he was driven (he says) to denouncing these vermin:

> "He spared the mouse, he praised the owl;
> But bats were neither flesh nor fowl"

—whereupon they called *him* a hireling,

> "With place and title, brother Bat."

It would be stretching a point to say that in claiming to have denounced political bats Coleridge is alluding to the Hely Addington passage, but we may safely cite it as a case in point; as evidence we may note that the same image-cluster bears similar political meanings in both passages. (Add also, not from verse located via the concordance, but from prose in the *Courier* of Dec. 3, 1814: most "men live like bats, but in twilight, and know and feel the philosophy of their age only by its reflections and refractions.")

[*Postscript:* Howard O. Brogan calls attention to the fact that the "lament of 1796" assigned to Coleridge in his *Poetical Works*, because signed by him in a letter of 1796, is actually an excerpt from Robert Burns's *Epistle to Robert Graham* (1791). This shows that Coleridge's first use of the snug statesman the authorship of a newly found essay (March 22, 1802: discussed below) which is a sequel to one of the essays (December 3, 1801) which Sara Coleridge identified by internal evidence.

When Coleridge departed from the coherence of his usual style, he knew that he was doing so. "Yes, Gentle Reader!" he exclaims (in a painful self-burlesque, the "Historie and Gests of Maxilian," which he contributed to *Blackwood's* in 1822), "the diction, similes, and metaphors, of the preceding paragraph, *are* somewhat motley and heterogene. I am myself aware of it. But such was the impression it was meant to leave." Alert to structural and postural tensions, he will say of the French Constitution that it exhibits "a metaphysical posture-master's dexterity in balancing"; of an unimpressive argument: "How will it fly up, and strike against the beam, when we put in the counter-weights!"; but of the assertion that Jacobinism and Royalism completely counteract each other, that it is "a childish application of mechanics to the subject, in which even as metaphors, the phrases have scarcely any intelligible sense (October 5, 1802).

For a mature application of mechanics, itself a good definition of Coleridge's way of keeping to the same law throughout his paragraph, observe this comparison of the French Empire to an avalanche (in a new essay of January 6, 1803, which requires little more than this passage for identification). I quote only the vehicular part of the long comparison:

The mis-shapen mass of snow, agitated on the Alpine summit, descends . . . harmless and unheeded; but accumulating, and accelerating . . . , its track is marked by ruin and desolation. . . . The same law that hurried it through its course . . . conducts it . . . to the spot where its impelling force is to be exhausted, and [where] it is itself to vanish before a milder temperature.[23]

---

image was a borrowed one, but does not affect the main argument, which depends chiefly on the nexus between the Addington passage and Coleridge's prose of 1814 and verses of about 1824. There is no denying, though, that my error neatly illustrates a common hazard. Misled by unquestioned "external evidence," one is inclined to turn up presumably supporting "internal evidence," concluding, with the aid of a concordance or otherwise, that a passage actually written by X contains a metaphor characteristic of Y. Can one avoid such pitfalls? I think so—if one pays more attention than I did to all aspects of the style of the misattributed passage.]

[23] If we look up "avalanche" in the concordance, we come upon Coleridge's one use of it in verse in "Hymn before Sunrise," published only four months earlier. The word is so familiar now that we are startled to see the poet having

3: The Signature of Style

I conclude with two examples of decisions illustrating the relatively high value I feel required to place on internal stylistic evidence. In both instances there has appeared no direct external evidence[29] and the indirect external evidence is somewhat negative: Coleridge was not in London at the time of the appearance of either piece, though in one case the probability of his having sent it in after leaving town, and in the other of his having left it with Stuart before he departed, is not difficult to accept.

The first decision concerns an essay of April 21, 1800, one of Sara's handful of really "conjectural" attributions, for which she has this apology: it "has, perhaps, fewer particular marks of his style than the others; but from the general flow of the composition I think it may have been from his pen, and it will be useful in throwing light on those that follow. . . ."[30] I agree that the essay has few particular marks of Coleridge's style, and I distrust both my own and his daughter's impression of so vague a quality as the "general flow of the composition." If it fell within the period "of Mr. Coleridge's attendance," as Sara admits it does not, its claim would be more impressive. The style seems really a little too good for Stuart—but not, perhaps, for some Mr. X he might have engaged to replace Coleridge. I will grant that it is easy to *suppose* that Coleridge wrote this; I will not be surprised when some external evidence comes in to restore it to the canon. On the internal evidence it cannot stand.[31]

The second decision concerns the essay of March 22, 1802, entitled "Mr. Addington's Administration," belonging to a period when it would seem that Sara's access was to very incomplete files of the

---

to define it in a footnote: "The fall of vast masses of snow, so called"—as he does also in a variant line of the poem,

"The silent snow-mass, loos'ning thunders God!"

In our prose passage the "mass of snow" is loosened by being "agitated" but is at first "harmless and unheeded"; in the poem it is at first "silent" and "unheard." In the poem the snow, like other phenomena apostrophized, obeys the bidding of God; i.e. it obeys "the same law" that hurries, conducts, etc. This is a fairly firm testimony of common authorship, analogously speaking.

[29] External evidence has now been found for the second; see "Postscript," below.

[30] Essays, III, 1019. In her notebook list of "Conjectured" pieces she summarizes the *ideas* in this essay but finds no metaphor to jot down.

[31] This conclusion is embarrassing, because I made some use of the essay of April 21 in making a case for the Washington essays; yet the case will stand without it.

paper. For I take this to be the climactic essay in a series begun early the previous December, a series of four essays, one printed as a leader, only the first of which Sara collected—with a note to the effect that the promised sequel did not appear. I feel sure that if she had seen the three essays that did appear, each crammed full of particular marks of her father's style, she would have accepted them without question.[32] I do accept them, but there is a stumbling block that must be stepped over carefully. This climactic paper, on Addington, appears in the newspaper about two weeks after Coleridge is known to have left London. And in one passage (which I will distinguish as a separate paragraph, for convenience) there is some comment on a particular exchange of hostilities in Parliament, with a reference to London gossip upon it, that took place during the week Coleridge was on his way north or with Sara Hutcheson in Durham. There is time for Coleridge to have corresponded with Stuart or even to have written the whole essay, drawing upon reports from London, and to have mailed it in. But a likelier hypothesis is that he wrote the essay before his departure and that the paragraph in question was added by Stuart or Lane before publication. The essay can be seen to have been complete without this paragraph, which consists of a fortuitously fresh illustration of Addington's ineptness, the theme of the whole. And indeed this hypothesis stands up very well under the closest scrutiny—i.e. the closest scrutiny of the internal evidence.

In the first place, there is good reason to believe that the essay on Addington was written in February, a month or so before its publication March 22. At the conclusion of the preceding essay in the series, a leader of February 23, it is promised for "to-morrow."[33] And it is announced in the editor's notice box on several subsequent days:

24 February: "The Character of Mr. Addington's Administration is delayed by the press of temporary matter till To-morrow."

25 February: "The article on Mr. Addington's Administration to-morrow also."

[32] It turns out that Sara did see the March essay and make extensive notes on it; she even intended to cite it in her preface in support of her belief "that the view of the Add[ington] administration taken in that paper [the *Post*] was substantially my fathers, & that the material of argu[ments] spun out of the paper from time to time afterwards [after he largely ceased contributing in 1800, as she supposed] was all pulled out of what was around his distaff at the beginning" (VCL: S MS F10.3, omitting deletions); but for some reason she decided not to print the essay or this part of her preface. See "Postscript," below.

[33] It is actually first announced Feb. 15 for "To-morrow, or the first open day"; the leader of Feb. 23 was to serve as introduction.

3: The Signature of Style

27 February: "While Mr. Addington labours under domestic calamities [the serious illness of his daughter], we shall delay inserting the Article we have promised. . . . we apprehend it might look like harshness and want of feeling on our part to [bring] it before the Public at present."

True, there had been one famous occasion when Stuart's promise for "to-morrow" had gone unfulfilled by Coleridge, the promised "Bonaparte" as a sequel to "Pitt" in 1800. But that was really an exception to the *general* rule that Coleridge's essays *did* appear after the editor's announcements. Incidentally, these Stuartian announcements, linking the Addington with the other essays, constitute a supportive bit of external evidence of Coleridge's authorship—or at least of his intended authorship.

In the second place, Stuart could never have written the whole essay, with its shrewdly psychological-political anatomy of the "temporising, fugacious policy" of a weak prime minister "alternately vibrating between" the war party and the peace party instead of "acting on a solid foundation." Addington is exposed as a surprisingly unopposed politician at the moment who, "previously to his closing the brazen Temple of *Janus*" [i.e. signing the treaty of peace], must have paid "his devotions to the two-faced God" by making private overtures to both parties; a man of such "small talent" that in order for him "to climb up into office" there had to be "the steps of the *accommodation ladder*, all, no doubt, pre-adjusted" [one finds in a Coleridge notebook of this era (*N*, ɪ, 655) the cryptic phrase: "accommodation ladder/clamp"]; a time-server who had run "before the wishes of the Grenvilles to obtain their support during the war" and "now . . . promised to run before the wishes of the Opposition after the Peace," but whose initial "unconstitutional measures and personal insults . . . had raised a wall of separation between them and the new Minister, which he could not overleap. To effect an union, he was obliged to shew a disposition to undermine, and, like Pyramus, to breathe his amorous wishes through it." No one could have written this essay for the *Morning Post* in 1803 but Coleridge. There can be no question of Stuart's or Mackintosh's having written it to complete the Coleridge series. Yet there is the paragraph in it which I think Coleridge did not write.

We need not suppose that Coleridge left the essay unfinished. The added matter comes in fairly far from the end, and its addition to an already complete essay is a very easy thing to explain. For this (hypothetically) inserted matter brings the essay up to date by reference to Addington's "late contest [i.e. on March 4 and 9] with Mr. Robson, on the subject of the bill for 19 *l.* 10. protested at the Sick and Hurt Office," an affair in itself "of no importance" but decisive "as a test of Mr. Addington's abilities." "In the city there is but one opinion." To make clear the nature of this affair in Parliament, let me adduce a modern parallel rather than attempt to summarize the long-forgotten Addington's harassment by the plaindealing Mr. M. B. Robson. Suppose a modern Coleridge to have gone off on vacation leaving in an editor's hands an almost hilariously critical analysis of "Mr. Eisenhower's Administration." And then suppose the imprudence of Mr. Sherman Adams and the oversights of the federal regulatory agencies to have erupted into the news as, in March 1802, did the questions of Mr. Robson and the alleged insolvency of the Sick and Hurt Office and other government offices. (Stuart gave so much space to the hecklings of Mr. Robson and a Mr. Jones, that the city called his paper "Robson's and Jones's Gazette," he protested later.) In short, assuming (as the notices imply) the existence of a completed essay on Addington, insertion of some allusion to the Robson business was obligatory upon any editor worth his salt. How fortunate, indeed, that the publication had been delayed. Mr. Addington might have gone through his whole dreary administration without stumbling into so neat an illustration of Coleridge's remarks about his inability to "repair an error, or cover a retreat."

But what about the signature of style in this passage now given so lightly to Stuart? Let me make affidavit to having had the impression, even before the Robson problem arose, that, figuratively speaking, this particular leaf lacked any discernible watermark. When I proofread my first transcription of this essay from microfilm, I queried in the margin certain grammatical constructions that I thought might be misprints or might throw some slight doubt on Coleridge's authorship of the essay, for I found the transcription itself to be accurate. Now, several years later, returning to this essay, arriving at the Robson hypothesis, and scrutinizing the text closely, I observed that the parts I had queried were all in the passage I now suggested attributing to the editor. Except in careless haste Coleridge would not have written: "the manner in which he took up the subject disclosed his state of intellects" (if "intellects" is not a misprint). In the previous paragraph he had written: "His intellect is too short-sighted" etc. I doubted the authenticity of "convicted of one error . . .

he denied some other fact"; I questioned a preposition ("in moving" for "by moving"); and I wondered whether Coleridge would have spoken of a mind as being "composed" of "small wares." (Though this *idea* was one he expressed, particularly of Mackintosh, the image Coleridge used was of the mind as a warehouse, stocked with, not composed of, small wares.)

Naturally, if never confronted with the Robson problem I should never have taken pains to attribute this particular passage to someone else than Coleridge; the weak grammar I might have shrugged at possibly with a footnote suggesting typographical error or careless editing. Doubtless a minute scrutiny of other Coleridge essays might turn up passages weak enough to assign to Stuart or Lane; but this would be a treacherous game, serving little purpose. The conjecture is resorted to here only under the duress of contradiction between the date of the passage in question and the overwhelmingly Coleridgean style of the rest. It is fortunately a fairly clear-cut situation; the hypothesis brings all the text into clearest focus and may be accepted as proved. It affords perhaps the most extreme example of my reliance on internal evidence: if the Robson passage *did* contain the stylistic signature of Coleridge, I should be forced to suppose that the essay (or a patch upon it) was sent in from the north some time after March 9.

As for the whole fabric of the essay on the Addington Administration, I should certainly be unwilling to give it up; yet the evidence for attributing it to Coleridge (along with the three essays of December and February with which it is tightly linked) remains primarily the quality of the style and the particular characteristics of thought and feeling revealed in the major metaphors—including that "accommodation ladder" clamped also to the Notebook.

Postscript

So matters stood when I wrote this paper in July. Then I made a serendipitous visit to the British Museum. There, in the famous scrapbook of Coleridge autographs known as Egerton MS 2800, of which I believed I had all the significant papers in photostat and which I was looking through almost idly, I saw the words "accomodation-ladder" [*sic*] among some jottings on a torn scrap of paper (folio 142 verso). The rest of the jottings (63 words in all, 21 of them Latin) may be described as suggestions for some of the ideas expressed in the March essay on Addington. As for the other side of the bit of paper (folio 142 recto) it contains 165 words which, with some deletions and incompletions, amount to a rough and perhaps first draft of a part of the related essay of February 23!

This bit of paper changes the whole demonstration, of course. Now we have manuscript evidence, solid external evidence, for the attribution of two of the four closely related essays. With the quality of internal evidence that exists (I have given only a few features of it here) there can remain no hesitation about admitting all four to the Coleridge canon. And I must in all candor admit that, confident as I was about the Addington essay, I feel pleased and relieved to have the support of *both* kinds of evidence after all: especially since I now find from Sara Coleridge's papers that she did examine and take notes on this essay and yet reject it, unaware of the two linked essays preceding it and of the notebook passage and manuscript fragment related to it, and unwilling to venture, for a period when it was her belief that her father "did not contribute largely to the M Post," an attribution based on ideas and style alone.[34]

[34] For an independent attribution of the Addington essay, on the basis of a rather different web of internal evidence, see John Colmer's article, reprinted below, No. 25—Eds.

4

Salmons in Both, or Some Caveats for Canonical Scholars[*]

By Ephim G. Fogel

NOT a quarter passes without the appearance of articles on canonicity in the scholarly journals, and many of these articles rely to a greater or lesser extent on internal evidence. It is clear, then, that Dr. Erdman has provided a forum for the discussion of a persistent problem in literary scholarship.[1] The contributions thus far challenge those who have dealt with the problem to examine their methods and to clarify their principles.

I share with the previous writers in the series the assumption that internal evidence may be profitably employed in attributing authorship. Like Professor Sherbo, however, I think it highly desirable that scholars who attribute or deny a work to an author do so for the right reasons ("Uses," p. 6). The purpose of the remarks that follow is to provide a framework for evaluating the arguments of Dr. Erdman, Professors Johnson, Lord, and Sherbo, and contributors yet to come. I shall first set forth characteristic methods of analyzing internal evidence and shall then examine in some detail the application of these methods in the present series; it will therefore be relatively easy for the reader of the *Bulletin* to compare the original contentions with my criticisms. My chief concern, even when I dwell on particular works, is with general questions concerning kinds of evidence and forms of inference.

---

[*] The present article originated in some comments made from the floor of the English Institute following the delivery of papers by Professors Arthur Sherbo and George de F. Lord, Sept. 3 and 4, 1958. It is reprinted from the *Bulletin of The New York Public Library*, LXIII (1959), 223–236, 292–308.

[1] Articles on attribution reprinted elsewhere in this volume will be referred to by the following abbreviations: No. 24 (Erdman, "Washington"); No. 21 (Sherbo, "Smart"); No. 26 (Johnson); No. 27 (Erdman, "Sonnets"); No. 1 (Sherbo, "Uses"); No. 2 (Lord); and No. 3 (Erdman, "Signature").

I

In his Dialogue on the Drama, [Dryden] pronounces with great confidence that the Latin tragedy of *Medea* is not Ovid's, because it is not sufficiently interesting and pathetick. He might have determined the question upon surer evidence; for it is quoted by Quintilian as the work of Seneca; and the only line which remains of Ovid's play, for one line is left us, is not there to be found. There was therefore no need of the gravity of conjecture, or the discussion of plot or sentiment, to find what was already known upon higher authority than such discussions can ever reach.[2]

It seems advisable to begin with some observations on the role of external evidence in establishing an attribution that relies, in significant measure, on internal evidence.

For all practical purposes, the canonical scholar, as Sherbo conveniently terms him, is never confronted with "a pure specimen," a work which must be attributed on the basis of evidence that is absolutely internal. He is confronted, rather, with a work that he knows or rationally believes to be the product of a given moment in history, a work with special physical (bibliographical, paleographical), linguistic, and cultural characteristics, bearing the marks of time and perhaps of circumstance. "Mother Midnight," for instance, is one of Christopher Smart's many pseudonyms; *Mother Midnight's Comical Pocket-Book* was published in Smart's lifetime and contains poems of a sort that Smart wrote. Of course, this "indirect external evidence" (Coleridge-Erdman) or "internal-external evidence" (Warren and Wellek) is not in itself indicative of authorship.[3] But it provides a minimal foundation for erecting a hypothetical attribution to Smart. If The New York Public Library had acquired a pamphlet dated in 1589 and entitled *Martin Marprelate's Comical Pocket-Book*, Professor Sherbo would surely have had no thought of pursuing such an attribution.

Few will quarrel with the proposition that direct external evidence may be equivocal. Even an apparently bona fide signature may be misleading; the sonnet by Lamb to which Coleridge signed his initials and the unacknowledged contributions by Coleridge or Wordsworth

[2] Samuel Johnson, in the life of Dryden, *Lives of the English Poets* (Oxford, 1946), I, 303. This is but one of Johnson's many acute observations on problems of authenticity.

[3] For the first term, see Erdman, "Signature," *ad init.*; for the second, Austin Warren and René Wellek, *Theory of Literature* (New York, 1949), 58.

to each other's poems are neat cases in point.[4] And the further we get from the author, the more questionable does external testimony become. A publisher may falsely attribute a work to a popular author in order to increase sales; an early editor may interlard his author's works with those of other men; a contemporary compiler of anthologies and florilegia may often guess at authorship and not seldom guess wrong; an industrious forger of documents and books may bedevil research for decades. Sherbo seems to feel that scholars are excessively skeptical about internal evidence and not sufficiently skeptical about the external variety.[5] But an experienced scholar will surely be intelligently skeptical about both types and will bring to bear upon *all* attributions a stringent analysis.[6] To pit external against internal evidence is to set up a barren and unprofitable dichotomy.

Yet this is just what Sherbo seems to be doing. He wishes to establish the "basic premise" that in questions of canonicity "internal evidence deals with essentials while external evidence deals with accidentals" and that "short of an unequivocal acknowledgment by the author himself, the value of internal evidence outweighs any other" ("Uses," p. 7; cf. "Smart," p. 283). Like Professor Sherbo's skeptical friends, we must deny him this premise, for it is certainly too sweeping. At times external evidence may of course be "ancillary," but at other times it may be preponderant, and that without "an unequivocal acknowledgment by the author himself." S. F. Johnson's article, for example, convinces me that the "Lines on the Portrait of a Lady" are by Coleridge. But I hardly think that external evidence plays a merely ancillary role in gaining one's assent to the attribution. The poem was written before Coleridge had achieved a distinctive style and is uninformed by any distinctively Coleridgian concepts. Hence, if it had appeared as one of a series signed G. V. and F. rather than T. C. and S., and in a Tory journal rather than in Coleridge's *The Watchman*, the verbal parallels which Professor Johnson skillfully adduces, and which

---

[4] For the sonnet by Lamb, see J. D. Campbell's edition of Coleridge's poems (London, 1893), 575; E. H. Coleridge's edition (Oxford, 1912), 85; Erdman, "Sonnets."

[5] "Smart," 283–284; "Uses," 7.

[6] For some admirable examples of such analysis, see R. C. Bald, "*The Booke of Sir Thomas More and Its Problems*," reprinted below, No. 10; the papers on authenticity and attribution by Giles E. Dawson, Gerald E. Bentley, and Herbert J. Davis in *English Institute Annual, 1942* (New York, 1943), 77–100, 101–118, 119–136 (Bentley's is reprinted below, No. 12); and William A. Ringler, Jr., "Poems Attributed to Sir Philip Sidney," reprinted below, No. 16.

now clinch the attribution, would be very weakly probative of Coleridge's authorship. In this instance, therefore, the external evidence of the place and time of publication, and of Coleridge's initials, may be called "essential," whereas the internal evidence turned up by means of the Coleridge concordance seems "ancillary." But, to repeat, the dichotomy implied by such terms can easily become invidious and misleading.

In the present series, the soundest attributions on grounds of internal evidence are, I think, Erdman's and Johnson's. It is worth noting, however, that the direct and indirect external evidence for their attributions ranges from good to very good and that each scholar sets it forth fully. To this statement, Dr. Erdman's impressive analysis of the March 22 piece on "Mr. Addington's Administration" (Signature") is no exception. Let us assume that Erdman had not discovered Coleridge's holograph notes in the British Museum. His attribution of the piece on Addington would then rest to a very large extent on internal evidence. Yet in that case one could also point to several facts which owe their probative value to something other than the signature of style:

1. The March essay on Addington is the climactic one in a series, the earlier numbers of which were probably written by Coleridge.

2. Given the small number of contributors to the *Morning Post*, there is a suggestive coincidence in the use of the odd phrase "accommodation-ladder" both in Coleridge's notebooks and in the March essay.

3. The illness of Addington's daughter and the *Post's* delay in the publication of further attacks out of solicitude for the politician's "domestic calamities" provide external justification for the hypothesis that Coleridge wrote the essay before he left London even though its publication was delayed until some weeks after his departure.

What Dr. Erdman modestly calls a "serendipitous" discovery has of course transformed a probable attribution dependent on good circumstantial and excellent internal evidence into a certain one: the probative weight of a few jottings in an indubitable autograph is in itself instructive.

Dr. Erdman's and Professor Johnson's discussions indicate, in short, that the canonical scholar, like others, must take account of *all* the evidence which bears upon his problem. And "all the evidence" includes, among other things, time, place, and circumstance of publication, stylistic features common to an age or a genre, the absence or presence upon the scene of others capable of writing the work in question, and the authenticity of the received texts with which the work is being compared. Professors Lord and Sherbo, on the other hand, seem to me to be insufficiently comprehensive in their examination of evidence and insufficiently attentive to several perhaps obvious propositions:

1. Unless one can show beyond a reasonable doubt that a given work *B* is by a known writer *A*, parallels between *B* and an anonymous work *X* have little if any value in proving *A*'s authorship of *X*.

Sherbo cites a poem which Wilbur Cross "hesitantly attributes" to Smart and then proceeds to use parallels between this poem and several in the *Pocket-Book* as arguments for attributing the pamphlet to Smart. Here, to be sure, Professor Sherbo concedes that he is pushing a method "to its extreme." But the concession does not diminish the flimsiness of the procedure and of the resulting inferences. Similar difficulties tend to weaken Lord's article. He concludes with an argument which depends on a similar description of the Earl of Sandwich in the anonymous "Second Advice" and in a pamphlet published more than ten years later (1678) which Pierre Legouis "lists as *possibly* Marvell's" (p. 43, above; italics added). Lord's article is open to a more fundamental objection. To extend the canon of Marvell's satires is perilous when the canon is so dubious to begin with. Aside from "Last Instructions," which we may grant is Marvell's, Margoliouth prints sixteen satires attributed to the poet.[7] Four of these total only fifty-five lines, forty-four of them in Latin. According to Margoliouth, two of the remaining twelve satires are "certainly spurious" (I, 215, 322, 325). Considerable doubt attaches to four others and to portions of a fifth (I, 288, 292, 296, 303, 305). There is no "definite proof" of the authorship of three satires which Margoliouth believes may be Marvell's (I, 301, 310, 317). And until we have a much fuller analysis of the evidence than Margoliouth offers, significant degrees of doubt seem to me to attach to the remaining two (I, 263, 289). One can hardly build firm inferences about Marvell's satiric style on such uncertain foundations. A more secure basis for comparison could be established by a literary and statistical analysis

[7] For these sixteen poems, see I, 137–140, 165–205 of his edition. The following comments on the twelve varyingly doubtful poems are derived from Margoliouth's discussions of authenticity at the places indicated.

of the ten authentic Marvellian poems in heroic couplets, the common
meter of the "Advices" and "Last Instructions." These ten poems total
over 1,500 lines, and many of them are satirical or political.[8]

2. Where external evidence is extremely weak or contradictory,
only a powerful argument based on internal evidence—on specific,
very unusual, and intricately connected parallels of thought and style,
for example, or on highly significant frequencies of linguistic
usage—can hope to establish probable authorship.

Margoliouth indicates that the external evidence for Marvell's
authorship of the "Advices" is dubious (I, 269),[9] and Professor Sherbo
concedes that the external evidence for his attributions is weak. So
far as *Mother Midnight's Comical Pocket-Book* is concerned, the evidence is actually contradictory.

A. The *Pocket-Book* was printed at the end of 1753 for J. Dowse
in the Strand. In the December 1750 issue of the *Midwife*, however,
Smart represents Mary Midnight as insisting: "All her Pieces will be
printed, as usual, for T. Carnan, in St. Paul's Churchyard . . . and
for no other person."[10] On this last statement Professor Sherbo comments ("Smart," note 3), "This, I should say, is one way to strengthen
one's pseudonymity should one wish to employ another bookseller."
But the full context, which Sherbo does not provide, shows that the
obvious purpose of Mary Midnight's pronouncement was to protect
the Smart-Newbery-Carnan interests against unauthorized imitators.[11]

[8] See Margoliouth I, 3–5, 83–87, 90–99, 103–119, 123–132; the poems in
couplets are used as a basis for comparison in Section III, below.

[9] Lord makes the external evidence seem far stronger than it is. The manuscript
received by Captain Thompson contained non-Marvellian poems, and Thompson
was an incompetent editor. Margoliouth (I, 213) calls his preface "a masterpiece
of confusion"; Hugh Macdonald states that he was "without critical judgment"
and included in his edition poems "which were known not to be by Marvell"
("Andrew Marvell's Miscellaneous Poems, 1681," *Times Literary Supplement*, July
13, 1951, 444). Margoliouth's rejection of the second and third "Advices" is
unequivocal (I, 270).

[10] Quoted in Edward G. Ainsworth and Charles E. Noyes, *Christopher Smart*
(Columbia, Mo., 1943), 45. The *Midwife* was one of the many enterprises of
John Newbery, the bustling "philanthropic bookseller" of *The Vicar of Wakefield*,
and was published under the imprint of his stepson Thomas Carnan. Smart was
very closely associated with Newbery and married his stepdaughter in 1753
(Ainsworth and Noyes, 36–73).

[11] The first number of the *Midwife* appeared in October 1750. In the December
issue Mary Midnight was already complaining about "good people who have
borrowed her Name to vend their Stuff," promising to satirize them in "the
Old Woman's Dunciad," which would "contain the *most choice* Collection of
Drivellers and *Humdrums* that ever was exhibited to publick view." Smart's

4: Salmons in Both: Some Caveats

Professor Sherbo is in effect suggesting that Smart was at this time playing a subtle and far-sighted double game: what seems like a warning against imitators is transformed, if we follow Sherbo, into a Machiavellian preparation for future pseudonymous printing of Mother Midnight material under the auspices of a bookseller other than Carnan or Newbery—a pseudonymous publication which the poet finally managed to effectuate about three years later, a few months after he had married his publisher's stepdaughter, Anna Maria Carnan.[12] As Sir Edmund K. Chambers says, "You can always explain away an historical record, with a sufficient licence of conjecture as to the *mala fides* of its origin."[13] But though poor Christopher Smart had a fair share of human frailties, scholars will perhaps wish to show more charity to the poet's memory than Sherbo's far-fetched theory seems to imply.

B. An acrostic poem on page 25 of the *Pocket-Book* which is entitled "The Author's Epitaph" spells out the name "Joseph Lewis." Sherbo disposes of this irritating fact by excogitating some bold assumptions. He suggests (page 286 below) "that Joseph Lewis is a ghost, that he never existed, but that if there was a Joseph Lewis, Smart usurped his obscure name (for who has seen any work by Joseph Lewis?) for his own purposes of mystification." At this point one remembers Professor Sherbo's admission, while engaging in a minor excursion on the identity of a Mr. Dowse who was "found dead upon a dunghill at an inn in High Holborn," that he "may be accused of excessive hypothesizing" ("Smart," note 1). He also admits that his ignorance of an eighteenth-century poet called Joseph Lewis does not constitute proof of Lewis' nonexistence. True enough. In every period there are obscure hacks on the fringes of literature and inglorious amateurs content to compose for their own or their friends' amuse-

---

enemy William Kenrick promptly brought out a fraudulent *Old Woman's Dunciad* "by Mary Midnight," purportedly printed for "Theo. Carnan," "containing/ The most choice Collection of *Humdrums* and *Drivellers*,/ that was ever expos'd to public View" (Ainsworth and Noyes, 45–46). This imposture impudently advised the public to beware of impostures and imitations such as Mary Midnight's warning in the *Midwife!* Incidentally, the emphasis on *Humdrums* may have something to do with the fact that the author of the *Comical Pocket-Book* is said to be Mother Midnight's grandson, Humphrey Humdrum.

[12] They were married before November 1753, possibly in June or July of that year (Ainsworth and Noyes, 72–73).

[13] "The Disintegration of Shakespeare," *Shakespearean Gleanings* (Oxford, 1944), 2.

ment. Some of these versifiers occasionally achieve the dignity of a printed signature appended to an undistinguished performance, transmitting to historians nothing more than a dim name. No Elizabethan scholar need be embarrassed by his failure to recognize "R: Hyther," "George Burgh, Cantabridg.," and "Simon Carril, Gen.," contributors of commendatory verses to Sylvester's Du Bartas. Hyther, writes Franklin B. Williams, Jr., is "a complete nonentity"; Williams does not maintain that Hyther never existed or that he is merely a mask for a better-known writer.[14]

Given the external evidence, scholars guided by economy of assumption will probably conclude that the *Comical Pocket-Book* is an anonymous imitation, possibly by one "Joseph Lewis," of Mother Midnight's contributions to the *Midwife*. It would take overpowering internal evidence, I think, to change this conclusion. But unfortunately, the internal evidence which Professors Lord and Sherbo offer in support of their attributions is weak, and the principle which they repeatedly invoke to justify the extensive citation of such evidence is dubious. In the following sections, I shall attempt to clarify the grounds of this judgment.

II

I tell you, captain, if you look in the maps of the 'orld, I warrant you sall find, in the comparisons between Macedon and Monmouth, that the situations, look you, is both alike. There is a river in Macedon; and there is also moreover a river at Monmouth. It is call'd Wye at Monmouth; but it is out of my prains what is the name of the other river; but 'tis all one, 'tis alike as my fingers is to my fingers, and there is salmons in both. [Fluellen, in *Henry V*, IV, vii, 24–31]

Fluellen's delightful analogy between the lives of Henry of Monmouth and Alexander of Macedon would be no more convincing if he had said that there were salmons and minnows and trout in the Wye, and salmons and minnows and trout in the river in Macedon. His interlocutor, Captain Gower, might well ask whether that particular combination of fluvial fauna was excessively rare. Fluellen's fallacy is rife in current literary scholarship. Investigators posit sources and influences, or discover intricate, hitherto unsuspected allegories, by an arbitrary excision of parallels, in disregard of a poem's total pat-

[14] "An Initiation into Initials," University of Virginia *Studies in Bibliography,* IX (1957), 164.

tern. Canonical scholars are by no means the most reticent representatives of Fluellen's method. Among this number, one must in my opinion include Professors Lord and Sherbo. Professor Lord enrolls himself in Fluellen's ranks tacitly, by his assumptions and procedures; Professor Sherbo is in effect an aggressive advocate of Fluellen's fallacy, challenging scholars to explain why they refuse to accept it. I shall try to use Lord's and Sherbo's particular arguments to illustrate the general character of the fallacious presuppositions and methods, and I shall contrast these with legitimate methods of attacking canonical problems.

We are concerned with the following question: how can one show that a dubiously attributed work, or an anonymous work without direct evidence of authorship, or a portion of a work by several authors (X), resembles one or more of an author's authentic works (A_1, A_2, A_3, . . . A_n) so closely that identical authorship is the most probable explanation of the resemblance?

There seem to be three main methods of arriving at a solution. They almost always occur in dyadic or triadic combination; for the sake of convenience, however, we shall discuss each one separately. The first method, which we may call "internal-external analysis," raises problems similar to those presented by the authentication of external evidence. The second and third methods aim to define the style, vocabulary, and other characteristics of X and A_n. The second, which we may call "literary analysis," relies mainly on judgment, taste, and inference, and is at its best an art. The third, which we may call "statistical analysis," relies on objective, quantitative indications and aspires to the mathematical and scientific. Each of the three methods has certain advantages and certain limitations.

Internal-external analysis attempts to assess bibliographical, paleographical, and philological evidence or to associate allusions in the text with contemporary persons and events so as to narrow the chronological limits of composition and to eliminate possible authors or admit them to candidacy. Bibliographical and paleographical evidence often plays a very important part in the attribution of works in manuscript. More pertinent to our concerns, however, is the analysis of contemporary allusions. It is employed by Lord when he argues that the second and third "Advices" satirize the same figures as does "Last Instructions"; by Sherbo when he associates the *Pocket-Book* and Smart's writings with Thomas Rosoman and Peter Hough of Sadler's Wells, with a trunkmaker at the corner of St. Paul's Churchyard, and with "Dr. Rock"; and by Erdman when he rejects the hypothesis of Coleridge's authorship of the August 19, 1803, article on Hatfield.

When we analyze contemporary references, our historical information must first of all be accurate. Secondly, we must interpret allusions correctly, both as to literal meaning and as to tone and intention, and fully, i.e., in relation to the whole context. I have not seen the *Pocket-Book*, for instance, and so I cannot evaluate its references to "Dr. Rock." Are they serious and sympathetic? If so, that fact tells against the presumed parallel with the note in Smart's *Hilliad*, which is certainly satirical. I have, however, examined all the verse satires discussed by Professor Lord, and it seems to me that he fails to take into account certain *patterns* of internal-external evidence and that several of his items of presumed evidence depend upon misreadings. As to the first objection, the meetings of the House of Commons are central to the spirit and structure of "Last Instructions" (see Section III, below), whereas the second and third "Advices" deal with Parliament very cursorily and concentrate upon the naval actions of 1665 and 1666. To Margoliouth (I, 270), this difference in emphasis is an important argument for the non-Marvellian authorship of the "Advices." But I should like to focus on Lord's misreadings.

Arguing that the second and third "Advices" are by the same hand, Lord finds the following link between the two. The third begins with an allusion to the Duke of York's love for the young wife of Sir John Denham, and "this reference was anticipated in 'Second Advice' by the poet's promise to draw 'Madame l'Édificatress' in his next. (Denham was Surveyor-General, the Royal Architect.)" But in the version I have before me,[15] the unknown poet of "The Second Advice" who assumes the mask of "Sir John Denham" makes no such promise. Throughout his poem, he parodies Edmund Waller's original "Instructions to a Painter," a fulsome panegyric on the Duke of York's naval action against the Dutch, and presents the Duke as an indolent, incompetent commander. When he finishes his account, he calls attention to the discrepancies between Waller's and his own ("Denham's") version of the facts:

> Now may Historians argue *con* and *pro:*
> *Denham* says thus; tho always *Waller* so:
> And he, good Man, in his long Sheet and Staff,

[15] In *Poems on Affairs of State*, "The Fifth Edition" (1703), 24–33; "The Third Advice" is on 34–45.

4: Salmons in Both: Some Caveats

This Penance did for *Cromwell's* Epitaph.
And his next Theme must be o'th' Duke's Mistress;
Advice to draw Madam *l' Edificatress.*

The parodist is not here promising "to draw 'Madame l'Édificatress' in his next." He is slyly predicting that *Waller* will do so, that the "good Man" whose "Advice" egregiously flattering the Duke of York is a kind of penance for his earlier eulogy of Cromwell will now have to compound his penance by writing still another panegyric, an "Advice to Draw the Duke of York's Mistress, Lady Denham." Lord has mistaken the parodist's parting thrust at the Duke and his flatterer for internal-external evidence of authorship.

More serious misreadings seem to me to occur in Lord's interpretation of references to George Monck, Duke of Albemarle. Most of "The Third Advice" is concerned with Monck, who is represented as the administration's drudge in every emergency. Quoting a passage from "Last Instructions" which includes the following lines,

> Often, dear Painter, have I sate and mus'd
> Why he [Monck] should still b'on all adventures us'd,

Lord states that the allusion "seems to show Marvell claiming 'The Third Advice' as his own creation" (p. 37). In this passage the poet ironically assumes a puzzled air, wondering why the administration constantly calls upon a commander and a Parliament that it despises. But even if the poet's *sitting and musing* about Monck is taken to be actual rather than fictional, it is surely not to be equated with his *writing* about him. And if we allowed this curious interpretation, we should still have to prove that the poet is referring to "The Third Advice" rather than to some other poem about Monck. But this would be a difficult task, I think, for although Lord says that "The Third Advice" and "Last Instructions" are "both rather equivocal" about Monck, the two poems adopt vastly different tones and attitudes toward him. More than half of "The Third Advice" is an irreverently comical and at times scatological description of both Monck and his wife. Introduced as "the *Monky Dutchess* all undrest," she climbs a ladder, careless of what the groom and coachman who support it see, and like a "*Presbyterian* Sibyl," in a prophetic fury, with her belly sounding and her udder bounding, snarls out a six-page bawdy, "viraginous" soliloquy. She several times refers in the following vein to a wound which Monck received in the buttocks:

79

the *Dutch* in hast prepar'd,
And poor Peel-Garlick *George's* Arse they shar'd.

And the poet in his own voice speaks of Monck with similar merriment and high spirits, pouring gay ridicule upon him even in the midst of praise.[16]

We may admit that Monck's political career was ambiguous. But if Marvell ever regarded Monck in the partly hilarious, partly contemptuous fashion of "The Third Advice," I can find no record of that fact. Quite the contrary. In 1653, he praises the three naval commanders, "those piercing Heads, *Dean, Monck and Blake*" ("The Character of Holland," line 150). After the Restoration, he sees General Monck often on business, writes to the mayors of Hull that Monck receives their petitions and their representatives (including himself) very favorably, and refers to the general in friendly fashion.[17] Not long after Monck's death, Marvell concludes a long familiar letter to his nephew William Popple with the following complaint:

The King would needs take the Duke of *Albemarle* [Monck] out of his Son's Hand, to bury him at his own Charges. It is almost three Months, and he yet lys in the Dark unburyed, and no Talk of him. He left twelve thousand Pounds a Year, and near two hundred thousand Pounds in Money. His Wife dyed some twenty Days after him; she layed in State, and was buryed, at her Son's Expence, in Queen *Elizabeth's* Chapel, And now,
    Disce, puer, Virtutem ex me verumque Laborem,
    Fortunam ex aliis. [March 21, 1670, Margoliouth, II, 302]

The view of Albemarle in "Last Instructions" is consistent with this record. Even the passage quoted by Professor Lord, though it has perhaps some slight ambiguities, mentions Monck's "Valour" and "*Herculean* Labours" (compare "Virtutem" and "Laborem," above), and looks upon Monck as an obstacle to Clarendon's drive for arbitrary power (lines 515, 520–523). A later passage (596–628) presents a sympathetic picture of Monck grief-stricken and enraged at the Dutch depredations, particularly at their seizure of the *Royal Charles*,

That sacred Keel, which had, as he, restor'd
His exil'd *Sov'raign* on its happy Board.

[16] The total effect is negative rather than "equivocal." So too thought Pepys, who on Jan. 20, 1666/7, borrowed "'The Third Advice to a Paynter,' a bitter satyre upon the service of the Duke of Albemarle the last year."
[17] See Margoliouth, II, 9, 62, 77–80, 237–239, 249.

4: Salmons in Both: Some Caveats

And still later the poet writes of the valiant Scot Douglas, who went down in flames with his ship:

> And secret Joy, in his calm Soul does rise,
> That *Monk* looks on to see how *Douglas* dies. [675–676]

Granted, then, that one can find Albemarles in both "The Third Advice" and in Marvell, they are by no means as "alike as my fingers is to my fingers," and it seems to me that Professor Lord has some explaining to do about the differences. To me these differences constitute one excellent argument for believing that the two satires are by different hands.

Suppose, however, that the contemporary allusions in two works are genuinely parallel. Whether that coincidence is probative of common authorship depends on the relative frequency of such allusions. Do Smart's contemporaries refer often or very seldom to Thomas Rosoman, Peter Hough, and "Dr. Rock"? What is the probability of any one literary man's mentioning all three names in the course of a sixty-four-page pamphlet such as the *Pocket-Book*? And from what data and mathematical operations are the answers derived? Professor Sherbo does not raise, let alone answer, such questions, but I imagine that the allusions he cites were not especially rare. Any literary man who frequented so familiar a place as St. Paul's Churchyard might refer to the trunkmaker at the corner; any versifier who had passed pleasant hours at Sadler's Wells might wish to commemorate its deceased proprietor Rosoman and that "well-known facetious Mortal," also deceased, Peter Hough.

Since contemporary references play a far greater role in Lord's essay than in any of the others in the present series, the question of the rarity of the particular allusions is in his case critical. Obviously, a great many of Marvell's contemporaries could and did refer scathingly to Clarendon. After garnering uncomplimentary references to the Chancellor from "Last Instructions" and the second and third "Advices," Lord himself concedes this point. "But the details of the other figures," he maintains, "are almost all, to the best of my knowledge, peculiar to these three poems, and though some bits and pieces may appear in contemporary sources other than political verse, there is scarcely a trace of them in the mass of verse satire which the 1660's produced" (p. 37). Let us test the *a priori* peculiarity of these satirical representations, however, by examining the details concerning Sir William Coventry.

After citing Bishop Burnet's and Pepys's high opinions of Coventry, Lord remarks: "That the three satires should represent as cheat, coward, and ruthless egotist a statesman and executive whose integrity, efficiency, and ability are witnessed by two such authorities increases the likelihood that the caricatures issued from one hand" (p. 32). But why not from different writers hostile to the administration or dissatisfied with the conduct of naval affairs? As Secretary of the Navy, Coventry—who, by the way, in a letter to Thomas Thynne "admitted himself to be a Trimmer" (Margoliouth, I, 278)—was an obvious target. Lord makes much of the fact that in all three satires Coventry is accused of selling offices. He fails to mention that Coventry's selling of offices was hotly discussed throughout the 1660's, that the charge was frequently aired in Parliament, before which Coventry frequently defended himself, and that the whole subject runs like a red thread through Pepys's comments on his superior. Here are a few characteristic entries from the *Diary:*

12 October 1663. At St. James's we attended the Duke, all of us. And there, after my discourse, Mr. Coventry of his own accord begun to tell the Duke how he found that discourse abroad did run to his prejudice about the fees that he took, and how he sold places and other things; wherein he desired to appeal to his Highness, whether he did any thing more than what his predecessors did, and appealed to us all.

14 June 1667. [Mr. Pierce] says that they are in great distraction at White Hall, and that every where people do speak high against Sir W. Coventry; but he agrees with me, that he is the best Minister of State the King hath, and so from my heart I believe.

28 October 1667. [Coventry] owns that he is, at this day, the chief person aymed at by the Parliament—that is, by the friends of my Lord Chancellor, and also of the Duke of Albemarle. . . . He says, he is so well armed to justify himself in every thing, unless in the old business of selling places, when he says every body did . . . [13]

"Every where people do speak high against Sir W. Coventry." I shall spare myself and the reader from the tedium of citing contemporary witnesses who supply parallels to the criticisms in the second and third "Advices" and "Last Instructions" of Arlington, Clifford, and the Duke and Duchess of York.

It seems obvious that three separate references to Coventry's or

[13] See also Pepys's entries of June 7, 1662, Oct. 30, 1662, May 24 and 31, 1663, June 2, 1663, Oct. 4, 1666, Jan. 18 and 20, 1666/7, Dec. 30, 1667, Mar. 1, 1667/8.

Arlington's malfeasance, whether in prose or in verse, are no more probative of common authorship than are three Opposition charges of malfeasance leveled against any administration from Clarendon's to Eisenhower's. Just as topical lampoons tend repeatedly to caricature a public figure's physical features,[19] so do they also tend repeatedly to satirize outstanding instances of his alleged misconduct. And once this tendency is acknowledged, Lord's internal-external evidence for Marvell's authorship of the second and third "Advices" falls to the ground. It seems likely that between June 1665 and November 1667[20] several poets hostile to the ruling group might concur in satirizing the real or presumed defects in appearance, wisdom, and probity of its chief members. And if the same constellation of figures does not occur in satires written after the fall of Clarendon, that is probably because new persons moved into top posts and new events furnished grist to the satirists' mills. Fluellen's fallacy, the "proof" of a thesis by carefully selected fragments of a total pattern, can vitiate historical as well as literary and statistical analysis.

III

Literary analysis attempts to indicate that the thought, structure, and style of X are overwhelmingly similar to or dissimilar from those of A_n. It seems likely that some intuitive judgment of essential similarity or dissimilarity precedes the application of more detailed and rigorous tests, whether circumstantial, statistical, or literary. But oracular judgments cannot be taken on faith, no matter who the oracle; on the Shakespeare canon, for instance, even Johnson and Coleridge were fallible. Eventually, the canonical scholar, however acute and well informed, must call attention to the particular and manifold resemblances or differences which underlie his instinctive impressions.

At its best, literary analysis is comprehensive. It refers to numerous

[19] Exaggerated representations of Clarendon's obesity or of Arlington's disfigured nose are thus no more indicative of identical authorship than are exaggerated representations of John L. Lewis' bushy eyebrows in political cartoons of the 1930's and 1940's.

[20] The dates, respectively, of York's victory at Lowestoft and Clarendon's flight to France. Mary T. Osborne's finding list, *Advice-to-a-Painter Poems: 1633–1856* (University of Texas, 1949), indicates that the four pseudo-Denham "Advices" and "Last Instructions" are the only "Advices" between these dates which satirize the administration. Since "Last Instructions" satirizes about sixty-five persons (Osborne, 37), it is all the more natural that many of them appear in the second and third "Advices."

and intricate combinations, to the total quality of the works being compared, to their conception, design, and manner. The evidence it yields is diverse, ranging from nuances of phrasing and delicacies of rhythm to startling peculiarities of thought and bold, characteristic arrangements and concatenations of parts. It is abundant in proportion to the length of the work; it is cumulative, since each subdivision of the work may offer additional instances of the author's particular style, unusual point of view, or characteristic ordering of materials. Yet literary analysis can yield valid results from a passage of moderate length. The celebrated additions by Hand D in *The Booke of Sir Thomas More,* for example, from which R. W. Chambers and Caroline Spurgeon derive their powerful arguments for Shakespeare's authorship, run to but 147 lines, a total which is gravely inadequate for the kind of thoroughgoing statistical analysis envisaged by G. Udny Yule.[21] And literary analysis can sometimes arrive at highly probable conclusions about a quite short passage—a sonnet or a paragraph of prose.

In the hands of a scholar who has a sense of proportion and a keen awareness of an author's configurations of thought and patterns of style, the literary method can be extremely effective. In his outstanding essay, R. W. Chambers draws remarkably close parallels to "D's" view of the consequences of disorder, and of various other matters, from the *Henry VI* plays, *Richard II, Henry IV Part II, Julius Caesar, Troilus and Cressida, Hamlet, Lear, Coriolanus,* and *The Winter's Tale.* As R. C. Bald emphasizes, "Chambers marshals his evidence to show not mere isolated parallels but whole sequences of thought and associated groups of images common to both D and Shakespeare."[22] Erdman's papers on the Coleridge canon also stress repeated "clusters of associated words" ("Sonnets"), "intimate and intricate connections" with particular authentic essays and with Coleridge's deepest habits of thought and imagination ("Washington"). This search for *Gestalten* rather than *Bruchstücke* is surely indispensable to any successful literary analysis.

In attributing an anonymous work, the canonical scholar should not overlook the larger features of literary art, an author's constructive

[21] Chambers, "Shakespeare and the Play of *More,*" *Man's Unconquerable Mind* (London, 1952), 204–249; Spurgeon, "Imagery in the *Sir Thomas More* Fragment," *Review of English Studies,* vi (1930), 257–270. If we generously assume seven words per line, the additions by Hand D total 1,029 words, just about 10 per cent of the minimum required by Yule for his analysis of nouns alone: see *The Statistical Study of Literary Vocabulary* (Cambridge, Eng., 1944), 281.

[22] "*More* and Its Problems," below, p. 170.

power, his ability to fuse action, character, diction, and other elements into a complex, unified whole. Thus Hereward T. Price refutes J. Dover Wilson's attribution to George Peele of the first act of *Titus Andronicus* by showing that the materials there are "severely controlled as never in Peele," whose powers of construction are extremely weak.[23] The continuous relevance of the speeches from the opening lines, the swift introduction of the leading characters and the clear portrayal of their interrelationships, the ironical theme of evil resulting from a perverse conception of good, the manner in which the actions of an individual implicate the whole political order—all this is beyond the art displayed in Peele's known plays but exactly in conformity with Shakespeare's principles of construction. Professor Price comments drily (p. 40): "Professor Wilson asserts that he has read through the whole of Peele for his vocabulary. It is also obvious that he has completely ignored Peele's [and Shakespeare's] dramatic technique."

Literary analysis has limitations, of course, and the scholar must observe certain precautions. It is not very useful when one is confronted with pieces that are undistinguished in thought and manner. Contemporary works in the same genre by different authors—two love-poems, let us say—may resemble each other more than two works by the same author in different genres—say, a satire and an amatory song. This is especially true in the earlier periods of our literature, when even the best authors tended to resort to commonplaces of thought and when they had fairly well-defined views of the style and diction appropriate to particular genres, and in the shorter literary forms, where individuality of treatment usually has less opportunity to manifest itself than it has in an extended treatise, a long narrative, or a drama. R. W. Bond, to choose a sobering illustration, believed that many unacknowledged lyrics by Lyly were buried in Elizabethan printed and manuscript anthologies; he felt that as an editor "impregnated as [he] necessarily was with [Lyly's] thought and phrase, [he] might enjoy the best chance of recognizing [Lyly's] hand. . . ."[24] Lyly, Bond argued, was in his prose "the recognized high-priest" of the following literary methods: "the continual strain after ingenious love-conceits . . . the constant habit of buttressing or illustrating an argument by appeal to natural phenomena, real or supposed . . . a proverbial and gnomic tendency, often verging on platitude . . . the

---

[23] *Construction in Shakespeare* (Univ. of Michigan Contributions in Modern Philology, No. 17, 1951), 37–40.

[24] "Lyly's 'Doubtful Poems,'" *The Athenæum* (May 9, 1903), 594.

use of antithesis."[25] Although Bond admitted that these methods were common to the age, he nevertheless proceeded, with the specious aid of isolated parallels of thought and phrase, to add to the Lyly canon scores of pieces never before attributed to him.[26] The results were painfully embarrassing. Only a few months after Bond saw his edition through the press, H. Littledale expressed doubt that Lyly had written a single line of the newly attributed poems and pointed out that some of the pieces which Bond had confidently claimed for Lyly were by Sidney, Spenser, Shakespeare, Robert Southwell, Anthony Munday, William Baldwin, John Higgins, and others. Bond was forced to confess that he had "overrated the importance of phrases" and allowed "too much to merely general sentiment."[27] He inserted errata slips in the unsold copies of Lyly's *Complete Works,* but the unhappily attributed pieces, and the copious notes defending their inclusion, still clutter the standard edition of an important Elizabethan writer.

The absence of a distinctive style from an anonymous work does not mean, however, that a given poet could *not* have written it. In the British Museum manuscript Harley 7392 (article 2), ff. 27ᵛ–28, there appears an amatory poem, "But this and then no more," with the attribution "FYNIS. G. O. R."[28] Puttenham quotes from the poem four times, ascribing one of the quotations to Sir Arthur Gorges and two to Sir Edward Dyer.[29] Helen E. Sandison at first was certain, on stylistic grounds that the poem could not be by Gorges; later, when it turned up in the manuscript "The Vanytyes of Sir Arthur Gorges Youthe," Professor Sandison was compelled to retract, and she has since printed it as an authentic piece in her edition of Gorges' poems.[30] Given the ambiguous external evidence before the discovery of "The

[25] *The Complete Works of John Lyly* (Oxford, 1902), III, 436–437.

[26] III, 433–502. The poems were printed, it is true, as "doubtful," but Bond wrote, "Of many I entertain no real doubt" (I, 387).

[27] In *The Athenæum* (May 16, 1903), 626. Littledale's criticisms are in the issues of Feb. 28, 1903 (274), and Apr. 4, 1903 (435–436). See also the unsigned review of Bond's edition, Feb. 14, 1903, 199–200. Later research has shown that the songs printed by Edward Blount in Lyly's *Six Court Comedies* (1632) are also apocryphal: see W. W. Greg in *Modern Language Review,* I (1905), 43–52, and John R. Moore in *PMLA,* XLII (1927), 623–640.

[28] Printed by Bernard M. Wagner, "New Poems by Sir Edward Dyer," *Review of English Studies,* XI (1935), 468–469.

[29] See *The Arte of English Poesie,* ed. Gladys D. Willcock and Alice Walker (Cambridge, Eng., 1936), 211, 227, 236, 237.

[30] See Professor Sandison's comments in *Review of English Studies,* XIV (1938), 449–452; *PMLA,* LXI (1946), 109–113; and *The Poems of Sir Arthur Gorges* (Oxford, 1953), xl, 26–27, 190–191.

Vanytyes," and given the absence of a very distinctive style in Dyer's and Gorges' known poems, one would have done well to be noncommittal as to authorship. On the other hand, no one after considering the results of Professor Johnson's concordance tests should refuse to admit "Lines on the Portrait of a Lady" to the Coleridge canon merely because "the poem is written in the insipid manner characteristic of much of the verse of the time."[31]

Good imitations, writes Samuel Johnson, "are, by the best judges, often mistaken."[32] Hence, the scholar who would prove that X and A_1 are by the same pen must take into account the possibilities that X is a reminiscence, plagiarism, imitation, or parody of A_1, or that X and A_1 are imitations of Y, or that two authors have each arrived independently at similar views and treatments of the same subject matter. This precaution is all too often disregarded. The disintegrators who find Peele's, Marlowe's, and other poets' hands in Shakespeare's earlier plays have failed to allow for Shakespeare's appropriation of others' phrases, sentiments, and techniques. Professor Lord does not give sufficient weight to similarities due to common imitation of Waller's "Instructions to a Painter." When "a good friend" objects that the parallels between the *Pocket-Book* and Smart's work "could be explained away individually and that the clear echoes of Smart's poetry could be coincidence or clever imitation," Professor Sherbo replies: "This is, I submit, to advance the implausible in the face of the eminently plausible" ("Uses," p. 10). But the objection is, on the contrary, entirely sound both in principle and in particular application. Professor Sherbo knows perfectly well that there *were* several imitations of Mother Midnight's poems before the *Pocket-Book* was printed.[33] Moreover, the very title page of the *Pocket-Book* suggests that it is yet another imitation, "Carefully Cook'd-up by Mother Midnight's merry Grandson . . . Humphrey Humdrum, Esq." And finally, Sherbo's own article on Smart concludes with a signal instance of failure to consider the present caveats. The parallels which Robert E. Brittain found between "The Benedicite Paraphrased" and Smart's "A Song to David" are far more startling than anything that Sherbo puts forward for Smart's authorship of the *Pocket-Book*. Both poems are in the same stanza, which Smart also uses for the *Psalms* and other poems. Both the *Benedicite* and Smart's *Psalms* expand one verse

[31] Lewis Patton's objection, as referred to in Johnson, below, No. 26.
[32] *Johnson on Shakespeare*, ed. Sir Walter Raleigh (Oxford, 1957), 73.
[33] See note 11, above.

of the original texts into one stanza of paraphrase, and both develop their expansions in similar ways. Furthermore, the tone and the rhetorical devices of each poem are very much alike. Unfortunately, Brittain did not ask whether the "Benedicite," which is in fact by James Merrick, might have influenced the later "Song to David."[34]

A writer's style will of course vary from one lustrum, occasion, genre, or subdivision to another. If in a play by Shakespeare one finds majestic poetry, bawdy prose, hair-splitting wit, and rattling doggerel, that does not mean, as the disintegrators would have it, that non-Shakespearian hands are at work. It means that Shakespeare, naïve bardolatry notwithstanding, had no wish to be continuously sublime and that he desired different effects in different scenes or speeches. Rigid expectations of a single manner are bound to distort canonical studies.

On the other hand, the style of an original talent is *sui generis*, and whatever lies at the heart of its mystery cannot be inferred from a few shreds and patches. A microscope may tell us many things about a bit of lint and a loose thread, a milligram of ink and a millimeter of paper, but such wisps and minims cannot tell anyone much about the shape and fit of the whole garment or the flow and formation of the whole script. "Stile," as Puttenham says, "is a constant & continuall phrase or tenour of speaking and writing, extending to the whole tale or processe of the poeme or historie, and not properly to any peece or member of a tale . . . [a] continuall course and manner of writing or speech [which] sheweth the matter and disposition of the writers minde, more than one or few words or sentences can shew."[35] Hence, when Professor Sherbo provides us with ten brief excerpts and asks us to identify those that are Johnson's, or when he asks "how many sentences that a majority of Johnsonians would declare his must predominate over non-Johnsonian sentences or parts of sentences before the whole [of an anonymous piece] would be accepted" into the Johnson canon ("Uses," pp. 11–13, 9), he is indulging in yet another manifestation of Fluellen's fallacy. One cannot subtract fragments and snippets that do not sound Johnsonian from those that do and give "An Essay on Elegies" to Johnson if there is a positive remainder. If the whole manner of the essay, its constant

---

[34] In their replies to Brittain, both Philip R. Wikelund and Alan D. McKillop make this point: see *ELH, A Journal of English Literary History*, IX (1942), 140, and *PMLA*, LVIII (1943), 582.

[35] *Arte of Poesie*, 148.

and continual tenor of writing, seems un-Johnsonian, it makes no difference that a half-dozen pieces and members resemble pieces and members in Johnson's authentic works. 'Tis not a phrase or clause we Johnson call, but the joint force and full result of all.

After reading and rereading "An Essay on Elegies," after making every allowance for lapses, "unbuttoned moods," and deliberate variety of effects, I can only say, This is surely not the voice, this is surely not the manner of the master. Most of the sentences lack the point and the cadence, the weight and the vigor, the exactness of diction and the clarity of outline of Johnson's prose. Some of them, like the last sentence in the essay (a limp and shapeless conclusion, that!) and the last in the third paragraph, are overburdened and sprawling. Others contain solecisms and infelicities that Johnson would probably have shunned: e.g., the use of "less" in the sense of "fewer," the crass sentence-fragment in the fourth and the clumsy failure of parallelism at the end of the second paragraph. But most important of all, the whole essay, in its diction, tone, and movement, strives constantly for a "gentlemanly" lightness of touch that seems foreign to Johnson's work. "As Pope *handsomely* says of his own," "*not to mention* our own Cowley,"[36] "the politer moderns *are for putting* [the plaintive muse's] *hair into papers*," "tho by that means, *many a putter together* of long and short verse in Latin, and many an alternate *rhymist* in English, had been *at a loss to know* what species of poetry he *writ in*": to me, all this sounds decidedly un-Johnsonian. How often, if ever, does Johnson use the phrases that I have italicized? Is he given to writing "writ" as a preterite or to ending sentences with a preposition? Since we do not have a concordance to Johnson's prose, it may be difficult, as Professor Sherbo protests, to give precise answers to such questions. But we do have Johnson's *Dictionary*, which Sherbo uses skillfully, along with other tools, to discredit Parr's attribution of the preface to Hampton's Polybius. It would do no harm if Sherbo used these instruments with equal ruthlessness against his own attribution. He would then find that the *Dictionary* recognizes "rhymer" and "rhymster" but not "rhymist," that it lists the nouns "putter" ("one who puts") and "putter on" ("inciter; instigator," with but two citations, both from Shakes-

---

[36] Since "our own Cowley" is linked with "the affected Italians, and ridiculous French poets," the phrase can hardly be chauvinistic or sentimentally patriotic (Sherbo, "Uses"); it is rather one of the essayist's many gestures toward urbane informality.

peare) but not "putter together," and that its definition and illustration of the verb "to put together" ("to accumulate into one sum or mass") do not seem to permit the sense "to compose," which of course underlies *X*'s breezy noun. So far as sentence-structure, grammar, diction, and the entire intrinsicate complex of style are concerned, the odds are heavily against Johnson's authorship of "An Essay on Elegies."

Professor Lord's attributions to Marvell seem more probable, on purely literary grounds and on the first approximation, than does Professor Sherbo's assignment of "An Essay on Elegies." Both the second and third "Advices" are vigorous, witty poems, and the former is at the same time sufficiently serious and responsible to justify careful inquiry into the possibilities of Marvell's authorship. Moreover, "Last Instructions" and the two "Advices" are mimeses of some length, cast in a special poetic convention, and involving imaginative, constructive, and technical powers beyond those called for by a brief essay or poem. Professor Lord is thus presented with a fine opportunity for the application of comprehensive literary analysis as a test of authorship.

Lord's remarks at the beginning of the final section of his essay are promising. He finds that the two "Advices" and "Last Instructions" display "similarities in structure, in imagery, in wit, in tone, and in diction" and that they "are the only ['painter' poems of the Restoration] which effectively use the convention and integrate the painter device with the subject matter" (p. 38). Unfortunately, however, Lord proceeds to cite as probative of Marvell's authorship interpretations of isolated images that seem no less forced and irrelevant than those that have been noticed earlier;[37] devices of diminution, irony, wit, and wordplay that are common to satires of all ages; and mythological allusions drawn from Ovid's *Metamorphoses*, a work familiar to anyone who in the fourth form of grammar school had copied it, construed it, parsed it, scanned it, recited it, imitated it, double-translated it, adorned it, amplified it, divided it, analyzed it, memorized it, and tried to "turn the same into most varietie of English verses."[38] This is not the integral criticism of parts in terms of wholes which

[37] Among other things, I have in mind Lord's curious notion that there is an intentional link between a reference to a microscope in one poem and a gibe at a dwarf in another, and that the allusions to Crete in the passages on Charles II are significantly parallel to those in the passage on Roger Palmer. See pp. 78–80, above, for an analysis of kindred misreadings.

[38] These exercises are prescribed for fourth-form students of the *Metamorphoses* in Charles Hoole's *A New Discovery of the Old Art of Teaching Schoole* (London, 1660), 161–162 (sig. G10^{r-v}).

Lord's introductory comments might lead one to expect; it is a Fluellen-like culling of fragments, a triumphant discovery of "salmons in both"—and such common salmons too.

If, in contrast to Lord's procedure, one studies the second and third "Advices" and "Last Instructions" as artistic wholes, one finds that, though all three are parodies of Waller's "Instructions," they nevertheless differ so radically in the use of the painter convention, in structure, and in style, as to indicate very strongly that they must be sired by three different fathers.

Marvell's authentic poems reveal a precise literary decorum, a severe sense of appropriateness, in accordance with which all elements subserve the poem's larger purposes and conform to its artistic presuppositions. His praise of Milton is characteristic:

> Thou hast not miss'd one thought that could be fit,
> And all that was improper dost omit.[39]

Now of the painter poems discussed by Professor Lord, "Last Instructions" is unique in its full exploitation of the values and its meticulous observance of the limits inherent in the "Advice" convention. When one asks a painter to represent the events of actual life, one cannot require him to depict speeches, for that is beyond a painter's art and scope. Waller himself realizes this when, after expressing in six lines of direct quotation the Dutch people's fear of York's forces, he apologizes:

> Painter! excuse me, if I have awhile
> Forgot thy art, and used another style.[40]

But the next two "Advices" violate the painter convention without troubling to apologize: "The Second Advice" gives in direct quotation an angry speech of twenty lines (131–150), and "The Third Advice" concludes with a six-page harangue by "the *Monky Dutchess*" which takes up at least half of the poem.[41] In contrast, "Last Instructions"

[39] "On Mr. Milton's *Paradise Lost,*" lines 27–28. See also the poem "On Doctor Witty's Translation of the Popular Errors" and the comments on Rev. Simon Ford's "advice" on the burning of London (Margoliouth, II, 296, 352; Osborne, *Painter-Poems,* 28).

[40] Lines 287–288, in G. Thorn Drury's ed. of the *Poems* (London, 1893), 186.

[41] Ed. 1703, 39–45. The poet, whoever he is, makes a clumsy attempt to tie this soliloquy to the "advice" convention: "Paint thou but her [the Duchess], and she'll paint all the rest." But this quibble on "paint" only underlines the indecorum.

does not contain a single line of direct quotation. It consists of a series
of tableaux which are both aptly satirical and genuinely pictorial. The
poet is aware at all points of the difference between his and the
painter's art and from time to time makes the distinctions overt:

> Dear *Painter,* draw this *Speaker* to the foot:
> Where Pencil cannot, there my Pen shall do't;
> That may his Body, this his Mind explain. [863–865]

> Express him startling next with listening ear,
> As one that some unusual noise does hear.
> With Canon, Trumpets, Drums, his door surround,
> But let some other Painter draw the sound. [907–910]

> And ghastly *Charles,* turning his Collar low,
> The purple thread about his Neck does show:
> Then, whisp'ring to his Son *in Words unheard.* . . .
>   [921–923; italics added]

The poet regards himself as a collaborator who must not push the
painter out of bounds, and he uses their collaboration to bring his
"advice" to a neat conclusion:

> *Painter* adieu, how w[e]ll our Arts agree;[42]
> Poetick Picture, Painted Poetry.
> But this great work is for our *Monarch* fit,
> And henceforth *Charles* only to *Charles* shall sit.
> His Master-hand the Ancients shall out-do
> Himself the *Poet* and the *Painter* too. [943–948]

It can be said, then, that "Last Instructions" thoroughly "integrates
the painter device with the subject matter," but "The Second Advice"
at one point fails conspicuously to do so, and "The Third Advice"
simply butchers the convention.

Because of its gross violation of decorum according to genre, because of the abyss between its treatment of Monck and Marvell's,
and because of many other considerations, we may exclude "The
Third Advice" from the Marvell canon. But the breach of decorum
in "The Second Advice," it may be argued, is after all more venial
and hence insufficient to eliminate that satire from candidacy. How
does "The Second Advice" compare with "Last Instructions" and with

---

[42] 1703: "How well our Arts"; Margoliouth: "how will."

Marvell's authentic poems so far as structure, style, and learning are concerned?

In order to satisfy myself as to the literary probability of Marvell's authorship of "Last Instructions," I have compared it carefully with all of Marvell's authentic poems in heroic couplets. In the details of style and in the larger elements of composition, it is of a piece, I find, with the authentic work. This original, superbly integrated poem, longer than any other now known to be Marvell's, is entirely worthy of him.[43] It commands with complete sureness a remarkable range of effects: ferocious satire and idyllic pastoral; the Spenserian allegory of the grief-stricken Medway and Thames and the Chaucerian genre painting of the Speaker of the House; the stylized tableau of young Douglas' immolation and the pictorial realism, the Rembrandt-like chiaroscuro, the supernatural chill of the windblown interview between Charles and the apparitions. Above all, its construction is masterly. An imaginatively conceived action, with parts proportioned and disposed so as to contribute to the harmony of the whole, unifies the historical events. And a consistent point of view, aware of complexities and enriched by a knowing irony, controls the action, characterization, description, tone, and all the other aspects of the poem. "Last Instructions" does not merely play a stream of witty satire over the surface of current events. It is distinguished by its deep and principled criticism of the health of "our *Lady State.*" It continually exposes the moral and political roots of recent military and diplomatic debacles, interpreting them as the inevitable results of rule by corrupt, incompetent courtiers who wish to isolate the king from his country and who constitute a rapacious faction in Parliament. Against this vicious and powerful group, the poet sets a divided and scattered parliamentary coalition, which, for all its inadequacies, nevertheless represents the country and the strongest elements of which are

> A *Gross* of *English Gentry*, nobly born,
> Of clear *Estates*, and to no Faction sworn;
> Dear Lovers of their King, and Death to meet,
> For Countrys Cause, that Glorious think and sweet:
> To speak not forward, but in Action brave;
> In giving Gen'rous, but in Counsel Grave. [287–292]

---

[43] Taken together with the internal-external evidence, the literary evidence makes Marvell's authorship highly probable. The poet is clearly a member of Parliament, and it seems very unlikely that any other poet then in Commons could have written the satire.

At every stage of its progress "Last Instructions" holds tenaciously to this point of view, supporting it by full accounts, at the beginning, middle, and end of the poem, of the conflict between the Clarendon-court faction and Parliament (lines 105–348, 469–478, 505, 518, 807–884, 988), enforcing it by a recurrent contrast between sturdy patriots and frivolous, cowardly, or venal courtiers, deepening it by a wonderfully effective mock-epical style,[44] driving it home by savage yet beautifully controlled satirical thrusts, and clinching it by its final reminder to Charles that the king and the country must be one, that "scratching *Courtiers* undermine a *Realm*," and that a monarch whose courtiers are independent, wise, courageous, and friendly to Parliament can rule without a private standing army.

I find this kind of originality, close-knit imaginative unity, fine proportioning of parts, continuous drive and relevance, and sharpness of diction and imagery in such Marvellian poems in couplets as "Tom May's Death," "The Character of Holland," "The First Anniversary," "On the Victory by Blake," and "Upon the Death of Cromwell." I do not find these qualities in "The Second Advice." It is commendable enough in itself, but next to "Last Instructions" an inferior performance. It is loosely structured, trailing after the chronology of actual events without imposing on them a unifying idea or artistic pattern. It is unoriginal in form: it follows Waller's "Instructions" closely even in the minutiae of its parody, e.g., in the use and placement of brief similes and in the Jove-Crete-Charles analogy of the address "To the King."[45] In range of learning and literary allusion, the poet of "Last Instructions" is much richer than the poet of "The Second Advice" (X). He alludes to Spenser, Chaucer, and chivalric romance, as X does not. His references to ancient and modern painters and the painter's art and to foreign geography and customs are more frequent, more concrete, and in most cases more apt than are X's. His classical learning is more dense and intimate. Indeed, the very diction and structure of the Latin verse-sentence have permeated his mind, so that his word order, like Marvell's, is much more heavily inverted and Latinized than X's. I have room to document but one item of the

---

[44] Cf. the traditional question to the Muse (147–150), the catalogue of the court faction and their opponents (151–306), the ironical comparision of Clarendon to Jove (355–360), the expansive or massed similes (551–560, 623–628, 677–690), the echoes of Virgil (693–696, 845–848).

[45] Most of Waller's similes are but two lines long, as are all the similes in "The Second Advice," with the possible exception of ll. 45–48. (In the 1703 ed. there is a period after l. 46, but this may be erroneous.)

last point: both Marvell and the poet of "Last Instructions" are fond of radical subject-object inversions, of which Marvell's friend Milton furnishes the most familiar English examples;[46] no such radical inversions occur in "The Second Advice." And finally "Last Instructions" differs from "The Second Advice" in versification. It has a greater percentage of run-on lines and a greater variety and boldness of pauses within the line; it also has a much lower proportion of multiple rhymes, being quite close in this respect to Marvell's authentic heroic couplets.[47] Nowhere in "Last Instructions" or Marvell's poems, moreover, do we get three pairs of multiple rhymes in succession, as we do in both the second and third "Advices."

On literary grounds, then, the probabilities are against Marvell's having written the second as well as the third "Advice." The evidence is insufficient to justify printing either of these poems as Marvell's "and thereby adding," as Margoliouth says (I, 270), "to the body of satires of doubtful authenticity which already pass under his name."[48]

IV

As we have seen, information about the relative frequencies of certain allusions and literary devices may be necessary to evaluate internal-external data or to check on subjective literary impressions. Statistical analysis of internal evidence can also be an effective method of attribution in its own right. It aims to give precise mathematical indications of such features as prosody, sentence structure, vocabulary, and linguistic usage, and it has the advantage of being applicable to works not notably distinctive in technique and style. Although no particular items in the vocabularies of X and A_n may be very striking, the relative frequencies with which ordinary terms occur may well be significant.

[46] E.g., "Thee, the Year's monster, let thy Dam devour" ("Last Instructions," 740; see also 31, 142–146, 289–290, 673–674). Cf. Marvell, in Margoliouth I, 91, ll. 55–56; I, 108, ll. 215–216; I, 112, l. 377; I, 124, ll. 31–32; and I, 127, l. 171. I have made no effort to list all instances.

[47] In Marvell's 1,520 lines of heroic couplets, I count 14 lines with multiple rhymes; this total includes the doubtful "endures-*Sewers*" ("The Character of Holland," 51–52) but not "prepare-prayer" or "pow'r-showre" ("On the Death of Cromwell," 185–186, 323–324). In the 990 lines of "Last Instructions," and the 364 of "The Second Advice," there are, respectively, 14 and 12 lines with multiple rhymes. In percentages, the proportions of multiple to masculine rhymes are as follows: Marvell, .9%; "Last Instructions," 1.4%; "The Second Advice," 3.3%.

[48] Cf. Osborne *Painter-Poems*, 28, n. 3.

Statistical studies require a careful definition of the population being investigated, an accurate count of possibly significant traits, and an adequate interpretation of the data thus assembled. Such analysis can be time-consuming even when the population under study has been narrowed down to two candidates and Anonymous. "If you want to show that the author of B (not the author of C) is also the author of A," G. Udny Yule points out, "you must show that the vocabularies of A and B are, not merely *alike*, but *more closely alike* than the vocabularies of A and C"; Yule finds that such a demonstration raises special statistical problems.[49] Obviously, the problems increase when there are a large number of candidates, for we must then show that one candidate's linguistic patterns are more nearly like X's than are those of all the other candidates. If by the use of electronic computers we could accumulate reliable linguistic frequencies for many authors of a given period, we might conceivably be able, in the absence of other evidence, to assign a dated anonymous work by comparing its linguistic frequencies with those already assembled. But would there not still be a reasonable chance that the anonymous work was written by a minor or obscure author not included in our computations? Would it not be necessary even then, as it is necessary now, to lighten the burden of proof by using external or internal-external evidence to reduce the number of candidates?

In any case, it does not require special training in mathematical or logical probability to see that the theory behind Lord's and Sherbo's citation of isolated parallels is untenable. Sherbo states that "a series of weak or minor arguments" depending on a series of "minor agreements" (or "commonplaces" or "coincidences") becomes, "in its totality, something other than the mere sum of those commonplaces . . . results in something more startling and rare than any one coincidence, however extreme it may be and however weak the individual coincidences may be" ("Uses," pp. 10–11), and Lord writes to similar effect. These formulations, and Sherbo's "analogy of the easily broken separate twigs and the much greater resistance of a number of these twigs bound together," are question-begging. They assume that we begin with items which can be called "evidence" or "arguments" (or "twigs"), however weak, and that these separately weak "arguments" or unimpressive "bits of evidence" or individually brittle "twigs" are not merely juxtaposed but are in some way united, so that a large sum or a strong bond results from the union. But commonplace parallels, unsupported by information about the relative fre-

---

[49] *The Statistical Study of Literary Vocabulary*, 247, ix.

quencies of the commonplaces in the work of potential candidates, fall into the category of "arguments" which R. W. Chambers calls "so unreliable as not to be arguments at all,"[50] zeros which add up to zero no matter how great their number. We do not have in Lord's or in either of Sherbo's essays a tidy, tight little bundle of twigs, but a random array of dead leaves, withered stalks, and bits of bark.

Is it not absurd, for example, to imagine that the mere occurrence in both Smart and the *Pocket-Book* of common nouns like "theme" and "caudle" is any kind of "evidence" for single authorship?[51] Or again, are the female breasts mentioned in both Smart and the *Pocket-Book* distinguished by any extraordinary features such as, say, a mole cinque-spotted? No, Sherbo admits, they have only the usual charms blazoned by poets from Ovid to Keats, "but no poet I know seems to have been so fascinated with this part of the female anatomy as Christopher Smart," and moreover one of the descriptions in the *Pocket-Book* occurs in a poem "in praise of Bessy's and Nancy's charms" and one should not forget "that Smart's wife's name was Nancy and she is frequent in his poetry." As to the first point, supposing it to be true, Sherbo makes no effort to show that the *Pocket-Book* and Smart are closer to each other in the fascinated frequency of their references to breasts than are Smart and other eighteenth-century poets. And as to the second, a poet who puts his wife's attractions into public comparison with Bessy's seems downright ungallant. But Sherbo is apparently not much worried about the dishonesty and grossness which he newly imputes to Smart while he is engaged in adding another item to the Smart canon.

Suppose we move from commonplaces to "uncommon agreements." Sherbo finds six of these in Johnson's work and in "An Essay on Elegies" ("Uses"), but none of them seems uncommon, even at first glance. The word "ditty," for example, is frequently applied to amatory poetry from the Tudor period onwards, and the phrase "amorous ditties" (Sherbo's sixth and final "uncommon agreement") occurs twice in *Paradise Lost* (I. 449, XI. 584).

What is involved here is more than a failure to check "ditties" in the *OED*, the concordances, and the dictionaries of quotations. It is a failure to grasp an important principle. An assertion of rarity is essentially a statistical assertion. In order to make it stick, the scholar will have to check frequencies with whatever means are available, from computers to laborious perusal of hundreds of poems and dramas.

[50] *Man's Unconquerable Mind*, 208.
[51] "Smart," 290–292; for the quotations in this paragraph, see pp. 288–290.

Thus R. W. Chambers, with the help of an assistant, checked all known dramas between 1580 and 1610, and found that the comic mispronunciation of *ergo* as *argo* or *argal* occurred only three times—twice in Shakespeare and once in Hand D's additions to *Sir Thomas More*. Such exact statements have a force that a subjective impression of rarity, even when it is the impression of a scholar as richly endowed as was Chambers, can never achieve. Yet Chambers immediately adds, in italics: *"But the occurrence of this word* ["argo"] *in itself is nothing, compared with the context in which we find it"* (p. 215). His case for Shakespeare's authorship does not depend on several genuinely uncommon agreements, but rather on complex stylistic and conceptual patterns in D and in Shakespeare.

A scholar who has not made a thorough check would do well to exercise the greatest caution in labeling usages "rare" or "uncommon." A widespread tradition can cause a seemingly odd phrase to occur in a variety of authors, as I once learned to my embarrassment. In arguing that two sonnets in the Fortress of Beauty triumph (1581) were by Sidney, I accumulated verbal parallels, one of which seemed especially striking. A speaker in the triumph refers to "the bowed knees of kneeling hearts," and Sidney, in his metrical version of Psalm 5, adds to the Biblical text the phrase "knees of my heart will fold." Professor William A. Ringler, Jr., who has since printed the two sonnets in his edition of Sidney's poetical works, was dubious about the value of parallels but agreed that the two rather strained metaphors of a heart with bending knees seemed sufficiently curious to be in some small degree probative of common authorship. When I happened to mention the conceit, however, to my colleague Jóhann Hannesson, curator of the Fiske Icelandic Collection, he informed me that the same metaphor occurred in a seventeenth-century Icelandic hymn.[52] Meanwhile, Professor Ringler had come upon several Elizabethan occurrences of the conceit, and he suggested, quite rightly, that I drop the verbal parallels altogether.[53]

[52] Stanza 9 of the twenty-fourth hymn of Hallgrímur Pétursson's *Passíusálmar*, or *Hymns on the Passion* (1666), adjures the soul to bend *"the knees of* flesh and *heart"* ("holdsins og hjartans kné"). Mr. Hannesson, who very kindly translated and commented upon the relevant portions of the hymn, points out that Stanza 8 of the hymn paraphrases and Stanza 9 applies the Gospel text describing the soldiers' mock homage of Christ: "and *they bowed the knee before him,* and mocked him, saying, Hail, King of the Jews!" (Matthew 27:29).

[53] On the Fortress of Beauty sonnets, see essay No. 17, below, and *The Poems of Sir Philip Sidney*, ed. Ringler (Oxford, 1962), 345–346 and 518–519.

4: Salmons in Both: Some Caveats

Properly used, statistical analysis holds great promise for canonical studies. New concordances produced by new techniques will lighten the burden of frequency checks and of other vocabulary studies.[54] Literary scholars cooperating with computer engineers may develop new methods of analyzing anonymous texts. And meanwhile, the scholar's unaided eye and brain can arrive at very convincing results. We may conclude the present section with a brief notice of an excellent series of articles, Cyrus Hoy's "The Shares of Fletcher and His Collaborators in the Beaumont and Fletcher Canon."[55]

Professor Hoy uses with admirable thoroughness criteria used earlier on a smaller scale by A. H. Thorndike, R. B. McKerrow, W. W. Greg, and others. Hoy counts all occurrences in the unaided work of Fletcher and his collaborators of about a dozen forms such as *ye*, *hath*, and various contractions (e.g., *'em, i'th'*). Some of the differences in usage frequencies are startling: the pronoun *ye*, for example, occurs over four thousand times in fourteen of Fletcher's unaided plays and only twice in fifteen unaided plays by Massinger. This virtually absolute opposition of preferences is "quite exceptional," however, "in the annals of the Jacobean collaborated drama" (VIII, 135); usually, the linguistic forms are present in the unaided work of each collaborator, but in different frequencies. If a number of linguistic forms occur in sufficiently distinct frequencies in the unaided work of a given writer, similarly distinct patterns of preferences should emerge in the portions of a collaborated play for which that writer is responsible. Professor Hoy marshals his evidence very skillfully. He moves systematically from the known, the demonstrably unaided dramas, to the unknown. He eliminates the possibility that the linguistic forms are due to compositorial intervention, takes account of the tendencies of known theatrical scribes to reproduce an author's linguistic preferences with greatly varying degrees of accuracy, and deals at length with the knotty problems posed by a play originally written by one dramatist and later revised by another. Where Beaumont, for instance, gave final touches to a play by Fletcher, Professor Hoy states frankly

[54] A series of Cornell Concordances, prepared with the aid of IBM computers, has been in progress since 1957. Already in print are concordances to the poems of Matthew Arnold (ed. Stephen M. Parrish [1959]), William Butler Yeats (ed. Parrish [1963]), and Emily Dickinson (ed. S. P. Rosenbaum [1964]).

[55] *Studies in Bibliography*, VIII (1956), 129–146; IX (1957), 143–162; XI (1958), 85–106; XII (1959), 91–116; XIII (1960), 77–108; XIV (1961), 45–67; and XV (1962), 71–90. [Only four installments had appeared when the present essay was first printed. The first installment is reprinted below, No. 14.—Eds.]

that his method runs into difficulties: Beaumont firmly changed Fletcher's *ye*'s to *you*'s; the frequencies of other forms in the unaided works of each dramatist are not essentially different; Beaumont's linguistic patterns tend to vary from one play to another (xi, 85–87, 90, 93). In certain plays, therefore, Hoy must rely upon metrical and dramatic rather than linguistic criteria.

It is for specialists in the Beaumont and Fletcher canon to pass final judgment on Professor Hoy's success in disentangling the various collaborators. I am impressed, however, by his heroic labors, his careful procedure, his awareness of complicating circumstances, and his scholarly objectivity. His study deserves to be consulted by anyone interested in the use of internal evidence.

V

"Let us, once and for all, stand up and be counted," writes Professor Sherbo. "If there are legitimate objections to the use of internal evidence, or to my presentation, let them be stated and examined" ("Uses," p. 22). There can of course be no objections to the proper use of any valid method of discovering truth; one can no more "be counted" against internal evidence than one can array himself against inductive logic. In the present essay, I have tried to indicate the fruitful *uses* of internal evidence by scholars such as Chambers, Erdman, Johnson, and Hoy, and what I consider the *abuses* of the method by Lord, Sherbo, and others. If the faults criticized were peculiar to the writers mentioned, they could be quickly forgotten. But they are on the contrary very widespread in canonical studies, and too many of us, transported by the mode, have at one time or another offended.

It is one thing to offend, however, and another to ask that the offense be approved by a vote of confidence. As I listened to Professor Sherbo's paper, and as I later read it, there were times when I felt that he wanted us to give canonical scholars carte blanche to succumb to a number of very seductive fallacies. "Partisan enthusiasm" can invigorate scholarship, but as Professor Sherbo recognizes, it can also obscure the scholar's vision. Trifles light as air are to the zealous confirmations strong as proofs of holy writ. Among such trifles few are more airy or more exhilarating than isolated parallels—salmons in both, or Coventrys and Albemarles in both, or caudles or amorous ditties in both, or hearts with bending knees in both. Understandably so, for these illusions marshal us the way that we were going. But they must be rejected as unreal mockeries even, paradoxically, when they are genuine. If our attribution depends entirely or very largely on such "evidence," we should resolutely refuse to impose it upon editors and readers. But if we nevertheless persist in clogging the channels of scholarly communication with Fluellen-like special pleading, our peers will have no choice but to reply to us as a duke once replied to the wild allegations of a partisan senator:

> To vouch this is no proof,
> Without more wider and more overt test
> Than these thin habits and poor likelihoods
> Of modern seeming.

Comments on the
Canonical Caveat[*]

By George de Forest Lord

What shall I say? Where's satisfaction?

. . . . .

If imputation, and strong circumstances,
Which lead directly to the door of truth,
Will give you satisfaction, you may have it.
(*Othello*, III,iii)

IN my original presentation I argued that two notable verse satires
of the Restoration, *The Second and Third Advice to a Painter*, should
be attributed to Andrew Marvell, who wrote the well-known "Last
Instructions to a Painter." My ascriptions were based primarily on
internal evidence: "Last Instructions" is a sequel and conclusion to its
two precursors; it takes the same views toward the same principal
public figures; it employs the painter convention in a similar way;
it alludes to the same myths; and it exhibits the same kind of wit.
I also drew to some extent on external evidence: on contemporary
statements that Marvell was the author and on the evidence of a manuscript compiled by the poet's nephew which, according to Marvell's
eighteenth-century editor, contained the second and third "Advices."
Finally, I used one bit of internal-external evidence to link "The Second Advice" with *Flagellum Parliamentarium*, a parliamentary blacklist of Court supporters which has sometimes been ascribed to
Marvell.

I was first drawn to the idea of Marvell's authorship of these two
poems after two years' study of the political verse written in the later
Stuart era. I had read several thousand such poems in miscellanies,

[*] A reply to the preceding essay by Ephim G. Fogel. Reprinted from the
Bulletin of The New York Public Library LXIII (1959), 355–366, with the author's
permission.

manuscripts, and broadsheets, and I was struck by the fact that the two "Advices" resembled "Last Instructions" far more closely in matter and manner than did any of the other political poems I had read—far more closely, indeed, than any of the verse satires printed as possibly or probably Marvell's in Margoliouth's excellent edition. I observed, furthermore, that no other painter poems of the Restoration—some thirty-five in number—bore any substantial resemblance to "Last Instructions." Those two closest in time and subject matter, the fourth and fifth "Advices," differ entirely in outlook. Their calumnious attitude toward Charles II contrasts markedly with the respect and loyalty expressed toward him in the three poems which now concern us.

The tacit principle behind my argument was that the coherence of many similarities of matter and manner, in the absence of serious discrepancies or inconsistencies, and with the addition of some external evidence, amounted to a probability that Marvell was the author of all three poems.

Professor Ephim Fogel has taken my arguments "to illustrate the general character of . . . fallacious presuppositions and methods" in the use of evidence. He attempts to show this by denying the significance of the similarities I have pointed to, by claiming that my literary analysis of the poems is insufficiently comprehensive, by offering statistical analysis of the verse to prove different authorship, by claiming for "Last Instructions" various literary virtues which he does not find in the "Advices," by pointing to alleged discrepancies in attitude, and by emphasizing the questionable authorship of *Flagellum Parliamentarium*.

Before we examine these points I should like to expose a misrepresentation of my method which Fogel makes early in his article (and therefore all the more prominently). On page 73 he gives as his first "caveat to canonical scholars" the principle that "unless one can show beyond a reasonable doubt that a given work *B* is by a known writer *A*, parallels between *B* and an anonymous work *X* have little if any value in proving *A*'s authorship of *X*." After objecting to my use of *Flagellum Parliamentarium* because there was some doubt as to Marvell's authorship, he observes:

Lord's article is open to a more fundamental objection. To extend the canon of Marvell's satires is perilous when the canon is so dubious to begin with. Aside from "Last Instructions," which we may grant is Marvell's,

Margoliouth prints sixteen satires attributed to the poet. Four of these total only fifty-five lines, forty-four of them in Latin. According to Margoliouth, two of the remaining satires are "certainly spurious." . . . Considerable doubt attaches to four others and to portions of a fifth. . . . There is no "definite proof" of the authorship of three satires which Margoliouth believes may be Marvell's. . . . And until we have a much fuller analysis than Margoliouth offers, significant degrees of doubt seem to me to attach to the remaining two. . . . One can hardly build firm inferences about Marvell's satiric style on such uncertain foundations. [p. 73]

It is surprising that a scholar who sets himself the task of schooling others in the use of evidence could so misrepresent the method I have followed. I built no inferences upon these "uncertain foundations." Fully aware that some degree of doubt attached to these satires attributed to Marvell, I concentrated my argument on the two "Advices" and "Last Instructions." To be sure, I referred to "Clarendon's Housewarming" as "a satire generally attributed to Marvell," and indicated that a pun on "an Hyde" in "The Third Advice" also occurred in that poem. This was the whole extent to which I employed this material in a paper which made more than fifty specific references to the three painter poems under discussion. From Professor Fogel's misconception of my argument one would suppose that I had drawn heavily on a body of material to which, in point of fact, I barely referred.

Such an error at the outset of his article does not augur well for Mr. Fogel's accuracy in treating the details of my case, as I shall show at appropriate points in my reply. But I should like now to consider his argument for the poetical superiority of "Last Instructions" to the "Advices." Although he recommends "the integral criticism of parts in terms of wholes" rather than the "Fluellen-like culling of fragments" which he accuses me of practicing, Fogel's critical survey of "Last Instructions" consists of little more than general statements to the effect that, like Marvell's "authentic" poems, "Last Instructions" reveals a "severe sense of appropriateness, in accordance with which all elements subserve the poem's larger purposes and conform to its artistic presuppositions" (p. 91). By contrast he finds "gross violation of decorum according to genre" in "The Third Advice" and "probative" differences in the versification of "The Second Advice." The first point depends on Fogel's mistaken idea that the painter convention limits the advising or instructing poet to quasi-pictorial techniques. I shall show later that the convention is not limited in this way and that "Last Instructions" does not observe the limitations: as Legouis observes, "Pas plus que son prédécesseur immédiat ni que Waller lui-même, Marvell [in "Last Instructions"] ne s'astreint à une poésie purement plastique."[1] In support of the second point Fogel offers statistics to prove that "Last Instructions" has a significantly lower percentage of multiple rhymes than "The Second Advice." As I shall show, his statistics are wrong, and the proportions are about the same.

The rest of Fogel's argument on style is largely devoted to more generalities about the "Spenserian allegory," "the Chaucerian genre painting," and "the Rembrandt-like chiaroscuro" which he finds in "Last Instructions." He concludes:

Above all, its construction is masterly. An imaginatively conceived action, with parts proportioned and disposed so as to contribute to the harmony of the whole, unifies the historical events. And a consistent point of view, aware of complexities and enriched by a knowing irony, controls the action, characterization, description, tone, and all the other aspects of the poem [p. 93].

The "Advices," on the other hand, "merely play a stream of witty satire over the surface of current events." If Fogel is right, prodigies have been performed in unifying this variegated poem, but he does not demonstrate his enthusiastic claims and fails to give that "integral criticism of parts in terms of wholes" which he promised. Nor is his denigration of the "Advices" substantiated by examples proving their lack of underlying gravity. As I shall show, the "Advices" have this high seriousness as well as the scurrility and humor found in "Last Instructions," while in literary quality they do not fall below their sequel.

"The Second Advice" parodies Waller's encomiastic poem and follows it closely in subject and structure. Fogel objects to the lack of originality here, but it seems essential in parody to be imitative. "Most of Waller's similes are but two lines long," Fogel observes, "as are all the similes in 'The Second Advice' " (No. 4, note 45).

But here again the parody follows its original in order to mock Waller's frigid and insipid comparisons. In its whole structure "The Second Advice" has the simple linear unity of the poem it parodies in covering events from the beginning of the naval war in the spring of 1665 to the temporary suspension of hostilities at the end of that

---

[1] Pierre Legouis, *André Marvell* (Paris, 1928), 330.

summer. Within this simple chronological structure one finds some brilliant portraits and tableaux—the sketch of Coventry (to which "Last Instructions'" portrait of St. Albans corresponds in position and importance), the Duchess of York's "sea masque" at Harwich, the moving tributes to Lawson and Marlborough (cf. "Last Instructions'" tribute to "brave Douglas"), and the tragicomedy at Bergen.

"The Third Advice" is patterned more loosely on its predecessors, but it, too, features the naval events of the summer and thereby gains satiric impact from the feeling that history is repeating itself. ("Last Instructions" gives corresponding prominence to the Dutch invasion of the Thames, for the same reason.) Like "The Second Advice" it uses the two-line mock-heroic simile, but not being as closely bound to a model as its predecessor it introduces a radical departure in the memorable figure of Lady Albemarle, who is allowed to complain of the government's ineptitude at length, particularly in connection with her overworked husband who is "Gen'ral at land, at sea, at plague, at fire" (line 432). Fogel objects that the poet violates the painter convention in allowing this coarse, absurd, and somehow admirable woman to speak her mind. He refuses to accept the little trick by which the poet tells the painter, "Paint thou but her and she will paint the rest," a line which, to my mind, indicates the poet's witty awareness of how artificial the convention is. The Duchess's appearance is concluded with a fine conceit which again has the convention (and a lot beside) in view:

> So Philomel her sad embroid'ry sung,
> And vocal silks tun'd with her needle's tongue.
> The pictures dumb in colors loud reveal'd
> The tragedies of courts so long conceal'd. [lines 451–454]

There is nothing better in "Last Instructions." The slatternly Duchess (a former seamstress) attains both wit and gravity as the modern counterpart of Philomel.

Fogel's second objection to the Duchess of Albemarle is that Marvell was a friendly business associate of Monck's and would not have depicted his lady as an "udder-bounding," "viraginous," "she-Albemarle." I shall discuss this question of attitude later, but perhaps it is worth observing here that Dryden directs some bawdy raillery at Charles II in the opening lines of *Absalom and Achitophel*.

The two "Advices" begin with introductions relating the satirical situation to the painter device, and they conclude with envoys respectfully urging the King to sack his evil counselors. "Last Instructions" does the same. The heart of both "Advices" is an account of naval and political affairs, with satiric portraits, elegiac passages, narrative summaries, and tableaux, among which mock-heroic similes and classical allusions are scattered. As is natural in topical satire, the structure of events determines the structure of the poems. The mood is mixed, but however gay or irreverent it may sometimes be, the dominant feeling is patriotic and serious.

How does "Last Instructions" differ from these two poems as a poetic organism? First, it is much longer (more than twice as long as "The Third Advice"), and its portraits and tableaux are proportionately more numerous and longer. Secondly, it has more classical allusions and longer similes. Thirdly, it includes more history. It covers those government and parliamentary affairs in the fall of 1666 and the winter of 1666–1667 which led to false expectations of peace, to the cheeseparing treatment of the navy, and finally, to the disastrous defeat at the hands of the Dutch. It concludes with the signing of the peace, the parliamentary post-mortems which blamed the scapegoat, Peter Pett (in the process recapitulating each debacle featured in the second and third "Advices"), and the removal from office of Clarendon. Fourthly, "Last Instructions" has a good deal more modal range than the two "Advices," chiefly in the "idyllic pastoral" and "the Spenserian allegory of the grief-stricken Medway and Thames," as Fogel describes them, and in the extended elegy on Douglas. Although these set pieces do contribute to the range of effects they are by no means integrated into the narrative and thematic structure of the poem. Granted that heterogeneity may be characteristic of satire, the excessively conceited passage on De Ruyter and the coy nymphs (echoing, incidentally, Enobarbus' description of Cleopatra) is exceptionally inappropriate to the prevailing tones and to the whole structure of the satire.

Partly because of its greater heterogeneity, "Last Instructions" has in fact much less unity than the "Advices." In the first three pages the poet has his painter sketch three long portraits: St Albans, the Duchess of York, and Lady Castlemaine. No connection is established between these figures, and only St Albans appears later in the poem. In the "Advices," on the other hand, all the leading characters portrayed—Coventry, Sandwich, Arlington, Clarendon, York, Albemarle, Lady Albemarle—take an active part in events. They are not, as here, sketched and then abandoned. "Last Instructions" is a brilliant satire, but it clearly does not have the careful integration of structure which Professor Fogel claims sets it apart from the "Advices."

II

Let us now examine in detail four areas of dispute in the argument: (1) canon, (2) subject matter, (3) style, and (4) attitude. At the end of my article I mentioned a striking resemblance between the descriptions of the Earl of Sandwich in "The Second Advice" and in a blacklist of the Court's parliamentary supporters entitled *Flagellum Parliamentarium*. This list, which has been attributed to Marvell, was compiled between December 1670 and the early months of 1673.[2] As I showed, "The Second Advice" refers to the British Admiral, in the context of the Dutch prizes which he rifled, as "the halcyon Sandwich," *halcyon* being used in the sense (unmentioned in the *OED*) of "cowardly." In *Flagellum Parliamentarium* the Earl appears as "the halcyon bulk-breaking Sandwich." The same rare epithet applied in the same context to the same person led to a strong assumption that the author of the pamphlet was the author of the poem. The fact that the pamphlet had sometimes been attributed to Marvell led me, therefore, to suspect still more strongly that Marvell had written "The Second Advice."

Since I wrote that article it has occurred to me that a comparison of the list of MP's attacked in "Last Instructions" with those attacked in the blacklist might be revealing. I found twenty-eight members satirized in the poem as venal henchmen of the Court. Twenty-two were named in *F. P.*[3] Considering the fact that party lines at this time were not clearly drawn, that votes in Parliament were jealously guarded from the public, that only a few such lists of Court supporters in the Cavalier Parliament are now known to historians, I was struck by the extent to which the poem and the pamphlet were in agreement. I was bothered nevertheless by the failure of the blacklist to mention the other six MP's attacked in "Last Instructions": Sir John Goodrick,

---

[2] These dates are taken from an article by E. S. de Beer, "Members of the Court Party in the House of Commons, 1670–1678," *Bulletin of the Institute of Historical Research*, xi (1934), 1–23.

[3] Sir Robert Paston, John Birch, Sir Stephen Fox, Edward Progers, Matthew Wren, Sir Francis Compton, Sir Heneage Finch, Sir Edward Thurland, Sir Jonathan Trelawney, Sir Courtenay Pool, Sir Thomas Higgons, Sir Frederick Hyde, Sir Salomon Swale, Sir George Carteret, Sir Gilbert Talbot, Sir John Duncombe, Lord Fitzharding, Sir Allen Apsley, Sir Allen Broderick, Sir Richard Powle, Lord Cornbury, Henry Coventry.

Robert Steward, Sir Henry Wood, Henry Brouncker, John Bulteel, and the famous Sir William Coventry. I then began to investigate possible reasons why these six might have been ineligible for a list of Court supporters made up in 1673. I then learned that Goodrick had died in 1670, Wood in 1671, Bulteel in 1669, and Steward some time before February 6, 1673. Brouncker had been expelled from Parliament in 1668, and Sir William Coventry had been dismissed from the Treasury and the Privy Council and sent to the Tower early in 1669. By 1673 he was writing a pamphlet attacking the government.[4]

This complete agreement with respect to the twenty-eight MP's means, then, that the author of "Last Instructions" (Marvell) is also, beyond a reasonable doubt, the author of *Flagellum Parliamentarium*. The occurrence in that pamphlet and in "The Second Advice" of the same highly distinctive description of the Earl of Sandwich then testifies strongly in favor of Marvell's authorship of "The Second Advice." Since the two "Advices" are so intimately related in thought, structure, style, metaphor, and attitude that they must unquestionably be the work of one man, it is probable that Marvell also wrote "The Third Advice."

III

Professor Fogel's chief argument in regard to subject matter of the three poems is that "meetings of the House of Commons are central to the spirit and structure of 'Last Instructions' . . . whereas the second and third 'Advices' deal with Parliament very cursorily and concentrate upon the naval actions of 1665 and 1666." He implies that because Marvell was an MP and treated parliamentary affairs at length in one satire, he would have been obliged to do the same in the others. "Last Instructions" to be sure devotes much time to the sessions of 1666 and 1667 which bore closely on naval affairs in the last year of the war, and one might reasonably expect some attention in "The Second Advice" to the parliamentary developments in the fall and winter of 1664 and 1665 which led to war, especially to the steps which led to the government's being voted the unprecedented sum of £2,500,000 on February 9, 1665. But while "The Second Advice" alludes to Sir Robert Paston's role in securing this sum, it gives nothing like the detailed narrative of parliamentary events one finds in "Last Instructions." This seems, therefore, to be a point against Mar-

---

[4] I am indebted to the parliamentary historian, Professor Basil D. Henning, of Yale, for much of this information.

vell's authorship until one realizes that he returned from a long diplomatic mission to Russia only at the end of January 1665, on the eve
of war.

As a sequel and conclusion to the two "Advices," "Last Instructions"
surveys the main events which made the Dutch War of 1665–1667
such an unmitigated disaster for England. Marvell summarizes these
miscarriages toward the end of "Last Instructions" in an imaginary
list of charges against Peter Pett, a naval commissioner:

> Whose counsel first did this mad war beget?
> Who all commands sold through the navy? *Pett.*
> Who would not follow when the Dutch were bet?
> Who treated out the time at Bergen? *Pett.*
> Who the Dutch fleet with storms disabled met,
> And rifling prizes, them neglected? *Pett.*
> Who with false news prevented the *Gazette?*
> The fleet divided? Writ for Rupert? *Pett.* [lines 769–776]

This passage touches on all the principal episodes covered in the sec-
ond and third "Advices": Clarendon's alleged responsibility for start-
ing the war ("Second," lines 135ff.); Coventry's sale of naval com-
missions ("Second," 25ff.); the Duke of York's failure to pursue the
Dutch after Lowestoft ("Second," 233ff.); Sandwich's failure at
Bergen and his rifling of captured merchantships ("Second," 243ff.);
Arlington's misinformation about the whereabouts of Beaufort's fleet
("Third," 281ff.); and Coventry's dispatch of an urgent order to Prince
Rupert "by the common post" ("Third," 310ff.). The choice in this
sardonic summary of just those episodes which are so prominent in
the two earlier poems suggests how closely linked "Last Instructions"
is to its two predecessors in narrative and attitude.

IV

To turn now to matters of style, let us take up Professor Fogel's
suggestion that "a more secure basis for comparison"—more secure,
presumably, than the comparisons I did *not* draw between the "Advices" and the satires dubiously attributed to Marvell—"could be
established by a literary and stylistic analysis of the ten authentic
Marvellian poems in heroic couplets, the common meter of the 'Advices' and 'Last Instructions'" (pp. 73–74). In pursuit of his own suggestion Mr. Fogel finds that "Last Instructions" differs from the "Advices" in having a much lower proportion of multiple rhymes and a
much higher proportion of run-on lines. He counts fourteen lines with
multiple rhymes in "Last Instructions," where there are, by my count,

sixty-eight.[5] He counts twelve lines with multiple rhymes in "The Second Advice" where I find twenty-four.[6] On the basis of his miscalculations Fogel concludes that the proportion of multiple to masculine rhymes, expressed in percentages, is 1.4 per cent in "Last Instructions" and 3.3 per cent in "The Second Advice." By my own calculations it is 6.8 per cent in "Last Instructions" and 6.7 per cent in "The Second Advice."

Fogel tries to clinch this part of his argument with the observation that "nowhere in 'Last Instructions' . . . do we get three pairs of multiple rhymes in succession, as we do in both . . . the 'Advices'" (p. 95). The facts, this time, are correct, but I do not find them very impressive in view of a ten-line passage of "Last Instructions" (lines 867–876) which contains six multiple rhymes with two pairs occurring in succession.

Fogel's suggestion that one might identify Marvell's *normal* use of enjambment in his "authentic" couplet verse seemed at first an appealing one: however, I found in *Fleckno* forty run-on lines out of 170 (about 23 per cent) and in *Tom May's Death* five out of 100 (5 per cent), with the other couplet poems— like the three painter poems under discussion—falling between the extremes. What, then, is Marvell's *normal* practice?

Although Fogel's statistical analysis of style turns out, on inspection, to be of little help, his conviction that "Last Instructions," unlike the two "Advices," shows a "meticulous observance of the limits inherent in the 'Advice' convention" seemed at first to be a formidable objection; both "Advices," as he says, contain direct quotations, and "when one asks a painter to represent the events of actual life, one cannot require him to depict speeches" (p. 91). But this statement is based on the misconception that in a painter poem the poet is limited to describing only what can be depicted. Were this true, the passages of "Last Instructions" which supply the thoughts or even the words (in indirect discourse) of various characters, would be equally inaccessible to the painter's art and would constitute an equal violation of the convention. How could Clarendon be *depicted* cursing his absent writing master to himself as he pens writs for a new Parliament (lines 469–472)? How paint the anxious English sailors ashore at Chatham "invoking" the boom which guards their ships from the

[5] The numbers refer to the first line of each pair of multiple rhymes: 59, 121, 189, 209, 245, 249, 265, 335, 355, 361, 367, 479, 483, 519, 549, 559, 563, 613, 629, 711, 713, 717, 769, 781, 789, 797, 815, 819, 867, 873, 875, 925, 973, 983.

[6] 59, 87, 101, 103, 129, 131, 141, 251, 265, 273, 275, 277.

Dutch—"Hold, chain, or we are broke" (line 592)? How represent the charges enumerated against Pett (lines 769–784)? Fogel appears to believe that the painter poem is confined to a verbal equivalent of what can be painted, but it should be obvious that the poet who addresses the painter may intersperse his descriptive tableaux with the thoughts and speeches of his characters to guide the painter in depicting their expressions.

All three of these painter poems, I feel, observe decorum, and integrate the form with the matter. Where speeches or internal monologues are recorded it is the poet who is doing the narrating, but all three poems show an adequate awareness of the convention. In this connection I noticed a resemblance between the miniature painter of "The Third Advice" who could "draw in little what we do in less" and the poet's recommendation to the painter in "Last Instructions" that he might need a microscope to discern "our compendious fame": in both, the painter's technique was adjusted to the satirical situation in the corresponding use of similar figures of diminution. It is this (I would think) clear resemblance to which Fogel refers as "Lord's curious notion that there is an intentional link between a reference to a microscope in one poem and a gibe at a dwarf in another" (note 37).

V

Let me conclude this rejoinder by considering now the disparities in attitude which Mr. Fogel feels distinguish the "Advices" from "Last Instructions," chiefly the latter's "deep and principled criticism of the health of 'our *Lady State*'" (p. 93). While I would readily grant that such underlying seriousness marks that poem, I cannot concede that it is lacking in the others. Patriotism, bitterness, scurrility, and humor run through all these poems in about the same proportions. Ultimately their mutual concern, in the words of "The Third Advice," is "the tragedies of courts so long conceal'd," and the revelations which they all make range between the comic and the tragic.

At its best satire achieves a middle state between gravity and humor by playing various attitudes against each other. Seriousness and wit are both apparent in these lines from "The Second Advice" and contribute mutually to the satiric effect:

> Then, Painter, draw cerulean Coventry,
> Keeper, or rather chancellor, of the sea;
> Of whom the captain buys his leave to die,
> And barters it for shame or infamy. [25–28]

5: Comments on the Caveat

In none of these poems does the witty stream of satire detract from the satirist's fundamental concern with the health of "our *Lady State*."

Mr. Fogel's chief point about the discrepancies in attitude is directed at the treatment of George Monck, Duke of Albemarle, in "The Third Advice" and "Last Instructions." He says, "if Marvell ever regarded Monck in the partly hilarious, partly contemptuous fashion of 'The Third Advice,' I can find no record of that fact" (p. 80). He cites various letters of Marvell and his poem on Blake's victory to show that the poet's attitude toward the General was respectful and admiring. But a sometimes hilarious attitude toward Monck in "The Third Advice" is no more incompatible with respect for him than Marvell's reference to Lord Clifford as a "tall louse brandishing a white staff" ("Last Instructions," line 18) is incompatible with his statement that "for quality, estate, and abilities, whether in war or peace" Clifford was "as capable and well deserving (without disparagement) as others that have the art to continue in offices" (*Growth of Popery and Arbitrary Government*, ed. Grosart, IV, 262).

But let me ask whether the treatment of Monck in "The Third Advice" is really "contemptuous." Whether the poet or the Duchess is speaking, the attitude I find uppermost is respect for Monck's prodigious courage and endurance. In one place, to be sure, Monck is chided for being foolhardy (lines 37–42), but this is the most severe criticism in the whole poem.

If raillery implies contempt, "The Third Advice" is contemptuous in having the Duchess of Albemarle allude playfully to the wound which her Duke received in the buttocks:

> Guard thy posteriors, George, ere all be gone;
> Though jury-masts, th'hast jury-buttocks none. [375–376]

But if this implies contempt, then what should we make of Dryden's sly raillery at the wounded Duke in so serious a tribute as *Annus Mirabilis* (lines 241ff.)? According to E. N. Hooker, "Dryden's raillery is admirable by the best standards of his age: it is a gentle thrust, serving to reveal or heighten certain admirable qualities in the object of raillery—in this instance, the Duke's unshaken courage." The thrusts in "The Third Advice" are less delicate, because they are delivered by the Duchess, but they serve the same purpose.

Fogel has found "a Fluellen-like culling of commonplaces" in the comparisons which I drew between "Last Instructions" and the two "Advices." He claims that the attitudes which these poems express toward public figures are satirical commonplaces which one might find in any antigovernment satire. But in their treatment of Clarendon, Coventry, Sandwich, Albemarle, Clifford, Arlington, the Duke and Duchess of York, Waller, Henry Brouncker, Sir John and Lady Denham, etc., the "Advices" and "Last Instructions" often agree in the smallest details. Where so many characters are involved, so many corresponding details are hardly coincidence. In both cases Coventry appears not only as the venal place-seller but as a coward—a charge for which there is no basis whatsoever. In both cases, out of all the possible charges that might be made against Arlington, his faulty intelligence service and his relationship to Bristol are emphasized. In both cases the same allusion is made to the Duchess of York's lost virginity and means for its restoration. The same point is made about Monck in both instances: an embarrassed Anglican government is forced to make this hated Presbyterian their military man-of-all-work.

Similar specific and corresponding configurations are found in the mythological allusions. The chief instance, perhaps, is the way "Last Instructions" and "The Second Advice" both use the myth of Minos, Pasiphaë, and the bull. Not only do they relate it to Charles II, but they also relate both the myth and the situation at court to the Venetian naval victory over the Turks which was the occasion for the archetypal painter poem on which Waller modeled his panegyric. The fact that every educated contemporary of Marvell's knew the *Metamorphoses* inside out has no bearing on the point.

In conclusion, Mr. Fogel's approach to satire seems at times too literal. When "Denham" says, as a parting shot at the end of "The Second Advice," that Waller's next poem must be "Advice to draw Madam l'Édificatress" (that is, the Duke of York's mistress, Lady Denham), and when "The Third Advice" opens with a reference to the affair and "Last Instructions" gives it great prominence, I find internal-external evidence of authorship. Fogel objects to my stating that in these lines the parodist ("Denham") is promising to draw Lady Denham in his next, on the grounds that he is really saying that *Waller* will do this. Does Mr. Fogel believe that the parodist felt either Waller or Denham could conceivably write a poem on this subject? Clearly the satirist (neither Denham nor Waller) *is* telling the reader in his sly way to expect something good on the Duke of York and his mistress in a later installment.

A Reply to Professor Fogel[*]

By Arthur Sherbo

I AM gratified that my plea for criticism has been heard; I am even more pleased that questions I have raised, particularly about Samuel Johnson's style, have evoked answers. F. V. Bernard has pointed out Johnson's use of "the former" and "the latter" in canonical pieces ("Errors in Boswell," *N&Q*, cciv [1959], 280–281) and has also written to me to point out four sentence fragments in the *Rambler* essays. (This evidence will serve to put in proper perspective Professor Fogel's assertion that Johnson "would probably have shunned" the "crass sentence fragment" in the fourth paragraph of the "Essay on Elegies.") Two other scholars have spotted sentence fragments elsewhere in the canon. That I am right or wrong about the "Essay on Elegies" and about *Mother Midnight's Comical Pocket-Book* is a matter of relative, not utter, indifference to me; at least matters are in the public forum at last. Indeed, I have the promise, possibly a threat, of a very good friend of mine of a full-dress reply to my argument for attributing the "Essay on Elegies" to Johnson. I think I can claim accomplishment of my mission.

Professor Ephim G. Fogel has had the chance to expand some objections from the floor on the occasion of the delivery of my and Professor Lord's papers, and it is with his objections to my paper, as well as an earlier piece on Smart, that I am concerned now. And I am also concerned, of course, about certain misunderstandings on Professor Fogel's part.

The first and most important misunderstanding that underlies Professor Fogel's arguments is his failure to recognize that my evidence for Smart's authorship of *Mother Midnight's Comical Pocket-Book* and Samuel Johnson's authorship of the "Essay on Elegies" is cumulative; it depends on a number of parallels, or coincidences, or even—in

[*] Reprinted with the author's permission from the *Bulletin of The New York Public Library*, LXIII (1959), 367–368; a reply to No. 4, above.

part—commonplaces that occur in the pieces mentioned and in the canonical works of both writers. It will not do, therefore, to isolate parts of the evidence and show they are weak; I acknowledge the weakness of certain bits of evidence. I know analogies are suspect, but the fact that a number of morsels of food, taken individually, will not take the edge off a man's hunger does not mean that, taken together, they will not, *ipso facto*, accomplish that end. Of course, one may wish to counter that morsels of no nutritive value whatsoever will not do the job either. Or, to adopt Professor Fogel's example, any number of zeros always add up to zero. Presumably, from Professor Fogel's title and his development of it, the fact that two rivers both contain "salmons" is worth nothing as evidence of kinship (and so, too, my "salmons"), but this is to ignore the very real fact that not all rivers contain "salmons." Allow me, then, at the very minimum, some positive value for my bits of evidence—and some of them are larger than "salmons"—and I repeat that as one increases the number of bits of evidence each bit takes on a little more value in its very appearance with the other bits. But I have said all this before.[1]

As a consequence of this vital misunderstanding Professor Fogel is at liberty to take some, *or parts of some,* of my arguments, which should be considered together, and show that they are not worth much. I am content to rest my case on this point by one example. Professor Fogel pitches upon the phrase "amorous ditties," selected by me as an uncommon agreement between the anonymous "Essay on Elegies" and Johnson's *Life of Cowley,* and shows that the same phrase occurs twice in *Paradise Lost.* This fact, he claimed, is enough to destroy any "assertion of rarity." I would only grant, initially, that this fact destroys any claim to *uniqueness* alone, not to rarity. But I would go much further and say that the phrase in Milton is not joined, as it is in the "Essay on Elegies," with (1) mention of false wit in Cowley, (2) misquotation of the same word in a line of Pope, (3) mention of the false wit of modern Italian writers, and (4) certain ideas on the naked, relatively unadorned, yet sublime style of the Bible. Most remarkable, of course, is the fact that these five agreements, and I will not gauge their individual rarity, are between the "Essay on Elegies" and one of Johnson's works alone—the *Life of Cowley.* And, it must be added, these are only five of seventeen agreements, major or minor, between the "Essay" and Johnson's known work. I find *no* disagreements. But Professor Fogel ays that the *style*

[1] "The Uses and Abuses of Internal Evidence," above, No. 1.

is not Johnson's, offering as evidence a negative impressionism which asks rhetorically if Johnson could be guilty of so many infelicities. I am willing to match impressionistic criticism with Professor Fogel; when my eyes *first* fell on the "Essay" I said, on the basis of style almost entirely, "This is Johnson's."

A second great shortcoming I find in Professor Fogel's criticism of my efforts is his lack of familiarity with the literature of the eighteenth century, especially with the minutiae of literary history in that century. He seems, to my mind, singularly blind to the many and varied *jeux d'esprit* in the century and to the delight that people took in them. Further, he attributes to the century a restraint and a regard for the proprieties that may have been true of some writers but was most certainly not true of a great many others. Thus, he is repelled by what he, not I, calls the "dishonesty and grossness" of Smart's referring to Nancy's breasts in a poem in the *Pocket-Book*, since Nancy, as I pointed out, was a diminutive of his wife's name. Here Professor Fogel disregards the conventions of love poetry and is ignorant of the canon of Smart's verse. Had he checked the page references I give to Smart's descriptions of female breasts ("Smart," p. 288), he would have found that in one poem, on Nancy's birthday, Nancy's breasts are called "two snowy heaps" where Cupid hoards up his "stores of choicest Love" (Callan, I, 201). In two other poems, both referring to Harriot Pratt, of whom he was enamoured, he asks to be let view "Thy parting breasts, sweet avenue" and he compares her breasts to the lily for their whiteness (Callan, I, 103 and 191). And in a poem to a still unidentified Miss A–n he writes: "What can those tumid paps excel, / Do they sink, or do they swell?" (Callan, I, 193). I would suppose Miss A–n's identity was known to some contemporary readers. The sensibilities of the eighteenth century are not Professor Fogel's.

In two places Professor Fogel says there were several "imitations" of Mother Midnight's poems before the *Pocket-Book* was printed and hence it too could be another imitation. What Professor Fogel, relying on second-hand sources, does not know is that Mother Midnight's *name* (see Professor Fogel's note 11) was usurped a couple of times, that her (i.e. Smart's) poetry was *parodied*, and that the one imitation I know of, *Mother Midnight's Miscellany*, is lamentably poor and obviously not Smart's. On more than one occasion Smart's poems were reprinted without his permission. Similarly, Professor Fogel's query whether references to Dr. Rock in the *Pocket-Book* are serious and sympathetic is based on his not having seen the *Pocket-Book*. Since I provide page references to the *Pocket-Book's* mentions of Dr. Rock, a letter of inquiry to The New York Public Library would have resolved his doubt. But Dr. Rock was a notorious quack, a fact a student of the eighteenth century who follows the learned journals or had read extensively in the century would know; there are no sympathetic references to him to my knowledge. And if Professor Fogel realized that a comparison between anybody and John H[i]ll (see my page 290) was never (almost never) complimentary, this, too, would have spared him any doubts. What is more, Professor Fogel does not seem to understand the methods and techniques of literary controversy in Grub-Street, else he would not make the statements he does in his section A (pp. 74–75). And, finally, if Professor Fogel were extensively read in the literature of the eighteenth century, he could answer his own questions about the frequency of the mention of such luminaries as Dr. Rock, Thomas Rosoman, Peter Hough, and the trunk maker at the corner of St. Paul's Churchyard. Goldsmith, for example, refers to the first; Fielding, to the last—but chances are heavy against any writers' referring to the four of them in the "course of a sixty-four page pamphlet." And when the laws of probability, call them mathematical or logical as you will, demand also that the presumptive writer have scattered references to these same four individuals elsewhere in his works, the odds against attribution of the work in question to anybody but this same presumptive author are overwhelming.

A few scattered remarks: Professor Fogel, as part of his argument that the *Pocket-Book* is an imitation of Smart's poetry, rather than by Smart, points to the pseudonymous author's identity as "Mother Midnight's merry Grandson," implying that the work is not, hence, by Mother Midnight herself. Let him look at my article ("Smart," p. 292) where, in a canonical work, Smart assumes the pseudonym "Master Christopher Midnight, My [Mrs. Midnight's] Great Grandson"; the transition from "great grandson" to "grandson," or vice versa, is not difficult—if one has a sense of humor. It is equally easy to become one's own pseudonymous nephew, as witness the authorship of the crambo song on "Lovely Harriote" by "Mrs. Midnight's Nephew." There is the fact, too, known to students of Smart's work, that he is, pseudonymously, both Ebenzer Pentweazle, of Truro, and Miss Nelly Pentweazle, daughter to Ebenezer. When one is in the presence of humorous poetry he must be continually, though not necessarily painfully, aware of that fact.

6: A Reply to Professor Fogel

Professor Fogel points to an acrostic poem in the Pocket-Book that spells the author's name as Joseph Lewis. What I might possibly concede, though I will not, is that one poem *is* by a Joseph Lewis, whose *non*-existence nobody can prove. But a closer attention to my article ("Smart," p. 292) would have told, or reminded, Professor Fogel that the author of the *Pocket-Book* slips, drops one of the two masks he is wearing, to the extent of referring to himself (Mother Midnight's Grandson) as "an old woman," continuing, and I quote myself now, "in language reminiscent of Mrs. Midnight, author of *The Midwife*"—even to the extent, I might add, of referring to her spectacles, one of the distinguishing features of the old woman.

Professor Fogel, *passim*, warns me that better scholars have come a cropper in canonical studies. He refers, among others, to Robert Brittain's attempt to claim a poem called "The Benedicite Paraphrased" for Smart; the poem is by the Reverend James Merrick. Since, Professor Fogel argues, Brittain had such a seemingly powerful case for Smart's authorship of the poem, and since his parallels between it and "A Song to David" are "far more startling than . . . Sherbo puts forward for Smart's authorship of the *Pocket-Book*," how weak presumably, by comparison, is my case for the *Pocket-Book*. It is again necessary to point out that many of Brittain's arguments, or at least those singled out as significant by Professor Fogel, are not so startling. The theme was not uncommon, the so-called "Song to David" stanza was by no means Smart's exclusive property, and the expansion of one verse of the original texts into one stanza of paraphrase was itself not uncommon, both for the Psalms and other religious poems and prayers—the Lord's Prayer, for example, being expanded to eight prose paragraphs for each verse. But "The Benedicite" is Merrick's, and there is little use in belaboring a dead horse. And the failure of some is no argument against the possible success of others.

Professor Fogel asks if it is not "absurd . . . to imagine that the mere occurrence in both Smart and the *Pocket-Book* of common nouns like 'theme' and 'caudle' is any kind of 'evidence' for single authorship?" Yes, it is, if one adds that "theme" is used in a particular way or context and that "caudle" had become a kind of trademark with Mother Midnight, ostensible midwife and real vaudevillian.

Professor Fogel will give no weight to Professor Wilbur Cross's hesitant attribution of a poem to Smart, even when I offer independent evidence to confirm the attribution. Given two anonymous poems, X and *X'*, the latter a part of a collection which shows certain affinities to the poetry of Smart, and the former claimed for Smart by Professor Cross, Professor Fogel refuses to concede that demonstrable similarities between *X* and *X'* lend weight to the theory that they are both by Smart. Professor Fogel might do well to look at "Newspaper Sonnets Put to the Concordance Test" (No. 27, below), the final footnote, and explain why, *external evidence apart,* he willingly accepts the method there when he denies me its application. And I might say, in anticipation of possible rebuttal, that Professor Johnson's case "An Uncollected Early Poem by Coleridge" (No. 26, below) referred to in that footnote, rests in part on the fact that the parallels between his anonymous poem and the Coleridge *Concordance* do not appear when checked against the Wordsworth *Concordance* alone. This is sufficient evidence for Professor Fogel despite the fact that the chief objection to the attribution to Coleridge was that "the poem is written in the insipid manner characteristic of much of the verse of the time" (p. 345). Again one finds Professor Fogel accepting here what he objects to in my own presentations, i.e. a failure to make an exhaustive search of *all* other authors writing at the times of publication of the *Pocket-Book* or the "Essay on Elegies."

It is not easy to discover from what cause the acrimony of a scholiast can naturally proceed. The subjects discussed are of very small importance; they involve neither property nor liberty, nor favor the interest of sect or party. The various readings of copies, and different interpretations of a passage, seem to be questions that might exercise the wit, without engaging the passions.

7

On "Multiple Rhymes": Some Clarifications

By Ephim G. Fogel

I DID not see Professor Lord's and Professor Sherbo's replies to my essay until the July, 1959, issue of the *Bulletin* was duly shelved in the Cornell University Library. Had I been given the opportunity of answering in the same issue, I should have disputed their new contentions in detail, for I continue to differ with them on matters of principle and procedure and on their particular arguments concerning *Mother Midnight's Comical Pocket-Book*,[1] the "Essay on Elegies," and the second and third "Advices." But since it was decided that my answer would be printed in a volume of which I am coeditor, extensive point-by-point rebuttal seems inappropriate. Moreover, the issues have been joined for some years now, and interested readers have perhaps decided for themselves whether, among other things, they should or should not allow Professor Sherbo, "at the very minimum, some positive value for [his] bits of evidence";[2] whether the "Essay on Elegies" and Johnson's prose are strikingly similar in spirit and style, or profoundly different; whether the attitude toward Monck which emerges from "The Third Advice" is in the main "rather equivocal" (Lord, p. 36, above), rather respectful (Lord, p. 113), bitterly satirical (Pepys, January 20, 1666/7), or partly hilarious, partly contemptuous, and on the whole negative ("Salmons in Both," p. 80).

---

[1] I have already pointed out (pp. 74–76 above) that the external evidence works against the theory of Smart's authorship of this pamphlet; having analyzed the contents of the pamphlet, I find that the internal evidence is even more damaging to that theory than appeared from Professor Sherbo's selection of parallels.

[2] Professor Sherbo's request is of course far from minimal: whether the "bits" have any positive value before being subjected to rigorous logical and statistical analysis is precisely the point in dispute. Needless to say, Professor Sherbo's *ad hominem* allegations about my ignorance of eighteenth-century culture can do nothing to settle the dispute in his favor.

Hence, although I should have preferred, under other circumstances, to deal with many questions of both general and particular interest, I am here deliberately restricting myself to a single, but important, feature of prosody.

In "Salmons in Both," I point out that both "Last Instructions" and Marvell's genuine poems in heroic couplets have much lower proportions of multiple to masculine rhymes than does "The Second Advice." In his reply, Professor Lord maintains that my statistics are seriously defective; for example, where I count fourteen lines with multiple rhymes in "Last Instructions," Lord counts sixty-eight. To call this discrepancy surprising is an understatement. Statistics on the proportions of multiple to masculine rhymes (or, in blank verse, of double and triple to masculine endings), long the staples of canonical scholarship,[3] are subject to fairly precise measurement. The statistics of certain other prosodic traits are inherently variable: in counts of mid-line pause, end-stopping, and enjambment, differences are unavoidable, since readers of verse differ in the placement and duration of pauses. But whether a rhyme or a blank-verse ending is masculine, double, or triple depends on the syllabification and stress of end-line words. And although syllabification and stress differ in different English-speaking communities (compare American and British pronunciation of such words as *laboratory* and *controversy*), they do not vary greatly within a given speech-community, still less within the discourse of a single speaker. Hence, when two scholars count multiple as against masculine rhymes in a poem written in a given place and time by a given author, their counts ought to agree rather closely, in spite of normal error due to imperfect attention or occasional phonetic ambiguity. The startling discrepancies between Professor Lord's counts and mine are therefore extremely puzzling—until one realizes that he understands the term "multiple rhymes" in two quite different senses, one a familiar sense, the other an unusual one. This confusion must be cleared up before one can resume fruitful discussion of the authorship of the second and third "Advices."

It is appropriate to begin with a few simple definitions and common historical observations. I use such terms as "rhyme" and "masculine rhyme" in the ordinary, familiar meanings found in current dictionaries, literary manuals, and textbooks such as Cleanth Brooks and Robert Penn Warren's *Understanding Poetry*. "The term *rime* . . . ," Brooks and Warren observe,

[3] See below, in the Annotated Bibliography, the studies of the authorship of *Henry VIII*.

is ordinarily used in the sense of **End Rime**, which is the identity in the riming words of the accented *vowels* and of all consonants and vowels following. . . . The forms of end rime may be classified as follows:

Masculine rime: The rimed syllables are the last syllables of the words in question, as in *surmount* and *discount*.

Feminine rime: The rimed syllables are followed by identical unaccented syllables, as in *delightful* and *frightful*. When only one unaccented syllable occurs after the accented syllable, there is an instance of Double rime, as in the above example. When two unaccented syllables, identical in the rimed words, follow the accented syllable, there is an instance of Triple rime. For example: *regretfully and forgetfully*.[4]

Because many authorities understand "feminine rhyme" to mean only double and not triple rhyme,[5] I use the less ambiguous term "multiple rhyme" to stand for both the double and triple forms. Thus the pairs *tickle-pickle* ("Last Instructions," lines 875–876) and *culminant-fulminant* (355–356) are both of them instances of multiple rhyme. In contrast, masculine rhymes are rhymes on *final and accented* syllables—e.g., *right-fight* ("Last Instructions," 5–6) and *matur'd-indur'd* (55–56). Occasionally, to be sure, the same word may be treated as a masculine or a double rhyme, and thus arises what Charles F. Richardson calls "the old monosyllabic-dissyllabic *fire: higher* question."[6] In giving statistics on the proportions of multiple to masculine rhymes ("Salmons," n. 47), I took the trouble to allow for such ambiguities:

In Marvell's 1,520 lines of heroic couplets, I count 14 lines with multiple rhymes; this total includes the doubtful "endures-*Sewers* . . . but not "prepare-prayer" or "pow'r-showre". . . . In the 990 lines of "Last Instructions" and the 364 of "The Second Advice," there are, respectively, 14 and 12 lines with multiple rhymes. In percentages, the proportions of multiple to masculine rhymes are as follows: Marvell, .9%; "Last Instructions," 1.4%; "The Second Advice," 3.3%.

Now these statistics, which indicate that multiple rhymes occur in "The Second Advice" at more than twice the frequency of occurrence in "Last Instructions," seem to me to have some bearing on the question of common authorship. As everyone knows, the use of

---

[4] (New York, 1950), 699–700.

[5] The term has long been used in this restricted sense: cf. *Elizabethan Critical Essays*, ed. G. Gregory Smith (Oxford, 1904), I, 205, and II, 221. For an even more limited definition of "feminine rhyme," see George Saintsbury, *Historical Manual of English Prosody* (London, 1910), 280.

[6] *A Study of English Rhyme* (Hanover, N. H., 1909), 117.

multiple rhyme in serious English poetry has been in dispute for centuries. Sir Philip Sidney used double and triple rhymes extensively in certain poems of the *Arcadia,* and his admirer Sir John Harington followed suit in his translation of *Orlando Furioso* (1591). But despite Sidney's potent authority, Harington was forced to admit that some critics of the *Orlando* "found fault with so many two sillabled and three sillabled rimes."[7] Some Restoration critics frowned upon the rollicking rhymes of Butler's *Hudibras:* Dryden, for instance, argued that "the double rhyme (a necessary companion of burlesque writing,) is not so proper for manly satire; for it turns earnest too much to jest," and later critics agreed with him.[8] Among Romantic poets, Shelley used multiple rhymes freely in his lyrics and Byron even more freely in his satires, but Coleridge declared that "double and trisyllable rimes form a lower species of wit."[9] The controversy persisted through the nineteenth, and has continued into our own, century.

Professor Lord cannot have had this historic controversy in mind when he turned to the question of multiple rhymes in "Last Instructions" and "The Second Advice," for he writes as follows (pp. 110–111):

[Fogel] counts fourteen lines with multiple rhymes in "Last Instructions," where there are, by my count, sixty-eight. He counts twelve lines with multiple rhymes in "The Second Advice" where I find twenty-four. On the basis of his miscalculations Fogel concludes that the proportion of multiple to masculine rhymes, expressed in percentages, is 1.4% in "Last Instructions" and 3.3% in "The Second Advice." By my own calculations it is 6.8% in "Last Instructions" and 6.7% in "The Second Advice."

It will be noted that Lord repeats the key term "multiple rhymes" and adopts my phrase "the proportion of multiple to masculine rhymes." If there are indeed 68 rhymes of the *tickle-pickle* and *culminant-fulminant* variety in "Last Instructions" and 24 in "The Second Advice," as against my count of 14 and 12, then Lord has without question shattered an important argument against common author-

[7] *Elizabethan Critical Essays,* II, 219; cf. II, 220–221. Cf. also Samuel Daniel on feminine rhyme, II, 383.

[8] Dryden, *Essays,* ed. W. P. Ker (Oxford, 1900), II, 105. Cf. Edward Bysshe, who believes that triple rhyme "ought wholly to be excluded from serious subjects" and approves Dryden's opinion that in heroic verse "even the double Rhymes ought very cautiously to find place" (*The Art of English Poetry* [London, 1705], 20–21).

[9] Quoted, without source, by Brander Matthews, *A Study of Versification* (Boston, 1911), 63.

ship, and my "miscalculations" are appalling. But when one turns to the lines cited by Lord ("Comments," n. 5), one learns that he has grouped two vastly different forms of rhyme under a single rubric. One form consists of multiple rhymes in the regular sense (*tickle-pickle, culminant-fulminant*), the sense understood by participants in the historic controversy mentioned above: of these rhymes Lord refers to the fourteen I counted in "Last Instructions" and the twelve I counted in "The Second Advice."[10] The sixty-six which Lord adds to my count, however, are rhymes of an entirely different and rather special sort. I quote the first five of Lord's thirty-three "additional" rhyming pairs:[11]

> Na*vy eats*–*the Cheats* ("Last Instructions," 121–122)
> in *rage*–in*gage* (189–190)
> Drun*kers drew*–Lea*ders knew* (209–210)
> the *round*–re*nowned* (245–246)
> the *Foe*–be*low* (249–250)

The reader will notice that these and the rest of Lord's "additional" pairs are in reality *masculine rhymes* on final and accented syllables, preceded by unaccented rhyming, or approximately rhyming, syllables.[12] Calling two different classes of rhyme by the same name and counting them as members of a single class has confused both the prosodic and the statistical points at issue. We need a distinctive name for Lord's sixty-six "additional" rhymes—"backward-extended masculine rhymes" seems like an accurate, if somewhat ponderous, descrip-

---

[10] The multiple rhymes in "Last Instructions" occur at lines 59–60, *able*-mal*leable*; 355–356, *culminant-fulminant*; 563–564, ten*able*-tenant*able*; 797–798, *Peeter-meeter*; 815–816, *Nation*-Convo*cation*; 873–874, *question*-di*gestion*; 875–876, *tickle-pickle*. The multiple rhymes in "The Second Advice" (*Poems on Affairs of State*, 1703) occur at lines 85–86 (Lord's numbering is 87–88), *Cable*-impenetr*able*; 99–100 (Lord 101–102), *Lyon-Arion*; 125–126 (Lord 129–130), *tender-render*; 271–272 (Lord 273–274), dis*aster-Master*; 273–274 (Lord 275–276), *proper-Copper*; 275–276 (Lord 277–278), Ammu*nition*-con*dition*.

[11] The italics indicate the rhyming syllables that Lord presumably had in mind.

[12] Some of these unaccented rhyming syllables are, when spoken in context, true rhymes, as in the third of the pairs above (*kers-ders*); some identical rhymes, as in the second pair (*in-in*); and some approximate rhymes, as in the first pair (*vy-the*). In context, these last syllables are pronounced [vɪ] and [ðə]. In the couplets cited by Lord, n.5, [ðə] is one of the rhyming members in seven other pairs of unaccented syllables (cf. "Last Instructions," 245–246, 249–250, 335–336, 549–550, 711–712, 713–714, 717–718). In "Last Instructions," 819–820 (*Dispatch-his Watch*), and "The Second Advice," 101–102 (*Dispute-his Lute*), the *s*'s of *Dis*- and *his* stand for different sounds, [s] and [z].

tive term[13]—and we need to separate them from multiple rhymes as ordinarily defined.

These two classes of rhyme have a fundamentally different end-line music: compare *culminant-fulminant* ("Last Instructions," 355–356) and *he brav'd-be sav'd* (361–362). Failure to appreciate this difference is evident in Lord's remarks upon my observation that "nowhere in 'Last Instructions' do we get three pairs of multiple rhymes in succession, as we do in both the second and third 'Advices.'" Lord writes, "The facts, this time, are correct, but I do not find them very impressive in view of a ten-line passage of 'Last Instructions' (lines 867–876) which contains six multiple rhymes with two pairs occurring in succession." Now the passage to which Professor Lord refers is instructive, for it contains, in sequence, a pair of backward-extended masculine rhymes, two pairs of ordinary masculine rhymes, and two pairs of ordinary multiple rhymes.

> Bright Hair, fair Face, obscure and dull of Head;
> Like Knife with Iv'ry haft, and edge of Lead.
> At Pray'rs, his Eyes turn up the Pious white,
> 870 But all the while his *Private-Bill's* in sight.
> In Chair, he smoaking sits like Master-Cook,
> And a *Poll-Bill* does like his Apron look.
> Well was he skill'd to season any question,
> And make a sawce fit for *Whitehall's* digestion:
> 875 Whence ev'ry day, the Palat more to tickle;
> *Court-mushrumps* ready are sent in in pickle.

Lord counts both the first pair and the last two as "multiple rhymes" ("six multiple rhymes with two pairs occurring in succession"). But the end-line music of lines 867–868 is quite different from that of lines 873–876. Plainly, the contrast between ordinary masculine rhyme and multiple rhyme is far more dramatic than the faint difference between ordinary masculine rhyme and backward-extended masculine rhyme. It cannot be supposed that, when Dryden criticized the "levity"

---

[13] If the unaccented rhyming syllables occur just before multiple rhymes (e.g., *desiring-retiring*), the combination may be called "backward-extended multiple rhymes." In all probability, many prosodists would regard unaccented rhyming syllables *preceding* accented rhymes as not in themselves true rhymes. In English prosody, there is a very strong tradition that end-rhymes, whether masculine or multiple, must begin on *accented* syllables. One should perhaps add that in a language full of monosyllabic function words and unstressed prefixes, rhyming or near-rhyming of unstressed syllables preceding a stressed syllable will often occur unintentionally; see the comments on [ðə] in n. 12.

of Butler's rhyme in *Hudibras* and charged that "the double rhyme" was unsuitable "for manly satire," he was talking about rhymes like *of Head–of Lead.*

There is no reason, of course, why one should not try to solve problems of authorship by accumulating statistics on backward-extended masculine rhymes. But in that case, one should explicitly define and illustrate this special class of rhymes; one should elucidate their significance for canonical studies, since discussion of such rhymes seems far from conspicuous in the history of English poetry; one should cope with the problem of unintentional occurrence (see note 13, above); one should certainly distinguish them from rhymes of the *tickle-pickle* variety. Finally, one should count them accurately. We have seen that my count of multiple rhymes is right, after all. But Professor Lord's count, once it began to include backward-extended masculine rhymes, should not have stopped at sixty-six of these in "Last Instructions" and "The Second Advice" but should have included several dozen more.[14]

Doubtless there is room for difference of opinion on the authorship of the second and third "Advices." But Professor Lord will perhaps agree that opinion should not be swayed one way or another by statistics which, in their present form, are not significant.

[14] For the sake of brevity, I limit myself to the omitted backward-extended masculine rhymes in "Last Instructions" only. I make no claim to completeness; indeed, I deliberately omit certain ambiguous cases, many of which occur when one is dealing, as Professor Lord often is, with approximate rhymes on unaccented syllables. If, however, one refers to actual pronunciation in context and to the kinds of "additional" rhymes which Lord finds in "Last Instructions," then it would seem that one should also include the following: Pain*ter see–for thee* ("Last Instructions," 3–4), *assay'd–a Maid* (53–54, 89–90), *he ran–began* (81–82), *the Face–smoother race* (85–86), *divide–decide* (111–112), *appear–the Rear* (185–186), Projec*tors chief–Eaters Beef* (207–208), Va*lour wise–surprise* (231–232), *assure–secure* (411–412), shor*ter reach–for each* (415–416), *abhors–Ambassadors* (451–452), *arise–the Skies* (551–552), *the Sea–a Flea* (587–588), love*ly chin–begin* (649–650), Ter*rour strook–danger shook* (705–706), unluc*ky hour–devour* (739–740), *a turn–adjourn* (839–840), *surround–the sound* (909–910), *does find–design'd* (927–928), *agree–Poetry* (943–944), *astray–the way* (959–960), *this while–his Isle* (967–968).

A Comment on the
"Multiple Rhymes" Question

By George de Forest Lord

THE disagreement between Professor Fogel and myself about "multiple rhymes" stemmed from a misunderstanding about the term. Professor Fogel was referring to feminine and triple rhymes only, while I included what he calls "backward-extended masculine rhymes" (which certainly function as a kind of double rhyme) as well. It is good that the misunderstanding has been cleared up at last, and I regret any confusion I may have unwittingly added to an already complicated question.

The incidence of feminine and triple rhyme *is* higher in "The Second Advice" than it is in "Last Instructions" or in the 1,500 lines of Marvell's undisputed pentameter couplets.[1] I agree that such a definable, countable stylistic feature *might* be an indication of authorship. I agree that "multiple rhyme" (feminine and triple rhyme) *is* "more dramatic" than "backward-extended masculine rhyme." But I am still unpersuaded by Professor Fogel's conclusions, drawn from the incidence of multiple rhymes, for several reasons. First, the sample seems too small to be of statistical value. Second, and more important, since multiple rhyme tends to have a burlesque or satirical effect, its incidence in Marvell's nonsatiric poems in pentameter couplets is no valid indication of his "normal" style. This leads to my third point: its incidence is inseparable from the tone of the passages in which it occurs. If there are more feminine rhymes proportionately in "The Second Advice" than in "Last Instructions," the obvious explanation is that one poem employs more burlesque effects than the other and

---

[1] Readers should be reminded that the texts of the "Advices" on which my articles were based in 1958 and 1959 differ materially from those printed in my *Poems on Affairs of State,* I (New Haven, 1963), and that therefore the figures and line numbers refer to seventeenth-century editions of the poems.

that, as the last of a series, "Last Instructions" amplifies the somber or hortatory notes that are present (though to a lesser degree) in "The Second Advice."

To recognize such differences in tone is not necessarily to posit two authors. We must take care lest in our jealous concern for a great writer like Marvell we reject on insufficient grounds poems that may fall below the standards we set for him. Would anyone deny that Marvell sometimes wrote in the low burlesque? Is there any *inherent* improbability that he wrote "The Second Advice"? It seems unwise to look for fixed "norms" in so demonstrably versatile and experimental a poet.

In ascribing the second and third "Advices" to Marvell I have not intended to rule out categorically and finally the possibility of different authorship. Ascription, especially in the case of deliberately anonymous or pseudonymous satirical styles, is a treacherous affair. In this case I still consider the evidence sufficient to justify a conclusion of "probably Marvell's."[2]

[2] See *Poems on Affairs of State: Augustan Satirical Verse, 1660–1714*, I (1963), 21.

II

STUDIES IN
ATTRIBUTION:
ENGLISH LITERATURE
TO 1660

Editorial Note to Part II

ALMOST invariably in medieval, and frequently in Renaissance, literature, the student of text or canon must have recourse to manuscripts. Accordingly, whereas Part I of the present volume was largely concerned with "printed documents of such provenience as to suggest possible attribution to an author of established canon," the first two essays of Part II take us into the complexities of multiple and polygraphic manuscripts.

In 1866, W. W. Skeat showed that the many manuscripts of *Piers Plowman* fall into three distinct groups: A, the earliest version, 2,579 lines; B, a revision and continuation of A, 7,241 lines; and C, a revision of B, 7,353 lines. Skeat assumed that all three versions (with the exception of a brief addition to A by John But, found in only one manuscript) were by the same author, William Langland. In 1906, John M. Manly challenged this assumption and instead postulated four separate authors (in addition to John But)—two authors in A, and one each in B and C. From that date until 1939, opinions on the question of single or multiple authorship tended to differ sharply; since World War II, the controversy, though not entirely inactive, has not been so prominent as it was earlier (see the account of recent *Piers* scholarship in the Annotated Bibliography, below), and critics have preferred to concentrate on problems of text and interpretation. Nevertheless, the debate about the authorship of *Piers Plowman* is the outstanding canonical dispute in Middle English scholarship of this century. The essay of 1919 (No. 9) by the late R. W. Chambers, one of the most active of the controversialists, affords a comprehensive summary of his case for single authorship and at the same time spells out some of the chief issues in dispute: the reliability of internal and external evidence for identifying the poet as "William Langland"; the relation between poet and persona (the dreamer of the poem) and the degree to which statements by the dreamer are to be interpreted biographically; Manly's hypothesis of a leaf missing in an A-archetype, which for that reason confused the poets of B and C; the meter, diction, and allegorical meaning of the three versions; the Biblical learning of A, B, and C; and their dialect. On this last point, Chambers has an austere warning: one must establish the text of *Piers Plowman* by an exhaustive analysis of the manuscripts before one can make valid deductions about dialect and thence about authorship. (But can one recover the original text, *Piers* editors now ask? And unless one takes a stand on authorship, can one even begin to edit?)

The complex problems presented by the Elizabethan manuscript play, "The Booke of Sir Thomas More," in which occur three pages in a handwriting claimed to be Shakespeare's, are summarized and brought to some conclusion in the late R. C. Bald's article (No. 10). Bald surveys and clarifies the evidence that bears on this fascinating attribution, inevitably controversial and abundantly productive of argument—paleographical, "bibliographical," theatrical, and literary. He insists upon a study of the whole manuscript, and, indeed, all its problems for light on the central one. He gives considerable weight, though in brief summary, to the test of style—both negatively, as eliminating playwrights other than Shakespeare, and positively, with emphasis "not on the isolated unit but on similar combinations of similar units." Bald calls attention to the progressive effect of increasing technical and literary knowledge in bringing the given problems into sharper focus and subtler discrimination.[1]

What can be done with "an array of parallels" is exemplified by Baldwin Maxwell's "Falstaff" paper (No. 11), which, though it parodies "identification" of dramatic characters rather than of authors, may be allowed to stand here for the vast host of speculative studies that have necessitated the sober caveats of the two essays that follow. Gerald Eades Bentley in an early English Institute essay (No. 12) and S. Schoenbaum in a recent one (No. 13) carry the dialogue concerning method into the area of Elizabethan, Jacobean, and Caroline drama, long the most active and still the most vexed field of canonical studies in English literature.

Bentley describes the field and its temptations and indicates that the problem confronted by the investigators of anonymous plays, "published" at several removes from their theatrical origins, is different from those faced by investigators of unsigned essays or lyrics. His

[1] One should note Harold Jenkins' compact survey of scholarship since 1911 on *The Booke of Sir Thomas More;* this survey appeared in a lithographic reprint (1961) of W. W. Greg's Malone Society edition of the play (1911) and was reprinted in the *Collections* of the Society, vi (1962, for 1961), 179–192. On the three possibly Shakespearean pages, Mr. Jenkins writes (p. 184): "An able and dispassionate re-examination of the evidence by R. C. Bald . . . concludes with a phrase More might himself have used, *et tu Shakespeare an diabolus,* and it is difficult to see what other verdict could be reached."

evaluation of the three most reliable—yet incomplete and often mis-leading—primary sources of external information about the plays contains both a warning against the neglect of these sources and an emphasis on their inadequacies (which often compel the scholar to turn to internal evidence despite its hazards). Schoenbaum examines "past failures and present limitations" in the use of internal evidence and stresses the great importance of conscious method. His seven caveats iterate the value of external and textual evidence, warn of the relative rarity of distinctive dramatic styles, especially in collaborative writing; and remind those who would rely on intuition of the logical distinction between convictions and evidence. In his fourth section Schoenbaum deals with the hazards of metrical evidence, imagery studies, and the favorite testimony of parallels, finding value in the latter only when they are properly employed. He deplores the neglect of the Golden Rules enunciated by Miss M. St. C. Byrne in 1932, and his concluding remarks, like Bentley's, underline the hypothetical nature of hypotheses.

The next two selections concern themselves with the minutiae of dramatic texts in order to determine authorship. Cyrus Hoy (in No. 14) applies statistics of language preferences in pronominal and contractional forms to the specific problem of distinguishing the work of Fletcher from that of Massinger. After analyzing both language preferences and such "accidentals" as spelling and hyphenation, Fredson Bowers (in No. 15) allocates scenes to the collaborative authors of *The Virgin Martyr*, arriving at results similar to those of previous scholars.

Sonnets and other poems attributed to Sidney, often on dubious or specious authority, are sifted in William Ringler's examination (No. 16), which illustrates, as do other essays in this volume, the variety of resources and tests a canonical scholar must have at command. In supplement, Ephim Fogel's "Addition" (No. 17) makes use of stylistic evidence within a zone of conjecture already rendered fairly narrow by external considerations.

The Three Texts of
*Piers Plowman**

By R. W. Chambers

ANY complete survey of the grammar of *Piers Plowman* is impossible till we know better than we do at present how far we can rely upon the different manuscripts, and how far we must treat the A, B, and C texts as the work of one man or of several. Meantime any definite facts that can be demonstrated as to any one of these questions will help toward the determination of all. All branches of the enquiry must proceed, tentatively, side by side.

As to certain facts there should be no dispute. *Piers Plowman* is extant in three main versions. The shortest (the A-text) was written not long after 1362. It is incomplete, and in most manuscripts breaks off suddenly at the end of Passus XI, leaving unanswered the problems which the dreamer, in bitter agitation, had raised. In three manuscripts, indeed, a short Passus XII has been added. But this passus makes no attempt to answer the questions and doubts of the preceding passus: it was apparently not finished, and one manuscript contains a conclusion which has been tacked on by one John But.

The second or B text follows the A text, with constant additions and alterations, till it reaches the end of A's Passus XI.[1] It then takes up the problems which had been there raised and abandoned, discusses them at great length, solves them, continues and concludes the search for *Dowel, Dobet* and *Dobest.* Its allusions to contemporary affairs fix the date of the B text after 1376–1377.

The C text is a new recension of the B text, made, as is shown by its allusions, at a date when the rule of Richard II was causing

* Excerpted from "The Three Texts of 'Piers Plowman,' and Their Grammatical Forms," *Modern Language Review,* xiv (1919), 129–151. Omissions are indicated by ellipses, but some footnotes are dropped silently.

[1] The temporary ending of the A text (Passus XII) is canceled, but motives and hints from it are utilized in several different places among the B additions.

dissatisfaction. It is not generally realized that there is no C text for the last two passus (*Dobest*), such trifling variations as exist being apparently due to the scribes.

Skeat never doubted that the three texts were the work of one man. . . . Professor Manly believes that we have in *Piers Plowman* the work of five authors: that the A text is the work of two men, A 1 writing as far as Passus VIII, line 130, and A 2 continuing to Passus XII, line 55: then comes the brief addition of John But. The B and C revisions Manly believes to be the work of distinct authors.

That John But added a few lines we all agree, though exactly how many it is not easy to say. Few Scholars have followed Manly in his rather arbitrary division of the A text into A 1 and A 2; but very many agree that B is a different writer, and I think most now regard C, at any rate, as a distinct person; though in the words of Dr. Bradley "some able scholars still believe C to be the original author himself." . . .

"WILL" IN A 1, A 2, B, AND C

The chief piece of evidence [for unity of authorship], albeit strangely neglected, is the fact that alike in A 1, in A 2, in the B additions, and in the C additions the name of the visionary is given as "Will," and John But, a contemporary, in his addition refers to the writer as "Will." Alike in A 2, the B additions, and the C additions, the tallness of "Will" is referred to.

The early editors, Whitaker and Wright, were inclined to regard "Will" as an imaginary figure of the dreamer, and this view has latterly been urged. . . . Now there are three passages in the B-text[2] and one in the A-text[3] where dreamer and writer seem so clearly identified as to make this theory very difficult. And further, *Piers Plowman* belongs to a group of dream-allegories, the conventions of which it shares. In these allegories dreamer and author are always identified, and a constantly recurring convention is *the introduction of the author's name into the text of the poem in ways identical with those in which "Will" is mentioned in "Piers Plowman."* . . . It may, of course, still be argued that A 2, B, and C, or any one of them, are the work of different authors who deliberately misused the name and reputation of the first "Will." But that the intention of these "Will" allusions is to claim all the texts as the work of one man, "Will,"

[2] B, xii, 16–19; xix, 1, 478.
[3] A, viii, 42–44.

is, I am convinced, demonstrable. It seems to me a mere anachronism to assume otherwise.

EXTERNAL EVIDENCE OF AUTHORSHIP

If this be so, the "Will" references constitute a claim for unity of authorship against which strong evidence must be brought if it is to be dismissed as an imposture.

On the other hand, these very "Will" references in the text rather seriously weaken the argument for unity of authorship, which has so often been drawn from the very numerous notes, headings, and colophons in which "William" or "Willelmus" is spoken of as the author. For since any fourteenth-century reader would have interpreted the "Will" in the text as the author, the "William" or "Willelmus" of the notes and colophons may be merely inference from such references in the text. . . .

Much more important is the fifteenth-century note to the effect that William "Langland" who made "Perys Ploughman" was a son of Stacy [Eustace] Rokayle, and that this Rokayle was a gentleman who held land under the Despensers at Shipton-under-Wychwood. Documentary evidence shows that the Rokayles *did* live near Shipton and *were* adherents of the Despensers. Peter de la Rokayle, the father of Stacy, and therefore (if we believe the note) the grandfather of William Langland, was pardoned in 1327 for adhering to Hugh Despenser. Why should details so specific and (so far as we can check them) so correct, have been invented? It is a mere anachronism to raise objections because William Langland does not take his father's name. Till a very much later date, younger sons might choose what surname they wished. Neither is there any discrepancy between the father's having held a farm at Shipton in Oxfordshire, and the sixteenth-century tradition that Langland was born at Cleobury Mortimer, fifty miles from Shipton. For Langland may have been born about the time of the Despenser troubles, when the lands of adherents of that family were being harried, and when there were the strongest reasons for the Rokayle family's being away from home.

We have accordingly no reason to doubt this information as to the surname and family connections of the "Will" whom the A 1, A 2, B, and C texts alike claim as the author.

RELATION OF THE B-TEXT TO THE A-TEXT

There is the strongest internal evidence that at any rate the A and the B texts are the work of one man. We have seen that in the

A text the search for *Dowel, Dobet,* and *Dobest* begins, but is abandoned suddenly, after the author has raised many difficult problems, to which he can find no satisfactory solution. The discussion was not resumed till some fifteen years later, when the B text was written. But before starting the B combination (Passus XI–XX), the dreamer explains how Lust of the Eyes, accompanied by Lust of the Flesh and Pride, prevented him for many years from wishing to know any more concerning *Dowel* or *Dobet* till he began to reach old age (B, XI, 45–50, 59). This is intelligible, if B be A, resuming that search for *Dowel* and *Dobet* which he had left unfinished some fifteen years before. But if B be not A? If B continued the work which A had left unfinished at his death, what *does* he mean by attributing the cessation of the search for *Dowel* to Lust of the Flesh, Lust of the Eyes and Pride? And if A be supposed to be still alive, the difficulty is equally great. Surely A might have objected to a continuator's not merely appropriating his unfinished work, but further stating that it was unfinished because "Lust of the Flesh clasped me round the neck." On the other hand, this is quite intelligible, if B be A. It has been the practice of visionaries throughout the ages to use stern and often exaggerated language about their own sins of omission and neglect.

But it is not only neglect to which B pleads guilty. In the next passus of the B text the dreamer is reproached by Imaginative, whose function it is to call the past to memory. Imaginative (Memory) tells the dreamer how he has often moved him to think of the wild wantonness of his youth, to amend it in his middle age. The chief wantonness specified is the wild speech with which the A text had broken off, from which Imaginative quotes verbally, and which he refutes.

Then, the difficulties having been settled, the search for *Dowel* and *Dobest* is resumed, according to a system which had already been twice sketched out in the unfinished and abandoned A text. It is by no means the case, as has been argued, that this B continuation is formless or devoid of system: very much the contrary.

In construction and "organization" the B text can be demonstrated to be not inferior to the A text. It adheres strictly to a plan which had been indicated fifteen years before.

THE "MISSING LEAF"

Certain crudities in the A text have been assumed by Professor Manly and Dr. Knott to be due to a lost leaf. B tried to remedy these crudities, but *not* on the assumption of such a lost leaf. So, it is argued, B cannot have been the original author, who must have seen what had happened. Now an error must be *obvious*, to be such that the original author cannot fail to detect it after fifteen years. But the loss of this leaf is so little obvious, that no one had suspected it, till Professor Manly assumed it. Those who have since discussed it are divided. . . .

All this disagreement does not prove Professor Manly wrong. The history of scholarship records many theories which have been almost universally modified or rejected, and have yet in the end been proved right. But can it reasonably be argued that Professor Manly is obviously and palpably right in offering a solution which is not accepted by ten out of eleven scholars? And the argument that B is not A lies, not in B's having overlooked an error, but in the belief that the error was so palpable and obvious that the original author *must* have seen exactly what had happened, and restored the original text. Yet none can agree what this original text was. . . .

OTHER ARGUMENTS

Alleged differences in metre, in diction, and in allegorical method, indicated by Professor Manly, have been the subject of distinct investigations by three different scholars. In each case the verdict has been the same: that there is no evidence for different authorship. Not only so, but all three find the evidence tending rather in favor of unity of authorship, so far as any conclusion at all can be drawn from the limited problem which each is studying. . . .

I propose to devote the rest of this paper to two aspects of the problem: the alleged difference in (*a*) scholarship and scholastic interests and (*b*) dialect. . . .

THE LEARNING OF A, B, AND C

It has been argued that A 1, A 2, B, and C cannot be the same man because of the difference in their interests, mental qualities and scholarship—that, for example, A 1 and A 2 differ in their "scholastic methods and interests," while C "is a better scholar than" A 2 or B.[4]

The Latin quotations, scattered so freely through all the texts, afford a good means of checking this argument. These quotations, mostly standing outside the verse, are a striking feature of A 1, which becomes even more marked later. Altogether (counting only instances where the Latin is quoted verbally) we have 29 quotations in A 1,

[4] Manly in *Cambridge History of English Literature,* ii, 18, 35.

36 in the (comparatively much shorter) A 2, 330 added in the B text, and 94 added in the C text—a large proportion considering that the C additions are not exceedingly bulky.

Now alike in A 1, in A 2, in the B additions, and the C additions, the Psalter is the book most frequently quoted (103 times in all: 8 in A 1, 6 in A 2, 71 in the B additions, 18 in the C additions). After the Psalter the book most quoted . . . is the Gospel of St. Matthew (79 times in all: 7 in A 1, 4 in A 2, 55 in the B additions, 13 in the C additions). Third comes . . . the Gospel of St. Luke (46 times in all: 5 times in A 1, 3 in A 2, 26 in the B additions, 12 in the C additions).

Alike in the A, B, and C texts the citations from the Psalms, St. Matthew and St. Luke are almost equal in number to those from all other sources put together.

Now, to find any parallel to this, we must go to certain devotional treatises, such as the *Prick of Conscience* or the *Imitation of Christ*. Even there, the parallel is not exact: for though the books most quoted are the Psalter and the Gospels, these books do not receive so exclusive an attention as they do in all texts of *Piers Plowman*.

Yet *Piers Plowman* is not a devotional treatise, but a satire, in the strict sense of the word: its subject is *quidquid agunt homines*: it takes us at the outset into the "fair field full of folk"—the wide world. It is, then, somewhat startling to find A 1, A 2, B, and C alike showing a love for just the books which appeal to a saintly recluse like Thomas à Kempis, isolated from worldly cares. And, if we "commit them with their peers," we find that A 1, A 2, B, and C agree in differing from their English contemporaries. The Bible is not to them a storehouse of narrative, as it is to Gower, or the poet of *Cleanness* and *Patience:* they neglect those treasuries of wordly wisdom from which Chaucer mainly drew his Biblical quotations, Ecclesiasticus and Proverbs: they care nothing for those profane authors whom the mediæval scholar loved to quote, Boethius, Seneca, Cicero, Ovid.

Mr. Prothero, in his *Psalms in Human Life,* has selected Dante, Langland, and Thomas à Kempis as the three mediaeval writers to whom the Psalms mean most. But even in Dante the Psalter is not, as it is in all texts of *Piers Plowman,* the book most quoted. In the *Convito* it is Proverbs (quoted 13 times); in the *Divine Comedy* and the *De Monarchia* it is St. Matthew (15 and 13 times respectively); in the *Vita Nuova* and the *De vulgari eloquentia* the Psalms are not quoted at all.

It cannot be argued that this exceptional preference for the Psalter is due to A 2, B, and C each imitating A 1.

There are avowed imitations of *Piers Plowman,* such as *Richard the Redeless, The Plowman's Crede, The Crowned King,* and *Death and Life.* Together they are nearly as bulky as the A text or the C additions. Yet, although ideas and mannerisms of *Piers Plowman* are often followed quite closely, they contain amongst them only one Latin quotation from the Psalter, against the 14 in the A text or the 18 in the C additions. For an imitator can easily imitate the phraseology and tricks of style of his original: but the imitator cannot emulate a habit of apt quotations from certain given works unless he, too, has his brain stored with passages from those works. This is why the quotations of *Piers Plowman* form so valuable a test of authorship.

The simplest explanation surely is that A 1, A 2, the B text, and the C text are what they profess to be—the work of one man. He was a man to whom the Psalter made a special appeal, and he knew his Psalter well, because he was a chantry clerk, and speaks of himself in the B text as one whose task it is to "say his Psalter and pray for those who give him bread" (B, xii, 16–17), and says expressly in the C text:

> The lomes [tools] that I laboure with • and lyflode deserue
> Ys *pater noster* and my prymer • *placebo* and *dirige*
> And my sauter som tyme • and my seuene psalmes.
>
> [C, vi, 45–47]

After the three favorite books, the Psalter, St. Matthew and St. Luke, we find a discrepancy. St. John is not quoted at all in A 1, is quoted twice in A 2, 19 times in the B additions, and 11 times in the C additions (proportionately a much larger percentage than the 19 times in B). But there is nothing in this growing affection for St. John which could lead us to argue any difference of authorship, unless it were supported by other discrepancies. And in other respects the remaining quotations are extraordinarily alike.

The Epistles are largely quoted, and in about equal proportions in A, B, and C (9 times in A, 40 in the B additions, 9 in the C additions).

The 40 quotations from the Epistles in the B additions are drawn from 22 different chapters. One may fairly suppose that these 22 chapters represent B's favorite reading out of the 121 chapters in the Epistles of the New Testament. It is noteworthy that the 9 quotations

A all come from the same 22 chapters from which come the quotations added by B: and so do 8 out of the 9 quotations in the C additions. This can hardly be due to imitation. In the four avowed imitations of *Piers Plowman* the Epistles are quoted textually once only, and then the quotation does *not* come from these chapters.[5]

Now, if the mental qualities and interests and scholarship of A, B, and C were really so different, it is just in points like this that we should expect the difference to be betrayed. On the contrary, what is betrayed is a striking similarity.

Let us now examine the assertion that C is a "better scholar" than A 2 or B. It is true that A 2 and B do agree in making an extraordinary blunder, which C does not make.

A [A 2] confuses *mecor (moechor)* with *neco:* he accordingly quotes the Latin of the seventh commandment, but translates it as if it were the sixth:

> For he [God] seith it hym selfe • in his ten hestis
> *Non mecaberis:* ne sle nought • is the kynde englissh.

B recasts the whole passage, but deliberately makes the same mistake:

> [God] seith "Slee nought that semblable is • to myne owen
> liknesse,
> But if I sende the sum tokne" • and seith *non mecaberis*
> Is, slee nought, but suffre • and al for the beste.

Note that B does not merely copy A's words, in which case he might also have copied his mistake mechanically. He has thought about the passage and rewritten it, repeating the error. Now surely there cannot have been many people in England who were under the extraordinary delusion that *non moechaberis* meant "slay not." This is no "vulgar error," but a highly individual one.

If, therefore, it is to be used at all in argument as to the authorship of A 2, B, and C, surely it tends to prove that A 2 and B are the same man. We are asked to believe, however, that, because C avoids the mistake, it proves C more learned. . . . True, C does avoid this mistake: but how? It is his practice to omit much that is found in the B text, and he misses out the whole passage of 39 lines in which

[5] Of course "B's 22 chapters" include a large proportion of the passages most open to quotation, but for comparison it may be noted that the Epistles are quoted some 70 times in Chaucer, and only 26 of these 70 instances come from B's 22 chapters.

this quotation is imbedded. We have accordingly no evidence whether C shares B's erroneous views on the meaning of *moechaberis,* or no.

But he shares other mistakes of A and B.

The A text misquotes "vengeance is mine" (*mihi vindicta et ego retribuam*) as *mihi vindictam et ego retribuam.* The B additions make the same erroneous quotation in three distinct places. One of these is adopted in the C text: and elsewhere, in the C additions, this somewhat overworked phrase is again quoted, also in the erroneous form. Too much must not be made of this, however, for this misquotation was a common mediaeval error. . . . But so far from C correcting B's errors in scholarship, C even follows B in making *post* govern the nominative case, or in taking *nebula* as accusative plural: *post maxima nebula* (B, xviii, 407; C, xxi, 454).

I think some of the parallels quoted above would be sufficient to establish a strong argument for A, B, and C's being the same man, even if they did not claim to be so. However that may be, they assuredly afford no ground for rejecting the traditional view.

THE DIALECT OF A, B, AND C

Nothing, probably, has done so much to support the view that A, B, and C are by different authors as the fact that the three texts, as printed by Skeat, are obviously in different dialects, which could never have been the speech of one and the same man. True, Skeat pointed out, over and over again, in his prefaces, that these dialectical discrepancies were not discrepancies between the A text and the B or C texts, but between the particular manuscripts selected. . . . But man, perhaps rightly, does not read prefaces. . . .

And however much the student may be aware, in theory, that the dialect is the dialect of the scribe and not of the author, nevertheless the dialect creates an atmosphere, which affects the reader unconsciously. . . .

[Attempts to prove that A 1, A 2, B, and C were written by different authors who employed different grammatical forms are invalid, Chambers maintains. Can one argue for multiple authorship on the grounds that A 1 uses only *ben* in alliteration, whereas A 2 uses both *ben* and *arn?* No, replies Chambers, because out of a mere four instances of such alliteration, chance alone could be responsible for the fact that A 1 alliterates twice on *ben,* while A 2 alliterates once each on *ben* and *arn.* And if *all* of the passages where *ben* and *arn* occur are taken into account in *all* of the manuscripts, then one finds "that

A 1, A 2, B, and C all used the form *ben* and the form *arn,* and C used *ben* much the more frequently." Again, although A, B, and C all have instances of alliteration on *heo* ("a provincialism current in the South and West"), all three use the alternative *she* most frequently. But since *she* was the regular London form at the time (Chaucer and Gower never use *heo*) and since all three versions of *Piers* (especially A and B) have references that identify them as London poems written primarily for a London public, it is remarkable that *heo* is preserved at all against the normal scribal tendency to remove such provincial features. Similar statements can be made about the use in A, B, and C of provincial *kirk* as an alternative to *church.* It would be remarkable, Chambers concludes, "if three successive writers, all writing (as it would seem) primarily for Londoners, should all use these same provincialisms. Anyway it is assuredly not the case that 'a careful study of the manuscripts' has shown 'that between A, B, and C there exist dialectical differences incompatible with the supposition of a single author,'" as Manly has contended.]

The Booke of Sir Thomas More and Its Problems*

By R. C. Bald

MS HARLEY 7368 in the British Museum is the damaged and much revised manuscript of an Elizabethan play bearing the title "The Booke of Sir Thomas More." It is known to have been in the collection of a certain John Murray of London in 1728; thence it passed into the library of the second Earl of Oxford, and with the rest of his manuscripts came into the possession of the nation in 1753. Nearly ninety years later it was first referred to in print in John Payne Collier's edition of Shakespeare, but in 1844 the play was edited for the Shakespeare Society by Alexander Dyce. The manuscript had already suffered from decay, but Dyce's transcript was a careful and reliable one. Since his time not only has the decay progressed but the manuscript has been repaired in a particularly unintelligent fashion. Holes were patched with gummed paper, and the leaves that showed signs of crumbling—six in all—were pasted over on both sides with a semi-opaque tracing paper. As a result Dyce's edition preserves many words and even lines that are no longer legible. Dyce's edition, like Hopkinson's (1902), was a limited one, and not until 1908, with the publication of C. F. Tucker Brooke's *Shakespeare Apocrypha*, did the text become generally accessible. In 1911 a facsimile of the manuscript was included by J. S. Farmer in his series of Tudor Facsimile Texts, and later in the same year the play was edited for the Malone Society by W. W. Greg. Greg's edition is likely to remain the definitive one; not only was the text prepared with exemplary care, but the various hands in the manuscript were first clearly distinguished

---

* Reprinted from *Shakespeare Survey*, II (1949), 44–65, with permission of author and publisher. At the end of this essay are transcriptions of the "Shakespearian" additions to *Sir Thomas More*, followed by four plates which reproduce portions of the manuscript.

and the relationship of the revisions to the original text was clarified.

In 1871 Richard Simpson contributed an article to *Notes and Queries* with the title "Are There Any Extant MSS in Shakespeare's Handwriting?" He answered his own question in the affirmative by citing the revisions in *Sir Thomas More* and by quoting passages from them which had a Shakespearian ring. A year later James Spedding, the editor and biographer of Bacon, wrote in support of Simpson, but pointed out that the passages which Simpson had cited were not all in the same handwriting and presumably not all by the same author. Thereafter no great progress was made in the discussion of Shakespeare's possible share in the play until 1916, when the former Director of the British Museum, Sir Edward Maunde Thompson, fresh from the writing of the chapter on handwriting for *Shakespeare's England,* turned his attention to the play. In his *Shakespeare's Handwriting* he attempted to prove, on palaeographical grounds alone, that the writer of the six authentic signatures of Shakespeare also wrote the three pages of revision in *Sir Thomas More* which are in the hand that Greg had designated by the letter D. His argument immediately aroused great interest; after the appearance of his book and all through the early twenties the correspondence columns of *The Times Literary Supplement* are full of references to the play of *Sir Thomas More.* The case for Shakespeare's authorship was further strengthened in 1923, when a group of scholars joined with Maunde Thompson in a series of essays, collected by A. W. Pollard and entitled *Shakespeare's Hand in "Sir Thomas More,"* in which every possible argument—palaeographical, "bibliographical," and literary—on behalf of Shakespeare was elaborated.

It may fairly be said that there was a widespread inclination on the part of scholars and general public alike to be convinced. The manuscript of a scene from a play in Shakespeare's handwriting was something which, for a variety of reasons, they had all desired to see, and the weight of authority to justify their faith was great. Naturally the Baconians demurred at being shown the Stratfordian in the very act of composition, and raised what objections they could. A few others were not convinced, and the part of devil's advocate was played by the acute but erratic S. A. Tannenbaum, whose palpable errors sometimes blinded his opponents to his real contributions to the discussion. Controversy, often heated, raged till about 1928. Thereafter the topic showed signs of exhaustion and, with one or two notable exceptions, the next decade produced little of comparable interest to the writings of the previous years. Since 1939 there has been no new contribution to the subject. Lest it should be thought that the issues were left in mid-air, a survey of the whole discussion seemed worth attempting in order to state clearly the real advance in our knowledge of Shakespeare which it achieved.

Unfortunately the three pages in the handwriting claimed to be Shakespeare's cannot be studied in isolation from the rest of the play. Not only is it necessary to have some understanding of the confused state of the manuscript, but other problems, such as the authorship of the other parts of the play, the extent to which it was revised, the date, and the company for which it was written, are all relevant to Shakespeare's possible share in it, and must be considered for the light they may throw on the central problem.

THE MANUSCRIPT

In its original state the manuscript of *Sir Thomas More* probably consisted of sixteen leaves, or eight sheets. It was a fair copy in a single hand occupying thirty-one of the available thirty-two pages, the last being blank. At an early stage in its history, though how early it is impossible to say, it was supplied with a vellum wrapper—a fragment of a thirteenth-century Latin manuscript—on which the title "The Booke of Sir Thomas More" was inscribed in large gothic letters. Signs of drastic revision of the original text are frequent in the manuscript: extensive passages are marked for deletion; at least two, and probably three, leaves have been torn out; and, in all, seven extra leaves as well as two smaller scraps have been inserted at different places. None of these is in the handwriting of the original scribe; no less than five different hands occur in the inserted material. The play has also been censored by Edmund Tilney, Master of the Revels from 1579 to 1610, and contains various deletions and notes in his hand.

The contents of the manuscript as at present bound up may be itemized as follows:

Folios 1 and 2. These two leaves are the early vellum wrapper. They are bound so that the remains of the original Latin text are the right way up, with the result that the title of the play, written in the wide lower margin of one of these pages, is now upside down at the foot of fol. 2b.

Folios 3–5 (hand S) are the first three leaves of the play, in the handwriting of the scribe responsible for the original fair copy. Greg designated him S (scribe) in his edition, but later was able to identify him as Anthony Munday.

Except for the first sixteen lines, all of fol. 5b is marked for deletion. After fol. 5 at least one, and almost certainly two, leaves were torn out.

Folio 6 (Addition I, hand A). This is a single leaf, written on one side only. It is evidently in the handwriting of the author, since it contains corrections and alterations which were clearly made during composition. In order to get all his material on to one side of the sheet the writer wrote the last seven lines vertically in the left margin. Two passages are marked for deletion.

Greg designated the hand of this page by the letter A. It has since been identified by Tannenbaum as that of Henry Chettle.

This leaf has been bound up in the wrong position. It is intended to replace a deletion much later in the play, on fol. 19a.

Folios 7-9 (Addition II) are three inserted leaves to replace the deletions on fol. 5b and the missing leaves. They contain three separate scenes (or rather, two scenes and the major portion of a third), and each is in a different hand.

Folio 7a (Addition IIa, hand B). This page contains an enlarged version of a short scene deleted on fol. 5b. This writer too has been anxious to crowd all his text on to a single page, and his last two lines are written upwards in the right margin. B has been identified by Tannenbaum as Thomas Heywood but, though the identification has been accepted by a number of competent authorities, it must, pending further evidence, remain uncertain.[1]

Folio 7b (Addition IIb, hand C) contains another complete scene and, at the foot, the opening stage-direction for the following scene, which begins at the top of the next page without any preliminary direction. C, the writer of this page, is nameless, but he has been identified by Greg as the theatrical scribe who wrote the plots of *The*

---

[1] The identification was considered and rejected by Greg, but has been accepted by C. J. Sisson, and by A. M. Clark in his study, *Thomas Heywood.* Difficulties in the way of accepting it are the differences in the length of ascenders and descenders in relation to the body of the letters in the two hands, and the fact that some of B's forms, notably his *th,* show certain signs of fluency and economy of effort absent from Heywood's. It is difficult to imagine a constant writer, as Heywood unquestionably was, abandoning these forms in later years, especially as there is no compensating gain in legibility. On the other hand, there is no question that the clown's part added by B is very much in Heywood's manner.

Seven Deadly Sins and *Fortune's Tennis*. There is little doubt that he also wrote the title of the play on the vellum wrapper. Tannenbaum has maintained that C was the dramatist Thomas Kyd, but the identification has not won general acceptance.

Folios 8 and 9 (Addition IIc, hand D) are the three pages (fol. 9b is blank) which have been claimed for Shakespeare. Fol. 8a begins a new scene without any introductory stage-direction, and the writer has crowded in his concluding words at the foot of fol. 9a. The scene does not end here, but continues near the top of fol. 10a.

Folios 10 and 11 (hand S). The original fair copy again. The first three lines of fol. 10a are deleted so that the text will be continuous with the insertion on the previous leaves. Several short speeches in hand B are inserted on fols. 10a and 11a.

A new scene begins about a quarter of the way down fol. 11b, but the whole of it has been deleted. It was probably a long scene and continued throughout the whole of the following leaf, but a leaf has been torn out after fol. 11.

Folio 11★ (Addition III, hand C) is a scrap, formerly pasted over the lower part of fol. 11b. It contains a single speech of twenty-one lines, and presumably was intended as the opening speech for the scene which begins on fol. 12a, but it is not clearly linked with it.

Folios 12 and 13 (Addition IV, hands C and E). These four pages seem to represent a revision of the scene which originally occupied fol. 11b, the missing leaf, and fol. 14a. As far as it is possible to estimate the number of lines involved, the revised version seems to be somewhat shorter than the original one.

C wrote three and a half of the four pages of this addition, but E inserted a few words in the upper part of fol. 13b and added a closing episode to the scene on the lower half of fol. 13b. E has been identified as Thomas Dekker.

Folio 14a (hand S). The whole page is marked for deletion; it contains the latter part of the scene replaced by Addition IV.

Folio 14★ (Addition V, hand C) is a scrap similar to fol. 11★, and was formerly pasted over the lower part of fol. 14a. This scrap, like the other, contains only a single speech (eighteen lines), but eight lines, written vertically in the right margin, partly in the original margin and partly on the margin of the scrap, provide a setting for it, and its own last line links it with the opening words on fol. 14b.

Folios 14b and 15 (hand S). Three pages in Munday's hand.

Folio 16 (Addition VI, hand B) contains an episode to be inserted at the conclusion of a scene which ends in the middle of fol. 17*a*. That a passage of fifteen lines on fol. 16*a* was deleted by the author during composition is shown by the fact that though the speeches in it are separated by short strokes they have no speakers' names prefixed.

The episode ends near the top of fol. 16*b*. Further down on the page appears the original draft of the lines copied by C into the margin of Addition V.

Folios 17–22*a* (hand S). The rest of the manuscript is in Munday's hand. On fol. 19*a* a long passage is deleted and was intended to be replaced by Addition I. On fol. 22*a* a passage of nine lines is deleted and is followed immediately by an expanded version, which concludes the play. It is likely that here, at least, Munday in transcribing revised his own work.

On the face of it, the manuscript presents the rather surprising appearance of a play in the autograph of a well-known dramatist which has been rehandled by no less than five different revisers. In his edition of the play Greg pointed out that the error of "fashis" for "fashiõ" (1. 1847) was scarcely one which an author would make, and so he regarded hand S as that of a copyist, in spite of the possible example of author's revision on the last page. But the keen ear of E. H. C. Oliphant detected three different styles in the original parts of the play, and he suggested the more reasonable theory that when first written it was the work of more than one author; Munday, as one of the part-authors, had undertaken the responsibility of fitting together the composite material and providing a fair copy.[2] On this hypothesis some at least of the revisers would be revising their own work. Further, if C was a professional theatrical scribe, it followed that the passages in his hand would almost certainly be the work of other men. The number of revisers is thus reduced to four, and, with Munday added, there is no need to suppose that more than five authors were ever concerned with the play. Re-examining the evidence in 1923, Greg decided that "the following conclusions in regard to the additions are at least plausible. A [Chettle, Addition I] is an author revising his own work. B on fol. 7*a* [Addition II*a*] is transcribing with small original additions the work of another writer; on fol. 16 [Addition VI] he is making an addition to a scene originally written by himself. . . . D [Addition II*c*] is a writer producing an entirely

[2] "Sir Thomas More," *JEGP*, xviii (1919), 226–235.

new version of a scene [written by the same author whose work in an earlier scene was revised by B]. E [Dekker, Addition IV] is a writer making an addition to his own revision [transcribed by C] of another man's original scene."[3] It would seem, then, that Munday, Chettle, and B (Heywood?) first collaborated on the play; Dekker may also have done so, or may have come in later as a reviser; D (Shakespeare?) was never anything but a reviser.

It was formerly taken for granted that the extensive revisions were undertaken at the insistence of the Master of the Revels,[4] but Greg first pointed out that this was not necessarily so; they could all have been theatrical revisions. In the margin of fol. 11*b*, at the beginning of the deleted scene which has been replaced by Addition IV, occur the almost illegible words: "This must be newe written." The hand is uncertain—possibly B's, according to Greg—but it is not Tilney's, and there is nothing in what remains of the canceled scene to suggest anything offensive to the censor. The writer is much more likely to have been someone of authority in the theatre who may have been dissatisfied with the original scene.[5] We can also watch B at work in the first scene of Addition II and on fols. 10*a, b,* and 11*a* of the original text. In Addition II*a* he was merely transcribing the earlier version and inserting speeches for a new character as he went along; in the following pages he was adding further short speeches for the same character. He was, in fact, trying to enliven a series of episodes by adding a comic part for the clown. These revisions at least have no demonstrable relation to Tilney's strictures, and there is no certain evidence that any of the other revisions were so related to them.

As theatrical scribe it was C's function, besides transcribing some of the additions, to fit them all clearly into their places and generally to prepare the manuscript for production. My impression is that C's first task was to transcribe on to a fresh sheet the part of Addition IV which is in his hand (the concluding episode in Dekker's hand was added later, but before the insertion of Addition V); the place of the new matter in the text was adequately indicated by the deletions on fol. 11*b* and by the producer's note alongside it: "This must be newe written." Next B inserted the clown's part, some of it on a new leaf (fol. 7) and some of it in the original text. A large cross opposite

---

[3] *Shakespeare's Hand in "Sir Thomas More,"* 46–47.

[4] E.g. Brooke, *The Shakespeare Apocrypha,* xlvii–xlviii.

[5] *If* the hand is B's and *if* B is Heywood, this would be an argument against an early date for the play. Heywood is not likely to have been in a position of such authority before 1600 at the earliest.

a deleted scene on fol. 5*b* and a similar one on fol. 7*a* make the relationship quite clear. These two crosses are probably not C's, but C seems to have recognized the existence of the symbol when he was called on to fit in another group of additions, and to have marked them with a set of symbols following on in series from the one already in use. Addition V is linked to its place in continuation of Addition IV by a cross within a circle, Addition VI to the main text by a cross within a double circle, and Addition I by a double cross.[6] If the evidence of this symbol-series is accepted, two things seem to follow. First, Additions III, which is out of series, and, for reasons to be considered later, II*b*, and *c*, belong to a yet later stage of revision. Secondly, the direction apparently added by C at the beginning of Addition V, "Mess/T Goodal," must, since it is enclosed by a surrounding line that also encloses the identifying symbol (a cross within a circle), be genuine, in spite of the charge of forgery that has been brought against it.[7]

It was also C's practice to add any necessary stage-directions or speech-prefixes to the additions he edited, and to link the additions to the main text by means of stage-directions (repeated if necessary) as well as by symbols. A good example of these activities can be seen in connection with Addition VI. On fol. 17*a* (original text), in the left margin alongside his cross in a double circle, he has inserted the direction "Enter To the players wth a reward"; at the top of Addition VI (a single leaf in B's hand without any original directions at all) he adds after the identifying symbol, with reference to the same entrance: "Enter A Servingman." Further down the page another necessary direction omitted by the author is inserted: "Enter Moore wth attendants w^t Purss & Mace." There is no exit at the end of the episode, nor has C troubled to supply one.

G's part in the three sections of Addition II is rather more complicated. Fol. 7*a*, in B's hand, opens without any entrance, but this pre-

---

[6] The statement in this sentence is an oversimplification but, I believe, a justifiable one. It should be noted that (i) owing to the damage at the foot of fol. 13*b* only part of the cross within a circle is visible; (ii) the double circle surrounding a cross is not really double, as C takes the second circle only a little more than half-way round the first; (iii) the top of fol. 6 has been damaged and the identifying symbol lost, though what seems to be a fragment of it is just visible in the top left-hand corner of fol. 6*a*. It was probably owing to the loss of the symbol that Addition I was bound up in the wrong place.

[7] S. A. Tannenbaum, "More about *The Booke of Sir Thomas Moore*," *PMLA*, XLIII (1928), 767–778; "Dr. Greg and the 'Goodal' Notation in *Sir Thomas Moore*," *PMLA*, XLIV (1929), 934–938; *An Object Lesson in Shaksperian Research* (1931).

sumably is supplied on fol. 5*b*, at the point at which the new scene
is to be inserted, by a direction added in the left margin by C: "Enter
Lincolne Betts williamson Doll." At the end of the first page (and of
the scene) C has added: "Manett Clowne." But overleaf begins
a new scene, transcribed by C, in which the clown has no part. This
scene ends near the foot of the page, and the last two lines contain
the opening direction for the next scene, since D's addition, which
begins on the following page, contains, like both those of B, no opening direction. C has been carefully through D's three pages, adding
one necessary entrance, and frequently altering the speech-prefixes
which D, who seems to have lacked a very precise knowledge of the
play, has from time to time left deliberately vague.

Addition II replaces the greater part of fol. 5*b* and two other
leaves, now missing, which followed it. As already explained, Addition
II*a* is the mere rewriting with the insertion of the clown's part of
a canceled scene on fol. 5*b*. This canceled scene is followed by a fragment of another scene in which some apprentices begin playing at
cudgels, but this too is deleted. Whether C's direction at the foot
of fol. 7*a*, "Manett Clowne," means that the clown was originally intended to intervene in the prentices' scene, or whether some other opportunity for his sallies was provided, cannot now be determined; subsequently D was called in to revise the insurrection scene, and the
intervening matter has disappeared. But the gap between II*a*, the
scene showing the beginning of the insurrection, and II*c*, showing
its pacification, was bridged by a brief scene, II*b*, which is made up
of reports of its spread and of the measures being taken to quell it.
This scene I suspect C, who transcribed it on the verso of the leaf
already used by B, salvaged from one of the leaves now missing. The
opening lines let us know what had happened in the prentices'
scene:

> ther was even now
> a sort of prentises playing at Cudgells
> I did Comaund them to ther m^{rs} howses
> but one of them Backt by the other crew
> wounded me in the forhead wth his Cudgell
> and now I feare me they are gon to Ioine
> wth Lincolne Sherwine and ther dangerous traine.

These lines are cut, partly it may be, as Greg has suggested, to meet
the possible objections of the censor, but also, surely, because they

contain a reference to an episode already deleted and involve a character who, though he had had a prominent part in the omitted scene, would now appear only in this one brief episode.

In summing up the state of the manuscript Sir Edmund Chambers remarked: "As it stands, the manuscript seems inadequate for prompt-copy. Besides perfecting the insertions, the book-keeper has still to supply a few missing entries and speech-prefixes. . . . In the text itself, many ragged edges have still to be joined."[8] True, in order to help the prompter, C has transferred a few directions in the original text to the left margin, where they would be more prominent.[9] Munday's directions, either centred or at the right of the text, do not stand out very clearly, and one cannot help feeling that a prompter would have been grateful for a few more such repeated directions. The appearance of Goodal's name at the beginning of Addition V suggests that the play had been cast,[10] but when one compares Addition V with Addition III one perceives that C had never properly fitted the latter into its setting. The manuscript could, indeed, have furnished copy for a tidy transcript to serve as a prompt-book, but the evidence seems to show that it was itself in process of being made ready for the prompter. But C never properly finished his job, and the unfinished state of the manuscript suggests that plans for production were abandoned.

The activities of Edmund Tilney are the most puzzling of all the problems of the manuscript. Tilney's bold hand is easily distinguishable, and some at least of his deletion marks can be identified from his habit of adding a marginal cross to the line he put alongside the passages to be omitted. But there are no deletions definitely attributable to him in any of the revisions, or in any of the surviving portions of the original text which have been replaced by revisions. Tilney's attentions were confined to three scenes only. Nearly all the first scene, showing the outrages committed by privileged foreigners

[8] *William Shakespeare: A Study of Facts and Problems*, I, 512.

[9] See W. J. Lawrence, "Was *Sir Thomas More* Ever Acted?" *Times Literary Supplement* (July 1, 1920), 421, where these directions are listed.

[10] Some surprise has been expressed at the appearance of Goodal's name at this point, though Chambers remarks that "there is equally sparse casting in other [manuscript] plays." It should be noticed that his name appears at the beginning of the scene which, of the whole play, would most have taxed the resources of the company. This suggests that Goodal was someone in the theatre whose ordinary occupation allowed only for occasional and exceptional appearances on the stage as a super; hence the note of his name. Was C himself Goodal? It is just possible.

on London citizens, is marked for omission; the third scene, in which the Privy Council is discussing grievances against the foreigners, has two passages marked, and "Mend y^{18}" written against the first of them. In the same scene Tilney has in one place altered "straunger" and in another "ffrencheman" to "Lombard."[11] The other scene to which Tilney objected comes considerably later in the play, and is the one in which Fisher, Bishop of Rochester, and Sir Thomas More demur at signing certain articles submitted to the Council by the King. Amusingly enough, there is no hint in the play as to what the articles were about, and the episode has been made as innocuous as one would imagine it was possible to make it. Nevertheless, the very suggestion of resistance within the Privy Council to the sovereign's wishes seems to have offended Tilney so much that he marked some thirty lines for omission and wrote alongside them "all alter."

The specific passages marked by Tilney for deletion or alteration are not very extensive, amounting in all to about 120 lines, but a note in the margin at the top of the first page demands much more drastic revision: "Leaue out ye insurrection wholy & ye Cause ther off & begin w^t Sr Tho: Moore att ye mayors sessions w^t a reportt afterwards off his good servic don being shriue off Londõ vppo a mutiny Agaynst ye Lubards only by A shortt reportt & nott otherwise att your own perrilles."[12] This would have allowed the second scene of the play to stand, but would have cut out everything else, including Addition II, up to the conclusion of the insurrection scene—a total of 497 lines—and presumably also the execution scene (sc. vii in Greg's numbering), since there would be no point in showing the rioters at the gallows if it was impossible to portray the events which had led up to their condemnation. This scene is 169 lines long, so Tilney's order would have involved the omission of a total of 666 lines, or over a quarter of the play.

There is no question that the revisions in Addition II do not carry out Tilney's instructions, and for this reason Greg believes that the play was censored after the revisions were made and abandoned be-

---

[11] Since the Battle of Pavia Lombardy has been under the control of Spain, and thus, in the latter part of Elizabeth's reign, was virtually enemy territory. During the same period, of course, England was in alliance with the French and Dutch against the Spaniards.

[12] In the introduction to his edition of the play (pp. xiii–xiv) Greg modernizes and punctuates, "upon a mutiny against the Lombards, only by a short report and not otherwise," but in view of the ensuing discussion in the text it should probably be "against the Lombards only, by a short report and not otherwise."

cause Tilney demanded such radical alterations after the many that had already been made. Sir Edmund Chambers admits the logic of this argument, but wonders at the temerity of the actors in submitting so chaotic a manuscript to the Master of the Revels. He continues:

My impression is that when Tilney had finished with sc. iii he realized that piecemeal reformation of this section of the play was hopeless, and that he then turned back to the first page, and wrote the note "Leaue out y⁰ insurrection wholy. . . ". He did not interfere with the harmless second section of the play, but in sc. x he crossed out the episode of More's resignation.[13]

This is helpful, and may well be a full explanation of what happened, but there is one odd feature of Addition II that has not previously been noticed. In the brief second scene (Addition IIb) on the two occasions on which the aliens are mentioned they are "Lombards" (ll. 82 and 104), whereas elsewhere they are, with one exception, either French or Dutch.[14] This discrepancy may merely be due to multiple authorship, though internal evidence seems to suggest that this scene (Addition IIb) is by the same author as the earlier council scene (sc. iii)—the very one in which Tilney had altered "straunger" and "ffrencheman" to "Lombard." In other words, it looks as if either the author or the transcriber was already aware of Tilney's objections to references to any foreigners but Lombards. One is tempted, therefore, to surmise that the play was submitted to Tilney not once, but twice; the first time he made only a few minor deletions in the early scenes, but altered the references to the aliens' nationality, and confined his attention mainly to the scenes on the missing leaves. He might well have objected to the staging of an apprentices' riot, have been dissatisfied with the original handling of the insurrection, and have insisted on seeing that his instructions had been observed in the revisions. So all references to the prentices had to go, and a more skillful dramatist than any of the original collaborators (D) was called in to refurbish the insurrection scene. When the play was re-submitted, Tilney proved, perhaps owing to recent political developments, even

---

[13] *William Shakespeare*, I, 503.

[14] It is somewhat surprising to find that in Addition IIa, on the other side of the leaf on which this scene is written, the added clown's part increases the number of derisive references to the French and Dutch; but if one thing emerges from a study of Tilney's dealings with this manuscript it is that he did not mark every detail to which he objected, but was content to issue general covering instructions.

more rigorous than he had been on the first occasion, and the actors, in spite of the fact that they had gone so far as to cast the play, decided that it was useless to attempt any further revision. This, admittedly, is almost all pure conjecture, but there is no specific evidence to contradict it. It is at least a possibility, and a possibility more satisfactory than the suggestion that the play was censored unrevised, "laid aside when Tilney sent it back, and taken up later by new writers, with different literary notions from Munday's, in the hope that the political cloud had blown by and that Tilney might now be persuaded to allow the main original structure to stand."[15]

COMPANY AND DATE

The men definitely known to have been connected with *Sir Thomas More* are Munday, Chettle, and Dekker, authors; C, scribe; and Thomas Goodal, actor. Heywood and Shakespeare must also be considered as possible part-authors.

Of the careers of C and Goodal little is known. The plot of *The Seven Deadly Sins,* in C's hand, dates from about 1590. According to Greg, it was written for Strange's men at the Curtain; according to Chambers, for the Admiral's men (or perhaps for a joint company) at the Theatre.[16] C's other extant plot, that of *Fortune's Tennis,* was written for the Admiral's men at the Rose about 1597 or 1598. Goodal, whose name appears in the plot of *The Seven Deadly Sins,* was thus a member of the Admiral's or of Strange's men about 1590; he is mentioned as a player in the parish register of St. Botolph in 1599, but there is no evidence of the company to which he then belonged.

Munday, Chettle, and Dekker were all members of the needy band of dramatists who did hackwork for Henslowe. Munday's literary career began in 1577, but he is not known as a playwright until a considerably later date. Weight must be given to Miss Byrne's contention that his other occupations probably gave him little time or opportunity for dramatic collaboration between 1588 and 1592,[17] and if we assign a date as early as 1592 or 1593 to his *John a Kent and John a Cumber* (which also survives in an autograph manuscript with a vellum wrapper, part of which came from the same Latin manuscript as that of *More,* and an engrossed title on it in C's hand), Maunde

---

[15] E. K. Chambers, *William Shakespeare,* I, 511–512.
[16] W. W. Greg, *Dramatic Documents from the Elizabethan Playhouses,* 17–19 and 41.
[17] "Anthony Munday and His Books," *Library,* I (1920–1921), at 243–245.

Thompson has argued on palaeographical grounds that *Sir Thomas More* must have been somewhat later.[18] Munday first appears in Henslowe's *Diary* in December 1597, and reappears on and off until December 1602. Chettle made his first appearance as a writer when he brought out Greene's *Groatsworth of Wit* in 1592 and followed it up in the same year with his *Kind Heart's Dream*. He is first heard of as a dramatist in Henslowe's *Diary* under the date February 25, 1598, but his autograph contribution to the manuscript play *John of Bordeaux* may be several years earlier. Chettle was at work for Henslowe with very few breaks from the beginning of 1598 until March 1603. Dekker, a younger man than either of these, also appears in Henslowe's pages for the first time at the beginning of 1598; he may have been writing as early as 1594, but it seems unwise to try to push back his career any further. And Heywood, who was twenty-one and fresh from Cambridge in 1594, published his first tentative effort in verse in that year, but makes his earliest appearance with Henslowe at an uncertain date toward the end of 1596.

The general trend of all this evidence is to suggest that *Sir Thomas More* was written for the Admiral's men, or at least for some company under Henslowe's management, at a date later than 1594, but it leaves unexplained how Shakespeare could have been connected with the play. This difficulty has caused Greg, in his most recent pronouncement, to push the date back to ca. 1593, when Strange's men, to whom Shakespeare then belonged, were in temporary association or amalgamation with the Admiral's.

In point of fact, almost every possible date between 1586 and 1605 has at one time or other been suggested. The more extreme limits can doubtless be ignored, and it is surely significant that there is no mention of the play in Henslowe's *Diary*. Allusions within the play itself are not very helpful. Disturbances against foreigners, though not on the scale of the insurrection which More is alleged to have pacified, are recorded for the years 1586, 1593, and 1595–1596, but one would expect the play to have been written at a discreet interval after, rather than on the heels of, such an outbreak. Ogle the wig-maker, alluded to in lines 1006 and 1148, is first heard of in 1571 and last heard of in 1600; he is "father ogell" in a note of Henslowe dated February 10, 1599/1600, so he was evidently then an old man. Another allusion, "Moore had bin better a Scowrd More ditch" (Addition IV, l. 215)

[18] "The Autograph Manuscripts of Anthony Mundy," *Transactions of the Bibliographical Society*, XIV (1919), 325–353.

has been taken as a reference to the scouring of Moorditch in May 1595, but it was also cleansed in 1603,[19] and doubtless at other times.

On the strength of such evidence, none of it really conclusive, the general tendency has been to date *Sir Thomas More* ca. 1595–1596. But it is difficult to ignore an objection raised by G. B. Harrison: if Shakespeare's hand is to be found in the play, the versification of the passages attributed to him is not that of the period of *Richard II*, but of *Julius Caesar* and *Troilus and Cressida*.[20] This argument, admittedly, involves assuming what is to be proved, but one way of testing a hypothesis is to inquire what its acceptance involves. Further, Harrison's evidence is not so rigid as to forbid a certain latitude; as valid a comparison could doubtless be made, say, with the versification of the choruses of *Henry V* as with that of Ulysses' speech on degree, but his general contention for a date ca. 1600 rather than ca. 1595 on metrical grounds is well founded.

Harrison's suggestion was followed up and elaborated by D. C. Collins,[21] who pointed out the significance likely to be attached to parts of the play in the period of Essex's rebellion. It is well known how the fall of Essex dashed the hopes of many Englishmen, and lines like these, to which Tilney has objected, almost certainly describe a widespread attitude at that time:

> I tell ye true, that in these daungerous times,
> I doo not like this frowning vulgare brow.
> My searching eye did neuer entertaine
> a more distracted countenaunce of greefe
> then I haue late obseru'de
> in the displeased commons of the Cittie. [ll. 318–323]

In the execution scene too there are lines, marked for omission, which could also have had a topical significance in February and March 1601, when first Essex and then his principal followers were led to the scaffold:

> God for his pittie help these troublous times
> The streetes stopte vp with gazing multitudes,

[19] See Percy Simpson, "*Sir Thomas More* and Shakespeare's Hand in It," *Library*, 3d ser., VIII (1916–1917), 79–96, and G. B. Harrison, *The Elizabethan Journals*, III, 317.

[20] "The Date of *Sir Thomas More*," *Review of English Studies*, I (1925), 337–339.

[21] "On the Date of *Sir Thomas More*," *Review of English Studies*, X (1934), 401–411.

Commaund our armed Officers with Halberds,
make way for entraunce of the prisoners.
Let proclamation once againe be made,
that euery householder, on paine of deathe
keep in his Prentises, and euery man,
stand with a weapon ready at his doore,
as he will answere to the contrary. [ll. 584–592]

Indeed, the political situation in February and March 1601 makes comprehensible not only Tilney's refusal to allow the stage to show two members of the Privy Council resisting the wishes of the sovereign—and Essex, of course, was a Privy Councillor—but also his insistence that the whole of the insurrection scene should be expunged from the manuscript of the play.

Theatrical history also tends to confirm a date of late 1600 and early 1601. The Admiral's men were acting at the Rose during the first half of 1600, but early in July they left it; presumably some at least of them went on tour. Meanwhile their new theatre, the Fortune, was being hurried to completion, but they were not able to occupy it until the end of November or beginning of December.[22] During this period Henslowe's payments for new plays are very few, and not until later do they pick up again. Chettle does not reappear in the *Diary* until March 31, nor Munday until October 10, 1601. It seems that during the building of the Fortune and until the novelty of the new theatre had worn off Henslowe made no attempt to provide full employment for his staff of dramatists. It would be natural for a group of them to try to find a market for their wares with the Lord Chamberlain's men.[23]

According to this hypothesis, then, *Sir Thomas More* was begun in the latter part of 1600. The collaborators must have thought that by joining with Munday, the ex-pursuivant and associate of Topcliffe, they could safely handle so delicate a subject as the life of More, and in such a way as to avoid offending the censor by any suggestion of Catholic bias. But the play did not entirely satisfy the company to which it was offered, nor, probably, the Master of the Revels, and revisions had to be undertaken. Even then a crucial scene was inadequate, and Shakespeare intervened to see what he could do with it. But meanwhile political events were moving fast; Essex launched his brief and futile rebellion; the Chamberlain's men, who had played

[22] *Henslowe's Diary*, ed, Greg, II, 63 and 94–95.
[23] On this presumption C must also have been available to help with the preparation of the manuscript.

Richard II with its deposition scene on the eve of the rebellion at the instigation of Essex's followers, were doubtless temporarily under a cloud, and the theatres were being closely watched. When the manuscript was submitted (or re-submitted) to Tilney soon after the execution of the rebels, he demanded further changes so sweeping that the play was abandoned.

THE HANDWRITING AND SPELLING
OF THE THREE PAGES

The parts of *Sir Thomas More* which it is possible with any show of reason to claim for Shakespeare are the three pages of Addition IIc, which are in the hand of their author (D), and Addition III, which is in the hand of C. As has been shown, there are bibliographical reasons for suggesting that these two insertions may be related, in that they both belong to the final stage of revision, but any attribution of Addition III to Shakespeare must rest mainly on internal and stylistic evidence. That for IIc, on the other hand, is based in addition on handwriting and on D's spelling habits as well.

The problem of identification of Elizabethan handwritings is complicated by the fact that most writers were accustomed to using at least two different hands—an English and an Italian one—and sometimes more. There was also a natural tendency in some writers to mix the forms of the two hands. In addition, certain writers used a signature notably different from their ordinary hands. When one adds the differences produced in a man's handwriting by lapse of time, and the difficulties resulting from the sparseness of the materials available for comparison, it will be seen that certainty is not always attainable.

The problem of Shakespeare's handwriting should be aprroached only after consideration of a number of other examples, such as can be found in Greg's *English Literary Autographs, 1550–1650*. One finds a writer such as Chapman signing his name indifferently in English or Italian script; others, such as Henry Porter or Sir John Davies, use signatures which furnish comparatively little information about the way in which they usually form the letters that make up their names. In other cases, such as those of Edmund Spenser, Gabriel Harvey, and Giles Fletcher the elder, only by reason of juxtaposition or authentication is it possible to identify two seemingly quite different hands as the product of the same writer. In yet others, like those of John Lyly and Joseph Hall, where the type of handwriting remains constant, causes such as lapse of years and variations in the degree of care in the writing, produce such differences even in signatures as would cause one, if there were any doubt as to the writer, to hesitate to make the identification. An extreme case, and one presenting in an exaggerated form some of the difficulties faced by the present investigation, is that of Christopher Marlowe. The *Massacre at Paris* scrap in the Folger Shakespeare Library is, if one accepts its genuineness, presumably an author's draft, yet its hand presents very little resemblance to the signature of Marlowe recently discovered.[24] The best one can say is that it is conceivable that the same hand wrote them both.

For a study of Shakespeare's handwriting there are only six unquestioned signatures and two other words: "By me." The earliest, of May 11, 1612, is attached to the deposition in the case of Belott *v.* Mountjoy in the Record Office; the next two, dated March 10 and 11, 1613, are affixed to the conveyance and mortgage of the Blackfriars property, and are preserved at the Guildhall and British Museum respectively; the other three are the signatures to Shakespeare's will, dated March 25, 1616: one signature is at the foot of each page, and the final one is prefixed by the words: "By me." All are considerably later than the manuscript of *Sir Thomas More*, and five out of the six were written in abnormal circumstances. The signatures to the will are clearly those of a man weakened by illness; they seem to have been written slowly and carefully, but with deliberate and perhaps painful effort. The signatures to the conveyance and mortgage have both been crowded on to the parchment strips (for the attachment of seals) inserted through slots in the deeds. Only the signature to the deposition was written with normal fluency. In the three signatures to the will the surname is written in full; in the other three it is abbreviated. The Christian name is unabbreviated in two of the signatures to the will and in that of the conveyance; in the others it is abbreviated to 'Wᵐ', 'Wiłłm', and 'Willm̃'. In all, these signatures contain seventy-six still legible letters; they give examples of the way in which Shakespeare wrote eleven minuscules and three majuscules.

Sparse as is this material for comparison with the addition to *Sir Thomas More*, it should be realized that the circumstances might be more desperate than they are. It can be fairly presumed that

[24] See J. Q. Adams, "The *Massacre at Paris* Leaf," *Library*, XIV (1933–1934), 447–469; J. M. Nosworthy, "The Marlowe Manuscript," *Library* XXVI (1945–1946), 158–171; Marlowe's signature is reproduced by John Bakeless, *The Tragical History of Christopher Marlowe*, I, opposite p. 208.

Shakespeare's signatures give us examples of his normal manner of forming the letters in his name;[25] this is evidenced by the signature at the end of the will, where there is no suggestion of any change of style from the words: "By me." Shakespeare and D both use the English hand with a minimum admixture of non-English forms, and there can be little question that the two hands are at least superficially alike in many respects. But it is clear that Shakespeare had no standardized form of signature to which he attempted to adhere. The signatures, even the three signatures to the will, vary considerably from one another; what is remarkable about them is the range of variant forms they display. They furnish more material for comparison than could be expected from such meagre specimens.

Several of the letters that can be compared, such as *e* and *y*, are of such standard forms that they show little individuality. In making his analysis, Maunde Thompson was on the watch for forms that might be regarded as showing personal peculiarities and in the signatures he found five which are also repeated in D:

(1) The "spurred *a*," illustrated in the deposition signature and in D's "that" at line 105. Other *a*'s in D can be found approximating this form (e.g. "are" in l. 107), but the one in line 105 is closest to that in the signature. What distinguishes these two *a*'s is that "the pen, descending in deep curve from the overhead arch, is carried to the left into the horizontal spur and then to the right *horizontally* till it ascends to form the second minim."

(2) "Shakespeare makes use in his few signatures of three out of the four forms of the letter *k* which appear in the Addition," and the unusual *k* in the second will signature, which is not the normal type of *k* with a crossbar, is paralleled by D's *k* in "knees" (l. 110).

(3) Though the form of the *p* in the mortgage signature is common enough, its formation is exceptional. First the downstroke, with its initial serif and its terminal upward lift, was made; then, beginning to the left of the downstroke the pen made a cross stroke to form the lower half of the loop, and the top of the loop was completed by a third stroke. The same formation can be observed in the initial *p*'s in each occurrence of "peace" in line 50 of the Addition.

---

[25] There is perhaps one exception to this statement. D usually, though not invariably, dots his *i*'s; in the signatures Shakespeare omits them. It should be added, however, that photographs seem to show a dot over the first *i* of 'William' in the first signature to the will, but it does not appear in the early facsimiles and may therefore be only a flaw or stain in the paper.

(4) The one Italian form found in the signatures is the long ʃ of the conveyance and mortgage signatures, and presumably also of the third will signature. It may be contrasted with the English ʃ of the second will signature. In the speech-prefix "seriant" at line 17, D uses the Italian ʃ, though of a somewhat different form. The ʃ and r in this word are the only Italian letters used by D.

(5) In the signature at the end of the will the m of "me" and the W of "William" have introductory upstrokes, in the lower part of which there is perceptible a preliminary downstroke which, in the W, is only partially covered by the upstroke and forms what has been called an "elongated needle-eye." A downstroke preliminary to a similar upstroke is visible in D at the beginning of such words as "wretched" (1. 75), "in" (1. 95), and "noble" (1. 144), and in line 130, at the beginning of "needs," the identical needle-eye effect of the signature is reproduced.

The peculiarities singled out by Maunde Thompson have not escaped criticism, and certain facts have been brought to light which weaken, though they do not destroy, his case. It has been pointed out, for instance, that Chapman uses a form of the "spurred a" capable of appearing in a form identical with that of the deposition signature;[26] Chapman, too, sometimes employs an initial upstroke preceded by a downstroke which produces the needle-eye effect,[27] though so far the phenomenon has only been found at the beginning of an initial A in his Italian hand. It is doubtful also if the k to which Maunde Thompson attaches importance is really a separate form. Further, it has been emphasized that Shakespeare's W's are different from D's (ll. 35 and 37), and that his B is unlike any made by D. In an effort to clinch the case against the identity of Shakespeare and D, Tannenbaum has drawn up what he calls "twenty-five points of essential difference" between the two hands.[28] They vary greatly in weight and importance, nor do they take any account of lapse of years or the abnormal circumstances in which five of the six signatures were written, though elsewhere Tannenbaum shows himself fully aware of the significance of these factors. He is capable too of citing for com-

---

[26] See R. W. Chambers, "Shakespeare's Handwriting in *Sir Thomas More*," *Times Literary Supplement* (Aug. 27, 1925), 557, and Greg's *English Literary Autographs*, Pl. xiib.

[27] S. A. Tannenbaum, *Shakspere and "Sir Thomas Moore,"* 16 and Pl. i.

[28] The phrase quoted is from *Shakspere and "Sir Thomas Moore,"* 15; the twenty-five points are in *Problems of Shakspere's Penmanship*, 199–211.

parison forms in D as unlike those in the signatures as possible and ignoring those which resemble the signatures, as when, in stating that the upward curve at the end of D's *i*'s is "almost invariably" different from Shakespeare's, he cites the words "this" and "his" in lines 101 and 102, but ignores "willd" in line 100, which furnishes a close parallel to the forms of the signatures.[29] The soundness of Tannenbaum's methods is thus open to suspicion, and he leaves one with the feeling that a really effective case on palaeographical grounds against Shakespeare's authorship of the Addition has yet to be stated.

Another argument in favor of the identity of the two hands has been advanced by Greg.[30] Five out of the eleven minuscules in the signatures and the Addition, he points out, assume several forms in both, and in both they are the same ones. "Such multiple agreement acquires considerable significance, even though the individual forms may be common." Of *e, h,* and *p,* there are two clearly marked varieties, as well as three *k*'s and three, or perhaps four, *a*'s. "Taken all together these agreements must be allowed to establish a case of some *prima facie* strength." How strong a case, however, is still not clear, for no information is available as to the probability of such agreements in more than one hand. Is it, in other words, a phenomenon for which the mathematical odds against its occurring twice are enormous, or is it something that might reasonably be expected to occur in the handwriting of a number of Elizabethans? But at least one does not have free scope to search for parallels for D throughout all England; D and Shakespeare were dramatists, and the range of search is restricted to the small group of dramatists writing at the end of Elizabeth's reign. On this fact the strength of Greg's case depends.

Greg has summed up his position in four propositions which may be accepted as the most authoritative statement yet made on the subject:

(1) The palaeographic case for the hand of Shakespeare and D being the same is stronger than any that can be made out for their being different.

(2) The hand of Shakespeare is more nearly paralleled in D than in any other dramatic document known to us.

[29] *Problems of Shakspere's Penmanship,* 203.

[30] "Shakespeare's Hand Once More," *Times Literary Supplement* (Nov. 24, and Dec. 1, 1927), 871 and 908.

(3) Setting Shakespeare aside, it can be shown that D was not written by any dramatist of whose hand we have adequate knowledge.

(4) On purely palaeographical grounds there is less reason to suppose that all six signatures were written by the same hand than there is, granting this identity, to suppose that the hand of the signature also wrote the addition to *More*.

It is true that these propositions have been attacked, and it has been stated categorically that, on the materials available for comparison, as good a case could be made for C or for Chapman as the writer of the Addition as for Shakespeare.[31] But no such attempt has been made, for the simple reason that any experienced eye can see that these hands are not the same. It would seem that no infallible criteria have been found for the identification of handwritings and that, after all, insufficient specimens of Shakespeare's hand have survived to put the issue beyond doubt. The palaeographical argument, which might have been conclusive, depends more than any other on a delicate balance of probabilities.

A line of argument allied to the palaeographical one has been developed by J. Dover Wilson.[32] Assuming that D is Shakespeare, can the forms of the letters he uses and the characteristic spellings he employs throw any light on the early printed texts of Shakespeare's plays? In three respects they can. An elaborate classification of misprints in the "good" Quartos which are probably due to misreading shows that similar misprints would be likely to occur from printer's copy in D's hand, and, in fact, modern editors of the Addition have been guilty of misreadings exemplifying four out of five of Dover Wilson's main classes. Secondly, misprints in the Quartos enable us to infer the spelling in the original manuscript which produced the misreading. For example, a misprint like "pallat" for "palace" (*Romeo and Juliet*, v, iii, 107) suggests: (i) that Shakespeare's *c* and *t* could under certain circumstances be mistaken for one another (how this could happen may be seen from a comparison of the *c* of "thinck" in line 138 of the Addition with the *t* of "what" in line 104); (ii) that Shakespeare, like many of his contemporaries, often omitted a final *e* after a palatal *c* or *g* (D does this frequently, though not invari-

[31] Tannenbaum, *Problems of Shakspere's Penmanship*, 190, and *Shakspere and "Sir Thomas Moore,"* 16. Cf. A. Green, "The Apocryphal Sir Thomas More and the Shakespeare Holograph," *Amer. J. Philology*, xxxix (1918), 229–267 at p. 253.

[32] "Bibliographical Links between the Three Pages and the Good Quartos," *Shakespeare's Hand in "Sir Thomas More,"* 113–141.

ably). Thirdly, spellings like "Iarman" (German), which is found in line 128 of the Addition, and the unusual "scilens" (silence) in line 50 have left traces in Shakespearian texts. "Scilens" never occurs in the text itself, but in the speech-prefixes of the Quarto of 2 *Henry IV* Justice Silence is either "Scilens" or "Silens"; the compositor would have normalized the spelling in the text, but when it was a proper name and a speech-prefix he left it as he found it.

Dover Wilson's method, in its concentration on a single hand, is much sounder than that of Leon Kellner in his *Restoring Shakespeare*, where Kellner illustrated his argument from a wide variety of Elizabethan hands, so that the reader ended up with the uneasy feeling that any letter might have been misread for any other, and that the liberty of emendation, instead of being restricted, was being granted new licence. Yet a great many of Dover Wilson's examples, as he is the first to concede, merely prove that Shakespeare, as we already know, wrote a fairly normal English hand and used spellings that are quite common in the period. But he is justified in stressing that the handwriting of the Addition is such as to be liable to cause the same groups of misreadings as are to be found in the Quartos, and that D's spellings reveal no habits at variance with those that can be inferred from the texts of Shakespeare. While the coincidence of the "scilens" spellings is spectacular, it is the accumulation of numerous small details that gives force to his argument.

Tannenbaum has attacked Dover Wilson's conclusion also.[33] He has a point, I think, when he affirms that certain misreadings in the Shakespearian texts are caused by confusion between *e* and the symbol for final *s* or *es* which can be confused with it, but which is not used by D. He also points out that D does not use flourishes such as that which concludes the *m* of 'William' in the conveyance signature, though such flourishes have, he believes, been occasionally mistaken for signs of abbreviation by the compositors who set up Shakespeare's plays. But he seriously underestimates one factor of which Dover Wilson is fully cognizant, and of which everyone is aware who has had to collate printed and manuscript versions of Elizabethan texts, viz. the extent to which compositors altered and normalized spellings found in manuscript. Once again we are justified in concluding that the case for the identity of D and Shakespeare "is stronger than any that has been made out for their being different,"

[33] "More about *The Booke of Sir Thomas Moore*," *PMLA*, XLIII (1928), 767–778 at pp. 774–778, and *Shakspere and "Sir Thomas Moore*," 44–63.

though Dover Wilson's evidence is admittedly only confirmatory and could scarcely be expected to stand by itself alone.

Finally, I have two crumbs to contribute to this part of the discussion. In order to Parallel D's spelling "Iarman," Dover Wilson cites from Shakespeare the misprint "Iamanie" from a speech of Dr. Caius in *The Merry Wives;* Tannenbaum retorts that "Iamanie" is comic dialect and that "*Iarman* is not to be found either in the Quartos or in the Folio." A quick check with the aid of the concordance produced the following result: "Iermane" (*Love's Labour's Lost,* III, i, 192, Q1598), "Iarman" (*2 Henry IV*, II, i, 158, Q1), "Ierman" (*Hamlet,* v, ii 165, Q2), "Iermans" (*Othello,* I, i, 114, Q1), and "a Iarmen on" for "a German one" (*Cymbeline,* II, v, 16, F.). We have no reason, then, to doubt that "Iarman" was a Shakespearian spelling. Secondly, the likelihood of graphic confusion between *x* and *y* has not previously been considered, but anyone familiar with Elizabethan hands who examines D's *y*'s in "Country" (l. 126) and "gyve" (l. 127), or the first *y* in "inhumanyty" (l. 140) will grant the possibility. It is therefore gratifying to find that in *Troilus and Cressida,* v, i, 16, the Quarto reads "box" where the Folio corrects to "boy."

STYLE, THOUGHT AND IMAGERY

Simpson and Spedding first suggested that Shakespeare had had a part in *Sir Thomas More* because of the Shakespearian tone of certain passages. It was the evidence of style that originally drew attention to the play, and had there been no resemblances with Shakespeare's acknowledged works there would have been no attempt to marshal other kinds of evidence. The thought and expression of the Additions are therefore of fundamental importance, and evidence of handwriting and spelling must be secondary to literary considerations. Unless the critical judgment is satisfied that these passages are such as Shakespeare could have written, there can be no question of admitting them to the canon, however Shakespearian the handwriting or spelling.

It would be easy to compile a list of earlier authorities who have been convinced that Shakespeare's style is to be found in the play, and oppose it with another list of names, equally authoritative, of those who have found no need to suppose that he had any part in it.[34] The early commentators like Simpson and Spedding were content

---

[34] See Green, "The Apocryphal Sir Thomas More," 255–257.

to quote a few passages, cite an occasional parallel, and leave the rest to the reader. But a much more intensive examination was made by R. W. Chambers in 1923, and his conclusions were reinforced a few years later by Caroline Spurgeon.[35] In his essay Chambers concentrates on Shakespeare's concept of political order and his attitude to the common people, as expressed in the Jack Cade scenes of *Henry VI*, in *Richard II, Julius Caesar, Troilus and Cressida*, and *Coriolanus*, finding not merely striking parallels of expression and imagery with the Addition, but complete consistency of attitude and thought as well.

It is true that since 1923 further study has brought out a certain element of commonplace in the ideas behind Ulysses' famous speech on degree in *Troilus and Cressida*,[36] so that there may be a tendency to underestimate the force of part of Chambers' argument. But Chambers himself reworked and extended his material in a second essay,[37] which, it seems safe to prophesy, will become a minor classic of Shakespearian criticism. This essay is readily accessible and involves few of the technicalities which have concerned us for the greater part of this paper, so there is no need to summarize it. It is sufficient to say that by means of a line-by-line commentary on the Addition, Chambers marshals his evidence to show not mere isolated parallels but whole sequences of thought and associated groups of images common to both D and Shakespeare.[38] Once again the emphasis is not on the isolated unit but on similar combinations of similar units. The validity of Chambers' method has only recently been strikingly confirmed in the results obtained by its application to the workings of Shakespeare's imagination as studied throughout the whole of the canon.[39]

[35] R. W. Chambers, "The Expression of Ideas—Particularly Political Ideas—in the Three Pages and in Shakespeare," *Shakespeare's Hand in "Sir Thomas More,"* 142–188, and Caroline F. E. Spurgeon, "Imagery in the *Sir Thomas More* Fragment," *Review of English Studies,* VI (1930), 257–270.

[36] Cf. A. O. Lovejoy, *The Great Chain of Being;* Theodore Spencer, *Shakespeare and the Nature of Man;* E. M. W. Tillyard, *The Elizabethan World Picture.*

[37] "Shakespeare and the Play of *More*," in *Man's Unconquerable Mind,* 204–249.

[38] Of particular interest is Chambers's vindication of his "sequences" against the mere collection and citation of isolated parallels, which renders untenable the arguments of L. Schücking, "Shakespeare and *Sir Thomas More*," *Review of English Studies,* I (1925), 40–59, and S. R. Golding, "Robert Wilson and *Sir Thomas More*," *Notes and Queries,* CLIV (1928), 237–239, 259–262.

[39] E. A. Armstrong, *Shakespeare's Imagination.*

Plate I. *The Booke of Sir Thomas More*, fol. 8*a*; Hand "D" (British Museum, Harl. 7368)

Plate II. *The Booke of Sir Thomas More,* fol. 8*b*; Hand "D" (British Museum, Harl. 7368)

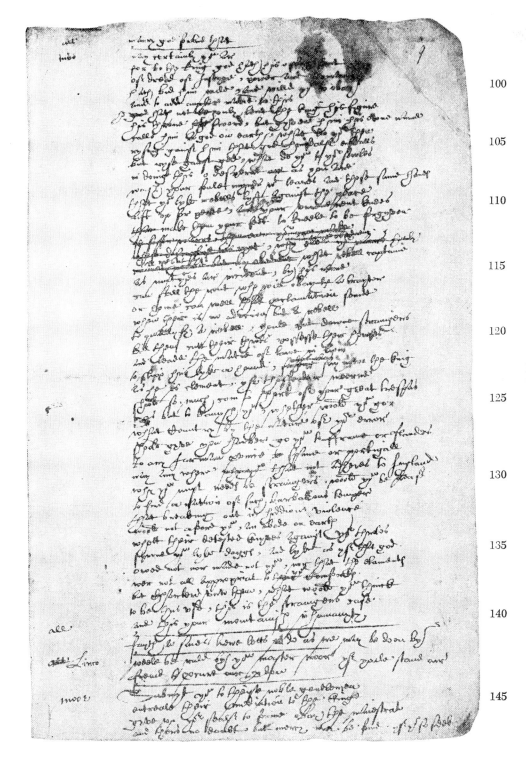

100

105

110

115

120

125

130

135

140

145

Plate III. *The Booke of Sir Thomas More,* upper half of fol. 9; Hand "D" (British Museum, Harl. 7368)

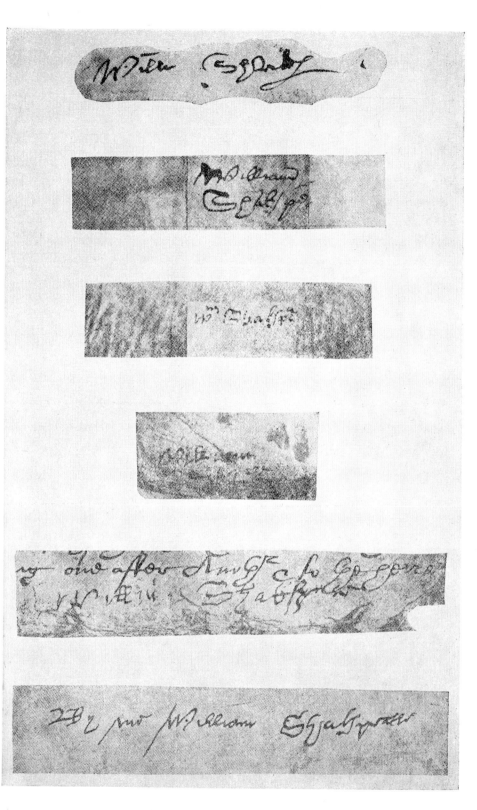

Plate IV. Shakespeare's Signatures

The "Shakespearian" Additions in
The Booke of Sir Thomas More
Addition II *c*

[*Note:* Deletions in the manuscript are printed between square brackets. Pointed brackets indicate readings supplied by Dyce for parts of the manuscript that are now illegible. Words in boldface type have been added by C.]

Lincolne	Peace heare me, he that will not see ⟨a red⟩ hearing at a harry	Fol. 8ᵃ
	grote, butter at a levenpence a pou⟨nde meale at⟩ nyne shillings a	
	Bushell and Beeff at fower ⟨nobles a stone lyst⟩ to me	
[other] **Geo bett**	yt will Come to that passe yf strain⟨gers be su⟩fferd marke him	
Linco	our Countrie is a great eating Country, argo they eate more in	5
	our Countrey then they do in their owne	
[other] **betts clow**	by a half penny loff a day troy waight	
Linc	they bring in straing rootes, which is meerly to the vndoing of poor	
	prentizes, for whats [a watrie] a sorry ꝑsnyp to a good hart	
[oth] **willian**	trash trash,: they breed sore eyes and tis enough to infect the	10
	Cytty wᵗ the palsey	
Lin	nay yt has infected yt wᵗ the palsey, for theise basterds of dung	
	as you knowe they growe in Dvng haue infected vs, and yt is our	
	infeccion will make the Cytty shake which ꝑtly Coms through	
	the eating of ꝑsnyps	15
[o] **Clown, betts**	trewe and pumpions togeather	
Enter Seriant	what say yoᵘ to t⟨he⟩ mercy of the king do yoᵘ refuse yt	
Lin	yoᵘ would haue ⟨vs⟩ vppon thipp woold yoᵘ no marry do we not, we	
	accept of the kings mercy but wee will showe no mercy vppõ	
	the straingers	20
seriaunt	yoᵘ ar the simplest things that eu' stood in such a question	
Lin	how say yoᵘ now prenty prentisses symple downe wᵗʰ him	
all	prentisses symple prentisses symple	
	Enter the L. maier Surrey	
	Shrewsbury	25
[Sher] **Maior**	hold in the kings name hold	
Surrey	frends masters Countrymen	
mayer	peace how peace I [sh] Charg yoᵘ keep the peace	
Shro.	my masters Countrymen	
[Sher] **Williamson**	The noble Earle of Shrowsbury letts hear him	30
Ge betts	weele heare the earle of Surrey	

10: "The Booke of Sir Thomas More"

Brief reference should also be made to the twenty-one-line speech of More which constitutes Addition III. It is in C's hand, but since C is known to be a scribe it is a fair assumption that he could have transcribed it from a scrap of paper in D's handwriting, just as he transcribed part of Addition V from the lines in B's handwriting on fol. 16b. But the argument for Shakespeare's authorship of this speech, which has been asserted by various writers,[40] depends almost entirely on stylistic evidence. An impressive number of parallels with Shakespeare's acknowledged work has been accumulated, and it seems reasonable, if the identity of D and Shakespeare is granted, to accept this speech also as his.

In conclusion, it may be said that if certain details of the argument for Shakespeare's share in *Sir Thomas More* seem less convincing than they did twenty years ago, the essential case remains substantially intact, and R. W. Chambers' paper of 1939 has given it added strength. With the increase of knowledge, too, not only of the handwriting, printing, and spelling of the Elizabethans but of their habits of thought as well we gain a fuller understanding of both Shakespeare and his fellow dramatists. And with every such advance the argument by elimination for Shakespeare's authorship of the Addition becomes stronger: it is increasingly more difficult to propose from among the dramatists of whose work we have knowledge an alternative to Shakespeare. Shakespeare, we perceive, possessed in a unique degree the capacity for rising above the immediate situation to a sense of the human and ethical issues involved in it; he seems instinctively to be able to link it with the best and most characteristic thought of his age. D also shows signs of this capacity, but who else among Shakespeare's contemporaries possessed it? Marlowe and Chapman, in a sense, and perhaps Jonson; but certainly not the Heywoods and Dekkers, however affecting their interpretations of single events may be, nor any of the rest of Henslowe's needy tribe. And dramatists like Marlowe, Chapman, and Jonson are too individual in style and outlook—by comparison with Shakespeare, too doctrinaire—to have written the Addition. To vary an old phrase which is penned in the margin of one of the other additions, *et tu Shakespeare an diabolus.*

[40] Simpson, in his original article, quoted part of this speech for its Shakespearian manner. For modern comment on it, see E. K. Chambers, *William Shakespeare*, I, 514–515; R. C. Bald, "Addition III, of *Sir Thomas More*," *Review of English Studies*, VII (1931), 67–69; H. W. Crundell, *Times Literary Supplement* (May 20, 1939), 297.

	and that yo^u sytt as kings in your desyres	
	aucthoryty quyte sylenct by yor braule	
	and yo^u in ruff of yor [yo] opynions clothd	
	what had yo^u gott; Ile tell yo^u, yo^u had taught	80

and that yo^u sytt as kings in your desyres
aucthoryty quyte sylenct by yor braule
and yo^u in ruff of yor [yo] opynions clothd
what had yo^u gott; Ile tell yo^u, yo^u had taught   80
how insolenc and strong hand shoold prevayle
how ordere shoold be quelld, and by this patterne
not on of yo^u shoold lyve an aged man
for other ruffians as their fancies wrought
wth sealf same hand sealf reasons and sealf right   85
woold shark on yo^u and men lyke ravenous fishes
woold feed on on another

Doll   before god thats as trewe as the gospell
[Betts] **lincoln** nay this a sound fellowe I tell yo^u lets mark him
moor   Let me sett vp before yor thoughts good freinds   90
                    on supposytion, which if yo^u will marke
                    yo^u shall ℙceaue howe horrible a shape
                    yor ynnovation beres, first tis a sinn
                    which oft thappostle did forwarne vs of vrging obedienc to aucthory⟨ty⟩
                    and twere [in] no error yf I told yo^u all   yo^u wer in armes gainst g⟨od⟩   95

all   marry god forbid that   Fol. 9ᵃ
moo   nay certainly yo^u ar
                    for to the king god hath his offyc lent
                    of dread of Iustyce, power and Comaund
                    hath bid him rule, and willd yo^u to obay   100
                    and to add ampler matie to this
                he [god] hath not [le] only lent the king his figure
                    his throne [his] sword, but gyven him his owne name
                    calls him a god on earth, what do yo^u then
                    rysing gainst him that god himsealf enstalls   105
                    but ryse gainst god, what do yo^u to yor sowles
                    in doing this o desperat [ar] as you are
                    wash your foule mynds w^t teares and those same hands
                    that yo^u lyke rebells lyft against the peace
                    lift vp for peace, and your vnreuerent knees   110
                    [that] make them your feet to kneele to be forgyven
                    [is safer warrs, then euer yo^u can make]
                    [whose discipline is ryot, why euen yor [warrs] hurly] [in in to yor obedienc]
                    [cannot ℙceed but by obedienc] tell me but this what rebell captaine
                    as mutynes ar incident, by his name   115
                    can still the rout who will obay [th] a traytor
                    or howe can well that ℙclamation sounde
                    when ther is no adicion but a rebell
                    to quallyfy a rebell, youle put downe straingers
                    kill them cutt their throts possesse their howses   120
                    and leade the matie of lawe in liom
                    to slipp him lyke a hound, [sayeng] [alas alas] say nowe the king

Linc	the earle of Shrowsbury	
betts	weele heare both	
all	both both both both	
Linc	Peace I say peace ar yo⁹ men of Wisdome [ar] or	35
	what ar yo⁹	
Surr	[But] what yo⁹ will haue them but not men of wisdome	
all	weele not heare my L of Surrey, [ ] no no no no no	
	Shrewsbury shr	
moor	whiles they ar ore the banck of their obedyenc	
	thus will they bere downe all things	40
Linc	Shreiff moor speakes shall we heare shreef moor speake	
Doll	Letts heare him a keepes a plentyfull shrevaltry, and a made my	
	Brother Arther watchin⟨s⟩ Seriant Safes yeoman lets heare	
	shreeve moore	
all	Shreiue moor moor more Shreue moore	45
moor	⟨even⟩ by the rule yo⁹ haue among yoʳ sealues	Fol. 8ᵇ
	Comand still audience	
all	⟨S⟩urrey Sury	
all	moor moor	
Lincolne betts	peace peace scilens peace.	50
moor	Yo⁹ that haue voyce and Credyt wᵗ the [mv] nvmber	
	Comaund them to a stilnes	
Lincolne	a plaigue on them they will not hold their peace the deule	
	Cannot rule them	
Moor	Then what a rough and ryotous charge haue yo⁹	55
	to Leade those that the deule Cannot rule	
	good masters heare me speake	
Doll	I byth mas will we moor thart a good howskeeper and I	
	thanck thy good worship for my Brother Arthur watchins	
all	peace peace	60
moor	look what yo⁹ do offend yo⁹ Cry vppõ	
	that is the peace, not ⟨on⟩ of yo⁹ heare present	
	had there such fellowes lyvd when yo⁹ wer babes	
	that coold haue topt the peace, as nowe yo⁹ woold	
	the peace wherin yo⁹ haue till nowe growne vp	65
	had bin tane from yo⁹, and the bloody tymes	
	coold not haue brought yo⁹ to [theise] the state of men	
	alas poor things what is yt yo⁹ haue gott	
	although we graunt yo⁹ geat the thing yo⁹ seeke	
[D] Bett	marry the removing of the straingers wᶜʰ cannot choose but	70
	much [helpe] advauntage the poor handycraftes of the Cytty	
moor	graunt them remoued and graunt that this yoʳ [y] noyce	
	hath Chidd downe all the matie of Ingland	
	ymagin that yo⁹ see the wretched straingers	
	their babyes at their backs, and their poor lugage	75
	plodding tooth ports and costs for transportacion	

173

as he is clement, yf thoffendor moorne
shoold so much com to short of your great trespas
as but to banysh yo{u}, whether woold yo{u} go   125
what Country by the nature of yo{r} error
shoold gyve you harber go yo{u} to ffraunc or flanders
to any Iarman pvince, [to] spane or portigall
nay any where [why yo{u}] that not adheres to Ingland
why yo{u} must needs be straingers, woold yo{u} be pleasd   130
to find a nation of such barbarous temper
that breaking out in hiddious violence
woold not afoord yo{u}, an abode on earth
whett their detested knyves against yo{r} throtes
spurne yo{u} lyke doggs, and lyke as yf that god   135
owed not nor made not yo{u}, nor that the elaments
wer not all appropriat to [ther] yo{r} Comforts.
but Charterd vnto them, what woold yo{u} thinck
to be thus vsd, this is the straingers case

all   and this your momtanish inhumanyty   140

[all] **Linco**   fayth a saies trewe letts [vs] do as we may be doon by
weele be ruld by yo{u} master moor yf youle stand our
freind to pcure our pdon

moor   Submyt yo{u} to theise noble gentlemen
entreate their mediation to the kinge   145
gyve vp yo{r} sealf to forme obay the maiestrate
and thers no doubt, but mercy may be found yf yo{u} so seek ⟨yt⟩

The Original of
Sir John Falstaff—
Believe It or Not*

By Baldwin Maxwell

IN recent years there have been many efforts by students of Elizabethan drama to lift the veil and to attempt not only to discover political significance in what had hitherto been considered harmless plots
but even to identify this or that member of a *dramatis personæ* as
some well-known contemporary personage. During the nineteenth century Fleay and his associates had carried that type of criticism not
only *ad absurdum* but even *ad nauseam*. It passed for a while into
bad repute. However, the opportunity it offers for delightful theories
and astonishing discoveries has proved too great for it to be abandoned. Certainly there must have been many an Elizabethan play with
a political purpose, many a contemporary figure satirized. But can
we by the method most in use today, the mere citing of parallels,
ever hope to identify a character? The advantages and the disadvan-
tages of such a method are the same as those of the old allegorical
interpretations: if an identification cannot be absolutely proved,
neither can it be disproved.

A friend of mine has recently set a student to compile a list of
the different identifications which have been made of characters in
Shakespeare's plays. Although the identifications have for the most
part been concerned with only a few of the major characters, the
student's list already, I am informed, numbers three hundred names.
Obviously they cannot all be right, if any; and by the law of chance
it would appear that any particular identification selected is wrong.

* Reprinted from *Studies in Philology*, xxvii, (1930), 230–232, with permission
of author and publisher.

11: The Original of Sir John Falstaff

How many persons have been identified as the original of Sir John Falstaff I have no idea. Enough, surely, so that one more suggestion can do no harm! Therefore I suggest—and I shall support my suggestion with a list of parallels, not general but specific and particular—that the original of Sir John Falstaff was none other than Robert Greene, Master of Arts.

In a court of law the prosecution labors to establish a motive. Such a motive is ready at hand, for had not Greene savagely attacked the young Shakespeare when he was struggling to establish himself as a dramatist?

Gabriel Harvey calls Greene the "Patriarch of shifters." "Who in London," asks Harvey,

hath not heard of his dissolute, and licentious liuing; . . . his vaineglorious and Thrasonicall brauinge: . . . his villainous cogging, and foisting; his impious profaning of sacred Textes: . . . his riotous and outragious surfeitinge; his continuall shifting of lodginges: his plausible musteringe, and banquetinge of roysterly acquaintaunce at his first comminge; his beggarly departing in euery hostisses debt; his infamous resorting to the Banckside, Shorditch, Southwarke, and other filthy hauntes: . . . his imployinge of Ball (surnamed, cuttinge Balle) [the notorious thief] . . . to leauy a crew of his trustiest companions, to guarde him in daunger of Arrestes. . . . ?

Each phrase applies equally well to Falstaff—the shifting, the boasting, the wild living and the outrageous surfeiting, the quoting of the Bible, the escaping scot-free in London, the frequenting of Shoreditch, and finally the surrounding of himself with a crew of companions and thieves.

Like Falstaff, or "Monsieur Remorse," Greene was frequently on the verge of repentance—a repentance soon laughed away by his associates. As Green tells us in his *Repentance:*

But this good motion lasted not long in mee; for no sooner had I met with my copesmates, but seeing me in such a solemne humour, they demaunded the cause of my sadness: to whom when I had discouered that I sorrowed for my wickednesse of life, . . . they fell upon me in ieasting manner, calling me Puritane and Presizian, . . . with such other scoffing tearmes, that by their foolish perswasion the good and wholesome lesson I had learned went quite out of my remembrance.

Compare the way Poins in Part I, I, ii, 124 ff., jests at Monsieur Remorse.

Both Greene and Falstaff, laboring in the vocation of thieving, carried their conycatching into their lovemaking. As Falstaff promised marriage, so Greene contracted marriage to gain possession of his wife's money. Moreover, Greene's wife was named Dorothy, or "Doll," as he addressed her in the letter written on his deathbed.

Greene and Falstaff have the same lack of generosity toward others, seen in the *Groats-Worth* and in Falstaff's remarks about Hal and Poins as soon as their backs are turned. Both lay the blame for their sins upon the company they have kept. As Falstaff warns the Prince against Poins and his other companions, so had Greene in the *Groats-Worth* warned Nashe. Both Greene and Falstaff make a ridiculous pretense to superiority and to social position.

Falstaff claims to have been attacked by an ever-increasing number of men in buckram; Greene claimed that he had been attacked or wronged by the actors, whom he called "buckram gentlemen."

The redeeming quality of both Greene and Falstaff is wit. "Glad was that printer," said Nashe of Greene, "that might bee so blest to pay him deare for the very dregs of his wit." Harvey called Greene "the Ape of Euphues." Falstaff at times speaks in perfect euphuism—not often, but, what is much more important, only at intervals (e.g., Part I, i, ii, 170 ff.; ii, iv, 456 ff.).

A final parallel is furnished by their dying broken and deserted. The Hostess alone is present to comfort Falstaff; according to Harvey, Greene died deserted by all save his compassionate hostess (Mrs. Isam, the shoemaker's wife) and two women, and it should be noted that throughout his account Harvey speaks of Mrs. Isam as "his hostisse."

So much for the parallels, though many others might be cited. Although it is only human for one to esteem his own suggestion, I believe very few of the identifications which have been offered have been supported by so convincing an array of parallels. If there is anyone who is still unconvinced that Robert Greene was the model for Sir John Falstaff, let him search the *Henry IV* plays for verbal parallels to the pamphlets of Greene. I promise him he will find many.

12

Authenticity and Attribution in the Jacobean and Caroline Drama[*]

By Gerald Eades Bentley

IN the corpus of the drama written in the reigns of James I and his son Charles I, there is to be found a large body of plays with no contemporary ascription of authorship. Among the extant plays are about one hundred anonymous pieces, and, among the plays of the period known by title or allusion only, there are well over a hundred more without authors. It is this large group of more than two hundred plays and titles of plays which have provided the happiest field for irresponsible speculation. Collier and Fleay and Sykes and Lawrence and Wilson have flitted about among the lonely orphans, assigning parents here and putative parents there, and Fleay even going so far as to grant on some occasions a temporary custody later to be revoked. Such mock-judicial activities are more reminiscent of Gilbert and Sullivan than of Malone, and entertaining though they may be and even, upon occasion, enlightening, they create havoc for the literary historian. After working painfully through the attributions of an anonymous play like *The Revenger's Tragedy* to Webster and to Tourneur and to Middleton and to Marston, the disgusted historian is tempted to lay down this principle: Any play first published in a contemporary quarto with no author's name on the title page and continuing without definite ascription of authorship for twenty-five years or more should be treated as anonymous world without end, Amen.

Yet such a principle, however satisfying to our seekers after absolute and final authority and however soothing to badgered and uncer-

[*] Reprinted from the *English Institute Annual 1942* (New York: Columbia University Press, 1943), 101–118, with permission of author and publisher. Two elisions are indicated.

tain historians, would certainly contribute to the perpetuation of error, for it would deny *Tamburlaine* to Christopher Marlowe and *The Woman Hater* to Beaumont and Fletcher. The logical corollary of such a principle—namely, that no play ascribed on an original contemporary title page to a dramatist and remaining unchallenged for twenty-five years should ever be removed from the canon of that dramatist—this corollary is equally dogmatic and equally erroneous. It would saddle Shakespeare forever with *The London Prodigal* and John Webster with *The Thracian Wonder.*

Principles such as those I have just proposed have been enunciated from time to time by dramatic historians. They have never been followed with any consistency even by their own originators.

It seems to me that one of the chief begetters of such misleading principles and of the many false or dubious ascriptions made by scholars in the field of the drama is the common tacit assumption that plays are an art form like the epic or the essay or the lyric. Now plays may be, and often are, great works of art, but plays in general are a business commodity, exhibited in seventeenth-century theaters just like the bears in Paris Garden, and in twentieth-century theaters just like the Dodgers at Ebbets Field. Plays have often been ascribed to authors for purely advertising purposes, just as cigars are given the names of popular heroes who never heard of them. Plays have also been acted and published anonymously, not as a rule because some noble author was trying to conceal his identity, as the Baconians and Oxfordians would have us believe, or because some established dramatist was ashamed of his product, as the historians have often suggested, but simply because the manager of the theater, on the one hand, did not think the dramatist's name on the play bills would attract any pennies to the box, or the publisher of the play, on the other, did not think the author's name on the title page would make any customer pick up the quarto at the bookstall.

Many teachers and scholars and critics apparently feel that it is beneath them to labor with such trash. If they feel so, there are two courses open to them: first, to ignore plays entirely—a consummation devoutly to be wished—and second, to pretend that plays are as respectable as any other literary form and to assign to their authors great concern for contemporary literary reputation, for accurate text, and for the opinion of posterity. The choice of this second course by many sensitive souls all too frequently lured onto the rocks of error by the siren song of Shakespeare has contributed largely to the piles of wreckage of old attributions and false notions of authenticity through which the historian of the drama must laboriously make his way.

So much for the sins of our fathers, and even of our brothers, which are visited upon us. What can we do ourselves which will not lay up trouble for the next generation of dramatic scholars and which may contribute something to an understanding of the dramatic achievements of the great Elizabethans and their successors?

To begin with the obvious, we can make sure that all contemporary sources of information have been examined and checked for every possible contradiction. The number of reputable scholars who have neglected this elementary chore is shocking. . . .

The contemporary sources themselves, however, though infinitely preferable to the impressionistic guesses and pseudoscientific analyses of modern scholars, are often misleading or flatly wrong. The chief repositories of contemporary statements of fact about plays of the first half of the seventeenth century are three. All scholars in the field use them with more or less confidence and would probably agree to list them in order of reliability as (1) the office-book of the Master of the Revels; (2) title pages of early editions; (3) the Stationers' Register.

Only scraps of the office-book of Sir George Buc have been preserved, but a large part of that of Sir Henry Herbert was copied out by Malone and Chalmers from Herbert's own manuscript before that invaluable document was lost around the end of the eighteenth century. Now Herbert was certainly in a position to know more about plays and playwrights, actors and theatres than anyone else in London, yet his extant records are woefully incomplete and not always accurate.

The incompleteness of the record is the first pitfall into which many a fair scholar has come a cropper. Most of Herbert's extant records of licenses for plays were printed by Malone in the third volume of his *Variorum* or by Chalmers in his *Supplemental Apology for the Believers in the Shakespeare-Papers*. Yet even Malone and Chalmers had copied out a number of licenses which they did not print, as is evidenced by manuscript extracts which have been written in the margins and on the flyleaves of books from their libraries. I once analyzed Herbert's records of plays licensed for the King's company and found reason to believe that we have extant records of the licensing of only a little more than half the plays Herbert really allowed for the company from 1622 to 1642.[1] Now obviously Malone and Chalmers had more interest in the plays of the King's company than in those licensed for any other troupe, for the King's men owned nearly all the plays of Shakespeare, Beaumont and Fletcher, Massinger, and Davenant, and a good part of those of Jonson. If Malone and Chalmers, then, neglected such a large part of Herbert's licenses for the King's men, what must be their average for the Queen's company or Prince Charles's or the Revels company? I very much doubt if we have records of so many as half the play licenses which are actually recorded in the manuscript of Sir Henry Herbert's office-book, wherever that elusive document may be.

Yet in spite of this probability, scholars continue to assume that our records of the office-book are complete. Again and again they argue that if we have no record of the license of a given play by a Jacobean or Caroline dramatist, then that play was licensed before 1622 or was surreptitiously acted after 1622 without the required license from the Master of the Revels. Much of Oliphant's work on Beaumont and Fletcher is marred by this assumption, and other Beaumont and Fletcher scholars frequently crash into the same pitfall along with students of Massinger, Shirley, Brome, and most of the other Caroline dramatists.

Yet even when a record of the play is to be found in Herbert's book, that record is not necessarily either complete or accurate. Take the lurid murder case which appears in our records of Herbert's licenses as "A new Tragedy, called, *A Late Murther of the Sonn upon the Mother:* Written by Forde, and Webster."[2]

The entry is dated only September 1624, but it occurs between entries for the third and the fifteenth of September. This laconic record has interested students of Ford and Webster for many years, and though the play itself is not extant much has been written of the appeal of such a subject to the two macabre geniuses of the Jacobean and Caroline theatre and of their selection of such material for dramatic presentation. Unfortunately for such happy speculation, there was a suit about this play, the documents of which were buried in the Public Record Office. Professor C. J. Sisson dug out the records, as he has so many others, and fifteen years ago printed them in *The*

---

[1] *The Jacobean and Caroline Stage* (Oxford, 1941), i, 101.
[2] *The Dramatic Records of Sir Henry Herbert,* ed. Joseph Quincy Adams (1917), 29.

Library under the lovely subtitle of the play, *Keep the Widow Waking*.[3] One of the authors of the tragedy testified in the suit and recorded his part in the play and the parts of his collaborators. That author was neither Ford nor Webster, but the redoubtable old Thomas Dekker, who testified that no brooding dramatist but the manager of the Red Bull theater selected the subject and then set Dekker to work on it with a gang of assistants to speed the composition. The whole group consisted of Thomas Dekker, John Ford, John Webster, and William Rowley. Herbert's record in this case not only left out the names of half the collaborators, but omitted the most important one, Dekker. Note that Dekker's importance in the piece is probably not exaggerated in the records of the suit. He was testifying in the case as one of the defendants; his object would have been to minimize, not to magnify, his part in the play.

Thus, neither the completeness nor the accuracy of our extracts from Sir Henry Herbert's office-book can be taken for granted, though, other things being equal, I should prefer his statements of date, authorship, and theatre to those of any other frequently used source.

The second most reliable source of our information about plays of the time is the title pages of contemporary editions, generally first quartos. In many instances these title pages are our only sources of information about the authorship and circumstances of production of a play. We accept them because no other information is available. Yet we know from the history of the Shakespeare Apocrypha, if from nothing else, that printers dishonestly or mistakenly printed the names of the wrong authors on their title pages. After Shakespeare's death, or, more accurately, after the appearance of the Jonson folio of 1616, title pages are somewhat more accurate than before, for playwriting became more respectable, and more dramatists showed at least a slight concern about the publication of their plays. Yet, even in the time of Charles I, title pages cannot be accepted without question.

In 1640, for example, there appeared a quarto with the title page,

THE CORONATION A COMEDY. As it was presented by her Majesties Servants at the private House in *Drury* Lane. Written by *John Fletcher*. Gent.

This play was reprinted in the second Beaumont and Fletcher folio of 1679. It is, however, quite suspicious that both the prologue and the epilogue for the comedy appear in Shirley's *Poems* of 1646. It

[3] *The Library*, 4th ser., VIII (1927–1928), 39–57, 233–259.

is even more suspicious that in the list of Shirley's plays entitled "A Catalogue of the Authors Poems already Printed" and published in Shirley's *Six New Plays,* of 1652–1653, *The Coronation* appears as one of Shirley's plays, with the note, "Falsely ascribed to *Jo. Fletcher.*" Finally, the case against the title-page ascription to Fletcher is complete when one notes that in Sir Henry Herbert's office-book under the date February 6, 1634/5 there appears the entry, *"The Coronation, by James Shirley, licensed."*[4]

Evidently the title page of the 1640 quarto is wrong, even though Shirley was alive and actively writing at the time of publication. This particular case is all the more curious since William Cooke, one of the publishers of the quarto, was Shirley's own chief publisher at the time and had already issued twelve of his plays. . . .[5]

Of the three primary sources of information about Jacobean and Caroline plays, we have left only the Stationers' Register, and it is probably the least reliable of the three. The difficulties arise not so much with the individual entries for single quartos as with those long lists of plays licensed after the closing of the theaters by Humphrey Moseley and Humphrey Robinson and Richard Marriot. These enterprising publishers certainly did own a large number of play manuscripts, for a great many of those they licensed were duly published by them in the course of a few years, but what about those they licensed but, so far as we know, never published? It is this group of titles which has created most of the confusion.

We can take for example the list of plays which Moseley entered on September 9, 1653. There appear to be forty-two items in this list, and the clerk of the Stationers' Company counted forty-two, for he charged Moseley 21 shillings for the entries. A number of these are without doubt perfectly *bona fide* entries and correct in their ascription of authorship, like the entries for Middleton's *Women Beware Women* and *No Wit No Help like a Woman's,* two plays which Moseley published together four years after the entry. There are also plays like *The Inconstant Lady* by Arthur Wilson. Neither Moseley nor anyone else published this play in the seventeenth century, but we know that Moseley's entry is correct, for there are several contemporary references to the piece, and we have three extant manuscripts of it.

[4] *The Dramatic Records of Sir Henry Herbert,* 36.
[5] Two further examples of false information on the title pages of Caroline plays are here omitted.—Eds.

But there are other entries in the list not so reliable, such as *The Merry Devil of Edmonton* by William Shakespeare, *Henry I* by Shakespeare and Davenport, *The Crafty Merchant, or The Soddered Citizen* by Shakerley Marmion, and *Alphonsus Emperor of Germany* by John Peele. We have good reason to believe that these four ascriptions of authorship are incorrect, but what of "*The History of Cardenio,* by Mr. Fletcher & Shakespeare" or "*The Foole without Booke* by Wm. Rowley"? And what about the ten plays assigned to Philip Massinger, all of them with subtitles, most of them now lost? This list has a very suspicious look because of the odd combination of titles and subtitles. In at least one instance, *The Judge or, Believe as You List,* the two titles do not belong together, for we have the manuscript of *Believe as You List* and there is nothing about a judge in it. In this case Moseley was obviously trying to get two plays licensed for one fee; we cannot tell how many more examples of this practice the list contains. Should each of the lost plays in the list be taken as a genuine product of the author named by Moseley? Should each entry be counted as covering two plays, and if so should each be taken as by the same author? I think there is no satisfactory and inclusive answer to these questions. Each particular item must be considered in relation to the known work of the ascribed dramatist, and even then the conscientious scholar will often be baffled by these entries of large blocks of plays. He can only give the titles recorded by Moseley or Robinson or Marriot with adequate warnings of the possibility of error which he sees.

Let us turn finally to the problems of disintegration and of attribution of authorship as they must be faced sooner or later by the dramatic historian. Disintegration is most familiar to us, I suppose, in the work of Fleay, Robertson, Wilson, and others on the Shakespeare canon and in the work of Boyle, Fleay, Gayley, Macaulay, Sykes, and Oliphant on the plays of the Beaumont and Fletcher folios. Shakespeare, as usual, stands apart because his work has been examined so much more thoroughly and persistently than that of any other English dramatist. If we are ever to be able to recognize with certainty the line of any dramatist and to distinguish the genuine from the spurious in his work, surely we ought to be able to do it by this time for Shakespeare. Yet I wonder how many of us, after reading the work of the disintegrators, can say with complete confidence, "These lines William Shakespeare assuredly wrote; these he definitely did not"?

Evidence for Authorship

If not for Shakespeare, how much less for Beaumont or Fletcher or Massinger or Ford? As I read the work of Oliphant and other students of the Beaumont and Fletcher canon, I am tremendously impressed with their industry, often enlightened by their observations about the style of various Jacobean dramatists, but seldom convinced of their success in separating the work of one collaborator from that of the other. Unless there is external evidence to show that a play was first performed after the death of Beaumont or that another dramatist was thought by his contemporaries to have contributed to a particular play, I think the dramatic historian must label most of the attempts at disintegrating the Beaumont and Fletcher canon "Not Proved."

The problems of attribution are more pervasive than those of disintegration, chiefly because of the large number of anonymous plays which we noted at the beginning. I think, furthermore, that one can point out in recent scholarship a number of thoroughly convincing demonstrations of the authorship of anonymous plays. Not that all modern scholars have got beyond Fleay's delightful guessing games. *The Times Literary Supplement* for March 23, 1922, carried a most entertaining example. W. J. Lawrence, to whose encyclopedic knowledge of the theatre we are all indebted, printed in that issue one of his more fanciful efforts. Beginning with the unknown Thomas Drue who wrote *The Life of the Duchess of Suffolk,* Lawrence identifies him, almost without evidence, with the T.D. who wrote *The Bloody Banquet,* and then with the Thomas Drew who was an actor in the Queen's company. This is the sort of attribution which nobody can deny, but which has little but its impetuosity to recommend it. It is characteristic of Mr. Lawrence's endearingly explosive style that the article should be entitled, "Found: a Missing Jacobean Dramatist."

More to be recommend as examples of the careful analysis of evidence for attribution are Cyrus L. Day's article in the *Publications of the Modern Language Association,*[6] called "Thomas Randolph and *The Drinking Academy,*" and the introduction by John Henry Pyle Pafford and W. W. Greg to the Malone Society reprint of *The Soddered Citizen* attributing that newly discovered manuscript play to John Clavell. Both these studies consider manuscript plays unknown before our time, and both set forth carefully considered reasons for assigning their authorship. Such discussions are welcome contributions to dramatic history. They present the evidence for and

[6] *PMLA,* xl.iii (1928), 800–809.

against the attribution in a conscientious attempt to approach the truth; they are not special pleas to carry away all opposition and get the name of "our candidate" established on the title page.

The problem of attribution is always one of a search for truth, and the honest scholar cannot make it over into a learned detective story. In the last analysis the essential difference between irresponsible and confusing attribution, like so much of Fleay's, and carefully reasoned presentation of evidence, like Cyrus Day's, is to be found in the scholar's conception of himself and his task. The work of the dramatic historian is not a game, and it is not a form of exhibitionism, and the scholar who tries to make it into the one or the other has betrayed a trust. Painstaking research and honest analysis of its results will bring answers to many of our present problems of attribution and authenticity. Others will probably never be solved, and the conscientious historian can only admit that he has failed in his search and has no solution to offer.

13

Internal Evidence
and the Attribution
of Elizabethan Plays[*]

By S. Schoenbaum

I[1]

THE investigator's task, as I see it, is to isolate and describe the special character of a literary work of unknown or doubtful authorship,
to show the extent to which a known writer's work partakes of that
special character, and from this evidence to arrive at an appropriate
conclusion. The enterprise is hazardous, for an author's individuality
never exists as pure essence, but is subtly alloyed by many interrelated
factors: literary conventions and traditions; personal, professional,
social, religious influences. And of all writers the dramatist is most
elusive, as he appears not in his own persona but in the manifold
guises of the personages that are his imaginative creations. All plays,
furthermore, are in a sense collaborations, shaped from conception
to performance by the author's awareness of the resources of actors
and theatre, the wishes of impresario or shareholders, and the tastes
and capacities of the audience.

The investigator working with the Elizabethan drama faces additional difficulties. Far removed in time from his materials, he may
be easily misled into fancying as original what a contemporary would
have instantly recognized as imitation. His task is not eased by the
fact that a great many plays of the period have perished, or by the

[*] Presented in somewhat different form at the English Institute in New York
on Sept. 8, 1960; reprinted from the *Bulletin of The New York Public
Library,* lxv (1961), 102–124, somewhat abridged, with the author's permission.
The author uses "the term 'Elizabethan' loosely, but conveniently, to include
the period until the closing of the theatres in 1642."
[1] The sections have been renumbered, since the introduction and Section I
are here omitted.—Eds.

related fact that plays generally were not held in very high literary esteem, especially before the appearance of the great Jonson Folio in 1616. Artistic individuality is scarcely to be expected in artifacts manufactured for a commercial market. That individuality neverthe-less blossomed—that the age produced not only Shakespeare, Mar-lowe, and Jonson, but also Chapman, Marston, Webster, and a number of other distinctive voices—is a remarkable assertion of the creative principle. But it should not blind the investigator to the parlous condi-tions of his labor—conditions that favor not the establishment of facts but the proliferation of conjecture.

I cannot then accept Arthur Sherbo's "basic premise" that, in ques-tions of authorship, "internal evidence deals with essentials while ex-ternal evidence deals with accidentals," and that "short of an unequivo-cal acknowledgment by the author himself, the value of internal evi-dence outweighs any other."[2] External evidence can and often does provide incontestable proof; internal evidence can only support hy-potheses or corroborate external evidence. So far as the Elizabethan drama is concerned, the justification for the use of internal evidence in determining a canon lies primarily in the inadequacy of the avail-able outward evidence. Our primary sources of information—the title pages of plays, the Stationers' Register, the Office Book of the Master of the Revels, the seventeenth-century catalogues—are pitifully incom-plete, misleading, or inaccurate. Famous "standard" attributions at times rest on remarkably fragile foundations. No record, for example, survives from Kyd's lifetime to connect his name with *The Spanish Tragedy*. The only external evidence that he wrote the age's most sensationally popular melodrama is Heywood's statement in his *Apol-ogy for Actors*, which appeared eighteen years after Kyd's death.

Yet *The Spanish Tragedy* is linked inseparably with Kyd's name. Justly so. For we recognize, with the play's most recent editor, that it stands in "a peculiarly intimate relation" to the closet drama *Cor-nelia*, translated by Kyd from Garnier, and that "the only reasonable way of accounting for the relationship is to say that the same man was responsible for both works."[3] In this case, as in others, the external evidence—by itself hardly overwhelming—is buttressed by the evi-dence of style. The responsible historian is of course aware of the gaps and contradictions in the records with which he works. Thus

[2] Sherbo, "The Uses and Abuses of Internal Evidence," above, No. 1.

[3] Thomas Kyd, *The Spanish Tragedy*, ed. Philip Edwards (London, 1959), p. xvii.

it is that Professor Bentley cannot subscribe to his own tempting formula, mentioned at the beginning of the previous essay, of everlasting
anonymity after twenty-five years. Such a principle, he is quick to
note, would not only deprive Marlowe of *Tamburlaine* but Beaumont
and Fletcher of *The Woman Hater;* it would thrust *The Thracian
Wonder* upon Webster and *The London Prodigal* upon Shakespeare.

Internal evidence used in fruitful conjunction with the meagre external facts stirs no controversy but provides, rather, welcome illumi-
nation of the obscurity in which we must too often work. But it is
another matter to suggest authors where the external evidence is pathetically insufficient (as in the case of *The Bloody Banquet,* with
its 1639 title-page ascription to "T. D.") or nonexistent (as with *The
Fairy Knight, Dick of Devonshire,* and many other plays). It is risky
to attempt the allocation of scenes in collaborations, even when all
the partners are known (Middleton, Rowley, and Massinger's *The Old
Law,* for example, which has come down in a wretched text); riskier
still when not all the collaborators are specified, as in the Beaumont
and Fletcher corpus, amply dissected by the disintegrators. Fraught
with even greater perils are the investigator's attempts to transform
into collaborations plays for which the outward evidence points to
single jurisdiction: Eberle finding Dekker in *The Family of Love,*[4]
Lucas and others seeing Webster in *Anything for a Quiet Life.*[5] But
most dangerous of all is the attempt to overthrow, by the weight of
internal evidence alone, an attribution for which there is external support: here we have the famous case of *The Revenger's Tragedy. . . .*[6]

II

The investigator who works without external evidence to bolster
his conclusions assumes the full burden of proof; he must anticipate
that his assumptions, methods, and claims will undergo the severest
scrutiny. It is a measure of the amateurism of Sykes and Lawrence
and the rest that they did so little to fortify themselves against this

[4] Gerald J. Eberle, "Dekker's Part in *The Familie of Love,*" in *Joseph Quincy
Adams Memorial Studies,* ed. McManaway, Dawson, and Willoughby (Washington, D. C., 1948), 723–738.

[5] John Webster, *Works,* ed. F. L. Lucas (London, 1927), iv, 66–68; H. Dugdale Sykes, *Sidelights on Elizabethan Drama* (Oxford, 1924), 159–172; Richard
Hindry Barker, *Thomas Middleton* (New York, 1958), 191–192.

[6] For a balanced view of the whole problem of attribution, whether by internal
or external evidence, see W. W. Greg's brief, disinterested statement in *A Bibliography of the English Printed Drama to the Restoration* (London, 1939–1959),
iv, xxi–xxii.

inspection. But even today, when there is less excuse, attribution studies frequently offer little or nothing in the way of description or defense of the methods employed. In some cases apparently no thought *has* been given to methodology, or so one would conclude from the cavalier violations of ordinary principles of logical procedure. . . . I cannot, therefore, really apologize for the elementary character of the procedures that I now recommend to canonical investigators. Such interest as these principles may have will lie primarily in the fact that they have to be stated at all. That they do need stating, the illustrations will, I trust, demonstrate.

(1) *External evidence cannot be ignored, no matter how inconvenient such evidence may be for the theories of the investigator.*

The Spanish Gypsy, claimed wholly or in part for Ford by Sykes, Sargeaunt, and others,[7] is credited to Middleton and Rowley on the title pages of the 1653 and 1661 Quartos. There is no reason to suspect fraud on the publisher's part: the flaunting of the names of the dramatists on the title page would not have stimulated sales, if one can judge from their contemporary reputations.[8] The attribution is, moreover, in keeping with the fact that the play was licensed for acting by the Lady Elizabeth's men (July 9, 1623). In the previous year the same company had performed the same authors' *Changeling*, which indeed is advertised by an allusion in the second act of *The Spanish Gypsy*.[9] The outward evidence of authorship is then fairly strong, and the play cannot be dislodged from the Middleton canon on the basis of subjective critical impressions—especially since some Middletonians have no difficulty in reconciling the play, on critical grounds, with the dramatist's acknowledged later work. Other instances might easily

---

[7] Sykes, *Sidelights*, 183–199; E. H. C. Oliphant, *Shakespeare and His Fellow Dramatists* (New York, 1929), ii, 18; M. Joan Sargeaunt, *John Ford* (Oxford, 1935), 41–57; Barker, *Thomas Middleton*, 208–209. I have myself in the past accepted too easily the arguments for Ford (Schoenbaum, *Middleton's Tragedies: A Critical Study*, [New York, 1955], 202, 247).

[8] It should be noted, however, that the same publisher, Richard Marriott, is responsible for the attribution of *Revenge for Honor* to George Chapman on the title page of the 1654 Quarto—although he had previously entered the play on the Stationers' Register as the work of Henry Glapthorne. The most plausible explanation *is*, in this instance, a dishonest commercial intention on the part of Marriott: the name of the famous translator of Homer, thus displayed, might well have been expected to spur the play's sales. But Middleton and Rowley are another matter.

[9] This point is made by G. E. Bentley, *The Jacobean and Caroline Stage* (Oxford, 1956) iv, 894.

be cited of the too casual treatment of relevant external facts. Most striking perhaps is Lucas' work on *The Fair Maid of the Inn*, which was licensed by Herbert in 1626 as Fletcher's composition and printed in the 1647 Beaumont and Fletcher Folio. Lucas includes the play in his standard edition of Webster, and divides it among Webster, Ford, and Massinger—thus eliminating Fletcher entirely.[10] It is Bentley's painful duty to point out that, contrary to Lucas' theories, the Master of the Revels was not an advertising agent, and the King's men, who produced the play and took a direct part in the preparation of the 1647 Folio, knew their business.[11]

(2) *If stylistic criteria are to have any meaning, the play must be written in a style.*

"Very few writers," remarks Miss M. St. C. Byrne, "are capable of anything so distinguished as a recognizable style, and the minor Elizabethan dramatists are definitely not among that happy band. Men like Munday and Chettle used blank verse as quickly, as slickly, and in as unremarkable a manner as the modern journalist uses his so-called prose.[12] The editors of the Oxford *Jonson* make much the same point about Jacobean prose dialogue.[13] Collaborations (which prompted the foregoing observations) and revisions are less likely to have stylistic individuality than the unrevised work of a single author. The partners may adjust their styles to one another; the reviser may imitate his predecessor. In *Eastward Ho*, Jonson, Marston, and Chapman—three of the age's most individualistic writers—pooled their talents to produce a play with remarkable consistency of texture. Whoever added to *The Spanish Tragedy* acquired, as Prior points out, mannerisms and characteristic images of the original author.[14] I do not envy the future investigator who attempts, on the basis of style,

---

[10] Webster's *Works*, IV, 148–152.

[11] *Jacobean and Caroline Stage*, III, 338; V, 1252–1253.

[12] "Bibliographical Clues in Collaborate Plays," *The Library*, 4th ser., XIII (1932), 22–23.

[13] "From the beginning of the seventeenth century there was a tendency for individual dramatic styles in prose dialogue to converge on one more or less established type; somewhat as a modern journal acquires a distinctive style to which all who write for it tend to conform" (Ben Jonson, *Works*, ed. C. H. Herford and Percy and Evelyn Simpson [Oxford, 1925–1952], IX, 637). And Jonas Barish, who has studied Elizabethan dramatic prose more closely than most students, similarly finds that "Elizabethan style, in the theatre particularly, tends toward anonymity" (*Ben Jonson and the Language of Prose Comedy* [Cambridge, Mass., 1960], 281).

[14] Moody E. Prior, "Imagery as a Test of Authorship," *SQ*, VI (1955), 383.

to distinguish between the work of William Faulkner and his collaborators on the screen play of *Land of the Pharaohs*.

Yet a recognizable style, and hence one that may be described,
is perhaps rather less rare than Miss Byrne would have us believe.
Even hacks like Chettle and Munday, with whom she is concerned,
may have occasional strange quirks of individuality. And when she
suggests that style is likely to answer our question only when we are
dealing with genius, Miss Byrne overlooks the startling distinctiveness
that really bad writing can have: Marston at his worst, for example.

The principle holds, however: no style, no stylistic evidence. A collection of stylistic commonplaces isolates nothing and persuades only
the gullible or those already convinced. Such collections—Sykes's
stock in trade—have unfortunately been the rule rather than the exception (*vide* Bentley). As preposterous as any are the attribution
studies of William Wells, who, after expressing learned disagreement
with Sykes, goes on to use similar "evidence" to assign *King Leir,
Alphonsus Emperor of Germany, The Troublesome Reign of King
John, Edward II*, and other plays to Thomas Kyd.[15] The number of
curious additions to the Kyd canon is, Wells grants, "large enough
to evoke hilarious incredulity among leading authorities with a too
conservative bent."[16] With this point I hesitate to quarrel.

(3) *The investigator must always work with reliable texts, prefera-
bly directly with the early editions or manuscripts.*

As in canonical investigation, the closest and most scrupulous
study of texts is required, the validity of this principle should be apparent. Yet Sykes evidently trusted to whichever edition came first
to hand. He used Hazlitt's *Webster* for *Appius and Virginia* and *The
Fair Maid of the Inn*, and the same editor's *Dodsley* for *The Second
Maiden's Tragedy, Lust's Dominion*, and other plays. He relied on
Dyce's *Middleton* for *Anything for a Quiet Life*, Pearson's reprint of
Chapman for *Alphonsus*, and (not without amply justified misgivings)
the Mermaid *Webster and Tourneur* for *The Revenger's Tragedy*. Of
these editions one, the Dyce *Middleton*, was an admirable achievement for its own time; but that time was 1840. Yet T. S. Eliot defers
to Sykes as "perhaps our greatest authority on the texts of Tourneur

---

[15] William Wells, "The Authorship of 'King Leir,'" *N&Q*, CLXXVII (1939),
434–438; "Thomas Kyd and the Chronicle-History," *N&Q*, CLXXVIII (1940),
218–224 and 238–243; and "'Alphonsus, Emperor of Germany,'" *N&Q*, CLXXIX
(1940), 218–223 and 236–240.
[16] "Thomas Kyd and the Chronicle-History," 219.

and Middleton."[17] So much for our greatest. Investigators continue, however, to rely upon unsuitable texts. In two recent books concerned with the Dekker canon, the data—often involving small details of style—are taken from the miserable Shepherd reprint of Dekker's plays, despite the fact that the first volumes of the superb Bowers edition have for several years been readily available.[18]

(4) *Textual analysis logically precedes canonical analysis.*

The wise investigator knows his own text and what evidence it may afford of corruption, revision, or collaboration. Apparently Lawrence did not know the Quarto of *Eastward Ho* when he suggested that before publication the play had undergone authorial revision, presumably by Jonson, so that offensive passages might be deleted and the gaps "neatly" closed.[19] The editors of the Oxford *Jonson* have since shown that the cuts were almost certainly the work of the publisher, and that, with the exception of the notorious passage on the Scots in Act III, the gaps were in fact not closed.[20]

Thus the canonical question bears an intimate relation to the textual problem. Further, an apparent matter of style may conceivably be an actual matter of text. Because the only extant early edition of Shakespeare's *Pericles* falls into sections of unequal merit, some authorities have assumed that the play is a collaboration. According to this view, the second author took over with the third act, when the style suddenly improves. But if Edwards is correct in suggesting that the 1609 Quarto represents a memorial reconstruction by a pair of reporters—the first responsible for the first two acts; the second, better skilled, for the last three—then we have no basis for regarding the original play of *Pericles* as anything but the work of a single dramatist.[21] Edwards' suggestion is of course only one hypothesis of many that have been offered to explain a particularly difficult problem. But it illustrates a possibility that other canonical investigators have failed even to consider.

[17] T. S. Eliot, "Cyril Tourneur," *Selected Essays* (London, 1951), 186.

[18] M. T. Jones-Davies, *Un peintre de la vie londonienne, Thomas Dekker* (Paris, 1958), 2 vols.; Barker, *Thomas Middleton.*

[19] W. J. Lawrence, *Pre-Restoration Stage Studies* (Cambridge, Mass., 1927), 363–364.

[20] Jonson's *Works*, IV, 495–498; IX, 637.

[21] Edwards, "An Approach to the Problem of *Pericles*," *Shakespeare Survey*, V (Cambridge, 1952), 25–49. In his New Shakespeare edition of *Pericles*, J. C. Maxwell considers and rejects the arguments in Edwards' "important article" (1956, xvi–xviii). Greg, however, regards them more favorably (*The Shakespeare First Folio* [Oxford, 1955], 98).

13: Attribution of Elizabethan Plays

In dealing wth the minute features of a dramatic text—spelling, linguistic forms, punctuation, and the like—the investigator has a special problem. He must recognize the possibility of compositorial intervention in the case of printed texts, and scribal intervention in the case of manuscripts. We know that compositors and scribes were capable of exercising considerable autonomy over certain features of the manuscripts they were reproducing. The impressionists—as I shall refer hereafter to the school of Oliphant and Sykes—do not often trouble themselves with considerations so hostile to romance, and it is not surprising that the skeptical reader should trouble himself as little with data gathered in a vacuum. On the other hand, an investigator like Cyrus Hoy, aware of the relevant bibliographical considerations, disarms us at the outset of his study of the Beaumont and Fletcher canon by forthrightly discussing the role of compositors and scribes.[22] Hoy's criteria for authorship—the presence or absence of certain pronominal and verbal forms and contractions—are simple enough and have been employed by previous students. Certainly they are not equally serviceable for all the collaborators traced in the Beaumont and Fletcher corpus. But these tests have never been handled with the like judgment and discretion, and for this reason Hoy's monograph has from the first commanded respect.[23]

(5) *For any author proposed, a reasonable amount of unquestioned dramatic writing, apart from collaborations, must be extant.*

The more plays the better; better yet if some precede and others follow the work under consideration, as a theory of imitation is then with more difficulty maintained. Oliphant suggests the possibility that Thomas Watson had a hand in *Thorney Abbey* (printed in 1662 as by "T. W."), and he goes on to advise that "anyone who wants a quite new field of Elizabethan study might first steep himself in a knowl-

[22] Cyrus Hoy, "The Shares of Fletcher and His Collaborators in the Beaumont and Fletcher Canon," *Studies in Bibliography*, VIII (1956), 137–142. [This essay is reprinted below, No. 14; for a complete listing of Hoy's articles, see n. 55 of essay No. 4, above—Eds.]

[23] It must be said, however, that Hoy is most effective when he relies upon linguistic criteria. When he turns (as indeed he must) to other kinds of evidence to supplement inconclusive linguistic findings, he drifts into stylistic impressionism. See, for example, Hoy's discussion of *The Laws of Candy* (*Studies in Bibliography*, XIII, 97–100), which he gives entirely to Ford. Hoy goes on to assign Ford a share in Act II, Sc. 1, of *The Fair Maid of the Inn*, on the very doubtful basis that "one passage therein echoes fairly closely a passage of similar import from III, 2, of *The Laws of Candy* . . ." (102–103). Thus, as so often in the work of Oliphant and company, one inference leads to another, supposition is based upon supposition.

edge of Watson's poetry and then read the dramas (and especially the unattached dramas) of the period prior to the middle of 1592, with an eye to determining his presence."[24] The value of the advice is lessened by the fact that not a single play survives that is known to be the work, in whole or in part, of Thomas Watson. Thus a whole new field of study remains unexplored.[25]

(6) *Intuitions, convictions, and subjective judgments generally, carry no weight as evidence.* This no matter how learned, perceptive, respected, or confident the authority. . . . [26]

The value of intuitions is that they are sometimes right. Their correctness is determined by the evidence. Nothing else counts.

(7) *Wherever possible, stylistic evidence should be supplemented by textual evidence.*

A playwright's individuality may find expression in a number of accidentals: his idiosyncrasies with regard to speech prefixes, stage directions, act divisions, the recording of entrances, and so forth; his peculiarities of spelling, punctuation, and abbreviation. As with linguistic preferences, the usefulness of the data depends entirely upon the fidelity with which scribes or compositors have followed the author's manuscript—provided they worked from author's manuscript. Because so little autograph dramatic manuscript has survived from the Elizabethan period, it is often impossible to do more than theorize about a playwright's habits with regard to these minutiae. Yet bibliographical evidence may at times provide a valuable corroboration of an attribution already probable on critical grounds. This is demonstrated in Bowers' textual introduction to Dekker and Massinger's *The Virgin Martyr*.[27] For Massinger there survives the holograph manuscript of *Believe as You List;* for Dekker we have only a single scene from *Sir Thomas More,* but valid inferences can be made from Dekker's printed texts. The 1642 Quarto was set by a single compositor, probably from the holograph papers of the two authors. Guided by such minute features of the text as the spellings *Cesarea* and *Cæsarea*

---

[24] E. H. C. Oliphant, "Problems of Authorship," *MP,* viii (1911), 439.

[25] The next—and ultimate—step is to attribute plays to persons for whom we have no literary remains whatsoever. That step has, indeed, been taken more than once.

[26] We omit a paragraph pointing out that T. S. Eliot singles out as characteristically Middletonian a passage in *The Changeling* from the last scene, which is very probably the unaided work of Rowley.—Eds.

[27] Reprinted below, No. 15.—Eds.

and the use of hyphens in compounds, Bowers effectively supplements the stylistic evidence for scene allocation.

Such textual evidence has not often enough been brought to bear on canonical problems. *The Puritan,* to cite but one example, has long puzzled scholars. Printed in 1607 as by "W. S.," it is certainly not by Shakespeare. A number of authorities feel it may be a Middleton work. The play is a comedy of London life acted by the Children of Paul's about 1606; at that time Middleton was the chief Paul's dramatist, and he was writing London comedies. There is some stylistic evidence for Middleton. No other plausible candidate for authorship has been proposed. But the case, as it stands, is inconclusive; further evidence is badly needed if the play is to be given even a conjectural place in the Middleton canon. Yet, although a number of investigators have made pronouncements about *The Puritan,* and although we have a sufficient quantity of dramatic manuscript in Middleton's hand, the 1607 Quarto has never been studied for spelling, punctuation, and other textual clues to authorship. Nor, for that matter, has it been studied for the related evidence of linguistic preferences.

The seven principles I have outlined do not exhaust the possibilities for cautionary advice to canonical investigators. Other strictures, at least equally wholesome, will no doubt occur to readers who have concerned themselves with attribution questions. The principles I have suggested derive from my own experience with particular problems and with the literature of attribution, which I have had to explore rather systematically in revising Alfred Harbage's *Annals of English Drama.* All seven reflect my dissatisfaction with the casual methodlessness of stylistic impressionism, the dominant mode of investigation during the past half century. That methodlessness is, I feel, largely responsible for the disesteem in which authorship studies are now held, at least in the area of Elizabethan drama.

III

It is not possible, in the compass of a single essay, to deal with very many—let alone all—of the tests by which investigators in their wisdom or folly have sought to prove authorship by style. Some of the criteria that have been employed are, in any case, too feeble even to require citation. But one or two tests, particularly that of parallel passages, certainly call for serious discussion, while still others, such as metrical investigations, may for present purposes be briefly considered.

"The danger of metrical evidence is that it is too often believed." So wrote Lucas some years back in his edition of Webster (IV, 250). After giving entirely persuasive reasons for regarding the tests with profound distrust, he goes on to apply them himself to *Anything for a Quiet Life* and *The Fair Maid of the Inn*, with results no happier than those of his predecessors. Today little danger exists of metrical statistics being too easily believed, except perhaps by their compilers. If the use of such evidence can be justified at all, it is only as corroboration for the assignment of scenes of collaborate plays in which the partners have been identified and are known to have widely differing metrical habits (e.g., Middleton and Rowley's *Fair Quarrel* and *The Changeling*). But even with such cases previous results testify to the need for extreme caution.[28]

Imagery studies have also yielded much dubious evidence. The hazards are nicely illustrated in the work of Marco Mincoff and the late Una Ellis-Fermor. Each made, unaware of the other, a detailed study of the imagery of *The Revenger's Tragedy*.[29] Mincoff concluded that the play was Middleton's; Ellis-Fermor, that it must be Tourneur's. Mincoff avoids certain pitfalls: he does not use imagery as the basis for pseudobiographical reconstructions, which must be reckoned as evidentially worthless. But skeptical readers will hardly be persuaded by his data, and the conflicting results achieved by two well-known scholars working on the same play and concerned with the narrowest possible field of author-candidates do not inspire confidence in the method. The strictures (discussed below) relevant to the test for parallels may be held to apply to image tests as well, and may provide some discipline. But the image-hunter faces special difficulties. The need for selection—few words do not convey an image of some kind—and classification inevitably enlarges the subjective factor in attribution work. The investigator is, moreover, hampered by our very limited knowledge of the images and image-patterns favored by the various minor Elizabethan dramatists. Detailed study of im-

[28] Metrical statistics for Rowley's plays have been derived from texts in which printers and editors have misdivided lines and printed prose as verse and verse as prose; see Dewar M. Robb, "The Canon of William Rowley's Plays," *MLR*, XLV (1950), 9–10. Robb justly concludes that "Metrical tests based upon such texts are worse than useless."

[29] U. M. Ellis-Fermor, "The Imagery of 'The Revengers Tragedie' and 'The Atheists Tragedie,'" *MLR*, XXX (1935), 289–301; Marco K. Mincoff, "The Authorship of *The Revenger's Tragedy*," *Studia Historico-Philologica Serdicensia*, II (1939), 1–87.

agery is a relatively recent critical preoccupation, and misgivings about applying its techniques prematurely to authorship problems would seem to be fully warranted.[30]

The foundation of most stylistic attributions during the past fifty years has not, however, been imagery or metrics, but the testimony of parallels: unusual correspondences of language and thought, generally in brief passages, between the doubtful play and the acknowledged works of the suggested dramatist. This test too has occasioned doubts and skeptical protests. "There is nothing more dangerous," E. K. Chambers declared, "than the attempt to determine authorship by the citation of parallels."[31] More recently, the editors of the Oxford *Jonson* have remarked upon "the illusory test of parallel passages" (IX, 636), and Bentley has deprecated, with customary vigor, the "parallel-passage 'evidence' of modern enthusiasts."[32] But in this instance the difficulties are, I feel, different in character and significance from those presented by the tests I have already touched upon. Most conservative editors, the Simpsons included, are able to use the evidence of parallels, and most conservative historians, Bentley included, can accept attributions based chiefly on such evidence.

In his account of the disintegration of Middleton's *Anything for a Quiet Life* by the impressionist quartet of Sykes, Oliphant, Lucas, and Dunkel, Bentley provides (IV, 859–860) an at times almost farcical but essentially sad chronicle of the misuse of stylistic evidence. That evidence consists mainly of parallel passages. Bentley's chief complaint is that "most of the passages are not parallel, and the words and phrases are by no means peculiar to Webster [Middleton's proposed collaborator]." The objection to commonplace or unparallel parallels occurs often in *The Jacobean and Caroline Stage*. It is a legitimate objection, but applies less to a method than to its abuses. For if the parallels are not parallel and the words and phrases are commonplace, the test, in a very real sense, has not been employed. . . .

[30] Certain of the pitfalls are usefully discussed by Prior in "Imagery as a Test of Authorship," 381–386. The complexities of definition and classification are ably surveyed by Edward B. Partridge in *The Broken Compass: A Study of the Major Comedies of Ben Jonson* (London, 1958), 19–36. Partridge believes that "imagery cannot be safely used to settle questions about the canon of an author" (p. 14).

[31] *William Shakespeare: A Study of Facts and Problems* (Oxford, 1930), I, 222.

[32] *Jacobean and Caroline Stage*, IV, 860.

Nor does the amassing of ungraded parallels prove anything. This truth was stated almost three decades ago by Miss Byrne.[33] At the same time she offered five Golden Rules, as she reasonably described them, for the improvement of parallel hunting. Miss Byrne observed that parallels vary in quality, and that correspondences of thought and phraseology are greatly superior to simple verbal parallels. She reasoned that parallel collectors may pass logically from the known to the anonymous or from the known to the collaborate play, but less securely from the collaborate to the anonymous work. She did not skirt the problem that even striking parallels may admit of more than one explanation: they may testify to common authorship, but they may also be the result of coincidence or of imitation, conscious or unconscious. Above all, Miss Byrne stressed the necessity for the careful grading of parallels, and for submitting them to negative checks to show that they cannot be duplicated as a body in acknowledged plays of the period. . . .

Allied to verbal parallels, and subject to some of the same strictures governing the admissibility of evidence, are the larger correspondences of thought and theme, characterization and dramatic technique. But parallels of this kind—which for convenience I shall call literary correspondences—also make special demands of their own. Their usefulness depends closely upon the investigator's capacities for literary analysis, and the precision with which he can formulate critical distinctions. In practice the canonical impressionists have been, as we might expect, critical impressionists, and the subjective element present in all criticism has been in their work pervasive and detrimental. Their inclination, insufficiently resisted, is to make oversimplified descriptive pronouncements and pass oversimplified value judgments. A scene is by Jonson because it is "masterful," by Middleton because "it has his irony," by Peele or Greene or Heywood because it is not very good. As evidence for Dekker's authorship of *Blurt, Master Constable,* Lawrence suggests that two songs in the play "have a good deal of that careless grace of style, what one might characterize artful artlessness, which marks Dekker's lyrics."[34] Apparently it did not occur to Lawrence that precisely the same observations might be made about any tolerable Elizabethan lyric, and the age produced a number of tolerable lyrics. The limited critical value of

[33] See n. 12, above.
[34] W. J. Lawrence, "Dekker's Theatrical Allusiveness," *Speeding Up Shakespeare* (London, 1937), 118.

this kind of impressionism is sufficiently obvious. As evidence its value is nil.

Yet verbal parallels and literary correspondences—defined correspondences, not mere impressions—may provide a basis for attributions acceptable to the responsible historian, critic, and editor. The evidence of style—largely of parallels—for the assignment of *The Queen* to Ford is most impressive.[35] Archer surely erred in assigning the play to Fletcher in his 1656 play list, and the error is satisfactorily explained by Greg. The attribution has gone unchallenged since Bang proposed it over half a century ago. An equally successful argument for attribution was made by Cyrus Day, who pointed out striking resemblances of phraseology, dramatic situation, and character portrayal between an anonymous seventeenth-century comedy, *The Drinking Academy*, and the known writings of Thomas Randolph, a distinctly minor dramatist who habitually pillaged his own works.[36] The literary correspondences are in this case satisfyingly concrete: the characters of Worldly, Knowlittle, and Cavaliero Whiffe in *The Drinking Academy* are equivalent to Simo, Asotus, and Ballio in *The Jealous Lovers*. The verbal parallels with nine of Randolph's acknowledged pieces are numerous and often unusual. There are no external facts to contradict the evidence of style, and Randolph's authorship of the play has been accepted by (among others) Hyder Rollins, Fredson Bowers, and G. E. Bentley.

IV

The results of any single test of authorship have to be viewed, of course, as part of a larger design. An investigator like Hoy, applying a limited number of linguistic criteria to the Beaumont and Fletcher canon, must at times supplement his findings with other kinds of evidence, and he recognizes fully that his own work depends in part upon the work of others before him. A case for attribution may well represent the patient efforts of a number of scholars over a long period of time. Each contributes his particular bits of evidence. The ultimate effect sought is a cumulative one, in which all the internal evidence—stylistic, bibliographical, and linguistic—converges inexora-

[35] See *The Queen, Materialien,* ed. W. Bang (Louvain, 1906), vii–ix, 41–57; also Sargeaunt, *John Ford,* Appendix I; Sykes, *Sidelights,* 173–182; and Bentley, *Jacobean and Caroline Stage,* III, 457–458.

[36] Cyrus L. Day, "Thomas Randolph and *The Drinking Academy*," *PMLA,* XLIII (1928), 800–809.

bly upon a single possible author-identification, an identification compatible with the known external information.

This cumulative effect no doubt is, as Sherbo and others have urged, something apart from and greater than the individual pieces of testimony of which it is composed, just as a building transcends the materials—the steel, concrete, wood, and plaster—that have gone into its making. But the architect of attributions must beware lest his materials be merely of the air, airy—the formulas of style and expression that are the common currency of an age. Thus the word "dilling," as the Simpsons complain with understandable irritation, "is not 'a Marston word' because it occurs once in the text of Marston . . . and 'well-parted' . . . is not exclusively a Jonson phrase when it is found in Shakespeare, Webster and Rowley, and Field."[37] Zeros, Ephim Fogel neatly puts it, no matter how great their number, add up to zero.[38]

Yet proper methods, employed by disinterested seekers after truth, may yield inconclusive results. Attribution proposals as firmly supported as those for *The Queen* or *The Drinking Academy* are, after all, rare, and the successful identification of the authors of collaborate plays rarer still. The investigator may find himself, sooner than he anticipated, at the frontiers of ignorance, which after so much expenditure of sweat and ink, remains a spacious domain. The words with which Baldwin Maxwell concludes his study of *A Yorkshire Tragedy* apply equally well to a number of other plays of anonymous or doubtful authorship. "A convincing identification of the author or authors . . . ," Maxwell writes, "if it is ever to be accomplished, must await our clearer knowledge of what were the peculiar characteristics of the various Jacobean dramatists."[39] The trend away from simple impressionism to a more analytical criticism (well exemplified by such recent work as Jonas Barish's *Ben Jonson and the Language of Prose Comedy*) may help to provide that knowledge with regard to the larger aspects of dramatic art. Electronic calculating machines will make possible on a wide scale the compilation of valuable statistical data—information about spelling, linguistic preferences, and other accidentals of style. They will also facilitate work on concordances. The few such tools now readily available—the Shakespeare, Kyd, and Marlowe concordances—have demonstrated how vulnerable is some of the

---

[37] Jonson's *Works*, ix, 636–637.
[38] See above, No. 4.
[39] *Studies in the Shakespeare Apocrypha* (New York, 1956), 196.

vocabulary evidence put forward by the impressionists. Further shocks will no doubt be felt as the stock of source materials for negative checks is increased. Cornell University has led the way in the pioneering application of electronic computers to literary research; others may be expected to follow.

But it would be excessively hopeful to assume that, even with better tools and more refined methods, students will be able to find answers—plausible explanations, I should say—for the majority of our vexing attribution problems. The investigator may be halted by unbridgeable gaps in his evidence; he may find himself faced with the stubborn reluctance of facts to dispose themselves conveniently in support of hypotheses. . . . [40]

There is a place for hypothesis as well as for demonstration, and in the field of Elizabethan drama, where the factual records are far from satisfactory, hypothesis assumes an especially important role. . . .

But if hypothesis is to be accorded its full value, it must be recognized and presented as such. Not only in authorship studies but in almost every specialty, we have encountered studies in which the evidence does not support the claims which the scholar's enthusiasm has led him to make. No doubt many a worthwhile speculation has been too easily dismissed because of the impatience that undue partisanship arouses. It is good, I believe, that we pay tribute now and then to the virtue of recognizing our limitations.

"Several things dove-tailed in my mind," writes John Keats in perhaps the most famous passage of his correspondence, "and at once it struck me what quality went to form a Man of Achievement, especially in Literature, and which Shakespeare possessed so enormously—I mean *Negative Capability,* that is, when a man is capable of being in uncertainties, mysteries, doubts, without any irritable reaching after fact and reason. . . ." The scholar no less than the poet must have his own kind of negative capability. He must know and accept the often frustrating limitations of the methods available to him if, in his quest to dispel illusions and errors, he is not to create new ones in their place.

---

[40] A summary of the "perplexities and frustrations" surrounding canonical study of the "most important Elizabethan play of disputed authorship," *The Revenger's Tragedy,* is here omitted for want of room.—Eds.

The Shares of Fletcher and His Collaborators in the Beaumont and Fletcher Canon[*]

By Cyrus Hoy

THE Beaumont and Fletcher canon consists traditionally of fifty-two plays, but it has long been recognized that of these only a small number represent the work of the two dramatists in collaboration.[1] The exact number has yet to be determined, but modern scholarship is agreed that less than twelve of the vast corpus of plays which are currently designated by Beaumont and Fletcher's names are indeed products of their joint authorship. Essentially, the some forty plays that remain represent the unaided work of Fletcher, or Fletcher's work in collaboration with dramatists other than Beaumont. Chief among these is Philip Massinger, whose share in the plays of the corpus can be demonstrated beyond any doubt, but there are others, and Beaumont-and-Fletcher scholarship from Fleay to Oliphant has suggested as candidates for the authorship of the non-Beaumont, non-Fletcher, non-Massinger portions of the plays in question, the names of virtually every dramatist known to have been plying his trade in Jacobean London. Among those whose names, with varying degrees of plausibilty, have been advanced, are Nathan Field, William Rowley, Middleton, Shirley, Ford, Webster, Tourneur, Shakespeare, Ben Jonson, Chapman, Daborne, and Robert Davenport.

[*] Reprinted from *Studies in Bibliography* (Papers of the Bibliographical Society of the University of Virginia), VIII (1956), 129–146, with permission of the author and publisher; subsequent parts of this study, not reprinted here, appeared in volumes IX (1957), XI (1958), XII (1959), XIII (1960), XIV (1961), and XV (1962).
[1] Throughout this study, in speaking of "the Beaumont and Fletcher canon" I refer to the plays published in the second folio (1679), including Beaumont's *Masque* but excluding Shirley's *The Coronation*.

14: The Beaumont and Fletcher Canon

Any investigation into the authorship of the plays which comprise the Beaumont and Fletcher canon will not, in the nature of things, consist merely in separating the work of Beaumont from the work of Fletcher. Quite apart from the problem of determining which among the fifty-two plays of the corpus are indeed Beaumont and Fletcher collaborations, there remains the sizable task of distinguishing the work of Fletcher from that of his various other collaborators apart from Beaumont. To distinguish any given dramatist's share in a play of dual or doubtful authorship, one must possess some body of criteria which, derived from the unaided plays of the dramatist in question, will serve to identify his work in whatever context it may appear. On this score, the question of authorship in the Beaumont and Fletcher canon is complicated at the very outset, for with the exception of his *Masque*, there is no play that can with any certainty be regarded as the unaided work of Beaumont. And while the *Masque* may afford a good enough indication of Beaumont's metrical habits, the poetic diction in which its verse is cast tends to preclude any widespread use of the linguistic forms—especially contractions—which comprise the particular body of criteria to be used as authorial evidence in the present study. Thus, in establishing evidence that can be used in determining the respective shares of the collaborating dramatists, it is necessary to proceed from the known to the unknown, the known in this case being the unaided plays of Fletcher (which, as will be seen, can be identified) and of Massinger (about which there is no problem of identification).

My purpose in the present study is to show (1) how the unaided plays of Fletcher can be singled out from among the other plays of the canon, and (2) how the pattern of linguistic preferences which emerges from Fletcher's unaided plays contrasts sufficiently with the language practices in the unaided plays of Massinger as to afford a basis for distinguishing the work of the two dramatists one from the other. It will be noted that the tests to be applied in this and subsequent studies tend not so much to overturn the usual assignment of shares in the plays of the canon as to confirm previous attributions by a more extensive use of linguistic evidence than has hitherto been brought to bear upon the works in question. This is particularly true of Fletcher and Massinger, whose shares have been assigned within reasonably specific limits since the days of Boyle and Oliphant; though it might be argued that tests of the present kind serve to base such assignments on rather more demonstrable evidence than has sometimes been used in the past, while they tend as well to define somewhat more precisely the extent of previous attributions. In the case of such dramatists as Field, Shirley, and Ford, it will be seen in a later article that linguistic evidence provides a more certain basis for assigning their share in the plays of the canon than has yet been available.

I

The criteria which I propose to apply in investigating the plays of the Beaumont and Fletcher corpus are of a linguistic nature. By linguistic criteria I mean nothing more complicated than an author's use of such a pronominal form as *ye* for *you*, of third person singular verb forms in *-th* (such as the auxiliaries *hath* and *doth*), of contractions like *'em* for *them*, *i'th'* for *in the*, *o'th'* for *on/of the*, *h'as* for *he has*, and *'s* for *his* (as in *in's*, *on's*, and the like). There is nothing particularly new in the use of criteria of this sort, and I can claim no originality for any of the linguistic tests that I apply in the course of this study. In 1901, A. H. Thorndike drew attention to the use of the colloquial contraction *'em* as a possible test of authorship.[2] Thorndike found the form to occur frequently in Fletcher, and not at all in Massinger, but since his evidence for Massinger was based on Gifford's edition—wherein *'em* is consistently expanded to *them*—his conclusions were vitiated, as he later pointed out in an errata slip. Nonetheless, the use of *'em* as opposed to *them* can afford a significant clue to distinct linguistic preferences, and the relevance of Thorndike's evidence remains, though it does not apply in quite such a clear-cut fashion to Fletcher and Massinger as he originally believed.

In editing *The Spanish Curate* for the Variorum Beaumont and Fletcher in 1905, R. B. McKerrow noted the marked preference for the colloquial form *ye* of the pronoun *you* in Fletcher's portion of that play, and W. W. Greg, in his Variorum edition of *The Elder Brother*, made the same observation with regard to that play. The extent to which Fletcher employs the pronominal form *ye* was noted independently by Paul Elmer More, who commented upon it in an article in *The Nation* in 1912.[3] In 1916, in an article in the *Publications of the Modern Language Association of America*, W. E. Farnham considered the use of such contractions as *'t* (for *it*, as in *to't*, *on't*, *in't*,

---

[2] *The Influence of Beaumont and Fletcher on Shakespeare*, 24 ff.

[3] Reprinted in *Shelburne Essays*, 10th ser., 3 ff. See also C. M. Gayley, *Francis Beaumont, Dramatist* (1914), 271–273.

etc.), *'s* (for *his* or *us*, as in *on's, to's*, etc.), *i'th, o'th'*, and the like, as a possible clue to authorship.[4] Most recently, in 1949, A. C. Partridge has applied linguistic evidence of this sort in his study of the authorship of *Henry VIII*, adding such additional criteria as are to be derived from the occurrence of the auxiliary *do* as a mere expletive in affirmative statements, and the use of the inflexional ending *-th* in the third person singular of notional and auxiliary verbs.[5] Linguistic tests of the sort that I have indicated have not, however, been hitherto applied to the question of authorship on any very considerable scale. The observations of both McKerrow and Greg were made incidentally in the course of editing single plays, and neither ever pursued the matter further. Paul Elmer More, after examining the occurrence of *ye* in fourteen plays, and pointing to the possible value that such evidence might have as an indication of Fletcher's share in the plays of the canon, added that work of the sort required for any detailed study of the subject was not much to his taste, and must be left to another. Farnham, who did not consider at all the occurrence of *ye*, dealt with *'t, 's* and contractions involving *the* (*i'th, o'th'*, etc.) in only eight plays. And Partridge, to the present time, has been concerned only with *Henry VIII*. Thus the various linguistic tests that have been proposed during the past half century have yet to be applied systematically to all of the plays which comprise the Beaumont and Fletcher canon.

From an examination of the language forms present in the plays of the canon, at least one distinct pattern of linguistic preferences is evident at once. This is chiefly marked by the widespread use of the pronominal form *ye*, together with the frequent use of such contracted forms as *i'th', o'th', 'em, h'as, 's* for *his*, and a markedly infrequent use of third person singular verb forms in *-th*. The pattern can be traced throughout fourteen plays: *ye* is used repeatedly from the beginning to the end of each, and this is enough to set them apart from every other play in the canon. They are: *Monsieur Thomas, Rule a Wife and Have a Wife, Bonduca, The Chances, The Island Princess, The Humourous Lieutenant, The Loyal Subject, The Mad Lover, The Pilgrim, Valentinian, A Wife for a Month, Women Pleased, The Wild Goose Chase, The Woman's Prize.* In no one of these does *ye* ever

---

[4] "Colloquial Contractions in Beaumont, Fletcher, Massinger, and Shakespeare as a Test of Authorship," *PMLA*, XXXI, 326 ff. Later studies of particular value are found in R. C. Bald, *Bibliographical Studies in the Beaumont and Fletcher Folio*, and in J. Gerritsen's edition of *The Honest Man's Fortune*.

[5] *The Problem of "Henry VIII" Reopened, passim.*

occur less than 133 times (in *The Woman's Prize*), and in the remaining thirteen plays its rate of occurrence is much higher than this, as high as 543 times (in *The Wild Goose Chase*). Elsewhere in the canon, *ye* never occurs with anything approaching this frequency. In certain plays (e.g., *The Knight of the Burning Pestle, The Nice Valour, The Coxcomb, A King and No King*), *ye* appears sporadically or not at all. In certain others (e.g., *The Spanish Curate, The Prophetess, The False One, Barnavelt, The Maid in the Mill*) the form appears, but it is to be found clustered in single acts or scenes, and does not occur throughout the length of an entire play. Thus, when *ye* is found to occur regularly throughout each of fourteen plays—and this in a manner that is not paralleled in any of the other thirty-eight plays of the canon—it seems reasonable to conclude that one is here in the presence of a distinct linguistic preference that can be of use in determining the work of the dramatist whose practice it represents.

To identify the dramatist whose linguistic practice is marked by the widespread use of *ye* is not difficult. He is clearly not Beaumont. The plays of the canon with which Beaumont's name is most closely associated—plays like *Philaster, The Maid's Tragedy, A King and No King, The Knight of the Burning Pestle*—are precisely those in which *ye* seldom or never occurs. Nor is Massinger the dramatist in question. An examination of Massinger's fifteen unaided plays shows that, in all of these, *ye* occurs but twice; in all other instances, Massinger employs the pronominal form *you*. And the contracted forms (*i'th', o'th'*, and the like) which are found to accompany the use of *ye* in the plays of the canon, are like *ye* itself conspicuous by their absence in the unaided work of Massinger, whose use of contractions is remarkably conservative. The assumption—a virtually inescapable one—is that the linguistic pattern characterized by a superabundance of *ye*'s must represent the pattern of Fletcher. For three of the fourteen plays in question (*The Loyal Subject, A Wife for a Month*, and *Rule a Wife*) there is external evidence for Fletcher's sole authorship,[6] and I have no hesitation in regarding them all as his unaided work.

That they are unaided work can, I think, be demonstrated by comparing the manner in which *ye* occurs in them with its occurrence elsewhere in the canon. As I have already observed, in these fourteen

[6] Entries in the Office Book of Sir Henry Herbert, Master of the Revels from 1622 until the closing of the theatres, twice refer to *The Loyal Subject* as the work of Fletcher (*The Dramatic Records of Sir Henry Herbert*, ed. J. Q. Adams, 22 and 53). In his record of plays licensed for acting, Herbert names Fletcher as the author of *A Wife for a Month* and *Rule a Wife* (28–29).

plays the occurrence of *ye*, and all the linguistic phenomena that accompany its prevalence (absence of third-person verb forms in *-th*, frequency of such contractions as *i'th'*, *o'th'*, *'s* for *his*), is constant in its appearance through every act and virtually every scene. In plays of the type of *The Spanish Curate* and *The Prophetess*, however, the linguistic pattern established by the occurrence of *ye* is to be found only within single acts, or within individual scenes within acts, at the end of which it is abruptly broken off. In such cases, it is usually preceded or followed by a pattern of a quite different sort; one in which, first of all, the occurrence of *ye* is sharply reduced, and in which a decrease in the occurrence of other contracted forms is accompanied by an increased use of the verb form *hath*. In a very great number of cases, the linguistic pattern which accompanies the pattern established by *ye* is that of Massinger. A comparison of the first two acts of *The Spanish Curate*, the first two acts of *The Prophetess*, and the first act of *Barnavelt*, to cite but three examples, will indicate the manner in which the two linguistic patterns alternate within the same play.

It is, I think, valid to conclude that when a play, of the type represented by *The Spanish Curate*, demonstrates in consecutive acts and scenes two such sharply opposed linguistic patterns as those characterized by the prevalence and the absence of *ye*, then that play must represent the work of two separate dramatists. On the other hand, when in a play of the sort represented by *The Loyal Subject* or *Monsieur Thomas* a single linguistic pattern is found to be maintained through virtually every scene of its five acts, there is, I think, no real room for doubt that that play is the work of a single author. Regarding the fourteen plays of this sort in the canon, the linguistic pattern which links them together as the work of a single dramatist is far too distinct in itself, and far too evident throughout each, to admit the possibility of a second hand intervening in their authorship. When a second hand appears in a scene that has been formerly dominated by the Fletcherian linguistic pattern, its presence is noticeable at once. If the second hand is that of a collaborator, then the pattern will be immediately interrupted, and will appear but sporadically throughout the play, as it does in such plays as *The Spanish Curate* and *The Prophetess*. If the second hand is that of a reviser, then the whole pattern will be obscured: *ye*'s will, for the most part, disappear, or their number will be greatly reduced, and the whole texture of Fletcherian accidence is altered. The canon affords an illustration of this in *The Night Walker,* originally one of Fletcher's unaided plays, but revised in its extant text by Shirley.

Since the Fletcherian linguistic pattern is so pronounced and so discernible wherever his unaided work is present, I cannot consider his unaided work to be in fact represented in any play where this pattern is not evident. Thus I cannot agree with all those who have previously studied the Beaumont and Fletcher corpus in placing *Wit without Money* among the plays of Fletcher's sole authorship. The linguistic pattern that emerges from this play resembles far more closely the pattern to be found in *The Night Walker* than the pattern which prevails in such plays as *Monsieur Thomas* or *The Wild Goose Chase.*

II

In evaluating linguistic criteria as a test of authorship, it is obvious that no linguistic form can be regarded as distinctive of a particular dramatist in any absolute sense; the extent to which he employs a given form may distinguish sharply enough his practice from that of two other dramatists, but not necessarily from that of a third. Thus emerges the necessity, in determining linguistic criteria for the work of any one dramatist, of singling out forms which are at once representative of his language preferences, while serving to differentiate his work from the maximum number of his known or supposed collaborators. The value to be attached to any body of linguistic criteria is, in the end, completely relative: all depends upon the degree of divergence between the linguistic patterns that are to be distinguished.

With regard to the linguistic patterns which distinguish respectively the work of Fletcher and Massinger, these, as has been observed, and as will be seen readily enough from the tables at the end of this study, are composed of language preferences which are of an essentially opposite nature. From this it is to be concluded that, in distinguishing the grammatical usage of two dramatists, a given linguistic form need not be present in an author's work to afford evidence for determining his share of a collaborated play. On the contrary, when his collaborator is found to employ that form, its absence in the work of the dramatist in question affords the best possible evidence for distinguishing the work of the two. In a play of Fletcher and Massinger's joint authorship, the fact that Massinger is known to make little or no use of the pronominal form *ye* constitutes evidence just as positive for his work as Fletcher's known preference for the form constitutes for his. Evidence of this sort is of the best, precisely because here the degree of divergence between the linguistic patterns that are being distinguished is as great as it can well be. The one pattern is marked by a strong preference for *ye*, with the use of the form averaging 50 per cent; the other reflects a tendency to avoid the form altogether.

Such clearly opposed linguistic preferences are, unfortunately, rare. The extent to which the work of two such collaborators as Fletcher and Massinger can be distinguished by the presence or the absence of a single linguistic form—pronominal *ye*—is, indeed, quite exceptional in the annals of the Jacobean collaborated drama. More often, such linguistic preferences as can be shown to exist in the work of two dramatists are of a more quantitative sort, with a given linguistic form present in the work of both, but present at a higher rate of occurrence in the work of one than in that of the other. In such a case, the value to be attached to any single linguistic form as evidence for authorship must depend upon the extent to which, in their unaided work, the one dramatist will tend to employ it and the other to eschew it. The less the degree of difference in the use which two dramatists make of the same linguistic form in their unaided work, the less will be its value as evidence for distinguishing their shares in a play of divided authorship. As two dramatists tend to approximate each other in their use of a given language form, the evidential value of that form is accordingly diminished.

Fortunately for any attempt to determine authorship on the basis of linguistic preferences, a single language form may be used by both of two dramatists and yet be of value in distinguishing their work in collaboration, provided only that that form can be shown to occur at a consistently higher rate in the unaided work of one dramatist than in that of the other. The value to be attached to the verb form *hath*, as it occurs in the unaided work of Fletcher and Massinger, is a case in point. *Hath* is to be found in the unaided plays of both dramatists, yet its occurrence in any single play of Fletcher's never equals its occurrence in any one of Massinger's plays. Similarly with *ye* in the work of Fletcher and Field: *ye* occurs with some regularity in Field's unaided plays, but its occurrence there never approaches the extraordinary frequency with which Fletcher employs the form. The evidence to be derived from linguistic preferences as sharply opposed as these is second in importance only to that which is the most significant of all: the evidence that is based upon language preferences which reveal themselves in the prevalence of a given form in the work of one dramatist and its absence in that of another.

Thus far, in considering the factors that must be taken into account in evaluating linguistic criteria, I have tried to emphasize the necessity for determining the extent to which a given language form does indeed point to a clear and unequivocal linguistic preference that will serve in distinguishing the work of two dramatists. It need hardly be said that no single linguistic preference will serve equally to distinguish the work of a given dramatist from that of all others. As I have already observed, a grammatical or linguistic practice that may tend to set a particular dramatist apart from two of his fellows will not necessarily set him apart from a third. It should be obvious that no piece of linguistic criteria can be evaluated in isolation; the significance which a single form may possess for distinguishing the work of any one dramatist will derive directly from the extent to which that form is present in the work of his collaborators. The frequent use of *ye, hath, i'th'*, or whatever in the plays of any dramatist is of no value in distinguishing his work from that of dramatists who employ such forms with equal or even approximate frequency. And no importance can be attached to the absence of a particular form from the work of any one dramatist unless it is known to occur in some noticeable degree in the work of another. The linguistic pattern that has been adduced for a dramatist on the basis of his unaided work will, of course, remain constant. However, the value of the evidence to be attached to the presence or absence of such linguistic forms as contribute to the distinctive nature of this over-all pattern will obviously shift in relation to the prevalence of those same forms within such other linguistic patterns as may be present with it in a single play. Or, stated in another way: if a given linguistic form is known to occur with approximately the same frequency in the work of dramatists A, B, and C, but does not occur at all in the work of dramatist D, then while that particular form will have no value as evidence for distinguishing the work of A, B, and C, it will have considerable value for distinguishing the work of any one of these from dramatist D. The use of the verb form *hath* in the plays of Massinger and Field will not serve to distinguish these dramatists from each other, but it may serve to distinguish both from Fletcher. And while the absence of *ye* from the plays of Massinger will have very little value in distinguishing his work from that of Beaumont, who seems to have employed the form at least as sparingly as Massinger himself, the fact that Massinger almost never uses *ye* will serve to distinguish his work not only from Fletcher's, but from that of Field as well.

Clearly, no linguistic form can be regarded as the exclusive property of a single writer. Just as clearly, however, writers can, and often do, demonstrate a preference for certain colloquial and contracted linguistic forms (a fact that is strikingly evidenced in the case of Fletcher and Massinger) and such preferences can often serve to set apart the work of one author from that of another. In a study such as this, the problem must be to distinguish what are, indeed, an author's preferential forms, and then to determine which of these can serve to differentiate his work from that of his associates. For such a purpose, the very best linguistic evidence will always consist in those forms which a given writer can be shown to have used with conspicuous frequency, but which those with whom he collaborated can be shown to have used ever so sparingly or not at all.

III

The language forms that constitute the greater part of my evidence for authorship consist, as will have been observed, of linguistic preferences which—in a great number of cases—are made manifest in only the most minute typographical features of a printed text. When one deals with such forms, and especially when one is preparing to attach any great importance to the frequency of their occurrence, the question is naturally raised as to the extent to which an author's choice of contractions is preserved in the transmission of his text. It is well known that certain seventeenth-century compositors possessed clearly defined spelling preferences which were imposed upon whatever text they might be setting, and one wonders just how far such compositorial preferences were carried. Would a compositor, for instance, venture to impose his own preferences among colloquial and contracted forms upon a text as well? If so, then any study such as the present one is the sheerest kind of folly, for the linguistic forms by means of which one is seeking to identify a given dramatist's share in a collaborated play might have been introduced into the text by any number of unknown compositors.

There is no reason, however, to believe that compositors took undue liberties with the contracted forms in the manuscript before them; there is, on the contrary, good reason for believing that they reproduced such forms with considerable fidelity. Both W. E. Farnham and Paul Elmer More have drawn attention to the extent to which the same contractions occur, with only slight variation, in the Beaumont and Fletcher quartos and folios. As Farnham has observed, it is clear from the verse that such contractions were intended by the author, and honored by the printer, because they are a necessary part of the metrical structure. And equally to the point is his further observation that differences in the use of contractions in the parts of a collaborated play are "too orderly to be ascribed to the vagaries of a printer."[7] No one can seriously consider the two linguistic patterns present in such a play as *The Spanish Curate,* coinciding as they do with the beginning of acts and scenes, to represent the language habits of two compositors. If such linguistic patterns did in fact represent the language preferences of two compositors, their occurrence would be found to accord with the bibliographical units of the printed text, and would not in any way be related to the act and scene divisions of the play itself. Finally, the manner in which the same linguistic preferences can be shown to persist throughout the unaided plays of a given dramatist, though the extant texts of these are the work of several different printers, affords the ultimate proof that language forms of the sort which can furnish evidence for authorship originated with the author himself, and are sufficiently preserved in a printed text. Fletcher's strong preference for the pronominal form *ye* is just as evident in the 1639 quarto text of *Monsieur Thomas,* printed by Thomas Harper, or in the 1640 quarto of *Rule a Wife,* printed by Leonard Lichfield, as in the remaining twelve plays of his unaided authorship, printed for the first time by Humphrey Moseley in the 1647 folio. The unaided Massinger canon presents what is perhaps an even stronger argument for this contention, for it is the product of even more diverse compositorial hands. Of Massinger's fifteen unaided plays, thirteen were published, and these represent the work of eleven printers. Yet the linguistic preferences which emerge from these are completely consistent within themselves, and what is equally striking, they are preferences which in no way contradict what we know of Massinger's language from the manuscript—in his autograph—of one of his unpublished plays. A study of the occurrence, in some one hundred plays, of the linguistic forms that are here employed as authorial evidence, convinces me that, in the greater number of cases, the use of such forms—either in the unaided plays of a given dramatist or in plays of divided authorship—is far too sys-

[7] "Colloquial Contractions," 332.

tematic to admit the possibility that their presence has been affected, in any truly significant degree, by compositorial intervention.

If, however, the evidence available would tend to absolve compositors from the charge of tampering with the contractions in the manuscript which they were set to reproduce, the same cannot, apparently, be said for certain scribes in their preparation of transcripts for the use of the theatre, the printer, or a private patron. The three scribal transcripts which exist for Fletcher's unaided plays demonstrate, on the one hand, a reasonable accuracy in reproducing the linguistic preferences of the author on the part of such a scribe as Ralph Crane and, on the other, the far more erratic practice of such a scribe as Edward Knight, with the practice of the unidentified scribe of *The Woman's Prize* falling somewhere between the two.

Crane prepared a private transcript of Fletcher's *The Humourous Lieutenant* (titled in his manuscript *Demetrius and Enanthe*). Since his text contains some seventy-five lines not present in the text of the first folio, the supposition is that Crane's transcript derives from Fletcher's original manuscript, whereas the folio text represents a promptbook containing theatrical abridgments. In his transcript, Crane introduces some thirty-four *ye*'s not present in the text of the folio, while he omits some fourteen *ye*'s which the folio text exhibits, but the difference of approximately twenty *ye*'s in the total occurrence of the form in the two texts is not great. It speaks, in fact, well for the care with which Crane reproduced his copy when it is compared with the wide divergence in the occurrence of *ye* in the two extant texts of another of Fletcher's unaided plays, *Bonduca*.[8]

The text of *Bonduca* is extant in a scribal transcript, prepared by Edward Knight, the book-keeper of the King's Company, from Fletcher's foul papers, and in the text of the 1647 folio, printed from the prompt-book. In the folio text, the pronoun *ye* is used 352 times; in Knight's transcript, the occurrence of the form has been reduced by more than half, to 147 times. The variation in the two texts in this respect is of significance because, on the basis of the first folio, the percentage of *ye*'s to *you*'s is the highest to be found in any play of Fletcher's unaided authorship. If, however, *Bonduca* survived only in Knight's manuscript, the play would present the lowest percentage

---

[8] For a careful study of Crane's characteristics as a transcriber, see R. C. Bald, *Bibliographical Studies in the Beaumont and Fletcher Folio of 1647* (Oxford, 1938), 95, but more especially his edition of Thomas Middleton's *A Game at Chesse* (Cambridge, Eng., 1929), 171–173.

of *ye*'s to *you*'s in all Fletcher, with the occurrence of the form falling markedly below its normal frequency in his unaided plays.

There is evidence of scribal intervention affecting the use of *ye* in another Fletcher play, *The Woman's Prize*, and there is good reason to suppose that the scribe responsible for the reduction in the occurrence of the form is once again Knight. Like *Bonduca*, *The Woman's Prize* is extant in two texts: an undated private transcript, prepared by an unidentified scribe, and the text of the 1647 folio. In the first folio text, *ye* occurs but 84 times, a number far below the usual occurrence of the form in Fletcher's unaided work. In the manuscript, *ye* is found 133 times, and while this still represents the lowest occurrence of the form in Fletcher, the increase of 49 *ye*'s makes for a rather more satisfactory basis for regarding the play as Fletcher's own.

There is external evidence which almost certainly has some bearing on the first folio text of the play and the linguistic forms which it exhibits. On October 18, 1633, the Master of the Revels, Sir Henry Herbert, suppressed a performance of *The Woman's Prize* (he refers to the play by its alternate title, *The Tamer Tamed*), which the King's Company had scheduled for that afternoon. On the following morning the promptbook was brought to him, whereupon he proceeded to purge it of "oaths, prophaness, and ribaldrye."[9] The play, Herbert explains, was an old one, evidently licensed during the mastership of one of his predecessors, which the King's Company had sought to revive, under a different title, without applying for a new license. Herbert was thereby deprived of his licensing fee, a matter about which he felt strongly, as he indicates in the entry in his Office Book, though he advances another and more public-spirited reason why old plays should not be restaged without the allowance of the Master of the Revels: "they may be full of offensive things against church and state; the rather that in former times the poetts tooke greater liberty than is allowed them by mee" (p. 22).

The upshot of the whole affair was that two days later, on October 21, Herbert returned the prompt copy, properly expurgated, to the players, accompanied by a note to Edward Knight enjoining him to "purge [the actors'] parts, as I have the booke." The players' capitulation to Herbert's demands was complete; two of their chief members apologized for "their ill manners" and asked his pardon, and the following month Fletcher's *The Loyal Subject*, which had been licensed by Sir George Buc in 1618, was submitted to Herbert for re-licensing.

[9] *Records of Herbert*, ed. Adams, 20.

Mr. R. C. Bald, in a most valuable discussion of the two texts of *The Woman's Prize*, points out that, while "the manuscript omits two whole scenes (II.i and IV.i), two passages of fourteen and seven lines respectively, and eight of three lines or less" that are included in the folio, the manuscript exhibits, on the other hand, "eleven passages . . . varying in length from half a line to nine lines," which the folio omits. It is Mr. Bald's opinion that the manuscript gives the play, which was originally performed in 1610 or 1611, "as cut for acting before Herbert's time," while "the folio gives a fuller version of the play, but observes the cuts that were made by Herbert in 1633."[10] To observe the cuts that Herbert demanded, it does not seem unreasonable to suppose that a new promptbook was drawn up, and if a new promptbook was prepared, it seems clear enough from Herbert's note of October 21 that the task would be performed by the bookkeeper Knight. From Knight's transcript of *Bonduca* we know how the Fletcherian *ye* diminished under his hand (see Bald, pp. 99–100), and I can account for the small number of *ye*'s in the folio text of *The Woman's Prize* only by supposing the manuscript from which that text derives to have been prepared by him. With regard to the scribal transcript, the supposition would be that the scribe responsible for it has been somewhat more faithful in reproducing the language forms that must have stood in the original. Since the manuscript text reflects more clearly than the folio the quality of the Fletcherian original, I have used it as the basis for the statistics set forth for *The Woman's Prize* in the linguistic tables at the end of the present study.

The possibility of scribal intervention should perhaps be considered in relation to two other of the plays which can be regarded as Fletcher's unaided work, *Rule a Wife* and *A Wife for a Month*. These, apparently Fletcher's last plays, exhibit after *The Woman's Prize* the least number of *ye*'s of all the fourteen plays that I consider to be his. The first folio text of *A Wife for a Month* gives clear indication of author's foul papers, but it is not impossible that the text has derived from a not too careful transcript of these. Two speeches are printed in alternately abridged and expanded versions, and there is a bad tangle in the second scene of the fourth act which clearly would have had to be set to rights before the manuscript behind the first folio text could have been used as a promptbook. But if Knight's transcript of *Bonduca* is any indication of his work for a private patron, he

---

[10] *Studies in the Beaumont and Fletcher Folio*, 60.

would not have been above letting such difficulties stand in a text which he prepared, if it were not to serve as a theatrical prompt copy. And if the total number of *ye*'s still present in the text of *A Wife for a Month* (176) does indeed represent a reduction from the original number, Fletcher's favorite pronoun has here been given much the same treatment as Knight accorded it in his *Bonduca* manuscript.

The substantive text of *Rule a Wife,* that of the 1640 quarto, probably derives, as Professor Jump has suggested, "either from a prompt-book or from a manuscript directly descended from a prompt-book."[11] The play was licensed for acting by Sir Henry Herbert on October 19, 1624, and four months later, on February 8, 1625, Herbert re-licensed *The Honest Man's Fortune,* for which Knight had prepared a new promptbook that is extant in his autograph. It would seem likely, then, since he was actively employed by the King's Company at this time, that Knight prepared the promptbook for *Rule a Wife* as well. There is evidence of a sort in the quarto of *Rule a Wife* that might be considered to link it with his work. The chief feature which the quarto and the *Bonduca* manuscript have in common is a frequent occurrence of the contraction *'um* (for *'em*). Since Knight employs *'em* throughout his manuscript of *The Honest Man's Fortune,* *'um* is not likely to represent his own linguistic preference And since the form is *'em* throughout the 1640 quarto of *Rollo, Duke of Normandy,* printed in the same house and in the same year as *Rule a Wife,* it seems improbable that the *'um* spelling is compositorial. I regard it rather as a Fletcherian form which Knight has reproduced forty-six times in his transcript of *Bonduca,* and—perhaps—thirty-two times in the manuscript behind the quarto of *Rule a Wife.* Seventeen times in the *Bonduca* manuscript, Knight uses the spelling *hir* for *her.* The *hir* spelling occurs twenty-nine times in the quarto of *Rule a Wife,* and it is the prevalent spelling throughout the manuscript of *The Honest Man's Fortune.* The evidence is admittedly not great, but combined with the fact that Knight was the probable person to have prepared a promptbook for the King's Company at this period, it seems at least possible that the diminished number of *ye*'s (213) in the quarto of *Rule a Wife* may be traced to his intervention in the transmission of the text.

IV

The following tables set forth the rate of occurrence, in the unaided plays of Fletcher and Massinger, of those linguistic forms which

[11] *Rollo, Duke of Normandy,* ed. J. D. Jump, xiii.

are of value in distinguishing the respective shares of the two dramatists in plays of divided authorship. I have omitted *The Faithful Shepherdess* from the number of Fletcher's unaided plays, for although it is undoubtedly Fletcher's own, linguistically at least it has nothing in common with any other of his unaided works. Its language is that of pastoral poetry, uncolloquial and somewhat archaic. It abounds in linguistic forms (most notably the third-person auxiliary forms *hath* and *doth*) which Fletcher seldom or never uses in his other unaided plays, while all the most distinguishing of his colloquial forms are either completely absent, or present in only a negligible degree. Nothing could be more misleading than to regard the language of *The Faithful Shepherdess* as typically Fletcherian.

Of the linguistic forms cited in the tables below, *ye* is much the most important for purposes of authorial evidence. Since Fletcher employs the form as both subject and object, direct or indirect, in either singular or plural number, the rate of its occurrence in his unaided plays is very high. In the fifteen unaided plays of Massinger, the form occurs but twice. Contractions in *y'* (*y'are, y'ave,* and the like) are much less frequent in Fletcher, and are of no value in distinguishing Fletcher's work from Massinger's. The two occurrences each of *y'are* in Fletcher's *Monsieur Thomas, Rule a Wife, Bonduca,* and *The Pilgrim,* for example, are matched by the two instances of the form in Massinger's *The Bondman.* The single instances of *y'ave* and *y'have* in, respectively, Fletcher's *The Chances* and *Bonduca* are paralleled by single appearances of the same forms in, respectively, Massinger's *A New Way to Pay Old Debts* and *The Guardian.* There is nothing to distinguish Massinger's use of contractions in *y'* from Fletcher's, and I have not included them among the forms cited in the following tables. Regarding the verb form *hath,* there is a distinct difference in the Fletcher-Massinger usage. In Fletcher, the form never occurs more than six times in a single play, and in two plays it occurs not at all. In Massinger, on the other hand, *hath* never occurs less than eight times in any one play, and generally it is found a good deal more often than this—as often as forty-six times in a single play. *Doth* comes in only one of the fourteen Fletcherian plays listed below, but since it appears but five times in Massinger, the distinction in the practice of the two dramatists on this point is not great. The contraction *'em* appears in all of Fletcher's unaided plays, from twenty-three times in *Women Pleased* to 130 times in *The Loyal Subject.* In certain of Massinger's plays, it will be noted, *'em* is to be found occurring as frequently as it does in certain of Fletcher's. But it seems significant

Evidence for Authorship

Linguistic tables for the unaided plays of Fletcher and Massinger*

Play	ye	hath	doth	'em	i'th'	i'the	o'th'	a	'is	h'as	t'	in's	on's	's (his) let's	's (us) of't
Fletcher															
M. Thom.	343	6		27	9		6			2	3			10	
R. W.	213	2		35†	20		12		5	7	3		1	12	
Bon.	352	1		95	14		10	4		10	4		1	27	
Chan.	290	2		44	12		4	4		10	2			20	
I. P.	258			64	7		8	1	8	5	1			14	
H. L.	367	5		80	28		11	2		11	3		3	11	
L. S.	424	3		130	13		10			4	2		1	10	
M. L.	308	6		25	16	1	4	15	4	7	3			17	
Pilg.	400	3		62	15		9			9	7			18	
Valen.	412	4		71	12		8	2		4	2			16	
W. M.	176			41	4		1		1	2	5		1	17	
W. P.	288	3		23	15		16			6	4		2	3	
W. G. C.	543	1		61	8		6		1	3	1		1	15	
W. Pr.	133	4	3	58	14		21‡			3	3			10	
Massinger															
D. M.		46		12		1					8			1	3
Bond.		8	1	15							1			2	
P. L.	1	21		7										1	2
R. A.		28		14		2				3				5	1
Pict.		35		52	5	3				3				1	4
Ren.		21		9										3	2
Bel.		36		26		1									
E. E.		31	1	26							2				5
M. H.		25		31		5					2				4
N. W.		16		36	2	1				1	2			1	4
G. D. F.		26		15											1
U. C.		23		16										1	1
B. L.	1	41	3	21	3	2					5	2		1	5
Guard.		26		47	7	4					4			3	9
C. M.		19		46	1	1					1				3

* Abbreviations (references to the folio, quarto, octavo, or manuscript text upon which all statistics in the present study have been based are given in parentheses after each title): *B. L.*, *The Bashful Lover* (O 1655); *Bel.*, *Believe as You List* (British Museum Ms Egerton 2828, ed. by C. J. Sisson, The Malone Society); *Bon.*, *Bonduca* (F 1647); *Bond.*, *The Bondman* (Q 1624); *Chan.*, *The Chances* (F 1647); *C. M.*, *The City Madam* (Q 1658); *D. M.*, *The Duke of Milan* (Q 1623); *E. E.*, *The Emperor of the East* (Q 1632); *Guard.*, *The Guardian* (O 1655); *G. D. F.*, *The Great Duke of Florence* (Q 1636); *H. L.*, *The Humourous Lieutenant* (F 1647); *I. P.*, *The Island Princess* (F 1647); *L. S.*, *The Loyal Subject* (F 1647); *M. L.*, *The Mad Lover* (F 1647); *M. H.*, *The Maid of Honour* (Q 1632); *M. Thom.*, *Monsieur* that all of these (e.g., *The Picture, The Guardian, The City Madam*) are late plays, licensed for acting after Fletcher's death in 1625.[12] In Massinger's early plays, which would presumably reflect his language practices at the time of his collaboration with Fletcher, *'em* is used a good deal more sparingly than in the unaided plays of Fletcher or in the later work of Massinger himself: seven times, for example, in *The Parliament of Love*, nine times in *The Renegado*, twelve times in *The Duke of Milan*. I tabulate the occurrence of the form for whatever value it may have as a piece of corroborating evidence for distinguishing the work of the two dramatists.

The evidence to be derived from the contraction *i'th'* is, on the whole, good. Despite the fact that the seven occurrences of the form in Fletcher's *The Island Princess* are equaled in Massinger's *The Guardian*, the form is found no fewer than four times in any of Fletcher's plays, and it may appear as many as twenty-eight times, while it is found in but five plays of Massinger's, and in none of these more than seven times. It may be worth noting that the five plays in which the form occurs are late ones, and that *i'th'* appears in no play of Massinger's written before Fletcher's death. A form, however, which Massinger tends to employ occasionally, but which occurs only a single time in Fletcher, is the contraction *i'the*. The contraction *o'th'*

---

[12] The eight Massinger plays which, on the evidence that is available, can be dated after Fletcher's death are: *The Picture*, licensed 1629; *The Emperor of the East* and *Believe as you List*, 1631; *The City Madam*, 1632; *The Guardian*, 1633; *The Bashful Lover*, 1636 (licensing dates are drawn from Herbert's Office Book). The date of *The Maid of Honour* and *A New Way to Pay Old Debts* is uncertain. Malone sought to identify *The Maid of Honour* with *The Honour of Women*, licensed by Herbert on May 6, 1628. If the reference to the taking of Breda in *A New Way* (I, ii) stood in the original version of that play—and there is no reason to suppose the contrary—then the play cannot have been written before that event occurred, on July 1, 1625 (W. Gifford, *The Plays of Phillip Massinger*, III, 503–504).

Thomas (Q 1639); *N. W., A New Way to Pay Old Debts* (Q 1633); *Pict., The Picture* (Q 1630); *Pilg., The Pilgrim* (F 1647); *P. L., The Parliament of Love* (Victoria and Albert Museum, Dyce MS 39, ed. by K. M. Lea, The Malone Society); *Ren., The Renegado* (Q 1630); *R. A., The Roman Actor* (Q 1629); *R. W., Rule a Wife and Have a Wife* (Q 1640); *U. C., The Unnatural Combat* (Q 1639); *Valen., Valentinian* (F 1647); *W. G. C., The Wild Goose Chase* (F 1652); *W. M., A Wife for a Month* (F 1647); *W. P., Women Pleased* (F 1647); *W. Pr., The Woman's Prize* (Folger Shakespeare Library, Lambarde MS).

† The form occurs 32 times as *'um* in the 1640 quarto text.

‡ The form occurs 10 times as *a'th* in the Lambarde MS.

affords evidence of a sufficiently clear-cut sort: the form occurs at least once in all fourteen of Fletcher's unaided plays; it occurs not at all in Massinger. The colloquial form *a* (for *he*) is found in six of Fletcher's plays, but appears in none of Massinger's. Of a similar nature is the contraction *'is* (for *he is*), present in five of Fletcher's unaided plays, but not present in Massinger. *H'as* (for *he has*) is found at least twice in each of the fourteen unaided plays of Fletcher, but it occurs only a single time in Massinger. The contraction *t'* (for *to*, before a following vowel or *h*) affords evidence of a sort for Massinger; it occurs at least once in ten of his fifteen unaided plays, but is found only a single time in Fletcher. Contractions involving *'s* for *his* occur chiefly in Fletcher following the preposition *in* and *on*. There are single instances in Fletcher of enclitic *'s* for *his* with four other prepositions (*at, for, to, up*); with an adverb (*than*); with a verb (*strike*). In Massinger, *'s* for *his* occurs but three times: twice in the contraction *in's*, once in the contraction *of's*. Only the uses of *'s* for *his* with *in* and *on* have seemed worth recording in the tables that follow.

As for contractions in *'s* for *us*, these occur most commonly in Fletcher with the imperative verb form *let*. I find only two occasions in which Fletcher has used enclitic *'s* for *us* after other notional verbs (*put* and *make*); elsewhere, he uses the form only after the preposition *on* (five times). In Massinger, *'s* for *us* is used only in the contraction *let's*, and even this quite normal form Massinger uses very sparingly. It is the only contraction in *'s* for *us* that I have recorded below. The enclitic use of *'t* for *it* with both prepositions and verbs (in contractions such as *in't, on't, for't, to't, is't*) is standard in the work of Elizabethan and Jacobean dramatists, and contractions of this sort are of no worth in distinguishing the work of Fletcher and Massinger, for their rate of occurrence in the work of each is virtually identical. In the tables shown on page 220, I have recorded only one form in *'t* for *it*, the contraction *of't*, and this only because the form does not appear in Fletcher, while it occurs from one to nine times in thirteen of the fifteen unaided plays of Massinger.

To summarize the chief features of the linguistic patterns of Fletcher and Massinger: the Fletcherian pattern is one which is marked above all by the constant use of *ye*; one which exhibits a strong preference for the contraction *'em* to the expanded form *them*; one which regularly employs such other contractions as *i'th', o'th', h'as,* and *'s* for *his*, and which makes sparing use of the third-person singular verb forms *hath* and *doth*. Stated numerically, it is a pattern in which the average rate of occurrence for the forms in question is as follows:

Contraction	Average occurrence per play
ye	322
'em	59
i'th'	14
o'th'	9
them	8
h'as	6
's (his)	5
hath	3

The full significance of these figures can best be realized when they are compared with the average rate of occurrence for the same forms in the unaided work of Massinger. There *ye* occurs twice in fifteen plays. *Hath* occurs at an average rate of 27 times. In the seven plays of Massinger's sole authorship written before Fletcher's death, and so reflecting most nearly the author's linguistic preferences during the period of his collaboration with Fletcher, *'em* is used an average of twelve times per play, *them* an average of twenty-three times. The contraction *i'th'* is found eighteen times in five of Massinger's unaided plays, all of which date after the death of Fletcher. *O'th'* does not appear in any of Massinger's unaided plays; *h'as* is found but once (in a post-Fletcher play); *'s* for *his* occurs twice (both times in a play written after Fletcher's death). In the linguistic pattern which emerges from the unaided plays of Massinger written during Fletcher's lifetime, it can fairly be said then that the Fletcherian *ye* has no parallel; that Massinger's average use of *hath* is nine times greater than Fletcher's: that the Fletcherian preference of *'em* to *them* is precisely reversed in Massinger; and that the contractions *i'th'*, *o'th*, *h'as*, and *'s* for *his* are completely absent from his work at this period. The linguistic patterns of the two are as nearly opposite as they could well be.

The Textual Introduction to
*The Virgin Martyr**

By Fredson Bowers

THE VIRGIN MARTYR by Dekker and Massinger . . . was
"reformed" and licensed by Buc for the Red Bull on October 6, 1620;
and was entered in the Stationers' Register to Thomas Jones on
December 7, 1621. Jones's edition, printed by Bernard Alsop and
dated 1622, would likely have appeared late in 1621 or early in
1622. . . .

The manuscript serving as printer's copy seems to have been a
collection of papers written in two different hands, in large part coinciding with conventional estimates of the division by authorship. This
manuscript was apparently not a theatrical one. No signs of professional intervention appear, and no one has troubled to remove the
redundant character identifications from Dekker's stage-direction
heading II.ii or the direction following II.iii.56.

It is evident that only one compositor set the type for this play:
an examination of spelling and typographical characteristics discloses
no such distinctions as can be remarked when more than one workman
is present. . . . [Hence] variable characteristics in the "accidentals"
that conform to the scene-division in the most conservative allocation
of authorship by scenes may safely be regarded as due to differences
in the respective portions of the underlying manuscript.

The question is, however, whether holograph papers constituted
the printer's copy or whether the manuscript was a transcript of some
sort of the holographs, either by one collaborator of the other's work,
or by an independent scribe of the work of one or of both. Ordinarily
the case would be undemonstrable and subject only to opinion. It

* Excerpted from *The Dramatic Works of Thomas Dekker*, edited by Fredson
Bowers (Cambridge University Press, 1958), III, 367–375, with permission of author and publisher. Omissions are indicated by ellipses.

is my own cautious conjecture that the amount of variation in *The Virgin Martyr* quarto may be too significant, and the kind of variation too minute, for us to believe that a scribal transcript formed the whole of the printer's copy. Minor variants like the double appearance of *Roome* (for *Rome*) in I.i., a Massinger scene, or of *Dorothæa* (for *Dorothea*) twice at II.ii.43, 49, in a Dekker scene, may have no significance that can be assessed when further repetition is wanting. On the other hand, when in five out of six appearances in scenes that are certainly Dekker's one finds the spelling *Cesarea* versus the invariable *Cæsarea* in Massinger scenes, and, statistically, a very high proportion of hyphenated compounds in Dekker versus a very low proportion in Massinger, one is justified in assigning these differences to the varying characteristics of the printer's copy according to the authorship of the scenes. Once this hypothesis is established, such other characteristics as the appearance a few times of the *apostrophus* I'am in Dekker scenes but never in Massinger's, or possibly a high proportion in Dekker of *ile* to *Ile* in Massinger, may assume a significance that otherwise might not be felt.

The conservative assignment of scenes may be referred to Gifford, who on critical grounds allocated to Massinger I.i; III.i, ii; IV.i, iii; and V.ii; and to Dekker II.i, ii, iii; III.iii; IV.ii and V.i. With the possible exception of IV.i, iii, the characteristics of the accidentals in the 1622 quarto agree with Gifford's literary allocation. We may, therefore, temporarily set aside these two scenes and survey the evidence found in the remaining.

In Massinger's undoubted scenes[1] we find the invariable spellings *Cæsarea, dietie* (for *deity*), *Emperour,* and *Gouernour* (except *Gouernor* in I.i). We also find some preference for *ere* (thrice) and *nere* (four times). On four occasions appears the form with the apostrophe *eu'n*. Although doubling of the vowel in pronouns may appear frequently in such contractions as *weele*, and so on, it is rare otherwise and is found only in *mee* (once). The contraction *ile* with lower-case appears only once. Contractions involving *it* are rare: *do't, of't, on't,* and *wer't* (once each). Hyphenation of compounds occurs only four times. Only a slight use is made of the dash, and relatively few exclamation marks are employed. Punctuation seems to have been so light as to cause the compositor occasional difficulty in interpreting the desirable pointing.

[1] In the present excerpt the details of location are omitted from the survey.—Eds.

In Dekker's undoubted scenes we find five spellings *Cesarea* to one of *Cæsarea,* the single *Emperor,* and two *Gouernor.* The word *deity* does not occur; no forms of *eu'n* with or without apostrophe appear; and there is only one *nere* and no *ere.* The doubled vowel in *mee* is printed twice, in *wee* seven times, in *hee* four times, in *shee* twice; and in *bee* six times. The contraction *ile* occurs ten times, and *i'me* once. Contractions of *it* are *doo't* twice, *on't* twice, *in't* once, and *ist* five times. A contraction of *his* as *'s* is *in's* (once). Other contractions are *ith'* five times, *to'th* thrice, *ath'* twice, *thou't* once, and *y'are* very frequently. The word *a* is used for *of* once. The *apostrophus* *I'am* appears thrice. In contrast to the four hyphenations in all of Massinger's scenes, nineteen are found in II.i, seven in II.ii, ten in II.iii, nine in II.iii, five in IV.ii, and ten in V.i. A marked use is made of the dash, and the exclamation point is liberally employed. Punctuation does not appear to be noticeably light.

When we survey the characteristics of IV.i, we find from Massinger's list the spelling *dieties,* which—since the word does not appear in Dekker's undoubted scenes—may or may not be compositorial; and we find the spelling *Gouernour.* On the other hand, from Dekker's list we have the somewhat doubtful value *shee.* More important, five exclamation marks are used, and three hyphenated compounds. What may be a typical Dekker spelling *bonefire* occurs (see III.iii.146), and in *Phlegmatike* a *k* spelling not found in the Massinger scenes but present in *Arithmatike* and *Zodiake* by Dekker. Stronger evidence comes in the contractions, however, for in this one scene we have *too't, i'th, doo't* (thrice), *bi'th,* and *too'th.*

In the language employed, a Massinger-scene phrase is repeated in *powers I serue.* Both writers have joined in applying the label *witch* of line 172 or *sorceress* of line 60 to Dorothea. Dekker had used the word *pash,* and had liberally *whored* Dorothea. More important, the phrase *proud Thing* applied to her was repeated from Dekker's II.iii, "Let not this Christian *Thing,* in this her pageantry / Of prowd deriding. . . ." At V.i. 74 Angelo, though with different intent, is called a *Thing.* The word *a* is used for *of* or *on,* a usage that an independent study made of Massinger's linguistic characteristics does not record as present in his unaided plays.[2]

In IV.iii we have what seems to be the characteristic Massinger-

---

[2] Cyrus Hoy, reprinted above, No. 14.

scene *eu'n* and a spelling *Karkasse* that is found later in V.ii.[3] The *power* Dorothea *serves* can, as in IV.i, be compared to Massinger's I.i.18. The idiom *to me* as in lines 12, 73, and 76 may be paralleled in Massinger's I.i.422, 425, although Dekker's II.iii.38 must be noticed. Massinger had applied *Apostata* to Dorothea, and to Antoninus, and the word is used in *Believe As You List.* On the other hand, although little weight may be placed on the spelling *bee,* the form *ile* might suggest Dekker, as might *ist* and the two exclamation marks. The two references to Dorothea as a witch are not distinctive. That she is a "prowd contemner / Of vs and of our gods" is very like Dekker's II.iii, quoted above in connection with IV.i. And Theophilus's comment on Harpax affected by Angelo, "He is distracted and I must not loose him" parallels Theophilus's remark to Harpax, "I will not loose thee then, her to confound" in Dekker's II.ii.

Since both the language and the accidental characteristics of IV.i resemble those found in scenes that are Dekker's, and the characteristics of Massinger scenes are so weak and uncertain, it may be that the scene should be assigned wholly to Dekker, to whom one would wish, surely, to give the British-slave speeches at the very least. . . . Hence if there are well-grounded signs of Massinger in IV.i, the characteristics of the printed text would suggest the conjecture that in this scene Dekker had rewritten a Massinger version.

It will be noticed that Dekker was responsible solely for scenes involving Hircius and Spungius, but that he was not confined to such scenes, on the evidence of II.ii and V.i; and in fact the lines devoted to Dorothea and her associates in II.i and II.iii outweigh the low-comedy sections. Thus if Massinger were responsible for all of Act I, and Dekker for all of Act II, and Act V were split between the two, we should expect something of an equal division of major responsibility in Acts III and IV. Act III, except for the Hircius-Spungius III.iii, is, indeed, Massinger's for the remaining two scenes. Thus we might expect Dekker to have been responsible for two of the three scenes in Act IV, and, so supported, add to undoubted IV.ii the IV.i scene in which his hand seems to be present.

The accidental characteristics of the Dekker scenes are very slight in IV.iii and perhaps ought not to be taken seriously were it not for the parallel language that Theophilus used of Harpax and possibly the reference to Dorothea as *prowd.* If Dekker may be associated

---

[3] That both points seem of doubtful value is explained in footnotes.—Eds.

with this probable Massinger scene on literary grounds, the evidence would suggest that he merely touched it up. Whether in the process he copied it out fair would be doubtful, certainly.

If then such variation in accidental characteristics between scenes as betray the hands of two different authors may be detected throughout the 1622 quarto, the question arises whether the single compositor set from the holograph papers of these two authors, from a transcript of both, or from a transcript of only one. . . .

16

Poems Attributed to
Sir Philip Sidney*

By William A. Ringler, Jr.

SIR PHILIP SIDNEY, with the graceful negligence that was expected of an Elizabethan gentleman, pretended to depreciate his literary labors. "Thinke not that I by verse seeke fame," he said to Stella (sonnet 90), "I wish not there should be Graved in mine Epitaph a Poets name." He did not prepare his writings for publication, and none appeared in print during his lifetime. Because he refused to publish, and because his literary holographs were lost through accidents of time, the text of his surviving works is uncertain, and even the authenticity of some of them is questionable.

Even while his verse circulated only in manuscript, Sidney was reputed one of the first poets of his time. He had sounded a new note in English poetry, one that appealed so greatly to his contemporaries that many lesser versifiers copied his rhythms, repeated his themes and tricks of phrase, and wrote poems of their own based on characters or situations in his *Arcadia* and other works. Anything associated with his name became precious, not so much because he was a poet, but because he was the ideal gentleman of his age and a national hero. As the editor of *A Poetical Rhapsody* said in 1602, Sir Philip Sidney's name would "grace the forefront" of any collection. *Sir Philip Sidneys Ouránia*, 1606, was a title devised to attract purchasers, though the publisher did add that it was "written by N[athaniel?] B[axter?]." In 1678, however, two London printers dishonestly issued a translation of Mlle. de la Roche Guilhem's *Almanzor and Almanzaida* with the statement that it was "Written by Sir Philip Sidney. And found since his Death amongst his Papers." So when Sidney died publishers and keepers of private commonplace books began

* Reprinted from *Studies in Philology*, XLVII (1950), 126–151, with permission of author and publisher. Omissions are indicated by ellipses.

an eager search for his writings; and they were frequently tempted to assign to him anything that sounded like his, because of the distinction added by his name.

The tendency to add to the Sidney canon has continued through the past three and a half centuries, during which time at least thirty poems, a bulk equal to about one-tenth of his authenticated verse, have been attributed to him. Critical examination will show that more than half of these could not possibly be from his pen, and that the authenticity of most of the rest is doubtful. But attributions once made were usually accepted, and in course of time collected editions of Sidney's writings included an ever increasing number of poems that probably are not his. The three-volume trade edition of his *Works,* 1725–1724, contained three attributed poems; William Gray's edition of the *Miscellaneous Works,* 1829, contained seven; A. B. Grosart's two-volume edition of the *Complete Poems,* 1873, contained twelve; and Albert Feuillerat's four-volume edition of the *Complete Works,* 1912–1926, contained fourteen. Collections of Sidney's writings are therefore cumbered with considerable literary baggage of questionable authenticity, which has been a source of error to his biographers and critics, who have accepted several wrongly attributed works as genuine. It is the purpose of this paper to determine which writings can properly be accepted as his and which are by other hands, and so to establish the canon of his poetical works.

At least 278 poems can be accepted without reservation as Sidney's, either because they were published under the supervision of his family or friends, or because they have a well-established manuscript tradition behind them. The 1598 *Arcadia . . . with sundry new additions,* published certainly with the approval and probably under the editorial supervision of his sister, the Countess of Pembroke, contains: (*a*) a patchwork version of the *Arcadia,* consisting of the incomplete "Revised" version and the last three books of the "Original" version, with 76 poems; (*b*) *Certaine Sonets,* with 31 poems; (*c*) *Astrophil and Stella,* with 108 sonnets and eleven songs; and (*d*) the "May Lady," with three poems. All these are certainly genuine. Five poems of the "Original" *Arcadia* (preserved in ten sixteenth-century manuscripts) that were not included in the "Revised" version, an additional "Certaine Sonet" found in the collection of miscellaneous poems at the end of two manuscripts of the "Original" *Arcadia,* and translations of the first 43 Psalms (preserved in fourteen sixteenth- and seventeenth-century manuscripts) are also certainly Sidney's work.

16: Poems Attributed to Sidney

Sidney himself assembled his miscellaneous poems, written on various occasions over a period of years, in a single collection, titled variously "Certaine Sonets" (1598 *Arcadia*), "Certein lowse Sonnettes and songs" (Bodl. è Mus. 37), and "Divers and sondry Sonettes" (Folger 4009.03). . . . The probability of there being any considerable number of miscellaneous poems that he did not include in *Certaine Sonet* is slight. Therefore the authenticity of any poem attributed to Sidney that is not included in the above collections must be viewed with suspicion; those who wish to assert Sidney's authorship of any such poem must make out a clear case, for the burden of proof rests upon them.

In the following pages I discuss the evidence for and against Sidney's authorship of all poems, not included in the authentic collections of his writings, that have at any time been attributed to him. For ease of reference I have numbered the poems according to the alphabetical order of their first lines, but sometimes discuss several of them together in a single group.

1. "All my sences stand amazed," 32 lines.
17. "Leave me O life, the prison of my minde," 10 lines.
22. "Some men will saie, there is a kinde of muse," 66 lines.

Mary Bowen, *MLN*, x (1895), 239–244, suggested that these three poems, included in Grosart's *Works . . . of Nicholas Breton*, 1879, might be by Sidney. No. 1 is preserved only in Brit. Mus. Add. 34064, f.23^{r-v}, whence it was printed by Grosart in his edition of Breton, I, t, 22. Miss Bowen suggests Sidney's authorship because of "certain intangible delicacies of phrasing . . . use of the feminine rime, and trochaic meter," and compares its rhythm with that of *Certaine Sonets*, No. 26, and Song ii of *Astrophil and Stella*. Miss Bowen does not specify what "intangible delicacies of phrasing" she has in mind, and Breton, who was a frequent imitator of Sidney, used feminine rime and trochaic meter in 16 of the 30 poems in his *Melancholike Humours*, 1600. Brit. Mus. Add. 34064 (Grosart's "Cosens MS"), contains in its first section, ff. 2–26, a collection of 49 poems that were probably all written by Breton. The poems are anonymous in the manuscript, but 32 of them appear in other contemporary collections (*Brittons Bowre of Delights*, 1591; *The Arbor of amorous Devises . . . by N. B. Gent.*, 1597; *Englands Helicon*, 1600; and Bodl. Rawl. Poet 85) either signed by or associated with the name of Breton. Until evidence to the contrary is produced, it would appear proper to assume that the other

17 poems, among which is No. 1, are also by Breton; certainly there is no acceptable ground for assigning No. 1 to Sidney.

No. 17 is preserved only in *The Arbor of amorous Devises . . . By N. B. Gent.*, 1597, B3ᵛ (ed. Rollins, p. 14), a publisher's miscellany containing "many mens workes," a large proportion of which are Breton's. Miss Bowen notes that one poem in this volume, "The fire to see," B3ᵛ–4, is by Sidney, and argues, "If one is Sidney's, why not more?" She compares the general theme of No. 17 with sonnet 72 of *Astrophil and Stella* and the last of the *Certaine Sonets*. Possibly the writer of No. 17 had in mind Sidney's "Leave me O love, which reachest but to dust" when composing his first line; but that is not sufficient reason for saying that Sidney is the author.

No. 22 appears in Brit. Mus. Add. 34064, ff. 20ᵛ–21ᵛ, whence it was printed by Grosart in his edition of Breton, I, t, 20. . . . Lines 37–66 are printed in *Brittons Bowre of Delights*, 1591, Dʳ⁻ᵛ (ed. Rollins, pp. 29–30); and Professor Rollins points out that lines 46–66 appear as stanzas 3, 5, and 6 of "A most excellent passion set downe by N. B. Gent." in *The Phoenix Nest*, 1593, I4-K. Miss Bowen bases her attribution to Sidney on the "similarity of thought" in *Astrophil and Stella*, sonnets 3, 6, and 15. R. W. Bond, *Works of John Lyly* (Oxford 1902), iii, 499–500, likewise using the test of similarity of thought, attributed the poem to Lyly. Professor Rollins, in his edition of the *Bowre* (p. 86), says that the "style and diction . . . strongly suggest Breton's authorship." A good case can be made out for Breton, none for Sidney.

2. "All things that are, or ever were, or shall hereafter bee."

This is the beginning of the first of 54 passages, totaling 204 lines, of metrical quotations in *A Woorke concerning the trewnesse of the Christian Religion . . . Begunne to be translated into English by Sir Philip Sidney Knight, and at his request finished by Arthur Golding*, 1587, a translation of Phillippe du Plessis Mornay's *De la verité de la religion chrétienne*, 1581. Grosart, i, 224–229, reprinted 12 of the first 16 passages, remarking: "I have not ventured to go beyond p. 83 of this 'begunne' translation; nor indeed was there any temptation to do so." Feuillerat, iii, 247–376, reprinted the preface and first six chapters, which contain 16 metrical passages.

There is no doubt that Sidney had something to do with this translation. Mornay's wife said in her *Memoirs* that Sidney had done her husband the honor of translating his book into English. In November

16: Poems Attributed to Sidney

1586, Fulke Greville wrote that Sidney "hathe most excellently translated among div[ers] other notable workes monsieur du plessis book agains[t] Atheisme, which is since don by an other" (PRO SP 12/195/33). Golding, in his dedication of the completed translation to Sidney's uncle, the Earl of Leicester, said that Sidney "began to put the same into our Language . . . and had proceeded certaine chapters therein" when he left England for the campaign in the Netherlands; but before leaving he committed the translation "unto my charge," and I have accordingly undertaken the "so great a taske" of completing it.

The question to be decided is how much of the translation is Sidney's and how much Golding's, and whether any of the verse can be attributed to Sidney. Professor Feuillerat compared the French text with the English and detected two methods of translation: "The one . . . manages to be faithful to the sense without being a slave to the letter . . . The other . . . servilely follows the foreign sentence and renders it word for word" (III, ix–x). Since Golding in his other translations used the word-for-word method, Feuillerat concluded that the more freely translated sections, the preface and first six chapters, were the work of Sidney.

But there is no difference discernible, either in method of translation or in style, between the earlier and later metrical passages, which are all laborious and clumsy renderings by a writer who had only a rudimentary sense of rhythm and no gift of phrase. Little attempt was made to reproduce the metrical forms of the originals; Sidney, in his translations from Horace, Seneca, and Montemayor in *Certaine Sonets*, was always careful to imitate their rhythmical peculiarities. More than half of the passages are in lumbering septenary couplets, Golding's favorite verse form, which he used in his translation of Ovid and frequently in the metrical sections of his other translations; Sidney experimented with the form only once, in Song vii of *Astrophil and Stella*, and was apparently dissatisfied with the result for he never used it again. Two passages are in anapestic tetrameter couplets, an old-fashioned verse form used by Golding in passages of his translations of Ovid and Chytraeus, but never used by Sidney. Certain peculiarities of vocabulary—such as the use of "everychone" as a rime word in chapters vi and xxxii—are typical of Golding's usage (cf. *Abrahams Sacrifice*, l. 778), but are not found in Sidney.

I believe we must assume that Sidney, in what little part of the work he did translate, left blank spaces for the passages of verse.

He worked in a similar manner when he revised his *Arcadia*, for the manuscript copy of his revision (Camb. Univ. Kk. 1. 5), dated 1584, is continuous for the prose, but in many cases contains only a blank space for the poetry, which he apparently intended to insert later. The rhythm and phrasing of the metrical passages of this translation are so overwhelmingly typical of Golding's manner, and so strikingly different from that of Sidney, that I can see no reason for attributing any of them to Sidney. . . .

4. "Are women faire? yea wondrous faire to see too," 26 lines.
12. "How can the feeble forts but fall and yeild at last," 30 lines.

These two poems are attributed to "P. Sydney" in the Crawford MS (pp. 59–61) . . . a commonplace book, largely composed of very late sixteenth- or early seventeenth-century verse, and containing some items written as late as 1625 and 1628.

No. 4 exists in ten other seventeenth-century copies, all anonymous. Seven of these stem from a twenty-line version of the poem. . . . In all of these the order of stanzas is the same and the verbal variants are unimportant; they derive from one another or from a common original, which I designate A. Four other manuscripts, of the second quarter of the seventeenth century or later, contain texts that can only be accounted for on the assumption that another version, which I designate B, probably an expansion and revision of A, once existed. B contained 24 lines and was formed by rewriting stanza 3 (which I designate 3*), adding a new stanza 6, and rearranging the stanzas (the numbers refer to their sequence in A) in the order 1 2 3* 5 6 4. Phillipps 9549 (Rosenbach Company, 1941 Catalogue, item 187), f. 6^{r-v}, is a careless copy which omits stanza 6 but is otherwise similar to B. The Crawford MS is also a rather careless copy of B (line 4 of stanza 3*, for example, has been badly garbled), which adds a final couplet found in no other version and reverses the order of stanzas 3* and 5. The remaining two manuscripts stem from another version of B (which I designate B*) that retained the stanza order of B, but had new versions of stanzas 5 and 6 (which I designate 5* and 6*). The Berkeley MS (Rosenbach Company, 1941 Catalogue, item 195), p. 15, is either B* itself or a fairly close copy; Brit. Mus. Egerton 2421, f. 15^v, follows the readings of B* but omits stanza 6* and rearranges the remaining stanzas in the order 1 5* 2 3* 4. This proliferation of variants, resulting in expanded and essentially new versions of the poem, is typical of what frequently happened to texts in seventeenth-century manuscripts. What the textual evidence shows concerning authorship is that the Crawford MS, the only one of eleven copies attributing the poem to "P. Sydney," is at best an imperfect copy of a copy of a copy, at least three removes from its original; it is highly improbable, therefore, that the attribution has a continuous manuscript tradition behind it. The poem does not appear to me to be in Sidney's manner; its cynical attitude toward women is different from his, which was usually one of admiration, or at least of respect. Since the poem was apparently quite popular, yet does not appear in any book or manuscript earlier than the seventeenth century; and since the Crawford MS, a comparatively late and derivative version, stands alone among ten other copies in assigning the poem to Sidney, I do not believe the attribution can be accepted.

No. 12 also appears, with no author indicated, in Brit. Mus. Harl. 7392, f. 71; and, signed at the end "M^rs M : R :," in Bodl. Rawl. Poet. 85, f. 114^r-v. The diction of this poem is characterized by thumping alliteration, which Sidney avoided, and by a series of lubricious *double entendres*, to which he never stooped. Rawl. Poet. 85 is a much earlier manuscript, and its attribution of the poem to "M^rs M : R :" is at least as acceptable as that of the Crawford MS to "P. Sydney." Since in addition the style and matter of the poem are different from Sidney's authentic work, I can see no adequate reason for accepting it as his.

5. "At my harte there is a payne," 36 lines.
24. "The darte, the beames, the stringe so strong I prove," 14 lines.

These two poems both appear in Bodl. Rawl. Poet. 85, ff. 24^v–26 and 9^v, above the initials "S P S." No. 5 is preceded by an unsigned sonnet by Gorges and followed by Breton's elegy on Sidney, signed "Britton." . . . The poem also appears, unsigned, in Brit. Mus. Add. 34064, ff. 16^v–17. . . . No. 24 is preceded and followed by authentic poems of Sidney, both signed "S P S." . . . Another copy, unsigned, is in Brit. Mus. Harl. 7392, f. 66.

Rawl. Poet. 85 is a poetical commonplace book compiled in the late 1580's and early 1590's, possibly by Robert Mills, who was first a student at St. John's College, Cambridge, and later a schoolmaster at Stamford. It contains 143 poems, 64 of which have the names or initials of their authors appended. These attributions, so far as they can be checked, are usually, but not invariably, accurate. For example, "The longer lyfe," f. 155^v, is signed "E[arl] of Surr[ey]," but in Tottel's Miscellany, No. 174 (ed. Rollins, I, 127), it appeared among the poems by Uncertain Authors; and "O more than moste fayre," f. 7ᵛ, is signed "Mʳ Dier," but was printed later as the eighth sonnet of Spenser's *Amoretti*. In addition to the two poems we are considering, this manuscript contains 23 poems certainly by Sidney; eleven are properly attributed to him by name or initials, nine are unsigned, one is signed "Incertus author," one is attributed to "Mʳ Nowell," and one to "Britton." Evidently the compiler had an extremely uncertain knowledge of what poems were by Sidney and what poems were by other authors. The manuscript also contains 15 poems by or probably by Breton, eight of which are assigned to him and seven of which are anonymous. Since the compiler wrongly attributed Song x of Sidney's *Astrophil and Stella* to "Britton," he may have erred in the opposite direction when he placed the initials "S P S" after No. 5, which also appears in Add. 34064, a collection of poems that are probably all by Breton (see above under No. 1).

There is nothing in the style or content of the two poems themselves to discredit Sidney's authorship. No. 5 is in trochaic tetrameters, a verse form that, so far as I have been able to discover, Sidney was the first English poet to use; but his innovation almost immediately became popular and was frequently imitated by Greville, Breton, and many others. No. 24 is a sonnet made up of a series of triads, similar to "Virtue, beauty and speech" in the *Arcadia*. But other Elizabethans also wrote similar sonnets, such as the popular "Her face, her tongue, her wit," by Sir Arthur Gorges, which immediately follows No. 24 in Harl. 7392. If Nos. 5 and 24 are similar to Sidney's work in his less inspired moments, they are equally similar to the work of several of his contemporaries. In view of the uncertain accuracy of the attributions of the only manuscript that directly indicates their authorship, I do not believe we are justified in saying more than that the two poems may possibly be by Sidney; and in the case of No. 5 I think the scanty evidence available slightly favors Breton. . . .

8. "Dick, since we cannot dance, come let a chearefull voice," 48 lines.

This is titled "A Dialogue between two shepherds, uttered in a pastorall shew, at Wilton," and was first printed on an unpaged insert sheet, SsII, among the *Certaine Sonets* in the 1613 edition of the *Arcadia*. . . .

16: Poems Attributed to Sidney

Grosart (I, xxv–xxvi) assumed that the 1613 edition of the *Arcadia* provides "the best text of the whole Writings of Sidney" because it "was *the* edition selected for her own library by the sister of Sidney." He bases his assumption on a copy of that edition, formerly in the possession of Richard Heber and now in the Widener Collection at Harvard, with a note on the title page: "This was the Countess of pembrokes owne booke given me by the Countess of Montgomery her daughter 1625" and below it in another hand the signature "Ancram" (i.e., Sir Robert Ker, created first Earl of Ancram in 1633). Professor W. A. Jackson, in a lecture of October 9, 1946, pointed out that the binding of this copy, flourished with M's and S's which Grosart thought were the initials of the Lady Susan, Countess of Montgomery, is a French binding that was originally made for a smaller book, and that the signature "is quite unlike any of the signatures of Ancram." It is therefore a sophisticated copy with perhaps a fabricated inscription, and so is inadmissible as evidence of any connection the Countess of Pembroke might have had with that edition. It is more probable that the Lady Mary had no connection whatever with this edition, for the 1613 printing of the *Arcadia* is the only one of the twelve issued between 1593 and 1674 that omits the preface of H. S., which informs the reader that the Countess of Pembroke had "begonne in correcting the faults" and "ended in supplying the defectes" of the 1590 edition. Instead, the 1613 edition relegates acknowledgment of her labors of revision to a cursory phrase in a note on another unpaged insert leaf, Ee5, placed in the body of the text at the point where the "Revised" version breaks off.

The 1613 *Arcadia*, however, was set up from a copy of the 1598 edition by someone who went to considerable pains to produce an accurate and consistent text. Many typographical errors were corrected, and lines 118–120 were added to "In faith good Histor" from a manuscript of the "Original" *Arcadia*; but there is is no evidence that the editor consulted any manscripts of Sidney's other works. The editor also noticed that the third of the *Certaine Sonets*, "The fire to see," appeared earlier in the text of the "Revised" *Arcadia*, 1598, Bb. He therefore dropped the poem from *Certaine Sonets*; this omission made the page endings of his edition different from those of the 1598 text from which the compositor was working. But by re-spacing the contents of the following three leaves the page endings were brought back into line at Rr6^v. The new poem, No. 8, was then printed on an unpaged insert leaf between Ss and Ss2, not as an after-thought, but to enable the compositor to keep the endings of the remaining pages even with those of 1598.

The poem is in poulter's measure, with heavy alliteration and fixed caesura, an old-fashioned meter and style used only once by Sidney in the burlesque "What length of verse" of the "Original" *Arcadia;* but as an apparently deliberate attempt to reproduce the crudities of earlier poetry, its rudeness is appropriate for a country "pastorall shew." The names of the interlocutors, Will and Dick, appear nowhere else in Sidney's writings; but line 28, "by two so black eyes the glittring stars be past," reminds us of the Mira of the two latest manuscripts of the "Original" *Arcadia* and of Astrophil's Stella. Sidney paid frequent visits to Wilton, the home of his sister the Lady Mary, and a letter of Sir Arthur Basset, dated February 1583/4 (printed in Butler's *Sidneiana,* p. 81), shows that he had a hand in arranging entertainments there. There is therefore no internal evidence to make us reject the poem, and two possible references that connect it with the Sidney circle.

The 1613 editor's whole handling of the text shows that he had an exceptional regard for accuracy. Sidney's brother Robert, his sister the Countess of Pembroke, and his friend Fulke Greville were all living in 1613. The activities of his family and friends in suppressing the unauthorized *Astrophil and Stella* of 1591, and in editing the 1590, 1593, and 1598 *Arcadia,* show that they went to considerable trouble to ensure the proper publication of Sidney's authentic literary remains. The fact that the poem was reprinted in all subsequent folio editions of the *Arcadia* indicates that they took no action to suppress it, and so possibly accepted it as genuine. The poem is probably by Sidney. . . .

11. "Her inward worth all outward Show transcends," 6 lines.

These verses, on a single sheet of paper 5¾ by 7 inches, are preserved in a small glass-covered case at Wilton House in Wiltshire. With them is a lock of blond, or faded auburn, hair and a second slip of paper on which is written, in a different hand, "This Lock of Queen Elisabeth's owne Hair was presented to Sir Philip Sidney by Her Majesty's owne faire hands, on which He made these verses, and gave them to the Queen, on his bended knee. Anno Domini 1573." They were first mentioned by James Smith, *Wilton and Its Associations,* Salisbury, 1851 (p. 218), as having been found by accident "in a copy of the 'Arcadia' preserved in the library" of Wilton House. They were exhibited at Salisbury, September 13, 1854, and a report of the discovery, with a transcript of the verses, in a "hand said to be Sidney's own," was printed in *N&Q*, 1st Ser., x (1854), 241 [and in two other contemporary journals]. Sidney's biographers . . . accepted the verses and the incident, though they indulged in various speculations concerning the date. Grosart (i, 224) printed the verses "from the autograph at Wilton," and remarked (i, xxxv) that this is the only surviving manuscript of any poem of Sidney's "in his own autograph"; Feuillert (ii, 340) included them in his appendix of doubtful poems.

By the kind permission of Lord Herbert, I was allowed to examine the lock of hair and two slips of paper at Wilton House and to compare the handwriting, letter by letter, with photostats of several examples of Sidney's holograph correspondence. Neither the handwriting of the verses, nor of the other slip of paper, bears the slightest resemblance to Sidney's; indeed, both have every appearance of being considerably later than the sixteenth century. Lord Herbert told me that Wilton House, and with it any papers of Sidney and his sister that may have been preserved there, was almost entirely destroyed by fire in 1647. Some of the reports mention that the verses were found in a "folio copy" of the *Arcadia* at Wilton House. There is no record of the existence of a folio *Arcadia* in Wilton House during the nineteenth century, and there is none there now. Sidney could not have presented verses in person to Queen Elizabeth in 1573, because he was on the continent continuously from June 1572 until May 1575. Since the verses are not in Sidney's but in a much later hand, and since the statement attributing them to him is clearly in error in matter of date, there is no reason to accept them as authentic. . . .

16. "Joyne Mates in mirth to me," 52 lines.
28. "Walking in bright Phoebus blaze," 78 lines.

These appeared as the first two poems in Francis Davison's *A Poetical Rhapsody*, 1602, B1–3ᵛ (ed. Rollins i, 7–12) with the heading, "Two Pastoralls, made by Sir *Philip Sidney*, never yet published." No. 16 was separately titled, "Upon his meeting with his two worthy Friends and fellow-Poets, Sir Edward Dier and Maister Fulke Grevill," No. 28, "Disp017rayse of a Courtly life"; both were signed "Sir Ph. Sidney." No. 16 was reprinted from *A Poetical Rhapsody* in the second edition of *Englands Helicon*, 1614, P5ᵛ–6ᵛ (ed. Rollins i, 203–204);

both were reprinted as Sidney's by Gray (pp. 205–211), Grosart (I, 191–196), and Feuillerat (II, 325–328).

Davison included the first lines of both poems in what is apparently his second manuscript catalogue of anonymous poems in *A Poetical Rhapsody* (Brit. Mus. Harl. 280, f. 105ᵛ; printed in Rollins' edition II, 61); but in his preface to the printed edition he apologized for "mixing . . . thinges written by great and learned Personages, with our meane and worthles Scriblings" because the printer wished "to grace the forefront with Sir Ph. Sidneys, and others names." He clearly believed the two poems to be by Sidney, and so must have included them by error in his manuscript catalogue of anonymous works.

Francis Davison (ca. 1575–ca. 1619) was the eldest son of William Davison, a friend and associate of Sidney and remotely related to him. He therefore moved within the periphery of the Sidney circle and was in a position to acquire manuscript copies of his poems. He dedicated the *Poetical Rhapsody* to William Herbert, Earl of Pembroke, eldest son of Sidney's sister, and included one of her poems in his collection. Certainly if Davison had had any doubt concerning the authenticity of the Sidney poems, he would not have placed them at the beginning of a volume dedicated to a member of Sir Philip's family. The style and content of both poems are entirely in Sidney's manner. The complex inversions of lines 37–46 in No. 16 are especially typical; and Sidney's correspondence shows that Greville and Dyer were his two closest friends and with him formed the "happy blessed Trinitie" celebrated in No. 16. His "Striving with my mates in Song," line 45 of No. 28, is also substantiated from other sources. His *Certaine Sonet* No. 16 is a reply to a sonnet by Dyer; and Greville's *Workes*, 1633, bore on their title page the legend, "Written in his Youth, and familiar Exercise with Sir Philip Sidney." Of all the poems of doubtful attribution, these two have the best claim to be accepted as genuine. . . .

20. "Philoclea and Pamela sweet," 86 lines.

This was printed with the heading, "A Remedie for Love. Written by Sʳ Philip Sidney, Heretofore omitted in the Printed Arcadia," at the end of the 1655 edition of the *Arcadia*, Iii4ᵛ–5ᵛ, and reprinted in the 1662 and 1674 editions. It has been included in all collections of Sidney's poetry since . . . .

The verses printed in the *Arcadia* are actually a debased version, omitting ten lines and containing inferior variants in forty of the remaining lines, of a poem headed "Description of three Beauties" in Sir J[ohn] M[ennes] and Ja[mes] S[mith's] *Musarum Deliciae,* 1655 (pp. 13–15), a collection of humorous verse by Mennes, Smith, and others. An anonymous version of the Mennes and Smith text, titled "A Songe," is in Phillipps MS 8270, ff. 125–126ᵛ (Rosenbach Company, 1941 Catalogue, item 194). Other versions of the Mennes and Smith text, in mid-seventeenth-century commonplace books, are Brit. Mus. Add. 25303, ff. 137–138; Brit. Mus. Harl. 6057, ff. 10ᵛ–11ᵛ; and Emmanuel College Cambridge, I. 3. 16, ff. 4–5ᵛ. All three are headed "An ould Ditty of Sʳ Phillip Sydneys," and all except the last add, "omitted in the printed *Arcadia.*"

The heading in the manuscripts, which probably led the publisher of the 1655 *Arcadia* to include the verses with Sidney's works, is merely humorous, part of the joke of the poem, which uses characters from the *Arcadia* as the basis for a play of wit. The Hudibrastic meter and scatologic humor are typical of the verse of Mennes and Smith, and quite different from that of Sidney. Internal evidence proves that the poem was written in the seventeenth, and not in the sixteenth, century. Line 60 of the manuscript versions refers to the "Old or New Exchange"; there was only one Exchange in London until 1609, when the New Exchange was built. The earliest *OED* entry for the term "puddle dock," meaning excrement (line 62), is 1648; Puddle Wharf or Dock, at Blackfriars, in the sixteenth century was a watering place for horses; apparently not until later in the next century was it used as "a laystall for the soil of the streets."

Austin Dobson, *N&Q,* 10th Ser., II (1904), 89–90, argued on the basis of the scansion of this poem that the name of the heroine of Sidney's *Arcadia* should be pronounced Pamēla. Since the poem is clearly not by Sidney, and therefore of no authority, the many Pamelas of today may continue to pronounce their names as they have been accustomed, with the stress on the first syllable. . . .

We may summarize the results of this investigation by classifying the 30 poems that have been attributed to Sidney as "probably," "possibly," "probably not," and "definitely not" authentic. In the case of 18 poems, more than half of those that have been attributed to him (Nos. 1, 2, 3, 6, 9, 10, 11, 13, 15, 17, 18, 20, 22, 23, 25, 27, 29, and 30), either the attributions have been made at a late date on erroneous impressionistic grounds, or there is positive proof that the poems could not possibly be of his authorship. These may be dropped with complete certainty from the canon of his writings. Evidence of style and content, or superior claims in favor of other authors, indicate that eight poems (Nos. 4, 5, 7, 12, 14, 19, 21, and 26) were probably *not* written by Sidney. Only one poem (No. 24) may be accepted as possibly, and only three (Nos. 8, 16, and 28), as probably authentic. These conclusions substantiate the evidence of the surviving manuscript copies of his works, and show that Sidney himself included nearly all his miscellaneous verses in the collection titled *Certaine Sonets.*

The editor of Sidney's complete poetical works should print the 278 poems that appear in the demonstrably authentic copies of his writings. In addition he should include Nos. 16 and 28 as Sidney's almost certainly, and No. 8 as his with a high degree of certainty. He should print No. 24 in an appendix clearly titled as containing poems only "possibly" by Sidney. There is no internal evidence to make us deny Sidney's authorship of this poem; but since it is assigned to him only in a single manuscript of uncertain reliability, the attribution must be viewed with considerable doubt. If the editor wishes absolute completeness, he may include Nos. 5, 14, 19, and 21 in a second appendix of "poems attributed to Sidney that are probably imitations." Their style is similar to Sidney's; but each has been attributed to him in only a single document of questionable reliability, and their content suggests that they were written by imitators rather than by Sidney himself. The other four poems I have listed as "probably not" by Sidney have been attributed to him (each only once) in documents of such uncertain reliability, and are so unlike his authentic work in manner and content, or the evidence in favor of other authors is so strong, that there is very little reason for including them in any collection of his works.

17

A Possible Addition to the Sidney Canon*

By Ephim G. Fogel

OF thirty poems "that have at any time been attributed" to Sidney, only four, Professor Ringler concludes in his cogent essay,[1] should be printed in a complete edition of Sidney's poetical works, and one of these four, he states, "The darte, the beames, the stringe,"[2] should be set apart "in an appendix clearly titled as containing poems only 'possibly' by Sidney." I should like to propose that two sonnets not considered by Ringler, Feuillerat, or other editors of Sidney's works have an even stronger claim to inclusion in such an appendix than does "The darte, the beames, the stringe."

The two poems occur in Henry Goldwell's pamphlet describing the Whitsuntide triumphs of 1581 in honor of the ambassadors of Queen Elizabeth's French suitor, the Duke of Anjou.[3] The challengers in these games were Sidney; Fulke Greville; Frederick, fourth Lord Windsor; and Philip Howard, Earl of Arundel. Calling themselves the Four Foster Children of Desire, they attacked the Castle or Fortress of Perfect Beauty—that is, "the Gallary or place at the end of the Tiltyard adioining to her Maiesties house at *Whitehall,* whereas her

* Reprinted from *Modern Language Notes,* LXXV (1960), 389–394, with permission. I am indebted to Professor William Ringler for valuable suggestions and criticisms and to Dr. Giles F. Dawson of the Folger Library for his helpful replies to my queries.

[1] See the preceding selection, No. 16.

[2] See *The Complete Works of Sir Philip Sidney,* ed. Albert Feuillerat (Cambridge, Eng., 1912–1926), II, 349. Hereafter, Roman and Arabic numerals in parentheses shall refer to volume and page number of Feuillerat's edition.

[3] *A brief declaratiõ of the shews . . . performed before the Queenes Maiestie, & the French Ambassadours . . . on the Munday and Tuesday in Whitson weeke last, Anno 1581* (London); STC 11990. Quotations are cited from photoduplicates of the copy in the Huntington Library. Goldwell's pamphlet is reprinted in John Nichols, *The Progresses and Public Processions of Queen Elizabeth* (London, 1823), II, 310–329.

person should be placed" (Goldwell, sig. A3ᵛ). In his dedication to Rowland and Brasebridge, Goldwell states that he has collected the "speaches, and chiefest inuentions, which as they bee, I present to your presence" (sig. A2ʳ), but he fails, unfortunately, to identify the authors of the poems or the prose orations. Malcolm W. Wallace, however, calls the reader's attention to the "true Arcadian" speeches of the triumph, which he attributes in its entirety to Sir Philip Sidney.[4] Morris W. Croll rightly differentiates between the Arcadian speeches made "on behalf of all the challengers" and the euphuistic speeches made on behalf of the defendants, and asks whether Sidney did not write the former.[5] Neither Wallace nor Croll sifts the evidence for the authorship of the challengers' speeches, however, nor does either mention the following two poems.

At the beginning of a triumph, a page approached the queen's "fortress" and sang as follows (sigs. A8ᵛ–Bʳ):

> Yeelde yeelde, O yeelde, you that this FORTE do holde,
>   which seated is, in spotlesse honors fielde,
> Desires great force, no forces can withhold:
>   then to DESIERS desire, O yeelde O yeelde.
>
> Yeelde yeelde O yeelde, trust not on beauties pride,
>   fayrenesse though fayer, is but a feeble shielde,
> When strong Desire, which vertues loue doth guide,
>   claymes but to gaine his due, O yeelde O yeelde.
>
> Yeelde yeelde O yeelde, who first this Fort did make,
>   did it for iust Desires, true children builde,
> Such was his minde, if you another take:
>   defence herein doth wrong, O yeelde O yeelde,
>
> Yeelde yeelde O yeelde, now is it time to yeelde,
> Before thassault beginne, O yeelde O yeelde.
>
> When that was ended, another Boye turning him selfe
>   to the *Foster* children and their retinue, sung
>   this Allarme.

[4] *The Life of Sir Philip Sidney* (Cambridge, Eng., 1915), 264. Friedrich Brie, *Sidneys Arcadia: Eine Studie zur Englischen Renaissance* (Strassburg, 1918), 291–294, states that both Sidney and Greville had a hand in the writing of the triumph and cites several parallels between it and various chivalric combats in the new *Arcadia*. But his remarks, like Wallace's, are too general to be probative of authorship.

[5] See Lyly's *Euphues,* ed. Morris W. Croll and Harry Clemons (London and New York, 1916), p. li, n. 4.

Allarme allarme, here will no yeelding be,
    such marble eares, no cunning wordes can charme,
Courage therefore, and let the stately see
    that naught withstandes DESIRE, Allarme allarme.

Allarme allarme, let not their beauties moue
    remorse in you to doe this FORTRESSE harme,
For since warre is the ground of vertues loue,
    no force, though force be vsed Allarme allarme.

Allarme allarme, companions nowe beginne,
    about this neuer conquered walles to swarme,
More prayse to vs we neuer looke to winne,
    much may that was not yet, Allarme allarme.

Allarme allarme when once the fight is warme,
    then shall you see them yelde, Allarme allarme.

The purpose of the remarks that follow is to bring together the detailed evidence that points to Sidney's authorship of the challengers' speeches and the two sonnets just cited.

Goldwell implies that Elizabeth's courtiers had a hand in the composition of the triumph.[6] Now three of the challengers—Sidney, Greville, and Arundel—were writers.[7] Hence each of them has a claim to be considered as the possible author of the challengers' speeches and of the sonnets. But Sidney's claim is by far the strongest. The most active poet and prose writer of the challengers, Sidney devised several entertainments and achieved a notable reputation as a maker of impresas.[8] In style, moreover, the challengers' speeches and the

---

[6] Goldwell states that after the French ambassadors came "to the English court, The Nobles and Gentlemen of the same . . . agreede among them to prepare a Triumphe, whiche was very quickly concluded, and being deuised in moste sumptuous order, was by them performed in as valiant a manner. . . ." He then adds that the Four Foster Children of Desire "made their inuention of the foresaide Triumphe in this order and forme following" (sig. A3ʳ⁻ᵛ).

[7] Lord Windsor, so far as I have been able to determine, was not.

[8] For Sidney's entertainments, see "The Lady of May" (II, 329–338) and "A Dialogue Betweene Two Shepherds, Utterd in a Pastorall Shew, at Wilton" (II, 323–324). A letter of February 6, 1583/4, from Sir Arthur Basset to Sir Edward Stradling suggests that Sidney is arranging a musical entertainment for a company of gentlemen at Salisbury on "the VIIth of March nexte" (Sidneiana, ed. Samuel Butler [London, 1837], 81). On Sidney's reputation as a deviser of impresas, see Edmund Molyneux in Holinshed's Chronicles (London, 1587), sig. 7L3ʳ; Henry Peacham, The Compleat Gentleman (London, 1622), sig. Cc4ʳ; and William Camden, Remaines of a Greater Worke (London, 1605), 165, 174.

sonnets are quite unlike the known works of Greville and Arundel,[9] but very similar to the prose and poetry of Sidney. Many of Sidney's favorite rhetorical devices occur in the prose of the challengers. Consider, for example, the characteristic use of the parenthetical interjection, so frequent both in the speeches of the Foster Children of Desire and in Sidney's works:

Whereto if you yelde, (O yelde for so al reason requireth) then haue I no more to say, but reioice that my sayings hath obteined so righ[t]full, and yet so blissefull a request. But if (alasse but let not that be needfull) BEAVTIE be accompanied with disdainfull pride, and pride waighted on by refusing crueltie. Then must I denounce vnto you (Woe is me, answere before it be denounced) that they determine by request to accomplish their claim. [Goldwell, Sig. A4ᵛ]

In the countrie of *Thessalia*, (alas why name I that accursed country, which brings forth nothing, but matters for tragedies? but name it I must) in *Thessalia* (I say) there was (well may I say, there was) a Prince (no, no Prince, whō bondage wholly possessed; but yet accounted a Prince, and) named *Musidorus*. O *Musidorus Musidorus*; but to what serve exclamations, where there are no eares to receive the sounde? [Sidney, I, 159; cf. IV, 98]

That anyone other than Sidney could then have written a prose so Arcadian seems doubtful.[10] Such close stylistic similarities, illustra-

---

[9] So far as Greville is concerned, the reader may easily check this judgment by consulting the *Poems and Dramas*, ed. Geoffrey Bullough, 2 vols. (New York, 1945), and *The Life of Sir Philip Sidney*, ed. Nowell Smith (Oxford, 1907). Arundel's works are more difficult to come by, being scattered in manuscripts and early printed books. A detailed list may be found in *The Venerable Philip Howard, Earl of Arundel*, ed. John H. Pollen and William MacMahon, Catholic Record Society, XXI (London, 1919), 324–330; specimens of his verse have been printed in Louise I. Guiney, *Recusant Poets*, I (London and New York, 1938), 226–228. Neither a long religious poem in 126 six-line stanzas ("O wretched man wᶜʰ louest earthly things") attributed to Arundel in Bodleian MS Rawl. Poet. 219, ff. 1–14ʳ and Folger MS 297.3, ff. 73ʳ–82ʳ, nor shorter poems attributed to him, bear a stylistic resemblance to the Fortress of Beauty sonnets. (Indeed, none of the attributed poems cited by Pollen, MacMahon, and Guiney are sonnets). Of Arundel's prose, I have read all the letters printed in Pollen and MacMahon's collection, the translation of Johann Justus (Landsberger), *An Epistle in the Person of Christ to the Faithfull Soule* (Antwerp, 1595), STC 14627, and Arundel's ("Callophisus'") challenge to a tournament at Westminster on January 22, 1580/1 (a copy of the challenge is in the Folger Library). None of these writings resembles the Arcadian prose of the challengers' speeches.

[10] In the spring of 1581, very few could have imitated the *Arcadia*, since very few had access to a manuscript of it. On Oct. 18, 1580, Sidney wrote to his brother Robert: "My toyfull booke I will send with Gods helpe by Febru-

tions of which could easily be multiplied, would seem to justify a conservative editorial decision to label the prose of the challengers as "possibly by Sir Philip Sidney." There is no reason to relegate to a more dubious classification the two poems imbedded in the prose. The following are arguments in favor of Sidney's authorship of the poems.

1. At the time of the Fortress of Beauty pageant, Sidney was the most active English practitioner of the sonnet form.[11]

2. The manner of the Fortress of Beauty sonnets is Sidneyan; both poems, and especially the first, display a use of *epizeuxis, polyptoton,* and other figures of repetition, which is quite like Sidney's practice. As for the matter, the conflict of Desire against Virtuous Beauty is of course a commonplace, but it is one that Sidney develops again and again in his amatory verse.

3. The second sonnet is a line-by-line reply to the first. Sidney wrote similar companion pieces in the old *Arcadia* and in "Certaine Sonets."

a. "Feede on my sheepe, my Charge, my Comforte, feede" and "Leave of my sheepe, yt ys no tyme to feede" (IV, 118–119).

b. "The Merchaunt Man, whome gayne dothe teache y[e] Sea" and "The Merchaunt man, whome many seas have taughte" (IV, 161–162).

c. "A Satyre once did runne away for dread," Sidney's companion piece to Edward Dyer's "*Prometheus* when first from heaven hie" (II, 308–309).

The first and third of these pairs are sonnets, as are the companion pieces in the Fortress of Beauty triumph. Moreover, the rhetorical pattern of "Feede on my sheepe" and "Leave of my sheepe" is extremely close to that of "Yeelde yeelde, O yeelde" and "Allarme allarme." In each case, the opening phrase constitutes a refrain which

---

ary" (III 132); the reference is doubtless to the first version of Sidney's romance.

[11] By the spring of 1581, Sidney had already written the twenty sonnets of the old *Arcadia* (IV, 25, 89, 91, 108–109, 118–119, 169–171, 179–180, 187, 189, 196, 202, 206, 216–217, 219, 236–237, 256, 347; see also a quatorzain in poulter's measure, IV, 27, and another in rime royal, IV, 117) and had very probably written most, if not all, of the thirteen quatorzains in "Certaine Sonets" (II, 301–302, 305–306, 308–309, 310–312, 322). Professor Ringler reminds me that the only other living Englishman who had written a comparable number of sonnets by 1581 was Thomas Howell: see the twelve sonnets and two quatorzains in *Howell's Devises, 1581,* ed. Sir Walter Raleigh (Oxford, 1906), 16–17, 25, 34, 38, 42, 45, 48–49, 55–56, 77–79, 85–86; two other sonnets in *Devises* are attributed to "E. L." and "I. K." (56, 97–98).

is repeated at the beginning of each of the main prosodic divisions—at lines 1, 4, 7, 10, and 13 of the *terza rima* sonnet "Feede on," and at lines 1, 5, 9, and 13 of "Yeelde yeelde."

In view of the evidence cited above, it would seem appropriate, pending discovery of positive proof or disproof of Sidney's authorship, for an editor of Sidney's complete poetical works to place "Yeelde yeelde, O yeelde" and "Allarme allarme" in a small appendix of poems "possibly by Sir Philip Sidney."[12]

---

[12] External evidence of Sidney's authorship of "Yeelde yeelde, O yeelde" may lie in a manuscript by Abraham Fraunce. An entry in the catalogue of the sale of Benjamin Heywood Bright's manuscripts at Sotheby's in 1844 reads as follows:

> 101 Fraunce (Abraham) Yeeld, Yeeld, O Yeeld: Omnia vincit
> amor. Venus est Dignissima pomo.
> > An Original and unpublished work by this singular writer,
> > addressed to Sir Philip Sidney.

So far as I can tell, none of Fraunce's extant works begins or has the title, "Yeeld, Yeeld, O Yeeld." I am informed by M. J. Kennedy of the British Museum that Item 101 was purchased for £4 by someone called "Rodd." This may be Thomas Rodd, bookseller, of 9 Great Newport Street, London, or Horatio Rodd, bookseller, of 23 Little Newport Street, London. The manuscript is not mentioned in Thomas Rodd's *Cat. of MSS & Ancient Deeds* (1845), the only catalogue of manuscripts by either Rodd which I have been able to examine. Further inquiries have failed to turn up the Fraunce item.

If we are to judge from the description in Sotheby's catalogue it would seem that Fraunce wrote a work, perhaps a lengthy poem (it seems unlikely that "Rodd" would have paid £4 for a short piece) with a possible mythological framework ("Venus est Dignissima pomo"), the title or the opening words of which were the same as the refrain of the first Fortress of Beauty sonnet. And it seems, furthermore, that Fraunce dedicated this work to his patron, Sir Philip Sidney. It is very possible that we have here a pointed example of Fraunce's habit of flattering imitation of works from Sir Philip's hand. The discovery of the manuscript purchased by "Rodd," or perhaps of a detailed description of it, may afford something very close to positive proof of Sidney's authorship of the Fortress of Beauty sonnets.

III

STUDIES IN
ATTRIBUTION:
ENGLISH LITERATURE
1660 to 1775

Editorial Note to Part III

ESSAYS in this section were chosen, from a field of many contenders, for the variety of problems and methods illustrated.

Sir Geoffrey Keynes's attribution of the continuation of Bacon's *New Atlantis* to Bacon's scientific continuator Robert Hooke (No. 18) constitutes a nice special case; for much hinges on the assumption that the secretive Hooke had exclusive knowledge of the early findings (about the cheese mites), made possible by a microscope of his own design. One could perhaps assign a more certain weight to the evidence if one could date with certainty the "accidents" alluded to by his biographer Richard Waller: "He was in the beginning of his being made known to the Learned, very communicative of his Philosophical Discoveries and Inventions, till some accidents made him to a Crime close and reserv'd." Yet if one of the Learned had borrowed Hooke's mites and lice for this earnest, nonsatirical treatise, would he also have borrowed Hooke's initials, "R.H."? A hypothesis that seems so strained will probably do little to weaken Keynes's attribution.

Akin to the studies of Hoy and Bowers in its single focus on a sharply defined set of data, David Vieth's paper (No. 19) explicates a method by examining the bibliographical evidence of collections of poems, within the context of chronological data.

Attributions of some circumstantially possible "uncollected" essays or poems on the grounds of similarities in style are very common. But R. S. Crane's attribution of an unsigned review to Goldsmith (No. 20) depends rather upon the limiting and crucial premise of the uniqueness "within the restricted group of the contributors to the *Critical Review* in 1760" of "this particular association of doctrines" and "the radical temper with which they were here expressed," plus the supporting evidence that the essay's borrowings from the *Encyclopedie* are limited to the one volume from which Goldsmith, in his undisputed essays of 1759, drew all but two of his borrowings from that same work.

In Sherbo's *Mother Midnight* essay (No. 21), which initiated the *Bulletin* series and is frequently alluded to, the discussion of method is applied to a booklet of miscellaneous nature and to parallelisms of miscellaneous quality. The argument is that certain parallels "are of such picayune details" as to suggest a single author's self-repetition rather than an imitator's close observation (see also No. 6).

Sherbo has raised the question whether a single sentence or phrase of Johnson's could be authenticated, and has answered it in the affirmative. To make such minute discriminations of authenticity is of course the province of the textual critic; but then, textual criticism is in one sense a continuous exercise in attribution on the microscopic scale. W. R. Keast in his scrutiny (No. 22) of Johnson's Preface to his *Dictionary* as it appears in the four folio editions printed in the writer's lifetime, attempts to distinguish between authoritative and un-authorized variants not only in phrases and single words, but also in such minutiae as punctuation and spelling. In such an enterprise, knowledge of composing-room and proofreading practices and of the handwriting (as well as the thought and style) of the author in question becomes highly relevant.

18

Robert Hooke
the Probable Author of
*New Atlantis Continued**

By Geoffrey Keynes

THE *New Atlantis Continued by R. H. Esquire*[1] is a book of considerable rarity and is not well known. The identity of the author, R. H.
Esquire, has been discussed, but has never been satisfactorily settled.
The name of Robert Hooke has been suggested, but there is no direct
evidence of his authorship, and even Archbishop Tenison in his
Baconiana, 1679, does not make any suggestion, giving the author simply as "R. H." (p. 36n.). Edmund Freeman in an article[2] discussing
the authorship remarks that Hooke was not famous at the date outside
scientific circles and might well be unknown to Tenison, so that his
evidence does not carry much weight.

After a dedication to King Charles and a preface giving arguments
in favor of monarchical government, the book begins by summarizing
the Argument of Bacon's *New Atlantis*, first published in *Sylva Sylvarum*, 1626. The narrative is then continued in the words of "the
stranger" who had been received in Bacon's utopia by the ruler or
Acadorem. The laws and customs of the country are described in some
detail and their humane and liberal character is emphasized, special

* Reprinted from *A Bibliography of Dr. Robert Hooke*, by Geoffrey Keynes
(Oxford: Clarendon Press, 1960), 2–4, with permission of author and publisher.
[1] *New Atlantis. Begun by the Lord Verulam, Viscount St. Albans: And Continued by R. H. Esquire. Wherein is set forth A Platform of Monarchical Government. with A Pleasant intermixture of divers rare Inventions, and wholsom Customs, fit to be introduced into all Kingdoms, States, and Common-wealths.
London, Printed for John Crooke at the Signe of the Ship in St. Pauls Church-
yard. 1660.*
[2] "A Proposal for an English Academy in 1660," *Modern Language Review*,
xix (1924), 291–300.

encouragement being given to "all ingenious persons," including authors of "all artificial inventions" (p. 53). There is nothing that could not have been written by Hooke and there are many points of similarity, as noted by Freeman, between the plans for the *New Atlantis* and Hooke's views as they are known from other sources, especially his enthusiasm at that time for cooperation in scientific and literary effort. Hooke was an exceedingly lively-minded and well-instructed young man of twenty-five in 1660 and was, moreover, about to publish an acute scientific treatise in the next year—the *Attempt for the Explication, by R. H.*, 1661. He had a profound admiration for Bacon. In a letter to Lord Brouncker he wrote in 1672: "I judge there is noe thing conduces soe much to the advancement of Philosophy as the examining of hypotheses by experiments & the enquiry into Experiments by hypotheses and I have the authority of the Incomparable Verulam to warrant me" (*Newton Correspondence*, I [1959], 202).

Hooke's authorship of the *New Atlantis* has been firmly rejected by Professor Andrade (personal communication), partly on the ground that Hooke would certainly not have described himself as *Esquire* on a title page in 1660. The word might, however, have been inserted by the printer or publisher, and the argument does not seem to me to be conclusive; much stronger evidence in favor of Hooke's authorship has hitherto been overlooked. Toward the end of the book the stranger is led by his guide, Joabin, into "a little closet at the end of that gallery" in which was "a little Ark containing rarities." He was next shown "a Selenoscope to view the Moon, Stars and new planets, and a rare Microscope, wherein the eyes, legs, mouth, hair and eggs of a Cheesmite, as well as the bloud running in the veins of a Lowce, was easily to be discerned" (p. 68). Reference to Hooke's *Micrographia*, not published until five years later, shows that exactly these details of the cheese mite and the louse are carefully described in consecutive sections of the book (pp. 212–214). A few pages farther on are descriptions of telescopes and their use in examining small stars and the surface of the moon. Whoever wrote the *New Atlantis* was clearly much interested in scientific knowledge and developments, and it seems unlikely that anyone but Hooke himself would have been familiar with these details, which could only have been seen through his newly designed microscope. If he had demonstrated his discoveries to another, it would probably have been to one of those among the early Fellows of the Royal Society, but there is no name in the list with the initials R. H. except Hooke himself.

18: *Hooke and* New Atlantis Continued

It seems to me to be more than likely that Hooke was in fact the author of the *New Atlantis Continued*. A copy of the book was entered in the catalogue of his library—no. 164 among "English books in 8°." He also possessed the 1674 edition of Bacon's *Sylva Sylvarum,* but he would certainly have been familiar with the book in another edition before this date.

19

Order of Contents as Evidence of Authorship: Rochester's *Poems* of 1680[*]

By David M. Vieth

THIS paper, as its title implies, explores a method. It discusses an example which shows how the arrangement of contents in a printed book or manuscript volume may indirectly provide evidence leading to significant conclusions. The example chosen is the earliest printed collection of the poems of John Wilmot, Earl of Rochester. First published shortly after Rochester's death in 1680, this collection quickly passed through at least ten interdependent editions, each giving the same sixty-one poems in the same order. Each of these editions attributes all its poems to Rochester, even though many of them were certainly written by other authors.

I

Previous studies of the 1680 editions have included a book by James Thorpe, an article by William B. Todd, and a paper which I read before the Modern Language Association at its meeting in 1954 and subsequently published as an article.[1] These studies have estab-

[*] Read at the Modern Language Association on Dec. 27, 1959; reprinted from the *Papers of the Bibliographical Society of America*, LIII (1959), 293–308, with permission of author and publisher.—Eds. For helpful criticism I am grateful to Mr. James M. Osborn.—D.M.V.
[1] James Thorpe, *Rochester's Poems on Several Occasions* (1950); William B. Todd, "The 1680 Editions of Rochester's *Poems*: With Notes on Earlier Texts," *PBSA*, XLVII (1953), 43–58; David M. Vieth, "The Text of Rochester and the Editions of 1680," *PBSA*, L (1956), 243–263, hereafter called "Text of Rochester." Bibliographical descriptions of the 1680 editions, as well as a facsimile reproduction of the Huntington edition, are provided in Thorpe's volume, to which Todd's article and my own stand as supplements.

lished the internal relationships among the ten editions and have identified the so-called Huntington edition as the first. Their concentration on questions of priority among the editions has, nevertheless, tended to obscure the far more pressing problems of authenticity raised by the sixty-one poems printed there. These problems of authorship are important partly because the collection of 1680, in addition to its spurious matter, contains the heart of the Rochester canon. The full scope of the problems can be appreciated, however, only by realizing that the 1680 editions served as ultimate sources for numerous texts and attributions in almost all the approximately forty other reprintings of Rochester's works during the century following his death. Thus the solution of these problems of authorship is a necessary first step in any systematic attempt to establish the Rochester canon, which has hitherto remained one of the most puzzling areas of inquiry in English literary scholarship.

This paper proposes to show that the order occupied by the sixty-one poems in the 1680 editions is an indispensable key to their authenticity. Lack of space will, of course, prevent presentation of the bulk of my evidence, which includes ascriptions in hundreds of early manuscript copies of the sixty-one poems. Such ascriptions, though not infallible, are generally more reliable than attributions in contemporary printed texts.[2]

II

Before the significance of the order of the sixty-one poems can be explored, it is necessary to summarize several points which were covered more fully in my earlier article, and to draw from them some further conclusions. These points all involve a Restoration manuscript miscellany, now in the Yale University Library and previously designated as the Yale manuscript.[3]

The Yale manuscript is a bound quarto volume transcribed in two late-seventeenth-century hands. Though the manuscript is unfortunately marred by seven gaps where leaves have been cut out, a glance at the second and third columns in the table at the end of this article will reveal that the extant portion in the first hand is

---

[2] This evidence will be found in full detail in my book *Attribution in Restoration Poetry: A Study of Rochester's "Poems" of 1680* (Yale Studies in English, CLIII, 1963).

[3] For a more detailed description of the Yale MS, see "Text of Rochester," 245–246, or *Attribution in Restoration Poetry*, 65–68.

unmistakably related in some fashion to the 1680 editions. It gives the same poems in the same order except that it includes eleven additional poems, omits one poem, and exhibits three small differences in arrangement. Textual evidence, as well as evidence of other kinds, shows that the Yale manuscript bears a collateral relationship to the Huntington edition, both being descended independently from a no longer extant archetype. Consequently, in order to evaluate the arrangement and ascriptions of the Yale manuscript and the Huntington edition, we must try to discover which of these two extant texts better represents the ascriptions and arrangement of the lost manuscript which served as their ultimate common source.

All available evidence indicates that the ascriptions given by the archetype are more accurately preserved in the Yale manuscript. The 1680 editions, as is well known, attribute genuine and spurious poems to Rochester indiscriminately. The Yale manuscript, by contrast, is more reliable in its ascriptions than most Restoration manuscript miscellanies, and in no case is there reason to suspect that it was influenced by the false attributions of the printed editions. Of the twenty-three ascriptions given explicitly in the Yale manuscript, all but two are supported by other contemporary evidence, especially by ascriptions in early copies of the poems which textual collation suggests are descended neither from the Yale manuscript nor from the printed editions. Moreover, only two of these twenty-three ascriptions are probably incorrect, and one of these two—for poem number 62 —was evidently distrusted by the scribe himself. Thus the ascriptions in the Yale manuscript, unlike those of the 1680 editions, possess some standing and may, indeed, be virtually identical with those of the archetype. Possibly, too, they correspond to the ascriptions given in the lost copy-text of the Huntington edition; the printer, of course, omitted any external indications that certain poems were not Rochester's.

The following tentative conclusion can therefore be formulated: *If the Yale manuscript ascribes a poem to some author other than Rochester, then an attribution to Rochester in the 1680 editions, or in sources descended from the 1680 editions, constitutes no evidence whatever that Rochester wrote the poem.* This conclusion would remove the last remaining arguments supporting the authenticity of nine poems which students of Rochester have already viewed as doubtful. These poems are numbers 44 through 46, which are three satires on Edward Howard; numbers 49 and 50, which are by Aphra Behn; numbers 56, 57, and 59, by John Oldham; and number 68, by Alexander Radcliffe. Similarly discredited is all external evidence that Rochester wrote poem number 52, the much-discussed "A Session of the Poets." For poem number 51, usually known as "Timon," all printed attributions to Rochester are disqualified, since the Yale manuscript assigns this satire to Sedley; Rochester's authorship is rendered probable, however, by evidence which lies outside the scope of this paper. More striking, perhaps, is the case of poem number 37, which has been universally accepted as Rochester's and has, indeed, been praised as one of his finest lyrics. The evidence supporting Rochester's authorship is limited, however, to the 1680 editions and sources descended from them, whereas the Yale manuscript assigns the poem to one of Rochester's archenemies, Sir Carr Scroope. Apparently this song is by Scroope, while the immediately following poem, as we shall see, is probably Rochester's obscene burlesque of Scroope's lyric.

In places where the Yale manuscript and the 1680 editions differ in their contents or arrangement, all known evidence indicates that again the Yale manuscript preserves the features of the archetype. This conclusion rests on what I have termed, in my earlier article, "linked groups" of poems. Such "linked groups" consist of poems which were gathered into manuscript pamphlets or loose sheets and passed from hand to hand in this form before being copied into manuscript miscellanies and commonplace books. Their existence is attested by surviving examples, as well as by the fact that groups of two to five poems often appear linked in the same order in several larger manuscript volumes. Four such "linked groups," which are shown in the table by double vertical lines, occur in places where the Yale manuscript and the 1680 editions exhibit differences in contents or arrangement, and in all four instances the Yale manuscript apparently preserves the grouping in its original state.[4] This result suggests that in

---

[4] [This footnote and the next are here inserted from "Text of Rochester," 250–251.—Eds.] (1) Group consisting of "Satyr" (p. 6) followed by "The Answer" ("Were I to choose what sort of Shape I'd weare"). The Yale MS gives both poems in this order, as do Harvard MS Eng. 623F, Harvard MS Eng. 636F, and Camb. MS Add. 6339. The printed editions omit "The Answer." This group might, however, have been formed independently by two or more scribes, since the second poem is an answer to the first.

(2) Group consisting of the songs beginning "How blest was the Created State" (p. 70), "While on those lovely looks I gaze" (p. 71), "Against the Charmes our Ballocks have" (p. 73), and "By all Loves soft, yet mighty Pow'rs" (p. 72), which occur in that order in Harvard MS Eng. 636F. The Yale MS gives the first two poems and part of the third in this order, with the remainder

the remaining cases where such differences occur, the order and contents of the archetype are represented by the Yale manuscript. Since the last poem in the editions, number 72, does not appear in corresponding position in the Yale manuscript, it probably was not included in the archetype, and it therefore presents an entirely separate problem of authenticity. The evidence fails to indicate whether Rochester wrote it.[5]

A further point is raised by the seven gaps in the Yale manuscript where leaves have been cut out. Since the Yale manuscript and the 1680 editions are so closely similar in contents and arrangement, it is tempting to suppose that the poems removed by the gaps were those which presently occupy the corresponding portions of the editions—except, of course, for the seventh gap, which involves a poem not

---

of the group removed by the fifth gap. The printed editions give the third and fourth poems in reverse order and insert between them the song beginning "Room, room, for a Blade of the Town" (p. 72).

(3) Group consisting of the three satires on Edward Howard beginning "Come on ye Critticks! find one fault who dare" (p. 88), "Thou damn'd Antipodes to common sense" (p. 90), and "As when a Bully, draws his Sword" (p. 89). The three poems occur in this order in the Yale MS and in *The Annual Miscellany: For The Year 1694,* 1694. The printed editions give the second and third poems in reverse order.

(4) Group consisting of "Ephelia to Bajazet" (p. 138), "A very Heroical Epistle" (p. 140), "On Poet Ninny" (p. 143), "My Lord All-Pride" (p. 144), and "A Familiar Epistle to Mr Julian Secretary of the Muses" ("Thou Common Shore of this Poetique Towne"). The printed editions include only the first four poems, but all five occur in this order in the Yale MS and Osborn MS Chest II, Number 14, and also in BM Egerton MS 2623, where they occupy a manuscript pamphlet by themselves. Moreover, a manuscript copy of the group probably served as copy-text for *A Very Heroical Epistle from My Lord All-Pride to Dol-Common,* 1679, which gives the second and fourth poems in order and includes a reference to the first poem.

[5] It is possible that this poem ["On Rome's Pardons"] was removed by one of the gaps in the Yale MS, or that it appeared in the copy-text for the first edition and not in the Yale MS, but its position at the end of the editions points instead to a familiar bibliographical situation. The last poem which the editions share with the Yale MS, "Captain Ramble," continues only through the first four lines on the recto of the last leaf of the earlier editions. If nothing else followed, most of the recto and all of the verso of this leaf would be left blank. Frequently an attempt would be made to fill such a space, but in the Yale MS, and presumably in the copy-text for the first edition, all the remaining poems would have been too long. It is therefore probable that "On Rome's Pardons" was taken from some other manuscript source because it was approximately the required length.

included in the editions. For the other gaps, the corresponding poems in the 1680 editions supply approximately the right amount of text, and in each case one or more of these poems is unusually obscene, which would explain the motive for their excision from the manuscript.

This assumption could remain only tentative, however, were it not for a peculiarity of the first hand in the Yale manuscript. The scribe, whose hand is very neat and regular, ordinarily writes exactly sixteen lines on a page, or the equivalent of sixteen lines where provision must be made for titles or spaces between stanzas. Thus a simple process of counting lines can determine whether the gaps in the Yale manuscript will accommodate the corresponding portions of text in the editions.

This test suggests that for five of the seven gaps, the contents of the Yale manuscript were as conjectured. Indeed, the first three gaps almost certainly did not remove any poem in its entirety. Similarly, the seventh gap probably removed only the missing parts of poems number 47 and 48, though it is barely possible that a single short poem intervened between these two. The sixth gap would be filled exactly by the missing parts of poems number 38 through 43. The probability that these poems occupied the sixth gap is increased because poem number 43, whose concluding lines are still extant in the Yale manuscript, is the last of a "linked group" of four poems.

It is apparent, however, that the contents of the fourth and fifth gaps were not identical with the corresponding portions of the 1680 editions, for in both cases the gaps are too large. An explanation of this discrepancy is suggested by the fact that elsewhere in its text, the Yale manuscript gives a total of eleven poems which are lacking in the editions. Thus the fourth and fifth gaps may have contained the corresponding poems in the editions together with some extra pieces. The fourth gap would have included poems number 17 through 22 and about seven more pages of text. The fifth gap is more complicated because it involves a difference in arrangement between the Yale manuscript and the 1680 editions, but the presence of a "linked group" at this point indicates the probable order of both the Yale manuscript and the archetype. The fifth gap, then, would seem to have contained the missing parts of poems number 34 through 36 and all of one additional short poem.

On the basis of these foregoing conclusions, the poems have been listed in the first column in the table at the end of the article in the order they presumably occupied in the archetype.

III

It is a paradox that although their attributions are unreliable, the 1680 editions are descended from an archetype whose poems were arranged in a careful, intricate order determined largely by their authorship. The only Rochester scholar who has sensed the meaning of this order is Thorpe, who noted that the contents of the 1680 editions might be divided into two groups, a section of thirty-three poems which are mostly by Rochester, followed by a section of twenty-eight poems which are mostly by other authors (pp. xxx–xxxi). The principles on which the archetype was organized can, however, be further clarified. Briefly, the first of the two major sections of the collection consists entirely of poems which the scribe evidently thought were written by Rochester or concerned Rochester in some way—that is, satires on him, poems which he answered, or poems written in answer to his. The second major section consists entirely of poems which the scribe evidently thought were written by miscellaneous authors other than Rochester.

Before these two sections can be discussed in detail, it is important to determine the point of division between them, which Thorpe may have located several poems too early. One method for establishing this point is provided by the fact that the section of poems by or concerning Rochester is further divided into two subsections. The first subsection, consisting of what might loosely be termed satires and translations, ends with poem number 15. The second subsection, consisting entirely of songs, includes poems number 16 through 38. The next few poems are clearly not songs; poem number 39, for example, is a burlesque in pentameter couplets of the manner of the heroic drama. It is reasonable to suppose that the end of the subsection of songs is also the end of the section of poems by or concerning Rochester, which would place the point of division between poems number 38 and 39.

This conclusion is supported by evidence of authorship supplied in other contemporary sources for the poems surrounding the point of division. Poem number 35, which Thorpe chose as the end of the first section, is the last of a "linked group" of four songs; this group appears in another early manuscript miscellany with all four poems ascribed to Rochester, and there is no reason to doubt the authenticity of any one of them.[6] Poem number 36 is unquestionably a satire on Rochester written by Thomas D'Urfey.[7] Though the fifth gap in the Yale manuscript causes a complication, poems number 37 and 38, which immediately follow the gap, would fit logically into the first section as a song by Scroope which Rochester burlesqued, together with the burlesque itself. At this point we enter quite different territory, for various contemporary sources assign all of the next dozen poems to authors other than Rochester. Indeed, poems number 39 through 46 may have been located together because of their connection with Buckhurst.

In the section of poems by or concerning Rochester, nine poems are probably not authentic because they are satires on Rochester, poems which he answered, or poems written in answer to his. Poems number 36 and 37 have already been mentioned. Poem number 3, which is omitted from the 1680 editions, is an answer to number 2, Rochester's "A Satyr against Mankind." Poem number 9, as Thorpe has shown (p. 174), is a satire on Rochester by an unknown author. Poems number 10 through 13 are a "linked group" of four satires involved in Rochester's poetical quarrel with Sir Carr Scroope; the first and third poems are by Rochester, while the second and fourth are Scroope's rejoinders. Poem number 25, which is an answer to number 24, may have been composed by Rochester's wife, since a manuscript draft in the process of revision survives in her handwriting.[8] The Yale manuscript unfortunately gives no ascription for this lyric.

Two other songs may be light-hearted lampoons on Rochester written by his cronies. Poem number 21, which is not extant in the Yale manuscript, depicts a typical day in the life of a Restoration rake such as Rochester. A contemporary anecdote, found in a letter dated from London early in 1673, describes how these verses were written as a satire on Rochester by his friend Buckhurst.[9] Poem number 17, also not extant in the Yale manuscript, is unlike Rochester's style, and it satirizes the sexual prowess of a person named Strephon, which was

[6] Harvard MS Eng. 636F, pp. 66–70.

[7] The poem alludes to Rochester's part in the notorious brawl at Epsom in June 1676, and it was claimed by D'Urfey in his authoritative *A New Collection of Songs and Poems. By Thomas D'urfey* (1683), 3.

[8] This draft is printed in Vivian de Sola Pinto, *Poems by John Wilmot, Earl of Rochester* (1953), 172–173.

[9] For this information I am indebted to Miss Lucyle Hook, [who has since presented it more fully in "Something More About Rochester," *Modern Language Notes*, LXXV (1960), 478–485].

a pastoral pseudonym commonly applied to Rochester. Though one early manuscript assigns this song to Rochester, another ascribes it more plausibly to Sedley.[10]

There is no real reason to doubt Rochester's authorship of the other twenty-nine poems in the first half of the collection. Evidently the scribe of the archetype thought they were Rochester's, and this conclusion clarifies and strengthens the case for their authenticity. Such additional evidence, to be sure, is scarcely required to prove that Rochester wrote poem number 2, "A Satyr against Mankind," or number 15, "Upon Nothing." Nevertheless, roughly half of the twenty-nine poems, especially the songs, have hitherto been assigned to Rochester on very flimsy evidence. The organization of the collection furnishes a much-needed warrant that they are probably genuine.

In the section of poems by miscellaneous authors, a question is raised by the presence of five satires which may have been written by Rochester. The probable explanation for this anomaly is that the scribe of the archetype did not *know* that the five satires might be Rochester's. Four of the five poems, numbers 55, 64, 65, and 66, appear in the Yale manuscript without ascription, while the fifth, number 51, is there ascribed to Sedley. Moreover, four of the satires continue to pose problems of authorship even today, so that the scribe's ignorance is understandable. Evidently the scribe did not intend to attribute to Rochester any poems in the second half of his collection. These arguments allow the formulation of another conclusion: *If a poem appears in the section of poems by miscellaneous authors, then an attribution to Rochester in the 1680 editions, or in sources descended from the 1680 editions, constitutes no evidence whatever that Rochester wrote it.* Thus, of the five satires, four which are printed in the editions can be assigned to Rochester only if other strong evidence is found.

This conclusion also disqualifies all remaining support for the authenticity of eight more poems whose authorship has been disputed. Poem number 39 is ascribed in another early manuscript to Buckhurst.[11] Poems number 40 through 43, a "linked group" of four verse epistles purportedly exchanged by Buckhurst and Etherege, were almost certainly composed by those two poets, as is shown by ascrip-

[10] Ascribed to Rochester in Harvard MS Eng. 636F, p. 10, and to Sedley in Bodl. MS Don. b. 8, p. 586.

[11] All Souls College, Oxford, MS Codrington 174.

tions accompanying the group in two other early manuscripts.[12] There is no longer any reason to suppose that Rochester wrote poem number 54. Poem number 60 is by Alexander Radcliffe, and number 63 may be the work of Etherege. Moreover, virtually all remaining evidence of Rochester's authorship is disqualified for poem number 48, which is the first of three poems by Aphra Behn.

The method outlined in this paper is not, of course, limited in its usefulness to the Rochester editions of 1680. For example, it can be profitably applied to later Rochester editions, notably those published in 1691 by Jacob Tonson and in 1707 by Benjamin Bragge. Similar methods might well prove valuable in solving problems raised by the early texts of other poets.

TABLE

The following table compares the contents, arrangement, and ascriptions of the Yale manuscript and the Rochester editions of 1680. The first column lists, by first lines, in normalized spellings, all poems appearing in these sources. The poems are listed and numbered in the presumptive order of the archetype.

The second column lists, in the order they occupy there, the poems in the 1680 editions. The presence of a poem in the editions is signified by its number in appropriate position. Since the editions assign all of their sixty-one poems to Rochester, individual attributions have not been indicated.

The third column lists, in the order they occupy there, the poems in the Yale manuscript (first hand only). Poems included in the Yale manuscript are signified by a note of the ascription given in the manuscript, or of the fact that the manuscript gives no explicit sign of authorship, or of the portion of the poem still extant in the manuscript. The seven gaps where leaves have been cut out are indicated to the left of this column. Poems marked "text not extant" are not actually present in the manuscript but presumably appeared on the excised pages. Ascriptions in the Yale manuscript occur at the beginning of a poem.

The fourth column specifies conclusions about the authorship of the poems. These conclusions are based on considerable evidence in addition to that presented in this article. [*Continued on p. 272.*]

[*Continued on p. 272.*]

[12] Harvard MS Eng. 636F, pp. 99–114; University of Edinburgh MS DC.1.3, pp. 72–74.

First Lines	1680 Editions	Yale MS	Author
(1) Dear friend I hear this town does so abound	(1)	Rochester	Rochester
(2) Were I who to my cost already am	(2)	Rochester	Rochester
(3) Were I to choose what sort of shape I'd wear	Not included	No ascription	Griffith or Pocock (answer to (2))
(4) Much wine had pass'd with grave discourse	(4)	Rochester (title and first 13 lines extant) [1st Gap]	Rochester
(5) Cloe by your command in verse I write	(5)	Rochester	Rochester
(6) Naked she lay clasp'd in my longing arms	(6)	Rochester (title and first 12 lines extant) [2d Gap]	Rochester
(7) O love how cold and slow to take my part	(7)	Rochester	Rochester
(8) As some brave admiral in former war	(8)	Rochester	Rochester
(9) Say heav'n-born muse for only thou canst tell	(9)	No ascription (title and first 8 lines extant)	Unknown (satire on Rochester)
(10) Well sir 'tis granted I said Dryden's rhymes	(10)	All extant except title and first 4 lines [3d Gap]	Rochester
(11) When Shakespeare Jonson Fletcher rul'd the stage	(11)	No ascription	Sir Carr Scroope (answer to (10))
(12) To rack and torture thy unmeaning brain	(12)	No ascription	Rochester

Linked Group

First Lines	1680 Editions	Yale MS	Author
(13) Rail on poor feeble scribbler speak of me	(13)	No ascription	Sir Carr Scroope (answer to (12))
(14) After death nothing is and nothing death	(14)	No ascription	Rochester
(15) Nothing thou elder brother ev'n to shade	(15)	No ascription	Rochester
(16) 'Tis not that I am weary grown	(16)	No ascription	Probably Rochester
(17) In the fields of Lincoln's Inn	(17)	Text not extant	Probably Sedley (satire on Rochester)
(18) Vulcan contrive me such a cup	(18)	Text not extant	Probably Rochester
(19) As Chloris full of harmless thoughts	(19)	Text not extant	Probably Rochester
(20) Quoth the Duchess of Cleveland to Mrs. Knight	(20)	Text not extant	Probably Rochester
(21) I rise at eleven I dine about two	(21)	Text not extant	Probably Buckhurst (satire on Rochester)
(22) Love a woman you're an ass	(22)	Text not extant	Probably Rochester
		[Probably several more songs were removed by this gap.]	
		4th Gap	
(23) Fair Chloris in a pigsty lay	(23)	No ascription	Probably Rochester

Subsection of satires and translations ← | → Subsection of songs

267

First Lines	1680 Editions	Yale MS	Author
(24) Give me leave to rail at you	(24)	No ascription	Probably Rochester
(25) Nothing adds to your fond fire	(25)	No ascription	Rochester or his wife (answer to (24))
(26) Phyllis be gentler I advise	(26)	No ascription	Rochester
(27) What cruel pains Corinna takes	(27)	No ascription	Probably Rochester
(28) Love bade me hope and I obey'd	(28)	No ascription	Probably Rochester
(29) To this moment a rebel I throw down my arms	(29)	No ascription	Probably Rochester
(30) How happy Chloris were they free	(30)	No ascription	Rochester
(31) All my past life is mine no more	(31)	No ascription	Rochester
(32) How blest was the created state	(32)	No ascription	Probably Rochester
(33) While on those lovely looks I gaze	(33)	No ascription	Probably Rochester
(34) Against the charms our ballocks have	See below	No ascription (title and first 4 lines extant)	Probably Rochester
(35) By all love's soft yet mighty pow'rs	(35)	Text not extant	Probably Rochester

5th Gap

Linked Group

268

First Lines	1680 Editions	Yale MS	Author
(36) Room room for a blade of the town	(36)	Text not extant	Thomas D'Urfey (satire on Rochester)
	(34)	[Probably one more song was removed by this gap.]	
(37) I cannot change as others do	(37)	Sir Carr Scroope	Probably Sir Carr Scroope (burlesqued in (38))
(38) I swive as well as others do	(38)	No ascription (title and first 4 lines extant)	Probably Rochester
(39) For standing tarses we kind nature thank	(39)	Text not extant	Probably Buckhurst
(40) Dreaming last night on Mrs. Farley	(40)	Text not extant	Buckhurst
(41) As crafty harlots use to shrink	(41)	Text not extant	Etherege
(42) If I can guess the devil choke me	(42)	Text not extant	Buckhurst
(43) So soft and am'rously you write	(43)	Last 6 lines extant	Etherege
(44) Come on ye critics find one fault who dare	(44)	Buckhurst	Buckhurst
(45) Thou damn'd antipodes to common sense	See below	Henry Savile	Possibly Henry Savile, Buckhurst, or Wycherley
(46) As when a bully draws his sword	(46)	Edmund Ashton	Edmund Ashton
	(45)		

5th Gap

6th Gap

Section of poems by or concerning Rochester and subsection of songs ←

→ Section of poems by authors other than Rochester

Linked Group

269

First Lines	1680 Editions	Yale MS	Author
(47) Since now my Sylvia is as kind as fair	Not included	Mulgrave (title and first 12 lines extant)	Mulgrave
	7th Gap	Last 10 lines extant	
(48) One day the am'rous Lysander	(48)		Aphra Behn
(49) Whilst happy I triumphant stood	(49)	Aphra Behn	Aphra Behn
(50) What doleful cries are these that fright my sense	(50)	Aphra Behn	Aphra Behn
(51) What Timon does old age begin t' approach	(54) (51)	Sedley	Probably Rochester
(52) Since the sons of the muses grew num'rous and loud	(52)	"Suppos'd to be written by Elk: Settle"	Possibly Settle
(53) Under this stone does lie	Not included	No ascription	Buckingham
(54) Have you seen the raging stormy main	See above	No ascription	Unknown
(55) At five this morn when Phoebus rais'd his head	Not included	No ascription	Rochester
(56) Now curses on ye all ye virtuous fools	(56)	Oldham	Oldham
(57) My part is done and you'll I hope excuse	(57)	Oldham	Oldham
(58) No she shall ne'er escape if gods there be	Not included	Oldham	Oldham
(59) Tell me abandon'd miscreant prithee tell	(59)	Oldham	Oldham

First Lines	1680 Editions	Yale MS	Author
(60) Rat too rat too rat too rat tat too rat tat too	(60)	No ascription	Alexander Radcliffe
(61) All human things are subject to decay	Not included	Dryden	Dryden
(62) A sad mischance I sing alas	Not included	"Suppos'd to be Written by Mr Shadwell"	Unknown
(63) How far are they deceiv'd who hope in vain	(63)	No ascription	Possibly Etherege
(64) If you're deceiv'd it is not by my cheat	(64)	No ascription	Probably Rochester
(65) Crush'd by that just contempt his follies bring	(65)	No ascription	Probably Rochester
(66) Bursting with pride the loath'd impostume swells	(66)	No ascription	Probably Rochester
(67) Thou common shore of this poetic town	Not included	No ascription	Possibly Buckingham
(68) Whilst duns were knocking at my door	(68)	Alexander Radcliffe	Alexander Radcliffe
(69) I sing the praise of a worthy wight	Not included	No ascription	Unknown
(70) From a proud sensual atheistical life	Not included	No ascription	Unknown
(71) As Colin drove his sheep along	Not included	No ascription	Possibly Buckhurst
(72) If Rome can pardon sins as Romans hold	(72)	Not included	Possibly Rochester

Linked Group

Section of poems by authors other than Rochester | Probably not in archetype

Evidence for Authorship

To the left of the first column, double vertical lines indicate the four "linked groups" of poems which occur in places where the Yale manuscript and the 1680 editions differ in their contents or arrangement. Also shown are the principal points of division in the archetype: (1) between the section of poems by or concerning Rochester and the section of poems by miscellaneous authors, and (2) between the subsection of satires and translations and the subsection of songs.

A Neglected
Mid-Eighteenth-Century Plea
for Originality and Its Author[*]

By R. S. Crane

THE second place in Hamilton's *Critical Review* for January 1760 was occupied by a vigorous and not too kindly discussion, in nine pages, of a book entitled *Critical Dissertations upon the Iliad of Homer*, by R. Kedington, D.D., Rector of Kedington, Suffolk (ix, 10–19). From the outset the anonymous reviewer took no pains to conceal his distaste for the work before him—a work the main purpose of which was, he tells us, "to vindicate those passages of Homer, which have been given up by all former commentators as absurd or immoral." To "prefer Homer to other writers," he remarked, "may indeed be allowable; but to talk of him as faultless, to say that his writings are more serviceable to an imitator than all other works put together; such assertions," he submitted, "savour strongly of little judgment, or much pedantic affectation." And of these vices, all too common among the race of critics, for whom there is "nothing so absurd which they have not been known to defend," Kedington's treatise seemed to him a peculiarly reprehensible example. "Homer is every where the divine Homer, the incomparable poet, the faultless writer, and the inimitable original for every good writer to draw after . . . ; every attack upon the old bard conduces to depreciate human nature, to arraign providence, minister to immorality, and indulge the unhappy sceptical turn of the age; every attack is not only vain, but almost impious, upon so divine a poem." Even Pope, who surely might be thought to have "be-praised the Grecian sufficiently" and to have

[*] Reprinted from *Philological Quarterly*, xiii (1934), 21–29, with permission of author and publisher.

seen "more in Homer than Homer knew," is to this panegyrist merely "a faithless asserter of his master's cause."

But to indulge in such extravagance is, the reviewer insisted, to build upon a false hypothesis from beginning to end; it is to assume that "objections to a work of genius diminish its value and render it contemptible," whereas in reality the rank of every artistic production is proportionate not to the fewness of its faults but to the number and quality of its merits; nay, we frequently observe that the more blemishes a work possesses the more abundant likewise are its beauties. Such, certainly, is the case with Homer. Faults he was bound to have, since in the age when he wrote "barbarity, ignorance, lust, and cruelty, were still in fashion; and, we may justly say, that heroism was never worse known than in those ages which were called heroic." These faults do not detract from his genius, and they were even, doubtless, sources of pleasure to his contemporaries; but it is vain to pretend that such things as "the love which Briseis bears to Achilles, the little tenderness even heroes have to their conquered captives, their being sacrified at a tomb to appease a dead warrior, speaking horses, and intriguing gods" do not, or should not, "fill us with ideas of contempt or horror." But if this is true, how absurd it is—the reviewer went on—and how nicely calculated to prevent all improvement in epic poetry—to prescribe, like Aristotle and twenty others, including Mr. Kedington, a strict imitation of Homer to every subsequent poet who would excel in this genre! Those who have followed this advice, with the single exception of Virgil, have all failed in their attempts; and the reason is, "not that Homer was inimitable, but because his successors copied their master even to the describing of manners which had been long antiquated, and of which they were consequently incapable of giving adequate descriptions." "From the prevalence of this rule, all our works of this nature seem to be cast in the same mould: the muse is invoked, she tells the tale, the episodes are introduced, armour rings against armour, games are described, and sometimes a shield; while all the conduct of the passions, and all the mixture of well-conducted intrigue are entirely left out of the question." Let our epic poets, then, give up this practice, imposed by critics, of "taking Homer, or Virgil, or any other celebrated name for a model"; let them "boldly follow nature in the dress she wears at present"; and the effects may be as happy as those which have followed our abandonment of the imitation of Sophocles and Euripides in tragedy. "In short," the reviewer concludes, "we could wish to excite men to leave those paths which have been already too much worn, and to strike out after nature, which is ever appearing in circumstances of variety."

These were brave words, and their appearance in the sober pages of the *Critical Review* in 1760 is bound to excite curiosity concerning the identity of their anonymous author. The problem, fortunately, is not as difficult as might at first appear. It is true that in ridiculing Kedington's idolatry of Homer, in denouncing critics as the chief obstacles to progress in literature, in insisting that writers should be valued for the abundance of their beauties rather than the fewness of their faults, in deprecating imitation of ancient models, and in urging modern poets to strike out new paths and to give their readers first-hand pictures of the distinctive manners of their own time, our reviewer was merely applying to his special purpose ideas to be found either separately or in partial combination in a considerable number of eminent critics, English and continental, of his own and the preceding age. Yet it can hardly be said that this particular association of doctrines, and still less the radical temper with which they were here expressed, had become, even by the beginning of the seventh decade of the eighteenth century, the common property of every chance reviewer or journalist of London. They were still the opinions of the more sophisticated and up-to-date among the literary class—uttered not without qualification and hesitation by Johnson, proclaimed as startling novelties only the year before by Young. Within the restricted group of the contributors to the *Critical Review* in 1760 it would be strange if there was more than one who held them with any conviction; and so it is natural, in seeking to give a name to our anonymous critic, to think at once of a writer—soon to become famous—who had been a regular purveyor of literary articles to this journal since January 1759, and who for a still longer period had been engaged in propagating precisely the same critical attitudes as appear in the review of Kedington. This writer was Oliver Goldsmith.[1]

From the time when, in a notice of Gray's *Odes* in 1757, Goldsmith had praised Pindar for adapting his poems to the genius of his countrymen and had chided Gray for building merely on the genius of Pindar without regard for the differences between ancient Greeks and modern English (*Works*, IV, 296–299), he had shown, in one writing

---

[1] For Goldsmith's contributions to the *Critical Review* between January 1759 and March 1760 see *Works*, ed. Gibbs, IV, 322–406, 409–412.

after another, a peculiarly outspoken hostility to literary "imitation" and excessive reverence for critical rules. The chief design of his first book, *An Enquiry into the Present State of Polite Learning in Europe* (published in April 1759), could be summed up, he told his readers, in the simple text: "Write what you think, regardless of the critics."

To break, or at least to loosen those bonds, first put on by caprice, and afterwards drawn hard by fashion, is my wish. I have assumed the critic only to dissuade from criticism. There is scarce an error of which our present writers are guilty, that does not arise from their opposing systems; there is scarce an error that criticism cannot be brought to excuse. . . . There never was an unbeaten path trodden by the poet that the critic did not endeavour to reclaim him, by calling his attempt innovation. . . . Thus novelty, one of the greatest beauties in poetry, must be avoided, or the connoisseur be displeased. It is one of the chief privileges, however, of genius, to fly from the herd of imitators by some happy singularity. [III, 512]

In other passages of the same work this antipathy to criticism as the great enemy of original attempts was coupled with a thoroughly relativistic theory of the relation which should exist between a poet and the peculiar manners of his nation and age. It is true, Goldsmith admitted, that "this is setting up a particular standard of taste in every country; this is removing that universal one which has hitherto united the armies and enforced the commands of criticism; by this reasoning the critics of one country will not be proper guides to the writers of another; Grecian and Roman rules will not be generally binding in France or England; but the laws designed to improve our taste, by this reasoning, must be adapted to the genius of every people, as much as those enacted to promote morality." But these were precisely the positions he wished to enforce; in other words, "every country should have a national system of criticism" (III, 533, 535). And not only every country, but every age as well: it is impossible, he pointed out, to discover any standard by which the relative merits of the ancients and moderns—in epic poetry, for example—can be justly compared, since both have, and quite properly, he thinks, "copied from different originals, described the manners of different ages."

Homer describes his gods as his countrymen believed them. Virgil in a more enlightened age, describes his with a greater degree of respect; and Milton still rises infinitely above either. . . . Had Homer wrote like Milton, his countrymen would have despised him; had Milton adopted the theology of the ancient bard, he had been truly ridiculous. [III, 530]

Hence the absurdity of idolizing ancient writers merely because they are ancient—an absurdity exemplified, as Goldsmith noted in another place, in the current English disposition to admire even the faults (as they appear to modern taste) of Shakespeare.

Let the spectator, who assists at any of these new revived pieces, only ask himself whether he would approve such a performance if written by a modern poet. I fear he will find that much of his applause proceeds merely from the sound of a name, and an empty veneration for antiquity. [III, 519]

That these were views which greatly preoccupied Goldsmith at this stage of his career is evident from the fact that the same or closely related opinions found frequent expression in his scattered journalistic writings during the middle and later parts of 1759 and in the early months of 1760. In June of the former year, for example, he reviewed the *Conjectures on Original Composition* in the *Critical Review;* and his notice, while hardly more than a summary, left little doubt as to his sympathetic agreement with Young's major positions (IV, 364–368). Again, in an essay "The Characteristics of Greatness," published in the *Bee* for October 27, 1759, he deplored the unwillingness of modern writers to deviate from others and follow unbeaten roads:

This enterprising spirit is . . . by no means the character of the present age: every person who should now leave received opinions, who should attempt to be more than a commentator upon philosophy, or an imitator in polite learning, might be regarded as a chimerical projector. Hundreds would be ready not only to point out his errors, but to load him with reproach. . . . Yet this is certain, that the writer who never deviates, who never hazards a new thought, or a new expression, though his friends may compliment him upon his sagacity, though criticism lifts her feeble voice in his praise, will seldom arrive at any degree of perfection. . . . An author who would be sublime, often runs his thought into burlesque: yet I can readily pardon his mistaking ten times for once succeeding. True genius walks along a line; and perhaps our greatest pleasure is in seeing it so often near falling, without being ever actually down. [II, 374–375]

Finally, in July 1760, he translated for the *British Magazine* one of the allegorical tales in Justus Van Effen's *Le Misantrope,* omitting a considerable portion of the original but retaining an amusing passage near the end in which Homer in Elysium was represented as much annoyed by the excessive eulogies of his commentators:

As he walked along . . . at every four paces he seemed to have an inclination to sleep, and his attitude in this respect was so natural, that the spectators seemed almost to sympathize; but, drowsy as they were, they still continued to cry out, "The divine old man! the incomparable poet! the marvellous genius! the admirable philosopher! the sublime orator!" In short, there was scarce a title of praise that was not lavished on the immortal Homer. It would have excited pity to see how much the old bard, who in the main was a man of good sense, seemed ashamed of so much unmerited praise. In vain he attempted to steal away from the crowd that was gathered round him; the commentators were a set of attendants not easily shook off; they even made him frequently blush with their fulsome adulations.[2]

It is clear, then, that an hypothesis identifying the anonymous reviewer of Kedington with Goldsmith cannot be dismissed as unworthy of consideration: as a regular contributor to the *Critical*, the opportunity to write the review was certainly his, and the basic opinions which it expressed were, without exception, opinions which he had long entertained.

But that is not all. If we look more closely at the text of the review, we discover between it and at least eight of Goldsmith's known writings, some earlier and some later in date than January 1760, a number of further resemblances of too precise a character to be easily explicable as accidents.

1. The reviewer in his second paragraph, after remarking that for Kedington "every attack is not only vain, but almost impious, upon so divine a poem," added: "In short, by the warmth of his defence, he seems almost as sanguine as that prince who sacrificed to the genius of Homer an unhappy critic, who objected to some exceptionable passages in the Iliad."[3] Goldsmith had alluded to the same story, in a different context, about three months before, in the *Bee* for October 27, 1759: "I have been told of a critic, who was crucified, at the command of another, to the reputation of Homer."[4]

2. The third paragraph of the review contained the following re-

[2] iv, 489. Cf. *Le Misantrope* (La Haye, 1726), i, 35.

[3] *Critical Review*, ix, 11.

[4] *Works*, ii, 363–364. The story may have been called to his mind by a passage in Justus Van Effen's *Le Misantrope* (ii, 129), a work from which he had borrowed a long passage for the *Bee* of the preceding week. See *Modern Philology*, xxiii (1926), 282–283.

flection on the motives which lead critics to write and publish extravagant eulogies of dead authors:

The praise bestowed on a writer of established reputation, is perhaps more frequently designed as a compliment to ourselves than the author: we only shew the rectitude of our own taste by a standard allowed already to be just: what advantages the public are to gain by praising Homer at this time of day, we know not; Mr. Kedington may reap some, since all must allow he has taste enough to relish those beauties which most men of taste have either relished, or pretended to relish before.[5]

Essentially the same conception of the psychology of critics was expressed by Goldsmith on two occasions, one earlier, the other later than January 1760. "The praise which is every day lavished upon Virgil, Horace, or Ovid," he had written in the *Critical Review* for January 1759, "is often no more than an indirect method the critic takes to compliment his own discernment. Their works have long been considered as models of beauty; to praise them now is only to show the conformity of our taste to theirs: it tends not to advance their reputation, but to promote our own."[6] And he was to return to the theme in November 1760 in a paper in the *Public Ledger* afterwards included in his *Citizen of the World*:

There are some subjects of which almost all the world perceive the futility; yet all combine in imposing [them] upon each other, as worthy of praise. But chiefly this imposition obtains in literature, where men publicly contemn what they relish with rapture in private, and approve abroad what has given them disgust at home. The truth is, we deliver those criticisms in public which are supposed to be best calculated not to do justice to the author, but to impress others with an opinion of our superior discernment. [*Works*, III, 358]

3. In his fifth paragraph the reviewer undertook to argue against what he regarded as the chief fallacy underlying Kedington's work—the assumption, namely, "that objections to a work of genius diminish its value and render it contemptible; and that Homer, to be great must be irreprehensible."

But the truth is [he went on], the merit of every work is determined, not from the number of its faults, but of its beauties: nay, we often find wherever the latter prevail, the former are generally seen in great abundance. To illustrate this thought from a sister art: The Italian schools of

---

[5] *Critical Review*, IX, 11.
[6] *Works*, IV, 325.

painting are by all allowed superior to those of France; and yet, if we examine the works of each minutely, we shall find their merits pretty much in this proportion: Raphael, and a great number of the Italians, who were famous for design, wanted the art of colouring: the greatest number of those who understood colours, erred grossly in design, Michael Angelo, Paul Veronese, and the greater masters of the Italian school having committed frequently the most gross absurdities. The French painters, on the other hand, have, beyond comparison, been more judicious in their composition: we never see in the pictures of Le Sueur, Poussin, and Le Brun, those ridiculous mistakes, or anachronisms, which betray an ignorance of history; they are always regular, just; and, still more, this regularity never offends against beauty: yet, should we from hence infer the superiority of the latter to the former, we should be very much deceived. The striking and visible graces of a single piece of Veronese operate more strongly upon us, than the most finished pieces of the correct Le Brun. The great beauties of every work make it inestimable; its defects are only arguments of humanity, not of weakness.[7]

Now the criterion of literary values enunciated at the beginning of this paragraph was one which Goldsmith had stated, in closely similar terms, at least twice during the year preceding January 1760. In his notice of Arthur Murphy's *The Orphan of China* in the *Critical Review* for May 1759, he wrote: "But, to do the writer ample justice, we will lay one scene against all his defects, and we are convinced that this alone will turn the balance in his favour. Works of genius are not to be judged from the faults to be met with in them, but by the beauties in which they abound" (iv, 353). So, too, in the essay "The Characteristics of Greatness," already quoted (*Bee*, October 27, 1759), where the thought is even closer to that of the review of Kedington: "The way to acquire lasting esteem, is not by the fewness of a writer's faults, but the greatness of his beauties; and our noblest works are generally most replete with both" (ii, 375). In these passages, it is true, we have only the principle without the illustrative comparison of French and Italian painting. But the idea was to recur once more in Goldsmith's writing and this time to be accompanied by a concrete example identical, except in one detail, with that in the review. In Chapter xv of *The Vicar of Wakefield* (1766) one of the characters is made to remark:

As the reputation of books is raised, not by their freedom from defect, but the greatness of their beauties; so should that of men be prized, not

---

[7] *Critical Review*, ix, 12.

for their exemption from fault, but the size of those virtues they are possessed of. The scholar may want prudence, the statesman may have pride, and the champion ferocity; but shall we prefer to these the low mechanic, who laboriously plods on through life, without censure or applause? We might as well prefer the tame correct paintings of the Flemish school to the erroneous, but sublime animations of the Roman pencil. [I, 130]

4. The eighth paragraph of the review began as follows: "In the times when Homer wrote, barbarity, ignorance, lust, and cruelty, were still in fashion."[8] With this may be compared a sentence from Goldsmith's review of Wilkie's *Epigoniad* in the *Monthly Review* for September 1757: "We have no reason to doubt but Homer, who lived in an age of ignorance, and consequently of credulity, believed, or at least was thought to believe, what he relates" (IV, 290).

5. In his eighteenth paragraph the reviewer ridiculed Kedington for the gravity with which he took up and answered an extremely trivial criticism on Homer's consistency in the episode of Dolon and the horses of Achilles.

The whole objection [he remarked], is in fact, a trifling one; such can no way lessen the beauty of a fine poem, even allowing them to be just; for when our imaginations are warm, and our passions raised, a reader of taste never stops at such minute imperfections. No, it is only the heavy critic who reads a poem with the same phlegm that he would a mathematical demonstration, that has leisure for such useless disquisitions: minute beauties are what raise his pleasure, and minute imperfections create his disgust.[9]

The same distinction between the aesthetic judgments of critics and of men of taste had been suggested by Goldsmith in a passage in his *Enquiry* (April 1759):

The ingenious Mr. Hogarth used to assert, that every one except the conoisseur was a judge of painting. The same may be asserted of writing. The public, in general, set the whole piece in the proper point of view; the critic lays his eye close to all its minuteness, and condemns or approves in detail. [III, 513]

It is impossible, I believe, to follow these parallelisms of detail between the reviewer and Goldsmith, as the latter is revealed not only in writings accessible in January 1760 but also in writings still to be written or published, without concluding that the hypothesis

[8] *Ibid.*, 13.
[9] *Ibid.* 16.

of the identity of the two has gained measurably in probability at the expense of any alternative hypothesis that one might devise to explain the more general similarities of idea and point of view.

But even this is not all. It has recently been shown that between March and November of the year preceding the publication of the review, Goldsmith had, on nearly a dozen occasions, enriched the content of his scattered contributions to periodicals by unacknowledged translations, some of them many pages in length, from the *Encyclopédie* of D'Alembert and Diderot.[10] Seven of the large tomes of this great work were accessible to him in 1759—had been accessible, in fact, since 1757; but for some reason, probably that he was too poor to afford them all, his depredations seem to have been confined during this period exclusively to Volumes I and V; and of these two it was Volume V (1755) which supplied him with the great majority—all but two, to be precise—of his borrowings. And he still had this fifth volume at hand at about the time the review of Kedington came out, since he translated two short passages from it for incorporation in an essay printed in the *Public Ledger* for February 21, 1760.[11]

Now the reviewer of Kedington also was a reader of the *Encyclopédie*—and, like Goldsmith, one not ashamed to conceal his debt. And the striking thing is that all his borrowings—five fairly long passages in translation plus a shorter one quoted in the original French—came from one volume, and that volume the fifth.[12] And the still more striking thing is that of the two articles in Volume V from which he pilfered, one—that headed "Ecole"—was an article upon which Goldsmith drew, probably at almost the same time, for an essay published in the *British Magazine* for February 1760.[13]

Is there any need to inquire further concerning our reviewer's name?

[10] See the *Times Literary Supplement* (May 11, 1933), 331.

[11] *Works*, III, 46, 47; cf. *Encyclopédie*, V (1775), 816–818.

[12] Cf. *Critical Review*, IX, 12, with *Encyclopédie*, V, 334b–335a; 12–13 with V, 825a; 13 with V, 829a, and V, 827a; 14 with V, 826b; 19 with V, 827b.

[13] *Works*, I, 386–387; cf. *Encyclopédie*, V, 333, 335.

Can *Mother Midnight's Comical Pocket-Book* Be Attributed to Christopher Smart?*

By Arthur Sherbo

THE desire to introduce a new work into the canon of a writer of merit often leads scholars to absurd extremes; at no time is the danger of committing an absurdity so great as when sole reliance is placed on internal evidence. One recalls particularly the abuse of this tool, method, or approach (call it what you will) in certain studies of Elizabethan plays of doubtful or composite authorship. And yet the value of internal evidence is great, greater indeed than the value set on its brother and helpmate, external evidence. Unfortunately, most modern scholars have tended to be so fearful of resting their case for a new attribution on internal evidence alone that they have often been guilty of oversights of major proportions. Ideally, of course, one should have both kinds of evidence, and the happy combination of the two, in sufficient strength, is usually enough to satisfy even the staunchest conservative. Most often, however, a bare attribution by an intimate of the author is enough to lend authority to an otherwise dubious addition to the canon. And almost no amount of internal evidence will exercise similar authority in the absence of such an attribution. All this is, obviously, in the realm of the general; it is only when one can come to the particular that judicious evaluation is possible. There are degrees of importance that can be accorded either or both kinds of evidence, depending on a number of circumstances. Perhaps a hypothetical example is in order at this point. Writer X has been dead more than three decades; the canon of his writings, many of them fugitive journalistic pieces hastily written and often not reread

* Reprinted from the *Bulletin of The New York Public Library*, LXI (1957), 373–382, with the author's permission.

by their author, is understandably not yet fixed. "Veterrimus" contributes a short letter to a newspaper affirming that he has heard Y, X's close friend, himself dead some fifteen years, state that such-and-such an anonymous essay in the *London Chronicler* was "indubitably" the product of his friend's "genius." This, such as it is, is considered sufficient external evidence, especially when coupled with some evidence of style and ideas, to warrant canonical consideration for the essay in question. And it is only just that it should be so considered. But the same internal evidence unallied with the tenuous authority of "Veterrimus'" recollection of Y's obiter dictum would hardly be allowed a hearing at the bar of present-day scholarship. Cancel "Vetterrimus" from the equation above and allow Y to speak *in propria persona* to the same effect; the authority is greater, of course, because the link to X is closer, but who, pray, constituted Y an authority on the anonymous products of his friend's "genius"?

I

Internal evidence concerns itself with style, ideas and areas of interest, verbal parallels and echoes, and peculiarities of spelling and (sometimes) punctuation. External evidence concerns itself with attributions by contemporaries or near contemporaries of the author, place of appearance or publisher (for article and book, respectively), and use of a pseudonym or distinguishing mark of some kind. My purpose in this study is to examine the value of internal evidence in determining the canonicity of a work which I take to be by Christopher Smart. The rare 64-page pamphlet entitled *Mother Midnight's Comical Pocket-Book* . . . by Humphrey Humdrum, Esq., 2nd edition, London, "Printed for J. Dowse,[1] opposite Fountain Court in the Strand,"

---

[1] J. Dowse, of whom so little is known, is worth a note. Plomer (*Dict. of Printers . . . 1726–1775*) says only that he was a "bookseller and publisher in London, opposite Fountain Court in the Strand, 1753. Publisher of pamphlets." Dowse sold the pamphlet *Critical Remarks on Sir Charles Grandison, Clarissa, and Pamela* (1754) and is characterized as "an obscure pamphlet-shop proprieter, not a prominent bookseller" by Professor Alan D. McKillop in his introduction to the reprint of the pamphlet for the *Augustan Reprint Society*, No. 21 (1950), p. ii. Since the name is an unusual one, the following obituary may be our man's. It appeared in the *Gentleman's Magazine* for January 1783 (LIII, pt. 1, 93): "Mr. Dowse, formerly a vocal performer of some celebrity at Vauxhall, Marybone-Gardens, Sadlers-Wells, etc. He was found dead upon a dunghill at an inn in High Holborn." Although I may be accused of excessive hypothesizing, I cannot resist linking this Dowse with Smart, and with the *Comical Pocket-Book*, on the basis of the Vauxhall and Sadler's Wells connection (see my second, numbered argument below).

n.d.,[2] is the work which I wish to claim for Christopher Smart. The miscellany—for the pamphlet is a collection of satirical and nonsatirical poems, epigrams, epitaphs, acrostics, and songs, with an occasional short bit of prose, usually introducing one of the poems—is listed in the *Gentleman's Magazine's* list for December 1753 (p. 593) and reviewed in the *Monthly Review,* x (January 1754), 74. The only remark of the reviewer is that the work "consists of scraps of foolish, illiterate verses, and prose of the same stamp." This judgment is unnecessarily harsh, as the *Pocket-Book* contains some entertaining bits, albeit there is no poetry of a high order of excellence. To my knowledge, the only modern scholar aware of its existence is Roland Botting. In his *Christopher Smart in London* he suggests that the work may be Smart's but rejects it for the following reason: "In view of its not having been published by Newbery or Carnan, it is doubtful that Smart had any connection with the *Comical Pocketbook*" (p. 40).[3] There is no discussion of the contents. No other student of Smart's work has seen fit to question Botting's decision. It must be further remarked that an acrostic poem, "The Author's Epitaph" (p. 25), spells out the name Joseph Lewis, and it is doubtless this fact which caused Halkett and Laing to attribute the pamphlet to him. They, incidentally, hesitantly date the publication as "1780."

Since "Mother Midnight" was Smart's pseudonym, one of very many, one is tempted to claim this fact as some slight external evidence, but Botting mentions a *Mother Midnight's Miscellany* (1751); which is probably the "poor faulty Pamphlet lately publish'd in her [Mother Midnight's] Name," disclaimed by Smart (p. 17 and note). There is not, hence, the slightest shred of external evidence for attributing the collection to Smart. Yet despite my awareness of the suspicion excited by attributions based solely on internal evidence I feel certain that Smart was responsible for the entire contents.

In the presence of a possible author in the person of one Joseph Lewis some proof of mistaken attribution is demanded. I have

[2] Recourse to the Union Catalogue reveals copies at the Massachusetts Historical Society in Boston and in the American Antiquarian Society in Worcester, Mass. I have photostats of the New York Public Library copy. There is also a copy in the British Museum, with the error of "Council" for "Comical" in the title.

[3] *Research Studies of the State College of Washington,* vii (March 1939), 3–58. In an advertisement in Volume i of *The Midwife,* p. 144, Mrs. Midnight says that only T. Carnan will print her "Pieces" as usual. This, I should say, is one way to strengthen one's pseudonymity should one wish to employ another bookseller.

searched long and diligently for any trace of a Joseph Lewis, eighteenth-century poet, without success. Further, I have asked a number of my friends, experts in the literature and ana of the century, for help in tracking him down. None could give me the slightest clue. This is hardly proof positive of Joseph Lewis's nonexistence, but, then, how does one prove the nonexistence of a Joseph Lewis? Since the *Comical Pocket-Book*, so the long subtitle runs, contains "the nicest and largest Dish of Novelties . . . Carefully Cook'd up by Mother Midnight's merry Grandson," it is clear that the author is warning that he is not to be confused with his grandmother, i.e. Christopher Smart. On pain of correction, I would suggest, therefore, that Joseph Lewis is a ghost, that he never existed, but that if there was a Joseph Lewis, Smart usurped his obscure name (for who has seen any work by Joseph Lewis?) for his own purposes of mystification. One need only accept "Joseph Lewis" as another of a bewildering number and variety of pseudonyms employed by Smart. The parallels in arguments 3, 5, 6, 9, and 13 and the last paragraph of 7 below are of such picayune details as to point to the author of the original pieces repeating himself rather than to a highly gifted and observant imitator.

What, then, is the exact nature of the internal evidence which makes an attribution to Smart possible? For sake of convenience I shall number each piece of evidence separately; the order followed is not in ascending or descending scale of importance.

1. The first poem in the *Comical Pocket-Book* is on tea drinkers; it is one of the better poems in the collection, consciously echoing Pope's *Rape of the Lock*. In the poem the tea drinkers indulge in a malicious exchange of gossip; at the conclusion of this school for scandal, the author writes:

> How much perverted now are female ways
> Since times of yore—in Bessy's golden days;
> When hearty food for spleen was a relief,
> And dames of honour breakfasted on beef;
> With pond'rous joints the groaning-boards were spread,
> And ev'ry damsel had her pound of bread. [p. 7]

Compare Smart's fable *The Tea Pot and Scrubbing Brush* (1752), in which, after the scrubbing brush has given several examples of the gossip and scandal owing to tea drinking, he continues:

> 'Twas better for each British Virgin,
> When on roast Beef, strong Beer, and Sturgeon,
> Joyous to breakfast they sat round,

21: Mother Midnight's Pocket-Book

Nor was asham'd to eat a Pound.
These were the Manners, these the Ways,
In good Queen *Bess's* golden Days. [i, 45][4]

The parallels are striking.

2. Smart's interest in the theatre and in actors and entertainers is well known. He wrote songs to be sung at Vauxhall Garden, and he moved in "theatrical" circles as producer of, and possible actor in, *The Old Woman's Oratory*, best described as early vaudeville. On pages 26–28 of the *Comical Pocket-Book* one finds a series of epitaphs on entertainers at Sadler's Wells.[5] The first is "Design'd for that well-known facetious Mortal, late of Sadler's Wells, P. H." P. H. is identified in the epitaph as "Peter Hough." I have recently (*Modern Language Notes*, LXXI [1956], 177–182) shown that Smart's catalogue of names in section D of *Jubilate Agno* is important for the probable light it throws on his past friends and associations, a name encountered in a newspaper or periodical calling to his mind a friend or acquaintance of the same name. The epitaph just cited allows me to identify another of these associations, for line D110 of *Jubilate Agno* (ed. Bond, 1954) reads "Let Hough, house of Hough rejoice with Pegasus The Flying Horse there be millions of them in the air. God bless the memories of Bsp. Hough & of Peter." Another of these epitaphs is for Thomas Rosoman, proprietor of Sadler's Wells from 1753 on. Rosoman was one of two witnesses to the contract between Smart and Richard Rolt and Thomas Gardner and Edmund Allen for the writing of the *Universal Visiter* (*TLS*, 1929, 474). And Rolt wrote for Sadler's Wells (*DNB*). What is more, Rosoman's was another name from the past to be recalled and recorded in *Jubilate Agno*, "God be gracious to Thomas Rosoman & family" (D156).

3. Reference is made in a short prose passage on page 39 to "the old trunk-makers, corner of Paul's-church-yard." Of Smart's two dedications of his *Horatian Canons of Friendship* (1750) one is to "my good friend, the Trunk-Maker at the Corner of St. Paul's Church-Yard." Smart refers to "trunk-makers" in an essay in *The Universal Visiter*, March 1756, page 137. The essay was claimed for Smart by me in *The Library*, 5th Series, x (1955), 203–205. In the last two of these references the trunk-maker is dependent upon writers for the paper

---

[4] Unless otherwise indicated, all references to Smart's poetry are to the edition by Norman Callan for the Muse's Library, 2 vols., 1949.

[5] It is worth noting a "Letter from an Eminent Tumbler [a fictitious one] at Sadler's Wells, to Mrs. Mary Midnight" in *The Midwife*, III, 7.

with which to line his products. See also *The Midwife*, I, 67, for another reference to trunk-makers as destroyers of literature, i.e. paper.

4. On page 37 as part of a poem entitled simply Song the Second,
in praise of Bessey's and Nancy's charms, there appears this stanza:

> Their panting breasts, that gently move,
>   Our am'rous bosoms fire;
> Those pretty rising alps of love,
>   Are all our soul's desire.

And in a *Letter to Caelia*, page 53, occurs the couplet:

> Each amorous, gazing youth doth not disown
> Love on thy snowy breasts hath fix'd her throne.

Now female breasts have always been likened to snow for their whiteness, and poets have had an observant eye for their rise and fall,
but no poet I know seems to have been so fascinated with this part of
the female anatomy as Christopher Smart. One recalls particularly the
youthful poem "To Ethelinda. On her doing my verses the honour
of wearing them in her bosom.—Written at thirteen," with its sexual
precocity and its description of the young Miss's breasts as "that ivory
throne" (I, 198). In another poem Smart speaks of "her breast the
throne of love" (I, 140). And if the reader wishes to trace Smart in
his descriptions, he may look at I, 79, 85, 103, 113, 131, 191, 193,
201 ("snowy heaps"), and 202.

At this point I should like to press the method of internal evidence
to its extreme by using parallels between a poem not universally accepted as Smart's and the poems quoted in the paragraph above as
another in my chain of evidence. Wilbur Cross hesitantly attributes
two poems in *The Covent-Garden Journal* to Smart (*Henry Fielding*,
II, 381–382). One, a song to Jenny Weston, bears many resemblances
to Smart's poetry, some of which are given by Cross; I will suggest
others after full quotation of the poem.

> Tho' Polly's and tho' Peggy's Charms,
> Each Youthful Poet's Bosom warms;
> None gives the Heart such fierce Alarms,
>   As Lovely Jenny Weston.

> No Violet, Jessamin, or Rose,
> Or spicy Gale that Afric blows,
> Does half such fragrant Sweets disclose,
>   As waft round Jenny Weston.

21: Mother Midnight's Pocket-Book

Let other Swains to Courts repair,
And view each glitt'ring Beauty there,
'Tis Art alone makes them so fair,
    But Nature Jenny Weston.

What Paint with her Complexion vies?
What Jewels sparkle like her Eyes?
What Hills of Snow so white, as rise
    The Breasts of Jenny Weston?

Give others Titles, Honours, Pow'r,
The Riches of Potosi's Shore,
I ask not Bawbles; I implore
    The Heart of Jenny Weston.

Possest of this, of this alone,
On India's Monarch I'd look down,
A Cot my Palace, and my Throne
    The Lap of Jenny Weston.

The song appeared in *The Covent-Garden Journal* for June 30, 1752. Besides the parallels to the descriptions of female breasts in the acknowledged canon of Smart's poetry, there is the use of "cot," appearing in three poems by Smart in 1752 (I, 128, 143, 151). "Polly" appears twice in poems by Smart in the same year and twice in *Jubilate Agno.* And there is a poem, "On Lovely Peggy," appearing in *The Midwife,* III (1753), 21, which begins "Though Peggy's Charms," suggesting at least the possibility that Smart had some hand in it. I would, understandably, not place too much weight on this last, but I would point out that the *Comical Pocket-Book* contains a poem "To Miss Mary Midnight," beginning "Polly, how cruel you are grown." To come back, however, compare lines 5–8 of the poem to Jenny Weston with stanza VI (p. 37) of the song on Bessy and Nancy in the *Comical Pocket-Book:*

No odour, from sweet vi'let beds,
    Nor Afric's fragrant spices;
As these two fair coelestial maids,
    So lovely and so nice is.

Again, these parallels need no pointing up. "To Health," a poem signed S and accepted as Smart's, in the *Universal Visiter,* March 1756 (pp. 140–141), contains "spicy Zephyrs" and "Afric." One should also observe the "spices—nice is" rhyme, the sort of rhyme made so popular by Ogden Nash but used often to good effect earlier by Christopher Smart and by one of his nineteenth-century admirers, Robert Browning. Nor should one forget that Smart's wife's name was Nancy and she is frequent in his poetry. And, of course, the "Hills of Snow so white, as rise / The Breasts of Jenny Weston" finds its counterpart in the "pretty rising alps of love," while "My Throne the Lap of Jenny Weston" is in slight degree similar to the line quoted from page 53 of the *Comical Pocket-Book*.

5. One of the epitaphs in the collection is for "Dr. Rock" (pp. 28–29); his name also occurs in the poem *Mother Midnight's Power of Gold* (pp. 9–10):

> And Rock can make your body whole,
> Tho' rotten to the bone.

A note in Smart's *Hilliad* contains a paraphrase of Dryden's epigram on Milton; one of the "three great wise men" is Rock: "Rock shone in physick, and in both John H- -ll" (p. 39). There is the strong probability that Arthur Murphy wrote or helped with the notes to the *Hilliad;* this fact, if proved, would not seriously affect my argument here. What is more, "Dr. Rocko" occurs in an essay in *The Midwife,* II, 25.

6. Another poem, pages 41–42, ends with the line "When beauty is their theme." In *A Song to David*, "God the eternal theme" and "God's the theme" appear, respectively, in stanzas 10 and 85. In Smart's version of the psalms one finds "Christ thy God and theme" (II, 494). And in the *Hymns and Spiritual Songs* occur "their Saviour for their theme" and "When Infinite's the theme" (II, 793 and 818).

7. There is a point at which the close student of a poet's work should be entitled to say that a particular poem sounds very much like the work of his man—and his opinion should command some respect. I would therefore ask that the reader remember the evidence already advanced for Smart's authorship of the *Comical Pocket-Book* in what follows. Smart wrote a few verse epistles which immediately came to mind as I read the poem on pages 52–53. The poem is introduced thus: "The author being t'other night at a merchant's house in the city, who entertain'd him in a very agreeable manner, after he'd done supper, wrote the following lines, in gratitude for the favour he receiv'd."

21: Mother Midnight's Pocket-Book

Sir,

At your kind cost, I'm proud to tell ye,
With ham and veal I fill'd my belly;
Permit this next to be inserted,
Bett's spinnet both my ears diverted;
Nancy's celestial voice has charm'd me;
Blythe Peggy's presence twice or thrice
Your kitchen chang'd to Paradice;
Dick with me ev'ry now and then
Kept from revolving back again:
Thus rarely blest, I'd have you know it,
I thought myself a happy poet;
For invitation, pot, and plate-full;
Expect to find me ever grateful;
For such an unexpected favour,
You'll always have my best behaviour;
May rigid fate, first time I faulter,
Provide a gibbet, cart, and halter;
This done, grant I may swing away,
Like Taffy, on St. David's day.

Notice the rhymes "tell ye—belly," "know it—poet," "plate-full—grate-ful." Compare with this Smart's poems, "To the Rev. Mr. Powell, On the nonperformance of a promise he made the author of a Hare," "Epistle to Dr. Nares," "An Invitation to Mrs. Tyler, A clergyman's lady, to dine upon a couple of ducks on the anniversary of the au-thor's wedding day," and "Epistle to Mrs. Tyler" (1, 206–210). It is in these four poems, incidentally, that Smart's Ogden Nashian rhymes occur.

"Taffy" of the last line of the poem quoted above is a common nickname for a Welshman; "Honest Taffy" speaks three lines of Welsh dialect in Smart's epilogue written for a performance of *The Conscious Lovers* in 1755. I must confess to not having encountered "Taffy" else-where in eighteenth-century poetry, and the *OED* does not give any examples of its appearance in poetry.

8. "A Castle built in the Air; or, The Author's Dream" (pp. 43–47) recalls the series on "castle-building" that Smart contributed to *The Student*.

9. Mary Midnight's very possession of a "pocket-book," the germ of the pamphlet's title, appears only once, to my knowledge, in *The*

Midwife (I, 177). A detail as small as this would be *best* known to Smart.

10. In the introduction to the *Comical Pocket-Book* the author refers to his grandmother "when she gave Caudle in the Hay-market" (p. 3). Caudle has unfortunately been identified as a performer;[6] it is actually "a warm drink, consisting of thin gruel, mixed with wine or ale, sweetened and spiced, given chiefly to sick people, esp. women in childbed; also to their visitors" (*OED*); and Mrs. Midnight is a "Midwife." (In *The Midwife*, III, 81 and 108, the author uses "caudle.")

11. On one occasion, the "Epigram by Sir Thomas More translated: The Long-nosed Fair" (1751), Smart assumes the pseudonym "Master Christopher Midnight, My [Mrs. Midnight's] Great Grandson." Humphrey Humdrum, author of the *Comical Pocket-Book* is, according to the title page and page 3, Mother Midnight's grandson. I intend here simply to emphasize my initial suggestion that Humphrey Humdrum, Mother Midnight's "grandson," is simply another pseudonym for Smart who had already been Mrs. Midnight's "great grandson."

12. On pages 22–23 of the *Comical Pocket-Book* the presumably male author of the pamphlet so forgets his identity as to speak of himself as "an old woman," continuing in language reminiscent of Mrs. Midnight, author of *The Midwife*.

13. On page 8 of the pamphlet, "Mother Midnight" is named as the writer of a "New Song" entitled "The True Patriot." Internal evidence corroborates the authorship as Smart's, a number of the naval heroes mentioned in the poem being encountered elsewhere in his writings. Smart, one may add, turned to the navy and some of its heroes for a few of his patriotic efforts. See, especially, the "Ode to Admiral Sir George Pocock" and "The King's Restoration," the seventeenth in *Hymns and Spiritual Songs*.

II

Some years ago Mr. Robert E. Brittain called attention to a poem in Dodsley's *Museum*, claiming it as Smart's.[7] It was almost immediately pointed out that "The Benedicite Paraphrased," the poem in question, was by the Reverend James Merrick.[8] What I am interested in is the final paragraph of Mr. Brittain's article.

[6] E. G. Ainsworth and C. E. Noyes, *Christopher Smart* (Columbia, Mo., 1943), 61.

[7] *PMLA*, LVI (1941), 165–174.

[8] *ELH*, IX (1942), 136–140, and *PMLA*, LVIII (1943), 582.

21: Mother Midnight's Pocket-Book

If the *Benedicite Paraphrased* be accepted as Smart's work, its significance is very great. It establishes once and for all that *A Song to David* is no miracle of insanity, but a perfectly logical development of Smart's natural bent. It suggests that *The Hop-Garden*, the *Midwife*, the clever epigrams and witty lyrics—in short, virtually all the poetry included in the 1791 "Collected poems"—are really extraneous from the main stream of his work. The period of confinement gave him rest and a chance to write as he pleased. His natural talent was for the composition of religious verse of an unusual and very high order, and that talent, first strongly apparent in the *Benedicite Paraphrased*, finds its ultimate expression in the great *Song*.

The arguments advanced for Smart's authorship were highly attractive, but, and here is the point I wish to make, they should have been ironclad and impregnable. Mr. Brittain was not only adding a poem to the Smart canon; he was using his attribution to formulate a new and revolutionary view of the whole of Smart's poetic output.

The attribution of the entire contents of *Mother Midnight's Comical Pocket-Book*, save a few songs and their accompanying musical scores, does not in the least change the picture of Smart's early years in London that has long prevailed. Such an attribution merely emphasizes certain well-known facts about this period in his life: he was incredibly busy and prolific; he was fond of, and was possibly forced to, various pseudonyms and mystifications; he was a ready and excellent composer of light verse; and, in the hurry of his writing, he often borrowed, now a phrase, now an idea, now a rhythm, from himself. There is no thought of claiming greater poetic stature for Smart on the basis of my attribution; I would simply add a few inches to his stature as a humorist.

The Preface to *A Dictionary of the English Language:* Johnson's Revisions and the Establishment of the Text[*]

By William R. Keast

SEVERAL studies of Johnson's revisions of his publications have disposed of the old belief that his care for his writings ceased when they originally left his pen. The interest of these studies has been chiefly in enabling us to see the process by which the final form of each text—the form in which we are familiar with it—was attained; only rarely has a knowledge of Johnson's revisions enabled editors to arrive at readings superior to those in the traditional texts. Johnson's revisions of his Preface to the *Dictionary of the English Language* present a more complex and instructive case. While noteworthy, like his other revisions, in displaying a great stylist at work, these revisions have an additional significance for the establishment of the true text of the Preface. For Johnson revised the Preface twice, making an independent set of alterations each time. And only one of these sets of revisions has been incorporated in the versions of the Preface printed since the eighteenth century.

Four folio editions of the *Dictionary* appeared during Johnson's lifetime. The first edition was published in 1755; the second closely followed, the first volume late in 1755 and the second early in 1756; the third edition was published in 1765; and the fourth in 1773. All the subsequent texts of the Preface contain variations from the first edition both in such "accidentals" as spelling and punctuation, and

[*] Reprinted, with permission of author and publisher, from *Studies in Bibliography* (Papers of the Bibliographical Society of the University of Virginia), v (1952–1953), 129–146, with abridgment as indicated by ellipses.

in "substantive" readings directly affecting the sense. It is the purpose of this study to record these variations; to indicate, on the basis of them, the relations among the several editions; to distinguish, so far as possible, between those variant readings which should be attributed to Johnson and those which should be attributed to the compositor or proof-corrector; and to suggest the editorial principles on which future editions of the Preface should be based.

I THE SECOND FOLIO EDITION, 1755–1756

The second edition departs from the first in thirty-one readings, of which fifteen are in the accidentals of the text and sixteen affect its substance. The accidental variants may be considered first, for they are not of great importance, and there is no clear sign that Johnson is responsible for any of them. . . .

Four of these changes . . . are simple corrections of errors in the first edition. All the errors are obvious, and the corrections merely bring the readings into conformity with the style of the remainder of the text. All could have been easily made by a careful compositor or an alert press-corrector, and the general excellence of the work on this edition suggests that the compositors were careful and the proof-correctors alert, for although these four errors were corrected, no new errors were introduced. I do not think, therefore, that these four changes need be attributed to Johnson.

Most of the remaining eleven changes are normalizations or easier readings. None seems clearly to be by Johnson, and in view of the relatively small number of substantive changes he made in the text for this edition, it is perhaps doubtful that his care extended to details of spelling and punctuation. I should be inclined to attribute these eleven changes in accidentals, therefore, to the compositor.

There are sixteen substantive changes in the second-edition text.

(11)[1] The first edition reads:

Such defects are not errours in orthography, but spots of barbarity impressed so deep in the *English* language, that criticism can never wash them away; these, therefore, must be permitted to remain untouched: but many words have likewise been altered by accident, or depraved by ignorance, as the pronunciation of the vulgar has been weakly followed; . . . . .

In the second edition the latter portion reads:

[1] I have numbered the paragraphs of the Preface, following the practice of the Hill-Powell edition of Boswell's *Life.*

. . . but many words have been altered by accident, or depraved by ignorance, ...

The omission of *likewise* may be a compositor's error, for it is easier to omit a word than to insert one. But I think this is Johnson's change, made because he saw that *likewise* was not quite accurate: alterations of the language from accident and depravations from ignorance are *errors*, and hence are *not* produced in a manner like that which accounts for the spots of barbarity referred to first; *likewise*, furthermore, dulls the antithesis, and weakens Johnson's charge that preventable damage is done by accidental or ignorant alteration. . . .

(38) The first edition reads:

As composition is one of the chief characteristicks of a language, I have endeavoured to make some reparation for the universal negligence of my predecessors, by inserting great numbers of compounded words, as may be found under *after, fore, new, night, fair,* and many more.

The second edition text omits *fair* from this list. This is surely Johnson's change. In defining *after, fore, new,* and *night* in the *Dictionary,* he calls attention to the use of each in composition and gives numerous examples—38 passages exemplifying compounds with *new,* some 30 compounds of *night,* 27 with *after,* and 73 with *fore.* But in defining *fair* he says nothing of its use as a compounding element, and he gives no compound words formed from it. We may speculate on the sequence of events underlying the inclusion of *fair* in the first edition. Johnson may have included it by mistake, although this is unlikely on the face of it, and the more so because the first four words in the list are in alphabetical order. It is most improbable that the compositor intruded a word. The likeliest explanation is that Johnson's manuscript contained a fifth example which the compositor misread as *fair;* in his revisal Johnson recognized *fair* as incorrect, without being able to recall the word he had originally written or troubling to add another. We can only guess at what the original reading may have been. Perhaps it was *semi,* which would fall correctly in the alphabetical series, which is treated in the *Dictionary* as a prolific source of compounds, and which could have been misread as *fair* in Johnson's hand.[2] . . .

[2] In "Some Emendations in Johnson's Preface to the *Dictionary,*" *Review of English Studies,* n.s., IV (1953), 52–57, I have given at greater length my reasons for conjecturing *semi* for *fair.*

(39) The first edition reads:

Of some forms of composition, such as that by which *re* is prefixed to note *repetition*, and *un* to signify *contrariety* or *privation*, all the examples cannot be accumulated, because the use of these particles, if not wholly arbitrary, is so little limited, that they are hourly affixed to new words as occasion requires, or is imagined to require them.

But *affixed* is wrong, for it means "to unite to the end, or *à posteriori;* to subjoin." Johnson therefore corrected the second edition text to *united* (having used *prefixed* earlier in the sentence, he did not want to repeat it).

(40) The first edition reads:

These [verbal phrases] I have noted with great care; and though I cannot flatter myself that the collection is complete, I believe I have so far assisted the students of our language, that this kind of phraseology will be no longer insuperable; . . . .

In the second edition Johnson changed *I believe I have* to *I have perhaps,* possibly with a view to continuing more consistently the modest tone of the preceding clause. . . .

(78) The first edition reads:

That many terms of art and manufacture are omitted, must be frankly acknowledged; but for this defect I may boldly allege that it was unavoidable: I could not visit caverns to learn the miner's language, nor take a voyage to perfect my skill in the dialect of navigation, nor visit the warehouses of merchants, and shops of artificers, to gain the names of wares, tools and operations, of which no mention is found in books; . . .

On rereading this passage Johnson was perhaps struck by the repetition in *warehouses:wares,* or perhaps by the imperfect balance which results from illustrating the contents of *warehouses* with one word and of *shops* with two. Whatever the reason, he made the phraseology at once more elegant and more particular by substituting for *wares* the words *commodities, utensils:* "the warehouses of merchants, and shops of artificers, to gain the names of commodities, utensils, tools and operations, of which no mention is found in books." . . .

(92) The first edition reads:

In hope of giving longevity to that which its own nature forbids to be immortal, I have devoted this book, the labour of years, to the honour of my country, that we may no longer yield the palm of philology to the nations of the continent.

Perhaps this seemed too categorical, especially for the peroration. Johnson revised it to read:

that we may no longer yield the palm of philology without a contest to the nations of the continent.

As will be seen, Johnson again made this change when he revised the Preface for the 1773 edition.

(93) The first edition reads:

. . . some who distinguish desert . . . will consider . . . that sudden fits of inadvertency will surprize vigilance, slight avocations will seduce attention, and casual eclipses of the mind will darken learning; . . .

In the second edition the words *of the mind* are omitted. I do not think Johnson made this change: it weakens the rhythm and obscures the meaning. The compositor accidentally dropped the phrase. . . .

Of these sixteen changes introduced in the second edition, two—those in (43) and (93)—are probably compositor's errors. The rest are probably by Johnson.

II THE THIRD FOLIO EDITION, 1765

In the third folio edition the text of the Preface has no independent textual authority. It is a page-for-page reprint of the second edition, and follows that edition in all the readings in which it departs from the first edition. The third edition introduces no new substantive readings. It departs from the second edition text in only twelve places: five of these are sporadic normalizations of spelling, three are slight changes in punctuation, of which one is indifferent and two obscure Johnson's syntax, and four are clear compositor's errors. The third edition may therefore be disregarded.

III THE FOURTH FOLIO EDITION, 1773

The fourth edition of the Preface is a page-for-page reprint of the first-edition text, varying from it in thirty-eight readings, of which twenty-one are accidental and seventeen substantive. Except for five of these readings, the text of the fourth edition does not repeat any of the variants introduced in the second-edition text nor any of the variants from the second edition introduced in the third. The five readings in which the second, third, and fourth editions agree against the first must therefore be examined in order to determine whether they imply dependence of the fourth-edition text on the second or third rather than, as the preponderance of the evidence would suggest, on the first. Four of the readings in which 1773 agrees with 1775–1756 and 1765 are in accidentals. . . . The first variant from the first-edition text in which the three later editions agree is a substantive change. In (92) as we have seen, Johnson originally said:

In hope of giving longevity to that which its own nature forbids to be immortal, I have devoted this book, the labour of years, to the honour of my country, that we may no longer yield the palm of philology to the nations of the continent.

In the second edition he had changed this to "that we may no longer yield the palm of philology without a contest to the nations of the continent"; this reading was repeated in 1765. The fourth edition reading is identical with the second, except that the phrase "without a contest" is set off with commas.

Do these five readings establish a textual connection between the second edition and the fourth, or between the third and the fourth? I do not think they do. The four changes in accidentals are all simple corrections of manifest errors, of the kind that could easily have been made by any careful workman, guided by the consistent practice in the rest of the text, whether or not he had a corrected copy before him. As to the alteration in (92), I think we must suppose either that Johnson in 1773 remembered having made this change in 1755 (and he may have done so because this is the beginning of the noble close of the Preface), or that he invented it anew (which he might easily have done, for once the need for some softening of the sentence is felt, the phrase inserted has a degree of inevitability). If we suppose instead that Johnson derived this reading from the second- or third-edition text, we must suppose what is almost inconceivable—that in all the other instances listed above in which these texts vary from the first edition Johnson rejected the reading of the intermediary text and returned by pure chance to the readings of the first edition. The agreement among the three later editions in these five places is to be attributed, therefore, not to a direct line of descent from one to another, but to the coincidence of simple and obvious corrections by compositors or proof-correctors (or, less likely, by Johnson) and to Johnson's chance recollection or repetition of one of his earlier revisions. The fourth-edition text is independently derived from the first edition.

The remaining thirty-three variations between the texts of the first and fourth editions may now be examined. Seventeen affect the accidentals of the text. . . . As in the second edition, [such] changes seem to be the occasional intrusion of the compositor or proof-reader. Johnson's revision was casual and did not extend to the minutiae of the text.

The text of the fourth edition contains sixteen changes in the substantive readings of the first edition. Readers familiar with the Preface will recognize these, because they have been incorporated in the standard text; one or two of them, I think, should not be attributed to Johnson. . . .

(34) 1755:

Words arbitrarily formed by a constant and settled analogy, like diminutive adjectives in *ish,* as *greenish, bluish,* adverbs in *ly,* as *dully, openly,* substantives in *ness,* as *vileness, faultiness,* were less diligently sought, and many sometimes have been omitted, when I had no authority that invited me to insert them; . . .

The reading *many sometimes* is clearly faulty, although Johnson had let it slip past him when he revised the Preface for the second edition: *many* words cannot with propriety be *sometimes* omitted. In 1773 Johnson solved the difficulty by deleting *many.* But the error in the first edition must be accounted for. I suspect that Johnson originally wrote *and may sometimes have been omitted,* and that the first-edition compositor misread *may* as *many.* If this was the original reading, it gives a sense preferable to that which results from Johnson's deletion of *many,* for the fourth edition text makes it seem that Johnson knows which of these words have been omitted, whereas the point is clearly that he does not know. A bold editor might introduce *may* into the text. . . .

(40) 1755:

There is another kind of composition more frequent in our language than perhaps in any other, from which arises to foreigners the greatest difficulty. We modify the signification of many verbs by a particle subjoined; as to *come off,* to escape by a fetch; to *fall on,* to attack; . . .

In 1773 "the signification of many verbs" is altered to "the signification of many words." This seems to be a compositor's error. This type of composition is confined to verbs, as is shown by the list of examples, all of which are verbs, and by Johnson's reference at the end of the paragraph to "combinations of verbs and particles." . . .

(69) 1755:

Thus have I laboured to settle the orthography, display the analogy, regulate the structures, and ascertain the signification of *English* words, to perform all the parts of a faithful lexicographer: but I have not always executed my own scheme, or satisfied my own expectations.

Johnson changed this in 1773 to read:

Thus have I laboured by settling the orthography, displaying the analogy, regulating the structures, and ascertaining the signification of *English* words, to perform all the parts of a faithful lexicographer: . . .

This change eliminates an awkward shift in construction in the original text, where *to perform* . . . must be taken not as the final member of a series, which it appears at first to be, but as a summary phrase. In improving the syntax Johnson did not notice, or chose to disregard, the new implication of the sentence—that he had in fact settled the orthography, displayed the analogy, etc.—an implication denied in the second clause, in the rest of the paragraph, and in the two paragraphs that follow.

(72) 1775:

When first I engaged in this work, I resolved to leave neither words nor things unexamined, and pleased myself with a prospect of the hours which I should revel away in feasts of literature, the obscure recesses of northern learning, which I should enter and ransack, the treasures with which I expected every search into those neglected mines to reward my labour, and the triumph with which I should display my acquisitions to mankind.

In 1773 the passage reads instead:

. . . and pleased myself with a prospect of the hours which I should revel away in feasts of literature, with the obscure recesses of northern learning, which I should enter and ransack; the treasures. . . .

The original reading is clear, and the change in 1773 produces some difficulty. In the first edition, *prospect* controls a series of four parallel elements—*hours, recesses, treasures,* and *triumph.* The *with* added before *the obscure recesses* in 1773 destroys this parallelism and appears to initiate a new one, less precise than the old, between *prospect* and *recesses;* and the added *with* must also be understood as preceding *the treasures* and *the triumph,* for Johnson, if he made this change, could not prefix a *with* to each of these because each is followed by a *with*-construction. This is all very awkward; it is also imprecise, for although Johnson could please himself in advance with the *prospect* of recesses of learning he intended to enter, he could not please himself with the recesses themselves, as the altered reading would have it, until he had entered them. If this is Johnson's change, he was careless, as he appears to have been nowhere else in the course of this revision. Despite the general accuracy of the compositor, therefore, I attribute this change to him rather than to Johnson.

(73) 1755:

I then contracted my design, determining to confide in myself, and no longer to solicit auxiliaries, which produced more incumbrance than assistance: by this I obtained at least one advantage, that I set limits to my work, which would in time be finished, though not completed.

In 1773 Johnson altered the ending to read "which would in time be ended, though not completed." This is an elegant change, and shows Johnson at his most fastidious. *To end* is defined in the *Dictionary* as "to terminate; to conclude; to cease; to fail," and *to finish* as "1. to bring to the end purposed; to complete. 2. to perfect; to polish to the excellency intended. 3. to end; to put an end to." The same nicety appears in the Advertisement Johnson composed for the 1773 edition: "Many are the works of human industry, which to begin and finish are hardly granted to the same man." . . .

(84) 1755:

When we see men grow old and die at a certain time one after another, from century to century, we laugh at the elixir that promises to prolong life to a thousand years; and with equal justice may the lexicographer be derided, who being able to produce no example of a nation that has preserved their words and phrases from mutability, shall imagine that his dictionary can embalm his language, and secure it from corruption and decay, that it is in his power to change sublunary nature, or clear the world at once from folly, vanity, and affectation.

In 1773 the lexicographer is made to imagine that he can "change sublunary nature, and clear the world at once from folly" etc. The change, which I take to be Johnson's, heightens the vanity of the lexicographer and perfects the parallelism of the last two clauses.

22: The Preface to Johnson's Dictionary

(88) In 1755, Johnson, commenting on Swift's proposal that words should not be allowed to become obsolete, says:

But what makes a word obsolete, more than general agreement to forbear it? and how shall it be continued, when it conveys an offensive idea, or recalled again into the mouths of mankind, when it has once by disuse become unfamiliar, and by unfamiliarity unpleasing.

The inversions at the end of this passage are changed in 1773 to the straightforward "when it has once become unfamiliar by disuse, and unpleasing by unfamiliarity." Since Johnson's style in his later prose tends to be less artfully contrived than in his earlier writing, I take this change to be his. . . .

On the basis of this comparison of the texts of the four editions of the Preface printed in Johnson's lifetime, the relationships among them may be summarized as follows:

1. The second edition, 1755–1756, was printed from the first; there is no sign that Johnson or the compositor returned to the manuscript—and a strong sign that they did not; compare the deletion in (38).

2. The third edition, 1765, was printed from the second: wherever the second edition varies from the first, the third edition follows the second; when the third varies from the second, it never returns to a reading of the first; the third edition introduces no readings which can be attributed to Johnson.

3. The fourth edition, 1773, was printed from the first, with revisions by Johnson independent of those he introduced into the second-edition text: the fourth edition does not follow the third in any of its variations from the second, nor, with the exceptions already accounted for, does it follow the second in any of its variations from the first.

We have, then, three texts of the Preface—since the text of the third edition may be disregarded—which possess textual authority. The second and fourth editions present texts independently revised, and contain substantive changes of importance. It does not appear from the number of these substantive changes that Johnson's revision of the Preface for either edition was systematic; this fact, together with the nature of the changes in the accidentals of the texts, suggests that he did not extend his attention to the details of spelling and punctuation, and that the changes in the accidentals are probably not by Johnson. Nor can all the substantive revisions in the two editions be automatically ascribed to Johnson; most of them are surely his, but some, as I have tried to show, may be suspected.

We need not be surprised at Johnson's failure to recall, in 1773, the revisions he had made in the Preface late in 1755. During the intervening eighteen years he had, as he wrote to Boswell, "looked very little into" the *Dictionary*,[3] and he had been heavily occupied with other writing. And the revisions made in 1755 were not on the whole so striking—with a single exception, perhaps—as to stick for years in the mind of a man who wrote and revised much. Nor need we, on the other hand, be surprised that Johnson, even if he had forgotten the changes made in 1755, did not once more notice at least the errors he had then corrected, if not the elegancies he had added, and correct them again in 1773. Both revisions were rather casual performances, not at all like his thoroughgoing work on the *Rambler*. He evidently read rapidly through the text, mending or improving where something happened to catch his eye.

The two sets of revisions therefore complement each other. Each represents, for certain passages in the Preface, Johnson's "final intention." And the editorial procedure to be adopted in the light of these circumstances is clear. There is no ground for adopting, as the copy-text for an edition of the Preface, the text of the fourth edition. This has been the procedure followed in all editions since 1773, on the familiar theory that the last edition published in the author's lifetime is the one most likely to contain his final intentions with respect to the work. Greg and Bowers have recently demonstrated that even for works whose textual history is more normal than that of the Preface to the *Dictionary* this is an editorial theory certain to produce corrupt texts.[4] For the Preface this theory has led, in all modern texts, to the exclusion of half of all the revisions made by Johnson, to the perpetuation of errors and stylistic defects which he had carefully expunged, and to the omission of several stylistic elegancies which he had added. Future editors must therefore adopt the text of the first edition as their copy-text and introduce into it the two sets of Johnsonian revisions from the second and fourth editions, together with

[3] *Life* II, 205; Feb. 24, 1773.
[4] See W. W. Greg, "The Rationale of Copy-Text," *Studies in Bibliography*, III (1950), 19–36, and Fredson Bowers, "Current Theories of Copy-Text, with an Illustration from Dryden," *Modern Philology*, XLVIII (1950), 12–20. Although I have not planned it as such, the present case may be regarded as another illustration of the correctness of the editorial procedure advocated in these two papers.

such changes in the accidentals from these texts as seem necessary for correctness or consistency. The editor will have to determine for himself which of the changes made in substantive readings in the second and fourth editions are authoritative; I have tried to indicate which are Johnson's, but I do not suppose that I have chosen correctly in every case. But the editor cannot avoid the responsibility of making a choice. The resulting text will be a composite, but only a composite text can reflect accurately the composite of intentions which influenced Johnson in 1755 and 1773.

IV

STUDIES IN
ATTRIBUTION:
ENGLISH AND AMERICAN
LITERATURE SINCE 1775

Editorial Note to Part IV

FEW methodically instructive canonical essays have been found concerning English literature after the 1820's, and too few in American literature for a separate section. Students of American literature appear to settle these matters expeditiously, with a plain paragraph or footnote—except on occasions when the arguments run to volume length. An instance of the more usual procedure is the candid admission appended by Leon Howard to an analysis which had assumed that "The Fiddler" was by Herman Melville:

NOTE:—"The Fiddler" was included (in a Melville volume in 1922) and its authorship remained unquestioned despite the fact that Francis Wolle, on the evidence of the *Harper's* Index, attributed it to Fitz-James O'Brien in his biography of O'Brien (. . . 1944). Aside from the weak evidence of similarity in theme to "The Happy Failure," I have found no reason for questioning this attribution and believe "The Fiddler" should be excluded from the Melville canon.—L. H., 1958. [From p. 216 of the 1958 reprint of Howard's 1951 biography of Melville]

At the other extreme, defying adequate summary, is the voluminous and unresolved debate on the authenticity and authorship of the Civil War "Diary of a Public Man," or the statistical argument of moderate compass, but too technical for the lay reader, such as Frederick Mosteller and David Wallace's article on the disputed *Federalist* papers.[1]

Fortunately, there are occasional exceptions that are not excessively brief, excessively long, or excessively technical. Robert Elias (in No. 23) is concerned with the rare problem which may be defined as the discovery of a novelist not known to have written anything but letters. The evidence is largely geographical and genealogical.

The group of Coleridge essays by David Erdman, John Colmer, and S. F. Johnson (Nos. 24–27) are printed as background to the symposium in Part I and as exercises in applying the test of style (including such matters as, in No. 24, "the imaginative control of a common metaphor") and the test afforded by concordances (Nos. 26

[1] "Inference in an Authorship Problem," *Jour. of the American Statistical Assoc.*, LVIII (1963), 275–309.

and 27). Colmer's attribution (No. 25) of the March 1802 essay is presented here because he works independently along quite different lines of internal evidence from those developed in No. 3. The subsequently unearthed external evidence of autograph notes (see No. 3, Postscript) serves as a control on both arguments.

Hoover Jordan's contribution (No. 28) to a debate long raging and recently brought to a different conclusion by Miss Elisabeth Schneider will, we hope, lead anyone interested in the particular case to turn to her readily available essay (*PMLA*, LXX, June 1955), for which unfortunately there was not room here.[2]

In the argument of Leonidas Jones (No. 29) much weight is supported by the apparently very slight reed of one author's habit of using familiar quotations. To view the argument as capable of sustaining the conclusion, one must stipulate that the external evidence (not exhibited in our excerpt) requires the author of the review in question to be either Keats or Reynolds, with no proponderance either way; it must be further stipulated that the search which turns up only two very unimpressive parallels in Keats has been truly exhaustive. (The presence or absence of quotations and literary allusions is also one of the tests applied in No. 28.)[3]

[2] See also the Annotated Bibliography, under "Hazlitt."

[3] For the periodical literature of the later nineteenth century, the standard work will be *The Wellesley Index to Victorian Periodicals, 1824–1900*, ed. Walter E. Houghton (University of Toronto Press and Routledge and Kegan Paul), which will refer to printed or manuscript authority for the attribution of anonymous or pseudonymous essays (about 90 per cent of the total). This invaluable guide will also contain bibliographies of contributors to the periodicals analyzed and an Index of Initials and Pseudonyms.

23

The First American Novel*

By Robert H. Elias

WAS *The Power of Sympathy* (Boston, 1789) the first American novel? It may well have been the first published in this country, but it was probably not the first novel written by an American citizen. Fourteen years earlier, if circumstantial evidence can be believed, Thomas Atwood Digges, of Warburton Manor, Maryland, had had *Adventures of Alonso: Containing Some Striking Anecdotes of the Present Prime Minister of Portugal* anonymously printed in two volumes by John Bew in London.

I

The principal clues leading to this discovery are to be found in two statements on the title page of The New York Public Library's copy of the book. The first statement, part of the printed title, is that *Adventures of Alonso* was "By a Native of Maryland, some Years resident in Lisbon."[1] The second, in pencil, is that it was "By Mr Digges of Warburton in Maryland."[2] If there is any doubt of the publisher's good faith in the first instance, that doubt is somewhat dispelled by the confidence apparently responsible for the identification in the second, and conviction is strengthened by the additional disclosure that the handwriting in question not only is typically late eighteenth century, but also closely resembles Thomas Digges's own.[3]

* Reprinted from *American Literature*, XII (1941), 419–428, with permission of author and publisher. A third and fourth section (428–434), not concerned with the authorship of the novel, and some documentary footnotes, are omitted.

[1] Oscar Wegelin (*Early American Fiction 1774–1830* [New York, 1913, 1925]) lists the book simply as "By a Native of Maryland." It is not included in Joseph Sabin's *Bibliotheca Americana* (New York, 1868–1936), or in Lyle H. Wright's *American Fiction 1774–1850* (San Marino, Calif., 1939).

[2] Mentioned by Robert B. Heilman, *America in British Fiction 1760–1800* (Baton Rouge, La., 1937), p. 70 and n.

[3] Digges's letters are to be found mainly among the Franklin papers in the Historical Society of Pennsylvania, the American Philosophical Society, and the

Yet even without the explicit information presented by this single title page it would be possible to make some reasonable inferences, from the contents of the book itself, as to the author's life and loyalties. It appears, to begin with, that he had first-hand knowledge of Portugal and the neighboring countries. Native words enter naturally into his sentences; familiarity with the region's physical aspects, distances, and topography characterizes his descriptions; and personal acquaintance with the events and the locale colors his political as well as fictional anecdotes. Moreover, a few of the characters with active roles seem to be persons who really existed and were known by the writer. In the New York Public Library copy of *Adventures of Alonso,* for example, someone many years ago identified Capt. J— (i, 70) and Mr. H— (l, 77) as "Jarvis" and "Hake." Capt. J—, in the story, is commander of an English frigate, and Mr. H—, a friend of Alonso's father, is "an English gentleman belonging to the factory" at Lisbon, who dies before the adventures are completed. At that time, contemporary accounts show, there were living at least two Captains Jarvis of the British navy, one of whom was kind to American prisoners during the Revolution, and two Messrs. Hake of Lisbon, one of whom was director of the bank and the other of whom died in Lisbon, July 30, 1772, at the age of twenty.

Furthermore, if it is fair to look for autobiography in the biography of the hero, the contents of the book indicate that the author was a son of respected parents and a Catholic and that he was educated in England near London in order to be taught something about mercantile activity; for Alonso, at the age of fifteen, "was . . . sent to an eminent boarding school in the vicinity of the capital, accompanied with a private tutor of the Roman Catholic religion" (i, 15), while his father, a merchant of good standing, hoped that "by living some time with a people, whose grandeur and opulence depended chiefly upon their commerce . . . [Alonso] would acquire higher and juster notions of what he was intended for" (i, 9). In addition, if Alonso's conduct can be said to represent the author's idea of heroic

---

University of Pennsylvania; the Hamilton, Jefferson, Madison, Washington, and Digges-L'Enfant-Morgan papers in the Library of Congress; the Lee papers at Harvard; the Emmet and Ford collections in The New York Public Library; the Rufus King papers in the New-York Historical Society; and the John Adams papers, at present sealed from the public. These, together with letters to and about him in some of the above collections, are the principal sources for information about Digges.

behavior, the attempt to smuggle diamonds out of Brazil and the endeavor to carry on contraband trade with the Spanish settlements bear the stamp of approval and intimate that, given the occasion, the author would have acted, or would act, in like manner himself.

Finally, there is the substantially more definite information to be gleaned concerning the writer's politics and nationality. Judged by the words he puts into the mouth of his protagonist, he reveals himself as either an Englishman sympathetic with the American struggle for equality or an intransigent American. Thus Alonso takes a stand against despotic government and finds fault with Pombal, the prime minister, for having ruined Portugal's commerce through deterrent taxes, through the creation of monopolies, and through unlawful seizure of property. And thus also, as if to bring the point home to the British reader, Alonso makes remarks obviously intended for consumption in the land where the book was published (1, 122–128). After terming the English people "a good sort" and "honest and sincere," he tells a group of acquaintances that "sensible people" believe Britain "ripe for a more arbitrary government" and that, "without some violent concussion in the state, to give play to the passions, and thereby restore the constitution to its first principles, the boasted freedom of England will soon be on a level with other states." Parliament is "venal," he warns, while the king's ministers place themselves above the laws.

The pre-sentiment of the loss of their liberties . . . ought to fill the mind of every Englishman with horror—They ought to contrast opulence, independency and happiness—the appendages of freedom—to despotism—the uncertainty of property, and all that train of evils which accompany arbitrary power. This picture they ought constantly have in view, in order to awaken their attention to their interest, prosperity, and welfare.

In sum, added to the explicit clues already cited, the internal evidence of *Adventures of Alonso* suggests that the author would in all likelihood have been a Catholic, have gone to England for his education, been interested in commerce, and of course have been before 1775 some years resident in Lisbon, where he would have made some friends. He would also, when the American conflict broke out, doubtless have opposed George III and his ministers, and might even have carried on contraband trade with the Colonies if he were not there himself fighting. If it can be shown that there was a Mr. Digges of Warburton, Maryland, who was some years resident in Lisbon before the publication of *Adventures of Alonso* and who, beyond that, fulfilled those other qualifications implied by the book, then his identification will have something solid for its foundation.

II

Without any question, Thomas Atwood Digges is the Mr. Digges of Warburton in Maryland who best embodies the characteristics of the anonymous writer. He came from an old Catholic family, originally of Kent, and could trace his lineage back to the time of Richard I, perhaps even to Alfred the Great himself. Among his more illustrious ancestors were Thomas, the mathematician; Sir Dudley, author of *The Compleat Ambassador* and Master of Rolls under Charles I; and Edward, royal governor of Virginia in 1656. His father, William, was a good friend of George Washington's, and Washington's letters and diaries show that the two families exchanged frequent visits and were on the most intimate of terms. Warburton Manor, the home of the Diggeses ever since Edward's eldest son had gained possession of it in the 1680's, now Fort Washington, was situated on the north side of Piscataway Creek and the Potomac nearly fronting Mount Vernon. Between these two estates, it is said, intercourse was maintained by a unique code of signals and by elegant barges imported from England, and Washington Irving relates that, when visiting William Digges, George Washington was "always . . . rowed by six negroes, arrayed in a kind of uniform check shirts and black velvet caps."[4]

Thomas was born at Warburton some time in 1741, according to the most reasonable calculations, the second of the six sons of Ann Atwood and William Digges.[5] Family tradition has it that he and a younger brother, George, were sent to Oxford for their education, and a portrait,[6] painted reputedly by Sir Joshua Reynolds and showing Thomas in the wig and gown of an alleged Oxford society, is invoked

---

[4] *Life of George Washington* (New York, 1855–1859), I, 321.

[5] The evidence is contradictory: cf. *D. A. R. Magazine*, LVII (1923), 130–131; copies of the wills of both old and young Charles Digges in Semmes Genealogical Collection, Maryland Historical Society; Jane Baldwin Cotton, *Maryland Calendar of Wills* (Baltimore, 1901–1928), VIII, 267–268; MSS: Digges to Jefferson, May 30, 1818, and Jefferson to Digges, June 15, 1818 (Jefferson papers, Library of Congress); Digges to Madison, Feb. 9, 1812, and Nov. 27, 1815 (Madison papers, Library of Congress). I am indebted to Mrs. Russell Hastings of New York for additional data.

[6] Owned by Mrs. Cecil Morgan, Macon, Ga., and reproduced in *D. A. R. Magazine*, LVII (1923), 126, and in Paul Wilstach's *Potomac Landings* (Garden City, N.Y., and Toronto, 1921), 100.

as proof. Although Oxford has no record of any Maryland Diggeses' ever having studied there, it may still be true that the two boys were schooled somewhere in England, even if not at Oxford, thus continuing the parallel with Alonso.

In any case, Thomas proved himself the most adventurous member of the family and was the only one of the Messrs. Digges of Warburton Manor to have gone to Lisbon before 1775.[7] Charles and Francis had died young; Henry perished at sea; and neither George nor Joseph left America until a few years after *Adventures of Alonso* was written and published. William Digges, the father, was of course perpetually present. But Thomas, on February 23, 1767, was in New York City getting ready to go to Lisbon. On that day he wrote Francis Street, a Philadelphia merchant:

I have . . . bespoken a passage in a Ship that will sail from this to Cadiz about this day week, and as it is not distant from Lisbon more than 30 or 40 leag[s]. it will not be very inconvenient to me; as I am told there are often opportunitys both by Land & water from thence to Lisbon[.] I could have wished to have seen you at Philadelphia, as I want some account given me of the nature of the Country to which I am bound & which I may probably stand in need of,   however I suppose there are many Englishmen in Cadiz, who can direct me w[ch] way to take for the most ready conveyance to Lisbon in which place there are some Gent[n]. to whom I am personally known & when I get among them I shall think myself snug enough. . . .[8]

If he acted according to plan, he must have gone on the ship *Earl of Hertford,* which the New York newspapers show cleared the customhouse on Monday, the twenty-third, but had not yet sailed on the twenty-sixth; and if the trip took what seems to have been the usual length of time, he must have arrived at his destination by the middle of May.

References in letters later written to Benjamin Franklin dem-

[7] The account of Digges's career is based on the MSS already cited in n. 3; on MSS in the Samuel Adams, George Bancroft, and Henry Laurens papers in The New York Public Library and the Franklin papers in the Library of Congress; on the published writings, correspondence, and diaries of John Adams, Franklin, Jefferson, Rufus King, Laurens, Arthur and William Lee, Madison, Washington, and George III; on the volumes of the American Revolution's diplomatic correspondence edited by Jared Sparks and by Francis Wharton; and on B. F. Stevens's *Facsimiles of Manuscripts in European Archives Relating to America 1773–1783* (London, 1889).

[8] MS, The New York Public Library.

onstrate that Thomas Digges actually did go to Lisbon. He said that Lisbon was a place where "I am well known & a little respected." He introduced William Burn "of the house of Messieurs Burn & sons of Lisbon" as "a particular Friend of mine" who had been helpful to Americans in Lisbon, "among whom I am a grateful example." And he offered to be of assistance to John Jay and William Carmichael, who were being sent to Spain, "a Country that I know well." Digges knew not only Lisbon, but, obviously, the surrounding country too.

How long he was there is not certain. If the death of Mr. H— in the novel is based on the death of young Hake, Thomas Digges was probably still in Lisbon on July 30, 1772. But he did not stay long after that, for some time in 1773 or 1774 he became a resident of London. In June 1775 the *London Magazine* and the *London Review of English and Foreign Literature* noted the appearance of the completely anonymous *Adventures of Alonso*. And then there is no word of him until almost two years later, when letters by, to, and about him in the correspondence of men active in diplomatic circles abroad during the Revolution reveal that he, like the author of *Adventures of Alonso*, was oppposed to arbitrary government and devoted to democratic principles and that, like Alonso himself, he was even a trader in contraband.

At the very outbreak of hostilities Digges made the most of opportunities to serve his country. As private agent, he furnished Arthur and William Lee with useful intelligence, fed and clothed imprisoned Americans, and shipped locks for guns and muskets to America, under cover of clearance for Spain. In 1778 he offered his services to Franklin, and on May 3, 1779, he went to Passy and swore allegiance to "the thirteen United States of America," thus becoming *de jure* the rebel that he had been and continued to be *de facto*. He now not only provided Franklin with the political and military news of the day and, in cooperation with William Hodgson, David Hartley, and the Rev. Mr. Wren, furnished prisoners with money, food, and clothes, as well as arranged the transfer of the sick from dank vaults to healthier quarters; but he also endeavored to keep the cartel ship afloat with exchange prisoners and to force the Admiralty to respect the agreements of English soldiers paroled by the Americans. Later, when John Adams arrived in Europe, he became the means of inserting pro-American propaganda in the British newspapers.

Throughout the period of battle and bickering Digges supported the American cause. He declared that "American Independency" was his "favourite wish"; he called the British blundering in provoking the war, in prosecuting it, and in blinding themselves to American sovereignty; and, occasionally, with the hope of terminating the conflict, he forwarded to Franklin peace proposals from minority members of Parliament. Moreover, his sincerity convinced men who knew him. Arthur Lee, in 1777, recommended him to Congress for an appointment; William Lee, early the next year, suggested he be named commissioner to Portugal; and Captain Conyngham praised him for his aid to Americans who had succeeded in escaping from English prisons. "Happy we to have such a man," Conyngham wrote Franklin in 1779.

Yet Digges's integrity has been questioned and his right to be called an American challenged. For this a misunderstanding with Franklin is largely responsible. When Franklin asked Digges for an accounting of the prisoners' money expended during 1779 and 1780, Digges could not render it, for the prudence that had prompted him to use some two dozen pseudonyms in his correspondence[9] had impelled him to place his papers "in a safe & distant quarter." This, of course, left Franklin only unsatisfied and suspicious; consequently, when Hodgson wrote in 1781 that Digges had gone to Bristol without providing certain necessary funds and was there secretly shipping goods to Boston on a vessel supposed to be bound for New York, Franklin was convinced that "If such a Fellow is not damn'd, it is not worth while to keep a Devil"; and both he and Hodgson proceeded to warn everyone against Digges. By the time Digges himself heard of this, it was too late: help he had given some indiscreet prisoners had resulted in the seizure of his papers, and he was now deprived of access to the evidence that could absolve him. Moreover, subsequent events, instead of clearing Digges, actually offered Franklin additional reasons for believing Hodgson and the worst. In an attempt to ask the favor of having his property restored, Digges did

[9] Sometimes he signed his own name or initials, sometimes no name, but usually it was one of the following, or their initials: B. B—d, Pierre J. Bertrand, Alexr. Brett, P—C., Wm. Singleton Church, Jacques Vincent Drouillard, P. Drouillard, V. J. Drouillard, Pierre J. Du Vall, Wm. Ferguson, Wm. Fitzpatrick, Donald Forbes, Wm. Forbes, Allen Hamilton, Arthur Hamilton, Wm. Hamilton, Alexr. Hammilton [sic], Alexr. McKinlock, A. McPherson, W. P., Wm. S. Ross, Wm. Russell, Robt. Sinclair, John Thompson, I. W—.

the ministry the favor of carrying a communication to John Adams, then in Holland, just at the time North fell from power; and, to some, Digges thus appeared to be in the pay of the British. When a few days afterward Digges returned to London, Shelburne so garbled the report of the interview with Adams that Adams was misled into believing Digges could not be trusted. Then, finally, as if another instance were needed, Jonathan Williams wrote Franklin on June 17, 1785, that Digges was in a Dublin jail in consequence of his "Folly & Wickedness." This all must have seemed but further proof of roguery at that time, and it has usually been accepted as such since.

As a matter of fact, the events from which Hodgson and Williams drew inferences only reaffirm Digges's loyalty to America, while the inferences themselves emphasize the price Digges had to pay for it. His valuable shipments of musket locks, clothing, and sail and tent materials to America in war time, naturally, because of the tremendous risk, demanded extreme caution and methods that might well have aroused Hodgson's suspicions; and his efforts after the war to send skilled craftsmen, indentured servants, and machinery from the British Isles to the United States made him liable to a fine and imprisonment that could explain his predicament in the Dublin jail. Personal ill-will and physical punishment were what men like Digges knew they had to endure. So, probably, when Digges was in Bristol subjecting himself to Hodgson's censure, he was supplying America with useful materials; and when he was behind bars in Ireland for what Williams considered follies, he was very likely paying for his endeavors to ship men and vital machinery to Franklin's homeland.

For some years after 1785, Digges remained abroad, and continued to furnish illustrations of his allegiance to the new nation. In 1792 he was still helping Englishmen and Irishmen to emigrate, having sent a score of "very valuable artists & machine makers" across the ocean in the course of the previous year. In 1793 he provided Jefferson and Thomas Pinckney with information concerning attempts to counterfeit coins for use in America. And in November and December of 1797 he assisted Rufus King in ferreting out some of the details of the Blount-Chisholm conspiracy to seize Spain's North American territories for the British. Finally, between April 10, 1798, when he shipped Washington a box of seeds and potatoes from London, and February 8, 1799, when he dined at Mount Vernon, Digges returned to Warburton Manor.

Whatever doubts existed as to his patriotism had in all likelihood been dispelled some time before. In 1794, on the basis of the bad reputation given him by Franklin and Hodgson, an attempt had been made to confiscate his estate, but, doubtless because of Washington's testimony, it had come to naught. The President had lightly dismissed the quarrel between Digges and Franklin as of little consequence and declared "that the conduct of Mr. Thomas Digges toward the United States during the War . . . and since . . . has not been only friendly, but I might add zealous." Certainly no doubt existed after Digges's return, for Washington had him over for dinner; Jefferson maintained a cordial correspondence with him, discussing agriculture, sheep-breeding, and political chicane; and the Madisons regarded him with friendly affection. Indeed, until but a few years before his death, he was active in the political circles of Jefferson, Madison, and other leaders, stamping out the remnants of the Tory party.

His final days were unhappy ones, however, and he may have died with a grievance against the government. He was not only plunged into the misunderstanding involving L'Enfant and the construction of Fort Washington at Warburton Manor, but he was also plagued with damages to his fisheries and farm caused by the work on the fort. It was in vain that he claimed reimbursement. The officials did nothing, and the depredations continued. When, in addition, storms dilapidated his house and illness and age weakened his body, he forsook Warburton for less troubled lodgings in the city of Washington, where, it seems, he died in the middle of December 1821. One of his nephews, John Fitzgerald, had written L'Enfant on December 6, requesting the return of an old pot that was being repaired at the shop and saying, "My Mother desires me to present her compliments & ask if you have heard how her Brother is—." By the twenty-fourth, another nephew, William Dudley Digges, was able to compose a letter beginning, "Since the death of my Uncle I have good reason to believe that I am entitled to the immediate possession of the estates of Warburton and Frankland. . . ." After that date there was some discussion about the disposal of the property, but the name of Thomas Atwood Digges was buried in silence, to be resurrected only by those historians who occasionally encountered it in the unfair fulminations of Franklin.

Yet this was the man who could have written *Adventures of Alonso*. His life and sentiments were identical with the author's as far as the author's life and sentiments can be detected in the book. Therefore, inasmuch as all the clues—the inferred, the inscribed, and the imprinted—lead to him, must we not conclude that he was *the* "Native of Maryland, some Years resident in Lisbon"?[10]

[10] This conclusion agrees with that reached in 1932 by Eugene D. Finch, of Phillips Exeter Academy, who is now completing a biography of Thomas A. Digges (see *American Literature*, xi [1939], 300). I did not discover until April 1939 that he and I were both doing the same thing, and then I learned that Dr. Finch had been working on the project since 1935. Inasmuch as my labors covered scarcely a year, I relinquished the larger subject, while he, in return, graciously consented to let me publish the facts about the authorship of *Adventures of Alonso*.

Postscript: Since publication of the foregoing article I have chanced upon Frank MacDermot's *Theobald Wolfe Tone* (London, 1939), which contains derogatory comments about a Digges, and two articles about Thomas Digges by William Bell Clark, which fully and sympathetically document Digges's activities in Great Britain ("In Defense of Thomas Digges," *The Pennsylvania Magazine of History and Biography*, lxxvii [1953], 381–438; "A Franklin Postscript to Captain Cook's Voyages," *Proceedings of the American Philosophical Society*, xcviii [1954], 400–405). But, contribute as they do to a more accurate account of Thomas Digges's character, they neither alter the evidence concerning his loyalty to the United States of America nor affect the inferences concerning the authorship of the novel.

24

Coleridge on George Washington: Newly Discovered Essays of 1800*

By David V. Erdman

SAMUEL TAYLOR COLERIDGE as a poet and as a lover of free-dom was passionately interested in America—its alligators, mosqui-toes, and savanna cranes; its "government *of* the people, and *for* the people"; its Wild Indians; and especially the freedom of some "cottag'd dell" on the banks of the Susquehanna where he and his friends might form an equalitarian society of intellectual farmers, "Pantisocrats," far from "the shame and anguish" of Britain at war with republican France. In 1794, when he proposed a tavern toast to George Washing-ton, he was at the height of whiggish enthusiasm and indiscretion. In 1809, fifteen years later, in an article on Spanish resistance to Na-poleon, he defended the idea of a popular junta by pointing out that Washington could not have united the insurgent Americans without the support of a Congress. In the years between, he wrote a great body of political verse and prose; yet in all his published work there is surprisingly little mention of the United States or of its leaders.

A rare exception is his reply to an apologist for Napoleon, who was arguing that no *new* government could afford to permit freedom of the press: "Did the writer never hear of the United States of America?" From the meagerness of such allusions in his own writ-ings, Coleridge's own readers are at times tempted to ask him the same question. Even the name Washington occurs in the indexes of the largest studies of Coleridge only once or twice or not at all. Never-theless some sort of treatise could be assembled of Coleridge's thoughts about Americans. And no one has supposed that Coleridge

* Reprinted from the *Bulletin of The New York Public Library*, LXI (1957), 81–97, with some correction and condensation.

if called upon would have been unable to elaborate the declaration in an article on Napoleon in the London *Morning Post,* April 21, 1800: "If his virtues be as great as his genius, he may do for the old world what Washington has done for the new." Conjecture, however, is not text.

It is exciting, then, suddenly to discover a previously unnoticed group of essays on Washington, two of them unmistakably by Coleridge and full of his familiar concepts and mannerisms. Beginning three months earlier than the Napoleon article, they appeared in the same newspaper, the *Morning Post,* during the period when Coleridge was its chief writer of political essays.

The first of the new-found essays, published on January 27, is a brief but penetrating character study and eulogy of Washington called forth by the news of his death in December. It presents him as the unostentatious president of a republic but at the same time a "commanding genius." Two slight editorial paragraphs followed on ensuing days. Then a second long essay appeared March 25, inspired by the publication of Washington's Last Will and Testament. Both the longer essays meet our expectation of what Coleridge *would* say in praise of the first President of the land of "Peace and mild Equailty," the land of "wizard Passions" coexisting beside "Virtue calm" (to quote from his Pantisocracy poems). And in theme they lead logically to the April comparison of Washington to Napoleon, for both prepare the thesis that Washington had virtues as great as his genius and in more stable combination than Napoleon. Together they constitute a portrait of Washington which matches (and supplies points of contrast to) both the well-known portrait, published on March 19, of William Pitt, war minister of Britain, who was cordially loathed by Coleridge and the *Morning Post,* and the preliminary portrait of Napoleon Bonaparte which lies scattered in editorial paragraphs of March 4, 11, 13, 14, and 15.

The first Washington essay, though only now recovered, did not go unnoticed at the time, for as late as the following September people were hearing about it and writing to the editor, who could only reply that it was out of print—*Morning Post,* September 20, 1800: "TO CORRESPONDENTS: The Eulogy on General Washington appeared in this Paper some months ago."

One wonders why the Eulogy did not survive in the Coleridgean clipping file to be placed where it belonged in Sara Coleridge's edition of her father's *Essays on His Own Times.* The answer may lie in another discovery. Eleven years after its first printing in the *Morning*

24: Coleridge on Washington

Post I find that an almost identical reprint of the Eulogy appeared in the London *Courier*, August 16, 1811. Now in that very year Coleridge had committed himself, in May, to a weekly supply of articles to the *Courier*, and by autumn he had begun to fall back on old material. An "Allegoric Vision" that he had written in 1795 was used on August 31. Part of an essay on the price of grain, first printed in the *Morning Post* of October 3, 1800, was used on September 19. The reappearance of the Washington obituary in the *Courier* this August is additional evidence that Coleridge wrote the original essay. A line in the *Courier* identifying it as a reprint from the "*Morning Post* June 27, 1800"—a mistake for January 27—means probably that Coleridge handed in a clipping on which the date had been scrawled not quite legibly.

The circumstantial evidence for Coleridge's authorship of the two essays of 1800 is therefore splendid. What clinches the attribution is the internal evidence—not only the style, the nuances of political and psychological outlook, but also the intimate and intricate connections between these unknown essays and several of the known essays of Coleridge's written in the same early months of 1800.

In the first essay on Washington, January 27, Coleridge speaks of the difficulty of "analysing the character of a commanding genius" and then proceeds to surmount that difficulty. In the first essay on Bonaparte, March 11, he calls the French ruler "a man of various talent, of commanding genius, of splendid exploit" "seated on the throne of the Republic," though seated by foul means. Finally, in his portrayal of Pitt, March 19, he makes the devastating discovery that in *him* there is "no one proof or symptom of a commanding genius." In this and other respects the analyses of Pitt, Bonaparte, and Washington are complementary and contrastive; it is impossible to read them all together and doubt they are by the same hand. I speak now of the two larger Washington pieces; the two shorter ones are almost too brief to make any assertion about, though, since it was Coleridge's practice to undertake "all" the articles on the topics he was assigned (peace, the French Constitution, Ireland), we may suppose that once George Washington became his assignment he had at least a supervisory hand in all the paragraphs about him. It will be instructive, in any case, to follow the whole sequence in chronological order from the desk-view of an eighteenth-century editor.

The first adjustment we must make is to the absence of cable or radio communication:

December 14, 1799. George Washington dies at Mount Vernon.

January 23, 1800. The first rumor reaches London, too late for the newspapers. At the coffeehouses, sources of journalistic "intelligence," all is confusion.

January 24. Some papers print obituaries, but the liberal *Morning Post* is unwilling to believe unwelcome rumors: "It was very currently reported in the city yesterday, that intelligence had been received of the death of General Washington on the 15th ult. after a short illness of thirty hours. Advice was yesterday received on the arrival of several vessels from America, and the intelligence was given as certain . . . but . . . we could not trace the report to its source, and we do not feel warranted in stating as a fact so great a loss to the cause of liberty, at a moment when it stands in need of every assistance." The editor and proprietor, Daniel Stuart, is probably also scurrying around for something to print to do the occasion justice. He could not prod Coleridge to an immediate response; in fact Stuart would later complain, with some exaggeration, that the hardest thing to get out of Coleridge was a swift response to a sudden occasion. Note that when Coleridge does respond on the twenty-seventh he begins with a sigh at his own indolence in this respect. It would be easy to spin meaningless rhetorical remarks, he says, but a genuine eulogy is not easy, a true analysis of the commanding genius is not to be managed by any hack.

The evening *Courier* of January 24 carries a pithy seven-paragraph character study of Washington, drawn largely but without acknowledgment from the recently published *Travels through the states of North America during the years 1795, 1796, and 1797,* by Isaac Weld (see the third edition, London, 1800, I, 104–107).[1]

January 25, Saturday. "The melancholy account was brought by a vessel from Baltimore, which is arrived off Dover."[2] The *Morning Post* is "sorry to confirm the intelligence"—and probably sorry to have nothing to go with it but two paragraphs silently lifted from the *Courier* of the previous day.[3] The *Times* honestly publishes an extract

[1] [I had not seen this day's *Courier* but deduced its contents from reprintings. I now find that the character study consists of eight paragraphs following two paragraphs of introduction.]

[2] This sentence the *Post* lifted verbatim from the *Courier;* it constitutes the second news paragraph preceding the obituary essay cited in the previous footnote.

[3] I.e., two paragraphs of the eight-paragraph essay. Daniel Stuart, owner of the *Morning Post,* had purchased the evening *Courier* in 1799. He did not become actively concerned in its editing until 1803, but the two papers rather freely drew upon each other; they were probably printed in the same shop.

from Isaac Weld. Other papers including the *Sun* and the *General Evening Post* draw upon Weld or upon the Weldian character study without acknowledgment. The *Morning Chronicle* manages an apparently independent essay.

January 27, Monday. Coleridge, over the weekend, has constructed his own obituary panegyric, making some use of what the other newspapers have done, but also going back to Weld for something the others have all seen fit to leave out concerning a native but submerged violence in Washington's personality.

Coleridge had read "Isaac Weld's Travels" when they first came out; "I find them interesting," he told Southey in a letter of September 25, 1799, "—he makes the American appear a most degraded & vile nation."[4] That impression was never altogether erased, and now, while endorsing no such sweeping disparagement of the American nation, his interest was partly in the question how, in the character of their great leader, the Americans so transcended their potential wildness if not vileness. The original passage in Weld is worth quoting:

Few persons find themselves for the first time in the presence of General Washington . . . without being impressed with a certain degree of veneration and awe; nor do these emotions subside on a closer acquaintance; on the contrary, his person and deportment are such as rather tend to augment them. There is something very austere in his countenance, and in his manners he is uncommonly reserved. . . .

The height of his person is about five feet eleven [six feet three actually]; his chest is full; and his limbs, though rather slender, well shaped and muscular. His head is small, in which respect he resembles the make of a great number of his countrymen. His eyes are of a light grey colour; and, in proportion to the length of his face, his nose is long. Mr. Stewart, the eminent portrait painter, told me, that there are features in his face totally different from what he ever observed in that of any other human being; the sockets of the eyes, for instance, are larger than what he ever met with before, and the upper part of the nose broader. All his features, he observed, were indicative of the strongest and most ungovernable passions, and had he been born in the forests, it was his opinion that he would have been the fiercest man amongst the savage tribes. In this Mr. Stewart has given a proof of his great discernment and intimate knowledge of the human countenance; for although General Washington has been extolled for his great moderation and calmness, during the very trying situations in which he has so often been placed, yet those who have been

[4] *Collected Letters of Samuel Taylor Coleridge*, ed. E. L. Griggs (Oxford, 1956) I, 530.

acquainted with him the longest and most intimately, say, that he is by nature a man of a fierce and irritable disposition, but that, like Socrates, his judgment and great self-command have always made him appear a man of a different cast in the eyes of the world. He speaks with great diffidence, and sometimes hesitates for a word, but it is always to find one particularly well adapted to his meaning. His language is manly and expressive. . . .

The obituary writers seized upon the comparison to Socrates while deleting altogether the speculation about the potentially fierce Washington born amongst savage tribes. The essayist for the *Morning Chronicle* defined Washington's character as "a majestic pile" utterly lacking in any "wildness" or "eccentricity." Even the author of the character-study in the *Courier* toned down Weld's "strongest and most ungovernable passions" to "strongest passions" and then omitted everything until he came to the phrase "like Socrates." For Coleridge, on the other hand, the suggestion of a polarity of passions and calmness was a most valuable clue. His editorial stock in trade was the exhibition of motives and the induction of psychological "principles." So he knew how to make rich use of the conception that "self-command" was the secret of the commanding genius. The most striking evidence of Coleridge's authorship of this Washington obituary, indeed, is the preciseness with which it fits, in concept and nuance, alongside the other "commanding genius" essays which we have always known as his, the portraits of Napoleon and Pitt.

The other writers described Washington as a man above his age, aloof from his time: but this was surely a mistaken view of the paragon of Democracy, of the man whose head resembled "the make of a great number of his countrymen." Coleridge swept the idea aside, and made the gesture of sweeping it aside serve for his own concluding theme, in this and subsequent essays. On the lookout for that which "fraternises man" (*Religious Musings*) he discerned sincerity, not hypocrisy, in Washington's "humanness" and "complete union of himself with the mass of his fellow-citizens" (I quote the March essay). But the core of the Coleridge essays is a product of psychological omniscience that seems to owe little to the factual sources but rather to come naturally from a poet and literary philosopher who made great use of a theory of the imagination as a shaping power. In a flash of genial revelation he saw that Washington had been a man of great imagination "capable of bodying forth lofty undertakings." (On March 19 he would define Pitt, on the other hand, as a leader *lacking* "the imagination to body forth" "one *single image*" of real value for his nation.)[5] Washington also must have "possessed from his earliest years" a "prophetic consciousness of his future being" and "a deep sense of internal power." (The extreme contrast here is that Pitt "was cast, rather than grew" so that *his* sense of power was *not* internally derived, since he had been brought up in the mold of his father's ambition with "a conscious predestination" from without that "compelled" him "into that which he *was to be.*")

On the whole the portrait of George Washington imagined by Coleridge comes out looking rather like his friend William Wordsworth, who felt himself a "dedicated Spirit" to whom "the unity of all," and the means of bodying forth lofty imaginings, had been revealed. A first impression, at any rate, is that Coleridge makes Washington seem more like Wordsworth than a cautious reading of the historical evidence would warrant. At least he sees the patriot General as a genius who achieves his successes in the way that a creative poet does; a full gloss on the Coleridgean analysis of Washington's genius would take us through the gamut of Coleridge's pronouncements on the esemplastic power.

Here is the first Washington essay, printed as the leading Monday editorial, deftly attached to a fresh item of Sunday news:

THE MORNING POST

LONDON. Monday, January 27.

The officers and sailors of the American ships in the port of London, yesterday paid a just respect to the memory of their deceased friend General Washington, by attending at St. John's Church, Wapping, in naval mourning. We dare not record his death without attempting to pronounce his panegyric. This mournful office is both our duty and our inclination; but we confess, that we feel our powers oppressed into sluggishness by the sense of its difficulty. To build up goodly phrases into rhetorical periods, and attach to the name of Washington all splendid generalities of praise, were indeed an easy task. But such vague declamation, at all times an unworthy offering to the memory of the departed, is peculiarly unappropriate to the sober and definite greatness of *his* character. Tranquil and firm he moved with one pace in one path, and neither vaulted [nor][6] tot-

---

[5] *Morning Post*, March 19, 1800, reprinted in *Essays on His Own Times*, II, 327.

[6] *Morning Post* reads "or," corrected to "nor" in *Courier* reprint of August 16, 1811.

tered.[1] He possessed from his earliest years that prophetic consciousness of his future being, which both makes and marks the few great men of the world, who combine a deep sense of internal power, with imaginations capable of bodying forth lofty undertakings. His feelings, constitutionally profound and vehement (and which, if uncounteracted by the majesty of his views, would have been wild and ferocious), gave him a perpetual energy; while the necessity of counteracting and curbing these feelings gradually disciplined his soul to that austere self-command, which informed and moulded the whole man, his actions, his countenance, his every gesture. Thus, sympathising inwardly with man, as an ideal, not with men as companions, he perfected in himself that character which all are compelled to feel, though few are capable of analysing, the character of a commanding genius. His successes, therefore, great in themselves, and sublime in the effects which followed them, were still greater, still more sublime, from the means, by which they were attained. It may be affirmed, with truth, that if fortune and felicity of accident were to resume from his successes all which *they* had contributed, more would remain to him than perhaps to any man equally celebrated: his successes were but the outward and visible language of that which had pre-existed in his mind. But this character and these praises others have approached or attained, who, great in the detail of their conduct for the purposes of personal ambition, had subdued and fettered their feebler passions, only to become more entirely the slaves of a darker and more pernicious influence.—In Washington this principle and habit of self-subjugation never degenerated into a *mere* instrument; it possessed itself of his whole nature; he ripened his intellectual into moral greatness, intensely energetic yet perseveringly innocent, his hope, the happiness of mankind; and God, and his own conscience, his end! Hence among a people eminently querulous and already impregnated with the germs of discordant parties, he directed the executive power firmly and unostentatiously. He had no vain conceit of being himself all; and did those things only which he only could do. And finally, he retired, his Country half reluctant, yet proud in the testimony which her Constitution and liberty received from his retirement. He became entirely the husband and the master of his family: and the lines which Santeuil composed for the statue of the great Condé in the Gardens of Chantilly were yet more applicable to the Father and Hero of the American Republic.

> Quem modo pallebant fugitivis fluctibus amnes
> Terribilem bello, nunc docta per otia princeps
> *Pacis amans,* laetos dat in hortis ludere fontes.

[1] On the human "propensity of moving in one path," see Coleridge's *Philosophical Lectures*, ed. Kathleen Coburn (London, 1949) 339, 341; also his letter of October 14, 1797 (*Collected Letters*, I, 350); and his play *Osorio* V.i. 8–9.

24: Coleridge on Washington

Washington thought, felt, and acted in and for his age and Country; the same temperance presided over his opinions as his actions. He sympathised with the moral and religious feelings of the great mass of his fellow-citizens, and was that sincerely, which others assuming politically have betrayed hypocrisy, when they meant to have exhibited condescending greatness. He neither rushed before his age and Country, nor yet attempted to under-act himself; his actions, from the least to the greatest, he inspired with one high and sacred charm, by being always in earnest! Posterity will adjudge to him the title of GREAT with more sound and heart-felt suffrage, because he appeared no greater!

A characteristic mark of Coleridge's authorship is the imaginative control of a common metaphor, first fixing the image ("firm he moved with one pace in one path"), then making precise use of it ("neither vaulted nor tottered") and then keeping it to govern the final paragraph ("neither rushed before his age and Country, nor . . ."). Also characteristic is the advertisement of his ability to treat a theme of "sober and definite greatness" in appropriately sober and definite style. If we are to be "compelled to feel" the greatness of both theme and treatment, we must sense that both are capable of being analyzed as more imaginatively organic than the mere building up of "goodly phrases into rhetorical periods" of "vague declamation." In the March essay on Pitt we are told that the essence of Pitt's *lack* of genius, political and otherwise, is his being "elemented in words and generalities," "specious generalities" and "general and abstract phrases," which build up a "super-structure" but prevent the man from being conversant with "realities" and "images of realities" (a phrase garbled in the 1850 reprinting).

The lines from Jean de Santeul, Latin poet of the Renaissance, may have been gathered when Coleridge was preparing a volume of translations of modern Latin poetry. The great Condé, in retirement at Chantilly after a brilliant military career, decrees pleasant fountains as if in Xanadu.[8] If there is an element of the "august & innocent" Wordsworth in this portrait,[9] there is also an element of Coleridge as he wished to be, perseveringly innocent yet as intensely energetic as Napoleon. There is also something of his later conception of Luther,

---

[8] Rough translation: "He at whose aspect, terrible in war, the very streams with their fugitive floods recently turned pale, now, a peace-loving leader, in cultivated leisure, decrees merry fountains to play in gardens." The text Coleridge used (there are numerous variants) is to be found in *Poetarum Hujus Seculi Principis Opera Poëtica* (Paris, 1695), 292.

[9] See *Collected Letters*, II, 1033–1034.

"at the head of an army of the faithful" and "so possessed by his own genius that he acted poems not wrote them."[10]

The picture of the "querulous" American people and their "discordant parties," presided over by a genius whose own "temperance" came from the fact that the "majesty of his views" presided inwardly over his own "profound and vehement" feelings, elucidates the paradox in Coleridge's characterization of the Americans in an editorial of September 25, 1802:

> The Americans are neither very amiable nor very enlightened, as a people; yet what Government on earth has presented such continued proofs of wisdom, moderation, and love of Peace? Nothing can be conceived more violent than the contentions of the Candidates, nothing more calm, dignified, and incurable [*sic*] than the conduct of the same men as Legislators and Magistrates.[11]

For the next two months the *Morning Post* kept an eye out for Washingtoniana. On February 5, in an editorial paragraph that may have had Coleridge's attention but bears no particular marks of his style, belated news of the December mourning of "the various classes of Americans" led to the observation that friends of freedom and virtue everywhere had been often "refreshed and soothed" by the sight of "Washington's virtuous and honest policy." On February 8 the *Post* reported the effort of a stubborn democrat named Felix Faulcon to make a speech of mourning for Washington in the new "Legislative Body" of France, which was empowered only to vote without speaking; the *Post* did not report the various official demonstrations of mourning decreed by Napoleon. On March 6 a page was given to a Funeral Oration on Washington "by Major General Lee, Member of Congress from Virginia."

Coleridge, meanwhile, had undertaken to dramatize the issues of the time in a pair of analytical portraits of the opposed national leaders, Pitt and Bonaparte. When the *Morning Post* of January 24 spoke of Washington's death as "so great a loss to the cause of liberty, at a moment when it stands in need of every assistance," the moment meant was the critical pause in the war between England and France following Napoleon's rise to political supremacy as Chief Consul. The most anxious question in the editorial essays written by Coleridge at the rate of two or three a week from early December to mid-April was whether Bonaparte would display virtues commensurate with his

[10] *Philosophical Lectures*, 309.
[11] *Morning Post*, Sept. 25, 1802; cf. *Essays*, II, 498.

genius or would prove to be one of those who, with Washington's "principle and habit of self-subjugation" but without his "moral greatness" or his hope for the happiness of mankind, had "subdued and fettered their feebler passions, only to become more entirely the slaves of a darker and more pernicious influence" (to quote the essay of January 27).

The first essay on Washington alludes thus to Bonaparte without naming him. In the final essay on Bonaparte, April 21, Coleridge still expresses a hope that the French commanding genius "may do for the old world what Washington has done for the new." But the dark hints have grown darker week by week, and the particular poignancy of the nostalgic eulogies of Washington derives from the sense of romantic irony, the feeling that the more clearly we see "*his* virtues" the more vainly we seek them in the great men now living. Pitt, the great man of Britain, is seen as a mere factotum mouthing specious and abstract phrases. The promised series of essays on "Pitt and Bonaparte" begins with "Pitt" March 19—and ends there, except for the unheralded and somewhat incidental discussion in April.[12] What does follow Pitt is Washington again—a happier subject than that "dwarf" of France. Unfortunately for Coleridge's reputation up to the present, it has never been known that he wrote anything more in this period, and the failure to fulfill his promise, "To-morrow of Bonaparte," has become a classic instance of his authorial "sluggishness."

As a matter of record we can watch, in the daily notices above the masthead, the *intention* to write of Bonaparte being defeated by the *necessity* to write of Washington.

March 21, Friday. "The CHARACTER of BONAPARTE, and many valuable favours, are omitted for want of room," and the room is given (three columns or about half the day's free space) to a transcript of "The Will of General George Washington," concluded the following Monday. A brief introduction is printed as the day's leading editorial, and it is probably to be attributed to Coleridge, since he had undertaken, as we shall see, to follow the publication of the Will with a special essay on it.

Leading editorial, possibly by Coleridge:

Yesterday we received sets of American papers, and from one of the 13th ult. we have extracted the first part of the Will of General Washington.

[12] [I now doubt whether Coleridge wrote the essay of April 21, though he probably supplied some suggestions for it. See essay No. 3, above, "The Signature of Style."]

The second part, which we shall give to-morrow, disposes of his most valuable property among his relations, and is less of a public or interesting nature. The first duty which General Washington felt appears to have been that of giving freedom to his Slaves, who, on account of intermarriages, could not, however, be set at liberty till the death of his wife. It is reported, that Mrs. Washington has since freed them all. The will next shews the General's anxiety for the education of the American youth; imputing much of the immorality and political feuds to the sending of the young men abroad to foreign Universities for their instructions, General Washington proposes to create an University in America, and bequeathes the property given him by the State as a reward for his services (a gift he never accepted) to found the institution.——It is deeply interesting to read of the disposition of the Earl of Buchan's box, of the pistols of La Fayette, &c.—but above all of the swords left to General Washington's nephews, not to be unsheathed but in self-defence, or in defence of their country.

March 25, Tuesday. After the printing of the second part of the Will on Monday, all these deeply interesting matters, from liberated and unliberated slaves to sheathed swords, are discussed on Tuesday in another and longer essay which is constructed as an extension and variation upon the themes of the original eulogy of January 27.

Now Coleridge finds all Washington's virtues expressed in the outward form of his Will and Testament, "all arising naturally and unostentatiously" and giving proof that the wisdom of a commanding genius can be united in one person with the "humanness" of a citizen among fellow-citizens. Once again it is Coleridge the literary critic and moral philosopher who finds in the style an organic "manifestation" of the man; who sees in this "last deliberate act of a life so beneficial to the human race" a "composition" of the sort to be expected from the genius whose "successes were but the outward and visible language of that which had pre-existed in his own mind."

The organic relations between this and the first essay, the similarities of sentiment and image, scarcely need pointing out; nor is there reason to elaborate further the many consistencies in thought and style between these essays and the authenticated works of Coleridge.

Feature editorial, certainly by Coleridge:

GENERAL WASHINGTON.

We would fain believe that the whole of General Washington's Will has been perused by no man without some portion of that calm and pleasureable elevation which uniformly leaves us better and wiser beings. It would have been deeply interesting, considered only as the last deliberate act of a life so beneficial to the human race; but independently of this sublime association, it is in itself an affecting and most instructive composition. Like all the former manifestations of his character, it gives proof that a true and solid greatness may exist, and make itself felt, without any admixture of wildness, without any obtrusive appeals to the imagination: it gives proof, consolatory and inspiriting proof, how many virtues, too often deemed incompatible with each other, a thinking and upright mind may unite in itself. It were scarcely too much to affirm of this Will, that all the main elements of public and private morals, of civil and domestic wisdom, are conveyed in it either directly or by implication. It is, indeed, no less than an abstract of his opinions and feelings, as a PATRIOT, FRIEND, and RELATION; and all arising naturally and unostentatiously out of the final disposal of a fortune not more honourably earned than beneficently employed. Appertaining to his character, as the American PATRIOT, more exclusively than the other pages of his Will, is the plan and endowment of a CENTRAL UNIVERSITY. The motives which impelled the General to this bequest, he has stated with such beauty and precision, as scarcely leave any thing for the philosopher or the eulogist to add. We can only subjoin to the advantages so ably enumerated, that such an institution must be eminently serviceable to America, as having a direct tendency to soften and liberalize the too great commercial spirit of that country, in as far as it will connect the pleasures and ambition of its wealthier citizens, in the most impressible period of life, with objects abstract and unworldly; and that while by friendships and literary emulations it may remove local jealousies, it will tend to decorate the American character with an ornament hitherto wanting in it, viz. genuine local attachments, unconnected with pecuniary interests.[13]

Of a mixed nature, partly belonging to the patriot, and partly to the master of a family, is the humane, earnest, and solemn wish concerning the emancipation of the slaves on his estate. It explains, with infinite delicacy and manly sensibility, the true cause of his not having emancipated them in his life time; and should operate as a caution against those petty libellers, who interpret the whole of a character by a part, instead of interpreting a part by the whole. We feel ourselves at a loss which most to admire in this interesting paragraph, the deep and weighty feeling of the general principle of universal liberty; or the wise veneration of those fixed laws in society, without which that universal liberty must for ever remain

---

[13] It distressed Coleridge's friend John Thelwall, and probably Coleridge himself, to think that America, the ideal country for utopian plans of retirement, was developing such "avidity for commercial aggrandisement" as to make one "tremble at the consequences . . . upon posterity" (*Monthly Magazine*, Sept. 1799, p. 618).

impossible, and which, therefore, must be obeyed even in those cases, where they *suspend* the action of that general principle; or, lastly, the affectionate attention to the particular feelings of the slaves themselves, with the ample provision for the aged and infirm. Washington was no "architect of ruin!"

In the bequests to his friends, the composition evidences the peculiar delicacy and correctness of his mind. The high value which he attached to his old friend, Dr. Franklin's legacy of the gold-headed cane, by bequeathing it, and it alone, to his brother, Charles Washington; the spy-glasses, left, with the modest parenthesis, "because they will be useful to them where they live;" yet not without stamping the value on those precious relicts, as having been useful to himself in the deliverance of his country; the wisdom of remitting the box to Lord Buchan, with the gentle implication of the impracticability and impropriety of performing the conditions, with which the box had been originally accompanied; that reverence for the primary designation of a gift, implied in the words "agreeably to the original design of the Goldsmiths' Company of Edinburgh," and which words were besides necessary, in order to prevent the interpretation, that he had remitted it from inability to find any man in his own country equally deserving of it with the Earl; the bequest of the bible, and of the swords, the first without annotation, the last with the solemnity of a christian hero; all and each of these we have dwelt upon, as evidences of a mind strong and healthful, yet with a fineness and rapidity of the associating power, seldom found even in those who derive sensibility from nervous disease. The gratitude, the deep and immortal gratitude, displayed in the declaration of the motives of his bequest to his nephew, Bushrod Washington, is of a still higher class of excellence; and the virtue is individualised, and has a new interest given it, by his attention to the very letter of an old promise, no longer in force. The accuracy with which the estates are marked out will aid the distant posterity of the present Americans, in their reverential pilgrimages to the seat of their great PATER PATRIAE. The attachment which he has shewn to all his relations; the provisions he has made for them all; and the attention to honourable causes of local preferment in these provisions; are circumstances highly noticeable. Highly noticeable too is the disjunction of this family attachment from that desire of the aggrandisement of some one branch of the family, so commonly adherent to it. He has weakened by evidence the best and almost the only argument for primogeniture, *in new countries.* One fact strikes us particularly in the perusal of this Will.—Of all Washington's numerous relations, not one appears as a placeman or beneficiary of the government—not one appears to have received any thing from their kinsman as President and Influencer of the United States, yet all have evidences of the zeal and affection of the President, as their kinsman. *It is not so every where.* There is something in the arrangement of the will, beyond any example, which we recollect, instructive and judicious. He commences with a positive or perfect duty, the payment of duties; then goes immediately to the most respectful and affectionate attention to his wife, which becomes more intellectual, more moral, from the circumstance, which he after notices, of his having remained without issue; he proceeds to his concerns as master of his family, and provides for the emancipation of his slaves; and having finished his most immediate and *most* sacred offices, viz. the domestic duties, he rises, *then,* and *not till then,* into the PATRIOT; and founds a central University. After his own family comes his country, and then his relations by consanguinity not of his own family—after these his friends; and all those whom fellowship in arms, or old acquaintance had endeared to him; and last of all, he proceeds to the circumstantial disposal of his estate. Throughout the whole, there reigns a *humanness* of feeling, a complete union of himself with the mass of his fellow-citizens, so as even to avoid references to any public characters in that country; and above all, an ardent wish for improvement, combined with reverential observance, and affectionate awe for present and existing customs and feelings. But Washington was too great a man to court singularity. The dwarf, that steps aside from the crowd, and walks by himself, may gain the whole crowd to turn and stare at him—Washington could attract their admiration, while he moved on with them, and in the midst of them.

In this peroration every note that is taken over from the first essay is pitched a dramatic range higher. The common sympathy becomes "a *humanness* of feeling, a complete union of himself with the mass of his fellow-citizens." The moving with one pace and neither rushing before nor under-acting becomes, still at the same pace, an attractive moving "on with them, and in the midst," while the retrograde motion, previously only suggested in "neither vaulted nor tottered" "neither rushed before," is now bodied forth in the dwarf that steps aside, walks by himself, and gets stared at—an image lingering in the author's mind when, two years later, he compares the "new Caesar" of France (about whom his hopeful doubts have fled) to the ancient "Caligulas, Claudiuses, Neros" with their trembling underlings (the crowd turned slaves) and sees no hope but in a new deluge of "men and freemen" that will "sweep away slaves and dwarfs."[14] Still later Coleridge recurs to the piety of Washington in retirement and the contrast between Washington's virtues and Napoleon's now manifestly iniquitous ambition:

[14] *Morning Post,* Sept. 21, 1802; see *Essays,* ɪɪ, 481–482.

Evidence for Authorship

If when a Washington, having purchased the *independence* of his country by far-sighted patience and enduring courage as a warrior, and then established and watched over her *freedom* with the wisdom of parental love, unmoved by the entreaties of his fellow-citizens, lest by yielding to them he should form a precedent injurious to their posterity, retires to the unambitious duties of private life, and disclaiming all titles but those given by domestic love and reverence, bows at length his dear and venerable head to the emancipating angel, and restores his spirit to that great Being, whose goodness he had both adored and imitated—if for such a man we collect all terms of honour and affection, and fondly involve his name in phrases expressive of his virtues [here Coleridge is virtually describing his own editorial eulogies], must we remain mute, and stifle the feelings which the *contrast* to all this must needs awaken in us? and even though this contrast should furnish a humiliating proof, that the slaves of iniquitous ambition can carry guilt to a height which dwarfs the best virtues of the best and most heroic of men in the comparison?[15]

This synoptic interminable sentence is related in several ways to the earlier essays. "Slaves" and "dwarfs" appear once more, functioning differently as words, but still in association with the contrast of Washington and Napoleon. And in many details of implication and connection which it would be tedious to demonstrate, this recapitulation of the qualities of the patient warrior retiring to unambitious domesticity is so tightly connected with the first eulogy and the essay on Washington's Will as to constitute an unconscious signature of their common authorship. Should any further testimony seem necessary, a more voluminous demonstration could easily be made of the idiosyncratic Coleridgean themes in the essay on the Will: the importance of interpreting "the whole of a character by a part, instead of interpreting a part by the whole"; the wisdom of venerating fixed laws "even in those cases, where they *suspend* the action" of "the general principle of universal liberty"; the dubiety of the "only argument for primogeniture, *in new countries*"; the evidence in Washington's strong mind of "a fineness and rapidity of the associating power, seldom found even in those who derive sensibility from nervous disease"; and, apropos of the plan of a central University, the good Wordsworthian as well as Coleridgean argument that campus life would soften the querulous if not incurable Americans by attaching their youthful impressions to "objects abstract and unworldly" rather than "pecuniary."

[15] *Courier*, Dec. 21, 1809; see *Essays*, II, 644–645.

24: Coleridge on Washington

In these and other reaches of their common path, there was manifestly a great meeting of minds when the editorial writer for the London *Morning Post*, though he had privately fed on honey-dew and drunk the milk of Paradise, perused with calm and pleasurable elevation the "last deliberate act," the "affecting and most instructive composition," of the great *Pater Patriae*. It left him not a sadder but a "better and wiser" man.

Coleridge on
Addington's Administration*

By John Colmer

IN a note in *PMLA* for June 1954, Mrs. David Glickfield summarized
the evidence for attributing to Coleridge the authorship of six articles
in the *Morning Post* in addition to those already included in the first
two volumes of Sara Coleridge's collection of miscellaneous prose
works, *Essays on His Own Times*.[1] At the end of one of these newly
discovered articles, one which discussed certain rumored Ministerial
changes and which appeared on February 23, 1802, Coleridge promised to analyze "the character and proceedings of the Minister" in
the next day's issue. The Minister in question was Addington. Having
searched the *Morning Post* files up to March 16, 1802, Mrs. Glickfield
concluded that this was one of Coleridge's characteristic unfulfilled
promises. In fact, an article entitled "Mr Addington's Administration" appeared on March 22, and evidence exists for attributing its
authorship to Coleridge.

It is true that he was not in London when the article was published, but this is of little consequence, as Mrs. Glickfield herself
admits in considering other articles. It is certain that a number of
Coleridge's contributions to the *Morning Post* were written when the
poet was living away from London; these were sent to the editor by
post. The three essays comparing the "Present State of France with
that of Rome under Julius and Augustus Caesar" were written in this
fashion, as were the two "Letters to Mr. Fox."[2] In addition it seems
likely that after visits to London he may have left articles with Stuart

---

* Reprinted from *The Modern Language Review*, LIV (1959), 67–72, with
permission of author and publisher.

[1] *PMLA*, LXIX (1954), 681–685.

[2] No. 1 was published on Sept. 21, 1802, no. 2 on Sept. 25, and no. 3 on
Oct. 2 (*Essays on His Own Times*, ed. Sara Coleridge, II, 478–514). The letters
To Mr Fox appeared on Nov. 4 and 9, 1802 (II, 552–585).

on the understanding that the editor should publish them or not at his discretion. Coleridge paid a short visit to London in the winter of 1801–1802 and contributed a number of articles to Stuart's paper. By March 19, however, he was with the Wordsworths in the Lake Country. "He seemed half-stupified," noted Dorothy; and there is no evidence to suggest that on his return to the Lakes his thoughts were directed to politics. The chief subject of conversation was "of going abroad."[3] The essay on "Mr Addington's Administration," published on March 22, had, I think, been written in London and left behind with Stuart.

Although the only external evidence for attributing this essay to Coleridge is the promise to write on this subject made at the end of the article of February 23, the internal evidence is strong.[4] The whole character study turns on the distinction that Coleridge had begun to make between genius and talent. The most systematic presentation of the distinction is to be found in *The Friend*.[5] Genius was there held to be essentially creative and showed itself as "originality in intellectual construction"; talent, on the other hand, was said to be "the comparative facility of acquiring, arranging, and applying the stock furnished by others and already existing in books or other conservatories of intellect."[6] The distinction was first made in the *Morning Post* essays devoted to Napoleon and Pitt, where it acted as a philosophical yardstick to measure their characters and respective abilities:[7] Napoleon was the man of genius, Pitt the man of talent. With great ingenuity Coleridge demonstrated how the education that Pitt had received from his father, an education in words, had inevitably destroyed genius and fostered talent. Pitt thus acquired a premature and unnatural dexterity in the combination of words, "which," declares Coleridge, "must of necessity have diverted his attention from present objects, obscured his impressions, and deadened his genuine feelings."[8] And to this form of training he attributed the two main weaknesses in the man: his love of abstractions; and the coldness of his affections seen alike in his private and public life. He held that

[3] J. D. Campbell, *Samuel Taylor Coleridge*, 128–129.

[4] I accept Mrs. Glickfield's claim that Coleridge wrote the essay of Feb. 23, 1802.

[5] *The Friend*, Section 2, Essay 1 (Bohn ed., 274–283).

[6] *Ibid.*, 280.

[7] For essays on Napoleon see *Essays on His Own Times*, II, 313–319, 384–388. 403–408; for the character of Pitt, II, 319–329.

[8] II, 320.

the generalizations propounded by the man of genius were based on a coherent system of thought, those of the man of talent were empty abstractions. In Pitt's case they were "Generalities—Atheism and Jacobinism—phrases, which he learnt from Mr. Burke, but without learning the philosophical definitions and involved consequences, with which that great man accompanied these words."[9] Pitt's method of thought and speech was neatly summed up as "Abstractions defined by abstractions! Generalities defined by generalities!"

Nothing in the actual character of Pitt or in his actions can fully explain Coleridge's bitter hostility toward him; it is only explicable if one recognizes that he became a symbol for all that Coleridge most despised in the world of contemporary politics: the whole machinery of secret influence and intrigue disguised behind the façade of a "decorous profession of religion"; the overbalance of the commerical interest; and the whole system of repression that had resulted from the "panic of property"[10] caused by the French Revolution. He came, too, in some sense to symbolize in his person not only a whole political system but an alien philosophy of life. He was the embodiment of Lockian empiricism; or to use a phrase from a later letter, he was a perfect "Little-ist," a man of mere talent.[11] Circumstances had molded him; he lacked the necessary imagination to mold circumstances. "He was cast, rather than grew,"[12] declared Coleridge; and behind that epigram lies a distinction that possessed the utmost importance for him. For the application of the distinction made between organic and mechanic growth to politics in general he was indebted to Burke, from whom he had learned to revere the processes of slow growth and the wisdom of antiquity, but for its application to men he was drawing on his own acute psychological observations; and it will be noticed that the standards that Coleridge applied to statesmen and works of art were related; men who were the product of outward circumstance and not of a principle working from within fell

[9] II, 326.

[10] *The Friend*, Section 1, Essay 5, 137, and repeated elsewhere, for example, *Biographia Literaria*, I, 142–143.

[11] Letter to T. Poole, March 23, 1801 (*Collected Letters of Samuel Taylor Coleridge*, ed. E. L. Griggs, II, 708–709).

[12] II, 320. His view of Pitt did not change. See MS note, *The Stateman's Manual* (1816), Brit. Mus. Ashley 2850, p. 52. "Mere Experience—I mean a Statesman so endowed—unenlightened by Philosophy is Cyclops with one eye, and that in the back of his head. Such a statesman was MR PITT—hinc naturae lacrymae!"

into the same category as works of art in which only a mechanical as opposed to an organic form could be detected.

The essay "Mr Addington's Administration" begins with a reference to the category "men of talent," actually to "men of small talent." "We easily forget, or forgive, or perhaps overlook," says the writer, "the faults and errors of men of small talent." This fact, according to the essay, explains why Addington's administration had not been considered objectionable by those who had been bitterly opposed to that of his predecessor, Pitt. The essay then illustrates the writer's attitude toward a "man of small talent," and forms a companion piece with Coleridge's "masterly and unanswerable"[13] character study of Pitt, which had appeared two years earlier in the same paper and had caused something of a sensation.[14] The writer noted how Addington imitated Pitt in debate.

There is a difference, however, between him and his model in this particular. Mr Pitt puzzles his audience by his ingenuity, Mr Addington by his confusion. The one renders himself unintelligible by his sophistry; the other is not understood, because that which is not clearly conceived, can never be clearly and definitely expressed. He never displays dexterity in debate, expansion or vigour of mind, a strong discriminating power, originality of thought, or richness of fancy. His intellect is too short-sighted to see beyond the point immediately before him, and hence, in the case of complexity, it is mere chance if one part of his argument does not contradict the other.

He felt that it was a national disaster that the destiny of the country had been placed in such unsuitable hands.

This is, perhaps, the most critical aera in our history, and it will require the most skilful talents to carry us through it. That Mr Addington is equal to the task, standing as he does, without system or principles to guide his conduct, embracing to-day what he rejected yesterday, confounded by the least difficulty, a Tory one hour, a Whig the next, changing with every new breeze; that he is fit to guide the helm no man of sense will believe.

Mr. Addington had made the dangerous experiment of being "all things unto all men in hopes that all men would be of one mind and temper to him," and had only succeeded in proving to the country his own unfitness for high office. With somewhat perverse ingenuity the writer suggested that his very faults had saved the country. Had

[13] *Complete Works of William Hazlitt*, ed. P. P. Howe, I, 112.
[14] Campbell, *Coleridge*, 108.

he possessed greater powers of mind "we should be now upon a dangerous sea with the double disadvantage of a bad pilot, and that pilot possessed of our utmost confidence." As it was, he had lost the people's confidence; they had recognized that he was a poor pilot. Two months later Canning reminded the nation that they would be obliged to look to Pitt if "again the rude whirlwind should rise." Then, prophesied Canning,

> The regrets of the good, and the fears of the wise,
> Shall turn to the pilot that weathered the storm.[15]

But his words and those of the leader writer in the *Morning Post* went unheeded: the incompetent Addington remained at the helm.

Apart from the comparison of the character of Addington with that of Pitt and the discussion of Addington's character in terms of the distinction between men of genius and men of talent, there is subsidiary evidence to support the contention that this essay was the work of Coleridge. In the article on rumored Ministerial changes, February 23, 1802, which Mrs. Glickfield has conclusively attributed to Coleridge and at the end of which had appeared the promise to analyze the "character and proceedings" of the Minister, Coleridge had introduced the conventional "ship of state" image. In the essay on Addington it is taken up again and developed with characteristic Coleridgean ingenuity. Further internal evidence can be found in the passage devoted to Addington's performance in debate. It reveals a concern for clear thought and expression and an acute understanding of the relation that exists between the two which is very reminiscent of the way in which, according to Charles Lamb, Coleridge had "combined political and grammatical science"[16] in an essay in the *Morning Post* attacking Lord Grenville's reply to the French overtures for peace in the winter of 1799–1800.[17] There he had asserted:

We think *in* words, and reason *by* words.—The man who, while he is speaking or writing his native language, uses words inaccurately, and combines

---

[15] On May 25, 1802, Pitt was persuaded to preside at a dinner to inaugurate the "Pitt Club." The club was the work of Canning, and for its first dinner he composed the verses, "The Pilot That Weathered the Storm," from which these lines are abstracted (H. W. V. Temperley, *George Canning* [1905], 64).

[16] *The Letters of Charles and Mary Lamb*, ed. E. V. Lucas (1905), I, 154.

[17] "Lord Grenville's Note," Jan. 22, 1800, *Essays*, I, 261–266. Sara Coleridge was unable to assign a definite date to this essay, as the issues for Jan. 22, 26, and 27 were missing from the file she consulted. Reference to a complete file in the British Museum shows that it appeared on Jan. 22.

them inconsequentially, may be fairly presumed to be a lax and slovenly reasoner. False reasoning is perhaps never wholly harmless; but it becomes an enormous evil, when the reasoning, and the passions which accompany it, are to be followed by the sacrifice of tens of thousands.[18]

Implicit throughout the whole examination of the British Note was the belief that language is the organ of thought and not its mere decoration. Implicit too was the belief that the character of a statesman might be accurately gauged by reference to his use of language. The same attitude toward language and thought is evident in the examination of Addington's character. Such reflections do not find a place in the ordinary day-to-day essays in the *Morning Post*. Their presence, taken together with the facts already noted, helps to strengthen the claim that Coleridge was the author of the *Morning Post* article entitled "Mr Addington's Administration" and that he did, in fact, fulfill the promise made in the earlier article of February 23, 1802.

[18] I, 261.

An Uncollected Early Poem by Coleridge[*]

By S. F. Johnson

IN the third number of Coleridge's *The Watchman*, March 17, 1796, there appear among others three poems signed respectively T., C., and S.[1] The poems are "Elegy," "The Hour When We Shall Meet Again," and "Lines on the Portrait of a Lady." In the standard edition of the poetical works, E. H. Coleridge includes the first two of these but nowhere mentions the third. He notes that the "Elegy" was first printed without signature in the *Morning Chronicle*, Sept. 23, 1794, reappeared in *The Watchman*, signed T., and was included in several collections of Coleridge's verse (1817, 1828, 1829, and 1834), although it was omitted from the edition of 1852 "as of doubtful origin."[2] He notes that "The Hour" was first printed in *The Watchman*, signed C., and included in the collections of 1797, 1803, 1844, and 1852.[3]

The third poem, signed S. in *The Watchman*, has never to my knowledge been reprinted, although Professor Lewis Patton has publicly wondered "if the third poem . . . is not also his."[4] Patton cites Coleridge's well-known partiality for his initials as the chief evidence for attribution. This partiality is apparent in the Silas Tomkyn (or Titus) Comberbacke escapade of 1793–1794, the signature C. T. S. at the end of *An Answer to "A Letter to Edward Long Fox, M.D."* (Bristol, 1795), and the transcription of his initials in the Greek alphabet, ΕΣΤΗΣΕ.[5]

---

[*] Reprinted from the *Bulletin of The New York Public Library*, LXI (1957), 505–507, with the author's permission.

[1] Pages 77–79.

[2] *The Complete Poetical Works* (Oxford, 1912), 69, 1178.

[3] *Ibid.*, 96, 1178.

[4] "The Coleridge Canon," *TLS* (Sept. 3, 1938), 570.

[5] See the present writer's "Reflection on the Consistency of Coleridge's Political Views," *Harvard Library Bulletin*, III (1949), 138 and plate Ib.

26: An Uncollected Poem by Coleridge

In his edition of *The Watchman*,[6] Patton cites the essential external evidence but adds that the internal evidence is inconclusive, since the poem is written in the insipid manner characteristic of much of the verse of the time. With the aid of *A Concordance to the Poetry of Samuel Taylor Coleridge*,[7] however, I have assembled some parallels from Coleridge's known early poems, sufficient I think to support attribution on internal evidence. The poem follows.

Lines on the Portrait of a Lady

Tender as the sweets of Spring
    Wafted on the Western gale,
When the breeze with dewy wing
    Wanders thro' the Primrose vale;

Tranquil as the hush of night
    To the Hermit's holy dream;
While the Moon with lovely light,
    Quivers on the ripling stream;

Cheerful as the Beams of Morn,
    Laughing on the Mountain's side;
Spotless as the Cygnet's form,
    Heaving on the silver'd Tide.

Who can paint this varied grace,
    Charms that mock the mimic art?
Yet, my Laura! these I trace,
    With the pencil of the Heart.
                         S.

Stanza I. "Tender" appears frequently in Coleridge, but "sweets" occurs only six times, four of these in early poems. "Wafted" occurs five times, all of them early, and once in a similar context: "And soft gales wafted from the haunts of spring." "Western gale" occurs twice. "Dewy" appears with "wing" or a synonym in two of the sonnets from the *Morning Chronicle*: "He bathes no pinion in the dewy light" and Fancy flings "Rich showers of dewy fragrance from her wing." "Primrose" is used twice, once in "primrose bower," but "vale" is frequently found.

---

[6] Dissertation, Yale University, 1937, p. 487 n. 31; Professor Patton has now prepared this edition for publication as Vol. II of *The Collected Coleridge* (London: Hart-Davis; New York: Bollingen, 1966).

[7] Ed. Sister Eugenia Logan (1940).

Stanza II. "Tranquil her soul, as sleeping Infant's breath" occurs in 1791. An "agèd Hermit in his holy dream" appears in Coleridge's contribution to Southey's *Joan of Arc*.[8] The moon's "lovely light" is mentioned in 1791. Ripples are rare in Coleridge, but water lilies ripple a stream in 1793, and there is another "rippling stream." The moon's light quivering on a stream is closely paralleled in 1793:

> What time the pale moon sheds a softer day
> Mellowing the woods beneath its pensive beam:
> For mid the quivering light 'tis ours to play,
> Aye dancing to the cadence of the stream.[9]

Stanza III. "Morn's first beams" are mentioned at the beginning of "Pain" (?1790), and "orient beam" occurs twice (?1795, 1796). "Cygnet" appears nowhere in the poems from which the *Concordance* was compiled, but swans heaving on water occur in two early poems: "Fair, as the bosom of the Swan / That rises graceful o'er the wave, / I've seen your breast with pity heave, / And *therefore* love I you, sweet Genevieve!" and "As these two swans together heave / On the gently-swelling wave. . . ."[10] "Silver" modifies lake or waters in several early poems (1792–1793), and a current "silver'd its smooth course beneath the Moon" in 1794.[11]

Stanza IV. The last stanza has relatively few parallels in Coleridge's other verse. He speaks of painting "the moment" and "the hour"; five of the eight adjectival uses of "mimic" are early; "Laura" appears in four poems (all by 1800); and "pencil" occurs twice, the first time in the phrase, "those purple berries / Her pencil!" The constructions "paint . . . grace" and "trace . . . charms" along with the rhyme, "grace . . . trace," occur in the first quatrain of the sonnet "To Mrs. Siddons," published in the *Morning Chronicle* in 1795 and now attributed to Coleridge by David V. Erdman.[12]

The verbal parallels here adduced strongly support the external evidence for Coleridge's authorship.[13] Those few passages for which

---

[8] 1796; later incorporated in "The Destiny of Nations," l. 331.

[9] "Songs of the Pixies," lines 85–88.

[10] "Lewti," 1798, as extensively reworked from the original by Wordsworth.

[11] MS variant of "Lines to a Beautiful Spring," l. 30.

[12] See essay No. 27, below.

[13] As a check on my method, I have looked for possible parallels in Lane Cooper's *Concordance to the Poems of William Wordsworth*. Except for the fact that Wordsworth does use "cygnet" a few times, the parallels are negligible; there are none of the verbal and phraseological echoes that are to be found in Coleridge's verse.

I have found no parallels are not impossibly remote from the normal manner of his early verse. The only elements that lack authority from the rest of his verse are the cygnet, the false rhyme in the third stanza ("Morn . . . form," but compare the rhyme, "thought . . . Court" in the third quatrain of the sonnet "To Mrs. Siddons," mentioned at note 12 above), and the rather infelicitous image of the heart's pencil. These may account for the fact that Coleridge never included the poem in a collection of his verse.

Newspaper Sonnets Put to the Concordance Test: Can They Be Attributed to Coleridge?*

By David V. Erdman

THE seven poems selected for examination had, of course, first passed the rough test of appearing to be potentially Coleridgean—externally, in date and place of publication; internally, in subject matter and style. It was then necessary to compare the questioned sonnets both with the known work of Coleridge and with the sonnets of contemporaries in the manner—William Lisle Bowles, Charlotte Smith, Charles Lloyd, Charles Lamb, and Robert Southey. . . .

What in effect a concordance does . . . is to demonstrate whether or not the words and word-clusters in the poem under consideration are idiosyncratic for the poet of the concordance. Thus, when we check a Coleridge poem against the Coleridge concordance,[1] we find (*a*) a few *unique* words, i.e. words not in the rest of Coleridge's verse; (*b*) a number of common or *neutral* words, i.e. words used elsewhere by Coleridge but without special prominence or distinctive association; and, nearly always, (*c*) a few words that may be called *magnetic*, i.e. words which stand in dynamic attractive relation to other words in Coleridge's vocabulary, so that our search in the concordance leads us to passages where clusters of associated words appear. To a limited extent, then, it is possible to make memory serve the same purpose, especially when we have a small body of works to consider. For example, with the questioned poems in mind (and on the desk) it does not take long to read through the published sonnets of Bowles in search of the positive evidence of associated word-clusters or the

* Excerpt from an article in the *Bulletin of The New York Public Library*, LXI (1957), 508–516, 611–620; LXII (1958), 46–49.

[1] *A Concordance to the Poetry of S. T. Coleridge*, ed. Eugenia Logan (1940).

negative evidence of a high proportion of unique words. But beyond that, the Coleridge concordance can be used in reverse; that is, we can employ it to test the poems of Bowles and Southey and the others. The striking result of a fairly extensive trial is that never do the sonnets of his contemporaries prove to be magnetic for the Coleridge vocabulary in any high degree. In an especially careful checking of Southey[2] only once did a sonnet of his ("The Evening Rainbow") pick up a cluster of associated words in the Coleridge concordance—and these turned out to belong to the sonnet "On Bala Hill," which was not Coleridge's in the first place but a variant of Southey's "Sonnet to Lansdown Hill" and had got into the concordance by mistake. (The parts of *The Fall of Robespierre* known to be Southey's had already been eliminated from consideration.) It seems a fair deduction that an anonymous poem that *does* elicit an impressive response from the concordance belongs to Coleridge—always provided we are considering only poems that are likely, from the external evidence of date and place of publication, to have been written by him, and assuming that we have ruled out the possibility of parody or deliberate imitation. (Even the deliberate imitator, however, does not prove capable of constructing a very strong magnet: witness the Shufflebottom poems by Southey and the contributions written by Lamb for Coleridge's signature.)

A drawback of this method is that it will not always work positively; that is to say, even for a known, signed Coleridge poem, the response of the concordance is sometimes largely unique and neutral, with no magnetic attraction to associated words. We might reject by the test a poem really his. And knowing this, we may be tempted to ascribe to Coleridge a poem that subjectively "feels like" Coleridge despite the weakness of magnetic evidence. On the other hand we must not forget that even the strongest of such evidence remains, in the final analysis, circumstantial.

My first candidate for admission into the Coleridge canon is a pseudonymous sonnet in the *Morning Chronicle* of January 29, 1795. During December and January, Coleridge had contributed a series of eleven numbered "Sonnets on Eminent Characters," signed "S.T.C.," and for good measure an "Address to a Young Jack-Ass," also signed. On January 29 directly under the last of the signed and numbered

[2] I am grateful to Charles H. Kegel for assisting me in a good deal of the spadework with Southey and Bowles.

sonnets (the one "To Richard Brinsley Sheridan, Esq.") I find an extra "Sonnet. To Mrs. Siddons," signed "FONTROSE." Now exactly a month earlier a sonnet to Mrs. Siddons had been printed in the series as Number VIII and signed "S.T.C." though actually supplied by Charles Lamb. The hypothesis suggests itself that this second or extra sonnet to the eminent Siddons is a belated one by Coleridge himself, who can sell it to the newspaper but must sign it with a pseudonym since his own name has already been attached to the one in the series.

January 29, 1795   London *Morning Chronicle*
SONNET.
———

TO MRS. SIDDONS.

'Tis not thy fascinating charms to trace,
    Thou sweet Enchantress! that I strike the shell;
'Tis not to paint each mild seductive grace,
    Which in thy polish'd form delights to dwell:

Thy brilliant eyes thro' Passion's maze that roll,
    Thy piercing glance, the lightning of thy smile,
Thy magic tones which thrill th'enraptur'd soul,
    And meek-ey'd anguish of her tears beguile.

No, SIDDONS! 'tis thy rich, creative *mind*,
    Thy bold conception of the fire-clad thought,
Which sportive wanders, free and unconfin'd,
    Where'er wild FANCY holds her fairy Court.

    May *real Sorrow* ne'er thy bosom swell—
Or thou e'er *feel* those Woes, which thou can'st *feign* so well!
                    —FONTROSE.

A large cluster of about twenty-five words leads us, with hardly any need of the concordance, to Coleridge's "Translation of Wrangham's 'Hendecasyllabi ad Bruntonam'" of the preceding autumn. Fontrose tells Mrs. Siddons that his aim is "not thy . . . charms to trace" nor to paint each grace in "thy polish'd form" nor in "Thy brilliant eyes thro' Passion's maze that roll . . . and meek-ey'd anguish of her tears beguile." Coleridge had addressed the younger actress, Miss Brunton, as a "Maid of unboastful charms" who was guided safely "through the maze" of youth and was mothered by "meek-eyed

Pity" who "lov'd thy kindred form to trace" while "Th'entrancéd Passions" kept vigil. The "lightning" of Siddons' smile seems a variant of the "raptures lighten'd from" Brunton's face. The matching words may be tabulated:

To Mrs. Siddons: charms to trace . . . Enchantress . . . grace . . . thy . . . form . . . eyes thro' Passion's maze that roll . . . lightning of thy smile . . . tones . . . thrill th'enraptur'd soul . . . meekey'd . . . tears . . . wanders . . . bosom . . . Woes.

Ad Bruntonam: charms . . . through the maze . . . soul . . . meek-eyed . . . bosom . . . thy . . . form to trace . . . smile wander'd . . . Tones . . . woe . . . thrill[ing] . . . Passions . . . raptures lighten'd . . . grace . . . tear's . . . roll . . . [chaste]-eyed . . . Enchant[ing minis]tress of . . . woe.

In other poems Coleridge had used Milton's "meek-eyed Peace" and added "meek-eyed Power." He never used "meek-eyed anguish" but often "anguished" eye or sigh; in seven of his eight uses of "anguish" he associates it with eyes or tears. In his current sonnet on Pitt we see "the Tear's . . . dew Roll its soft anguish" while the "tones" of Mercy are "meek."

As for the Enchantress Siddons' "polish'd form" and "brilliant eyes," Coleridge would shortly write of "Meek" Sara's "polish'd Sense" as comparable to a "serenely brilliant" star. He had once called upon a "Sorc'ress" to summon a "dewy brilliance" to the "eyes" of Love. And he knew many an "Enchantress"; in a year or so he would hail Mrs. Robinson as a "mild Enchantress." From the eyes that roll with piercing glance the concordance leads us to "Eyes whose holy glances roll" in contemporaneous lines "To a Young Lady." "Passion's maze" lines up with "Passion's stormy day" and "Passion's drooping Myrtles" in the present sonnet series and, in the following year, "youth's perilous maze" and "manhood's maze," and later "fancy's maze."

"Enraptured soul" is frequent in Coleridge and, surely, elsewhere. Few of the units of this vocabulary are unique with Coleridge. But again see how the cluster of "magic tones which thrill th'enraptured soul" draws us to another cluster in the contemporaneous lines "To the Rev. W. J. Hort," where we hear the "passion-warbled strain" of a flute teacher "still'd with magic spell to roll The thrilling tones that concentrate the soul." Here are the shared words:

To Mrs. Siddons: thy . . . each . . . form . . . dwell . . . Passion's . . . roll . . . Thy magic tones . . . thrill [th'en]raptur'd soul . . . [meek]-ey'd . . . tears . . . wander[s], free . . . wild.

To the Rev. Hort: thy . . . passion . . . each form . . .magic . . . roll . . . thrill[ing] tones . . . soul . . . [chaste]-eyed . . . [im]passion['d] . . . wild . . . Free[dom] . . . dwell . . . Wander[ing] . . . thrill[ing] . . . Thy . . . form . . . raptur'd tear.

Another of Coleridge's maze-piercers is his Godwin, in the ninth sonnet of the *Morning Chronicle* series, whose eye shoots *glances* keen "thro' the windings of oppression's dark machine"—even (note the magnetic association) during "Passion's stormy day."

The thought which sportive wanders free "where'er wild Fancy holds her fairy Court" leads to another cluster of associations. Siddons' "fire-clad thought" has come up from the "fire-clad meteors" that fly about in Coleridge's facetious "The Nose." In "Destiny of Nations" "Fancy" opens the mind that sees meteoric lights "dance sportively." "Wild Fancy" in an early poem is asked to prolong the "notes" of her "passion-warbled song" (cf. the "Hort" poem), and these become "mazy notes" in revision for the *Poems* of 1796. The mutual attraction among words in a cluster is surprisingly strong: if we look up any of these—fairy (faery), fancy, and even "where'er"—we are led to all the others; and they are frequently together in the Coleridge of this period. Indeed the unity of this whole maze of associaton is such that it is difficult to think of Fontrose as anyone but Coleridge himself. Could any imitator so implicate himself—and place at the center the Coleridgean "rich, creative *mind*"? The phrase is Coleridgean in content and impress—yet not to be found in the concordance: the poet will not use such a phrase more than once, as he will not build more than one "stately pleasure dome."

The contrast italicized in the closing couplet—real sorrow vs. feigned—is characteristic, and the concordance reminds us that Coleridge *would* italicize *feel*. (The alexandrine, by the way, is common for Coleridge, Bowles, and Southey.)

A rapid survey indicates that the vocabulary of this poem is largely shared by Bowles and Southey but only singly, for none of these particular clusters is to be found in their verse. On the other hand the number of unique words in this sonnet is even below the average for poems in the Coleridge corpus, and most of these ("fascinating," "strike," "seductive," "conception," "unconfin'd") do occur in other forms. "Strike the shell" (line 2) is unique, but we may note that Coleridge, when copying out some lines from Bowles to put at the head of his sonnet to that Eminent Character, changed Bowles's "If his weak reed at times or plaintive lyre He touched" to the more forceful "If his weak harp at times or lonely lyre He struck."

27: Sonnets and the Concordance Test

Before we conclude that the Siddons sonnet which Coleridge did *not* sign is his, however, we should examine the one which he *did* sign but which is not his. Can we tell them apart?

In the sonnet to Mrs. Siddons in the *Morning Chronicle*, December 29, 1794, which "may have been altered by Coleridge, but was no doubt written by Lamb," because Coleridge twice put Lamb's signature to it,[3] we find several Coleridgean words, chiefly paralleled in the contemporaneous "To an Infant." Both poems picture a child affrighted, clinging to a mother/grandam. Coleridge's child has "eager grasp," Lamb's has "eager wondering," a phrase which Coleridge uses later in his "Ode on the Departing Year." But we find no cluster of related words. "Spell," "mandate," "grandam," "beldame," "murky," "midnight," "murder'd," "hags" are all in the concordance, but their quality is neutral, leading to no vein of ore. "Sad heart" is a common phrase; he never used "Cold Horror" but had recently written "Black Horror." "Perturb'd" he would use only once; "perturb'd delight" he never wrote of, though in "Dejection" he would imagine a tale of a child at midnight as one of "affright . . . tempered with delight." Strong positive evidence is conspicuously lacking.

But now observe the idiosyncracies of Lamb's usage that remain and that mark off this poem as his, not Coleridge's. Diction foreign to Coleridge's practice appears in: "Listens strange tales" (Coleridge never wrote of "strange tales"—but the important point is that he would use a preposition, "listens *to*"); "mutter'd to wretch by necromantic spell" (Coleridge would not omit the article before "wretch," nor does he ever mutter *to* anyone or use the word "necromantic"); "hags, who . . . ride the air" (he always says "ride *on*"—never, as it happens, "on the air" but once "on the blast"); "mingle foul embrace with fiends of Hell" (again Lamb in Miltonic fashion omits the preposition; Coleridge would insist on "mingle *in*"); and finally the adverbial "dear" in "lov'd each other dear" is not to be found in Coleridge, nor the inversion "mandate fell" (although once thirty years later he uses the double epithet "Dragon foul and fell").

Despite much shared vocabulary, then, we have no difficulty in distinguishing the work of Lamb from that of Coleridge—even when Lamb is trying to pass for Coleridge (which may account for the few parallels with "To an Infant").

At this point, since we have a Wordsworth concordance, let us see whether the Fontrose sonnet could have been his work—not that there is any actual likelihood. What we find is that the separate words

[3] See note in *Poems*, ed. E. H. Coleridge (Oxford, 1912), 85.

are in his vocabulary but that the phrases, in the main, are not, and that when Wordsworth uses the "same" words, his connotations are very different. For example, eyes are never "brilliant" for Wordsworth, though other things are; he sees "polish'd" objects, but never the Coleridgean "polish'd wit" or "polish'd form." He has passion and some mazes, but these are mostly literal and never anything like "Passion's maze." When Wordsworth "pierced the mazes of a wood" (in the late text of *Descriptive Sketches*) he did it with his legs, not his eyes, and not metaphorically (Coleridge's one literal maze is the "margin's willowy maze" of the "Sonnet to the River Otter," replacing a willowy "stream" supplied by Lamb; the image was clearly a favorite of Coleridge's at this time). In Wordsworth, eyes do not roll, though once someone's "eye-balls" do. Coleridge's "meek-eyed" personifications, Mercy, Pity, Anguish, stand in contrast to Wordsworth's one use of the epithet in "meek-eyed woman." Wordsworth's Fancy is "sweet," "proud," or "maturer"; not "wild" (except in a very late poem). The total impression made by the Fontrose sonnet is of nothing characteristically Wordsworth's as against much characteristically Coleridge's. In one place, however, "Fontrose" uses a phrase to be found in the *Descriptive Sketches* and possibly derived thence. Wordsworth had written of the "fire-clad eagle's wheeling form" before Coleridge wrote of the "fire-clad" nose or Fontrose of "fire-clad thought." Doubtless Coleridge could have told us of the history of the phrase; he was careful to acknowledge borrowing "green radiance" from Wordsworth's *An Evening Walk*.[4] . . .

[4] Mrs. Henry Sandford, in *Thomas Poole and His Friends* (1888), i, 124–125, prints "a rude and halting copy of verses" by Poole dated Sept. 12, 1795, hailing "Coleridge" in nine quatrains full of phrases and sequences of impressions from Coleridge's verse of the preceding months, such as "To the Nightingale" and "Religious Musings." Oddly enough, Poole's poem contains the following: "I love to . . . see the passions in thine eyeballs roll" and "I hear thee . . . dispell The murky mists of error's mazy reign." The mists are from "Religious Musings," but the conjunction of "passions" "roll" and "mazy" could indicate that Poole knew the Fontrose sonnet, as would not be unlikely.

28

Thomas Moore and
the Review of *Christabel**

By Hoover H. Jordan

NO one knows who wrote the September 1816 critique of *Christabel* in the *Edinburgh Review*. Hazlitt is usually thought to have been involved, at least to some extent, and Jeffrey too, despite his disclaimer of authorship. The only others seriously considered as possibilities are Henry Brougham, whose claims were advanced some twenty years ago by P. L. Carver,[1] and Thomas Moore, whose name was only recently linked with the review by Miss Elisabeth Schneider.[2] Necessarily the only way in which this mystery can be dispelled is by the discovery of external evidence which ascribes the authorship beyond cavil, but at the moment such evidence is lacking. One clearly must share Miss Schneider's conclusion: "It [external evidence] is not sufficient, as biographers long ago recognized, to fix the authorship upon anyone, and the scraps of information that have been added here about Moore are by no means conclusive" (p. 423).

This absence of valid external testimony has often occasioned the argument in favor of one candidate or another to proceed by means of internal evidence, which is vexatious to use effectively. Indeed, further discussion employing it might be deemed needless, were it not that Miss Schneider's challenging of the older, conventional theories of authorship urgently requires a new and more careful analysis of internal evidence before the merits of her argument can be established. Her thesis is unorthodox both in its description of the style of the review and in its conception of Moore as a man and a critic.

* Reprinted from *Modern Philology*, LIV (1956), 95–105, with permission of author and publisher.

[1] "The Authorship of a Review of *Christabel* Attributed to Hazlitt," *JEGP*, XXIX (1930), 562–578.

[2] "The Unknown Reviewer of *Christabel*: Jeffrey, Hazlitt, Tom Moore," *PMLA*, LXX (1955), 417–432.

Consequently, it presents the reader a choice: he must believe that it fits together by Procrustean methods an unusual conception of the *Christabel* review and of Moore or that a long series of close readers of Jeffrey, Hazlitt, and Moore—a century and a half of them from Lord Byron to P. P. Howe—have been unable to identify characteristic ideas and stylistic traits of these three writers. The history of such controversies does indeed teach that judgments on style are often highly impressionistic, highly unscientific, and hence subject to gross errors, but the same history also teaches the necessity of validating to the utmost any generalized observations about internal evidence. Unhappily, however, not once in the course of this old controversy has anyone presented a really thorough analysis of style and content.

The following remarks, therefore, attempt to offer a more detailed analysis of internal evidence than has hitherto been presented and ultimately to show the good sense of Mr. P. P. Howe's opinion that the review has "something of Hazlitt and a good deal of Jeffrey."

A reasonable beginning, no doubt, is to examine the review for traces of Hazlitt's usual style and ideas. Though the final paragraph of the review is the most interesting in this regard, it is perhaps well to begin with the clauses in the penultimate paragraph, reading, "and even these are not very brilliant; nor is the leading thought original." Miss Schneider has said of this sentence: "Brilliance was never Hazlitt's criterion of excellence." On VIII, 48,[3] however, Hazlitt contends that brilliance is often essential to writing and is dismayed by critics who attack a work because it is "made up entirely of 'brilliant passages.'" As examples of his own practice in reviewing, he remarks on IX, 244, that Moore's "fancy is delightful and brilliant"; on XI, 73, that Byron has "brilliancy of . . . style and imagery"; on XI, 170, that Moore's poetry is "brilliant and agreeable." Further, on XI, 35, he comments on how Coleridge's poetry and conversation rise above his prose where "hardly a gleam [a word used in the *Christabel* review] is to be found in it of the brilliancy and richness of those stores of thought and language that he pours out incessantly." Such evidence would seem to indicate that Hazlitt did often use brilliance as a criterion of excellence.

The second part of the quoted sentence, "nor is the leading thought original," offers no real clue in wording; Hazlitt repeatedly

[3] All Hazlitt citations refer to the Centenary edition, *The Complete Works of William Hazlitt*, ed. P. P. Howe (London and Toronto, 1932).

spoke of originality,[4] but so did most reviewers for the *Edinburgh Review*. Nor is it possible to find a real clue in the sentence which opens the final paragraph; in it the reviewer damns all the couplets of *Christabel* except for the few which he quotes, but again it should be added that this trick of wholesale condemnation was well known to Hazlitt as to other *Edinburgh Review* contributors. Hazlitt, for instance, declared of William Pitt (IV, 127): "He has not left behind him a single memorable saying,—not one profound maxim,—one solid observation,—one forcible description,—one beautiful thought,—one humorous picture,—one affecting sentiment. He has made no addition whatever to the stock of human knowledge." Of Southey's "New Year's Ode" (VII, 26): "We have turned over the Ode again, which extends to twenty pages, in the hope of finding some one vigorous or striking passage for selection, but in vain"; and of Coleridge's *Lay-Sermon* (VII, 115): "If, on committing the manuscript to the press, the author is caught in the fact of a single intelligible passage, we will be answerable for Mr. Coleridge's loss of character."

The anonymous reviewer's next remark is that *Christabel* would not be reckoned "poetry, or even sense" if found "upon the window of an inn." As Thomas Hutchinson observed of this phrase,[5] Hazlitt at least three times repeated with relish (once in his essay on Thomson and Cowper, again in that on Coleridge's *Statesman's Manual*, and then in "My First Acquaintance with Poets") the story of a well-thumbed copy of Thomson's *Seasons* lying "in the window of a solitary alehouse," which elicited the exclamation from Coleridge, "That is true fame!" Though Col. Prideaux and others have tried to minimize this point, the phrase does, nevertheless, have "something of Hazlitt" in it.

The unknown reviewer then proceeds to attack *Christabel* as a "mixture of raving and driv'ling, extolled as the work of a *'wild and original'* genius, simply because Mr. Coleridge has now and then written fine verses, and a brother poet chooses, in his milder mood, to laud him from courtesy and from interest." *Raving* and *driv'ling* are words frequent in the Hazlitt vocabulary. Southey, for instance, "dotes, and raves, and drivels" (VII, 204), and Coleridge indulges in "slimy, drivelling abuse of Jacobinism" (XIX, 210). The concession that

---

[4] For example, in one essay alone, "On the Living Poets," he spoke of originality at least five times: V, 154, 156 (twice), 162, 163.

[5] *N & Q*, 9th ser., XI (Feb. 28, 1903), 171–172. Col. W. F. Prideaux's less effective answer (269–272) should also be read.

Coleridge has written fine verses is one which Hazlitt always freely made, and the reference to the "milder mood" of Byron is consistent with Hazlitt's conception of Byron. He finds Byron's characters, for example, "sullen, moody, capricious, fierce, inexorable, gloating on beauty, thirsting for revenge" (xi, 73). Hazlitt even used the same wording in asking why Byron should praise Napoleon, "Why should Lord Byron now laud him to the skies?" (v, 154). The final turn of the reviewer's sentence is typical of Hazlitt's customary balanced sentence construction, "from courtesy and from interest."[6]

The reviewer's next sentence is true Hazlitt: "And are such panegyrics to be echoed by the mean tools of a political faction, because they relate to one whose daily prose is understood to be dedicated to the support of all that courtiers think should be supported?" Not only did Hazlitt attack Coleridge repeatedly on this score, but the very wording is typically Hazlitt. *Panegyric* is common with him, especially in such epithets as the "ministerial panegyric" (vii, 212) or "the *hired panegyrist* of the court" (xix, 116). The word *tool* occurs over and over in Hazlitt: "tools and puppets in the hands of power" (iv, 152), "regular-bred courtiers, trammelled tools of despotism" (vii, 132), "a tool in the hands of a minister" (vii, 140); Southey is a "servile court-tool" (vii, 169); false patriotism is "the watchword of faction, the base pander of avarice and pride, the ready tool in the hands of those" (vii, 68). *Courtiers,* in the reviewer's scornful sense, is a frequent word with Hazlitt, as, indeed, one can see from the previous quotations: "Nor do we like poets turned Courtiers" (iv, 152); in his essay on court influence, he attacks both Coleridge and Southey as the "Court-party" (vii, 238).

The anonymous reviewer concludes his paragraph with the wish that, if patronage is to be dispensed, "the good old system of rewarding their champions with places and pensions, instead of puffing their

---

[6] It should not be overlooked that Hazlitt is a master of the balanced sentence. Here is a typical passage (Hazlitt is speaking of Moore): "He is neither a bubble nor a cheat. He makes it his business neither to hoodwink his own understanding, nor to blind or gag others. He is a man of wit and fancy, but he does not sharpen his wit on the edge of human agony, like the House of Commons' jester, nor strew the flowers of fancy, like the Jesuit Burke, over the carcase of corruption, for he is a man not only of wit and fancy, but of common sense and common humanity. He sees for himself, and he feels for others. He employs the arts of fiction, not to adorn the deformed, or disguise the false, but to make truth shine out the clearer, and beauty look more beautiful" (vii, 288). Whole essays of his are written in this style.

bad poetry" is to be preferred. Again these are Hazlitt phrases. I have noted eight uses of the exact phrase "places and pensions" in a cursory examination of Hazlitt, as, for instance, in the essay on Coleridge in *The Spirit of the Age*, "places and pensions, when the critic's praises, and the laurel-wreath were about to be distributed" (xi, 37).[7] In addition, there are several more modifications of the phrase, as in "gentlemen-placemen and pensioners" (vii, 263–264). Of further note is Hazlitt's preference for alliterations, especially those using the letter *p*, as in "to prince and people, and to exchange their principles for a pension" (iv, 152). Here in the *Christabel* review is "places and pensions, instead of puffing their bad poetry." Puffing also often incurred Hazlitt's wrath, and to it he devoted an essay, "On Patronage and Puffing." Then, too, the general charge contained in this closing passage of the review is one which Hazlitt several times leveled at Coleridge. In reviewing Coleridge's *Lay-Sermon*, he says: "He gives up his independence of mind, and yet does not acquire independence of fortune" (vii, 118); on Coleridge's Lectures: "You see him now squat like a toad at the ear of the *Courier*" (xix, 210); and "He who began his career with two Sonnets to Lord Stanhope and Mary Wolstonecraft [*sic*], in the *Morning Chronicle*, should end with slimy, drivelling abuse of Jacobinism and the French Revolution, in the *Courier;*—that, like some devoted fanatic, he should seek the praise of martyrdom by mangling his own soul with a prostituted, unpaid-for pen, and let out his last breath as a pander to that which would be a falsehood, but that it means nothing" (xix, 210).

A few other passages in the *Christabel* review savor of Hazlitt in idea and specific word. The opening paragraph refers to poets as "that once irritable race"; Hazlitt, too, made several comments on the irritability of writers: on xii, 318, Hazlitt observes, for instance, that men of science have less "*wear and tear* of the irritable fibre" than do men of letters, and on vii, 197, that Southey "does not form an exception to *irritabile genus vatum*." Also the unknown reviewer charges that *Christabel* is characterized by "sudden transitions—opening eagerly upon some topic, and then flying from it immediately." Observe that almost simultaneously with the appearance of the *Christabel* review Hazlitt was writing of Coleridge, in the remarks on the *Lay-Sermon:* "His mind has infinite activity, which only leads him into numberless chimeras. . . . He is no sooner borne to the ut-

[7] For other examples, see vii, 110, 181, 187, 188, 192, 198, 251.

most point of his ambition, than he is hurried away from it again by the same fantastic impulse" (vii, 117). In his essay on Coleridge in *The Spirit of the Age* Hazlitt expands this point at length.

Here and there are further touches of Hazlitt. The reviewer's contempt for Coleridge's "miserable piece of coxcombry and shuffling" is stated in language with which readers of Hazlitt are familiar, numerous examples of which can be quickly culled by leafing through a few of his reviews; Southey, for example, is guilty of "intellectual coxcombry" (vii, 202) and "shuffling evasions of common-sense" (vii, 200). The reviewer's attack on "The Pains of Sleep" as "mere raving, without any thing more affecting than a number of incoherent words, expressive of extravagance and incongruity" contains four words usual in Hazlitt—*raving, affecting, extravagance,* and *incongruity.*[8] Finally, to bring this part of the discussion to a close, there is the question about the use of innuendo by the *Christabel* reviewer. Miss Schneider, who finds several innuendoes, absolves both Hazlitt and Jeffrey from responsibility on the ground that they do not use innuendo, and so she finds evidence of Moore's authorship. What these innuendoes are is not wholly clear—presumably the jocular reference to Geraldine's drunkenness and that bearing on the seduction of Christabel. The first of these two is, without question, a genuine innuendo, suggesting that the glitter in Geraldine's eye is from drunkenness occasioned by a second draught of wild-flower wine. As Moore is not particularly given to toying with this sort of subject, no doubt Professor Schneider wishes to call attention more especially to the supposition about seduction. Here is the sentence in question: "Upon this the Baron falls into a passion, as if he had discovered that his daughter had been seduced; at least, we can understand him in no other sense, though no hint of such a kind is given, but, on the contrary, she is painted to the last moment as full of innocence and purity" (p. 63). Is this innuendo or outright statement? The reviewer, to be sure, pro-

---

[8] These words, used in this same sense, are very frequent in Hazlitt. See the following for examples: *raving,* vii, 34, 135, 204, 226, 255, 290 (Coleridge, "raving like a Bedlamite," and Southey "dotes, and raves, and drivels"); *affecting,* iv, 268, 283, 303 ("they are equally affecting, if it is affecting to shew *what a little thing is human life*"); *extravagance,* v, 161, 162 (twice), 163 (the "renegado extravagances" of the Lake school, this "extravagant or childish" new poetry); *incongruity,* iv, 72; vi, 203; xvi, 265, 273 (Shelley "ransacked his brain for incongruities" and erred in "disjointedness of the materials, the incongruous metaphors, and violent transitions").

ceeds to accuse Coleridge of using innuendo in the poem, but his own statement, even if it be classified as innuendo, pales in comparison to Hazlitt's remark in the *Examiner* on *Christabel*: "There is something disgusting at the bottom of his subject, which is but ill glossed over by a veil of Della Cruscan sentiment and fine writing—like moon-beams playing on a charnel-house, or flowers strewed on a dead body" (xix, 33). Though in a sense Hazlitt calls Coleridge's subject "something of the 'charnel-house,'" as Professor Schneider observes, yet by the use of the word *like* he does not specify the nature of the something disgusting and only hints. Hutchinson (p. 171) offers a good discussion of what Hazlitt's suspicions were.

In summation, internal evidence does not demonstrate that Hazlitt wrote this review in its entirety, but, on the other hand, it does indicate that in idea and wording some contribution was possible from him. Furthermore, it indicates that such an attack would not have offended his sensibilities. His reviews of the *Lay-Sermon* (September 8, 1816) and the *Statesman's Manual* (December 29, 1816) have a ferocity which makes the *Christabel* review seem temperate.

The justice of Mr. Howe's opinion that the review contains "something of Hazlitt and a good deal of Jeffrey" is further illuminated by a careful reading in terms of Jeffrey's customary ideas and known habits of expression. For instance, the opening sentences of the review mention Byron's praise of *Christabel* and question his judgment: "some of his latest *publications* dispose us to distrust his authority, where the question is what ought to meet the public eye." The same sentiment Jeffrey was expressing about such poems as "Fare Thee Well" in his December, 1816, review of the third canto of *Childe Harold's Pilgrimage* and *The Prisoner of Chillon, and Other Poems*: "It is painful to read them—and infinitely to be regretted that they should have been given to the public . . . not even the example of Lord Byron, can persuade us that they are fit for public discussion." Then, too, like Hazlitt, Jeffrey is aware of the irritability of poets, calling them "the most irritable and fantastic of all men of genius," but later qualifying this sentiment, "The smaller only—your Laureates and Balladmongers—are envious and irritable."[9]

Like the *Christabel* reviewer, Jeffrey is much concerned with the

---

[9] *Edinburgh Review*, xxxi (1816), 464. All ensuing references concerning Jeffrey are to the *Edinburgh Review* and are to essays which he acknowledged as his.

"new school" of Lake poets, whom he dubs silly, unintelligible, childish. The unknown reviewer uses the words "unmeaning or infantine"; to the best of my knowledge Hazlitt does not employ *infantine* in any of his reviews, but Jeffrey applies it at least twice to Southey, calling his style "infantine" (vii, 17) and his phrases full of "affected simplicity and infantine pathos" (xxv, 30). The unknown reviewer also adds in the second paragraph, concerning the Lake poets, "we had been admiring their extravagance for many years." Jeffrey had, of course, been reviewing Southey since the turn of the century and had remarked in his first review on the "most wild and extravagant fictions" of Southey. The charge brought against *Christabel* of unintelligibility is a standard kind of judgment by Jeffrey (as by Hazlitt). He had, for example, berated Southey in 1802 for "a veil of mysterious and unintelligible language, which flows past with so much solemnity, that it is difficult to believe it conveys nothing of any value" (i, 70).

Professor Schneider has difficulty believing that the flippant summary of *Christabel* could have been written by Jeffrey. "It has none of the authoritative Johnsonian air maintained by Jeffrey." Though Jeffrey was often Johnsonian, it is interesting to note how often he dropped such an air and, indeed, in this regard to accept Mr. Howe's invitation to read Jeffrey's review of the *White Doe of Rylstone*. There we find comments such as these, which seem relevant to this discussion:

> Mr. Wordsworth seems hitherto to have been unlucky in the choice of his liquor—or of his bottle holder [Jeffrey is referring to poetical intoxication]. In some of his odes and ethic exhortations, he was exposed to the public in a state of incoherent rapture and glorious delirium, to which we think we have seen a parallel among the humbler lovers of jollity. In the Lyrical Ballads, he was exhibited, on the whole, in a vein of very pretty deliration; but in the poem before us, he appears in a state of low and maudlin imbecility, which would not have misbecome Master Silence himself, in the close of a social day. [xxv, 355–356]
>
> One, who it seems is an Oxford scholar, conjectures that she may be the fairy who instructed Lord Clifford in astrology. [xxv, 357]
>
> The poor lady runs about indeed for some years in a very disconsolate way in a worsted gown and flannel nightcap; but at last the old white doe finds her out, and takes again to following her—whereupon Mr. Wordsworth breaks out into this fine and natural rapture. [xxv, 362]

Like the *Christabel* review, this article employs highly ironical praise—"fine and natural rapture," "sweet nursery phrases," "natural and luminous apostrophe to his harp," "lofty and dispirited strains," "this exquisite address," and so on.

But the *White Doe* review is by no means the only example of levity in Jeffrey. In reviewing *Thalaba* (I, 75), he uses the pert "old lady" epithet to describe the widow and intersperses jocular comments, such as "a ring, inscribed with some unintelligible characters, which he is enabled to interpret by the help of some other unintelligible characters" (which sounds a bit like the unknown reviewer's "as to outdo all his former outdoings"). His famous review of *The Excursion* follows the same plan of summary and flippant comment. There we hear of Wordsworth's "own delightful simplicity," "his luminous and emphatic harangues," "that rapturous mysticism which eludes all comprehension," "the author's own sublime aspiration after the delight of becoming *a Motion,* or *a Presence,* or *an Energy* among multitudinous streams"; "*we* have not ingenuity enough to refer the conglobated bubbles and murmurs, and floating islands to their vital prototypes"; "his daintiest ravings"; "a few descriptions of baby-houses, and of old hats and wet brims"; "a man who went about selling flannel and pocket-handkerchiefs in this lofty diction, would soon frighten away all his customers; and would infallibly pass . . . for a madman"; and so on. Further examples of Jeffrey's levity can be found in the reviews of Southey and of Montgomery's *The Wanderer of Switzerland and Other Poems.*

In the anonymous reviewer's remarks on the meter of *Christabel* is a touch which fits Jeffrey, not Hazlitt. Reference is there made to readers of English poetry "whose ear has been tuned to the lays of Spenser, Milton, Dryden, and Pope." Hazlitt would agree on Spenser and Milton, hold qualifications on Dryden, and disclaim Pope, whose rhythms he called "sing-song." But all four stood high in Jeffrey's estimation.

P. P. Howe has called special attention to the *Christabel* reviewer's paragraph, second to the last in the review and beginning "Upon the whole," which he thinks suitable to Jeffrey. It is indeed. The remarks on the Lake school follow those of Jeffrey. Even the particular slur on the *White Doe* and the laureate odes is true to Jeffrey's opinions. In speaking of Wordsworth and Southey, Jeffrey is much concerned (like the unknown reviewer) with their throwing away their talents on mean subjects, "baby-houses" and "hat brims," and with their "false theory of poetical composition," on which he discourses freely in the review of *The Excursion.*

One additional test of authorship Jeffrey meets well—the test of word frequency. A spot check will quickly show how key words from the *Christabel* review abound in Jeffrey's writing: *wild, extravagant, piece, incongruity, boldest, raving, feeling, fancy, brilliant, original,* and so on.

Using this same kind of internal evidence, let us proceed to the possibility of Moore's having written the review. First, one must be clear about Moore's attitude toward the Lake poets, because the *Christabel* review includes indirectly both Southey and Wordsworth in its condemnation. Wordsworth, in Moore's estimation, was the leading poet of the day. Moore spoke of "his great powers," called him "the great poet of the Lakes," a "capacious mind, like the great pool of Norway," "one of the very few real and original poets that this age . . . has had the glory of producing," and deeply lamented "the injustice this age does him" and the "no small disgrace to the taste of the English public" that his works had not sold more widely. His memoirs and other writings are uniformly respectful toward Wordsworth, except on the score of Wordsworth's self-centeredness in conversation; on other personal counts he regarded Wordsworth as "manly." Moreover, toward Southey, Moore did not display such disapprobation as the unknown reviewer reveals. Addressing an audience in Dublin in 1818, Moore called *Roderick* "one of the noblest and most eloquent poems in any language." When Moore finds fault with Southey, it is chiefly on political and religious grounds, not on literary, though he is disappointed that a man of Southey's talents would turn to writing birthday odes. But he is by no means unappreciative of Southey's great abilities as a poet.

Second, Moore strenuously rejected the standard offered by the unknown reviewer, who requested Coleridge to "show us how these lines agree either in number of accents or feet." In his biography of Sheridan, for example, Moore attacked that sort of prosody "upon which, in the system of English education, a large and precious portion of human life is wasted" and asserted his long-time belief that poetry "is made by the ear" rather than by rule and the tally of syllables.[10] Excessive regularity irked him. In his *Memoirs* he declared: "Milton . . . is the truly musical poet, and Milton was a musician, which neither Pope nor any of his monotonous imitators are. The genuine music of poetry is to be found in the olden time, and we, in

[10] *Memoirs of the Life of the Right Honourable Richard Brinsley Sheridan* (London, 1825), I, 268 ff.

these days, would revive its note, if the lovers of the Popish sing-song would let us."[11] In *Lalla Rookh* through Fadladeen he ridicules making verses tally and offers there the line "Like the faint, exquisite music of a dream" as the sort of line which he thought the ear rejoices in but which could not be tolerated by eighteenth-century critics because of the "syllabic superfluities." In his *Memoirs* he delights in his creation of "extraordinary metres" in such poems as "At the mid hour of night" and "Through grief and through danger" (ii, 178); not on such grounds did he quarrel with Wordsworth and Southey or, so far as we know, with Coleridge. In any event he did not share the unknown reviewer's interest in the tallying of verses.

Third, Moore (like Hazlitt) would never list Spenser, Milton, Dryden, and Pope as the great musicians of the language. He thought Milton "the truly musical poet" but had little respect for Pope on that score. Dryden he did think well of as a harmonious writer. His opinion of Spenser is not recorded; certainly, Spenser was not one of his favorites. The selection of these four names is not characteristic of Moore, and, indeed, the likelihood is that Shakespeare would have appeared in any combination of names that he would formulate, as Shakespeare was the pinnacle of literary achievement in his estimation. Nor is it the least likely that Moore would have coupled Dryden's *Ode* with *Paradise Lost;* his admiration for *Paradise Lost* was great, but in his writings I find no mention of Dryden's *Ode.* He did say, however, very directly that Virgil, Racine, and Dryden fall short of Milton by their deficiencies in sublimity and imagination (ii, 344).

Fourth, the *Christabel* review does not stylistically suit Moore. A check of Moore's known reviews is interesting in terms of those key words that abound in the *Christabel* review and in Hazlitt and Jeffrey, words like *extravagance, raving, drivelling, shuffling, incongruity.* Most of these simply are not present in Moore, and the few that can be found are so infrequent as to offer no evidence worth mentioning. But of further interest is the fact that the *Christabel* review lacks allusion and quotation (except from *Christabel* itself). Miss Schneider finds in this stylistic trait evidence of Moore's workmanship and suggestion that Hazlitt did not write the review: "Hazlitt thought so naturally in allusive quotation that scarcely a paragraph of his writing is without its nostalgic borrowed (and acknowledged) phrase" (p.

[11] *Memoirs, Journal, and Correspondence of Thomas Moore,* ed. Lord John Russell (London, 1853–56) ii, 344.

427). Very true, but the statement applies almost equally well to Moore. In his review of Lord Thurlow, for instance, he quotes from or alludes to a score of writers—Shakespeare twice, Lucan, Lucretius, Aristophanes, Sheridan, Dante, Cowley, Boileau, Linnaeus, and so on.[12] In his review of the dramas on Anne Boleyn are similar quotations from or allusions to Voltaire, Southey, Kemble, Aristotle, Virgil, Scaliger, Apuleius, Dr. Johnson, and others (pp. 117–144). His usual style is to stud his sentences with reference. His style also features much imagery and many plays upon words (there are at least four conspicuous examples of this playfulness in the review of Lord Thurlow); these traits are lacking in the *Christabel* review.

Fifth, in all but one of his known reviews Moore finds some praise to accord the author. The exception is that of Overton's *Ecclesia Anglicana,* a work which contains a harsh attack upon the Roman Catholic church in Ireland and an equally violent defense of the Protestant establishment in Ireland. In his other reviews, however, he found something pleasant to say even for such minor writers as Thurlow, Grover, and Milman, for whom he felt no admiration. The *Christabel* reviewer lacks such charity.

Sixth, evidence is lacking to show that the relations between Moore and Byron were strained at this time, but it is clear that the *Christabel* reviewer is hostile toward Byron or at least indifferent toward him. He accuses Byron twice of self-interest in praising Coleridge—"what is thus lavishly advanced may be laid out with a view to being repaid with interest," as the opening paragraph expresses the matter. To accuse Moore of writing the sentence is to accuse him of two ethical improprieties. First, in his letter asking Moore to review *Christabel* praisingly, Byron had explained carefully that his motives in making the request were entirely honorable: he thought well of the poem, he knew Coleridge to be in distress, he regretted Coleridge's harsh treatment by the critics, and he thought praise might occasion Coleridge "to explode most gloriously" as a poet.[13] Moore would have been in a most ungenerous mood to have denied the honesty of these sentiments and to have accused Byron of another motive entirely. Second, if one assumes the review to have been written in July or August 1816, the date is significant. Earlier in the year Byron had experienced

[12] Thomas Moore, *Prose and Verse,* ed. Richard Herne Shepherd (New York, 1878), 35–54.
[13] *The Works of Lord Byron: Letters and Journals,* ed. R. E. Prothero (London, 1899), III, 232–233.

his marital difficulties, over which Moore had been greatly concerned, and then had left his homeland, feeling much alone in the world and thinking of Moore as one of the few who were faithful to him. As evidence does not show any coolness on Moore's part, it is a bit difficult to think of his attacking Byron at such a time. Then, too, in the last analysis the reviewer seems to speak as reviewer, not as a poet addressing his fellows, though, of course, a poet might assume such a guise. In the opening paragraph the reviewer states: "We are a little inclined to doubt the value of the praise which one poet lends another. It seems now-a-days to be the practice of that once irritable race to laud each other without bounds." This statement should be considered in the light of the fact that Moore was at the moment prepared to dedicate *Lalla Rookh* to Rogers (though the poem was not to be printed until the next spring), that a few years later he was to dedicate *Fables for the Holy Alliance* to Byron, that Byron had already lavishly praised Moore in the dedication of *The Corsair,* and that Byron had previously dedicated *The Giaour* to Rogers. Under the circumstances Moore was scarcely in a position to doubt the value of the praise which he, Byron, and Rogers were lending one another. Byron, who had probably read every word which Moore had printed, was, indeed, so far from connecting Moore with the review that he spoke of it several times to Moore in letters and never seemed to doubt that it was from the pen of Jeffrey.

One further consideration about Moore's authorship needs mention, though it is not exclusively a matter of internal evidence —namely, the characterization of Moore which Professor Schneider has delineated to make him seem likely as the reviewer. Her contention, to which all should assent, is that "biography and biographical scholarship need not be a form of protective custody in which one shelters one's adopted child by calling the neighbor's son a thief or bully," but it is worth asking whether she has not made Moore the neighbor's son at whom to hurl invective. Her impressions of the style of the *Christabel* review accord with her impressions of Moore as author. Accordingly, she portrays him as "puerile," a "pert" and "corny" wit, a "spoiled darling of the public," "an overpopular entertainer who assumes that whatever he says will be thought amusing," "a dart-thrower" whose "barbs are blunt," a writer whose style is "lax and dead in spite of its levity," whose "sentences and whole passages flounder . . . from failure of intellectual energy," whose writing lacks "speaking intonations and inflections," who is "careless and cold" because he will indulge in "light-hearted cutting-up of a poem for the amusement of the reviewer and his readers" and cares nothing, therefore, for literary matters, who couples Dryden's *Ode* and *Paradise Lost* presumably because he lacks "taste or literary standards." As a description of the style of the *Christabel* review, this is unorthodox impressionism; traditionally, the manner of writing has seemed quite consistent with the style of such capable authors as Hazlitt and Jeffrey. But the description is equally unorthodox as a characterization of Moore. Criticisms of his prose style from those by Sydney Smith and Macaulay to that by H. M. Jones have not described it as lax, dead, and floundering; rather the usual comment is that it is alive, effervescent, coruscating to excess. That his wit is "corny" is again not a usual opinion; Hazlitt's judgment on him as "the greatest wit now living" comes closer to orthodoxy. But the fundamental misunderstanding is that of Moore's literary standards, in the contention that, unlike Hazlitt or Jeffrey, Moore did not take poets or poetry seriously and was simply a drawing-room entertainer. A proper answer to such a contention demands far more space than is available in this article, but perhaps one passage out of many will help to set this matter a bit straighter. Moore writes:

The true province of poetry is to embellish and dignify this life, and shed a light over the future, and the poet who employs his art in blackening and degrading human nature, and throwing the darkness of eternal death over the prospect before us, runs counter to the purposes of his high calling. . . . The *ton moqueur* was never yet the tone of a lofty genius, and it was what alone, perhaps, prevented Voltaire from being a great man. Even he avoided it in his loftiest efforts.[14]

The known writing of Moore reveals no flippancy toward great writers. His own canons of taste placed Shakespeare, Dante, and Milton on the highest level, and of his contemporaries he has no "pert" attitude toward Wordsworth, Southey, Byron, Shelley, Crabbe, Landor, or, indeed, any writer of manifest ability. The truth is that we simply do not know enough of his ideas about Coleridge to make an acceptable résumé of them. That he did not approve of some points of Coleridge's character is not strange; neither did Wordsworth or Southey. That he called a critical idea of Coleridge's "absurd" does not show contempt for Coleridge, as Miss Schneider implies, and is assuredly no measure of his general opinion of Coleridge, for the idea quoted is absurd; Coleridge was asserting at the time that skillfully

[14] *Prose and Verse*, 414.

constructed verses can be read faster than unskillfully constructed ones, and, as he could read three verses of "Whistlecraft" for every two of "Beppo," the lines of Frere were in that measure superior in construction to Byron's. Moreover, at a later time, in 1833, when Coleridge read Moore some of his poetry, Moore found it "very striking."[15] That Moore was hostile to Coleridge, flippant toward him, or ignorant of his ability cannot be proved by materials now available in print.

The only legitimate internal evidence connecting Moore with the *Christabel* review seems to be the use of the word *couplet,* which Professor Schneider has happily noted. Nonetheless it is odd that nowhere except in the reviews noted by Miss Schneider does Moore use the word *couplet* in anything but its orthodox sense despite innumerable opportunities. It is also apparent that this particular use of the word is not confined to Moore. Leigh Hunt, for instance, in his *Specimens of British Poetesses* uses *couplet* to refer to two unrhymed lines.[16] How many others used it in this sense is hard to say, particularly when it is remembered that a number of writers reviewing for Jeffrey wrote so little about poetry that their usage in such matters cannot well be surveyed. In addition, any list of *Edinburgh Review* contributors does not embrace those usually unknown learned men to whom Jeffrey submitted manuscripts for comment and revision. To find out whether others besides Moore used the word *couplet* in this sense, therefore, is next to impossible.

In the last analysis, this inquiry has been simply an attempt to employ the procedures of internal evidence with greater care than has hitherto been used in the discussion of this controversial question; it has not presumed to establish the authorship of the *Christabel* review beyond argument. It does not demonstrate that one man wrote the review—and certainly such a review is not a formidable task for one man—or that several were involved, though this latter possibility remains. P. P. Howe observed that on one occasion Jeffrey corrected and added to a manuscript by James Mill that had already been revised by Dr. Ferrier of Manchester; it is not inconceivable that the *Christabel* review was written under such circumstances. But, despite the treacherous nature of internal evidence, it does in this circumstance seem to work against Miss Schneider's thesis. The *Christabel* review shows almost nothing representative of Moore's ideas or style, but it does have "something of Hazlitt and a good deal of Jeffrey."

[15] *Memoirs,* VII, 8.
[16] *Leigh Hunt as Poet and Essayist,* ed. Charles Kent (London and New York, 1889), 352.

Keats's Theatrical Reviews
in the *Champion**

By Leonidas M. Jones

. . . EXAMINATION of external evidence leaves the question of the authorship of the review of *Richard, Duke of York* unresolved.[1] Either Reynolds or Keats may have written it, but no information from outside the article itself provides a basis for a definite attribution. Internal evidence, however, shows clearly that Reynolds wrote the article. Earlier critics have been easily misled by reading the review, for the ideas and prose styles of Keats and Reynolds were very similar. The article sounds very much like Keats, but a large proportion of Reynolds' other prose does also. Nevertheless, there are a number of factors in the essay that point to Reynolds, and Reynolds alone. Throughout his life he had a habit of picking up quotations from his reading and quoting or paraphrasing them in his work. The following comparisons of quotations and passages from *"Richard, Duke of York"* with similar quotations and passages from other essays, known to be by Reynolds, identify the author of the doubtful essay.

The author of *"Richard, Duke of York"* wrote, "What might almost be deemed an airy nothing acquires at once a local habitation and a name." In an earlier article Reynolds had praised "the glorious faculty that 'Turns them to shapes and gives to airy nothing / A local habitation and a name.'"[2] Years later he wrote in the *London Magazine*

* Excerpted, and reprinted from the *Keats-Shelley Journal*, III, (1954), 55–65, with permission of author and publisher.

[1] Keats wrote his first theatrical review, entitled "Mr. Kean," for the *Champion* of Dec. 21, 1817. A second review, *"Richard, Duke of York,"* in the *Champion* of Dec. 28, 1817, had been erroneously ascribed to Keats until the present essay, the first part of which surveys the misleading external evidence. The opening of the review is reprinted at the end of this essay.

[2] "Popular Poetry, Periodical Criticism, &c.," *Champion*, Oct. 13, 1816. The article is unsigned, but can be attributed to Reynolds because of a reference to a vacation in Exeter from which he had just returned.

that a successful actor "gave to airy nothing a local habitation and a name."[3]

In *"Richard, Duke of York,"* there is the brief quotation, "in his habit as he lived." A year later Reynolds repeated the quotation in the *Scots Magazine.*[4]

The alteration of a quotation to make it fit a particular case was a favorite device with Reynolds. The author of *"Richard, Duke of York"* changed a quotation so radically that it was hardly suitable when he wrote that "Wallack, as *Young Clifford,* 'towers above his sex.'" Six months earlier Reynolds had used the quotation more appropriately, "She towers above her sex."[5] In the *London Magazine* he repeated the quotation twice (Nov. 1821, May 1822).

In *"Richard, Duke of York,"* a quotation is paraphrased to describe Kean's enactment of the death scene, "It is an extinguishment, not a decay." Reynolds had given the quotation directly in an earlier article on John Philip Kemble's retirement from the stage, "He was 'extinguished not decayed'" (*Champion,* June 29, 1817).

Two other passages, which are not quotations, show an unusual similarity in metaphor and diction to passages which are undoubtedly by Reynolds. The author of *"Richard, Duke of York"* said of Shakespeare's poetry, "It is of the air, not of the earth." In the earlier article Reynolds had written of Kemble's retirement from the stage, "He now appears to us to be of the air,—to have vanished from the earth." In describing the poetry of Shakespeare's histories, the author of *"Richard, Duke of York"* employed an unusual personification, "It is poetry!—but oftentimes poetry wandering on the London road." Less than two months earlier Reynolds had used a similar personification to describe the songs in *The Beggar's Opera,* "They seem to be a poetry that has seen better days: a poetry seduced!" (*Champion,* Nov. 2, 1817).

[3] "The Drama," *London Magazine,* v (Mar. 1822), 292.

[4] "Mr. Hazlitt's Lectures on the Comic Genius of England," *Scots Magazine,* Feb. 1819, p. 144. This unsigned article . . . can be assigned to Reynolds without question, for he incorporated into it an earlier paper which he had signed with his initials in the *Champion,* June 16, 1816, p. 190.

[5] "Dramatic Review," *Champion,* June 8, 1817. Compare Addison, *Cato,* I.i.147, "The virtuous Marcia tow'rs above her sex." It has long been known that Reynolds was the chief theatrical critic for the *Champion* from Dec. 1815 through Dec. 1817. I have confirmed by internal evidence Reynolds' authorship of all the reviews cited in this article in a doctoral dissertation at Harvard, "The Essays and Critical Writing of John Hamilton Reynolds" (1952), but it would obviously be impossible to reproduce all the evidence for every review in the present paper.

Evidence for Authorship

The repetition of brief quotations furnishes strong evidence of Reynolds' authorship. On the other hand, a comparison of the essay with Keats's work reveals only two minor parallels. The author of "*Richard, Duke of York*" described the civil wars as "pelican strife," while Keats once referred to his creditors as "Pelican duns."[6] The similarity may be discounted as mere coincidence, however, since Reynolds used the metaphor four times. He referred to Lear's "Pelican daughters" twice (Feb. 2, 1817; Dec. 1818), and to his "pelican children" once (April 1823). On another occasion he described criticism as "a pelican thing, that feeds upon the bosom that hath bred it" (May 1817). The only other parallel between the doubtful essay and Keats's work is the quotation, "as musical as is Apollo's lute," which the author applied to Kean's voice. A year and a half later Keats quoted the passage from *Comus* in which the line occurs (*Letters*, p. 317). Again the similarity is probably due to coincidence, for Reynolds also quoted a passage including the same line (Jan. 7, 1832). Thus, despite the two minor items which suggest Keats, the preponderance of the internal evidence indicates quite clearly that Reynolds was the author of "*Richard, Duke of York*."

. . . The review of *Richard, Duke of York* is somewhat better than the average critical essay by Reynolds, but a large number are equally fine, and a great many offer even better examples of his witty and imaginative prose.

Review of RICHARD, DUKE OF YORK (opening paragraph)

From the *Champion,* December 28, 1817

(Here attributed to John Hamilton Reynolds)

The Committee of Drury Lane have thought proper to give the name of Richard to the last-born of their ancient house, without considering that they have a child still living that bears the same title: a confusion has very naturally arisen in the minds of those, who have been introduced to both, as to *which is which*—and we will venture to say that more than half of the spectators believe, in the innocence of their hearts, that there are not two Duke Richards, but one Duke Richard. " 'Tis yet to know" with many, that this same Duke of York is the father of their old, savage, crafty and courageous favourite, Richard the Third. The present ingenious compilation, or rather the essence of three of Shakespeare's historical dramas,—only

[6] *Letters*, ed. M. B. Forman (3rd ed.; 1947), 35.

throws us back into the breaking of the stormy day of the Lancastrian strife. We have on the stage been used to the noon-tide of the struggle, and to its tempestuous night. It is the morning of the Plantagenets. The white rose is but just budding on the tree,—and we have known it only when it was wide dispersed, and flaunting in the busy air, or when it was struck, and the leaves beat from the stem. Perhaps there is not a more interesting time in history, than this pelican strife,—for it has a locality which none of us can mistake, at the same time that it relishes of romance in its wildness and chivalrous encounters. We read, of royal deeds of valour and endurance, and of the personal conflicts between armed and youthful princes under waving and crested banners,—till we might almost think the most knightly days were come again;—but then we read of Tewkesbury and Gloucester,—and of cities and towns which lie all about us; and we find the most romantic occurrences realized in our minds. What might almost have been deemed an airy nothing,—acquires at once a local habitation and a name. The meeting with such places as the Temple Hall and Crosby House, flatly contradicts the half-formed notion that " 'Tis but our fantasies," —and we readily "let belief take hold of us." We have no doubt but that Shakespeare intended to have written a complete dramatic history of England,—for from Richard the Second to Richard the Third the links are unbroken. The three parts of Henry 6th fall in between the two Richards. They are written with infinite vigour, but their regularity tied the hand of Shakespeare. Particular facts kept him in the high road, and would not suffer him to turn down leafy and winding lanes, or to break wildly and at once into the breathing fields. The poetry is for the most part ironed and manacled with a chain of facts, and cannot get free:—it cannot escape from the prison house of history, nor often move without our being disturbed with the clanking of its fetters. The poetry of Shakespeare is generally free as is the wind;—a perfect thing of the elements:—winged and sweetly coloured. Poetry must be free! It is of the air, not of the earth,—and the higher it soars, the nearer it gets to its home. The Poetry of "Romeo and Juliet," of "Hamlet," of "Macbeth," is the poetry of Shakespeare's soul,—full of love and divine romance;—It knows no stop in its delight, but "goeth where it listeth:"—remaining however in all men's hearts a perpetual and golden dream. The poetry of *Lear, Othello, Cymbeline,* &c., is the poetry of human passions and affections,—made almost ethereal by the power of the Poet. Again, the poetry of *Richard, John,* and the *Henries,* is the blending of the imaginative with the historical:—it is poetry!—but oftentimes poetry wandering on the London road. We hate to say a word against a word of Shakespeare's,—and we can only do so by comparing himself with himself:—on going into the three parts of *Henry the Sixth* for themselves;—we extract all dispraise and accusation,—and declare them to be perfect works.—Indeed they are such. We live again in the olden time.

The Duke of York plucks the pale rose before our eyes. *Talbot* stands before us,—majestic,—huge,—appalling,—"in his habit as he lived." *Henry,* the weak, careless, and good *Henry,* totters palpably under his crown. The temple hall is in our sight. By way of making some reparation for having put these plays last in our estimate,—and for the real pleasure of contradicting the critical remarks which we in our petty wisdom have urged,—and for the simple and intense delight we take in copying, and feeding upon, noble passages in Shakespeare,—we will here give one of the speeches of *Richard, Duke of York,* which is in itself rich enough to buy an immortality for any man. . . .

V

DETECTIONS
OF FORGERY

Editorial Note to Part V

WE do not intend more than a token reconnaissance into the inferno of Frauds and Forgeries. The selections that follow are but a small sampling of recent extensive investigations, and are included here mainly to reinforce some earlier caveats. Forged writings, of course, are texts that are not texts by authors who are not the stated authors. We do not here refer to ghostwritten speeches, essays, or books (though that class of writings, with all the possible degrees of acknowledged and unacknowledged "aid" in composition, poses interesting questions for canonical scholars). As we define it, a literary forgery is a passage which was not written in its present form by the author to whom it is attributed and which has been attributed fraudulently, without that author's knowledge or consent.

Such a definition comprehends writing shuffled together from portions of an author's genuine work and arranged so as to appear to be a "hitherto unknown" piece by that author. With forgeries of this class, such as the "Letters" allegedly by Lafcadio Hearn (see essay No. 31), the method of exposure consists chiefly in showing how the forger mingled the genuine excerpts with spurious materials in a false composition. In the case of the pseudo-Hearn "Letters," method eventually triumphed. But it is sobering to note that some scholars, and even Hearn's own son, reading unmethodically and thereby overlooking the echoes of Hearn's critics and biographers, as well as the changed context, function, and dates of the authorial components, could be deceived into accepting a fraudulent mosaic because of the authenticity of many of the fragments.

On the other hand, the most convincing evidence of the fraudulence of the "Horn Papers" (see essay No. 30) is their inauthenticity as artifacts (e.g., their artificially aged ink and paper). But the internal-external evidence of anachronisms, and the internal evidence of style, also count heavily against the "Papers." (One should note that for the close dating of usage, the investigators rely more confidently than is advisable on the *Oxford English Dictionary* and the *Dictionary of American English*.) From a long report—itself the digest of a much longer one—we excerpt discussions of laboratory, historical, and stylistic evidence. With this type of forgery, it is difficult to apply internal tests other than those of self-consistency and historical accuracy: the nonexistence of authentic writings by the purported "author" may make comparison impossible, as may the unavailability of comparable texts written by the suspected forger in his own name. The Horn forger facilitated detection, however, by ascribing his pseudo-archaic documents, in Chattertonian fashion, to several different persons. Hence, the very consistency of the documents with respect to certain linguistic idiosyncrasies was yet another serious blow to the hypothesis of their integrity.

A more sophisticated forgery, lying outside our province but an instructive text for all canonical critics, was that of the recent Rimbaldian "La Chasse spirituelle."[1] This poem was fabricated so successfully that, like the false Vermeer paintings, it fitted, if anything, too perfectly into the received canon. Once the forgers publicly announced the game they had been playing, the rush to expose "La Chasse" as a "gross" falsehood produced an assortment of retrospective investigations of authorship in which critics reached the foregone conclusion, but more often than not by the abuse of evidence and the misapplication of historical, stylistic, and other canonical tests. Whether in the detection of nonauthorship or of authorship, the exercise of sound method and sober logic is indispensable.

[1] See Bruce Morrissette, *The Great Rimbaud Forgery: The Affair of "La Chasse spirituelle"* (St. Louis, 1956).

30

The Mystery of
the Horn Papers*

By Arthur Pierce Middleton and Douglass Adair

ALMOST anyone who saw the substantial three volumes entitled *The Horn Papers: Early Westward Movement on the Monongahela and Upper Ohio, 1765–1795* lying on a library table probably accepted them as an unusually impressive collection of data on local history. The respectable bulk of the books, the discreet gold lettering of the title on the black cover, give no hint of the furor excited by their publication. Everything about their external appearance is reassuringly undramatic. Yet the printing of these solid-looking volumes divided a local community into opposing camps, agitated an entire region in fierce partisan debate, and, in time, attracted the incredulous attention of the whole American historical profession.

If our same hypothetical observer, in idle curiosity, had leafed through the first two volumes of *The Horn Papers*—the volumes that provoked the bitter controversy—he still would have seen little to arouse his excitement. Here he would have found the diaries of Jacob Horn and his son Christopher, whose entries, dated from 1735 to 1795, fill approximately sixty printed pages. Published with the diaries is the fifty-page court docket, dated 1772–1779, of what is described as "the first English court held west of the mountains" (i, 328). Also printed here are miscellaneous papers, court orders and maps of the Ohio region during the last half of the eighteenth century. The last 265 pages of Volume i of *The Horn Papers* contain fifteen chapters written by W. F. Horn (a descendant of the above-men-

* This article is based on the report of the committee sponsored by The Institute of Early American History and Culture. The detailed statement of the committee's findings is on file at The Institute and may be consulted there. The present excerpt has been made, with permission of authors and publisher, from *The William and Mary Quarterly: A Magazine of Early American History*, 3rd ser., iv (1947), 409–445.

tioned diary-writing pioneers who now lives in Topeka, Kansas) on the early history of southwest Pennsylvania and the adjacent counties of northwest Virginia and Maryland. These chapters, with such titles as "Indian Wars and Massacres," "Early Forts," "Forgotten Towns," "First Courts and Court Houses," are based in large part on the data contained in the diaries and court records printed in the first 140 pages of the volume. Volume II is made up of more than five hundred family histories and genealogies of the early settlers in the region, and these, too, depend on the Horn diaries and records for their validity. On cursory examination, therefore, *The Horn Papers* look like just another example of the standard type of local history issued by so many county and state historical societies during the last century. As such, *The Horn Papers* appeared to be an extremely valuable publication, not only for students of local history but also for professional scholars, who draw much material required for building up a more comprehensive picture of the American past from works of this type.

Nevertheless the appearance in print of these innocuous-seeming historical data in 1945 drew forth a charge almost unprecedented in the annals of American scholarship. Made by Mr. Julian P. Boyd, Librarian of Princeton and recognized authority on the history of western Pennsylvania, this charge appeared in the July 1946 issue of the *American Historical Review*, which as the official publication of the American Historical Association is the most influential historical journal in the United States. Mr. Boyd wrote, after a careful examination of *The Horn Papers:*

I think the conclusion is inescapable that large parts of the documentary materials in the first two volumes, including diaries, maps, court records, memorandums, and even lead plates and hieroglyphs, are sheer fabrications. I do not know of any similar publication of fabricated documents among all the thousands of documentary publications issued by American historical societies.

This suspicion of forgery—the most serious charge that can be leveled at any historical writing—focused attention on the mystery of *The Horn Papers;* but it did not solve that mystery. Mr. Boyd felt sure that part of the materials was manufactured—but some of the documents had the ring of authenticity, and he confessed that the true and false were so intermingled that it was difficult to separate them. The situation was further complicated by the opinion of two other professional historians—also experts on frontier history—Dr.

30: The Mystery of the Horn Papers

Paul Gates and Dr. Julian P. Bretz, who rejected the idea that the Horn documents were fabrications.[1] There was no reason to doubt that in the main they were authentic eighteenth-century documents, badly edited by amateurs whose chief sin was lack of scholarly training. It was this slovenly editing, Mr. Bretz and Mr. Gates believed, that had misled Mr. Boyd and aroused his suspicions. . . .[2]

The committee appointed to investigate *The Horn Papers* began their analysis of the published volumes with an impartial mind. It was soon discovered that the materials published in Volumes i and ii furnished internal evidence that bore out Mr. Boyd's judgment.

I

The *prima facie* reasons why portions of the documentary material in *The Horn Papers* appeared to be spurious are: (1) evidences of ineptitude in copying the original manuscripts; (2) anachronistic and doubtful words and phrases; (3) biographical anomalies; (4) historically incorrect or doubtful statements; (5) internal discrepancies; and (6) internal similarities of documents purporting to be of different authorship.

A glance at *The Horn Papers* reveals that the documentary material was carelessly presented. Although the original manuscripts are said by Mr. Horn to have been in very poor condition and partially illegible when he copied them in 1891, there are few or no indications of omissions, of conjectural reconstructions of damaged pages, or of illegible or doubtful words. These deficiencies, although more heinous in connection with the documentary material, are by no means confined to it. The secondary material, containing many quotations from supposed primary sources, is usually without citation, and never with an adequate citation. This leads one to surmise either that the copyist was completely unfamiliar with accepted editorial techniques or that he had reason to conceal the source of his information.

Although editorial ineptitude puts the careful scholar on his guard when considering specific details, it is not necessarily evidence against the authenticity of a document as a whole. Much more important evidence is the frequent appearance of anachronistic and doubtful words and phrases, for it is well known that "anachronisms are the rock on which counterfeit works always run most risk of shipwreck."[3]

---

[1] *Pennsylvania History,* xiii (1946), 309–310.
[2] At this point eighteen pages of the original article have been omitted.—Eds.
[3] James Anson Farrer, *Literary Forgeries* (London, 1907), 2.

Evidence for Authorship

The documentary material in *The Horn Papers* abounds in such words and phrases, some of them quite impossible for the eighteenth century[4] and many others highly dubious.[5] Scarcely a page is devoid of them. Similarly, many passages in the diaries have the ring of nineteenth-century rather than of eighteenth-century phraseology.[6] Others reveal virulent opposition on the part of Jacob Horn and his fellow pioneers to the king, parliament, and the royal government of Virginia—an attitude unknown when the frontiersmen were dependent on British power to defend them against the French and Indians.[7] It is well known that this opposition developed after 1765, not in the 1740's and 1750's.

An authentic diary would state the truth throughout, not just in a majority of its entries. It would be true, in all instances where the writer was in a position to know the truth. A genuine diary might, indeed, contain a false statement because the writer was misinformed, because he recorded hearsay that was in error, or because his judgment was faulty. But an authentic diary would under no circumstances

[4] Examples: "trail," used frequently in the Horn diaries as early as 1735, to mean a path or road, belongs to a later period—the earliest reference to it in the *Oxford English Dictionary* and the *Dictionary of American English* is dated 1807; the word "stow[a]way," used in the Jacob Horn diary in an entry for 1738, first appears in the *Oxford English Dictionary* in a reference dated 1834. Other undoubtedly anachronistic words and phrases in the Horn documents are "tepee" (1740), "Virginia Blue-bloods" (1748), "braves" (1748) for Indian warriors, and "Ranch" (1748) in the expression "Gist's Mule Ranch."

[5] Examples of doubtful words and expressions: "hometown" (1736), "fur trade house" (1739), "frontire spirit" (1739), "the wilds of Baltimore's Colony" (1739), "race hatred" (1772). The committee has on file a full list of such anachronisms of which the above is but a small sampling.

[6] Examples: "black pirates with a just claim only to the Devils own region" (applied to Christopher Gist's Baltimore creditors, 1770), General Washington referred to in 1777 by the Napoleonic title of "the First Consul of the Colonies," the Pennsylvanians referred to as "a body of long hair, big hatted set of loud talkers for freedom and peace" (1782) and as "long whiskered peace loving brethren from the Susquehanna" (1782).

[7] Examples: "the small Snow Creek Settlement are outside of Virginia Colonial directions. All men are their own masters, and say their own laws . . . I Jacob Horn, fear God, and his Holy Laws, but fear no man . . . Snow Creek . . . is beyond the Colonial Claims of Virginia . . . it is solely the land of the settlers, and no king, or colony hath a say over it" (1742); "I Jacob Horn am a loyal Virginia subject, so long as the King and Parliament set down no Ords" (1745); "I Jacob Horn, declare the King and Colony hath no jurisdiction over any part of this frontire settlement" (1748); Canon "declared Parliament Acts to be more of speech than of force" in Virginia (1750); "John Canon . . . heeds not the threats of the King nor the Acts of Parliament" (1750); "I, Jacob Horn, first, Virginia next, and Parliament when it is good to my will" (1754).

record the appearance and activities in the writer's company of a person when that person is known to have been elsewhere or after he is known to have died. A single instance of this kind would cast doubt on the authenticity of a diary even though every other entry were correct, for it would unquestionably demonstrate that the document had been tampered with. *The Horn Papers* contain not one but many such biographical irregularities, which form, perhaps, the most important single body of *prima facie* evidence against the manuscripts.[8] Closely associated with biographical errors are the many historically incorrect or doubtful statements, which, though too numerous to consider individually, have the cumulative effect of discrediting the Horn documents. A few instances might, after all, be the result of an occasional interpolation, an inexact rendering of an illegible text, or a typographical error in transcription or typesetting. But hundreds of statements of doubtful character scattered widely through the documents render it improbable that any such extenuating circumstances might account for these errors.[9]

Also damaging to *The Horn Papers* are the internal contradictions in the documentary material. Christoper Horn variously recorded Gist's death as having occurred from November 1768 to October 1770. The references to the date of the battle of Flint Top reveal that the author of both the Jacob and Christopher Horn diaries was completely unfamiliar with the Julian Calendar (in universal use in the British colonies until 1752) and that, as a result, the references are considerably at variance. Moreover, the ignorance of the calendar change resulted in situations such as the appearance in Williamsburg of Buck Eckerlin and his brother in October 1748, after having witnessed a battle on the frontier that was not supposed to have taken place until the following month.

From a purely stylistic point of view, there is evidence that the diary of Jacob Horn, the notes of Christopher Horn, the diary and daybook of John Horn the elder, and the Camp Cat Fish docket were

---

[8] Christopher Gist appears frequently in the Horn diaries during the years 1759–1769, and his death from eating a surfeit of wild grapes and red plums is recorded at "Laural Hill, or Little Haystack Knob" in 1769. But from unimpeachable contemporary documents we know that Gist died of smallpox *en route* from Williamsburg to Winchester, Virginia, in 1759. Other biographical impossibilities in *The Horn Papers* involve Thomas Cresap, John Canon, Dr. Samuel Eckerlin, and Jonathan Hager.

[9] A full list of impossible statements of this type is on file with the Institute of Early American History at Williamsburg.

probably written by the same person. In the writings of both Jacob and Christopher Horn the eccentricities are identical: the same misspellings,[10] the same use of anachronistic words,[11] the same use of doubtful words and phrases,[12] and the same historically incorrect or dubious statements.[13] Another similarity between the Jacob Horn diary and the Christopher Horn notes is the fondness of both for recording prophetic words of Gist and Canon. On the other hand, each of these documents is written in the same peculiar literary style—an ill-matched combination of extraordinary linguistic crudities or pseudo-archaisms and outbursts of romantic sentiment couched in graceful nineteenth-century language.

On the other hand there was a weight of evidence favorable to *The Horn Papers;* otherwise there would have been no disagreement about them. The mere bulk and complexity of the collection of papers, the impressive number of collateral artifacts, the absence of any pecuniary or other compelling motive for forgery, the unquestioned sincerity of the sponsoring society, the many statements in the manuscripts that agree with generally accepted facts all strengthened the opinion that some of the Horn documents were genuine.

II

In view of this conflicting testimony the investigation entered a second phase. *The Horn Papers* certainly could not be accepted as genuine in their entirety. The search now concentrated on the problem of discovering if any were unimpeachable. It was hoped by expert examination of the physical objects—the eighteenth-century manuscripts, the lead plates, the maps, the other artifacts—to rescue some bona fide material.

The original papers upon which *The Horn Papers* are based were, according to Mr. W. F. Horn, boxed up by Christopher Horn in 1795 and the chest handed down in 1809 to his son, John, and by him in 1856 to his grandson, Solomon. In 1882, Solomon Horn moved west and took it with him to Doniphan County, Kansas. Mr. Horn reported that when the chest was opened in 1891 at Troy, Kansas, by his father and himself, it was found to contain the family records and maps as

---

[10] "malitia"; "controll"; "corte"; and "storey."

[11] "blue Bloods"; "trail" (meaning path); "tepee"; and "brave" (Indian warrior).

[12] "wilds of," "Great Spirit," "black leaf tobacco."

[13] Gist's death in 1769; the incredible slaughter of Indians at Flint Top in 1748; John Canon described as a nephew of Lord Dunmore.

well as a number of artifacts—small wooden boxes, tools, objects of shell and stone, and glassware. Mr. Horn also asserted that the papers, being in a poor state of preservation—or, to use his words, "very much moth-eaten"—were partially illegible. But the introduction of *The Horn Papers* states that "many, including the court docket, were preserved," and the impression that a substantial portion of the original manuscripts had survived was sustained by statements in the promotional literature. The committee, however, learned from the President of the Greene County Historical Society that only the court docket and three of the maps purported to be original; everything else in the Society's possession was a copy made by W. F. Horn in 1891 of original papers no longer extant. In addition the Society had had two supposedly original items: (1) a torn portion of Lord Dunmore's receipt to Jacob Horn for the return of his commission as justice at Camp Cat Fish; and (2) a perspective map on birch bark of the site of Turkey Foot Rock made by Jacob Horn in 1751. Shortly after the Horn papers were deposited with the Society, the surviving fragment of the receipt vanished. Thereafter, the Society took steps to reproduce photographically the remaining papers, a timely precaution, for almost immediately thereafter the birch bark map also disappeared in an inexplicable manner. That left only the court docket, the three maps, and the artifacts. The manuscripts, purporting to be original, upon which *The Horn Papers* are based, amount to 56 of the 141 pages of primary material contained in the work.

The court docket together with several maps and a number of sheets of Mr. Horn's transcript of 1891 were accordingly sent by the Greene County Historical Society at the committee's request to Mr. Arthur E. Kimberly, of Washington, D.C.,[14] for scientific analysis. Mr. Kimberly's report follows:

This is a report of the examination of the alleged docket of "Camp Cat Fish Corte," three manuscript maps purporting to be of the period 1770–1790, and seven sheets of manuscript in the handwriting of W. F. Horn which are said to have been copied from diaries kept by various members of the Horn family about 1770. The docket and maps are discussed in detail below.

The alleged docket is an octavo volume two inches in thickness in an oversize leather covered board jacket which is obviously not the original cover, if such a cover ever existed. The pages are blue, laid 100 per cent rag paper watermarked "Henry & Co." or "Lacourade." Neither of

[14] Mr. Kimberly, who is on the staff of the National Archives, acted in a private capacity.

these watermarks is known to have been in existence during the period under consideration. The end papers and the edges of all the pages have been discolored, apparently with the same ink used in the text. The cord used in sewing the signatures together is clean and strong and the style of sewing is modern.

The text of the docket was written with a metal pen (first marketed in England in 1803) using non-ferrous blue-black ink of a type originating in Germany about 1836. This ink turns brown and tends to smudge when brought in contact with an alkali. If a sponge dampened in ammonia had been used to give the appearance of age, the observed smudging of the writing and bleaching of the paper could be explained. In some cases the first line or two on a page were not treated and so survive "unaged." Minor corrections made after "aging" also exhibit a blue color.

The largest map (10½" × 13¾") bearing the legend "MDCCLXV— Louis Map of MDCC LI by Doughty" is drawn in pencil and ink on comparatively modern paper (1860 or later). Both blue and brown ink notations are shown and the entire map has been given an ink (brown) wash followed by a coat of wax. The blue ink notations were made after the map was waxed.

The second map (5½" × 8⅞") number "39" is of the same general character as the above, but has no wax coating. The ink is of the type used in the docket, the body of the map being brown while river banks and a trail are drawn in blue.

The smallest map (3½" × 6") bearing the legend "Gist Map of MDCCL C. Horn" is on rag, laid paper and is drawn in pencil and brownish red ink. Faint ink lines have been overdrawn with modern lead pencil and the words "Cat Fish" have been added in the same pigment. Pin holes in the upper left and lower right corners suggest that this item might be a tracing.

Excerpts of the Horn diaries in the admitted hand of W. F. Horn are written in ink of the same type used in the docket and maps. The color of the ink varies from blue to brown indicating that these specimens were used in experiments on artificial aging. The handwriting resembles that of the docket in many respects.

In view of the results set forth above, it is my opinion that:

(1) The docket and maps were not produced during the period 1760–1800 as stated but were manufactured at a considerably later date.

(2) One person . . . produced all of the items examined.

(3) Although the precise determination of the age of ink inscriptions of this type is difficult, it is most probable that these writings were produced no earlier than 1930.

Washington, D.C.
April 25, 1947   [*signed*] Arthur E. Kimberly

31

Letters to a Pagan
Not by Hearn[*]

By Albert Mordell

IN 1933 Robert Bruna Powers published in Detroit, in a limited edition, a volume called *Letters to a Pagan by Lafcadio Hearn*, containing twenty-eight letters alleged to be from Hearn to Countess Annetta Halliday Antona, addressed as "Pagan." The first letter, undated, purportedly from New Orleans, would have to be assigned to the year 1878, since it refers to the dengue fever which we know that Hearn had then contracted. The book contains altogether eleven letters from New Orleans, of which the third is dated 1882 and the last 1887; nine from the island of Martinique, of which eight are dated 1887 and one 1889; one from New York in 1890; and seven from Japan, of which the first is assigned to Yokohama, 1890, and the last to Tokyo, 1901.

In some quarters these letters have been accepted as genuine letters by Hearn. No less a person than his own son, Kazuo, the eldest, has translated them into Japanese. They have been cited by some scholars and translated into French; on the other hand their authenticity has been privately denied by several Hearn scholars. Let us then examine these letters and see if from internal evidence they could be by Hearn.

On a first reading of these letters the impression is that they reveal the familiar characteristics of the author. Here are the same ideas and style, the same favorite notions and prejudices, the same literary allusions, as are found in his writings and published correspondence. Moreover, there is inserted in the book a facsimile reproduction of a two-page letter from St. Pierre, dated 1887, on yellow paper such as Hearn used in his early days because his poor eyesight could not endure the glare of white. (No facsimile, however, of an addressed envelope with a canceled stamp is given.) In a Foreword the publish-

[*] Abridged from the two-part article in *Today's Japan*, IV, No. 11 (Nov.–Dec. 1959), 7–18, V, No. 1 (1960), 89–98, with permission of author and publisher.

er states that Annetta Halliday, the recipient of these letters, was a woman who had known Hearn as a child in Cincinnati during the 1870's, had married an Italian Count named Alessandro Giuseppe Valerio Antona, and was living in Detroit. She is said to have kept a girl's diary of many of her experiences with Hearn.

The first question as to the authenticity of these letters arises from conflicting indications of her age. In one of the letters (p. 40) Hearn is represented as saying, "I was an inhabitant of this world almost a generation before you entered it," which would imply that she was about twenty-eight years younger—hence born about 1878 (about the time the letters begin!)—but in the Foreword we are told that the friendship began in Cincinnati in 1871, when she was a child and he a book agent who told her ghost stories.

Let us examine the letters themselves. We note that there are numerous fairly long passages to be found verbatim in essays and published letters of much later date. As repetitions, these are suspiciously clumsy and often irrelevant; they are also frequently inaccurate and anachronistic.

In the first letter, from "Hearn" in New Orleans to "Pagan" in Cincinnati, we read (page 15):

The city is sprinkled on lamp posts and piazza pillars with signs Décédé, Décédé. Soon it may read,
"Ce matin à trois heures,
Lafcadio
Natif de . . ."
They are firing off cannon every day as a prevention, but it usually brings rain. It is not yellow-jack with me,—as yet, just dengue, and there is no help for it but lemon juice.

Here is what Hearn wrote in 1878 to his friend Henry E. Krehbiel, the music critic, then also living in Cincinnati:

I had another attack of dengue, but have got nearly over it. I find lemon-juice the best remedy. All over town there are little white notices pasted on the lampposts or the pillars of piazzas bearing the dismal words:
Décédé
Ce matin à 3½ heures
Julien
Natif de . . .
and so on. . . . Somebody is advocating firing off cannon as a preventive. . . . It brings on rain. . . .[1]

[1] Elizabeth Bisland, *Life and Letters of Lafcadio Hearn*, I, 185–188.

31: Letters to a Pagan *Not by Hearn*

There is no reason why these similar passages could not have been written independently to different correspondents. So far, so good. But as we read on in this first letter to Pagan, we find this sentiment in connection with the fear of death: "How the human soul fears to break through its chrysalis even though Infinite Peace lies dimly beyond." Eleven years later, in 1889 in a letter to Dr. George M. Gould, Hearn used almost the same language in describing poetry as touching what science cannot, "the fluttering of the Human Soul in its chrysalis, which it at once hates and loves, and strives to burst through, and still fears unspeakably to break,—though dimly conscious of the infinite Ghostly Peace beyond" (Bisland, I, 461).

The repetition of this metaphoric language, for matters unrelated to each other, is rather surprising over a great lapse of years.

A couple of sentences later in the Pagan letter occurs this passage:

If I obtain oblivion, that which you know of me, whatever we may call it, will surely become a revenant, but not, (no, no, Pagan) not in the form of a bat, for I know your repugnance. I should not like you to beat me away with cries of disgust, and I should be tempted to fasten my teeth into your little wrist gently though, not to hurt you, and hang on until you stroked my head.

The clue to this apparent nonsense is supplied by another letter of 1889 to Dr. Gould (I, 465–466). A bat entering his room reminded Hearn of one that had done so in Martinique when he was in the village of Grand Anse with his friend Arnoux (in June 1888). It had been suggested that the bat was Hearn's former landlady coming to visit him; the bat interrupting the letter, Hearn wrote to Gould, might be the soul of his Martinique washerwoman, recently dead:

I caught it in my hat, and it revealed its plain nature by burying its teeth in my fingers; . . . but I tried to caress its head, which felt soft and nice. But it showed its teeth. . . .

In Hearn's book *Two Years in the French West Indies* (1890), in an essay called "Un Revenant," he says that Martinique has been called "Le Pays des Revenants."

We now ask ourselves how Hearn in New Orleans in 1878 knew of the superstition of revenant bats which he first learned about in Martinique in 1888? How does he happen to give Pagan in 1878 an imaginary description of a caressed bat which tallies with the description he would write in 1889 of an experience of 1888? There is no conclusion other than that the composer of the 1878 letter copied from the genuine letter of 1889.

Another amazing coincidence is the use of identical language in a description of the "green masses" of "frondage" in New Orleans, in the 1878 letter, and in a description, first published by Hearn in 1887, of the scenery of Trinidad. Another is a passage advising "Pagan" to "write to Maisonneuve and Cie, Paris, for the Oriental catalogue. You will find all you want of Egyptian music there"—which parallels Hearn's advice, in a letter of 1883, to Krehbiel, who we know was interested in Egyptian music: "I find in my oriental catalogues Villoteau: *Memoirs sur la Musique de l'antique Egypte.*—Paris: Maisonneuve & Cie, 1883 (15 fr.)" (I, 285).

Thus we see that the first letter is made up of scraps from Hearn's books and genuine letters, and reeks with anachronisms. The second and third letters also contain passages that seem derived from genuine letters to Krehbiel.

The third letter, dated May 1882 from New Orleans, deals with subjects found in a letter to Krehbiel in 1880, with similar details about double flutes, Overbeck's *Pompeii*, etc., and speaks of showing Pagan's manuscript to Krehbiel—who was then not in New Orleans but in New York. But the person who composed the 1882 letter misunderstood the 1880 letter and made Hearn guilty of a serious blunder in the dates and details of a reference to his translation of "King Candaules" and other stories from Gautier. It becomes clear that the 1882 letter is an artificial rehash of the 1880 letter to Krehbiel.

In other letters Hearn is made to incorporate passages from the works of modern critics, biographers, and editors. I am personally flattered to find that Hearn is made to copy matters from an Introduction I wrote to a book of selections from his fugitive writings twenty years after his death. The following suggestion, for example, was original with me:

Possibly some day Cincinnati and New Orleans will honor themselves by erecting statues to this greatest literary man who ever abode in those cities.[2]

When I made this suggestion, Hearn had an international reputation, having being translated into Japanese, French, German, and other languages. He had been dead twenty years; there was a uniform edition of his works in sixteen volumes; there were already several

[2] *An American Miscellany* (1924), I, lxxvi.

biographies of him. Hearn was famous, though not regarded as a literary star of the first magnitude. The idea arose out of my admiration for Hearn. The suggestion about the statues has not so far been adopted.

In the eighth letter to Pagan, September 1884 (p. 34), Hearn is depicted as having the same thought: "Perhaps some day Cincinnati and New Orleans will set up a monument to the greatest literary man who ever lived in these cities." But what had Hearn done up to that time? A volume of translations from Gautier in 1882 and a volume of adaptations of stories with no pretense to originality, *Stray Leaves from Strange Literature,* published in June 1884. What did he really think of himself and of these books before the date of this letter? Fortunately there is testimony in his genuine letters. The Gautier volume, he said, had "divers inaccuracies and errors." The *Stray Leaves* volume he felt was "not a gorgeous production, only an experiment." What was his general opinion of himself in 1883? "Knowing that I have nothing resembling genius and that my ordinary talent must be supplemented with some sort of curious study in order to place it above the mediocre line, I am striving to woo the Muse of the Odd," etc. (I, 290–291).

The fact that Hearn is made to add, "You who always say I am overmodest, does that appeal to you?" should not mislead us. No, I am afraid the pseudo-Hearn must have read my suggestion—though the real Hearn died twenty years before it was made.

Strangely enough there is another parallel in the same letter. In my Introduction I had written:

Hearn was attracted by any tale in real life or fiction that dealt with inter-marriage between the races. The story of Baudelaire's marriage to a dark woman appealed to him and the greatness of Loti was enhanced for him because Loti's plots dealt with the loves of white men and women of other races.

"Hearn" writes to "Pagan" on page 34 of the 1884 letter:

I am attracted to anything that deals with intermarriage between the races. Perhaps this accounts for my fondness for Loti's plots of the loves of white men and women and other races and breeds. Baudelaire married a dark woman.

And there are still other borrowed matters, including a list of Hearn's literary admirers in the eighties—but Hearn is made to say that he has "pleasant memories of them all," though he would not have had of Stoddard or Cable at that time—and a list of editors of the newspapers he worked under in Cincinnati and New Orleans—getting the name of one of them wrong. Indeed four passages that I wrote in 1924 are lifted by the composer of two of Hearn's letters to Pagan dated September 1884 and December 1890.

On another occasion it seems that Hearn was mistaken about the nature of a literary composition of his own. In the collection of his newspaper writings called *Occidental Gleanings*, I included an article from the Cincinnati *Commercial* for April 9, 1878, called "Black Varieties" with the subtitle "The Minstrels of the Row." (I identified it as Hearn's from internal evidence and also because his newspaper editor on the paper, Edwin Henderson, whom I met in Cincinnati, said to me when I mentioned the article, "That is Hearn all over.") In the sixth letter to Pagan, dated 1883, the pseudo-Hearn refers to "the Minstrel Show I wrote in that same town [Cincinnati] and called it *Black Varieties*." But the newspaper article was simply an eyewitness account of a visit Hearn paid to a theatre on the levee in Cincinnati where a Negro performance was going on. I fear the writer of the letter was led to create the legend of Hearn's writing a minstrel show by his faulty reading of the title and subtitle of the article I had discovered and reprinted.

The same letter shows another strange lapse. "Hearn" tells "Pagan" in 1883, "You know I am now on the Editorial Staff of the T-D" (*Times-Democrat*). Well, it took him a long time to find it out or to tell it to Pagan. He had been on the editorial staff during the whole of 1882, while he had supposedly sent her one letter in that year followed by two others in 1883 before the present one.

Hearn in some of these letters is made to repeat mistakes of his biographers and editors, and worse, invent fictitious and libelous episodes to supply gaps in his biography. In a long autobiographical letter dated Martinique 1887 (pp. 68–75) he attempts to clear up his mysterious life in London, and he writes to Pagan that (as his biographers well know) this period was a sealed chamber to all but a few. The pseudo-Hearn repeats in this letter, however, an early biographer's erroneous account of his having been a student in a monastery in Wales; has him in London in 1869 when he was really in New York; and even uses two of the biographer's double adjectives, "travel-stained, poverty-burdened."[3]

[3] Compare Milton Bronner, ed., *Letters From a Raven* (1907), 22.

31: Letters to a Pagan *Not by Hearn*

In this letter an error of some of Hearn's biographers, namely, that he spent two years in New York before going to Cincinnati, is repeated. The letter tells of occupations in New York, waiter, dishwasher, vendor, which were really occupations he followed in Cincinnati. "Hearn" then relates two apocryphal stories of having seduced a girl in London and having been arrested as a pickpocket there. "And so, dear friend," he concludes to "Pagan," as if to help future biographers, "the lost months of my life like the hidden years in Christ's, have been stripped of secrecy and bared to view,"—Hearn the agnostic alluding thus to Christ!

The author of the letters to Pagan is made to solve another mystery that has puzzled biographers. The question, first raised by Eugene Field, as to whether Hearn had ever written a book called *Perfume of Women*, was discussed by E. L. Tinker (*Lafcadio Hearn's American Days*, 1924), who found the evidence tenuous. No one has ever seen the book, which was said to be limited to thirty copies and was supposed to be pornographic. The bookseller Hawkins once said that he had such a book in his safe, later that he had never heard of it. No copy was found in his safe after his death. As if to dispel these doubts, "Hearn" writes in 1885 (p. 38):

Pagan, I have written a book, no, not a real book, more of a brochure, to amuse my male friends. You will not see it, so you shall not be shocked, but Hawkins proposes to burn it if he outlives me. I call it *Perfume of Women*.

In some of the letters "Hearn" avails himself of his biographers' research into matters on which the real Hearn was not informed, such as his own ancestry. In several he draws upon passages in essays written by the real Hearn many years later. But the composer of the letters may have thought he could repeat Hearn's exact statements because on some occasions Hearn *did* repeat himself. I myself had said that Hearn's lectures on literature at times were made up from old literary editorials and that "he repeated himself in later life and often plagiarized from himself." The biographer Nina Kennard made a similar observation. But the repetitions in these letters are entangled in absurdities and incongruities and anachronisms.

The style at times seems, when not directly copied, like an imitation, instead of Hearn's real style. Slips are made that would be strange for a writer so careful as Hearn was of his English. An 1887 Pagan letter speaks of filmy fogs that come "felinely, like a cat" (p.

59), an unpardonable pleonasm. And the singular thing about this comparison is that it appears to be an anticipation, by a generation, of Carl Sandburg's rare comparison in the frequently quoted poem called "Fog." The pseudo-Hearn also appropriates a simile from a poem by Sara Teasdale, "Let It Be Forgotten," published sixteen years after Hearn's death. The poem concludes with the lines:

> 'As a flower, as a fire, as a hushed footfall
> In a long forgotten snow.

"Hearn" says to "Pagan": "Let it be forgotten as a silent footfall in a long-forgotten snow" (p. 105).

An instructive comparison can be made to two groups of authentic letters written by Hearn in the 1870's and 1880's. They do not sound like the letters to Pagan. Nothing in them is found that reappears in his books or other letters.

We have to conclude then that the letters attributed to Hearn in *Letters to a Pagan* are spurious, made of garbled passages from his genuine letters and essays, full of inaccuracies and anachronisms, repeating mistakes of some biographers, and copying passages from articles and books about Hearn composed after his death. One letter charges Hearn with flagrant crimes he is not known to have committed. I consider it a literary service to present and future students of Hearn to warn them of the inauthenticity of this volume.[4]

[4] I shall conclude by stating that two letters to Pagan dated May 1887 were sold at auction as genuine in 1938—one signed "Paddy," a name Hearn dropped in 1869 when he came to America and did not use even on letters to his brother, who knew him by that name.

ANNOTATED
BIBLIOGRAPHY OF
SELECTED READINGS

Editorial Note

AS we have stated in the preface, we regard the Annotated Bibliography as an important part of this book. The aim of the bibliography is to call attention to, and, whenever practicable and advisable, to give specific, compact descriptions of, selected studies in authorship printed between about 1940 and 1960. We have sometimes gone beyond these limits, especially in the following categories: (1) Discussions of the canons of major writers before 1660—here we have offered a conspectus reaching back to the beginnings of scholarship on a given question (see in particular the Shakespeare entries, below). (2) Essays of special interest, such as those by M. St. Clare Byrne in *The Library*, 4th Series, xiii (1932), and R. C. Bald in *Bibliographical Studies in the Beaumont and Fletcher Folio of 1647* (1937). (3) Recent developments in statistical studies and computer applications. (4) Continuations of controversies first aired in the *Bulletin of The New York Public Library*, in its series on internal evidence and in related articles.

Even when we have stayed within the chronological limits specified above, we have had to be severely selective. It was not feasible, of course, to include all essays on problems of attribution printed between 1940 and 1960. (In addition to consulting the *Cambridge Bibliography of English Literature* and the various period bibliographies in scholarly journals, the reader interested in completeness may readily track down omitted entries in the *International Index to Periodicals*, under the headings "Authorship, Disputed," with cross references to specific authors, and "Authorship," with various subject references.) Although we recognize that we may have overlooked valuable essays, we hope that our principles of selection have been reasonable. Obviously, the normal distribution of canonical studies in English literature has weighted the balance in favor of works written before 1660. The older literary canons have in general presented more problems than the more recent ones, and since scholarship in the older canons began earlier, there have been greater opportunities to define issues, test arguments, and improve methods. Apart from such historical considerations, our selections have been influenced by the inherent interest

397

of the subject (we have favored Shakespeare at the expense of other playwrights), by the thoroughness and originality of the study itself (we have preferred articles to notes, and novel methods or applications to familiar ones), by the concreteness, though not necessarily the conclusiveness, of the arguments (some internal evidence, like that for assigning the "non-Marlovian" scenes in *Doctor Faustus*, seems too indefinite and uncertain to be of much interest), and by illustrative vividness, whether of good or bad procedure (a jewel needs a foil to set it off). With a few rare and obvious exceptions, we have had to exclude reviews of books. Throughout, want of space has imposed hard choices. In the section on English Literature before 1500, for instance, we had room for but one debate about single versus multiple authorship. The decision to include the debate about William Langland meant that we had to omit the debate about the *Pearl* Poet.

The survey of the *Piers Plowman* controversy is by Sumner J. Ferris, the rest of the Annotated Bibliography by the editors. Ephim Fogel is responsible for the entries before 1660 and David Erdman for those after that date, but each editor has contributed some entries in the other's area. We leave the identification of these insertions to readers who have exhausted other problems of attribution.

Note. The order of entries within each period is alphabetical by author or pseudonym. Under each author the items are listed chronologically. It should be noted further that the period between 1500 and 1660 is subdivided into "Nondramatic Literature" and "Elizabethan Drama."

English Literature to 1500

ATHELSTAN'S *ORDINANCE*

Sisam, Kenneth. "The Authenticity of Certain Texts in Lambarde's *Archaionomia* 1568," in *Studies in the History of Old English Literature* (London, 1953), 232–258; reprinted from *MLR*, xvii (1923), 100ff.

Sisam refutes the hypothesis of a lost MS source for the English text of Athelstan's *Ordinance* in Lambarde's *Archaionomia* of 1568 (requiring the anomaly of two independent drafts of a law text); he accounts for the unidiomatic grammar and syntax by supposing that Laurence Nowell, Lambarde's teacher, composed an Old English text from the Latin. This study is apparently an exhaustive reply to twenty-one points made in defense of authenticity. The 1923 article was objected to by F. Liebermann in *Anglia-Beiblatt*, xxxv (1924), 214–218; Sisam's reply is included in *Studies*.

Whitelock, Dorothy. "Appendix: On the Supposed Lost Manuscript used by Lambarde," *EHR*, lvi (1941), 19–21.

"Mr. Sisam's views received remarkable confirmation when the British Museum acquired a transcript of Nowell (see R. Flower, 'Laurence Nowell and the Discovery of England,' *Proceedings of the British Academy*, xxi, esp. n. 16)."

BARBOUR

Coldwell, David F. C. "Wyntoun's Anonymous Contributor," *JEGP*, lviii (1959), 39–48.

The anonymous contributor of several thousand lines of vigorous Scottish verse, taking up history where John Barbour's *Bruce* left off, to the otherwise grave Chronicle of Andrew of Wyntoun was most probably Barbour himself. Coldwell finds no good reason why Barbour should not have been the author; much cumulative evidence of parallels in word-choice, in spirit, in thought, in literary technique, lead to the conclusion that Barbour or else "a disciple not much younger than Barbour, yet possessed of a bibliomaniac attachment to the letter of the *Bruce*" must be the author. Varying degrees of force in kinds of internal evidence are recognized.

CHAUCER

A greater volume of apocryphal works has been attributed to Chaucer than to any other English writer. For hundreds of years, *The Testament of Love* by Thomas Usk, *The Complaint of the Black Knight* by John Lydgate,

Annotated Bibliography

The Testament of Cressida by Robert Henryson, *The Flower and the Leaf,*
The Cuckoo and the Nightingale, La Belle Dame sans Mercy, and other
substantial compositions swelled the so-called *Works of Chaucer* to more
than twice the bulk of the writings today accepted as canonical. As F. N.
Robinson states—*The Works of Geoffrey Chaucer* (Boston, 1957), xxviii—
"Skeat's Oxford Chaucer (six volumes, 1894) and the Globe Chaucer
(1898) were the first modern collected editions from which such spurious
works were rigorously excluded." The processes of accretion and rejection
are traced in some detail in Eleanor P. Hammond's excellent *Chaucer: A
Bibliographical Manual* (New York, 1908), 51–69, 114–149; in John Edwin Wells's *A Manual of the Writings in Middle English, 1050–1400* (New
Haven, 1916), 617–623 (see also the nine supplements to 1951); and
more recently in Francis W. Bonner, "The Genesis of the Chaucer Apocrypha," *SP*, xlviii (1951), 461–481. The three fullest 20th-C. discussions
of the authenticity of individual works are Hammond, *Manual*, 408–463
(see also s.v. "Authenticity" the discussions in alphabetical order of the
canonical works, pp. 354–405); W. W. Skeat, *The Chaucer Canon* (Oxford,
1900); and Aage Brusendorff, *The Chaucer Tradition* (London and Copenhagen, 1925). Because of the importance and the illustrative character of
the history of the Chaucer apocrypha, a brief summary may be useful to
readers of the present volume.

Several of Chaucer's own statements encouraged the growth of the
apocrypha. In listing the works he had composed (Prologue to *The Legend
of Good Women,* headlink to *The Man of Law's Tale,* and the "retracciouns"
at the end of *The Parson's Tale*), Chaucer named some that do not seem
to have come down to us (e.g., "the Wreched Engendrynge of Mankynde,"
"Orygenes upon the Maudeleyne," "the book of the Leoun") and named
others in very general terms. John Lydgate in his Prologue to *The Fall of
Princes* repeated the list of works claimed by Chaucer himself, added one
or two puzzling allusions (e.g., to "Daunt in English"), and ended by
noting that "my maister, in his dayes / Made and compiled ful many a
fresh ditee / Complaintes, ballades, roundles, virelaies / Ful delectable to
hearen and to see." Since the acknowledged genius of Chaucer encouraged
imitations, often anonymous, many of these were ascribed to the master by
careless admirers. It is not surprising that scribes and readers tended to
credit, say, a poem on Mary Magdalen to Chaucer on the strength of
stylistic resemblance and the Chaucerian reference to "Orygenes upon the
Maudeleyne." Chaucer's vague references to "othere bookes of legendes of
seintes, and omelies, and moralitee, and devocioun," to "balades, roundeles,
vyrelayes," and to "many another book, if they were in my remembraunce,
and many a song and many a leccherous lay" (cf. the echoes by Lydgate,
above) afforded an even broader scope for canonical conjecture.

Few of those who augmented the canon paid very close attention to internal evidence. Speght, to be sure, rejected some pieces on linguistic grounds (1598): "[other works] I have seene without any Authours name, which for the invention I would verily judge to be Chaucers, were it not that wordes and phrases carry not every where Chaucers anitquitie." But only a systematic study of Chaucer's grammar and prosody could provide a firm basis for discrimination, and since such a study did not get under way until almost three hundred years after Speght's edition, judgments of authenticity were in the meantime bound to be uncertain. Both John Stow (1561) and Speght (1598, 1602), for example, printed as Chaucer's *The Court of Love*, a late 15th-C. or early 16th-C. imitation of a medieval poem, by an unknown author who, as T. R. Lounsbury puts it, combined "a modern grammar with an archaic vocabulary," and who invented morphemes unknown to Middle English (cf. Skeat, *Canon*, 127–135).

On the other hand, the rejection of spurious pieces from the canon owed much to the accumulation of data about Chaucer's grammar, phonology, diction, and prosody. Thus the first scholar to present a detailed historical account of Chaucer's language and versification was also the first to reject a large body of apocrypha. We refer, of course, to Thomas Tyrwhitt, whose edition of *The Canterbury Tales* appeared in 1775–1778. Although, in Miss Hammond's words (*Manual*, 211), Tyrwhitt "formed his [canonical] judgments . . . mainly upon his notions of Chaucer's style," those notions must have been strongly reinforced by his study of Chaucer's syntax and prosody, and Miss Hammond concludes, "It is perhaps upon the canon . . . that the results of Tyrwhitt's labors are most conspicuous and most permanent." (For the rejection of *The Testament of Cressida*, *La Belle Dame sans Mercy*, and other works, Tyrwhitt cited non-Chaucerian ascriptions in books and MSS.)

By applying internal evidence, Henry Bradshaw and other 19th-C. scholars eliminated several apocryphal works retained by Tyrwhitt. In 1868 Bradshaw rejected *The Court of Love*, *The Cuckoo and the Nightingale*, *The Flower and the Leaf*, *The Isle of Ladies*, *The Romaunt of the Rose*, *The Complaint of the Black Knight*, and various shorter poems. Bradshaw "appealed to what is known as the 'y-ye test,' that is, to the fact that Chaucer in his admittedly genuine works did not rime together words which etymologically end in -y and words which end in -ye, e.g., *trewely* with *folye*" (Hammond, *Manual*, 67). Such rhyme tests and certain grammatical criteria were disputed by some but applied by others, conspicuously by Skeat. The discovery of the true authorship of *The Testament of Love* makes a fascinating story (Hammond, 458–459; Skeat, *Canon*, 97–99), which deserves brief mention. Bradshaw questioned Chaucer's authorship in the first half of the 1860's. Hertzberg pointed out in 1866 that Chaucer would not have referred to himself by name (*Testament*, Book III, ch. 4) as one who "in witte and in good reson of sentence . . .

passeth al other makers." Skeat pointed out in 1893 that the first letters of the chapters in the *Testament* yielded the sentence MARGARETE OF VIRTW HAVE MERCY ON THSKNVI: the last word he interpreted as an anagram for the name of the presumable author, Kitsun. But Henry Bradley, who believed that Usk was the author, showed by a close examination of the sense of the text (1897) that certain leaves had been misplaced and that these when properly rearranged yielded not THSKNVI, but THIN VSK (i.e., "thine Usk").

One recent scholar has been conspicuous for his emphasis on external evidence. Aage Brusendorff's stated purpose in *The Chaucer Tradition* (London and Copenhagen, 1925) is "to examine the way in which the knowledge of Chaucer's personality and writings was handed down by the first two generations of the XV century, in order to show that our information, scrappy though it is, represents a fully authoritative tradition, which yields some important biographical facts about the poet and offers the sole reliable basis for a true bibliographical canon of his works." Brusendorff regards as decisive the testimony transmitted by Lydgate and by Lydgate's associate John Shirley, scribe, booklender, and publisher. (On the significance of Shirley for the canon of Chaucer and of early 15th-C. poets, see Hammond's *Manual*, 515–517, and her *English Verse between Chaucer and Surrey* [Durham, N.C., 1927], 191–197.) Brusendorff argues that a Thomas Chaucer who must be the poet's son (this view is generally accepted) was Lydgate's patron and must have passed on to him reliable information about Geoffrey Chaucer and his works. And Shirley's testimony, in turn, is also of special authority because of his close relationship with Lydgate. Brusendorff also sets forth complicated hypotheses about such matters as the state of Chaucer's text and the poet's share in the translation of *The Romaunt of the Rose*. *The Chaucer Tradition* met with a mixed reception; see the reviews listed in Dudley D. Griffith, *Bibliography of Chaucer: 1908–1953* (Seattle, 1955).

Because of the labors of scholars from Tyrwhitt to Bradley, only one possibly dubious work of any considerable length remains in 20th-C. editions of Chaucer. The poet's statement that he "translated the Romauns of the Rose" (*Leg. of Good Women*, G, 255) seems to be corroborated by Lydgate and Deschamps, and the unique M.E. version of that poem is printed in various modern editions, including both of Robinson's (1933, 1957). Chaucer's authorship of this fragmentary translation was questioned, however, in the late 1860's; Francis J. Child stated in 1870 that the treatment of the translation changed at about line 5814; Max Kaluza in 1890 pointed out that the division was really tripartite. Of the three fragments (A, 1–1704; B, 1705–5810; C, 5811–7696), A is today generally accepted as Chaucer's; B is rejected, in large measure because of the frequent occurrence of Northern dialectal forms; and C is considered rather doubtful, though defended by some as Chaucerian (cf. Hammond, *Manual*, 450–454: Robinson [1957], 564–565, 872). Brusendorff (*The Chaucer Tradition*, ch. 5) offers the ingenious—and coolly received—hypothesis that all three fragments are the remains of what was once a complete Chaucerian translation set down from imperfect memory by an early 15th-C. writer from the northern Midlands.

Given the previous history, one can well understand the reluctance of scholars to add a work to the Chaucer canon. The following entries deal with two additions proposed since 1935, "An Holy Medytacion" and *The Equatorie of the Planetis.*

Wretched Engendering

Brown, Carleton, "Chaucer's *Wreched Engendring*," *PMLA*, L (1935), 997–1011.

Brown's thesis is that the poem "An Holy Medytacion" (hereafter *HM*) attributed to Lydgate in a 15th-C. MS (see under Lydgate, below) is the lost "Wreched Engendring" to which Chaucer refers in *The Legend of Good Women*, G:

> "He hath in prose translated Boece,
> And of the Wreched Engendrynge of Mankynde,
> As man may in pope Innocent yfynde." [413–415]

The reference is to Innocent's *De Contemptu Mundi, sive de Miseria Conditionis Humanae* (hereafter *DCM*). *HM* is a translation of a 13th-C. Latin poem *De Humana Miseria Tractatus* (hereafter *Tractatus*), which in turn is a translation of *DCM*. After stating that Chaucer's phrase "in prose" applies only to the Boethius and after trying to explain away Chaucer's reference to Innocent's work rather than to the *Tractatus*, Brown offers the following arguments:

1. John Shirley's ascription of *HM* to Lydgate is unreliable (see under Lydgate, below). In the Trinity MS, *HM* is second in a group of five pieces, of which the first, fourth, and fifth are by Chaucer.

2. Two full columns of examples show that the author of *HM* uses rhymes used by Chaucer.

3. Chaucerian phrases such as "lat see" and "ye gete na-more of me" occur in *HM*.

4. To imitate Chaucer's style successfully while translating the Latin *Tractatus* "would have been, one may well believe, an impossible *tour de force.*"

5. Though translated from the *Tractatus*, the description of springtime in *HM* is "an adumbration of the Canterbury prologue."

Brown's article initiated a flurry of controversy. J. S. P. Tatlock indicates his skepticism in "Has Chaucer's *Wretched Engendering* Been Found,"

MLN, LI (1936), 275–284. Though he concedes that Chaucer's authorship of *HM* is possible, he emphasizes Chaucer's words "in prose" and "in pope Innocent," and argues that *HM* is "mostly . . . of a different mood and temper from Innocent's *DCM*." The author of *HM* specifically avoids the "wretched engendering of mankind," i.e., "the odiousness of conception and gestation," to which Innocent devotes the first five chapters of his work and with which the *Tractatus* also deals. Moreover, almost half of *HM* is original material not in the *Tractatus*, whereas when Chaucer used "translation," he meant a rather faithful following of a foreign work. Tatlock goes into the possibilities that *HM* is by Lydgate or by "a sensitive though not talented admirer" of Chaucer. Such imitation is not "an impossible *tour de force*."

In "Did Chaucer Write *HM*?" Germaine Dempster (*ibid.*, 284–295) seconds Tatlock's objections and adds others of her own. Using contemporary non-Chaucerian poems, she shows that they have a greater frequency of "Chaucerian" rhyme-pairs than Brown cites from *HM*. She suggests that the absence of an ascription to Chaucer is significant, since Shirley in the Trinity MS ascribes to Chaucer nine of ten poems today accepted as genuine and to Lydgate twenty-eight of twenty-nine canonical poems. She finds in *HM* an un-Chaucerian spirit of professional preaching and of moralizing, emotional and intellectual poverty in dealing with the central concerns of Christian faith, and un-Chaucerian phrasing and vocabulary. Somewhat paradoxically, perhaps, Mrs. Dempster also argues that the "very frequency of characteristically Chaucerian phrases . . . is the clearest earmark of imitative work. . . . No other indication of unauthenticity is as decisive as an overdose of the easily imitable."

In "An Affirmative Reply" (*ibid.*, 295–300), Brown cites from Chaucer rhymes and phrases similar to those that Tatlock and Dempster call un-Chaucerian. "Engendering," he believes, should not be limited to procreation: "Chaucer had in mind rather man's existence as conditioned by his [sinful] inheritance from Adam." *HM*'s omission of the details of procreation shows Chaucer's good taste.

Germaine Dempster's "Chaucer's *Wretched Engendering* and *HM*," *MP*, XXXV (1937–1938), 27–29, is a concise "resketching" of the arguments against Brown's attribution. The essay, Mrs. Dempster says, "has been read by Professor Tatlock and can be taken as our joint work."

In "Chaucer's *Wreched Engendrynge*" (*ibid.*, 325–333), Beatrice Daw Brown (Mrs. Carleton Brown) restates and in some cases refines upon her husband's arguments. Among other matters, she suggests that *HM*, presumably an early work, should be compared with early works in the Chaucer canon; she believes that in such a poem in couplets as Chaucer's "Legend of Ariadne," which Lowes thought was early work, the style is similar to that in *HM*.

In "The Vocabulary of *HM*," *PQ*, xvii (1938), 359–364, Mildred Webster selects at random fragments of 180 consecutive lines from poems by Chaucer, Gower, Occleve, and Lydgate and compares them with the 180 lines of *HM* for vocabulary held in common with Chaucer. (The percentages derived for the Chaucerian fragments total less than 100, since words that occur nowhere else in the canon are not counted.) Miss Webster's conclusion is that the vocabulary of *HM*, 99.4% of which occurs in Chaucer, "is more consistent with Chaucer's practice than with the practice of Lydgate, Gower, or Occleve." She fails to check, however, to what extent *HM* would agree with the Lydgate fragments, say, as against the fragments by the other three authors. Neither does she allow for margins of error; one notes that the percentage derived for *HM* is closer to the percentages for two fragments by Gower (98.95, 98.6) and one by Lydgate (98.38) than to that for a fragment of Chaucer's portion of the *Romaunt of the Rose* (98.3). Furthermore, Dorothy Everett observes (*YWES* for 1938, p. 63) that Miss Webster's "grouping of words is sometimes odd. For example Gower's *noman* is said to be 'non-Chaucerian,' though *no man* is frequent in Chaucer."

Robinson (1957) does not reprint *HM;* he states (p. 845) that "the Wreched Engendrynge" is "apparently a lost translation, complete or partial" of *DCM*, and he cites without comment the articles in the controversy initiated by Brown.

Equatorie

Price, Derek J. *The Equatorie of the Planetis* (Cambridge, Eng., 1955).

See esp. ch. 11, which suggests that the text and the first set of tables of *The Equatorie* (Peterhouse MS, 75.I) "are a Chaucer holograph of about 1392." Since the materials with which one can compare *The Equatorie* are limited, Chaucerian authorship is put forward not as definitely proved but rather as a tentative explanation that can best account for "the facts and indications": (1) The MS is an author's holograph, with an autograph date of 1392, and examples for the year 1391 (as in Chaucer's *Treatise on the Astrolabe*). (2) The ascription of the work to Simon Bredon (in a 16th-C. hand) must be wrong, since Bredon's will was proved in 1372. (3) The name "chaucer," which occurs in the same hand as the rest of the text proper, is very similar to the "chaucer" in a PRO document of 1378, thought by scholars to be a Chaucer holograph. (4) *The Equatorie* has many coincidences of phrasing with Chaucer's *Astrolabe*. (5) Linguistic analysis by R. M. Wilson indicates that the dialect is the same as Chaucer's, the English of London or southern Midlands, and that nothing in the style or language is "definitely against Chaucerian authorship."

Reviews 1. Curt S. Zimansky, *MLN*, lxxi (1956), 70–76. "At the least, the evidence is as probable as that for Shakespeare's hand in *Sir*

Thomas More." But Zimansky believes, as does Norman Davis (below) that acceptance of Chaucer's authorship will have no important effect on the textual criticism of the poetry.

2. Robert W. Ackerman, *PQ*, xxxv (1956), 220–223. The "chaucer" note is "the strongest piece of evidence brought forth in the book," but there is "no clear parallel of intent and perhaps of method in *The Astrolabe* and *The Equatorie*." We must wait for new and more positive evidence of authorship.

3. A. C. Crombie and N.[orman] D.[avis], *RES*, n.s., ix (1958), 179–183. Davis argues that Chaucer's poetry does not always provide a safe basis for canonical inferences. Certain linguistic forms in *The Equatorie* (e.g. forms of the word *work*) differ rather consistently from the forms in Chaucer's poetry. Chaucer obviously had some connection with *The Equatorie*, but "we may never know for sure what part he had" in it.

4. Roland M. Smith, *JEGP*, lvii (1958), 533–537. Smith says that Price's caution about authorship (and F. N. Robinson's in not admitting the *Equatorie* into his ed., 1957) is proper. He reviews Chaucer's possible associations with the Oxford scene. The final verdict must await evidence which may yet turn up, since medieval MSS on astronomy are so plentiful.

See also Smith's comments on Herdan, below.

Herdan, G. "Chaucer's Authorship of *The Equatorie of the Planetis*: The Use of Romance Vocabulary as Evidence," *Language*, xxxii (1956), 254–259.

The Romance language of Chaucer's works, as counted by Joseph Mersand (1935) and re-examined by G. Udny Yule (1944), varies, Herdan finds, according to the logarithm to the base 10 of the total words in the text. The formula may be expressed

$$P_v = 10 \log_{10} N,$$

where P_v is the percentage of Romance vocabulary, and N is the total number of words. Since Herdan estimates 6,048 words in the printed text of *The Equatorie* and since the logarithm of that total is 3.78, one would expect 37.8% Romance words in the work if it is by Chaucer. Herdan's count of words in the glossary shows an actual Romance percentage of 37. "The good agreement between theory and observation provides evidence for Chaucer's authorship of the *Equatorie*." This argument appears in slightly different form in Herdan's *Language as Choice and Chance* (Groningen, 1956), 17–22.

Norman Davis, p. 182, n. 1, and Roland M. Smith, p. 535 (see above), criticize Herdan for comparing the prose *Equatorie* with Chaucer's poetry rather than with his prose, which, as scholars have pointed out, has a higher percentage of Romance words than the poems. Joyce Bazire (*YWES* for 1956, p. 101) objects that "Herdan has not indicated what the margin of error may be" and mentions other limitations of his statistics.

CYNEWULF

Philip, Brother Augustine. "The Exeter Scribe and the Unity of the *Christ*," *PMLA*, LV (1940), 903–909.

Since 1853, when F. Dietrich suggested that the first three poems in the Exeter Book are a single poem, all scholars have not agreed. The scribe's scheme of spacing, capitalization and end-marking is discussed (and illustrated) to make the point that he regarded the three as independent poems. It is recalled that the title is a modern invention. (See next entry.)

Mildenberger, Kenneth. "The Unity of Cynewulf's *Christ* in the Light of Iconography," *Speculum*, XXIII (1948), 426–432.

This scholar surveys earlier controversy (including criticism of the argument that the Exeter scribe was consistent); he finds "an ideological foundation for claims of unity" in the pictorial record of a tradition in which the three themes in the *Christ*, Advent, Ascension, and Judgment, are treated in threefold unity—a tradition known in 8th-C. Northumbria.

HILTON

Hodgson, Phyllis. "Walter Hilton and 'The Cloud of Unknowing': A Problem of Authorship Reconsidered," *MLR*, L (1955), 395–406.

Miss Hodgson gives a thorough demonstration of the fundamental differences between two bodies of writing that have many apparent similarities, in this case "The Cloud of Unknowing" and the works of Walter Hilton. (Several previous discussions of the case are cited.) Similar wording with different meaning might be explained as change in one author's views, but could an author have "deliberately and consistently redefined his epithets, giving them fresh associations"? Passages traceable to a common stock are not significant in similarity but in divergency; strong differences are seen in use of common images, in sentence structure, and in word patterns.

LANGLAND

See *Piers Plowman*.

LYDGATE

MacCracken, Henry Noble, ed. *The Minor Poems of John Lydgate*, EETS, extra ser., CVII (1911).

See the section on "The Lydgate Canon and Index to the Canon," pp. v–lviii, in which are discussed, briefly, Lydgate's rhyme, meter, and style. MacCracken believes that "internal evidence gives doubtful results" (p. v), yet feels that because of the uniformity of Lydgate's practices, "tests of rhyme, rhyme-tag, metre and phrase should be applied with almost absolute precision" (p. vi). On pp. 43–48 is reprinted "An Holy Medytacion" (hereafter *HM*), attributed to Lydgate by John Shirley in Ashmole MS 59. (On Shirley see the headnote on Chaucer, above.)

Carleton Brown lists *HM* as "by Lydgate" in *A Register of Middle English Religious and Didactic Verse*, II (Oxford, 1920), 28. In 1925, however (*MLN*, XL, 282–285), Brown rejects *HM* from the canon—no great loss to Lydgate, he feels—because Shirley's ascriptions in Ashmole 59 are not entirely reliable; because the opening of *HM*, like much of the poem, is a direct translation from a 13th-C. Latin poem and not, as might be supposed, an imitation of the Prologue to the *Canterbury Tales;* and because *HM* contains instances of "penultimate or antepenultimate rhyme of words in -oun," one of MacCracken's tests for spuriousness. In 1935 (*PMLA*, L, 997 ff.), while arguing that *HM* is by Chaucer (see above), Brown states that MacCracken's rhyme test is invalid, since Brown's partial check has revealed sixty-seven instances in Lydgate of the supposedly excluded rhyme. But he still firmly believes that *HM* is not by Lydgate, and he is supported in this view (p. 1009) by Henry Bergen, editor of Lydgate's *Troy Book* and *Fall of Princes*. In the post-1935 debate on Chaucer's *Wretched Engendering* (see above) Tatlock suggests, without pressing the point, that *HM* may after all be Lydgate's.

MIDDLE ENGLISH ROMANCES

Baugh, Albert C. "The Authorship of the Middle English Romances," *MHRA Annual Bulletin of the Modern Humanities Research Association*, No. 22 (Nov. 1950), 13–28.

From scattered hints and passages, from subject matter, sometimes from tone, it can be deduced that the Middle English romances were only sometimes composed by the minstrel who recited them, more often by court poets, even scholars, and quite often by clerics.

LAURENCE NOWELL

See "Athelstan's *Ordinance*."

PIERS PLOWMAN

Chambers, R. W. See essay No. 9.

[The following summaries of studies in the authorship of *Piers Plowman* are by Sumner J. Ferris.]
The Vision of William Concerning Piers the Plowman . . . by William Langland, ed. W. W. Skeat (2 vols., Oxford, 1886).
Piers the Plowman: A Critical Edition of the A Version, ed. Thomas A. Knott and David C. Fowler (Baltimore, 1952).

Piers Plowman: The A Version. Will's Visions of Piers Plowman and Do-
Well, ed. George Kane (London, 1960).

The authorship of Piers Plowman (hereafter PP in all occurrences) was
at one time acrimoniously disputed, though it is no longer a major subject
of controversy in M.E. studies. Its earlier history, only briefly alluded
to here, can be traced in detail in M. W. Bloomfield, "Present State of PP
Studies," Speculum, XIV (1939), 215–232, and Wells, Manual and Supplements (see Chaucer above), ch. 4, sec. II, No. 51, 244ff. In 1866 Skeat
first clearly demonstrated the existence of three versions of PP: A (to use
his designations) apparently the first, B a revision of A, and C a revision of
B. In the introduction to his ed. (originally published by EETS, 1867–
1884) he largely rather assumed than demonstrated that all three (with an
exception to be noted) were by one and the same author; and he took this
author to be the "Will" who is the dreamer-narrator of PP and identified
him with the William Langland (otherwise unknown to history) mentioned
in a note (in a medieval hand) to a C MS. In particular, Skeat saw an anagram of Langland's name in B, XV, 148—"I haue lyued in londe, quod I ·
my name is longe wille"—and reconstructed the poet's life from apparently
autobiographical remarks in the three versions.

J. M. Manly was the first really to urge the case for multiple authorship,
which he did in a series of publications from 1906 to 1910, when he retired from the field unconverted (see T. A. Stroud, "Manly's Marginal
Notes on the PP Controversy," MLN, LXIV [1949], 9–12, but cf. George
Kane in MLR, XLIII [1948], 1, n. 3). Manly contended that A was really
two separate poems—the Vision of Piers Plowman proper, etc., in the Prologue and first 8 passus, and the Vita de Do-Wel, Do-Bet, and Do-Best in
passus 8–12—each by a different author, and that B and C were written by
still two other poets. (To one John But various critics assign various shares
of A, XII.) Manly's principal argument is that there would seem to have
been a "lost leaf" in the ancestor of A (and thus in the MS used as the
basis of the revision into B), a loss which, in this view, caused an omission
of Wrath from a series of Seven Deadly Sins and the inappropriate placing
of Robert the Robber under the Sin of Sloth—two errors, Manly believed,
that B and C do not cope with satisfactorily. Moreover, Manly professed to
see a progressive deterioration in the quality of the three versions, successive misunderstandings of A by B and of B by C, and important and irreconcilable "differences in diction [and dialect], in metre, in sentence
structure, in methods of organizing material, in number and kind of rhetorical devices, in power of visualizing objects and scenes presented, in topics
of interest to the author and in views on social, theological and various
miscellaneous questions" in the work of the four authors (CHEL, II [1908],
ch. 1). For Manly "Will" was an entirely fictitious, assumed personality
and the surname "Langland" probably due to a scribe's misunderstanding

of the very line Skeat cited. Manly was answered, point for point, by many critics—most notably in the early years by J. J. Jusserand and (over thirty years' time) by R. W. Chambers and J. H. G. Grattan, who pointed out the inadequacy of Skeat's texts (esp. *A*) and promised new eds. of all three versions, which they said would decisively disprove Manly's various contentions. (Only now are these eds. beginning to appear: *A* by George Kane, *B* to be by E. T. Donaldson and Kane, and *C* by A. G. Mitchell and G. H. Russell.) Manly's position was taken, though often modified or refined, by T. P. Dunning (who later recanted; see *Medium Ævum*, xii [1943], 45, n. 1), Samuel Moore (who argued that there is no necessary presumption of single authorship), and Thomas Knott; otherwise chiefly by Manly's students and colleagues such as Mabel Day. But most critics of *PP* not directly concerned with the authorship controversy (e.g., of late, A. C. Spearing, John Lawlor, and Elizabeth Salter) either assume or have been persuaded of the truth of the theory of single authorship. J. R. Hulbert, in "*PP* after Forty Years," *MP*, xlv (1948), 215–225, not in the main adducing new arguments, has attempted a restatement and defense of Manly's views. He contends, *inter alia*, that there are striking and obvious literary differences among the three versions; that what may seem to a modern reader to be peculiarities of subject, attitude, etc., in these three versions often prove to be medieval commonplaces; and that Manly's opponents, notably R. W. Chambers, mask the weakness of their case by means of logical and rhetorical slipperiness. The first contention, as Hulbert admits, is a matter for personal judgment; but the second is no more a proof of multiple authorship than of single authorship; and the third might be said to apply at times to critics of both persuasions.

For a few years there were a number of close comparisons of the versions of *PP*, in attempts to prove either single or multiple authorship. (The attribution to William Langland remains, as it has always been, a lively side issue.) Bernard F. Huppé, in "The Authorship of the A and B Texts of *PP*," *Speculum*, xxii (1947), 578–620, seeks to show by this means that the *B*-poet did not misunderstand *A*, as Manly had said, and that the same author probably wrote both versions. He argues that the *B* revision of the Prologue and first eight passus appears to be by the author of *A*; that because *A* stops abruptly after the Vita de Do-Wel and before the promised Vita de Do-Bet and Vita de Do-Best (since Chambers, a generally but not universally held opinion), the author would seem to have been interrupted while writing this part of the poem; that this interruption was due in large measure to the political crisis of 1376–1377 (cf. the Rat Parliament in *B*, Prol., 146–207, usually taken to be a fable of the Good Parliament of 1376), which caused a "deepened pessimism" in the author; that he rewrote the *A* version in this mood, completing the Vitas, making the new version more topical, achieving in it a greater sense of unity and clarity, and adding a continuation quite in keeping with what he had already written.

An important, posthumously published article by R. W. Chambers, "Robert or William Longland?" *London Mediæval Studies*, I, pt. 3 (1948, for 1939), 430–462, has been neglected by some students (possibly because it was published after World War II, in an irregularly issued journal, but bound in a volume dated "1937–39"). Chambers begins by examining a cluster of 16th-C. passages by John Bale and others, including one in Huntington Library MS Hm 128, which ascribe *PP* to "Robert Langland"; Hm 128 also contains an earlier ascription, "Robert, or *William* langland made pers ploughm*an*." Skeat assumed that this was a 15th-C. note, but bibliographical analysis by experts at the Huntington Library has proved that the inscription must have been written some time after the MS was rebound, probably about 1540. Furthermore, this late ascription almost certainly arose from a corruption of the opening line of *Vita de Do-wel*, "Thus i-robed in russet · romed I aboute," to "*And y Robert in rosset gan rome abowhte*," a line which actually occurs (with minor variations) in two MSS. We can therefore understand why Bale and other early antiquaries assumed that "Robert" was the author's Christian name and that Will the Dreamer was "a purely imaginary personage." But there is no reason, Chambers urges, for us to follow these early scholars in their error. In *PP*, as in the allegorical dream-visions of the 13th and 14th C. by Dante, De Lorris, De Meun, De Deguileville, Ruteboeuf, Huon de Meri, Raoul de Houdan, Chaucer, and Gower, the author claims to be the dreamer. Some of the circumstantial details in these author-dreamer identifications may be conventional and fictitious; but other details, including the name of the poet, can only be actual. And so it is with *PP*: the literary convention would lead us to expect the author-dreamer to record his name, and Langland does so in several places—notably in *A*, VIII, 42, "Then were merchants merry, and gave Will *for his writing* woollen clothes," and in *B*, XV, 148, "I have lyued in londe, quod I · my name is longe wille"; Chambers also cites *B*, XII, 16, where the dreamer is addressed as a poet, one who "meddles with makings," and he compares the dreamer-*writer* identifications at *B*, XIX, 1, 478. Chambers regards Manly's admittedly unique interpretation of "long will" as "long experience and observation" as an arbitrary attempt to explain away evidence of authorship. And finally Chambers points out, "there is a vital piece of external evidence" in the *C*-MS memorandum, in a contemporary hand, about will*ielmi* de Langlond," son of "Stacy de Rokayle" and author of *PP*. "It is the mere wantonness of skepticism," Chambers concludes, "to refuse to attend" to this external evidence.

E. T. Donaldson's *PP: The C-Text and Its Poet* (New Haven, 1949) is primarily an attempt both to rehabilitate the reputation of *C* (whose in-

feriority to *A* and *B* had been conceded even by advocates of single authorship) and, though only secondarily, to show that the author of *B* (and of
A) was the author of *C* too. Donaldson argues, for example, that the *C*-poet
knew *B* as thoroughly as only the author of *B* would have been likely to;
that there are no inexplicable inconsistencies between *B* and *C*; and that
the art of *C* (in respect to alliteration, etc.) is strikingly similar to that of
B. Most important, however, is the demonstration, largely by means of an
investigation of what the *C*-poet meant by "commune," that there seem to
be no significant differences in political attitude between *B* and *C* (though
some may feel uneasy at Donaldson's largely philological approach to a
historical problem). Donaldson accepts William Langland as the author
and finds sufficient autobiographical data in *PP*, whose historical accuracy
can be confirmed from other sources, to conclude that Langland was, as
Will seems to be, "a married clerk, of an order certainly no higher than
acolyte, who made his living in an irregular fashion by saying prayers for
the dead or for the living who supported him" (p. 219). Not all of Donaldson's arguments are equally persuasive, but he does show that the *C*-poet
must have known *B* remarkably well; and it would be difficult to imagine a
medieval author creating an entirely fictitious persona with such circumstantiality and such accuracy of detail in that circumstantiality.

The relevant portions of Howard Meroney's "The Life and Death of
Longe Wille," *ELH*, xvɪɪ (1950), 1–35, are epigrammatic, allusive, and
sometimes cryptic. For him the anagram in *B*, XV, 148, that Skeat found in
"I haue lyued in londe, quod I · my name is longe wille" does not exist.
The line is properly to be understood in the light of the discourse on
charity in I Corinthians 13 (of which the opening of *B*, XV, is a paraphrase): the first half being equivalent to *factus sum vir* (v. 11), the second to *Caritas patiens est* (v. 4). "Longe wille" is thus a Biblical allusion,
equivalent to *Longanima;* and the "hero's epithet thus means 'Long Suffer-
ing' or 'Great Desire'"—as Manly had in part suggested. Moreover, for
Meroney, *A* "is an abridgement for a nonclerical audience by a redactor
of the B-Version, who abandoned his project when the poem became too
esoteric"; that is, *B* is the first version, not *A*. Meroney goes on: "I would
state the grounds of my conclusion thus: (1) The Latin is handled in such
a way that omissions by A are more likely than additions by B; (2) by the
same token, strange words of Romance origin and odd turns of English expression are so handled that their avoidance by A is more likely than their
introduction by B; and, finally, (3), many differences between the texts
indicate that the writer of A has failed to comprehend the original." Further, "One group of meddlers, call them the A-continuators, farced up a
spurious Passus A XII" that the A-reviser had failed to get to.

D. C. Fowler, in "The Relationship of the Three Texts of *PP*," *MP*, ʟ
(1952), 5–22, inaugurated the only real controversy about the authorship

of *PP* in recent years. Fowler proposed that errors in the *A*-MSS caused by scribal corruptions (due to line-skipping and attempts to compensate in various ways) were present in the archetypes of *B* and *C* and therefore presumably in their authors' copies of *A*. From a comparison of seven such seemingly corrupt passages in the *A*-MSS with corresponding passages in *B* and *C* (that is, in the established *texts*), Fowler concludes that the latter two are based on "corrupt originals" of *A* and are therefore by different authors from *A*—since the *A*-poet would presumably have used a "pure original" as the basis of his revisions. But Donaldson, in "The Texts of *PP*: Scribes and Critics," *ibid.* (1953), 269–273, takes issue with "several faulty assumptions" of Fowler's—notably that "the reconstructable *A*-text will . . . reproduce the author's autograph" (see the note on Kane's ed., below) and that it is possible to determine, as Fowler attempted to do, "whether any given alteration is the work of a scribe and not the conscious revision of a reviser," "without overt use of literary judgment" (and therefore without prejudice). Donaldson defends several of the seven passages in *B* and *C* as quite possibly the product of such conscious revision and finds "as much reason to ascribe the changes Fowler discusses to an aspect of the many-faceted miracle of creation as to the errors of intervenient scribes." And A. G. Mitchell and G. H. Russell, in "The Three Texts of *PP*," *JEGP*, LII (1953), 445–456, handle Fowler even more roughly, examining each of the seven parallel passages and finding Fowler's arguments in all cases variously "vague," "impossible," "highly improbable," etc. They conclude that Fowler nowhere establishes proof that the *B*- and *C*-poets used a faulty *A*-text and warn: "It is not always necessary to assume that the *A*-archetype must be correct as against the *B*-archetype. The *A*-reading may be an error that stood in the *A*-archetype, but not in the *A*-autograph or in a copy between the *A*-autograph and *A*-archetype upon which *B* is based." Fowler's case must be considered disproved.

Fowler's *PP: Literary Relations of the A and B Texts* (Seattle, 1961) contends that between *A* and *B* "there is a fundamental difference in spirit. The God of the *A*-text is St. Truth; the God of the *B*-continuation is St. Charity" (p. 118); and that *A* "gives aid and comfort to those desirous of revolutionary action against the social order," whereas *B* "calls for a revolution, not of society, but . . . within the individual," two views that "are perhaps not ultimately irreconcilable [but] nevertheless stand in significant opposition" (p. 205). The Dreamer, moreover, is not the author but an ironically handled, entirely fictitious character, who serves like Parsifal as "God's Fool." The true author of *B* was rather "a learned man, a member of the secular clergy, a fearless opponent of corruption in and out of the Church, a friend of the aristocracy, and a relentless opponent of the friars," quite possibly "John Trevisa, Vicar of Berkeley and chaplain to Thomas Lord Berkeley in the second half of the fourteenth century" (p. 186), best known to us as the translator of Higden's *Polychronicon*. Fowler adduces some similarities of attitude and concerns between Trevisa and the author of *B*, but admits that his only firm evidence is that Trevisa was probably Cornish, that apparently few clerks were, and that part of the Creation scene (*B*, XI, 332–353) in *PP* is "almost certainly derived from the Cornish [drama] *Origo Mundi*" (p. 204; cf. pp. 67–68). Fowler will probably fail to convince the unconverted. The differences between *A* and *B* are there, but to a critic of the opposing school may not be of major importance or may represent simply a change of intention by a single author for his poem. The first-person narrator of a dream-vision may seem obtuse and yet represent the author (Chaucer, e.g., in the *Book of the Duchess*). Fourteenth-century chroniclers and controversialists naturally cover much of the same material, with much the same attitudes; and the Creation scenes in *PP* and the clerically composed *Origo* may well go back to some common (Latin?) source or to a tradition not yet identified.

The Knott-Fowler edition of *A*, based on familiar Lachmannian principles of recension, briefly raised hopes that when texts of all three versions had been soundly established, conclusive stylistic comparisons of their diction, alliteration, etc., could be carried out. But in his definitive edition of *A*, Kane has demonstrated (pp. 53–114) that it is impossible to determine any genetic relationship among the *A*-MSS and that consequently not even the best critical edition of this version can represent either the author's autograph or the archetype of *A*. (Something of the sort seems to be true of *B* as well; see Donaldson, "MSS R and F in the B-Tradition of *PP*," *Trans. Conn. Acad. of Arts and Sciences*, xxxix [1955], 177–212.) Since an editor must therefore rely on the best, but necessarily imperfect, MS and his trained judgment in establishing a text of *A* (see Kane, pp. 115–172) and since Kane uses, for example, metrical regularity as one of the bases of deciding among variant readings, it would seem to have become extremely difficult to apply detailed and definitive tests of the language or style of *A*, *B*, and *C* in deciding between single and multiple authorship. (It may be pointed out that neither edition attributes *A* explicitly to Langland, but that the full title of Kane's—*Will's Visions of . . . Do-Well*—implies a theory of the incompleteness of *A* such as Huppé holds but Fowler, e.g., rejects: see the latter's review of Kane's edition in *MP*, LVIII [1961], 212–214.)

In sum, the recent advocates of single authorship for the three versions of *PP* have been more numerous, more convincing, and more resourceful than the advocates of multiple authorship. Future students of the question might perhaps try some new approaches. Philologists have illumined much of what is dark in the poem; one wonders what a trained medieval historian could contribute to the understanding of the attitudes evinced and the events reflected in each of the three versions. Perhaps the rapidly developing field of stylostatistics (with the proviso noted above) may offer some aid. But otherwise, as Donaldson has repeatedly emphasized, literary judgment must decide the issue (though Manly was an outstanding cryptanalyst, with the ability to find patterns and solve problems unnoticed by other men); and to date most of the best literary judges of *PP* have thought all three versions to be by the same author.—S. J. F.

George Kane's *PP: The Evidence for Authorship* (London, 1965) came to hand after the present Annotated Bibliography was set in type. To the student of attribution, the theoretical interest of Professor Kane's important study lies in its strict subordination of internal evidence to external evidence and to evidence derived from literary history. The organization of Kane's monograph is a direct consequence of this subordination. To the student of *PP* in particular, the practical interest of the monograph lies in its deliberately nonforensic manner and in its minute analysis—more complete and thoroughgoing than that of Kane's mentor, R. W. Chambers—of the external and literary-historical evidence for unitary authorship. Kane states that he and the other editors of *PP* were agreed at the outset of their work on the hypothesis of single authorship; now, an investigation stimulated by the appearance of David Fowler's study of 1961 (see above) has led to an unexpected positive result which, Kane believes, "has materially reduced the hypothetical element in our editorial position."

Professor Kane's first chapter is entitled "The Rationale of Ascription." Kane feels that by using the debate form, *PP* controversialists on both sides put "a premium on skill of advocacy rather than judiciousness" (cf. Dr. Ferris, above). Kane even omits a chronological summary of the arguments from internal evidence, in order to avoid reproducing a "give and take of disputation" which would be inconsistent with his intention "not to answer arguments but to test them." As a preliminary to the desired objective assessment of the evidence for and against the theory of single authorship, he briefly disposes of the "illusory" hope that a "scientific" determination of the text will provide decisive arguments derived from dialect, alliteration, and similar details (see Donaldson, Mitchell, Russell, and Kane, 1953 and 1960, above); he disposes, too, of the biographical argument, which has sometimes been "remarkably naïve" and has in general amounted to little more than a declaration of faith by both advocate and adversary of single authorship. One is left, then, with the central contention that the internal evidence derived from the three versions of *PP* is contrary to the external evidence of single authorship. Kane believes that it is essential to make and maintain the distinction between the two classes of evidence. External evidence, whether it is ultimately shown to be true or false, exists absolutely and "is a kind of physical fact," whereas internal evidence is logically to be regarded from another point of view. One must often have recourse to it and one may have to give it great weight. But it "is a critical postulate" and has "a contingent character," since it depends "for its existence on being identified as such by someone, and for its validity upon, first, the correctness of the identification, and second, the quality of the reasoning applied to it." If arguments for multiple authorship of *PP* from internal evidence are "critically, logically and historically compelling," the note in Trinity College, Dublin, MS D.4.1 "ascribing *PP* to Langland can be disregarded as referring at best to some one of the versions; if not it must be re-examined, since the possibility of its truthfulness has not been excluded."

Accordingly, in ch. 2 Kane examines the internal evidence adduced against single authorship and finds it seriously defective. There are, admittedly, differences between the three versions. *A* for instance, is better organized, more consistently visual, and less abstract than *B*, but these differences, where they have not been exaggerated, are to be explained by the different, and more difficult, undertaking of *B* as against *A*. Kane denies the hypothesis of a lost leaf. Certain alleged "discrepancies" between *A* and *B* are chimerical, and the rest can be attributed to "imperfect assimilation by a single author," and to the obviously unfinished character of *A*. In general, Kane concludes that the arguments for multiple authorship are neither necessary nor logical (some of them, indeed are characterized by extreme and even absurd special pleading) and that they have failed to demonstrate the antecedent probability that the hypothesis of multiple authorship is a better explanation of the differences apparent in *PP* than is revision by a single poet who, like most thoughtful writers, changed and developed over a period of time.

Kane has thus prepared the way for re-examination of the external evidence (ch. 3), which "takes the form of a number of ascriptions either physically distinct from the poem or otherwise unmistakably distinguished from its text." Of these the most important is the inscription at the end of a copy of the *C* version, Trinity College, Dublin, MS D.4.1: "Memorandum quod Stacy de Rokayle pater willielmi de Langlond qui stacius fuit generosus & morabatur in Schiptoun vnder whicwode tenens domini le Spenser in comitatu Oxoniensi qui predictus willielmus fecit librum qui vocatur Perys ploughman." Kane first shows that the attempts to weaken this ascription are ill-founded:

(1) Manly, following Skeat, who had not seen the MS, described the inscription as written "in a 15th-C. hand (but not early)"; but the best-informed modern paleographers date the hand as belonging to about 1400. The writer of the ascription could thus have had firsthand knowledge of the identity of the author. Moreover, the inscription is one of a series on the same leaf which displays "a considerable interest in the affairs of the

South Wales Border, and a good deal of local knowledge" (E. St. John Brooks, "The *PP* MSS in Trinity College, Dublin," *The Library*, 5th ser., vi [1951], 150).

(2) The argument that William Langland could not have been the name of the poet of *PP* if that poet were the legitimate son of Stacy de Rokayle is invalid. Students of British surnames have shown that in the 14th C. many surnames were not yet fixed and hereditary and that men were often named after a locality rather than after their fathers.

(3) The argument that William Langland must be a fictitious person since no such name has yet been discovered in Shropshire is invalid on both logical and historical grounds. As to the logical grounds, the *"argumentum e silentio* must rest in a situation like the present one upon three distinct assumptions: that all records have survived; that surviving records are comprehensive; and that the search in question" has been efficient. If any one of these assumptions is uncertain, the argument from silence is seriously weakened. As for the historical evidence, the muniments of the Childe family preserved in the Birmingham Reference Library contain legal documents dating from 1399 to 1581 and referring to various persons in Shropshire by the name of "Longland" (variously spelled); two of the Longlands named in 1524 and one named in 1577 bear the Christian name "William."

"The sum of these implications," Kane states, "is then that a William Langland, the son of Stacy de Rokayle, not merely existed but was known by the writer of the Trinity College, Dublin, ascription to have been concerned with writing poetry." Furthermore, two other ascriptions, that by John But in *A*, XII, 99–104, and an explicit in Liverpool Univ. Lib. MS F.4.8, agree that the poet's Christian name was William. Although one cannot exclude the possibility that this identification is derived from Will the Dreamer of the poem itself, But's lines also refer to the circumstantial detail of the poet's sudden and unexpected death.

Kane then explains away what appears to contradict the evidence of the Trinity College, Dublin, MS:

(1) Five *C* MSS state at the end of Passus X: "Explicit visio Willielmi .W. de Petro le plouhman." The ".W." could refer to an alternate surname of Langland (possibly "William Wychwood," after a locality with which Stacy de Rokayle was connected), or it could imply that the author was a William with a surname other than Langland. But the likeliest explanation is that the ".W." is the error of a single scribe writing in the exclusive common ancestor from which all five MSS having the explicit most probably descend.

(2) Analysis of agreements in biographical and other circumstantial data in various 16th-C. passages (see Chambers, 1948 for 1939, above) suggests that the ascription of *PP* to "Robert Langland" originated in an

inadequate early Tudor search for the identity of the poet, and that the ascription to "Robert" descended from a single exclusive common ancestor, the writer of which was probably misled by the "yrobed-I Robert" sophistication. Kane shows that the presence of this corruption caused at least two MSS to sophisticate a later line in the same passus (*B*, VIII, 124; *A*, IX, 118) which identified the dreamer as Will. The authority of the 16th-C. ascription to "Robert" is thus too light to overweigh that of the ascription of ca. 1400 to "Will."

But did one man, whether he was called "William Langland" or by some other name, write all three versions of *PP*? The rubrics in the MSS, Kane answers, show that the designation *PP* was applied to the entire poem, both the *Visio* and the *Vita* being regarded as parts of a single whole and the *A* version being regarded as incomplete unless it was followed by either *B* or *C* or both. "There is no evidence of an ancient view of multiple authorship, but some that single authorship was taken for granted."

Ch. 4, "Signatures," deals with "the implications of the fact that the first-person narrator in each of the three versions" is called Will. This is "neither external evidence of authorship, since the name is an element of the text, nor internal evidence, since its existence is absolute, not contingent on identification by the critical faculty." Kane's previous chapters have narrowed the problem of the names to the question: are the names in the poems deliberate signatures of the William Langland whom sound external evidence, uncontradicted by countervailing internal evidence, shows to be the author of *PP*? The answer is both a matter of literary history—the common practice in 14th-C. dream-visions—and of literary criticism: do "the disposition and function of the name in the three versions and the activities imputed to its bearer appear designed to encourage at least nominal identification of dreamer and poet?" Kane sets forth an array of evidence even more massive than Chambers' (see above) showing that 14th-C. poets used a variety of signatures—open, anagrammatic, punning, and so forth—in order to identify themselves as authors of many different kinds of poems, not merely dream-visions. In fact, Kane does not know of a single "substantive 14th-C. poem of known authorship recounting a dream-vision in the first person where the dreamer bears another name than the poet's." To insist that the dreamer Will "is a total fiction with another name than the author" is therefore "to posit a very remarkable exception." On the contrary, as Kane argues by detailed literary analysis of relevant passages, "the Dreamer Will represents an aspect of the author's developing conception of his own work." In *A*, the name "Will" is gradually particularized, as it is introduced on three separate occasions, in such a way that the reader is encouraged to make two deductions: that the name of the dreamer is also that of the author, and that author and dreamer are not to be identified completely. In *B*, references such as that at XIX, 1,

478, seem intended to diminish the distance between dreamer and writer. In *C*, the dreamer is named "Will" early (II, 3–5; the variants in some MSS are held to be nonauthorial), as if the author, in this redaction, wishes to introduce his signature as quickly as is convenient; in *C*, too, the dreamer emerges early as both sinner and censor, with a humility and personal involvement appropriate to his offences. "The presence of three signatures in each version," Kane concludes, "implies a systematic claim to authorship," and the cryptogram in the much-discussed line "I haue lyued in londe" (*B*, XV, 148), following what "was demonstrably a 14th-C. practice," is intended to give the author's full name, in a form that would be obscure to some readers, but clear to others. [One might add that this practice of revealing to the esoteric reader biographical information that was at the same time concealed from the exoteric reader was continued in Renaissance poetry and romances.]

In his brief "Conclusion" (ch. 5), Kane sums up his findings and affirms that in default of a sworn legal deposition by William Langland, "the common effect of [the] external and historical evidence is entirely unambiguous" and that its "single, unmistakable import" is entirely opposed to the theory of multiple authorship.

Although it is disputable in some of its formulations and details, Kane's is undoubtedly the most cogent and coherent argument on the *PP* question to date. It may indeed bring the controversy to a complete halt, unless some startling new external evidence should set it in motion once again. One may safely predict that it will consolidate an already dominant opinion concerning *PP*. Regarded from the point of view of the student of attribution rather than of the medieval specialist, the present state of the *PP* controversy appears as a counterpart to the present consensus about *Henry VIII* (see below, under "Shakespeare"). If the Elizabethan controversy suggests that internal evidence must in some cases overrule apparently authoritative external evidence, the medieval controversy suggests that external and historical evidence must in other cases establish an overwhelming presumption of authorship which tends to diminish radically the force of contrary arguments from internal evidence. Both lessons are equally salutary.—Eds.

WULFSTAN

Whitelock, Dorothy. "Wulfstan and the So-called Laws of Edward and Guthrum," *EHR*, LVI (1941), 1–21.

This study corrects the date of a code inaccurately called Laws of Edward and Guthrum (EGu), on evidence of the code's strong influence only after 1008 and its content and style; notes linguistic and stylistic correspondences between EGu and some other codes and the writings of Wulfstan; presents the most likely explanation in his having had a hand in the compilation; and reconstructs "the probable course of events" though "aware that it stops short of proof."

Whitelock, Dorothy. "Wulfstan and the Laws of Cnut," *EHR,* LXIII (1948), 433–452.

This article attributes both an earlier and later version of Cnut's laws to Wulfstan, on complex evidence of style, method of work, opportunity, sources, exemplification of Wulfstan's views, and preservation among Wulfstan MSS.

Bethurum, Dorothy. "Six Anonymous Old English Codes," *JEGP,* XLIX (1950), 449–463.

The redating of a number of documents removes difficulties in the way of recognizing "Wulfstan's highly characteristic style" in six codes preserved in MSS with close associations with Wulfstan (early 11th-C.). The evidence "merely on stylistic grounds" is presented as conclusive—and presented in some detail. "The alternative . . . is thinking that some very skilful imitator of his style, who knew also the range of his interests and had the same connection of subject and unrelated phrase . . . reworked these pieces in time for three of them to be put into Wulfstan's own commonplace book. . . ."

English Literature 1500 to 1660

BRYAN

Daley, A. Stuart. "The Uncertain Author of Poem 225, Tottel's *Miscellany*," *SP*, XLVII (1950), 485–493.

Starting with a possible anagram in the initials of stanzas (T-A-W-I-T interpreted as T.WIAT or WIATT), a detective pursuit is made for a poet who was an associate of Wyatt and suited the possibly autobiographical clues of the poem: Sir Francis Bryan is found to make a strong claim.

CLEVELAND

Withington, Eleanor. "The Canon of John Cleveland's Poetry," *BNYPL*, LXVII (1963), 307–327, 377–394.

In an analysis of 66 poems more or less doubtfully ascribed to Cleveland at one time or another, this scholar concludes: "My distrust of internal evidence will be obvious. It is not that I disagree with Berdan's tests for Cleveland's manner. It is just that this manner was tremendously popular and . . . successfully imitated. . . ."

Woodward, Daniel H. "Notes on the Canon of John Cleveland's Poetry," *BNYPL*, LXVIII (1964), 517–524.

Supplements Miss Withington's essay.

DANIEL

Gottfried, Rudolf B. "The Authorship of *A Breviary of the History of England*," *SP*, LIII (1956), 172–190.

Though printed over Ralegh's name (1693), the *Breviary* was found to reappear "almost word for word" in Samuel Daniel's *History*. Gottfried first sorts out the MSS for the best text, establishes a date (1612), and evaluates the weak claim of Ralegh, before supporting the claim of Daniel by a lengthy array of parallels.

DONNE

Langston, Beach. "A Donne Poem Overlooked," *TLS*, Jan. 18, 1936, p. 55.

Commendatory verses signed "IO:DONNE" are found in John Smith's *History of Virginia*, 1624.

REPLIES: "A Donne Poem?" *TLS*. Jan. 25, 1936, p. 75. B. H. Newdigate has sent a note of the same discovery to the *London Mercury* (Feb. 1936); John Hayward observes that the poem was not overlooked by editors, just not accepted; he suggests John Donne the younger—or John Done. *TLS,* Feb. 1, 1936, p. 96. I. A. Shapiro makes four points against Donne's authorship. B. H. Newdigate calls attention to his *Mercury* article (*TLS,* Feb. 8, 1936, p. 116). Roland B. Botting, compiling a concordance of Donne's poems, states that this poem has ten words not to be found in Donne's poetry, also different orthography and untypical use of stanza and of feminine rhymes (*TLS,* Mar. 14, 1936, p. 224).

MARVELL

Lord, George de Forest. See essays Nos. 2, 5, 8.

Fogel, Ephim G. See essays Nos. 4, 7.

Wallace, John M. "The Date of John Tatham's *The Distracted State,*" *BNYPL,* LXIV (1960), 29–40.

As the title indicates, this essay, the tenth in the *Bulletin* series "The Case for Internal Evidence," is concerned with the use of such evidence to solve a problem of chronology. Wallace prefers "a tentative probability on general grounds to an insistently-argued mechanical 'proof.'" In this context, he comments briefly on the earlier authorship controversy: "I am in only partial agreement with Professor Fogel . . . on the validity of accumulated minor testimony. Professor Lord's impressive case for attributing the second and third 'Advices' to Marvell depends mainly, in my opinion, on his statement that they are much superior to the numerous other contemporary satires he has seen (a statement which would be true also of Marvell's commonwealth poems), on his observation of very similar materials and a common loyalty to Charles in these poems and 'Last Instructions,' and on his recognition of a use of Ovid which distinguishes all three of them."

Lord, George de Forest, ed. *Poems on Affairs of State: Augustan Satirical Verse, 1660–1714. Vol. I: 1660–1678.* (New Haven, 1963).

Lord prints as Marvell's the second and third "Advices," "Last Instructions," "Further Advice to a Painter" (1671), and five other poems. For criticism of seven of these attributions, see the next item, below.

Wallace, John M. "Restoration Satire," *The Yale Review,* LIII (1964), 608–613.

In this review Wallace praises the annotations and other features of Vol. I of Lord's edition of *Poems on Affairs of State* (see the previous item), but has "a bone to pick with [Lord] about his attribution of poems to Marvell. . . . I do not consider the evidence for more than two of [the nine poems attributed to Marvell] to be securely based: 'Last Instructions' and 'Upon Blood's Attempt to Steal the Crown.' . . . The second and third 'Advices' . . . were the subject of his controversy with Professor Fogel four years ago [see essays Nos. 2, 4, 5]. He now refers readers to these articles, and on the strength of them writes of the poems confidently as Marvell's in this edition. I now think Fogel was right, and the vast superiority of 'Last Instructions' to the second and third 'Advices' could be easily demonstrated. . . . The evidence ought to be strong indeed before we make [Marvell] the author of very inferior work. It is to be hoped Professor [J. Max] Patrick in his forthcoming edition [of Marvell's poems] will be extremely circumspect."

OVERTON

Wolfe, Don M. "Unsigned Pamphlets of Richard Overton: 1641–1649," *HLQ*, xxi (1958), 167–201.

In an impressive introductory essay Wolfe discusses eight "criteria for identification of Overton's pamphlets" and grades them from "most conclusive" to "least conclusive" (the latter consisting of "correlative evidence only"). Getting down to specific attributions, however, he inclines to be satisfied with the lesser or least conclusive types of evidence and to ignore the caution of his introduction. On the other hand, in some instances (e.g. item 2, *The Passionate Remonstrance*) evidence felt as "unmistakable" appears to fall outside the graded criteria altogether.

PEELE

Parks, George B. "George Peele and His Friends as 'Ghost'-Poets," *JEGP*, lxi (1940), 527–536.

Eight of nine testimonial poems ascribed to nine eminent men of action, in *A True Reporte* (1583), are declared to be professional in style, probably the work of a single poet. The "G.P." of the dedication is deduced to be, not George Peckham, as always supposed, but Peele. The argument is circumstantial and deductive; evidence of style is cited but not brought into demonstration. See also "Peele" under "Elizabethan Drama," below.

RALEGH

See above, under "Daniel."

SIDNEY

Ringler, Jr., William A., and Fogel, Ephim G. See essays Nos. 16 and 17. See also the notes in *The Poems of Sir Philip Sidney*, ed. William A. Ringler, Jr. (Oxford, 1962), 349–358, 517–519.

SPENSER

Apart from the question whether "The Doleful Lay of Clorinda" in Spenser's "Astrophel" (lines 217ff.) is by Spenser himself or by Sir Philip Sidney's sister, the Countess of Pembroke, the only canonical question which in recent years has occasioned any extended discussion among Spenser critics is whether or not the English version of the *Axiochus* is by the poet. Since the discussion of the stanzas in "Astrophel" has failed to generate especially interesting arguments, the following entries are restricted to the problem of the *Axiochus*. For a review of the scholarship on this question, see Gottfried, 1949, below. Throughout the entries, the names "Mundy" and "Burbie" have been regularized.

Axiochus

During the 18th C. there were references by Thomas Osborne, John Upton, and others to a translation of the pseudo-Platonic dialogue *Axiochus* by Spenser. In the 19th and 20th C., scholars were unable to locate the work, and some were dubious of Spenser's connection with it. The *CHEL*, IV, 439, has the curious entry: "Axiochus, a Dialogue, attributed to Plato, translated by Edm. Spencer. Edinb., 1592. This was translated also by A. Mundy." No copy printed in Edinburgh or attributing the *Axiochus* to Mundy is now known. In 1932, however, Frederick M. Padelford obtained a 1679 folio of Spenser's works with which was bound the *Axiochus*, printed at London in 1592 for Cuthbert Burbie and *"Translated out of Greeke by Edw. Spenser. Heereto is annexed a sweet speech or Oration, spoken at the Tryumphe at White-hall before her Majestie, by the Page to the right noble Earle of Oxenforde."* The *Axiochus* contained an unsigned dedication to Benedict Barnam, Alderman and Sheriff of London; an address to the reader gave the translator's full name as "Edward Spenser." Padelford's copy lacked the "sweet speech" mentioned on the title page, but a copy containing the speech turned up in 1936 and was purchased for the Carl H. Pforzheimer Library. Meanwhile, Padelford had printed the translation as Spenser's in 1934. The arguments about authorship appear below. Among scholars who do not argue the case, Alexander C. Judson, *Life of Spenser* (Baltimore, 1945), p. 161, is benevolent toward Padelford's "natural assumption" but otherwise neutral; and C. S. Lewis, *English Literature in the 16th Century* (Oxford, 1954), p. 678, rejects Spenser's authorship.

Padelford, Frederick M., ed. *"The Axiochus of Plato"* by Edmund Spenser (Baltimore, 1934), 1–29.

The translation is Spenser's, but from a Latin rather than a Greek version. Since the poet's full name had not appeared in any of his works printed before 1592, it is not surprising that the first name appears on the *Axiochus* as "Edw." rather than "Edm." Some of Spenser's favorite words and characteristic phrases occur in the translation. As in Spenser's *View of the Present State of Ireland*, the prose sometimes falls into rhythmical and iambic five-stress patterns, "further evidence, if such were needed," of Spenser's authorship. The work is early (cf. especially the youthful qualities of "the snatches of poetry"), perhaps "well prior to . . . *The Shep-heardes Calender*" (1579). The euphuistic style of the translation could have been influenced by rhetorical devices found in works printed before *Euphues* (1579). The "sweet speech" was possibly by Spenser too. The literal 1607 English translation of Philippe du Plessis de Mornay's French version of the *Axiochus* may be the one attributed to Mundy in *CHEL*, IV, 439.

Freyd, Bernard. "Spenser or Mundy? A Note on the *Axiochus*," *PMLA*, L (1935), 903–908.

Freyd doubts the ascription to Spenser and asks: Why *Edward* Spenser? Many prose works have the iambic rhythms Padelford calls "Spenserian." Spenser disliked euphuism, and the translation is not beyond the powers of lesser writers. Spenser would have translated from Greek rather than Latin, and he was not a "servant" of Oxford. The external evidence is not weighty enough for the attribution to Spenser. On the other hand, Burbie often published Mundy's work, and Mundy may well be the translator of the *Axiochus*. His spelling peculiarities appear there, and he might have incorporated phrases "from the newly popular" poet Spenser.

Padelford, Frederick M. Reply to Bernard Freyd, *PMLA*, L (1935), 908–913.

The only "external evidence to which I give weight" is the attribution on the title page and in the address to the reader. As for "Edward," even William Camden, probably a personal friend of Spenser, called the poet by that name. We have no certain knowledge of Spenser's command of Greek. Since the "sweet speech" is missing, conjecture about its authorship is futile, but Spenser addressed one of the dedicatory sonnets of *The Faerie Queene* to Oxford. The spelling peculiarities noted by Freyd occur also in Spenser. *The Shepeardes Calender* has euphuistic devices. The "musical and flowing style of the whole translation" is Spenserian. Mundy's style is completely different, and his translations "are pure hack-work."

Jackson, William A. In *The Carl H. Pforzheimer Library: English Literature, 1475–1700* (New York: privately printed, 1940), III, 995–998.

These pages contain a bibliographic description of the *Axiochus* and a photographic reproduction of the "sweet speech." Some sheets were printed by John Charlewood; others "possibly" by Edward Allde. "Failing direct testimony," Padelford's case for Spenser as author of *Axiochus* "will probably be accepted by Spenser scholars generally." But the "sweet speech" is probably by John Lyly. Bibliographic analysis indicates it was added as an afterthought. External and internal-external evidence identifies the triumph as that of January 22, 1581. Spenser was not a "servant" of Oxford and was at that time in Ireland. Either Mundy or Lyly could be the author, but "the unusual ease of rhythm of the *Speech*, together with its marked euphuism, incline the verdict to John Lyly without much question." Burbie could have acquired both translation and speech as "unconsidered trifles in transcripts which had long since passed out of their authors' hands."

Swan, Marshall W. S. "The *Sweet Speech* and Spenser's (?) *Axiochus*," *ELH*, xi (1944), 161–181.

Neither the *Speech* nor the *Axiochus* is Spenser's. Ponsonby published Spenser's works. Burbie and the probable printers of *Axiochus*, Charlewood and Danter [not Allde], were piratical. The printed attribution is therefore not reliable. In January of 1581 Spenser was in Ireland and probably had no connection with Oxford. Mundy, on the other hand, wrote many civic pageants, and dedicated eight or more works to Oxford, three of them by 1581. As a printer's apprentice, Mundy worked for a master with a shop next to Burbie's, and Burbie printed works by Mundy in 1592 (the year of the *Axiochus*), 1595, and 1596. Between 1577 and 1592, Charlewood "printed a dozen works" by Mundy. Spenser sought noble, Mundy middle-class, patronage; Mundy, Barnam, and the parents of both were members of the Draper's Company. In his dedication, the writer states that he and Barnam "were Schollers together": Mundy and Barnam were about the same age, but Spenser and Lyly were about seven and six years older and Burbie about eight years younger. None of Lyly's 42 works are separate translations, and only four of them have even a remote connection with Burbie. The misattribution to Spenser may have resulted from connivance between Burbie and Mundy or from other causes.

Gottfried, Rudolf, ed. *Spenser's Prose Works, Variorum Spenser,* ix (Baltimore, 1949).

Gottfried reprints the *Axiochus* between two letters from Spenser to Harvey and Spenser's dialogue *A View of the Present State of Ireland*. In App. II (487–496), Gottfried sums up discussion of the *Axiochus* from 1744 to 1944. Although he agrees with Swan that Mundy is probably the author of the "sweet speech," Gottfried points to the large number of parallels (many of them not mentioned by Padelford) between the *Axiochus* and Spenser's poems and *A View*. Although Swan has written to Gottfried that "many of [the parallels] can also be traced in other Elizabethan writers," Gottfried finds that "no one other Elizabethan writer . . . supplies so many or such significant parallels with *Axiochus* as Spenser does."

Wright, Celeste Turner. "Anthony Mundy, 'Edward' Spenser, and E. K.," *PMLA*, lxxvi (1961), 34–39.

Having previously expressed the view that Mundy is the author of the *Axiochus* and that the attribution to Spenser is fraudulent (*SP*, lvi [1959], 162), Professor Wright, author of *Anthony Mundy* (Berkeley, 1928), offers further evidence. Mundy, she suggests, knew Burbie as early as 1588, when Burbie was apprenticed to William Wright, who distributed Mundy's

Palmerin d'Olivia. "Furthermore *Gerileon*, the Mundy-Burbie book immediately following the *Axiochus*, also smacks of the fraudulent: it features a puff misleadingly signed T. N.—as if to trade on the popularity of Thomas Nashe." Mundy's *Mirrour of Mutabilitie* (1580) has Spenserian touches; one of his probable lyrics ("Beauty Sat Bathing") is dedicated to "Colin Clout," i.e., Spenser; and Mundy is probably the "Palinode" of Spenser's *Calender* ("July," 179–188). The article explores other possible links with Spenser through various figures, including Hugh Singleton, the publisher of the *Calender,* and Edward Knight, possibly the "E. K." who annotated that work.

SUCKLING

Beaurline, L. A. "The Canon of Sir John Suckling's Poems," *SP*, LVII (1960), 492–518.

A "preliminary study" of the various kinds of "slight and insubstantial" evidence confronting an editor of Suckling, this article discusses the major problems of authorship, confirms a few additions to the canon, rejects several, indicates the need of "a great deal more work . . . before we can establish the canon of the poems."

See also the same author's "New Poems by Sir John Suckling," *SP*, LIX (1962), 651–657.

ELIZABETHAN DRAMA

The abbreviations of Shakespeare's [Shak.'s] works follow those in C. T. Onions, *A Shak. Glossary*, p. x, with a few slight, self-evident changes. Other abbreviations are as follows:

A: The "Shakespearean" [Shak.'n] portion of a play of disputed authorship.
B: The "non-Shak.'n" portion of such a play.
Chambers: E. K. Chambers, *William Shak.: A Study of Facts and Problems* (Oxford, 1930), I.
E2: Marlowe's *The troublesome raigne and lamentable death of Edward the second.*
E3: Anonymous, *The Raigne of King Edward the third.*
Eliz.: Elizabethan.
Folio: The Shak. First Folio, 1623.
Munro: John Munro, ed., *The London Shak.* (6 vols.; London, 1958).
NSS Trans.: New Shak. Society Transactions.
Q.: Quarto. Q1, Q2, etc.: First Quarto, Second Quarto, etc.
Shak.: Shakespeare (and variant spellings).
Shak.'n: Shakespearean (and variant spellings).
Sir TM: The Booke of Sir Thomas More.
TNK: The Two Noble Kinsmen.

"Eliz." is here a convenient inclusive term for Tudor and Stuart drama to 1642. The largest number of entries is, of course, for Shak.; the items under that heading may be consulted for problems and procedures that may also apply to other Eliz. dramatic canons. Moreover, many of the discussions about the canon of Greene, Peele, Marlowe, Nashe, and Lodge, and some of the discussions about the canons of Fletcher, Chapman, and Massinger have been entangled in the controversies concerning the Shak. canon. Only a limited sampling of studies (mostly since 1950) of a few non-Shak.'n canons is here possible. Inclusion does not of course imply endorsement; the entries indicate recent methods and arguments, some more reliable and persuasive than others.

For surveys of Eliz. dramatic attribution to 1923, see E. K. Chambers, *The Eliz. Stage;* for studies after that date, consult *CBEL* and *Supplement* (1957) and the annual bibliographies in *SP*. For drama after 1603, the indispensable guide is G. E. Bentley, *The Jacobean and Caroline Stage,* Oxford, 1941–1956 (5 vols.; vols. vi and vii are in press). In vols. iii–v, Bentley discusses each playwright, in alphabetical order, and reviews what is known and has been inferred about each of the plays. Bentley will discuss anonymous plays in his final volumes. Also of major importance is Sir Walter W. Greg's monumental *Bibliography of the English Printed Drama* (4 vols., Oxford, 1939–1959). A broad review of the whole field by S. Schoenbaum, *Internal Evidence and Eliz. Dramatic Authorship: An Essay in Literary History and Method* (Evanston: Northwestern Univ. Press), is scheduled to appear early in 1966.

GENERAL STUDIES

Oliphant, E. H. C. "How Not to Play the Game of Parallels," *JEGP*, xxviii (1929), 1–15.

Some golden rules are formulated by an author who at times broke them. Parallels should be of thought as well as of expression, should not be commonplace even if they meet this criterion, should not be duplicated in other writers, and should be corroborated by literary style. One must eliminate possibilities of imitation and coincidence, and take into account not only resemblances but also differences that militate against one's argument. Oliphant gives detailed criticism of the parallelists H. Dugdale Sykes and S. R. Golding, who magnify trifles and multiply weak parallels ("mere weight of numbers counts for nothing"). Even dramatic resemblances can be deceptive: "The really significant repetitions are those which repeat little tricks of expression that no one would think of copying."

Byrne, M. St. Clare. "Bibliographical Clues in Collaborate Plays," *The Library,* 4th ser., xiii (1932), 21–48.

See Schoenbaum, essay No. 13. Distinctions of style may help to isolate the shares of an author of genius but are of little value in separating the scenes of commonplace writers like Chettle and Mundy in the two parts of *Robert Earl of Huntington*. Here bibliographical data, such as latinized stage directions, use of a dash after a broken speech, peculiar spellings, and inferences from a known script with a tendency to degenerate into illegibility, may provide a real, though limited, check on one's inferences. Analytic bibliography warns one "that alternative explanations are nearly always possible when collaboration is in question."

Bald, R. C. "The *Locrine* and *George-a-Greene* Title-Page Inscriptions," *The Library*, 4th ser., xv (1934), 293–305.
Bald refutes S. A. Tannenbaum's arguments (in *Shak.'n Scraps*, chs. 2–4) against assigning the inscriptions to Sir George Buc; disposes of Tannenbaum's argument for forgery by showing that all the alleged signs of forgery exist in authentic Buc MSS; and makes important comments on handwriting.

Dawson, Giles E. "Authenticity and Attribution of Written Matter," in *English Institute Annual, 1942* (New York, 1943), 77–100.
Paleography and related problems in evaluating manuscripts and annotations in printed books of the Eliz. period are discussed, with particular comments on Ben Johnson, John Barclay, the forgeries of John Payne Collier, and, most interesting of all, a very possibly authentic signature by Shak. in a copy of William Lambarde's *Archaionomia* (1568). "Each individual problem," the author emphasizes, "presents new aspects and must be attacked in its own way." [On the signature in Lambarde, see Huber and Sisson under *Sir TM*, below.]

McManaway, James G. "Latin Title-Page Mottoes as a Clue to Dramatic Authorship," *The Library*, 4th ser., xxvi (1945), 28–36.
Many popular playwrights (Heywood, Middleton, Webster, Jonson) use Latin mottoes on their plays. Jonson's mottoes vary with the subject matter; Heywood and other playwrights use the same motto for different plays. The anonymous *Dick of Devonshire* has been ascribed to Heywood, but it has a motto different from his. If two or more anonymous plays with important resemblances "also bear the same Latin motto on their title-pages, they may with reasonable confidence be attributed to the same author."

Greg, W. W. "Authorship Attributions in the Early Play-Lists, 1656–71," *Edinburgh Bibliographical Society Transactions*, ii, pt. 4 (1946), 305–329.
Detailed analyses are given of attributions in the lists of Richard Rogers and William Ley, 1656 ("at least three times as likely to be wrong as right"), Edward Archer, 1656 (his original attributions are "in two cases out of three either careless blunders or irresponsible guesses"), and Francis Kirkman, 1661 and 1671 (more careful than the previous compilers, but his

results "can only be described as disappointing"). Specific attributions to Shak., Peele, Middleton, and other Eliz. dramatists are discussed.

Schoenbaum, S. See essay No. 13.

BEAUMONT AND FLETCHER

Bald, R. C. *Bibliographical Studies in the Beaumont and Fletcher Folio of 1647*, Supplement to the Bibliographical Society's Transactions, No. 13, 1937 (Oxford, 1938).

This monograph contains information of fundamental importance to students of the Beaumont and Fletcher canon, and indeed of other Eliz. canons. It discusses collection of the copy, including acquisition of plays after the contents had been decided and printing had begun; the printers and the printing of the Folio (see the useful "Tabular Summary," pp. 38–39); the texts of the manuscript versions of five plays and their relations to the printed texts; the role of scribes and censorship; the nature of Fletcher's foul papers of *Bonduca;* varying act and scene divisions and stage directions; Massinger's punctuation of stage directions as a clue to authorship (cf. pp. 112–113); textual confusion and revision; similar misreadings of authors' hands in *Hamlet* Q2 and the Beaumont and Fletcher plays; scribal intervention as to *you-ye* and other linguistic preferences; and finally the nature of the printer's copy (degrees of evidence for prompt-book copy, evidence for copy prepared by Ralph Crane, etc.). "There is little doubt that, as [the publisher] Mosely states, the book was in the main printed from what were regarded as the best and most authentic texts—those which had been used by the King's Men for the performance of the plays."

Hoy, Cyrus. See essay No. 14.

DEKKER

Bowers, Fredson. See essay No. 15.

MASSINGER

For Massinger's shares in the Beaumont and Fletcher canon, see Cyrus Hoy, essay No. 14.

Jones, Frederick L. "An Experiment with Massinger's Verse," *PMLA*, XLVII (1932), 727–740.

Jones has examined 172 plays by 33 known and some unknown authors to collect statistics about verse lines ending with *of* and *to*. "The important points of this investigation may be summarized as follows: (1) Throughout his career as a dramatist Massinger concludes many of his lines with *of* and *to* when these words are part of split phrases. (2) Among 19 of his contemporaries, 13 distinctly avoid this practice. (3) As a test to indicate

Massinger's verse, this characteristic, when found in plays revised by him or in which he is a collaborator, has almost invariably indicated some of the portions which scholars, studying the plays from entirely different points of view, have confidently assigned to Massinger. Alone, such evidence can never be convincing; with other metrical tests, qualities of style, ideas, and methods of phrasing, the data of the *of* and *to* test may be found useful as corroborative proof."

MIDDLETON (?), TOURNEUR (?)

The entries under this heading are concerned solely with *The Revenger's Tragedy* (hereafter *RT*), published anonymously in 1607, first attributed to Tourneur in 1656 and to Middleton in 1911. For a full survey to 1954 of pertinent canonical studies, see S. Schoenbaum, *Middleton's Tragedies* (New York, 1955), chs. 5–7; for a supplementary account of *RT* studies through 1960, see *BNYPL*, lxv (1961), 120–122, where Schoenbaum concludes "that the question remains unanswered because it is unanswerable." Our entries begin in 1960. (*AT* stands for *The Atheist's Tragedy*, by Tourneur.)

Ekeblad, Inga-Stina. "On the Authorship of *RT*," *ES*, xli (1960), 225–240.

In order to clarify the problem of authorship, one must approach the play as a whole and in relation to "relevant dramatic traditions." Though different in form and execution, both *RT* and *AT* are based on "traditional Christian morality." In *RT*, revenge-play devices are used for a moral purpose or with satiric intent. But in the comedies Middleton wrote before and soon after *RT* the satire is not "deepened by an inherent moral purpose." Middleton is concerned, rather, with effects, with "purely dramatic possibilities inherent in plot and character." Since the dramatic method is diametrical to that of *RT*, Tourneur has the better claim.

Price, George R. "The Authorship and Bibliography of *RT*," *The Library*, 5th ser., xv (1960), 262–277.

The first half of this essay (to p. 270) examines the texts of *RT* and *AT* (which last is indisputably Tourneur's) for their graphemic traits (analysis indicates that the printer's copy for each text was probably the author's holograph) and finds cumulative evidence in favor of Middleton's authorship: e.g., the identification of minor characters by the use of mere numerals as speech headings; characteristically light punctuation (Tourneur's is heavy); characteristic spellings found in Middleton's holograph and printed works; odd use of the apostrophe (*e'm* for *'em*). Price criticizes Allardyce Nicoll's inferences about *RT* (*Works of Tourneur*, 1929).

Murray, Peter B. "The Authorship of *The Revenger's Tragedy*," *PBSA*, lvi (1962), 195–218.

Murray applies a series of linguistic tests such as Hoy's (essay No. 14, above) to *RT* and works by Middleton and Tourneur. He eliminates stylistic decorum and the printing house as sources of difference. The statistical correlation is very strongly in favor of Middleton as author of *RT*. Application of the chi-square test of significance indicates that the odds are 2,000 to 1 against the chance of an accidental correlation of this sort "between Middleton's work and a play he did *not* write."

Nicoll, Allardyce. "*The Revenger's Tragedy* and the Virtue of Anonymity," in *Essays . . . in Honor of Hardin Craig*, ed. Richard Hosley (Columbia, Mo., 1963), 309–316.

Although the pursuit of problems of Eliz. dramatic authorship is necessary and has some value, it can distract attention from the central issues—the artistic organization of a work and its place in the dramatic tradition. It may be wise to follow W. W. Greg's suggestion "to forget that these plays had authors at all." Nicoll illustrates his point by surveying the debate about the authorship of *RT*.

PEELE

Sampley, Arthur M. "Plot Structure in Peele's Plays as a Test of Authorship," *PMLA*, li (1936), 689–701.

Dramatic structure, which "appears to be as much a constant as style or characterization," can provide a strong negative test for authorship. Peele's known dramas have "a discursive, haphazard, chronicle type of structure" with additional elements "of weakness [in] the incoherent development" of the separate plots of a given play and in the disproportionate emphasis given to certain scenes. Such well-constructed plays as *Titus Andronicus, King Leir,* and *Alphonsus Emperor of Germany* are not therefore likely to be Peele's, as H. Dugdale Sykes and J. M. Robertson believe. On the other hand, the structural test is "not quite so strong when applied positively," and Peele "cannot be held responsible for all the poorly constructed anonymous dramas of his period." (See below under Shak., *H6* and *Titus*.)

See also "Peele" under "Nondramatic Literature."

SHAKESPEARE

The entries that follow are not concerned with the nonliterary question of Shak.'s identity but with scholarly and critical questions about the Shak. canon. This bibliography, then, does not mention works of writers who ask, "Was Shak. really Shak., or was he Bacon or Oxford or Marlowe?" (For recent discussions of non-Stratfordian hypotheses, see the chapters on the Baconians and Oxfordians in *The Cult of Shak.* [London, 1957], by F. E. Halliday, who aptly calls the theories "matter for a psychologist and a May morning"; *The Shak.'n Ciphers Examined* [Cambridge, Eng., 1957] by William F. and Elizabeth S. Friedman; *The Poacher from Stratford* [Berkeley, 1959] by Frank W. Wadsworth; and *The Shak. Claimants* (New

York, 1962) by H. N. Gibson.) It deals, rather, with writers who ask: "Which works attributed to Shak. but outside the Folio belong in the canon? Which, if any, parts of plays in the Folio are by a non-Shak.'n hand?"

Entries are here given for ten plays, six printed in the Folio (*1,2,3H6, Titus, Shrew, H8*) and four outside of it (*E3, Sir TM, Per., TNK*). Disregarded are those non-Folio plays now generally considered apocryphal and no longer involved in significant controversy—i.e., *Arden of Feversham, *Locrine, Mucedorus, Sir John Oldcastle, *Thomas Lord Cromwell, The London Prodigal, *The Puritan, *A Yorkshire Tragedy, The Merry Devil of Edmonton, Fair Em,* and *The Birth of Merlin.* (All eleven of these are reprinted, with useful discussions of authenticity, in C. F. Tucker Brooke, *The Shak. Apocrypha* [Oxford, 1908]; see also Chambers, 532–542, and, for the four asterisked plays, Baldwin Maxwell, *Studies in the Shak. Apocrypha* [New York, 1956].) Similarly disregarded are the books and articles of those who find one or more non-Shak.'n hands in every Folio play (on the disintegrators, see Chambers, 214–235, and the same author's *Shak.'n Gleanings* [London, 1944], 1–34, 76–97). Also excluded are discussions of possibly unauthentic but relatively brief passages like the Hecate scenes in *Mac.* (III.v; IV.i.39–43, 125–132).

For five of the ten chosen plays (*Titus, Shrew, Per., Sir TM,* and *E3*), the entries are almost entirely from 1950 onwards, and the summaries of previous scholarship are necessarily brief. (For the scholarship to about 1929, see Chambers, chs. 9 and 10; to about 1950, the documented introductions to the individual plays in Munro; and to various other dates of publication, the separate titles in the New Shak. ed. [Cambridge, Eng.] and the New Arden Shak. [London and Cambridge, Mass.]. For an excellent survey of the problem of authenticity in Shak., see Chambers ch. 7.) *1,2,3H6* (referred to collectively as *H6*), *H8*, and *TNK* are treated in greater detail. *H6* is worth special attention because systematic study of the Shak. canon begins with criticism of this early trilogy and because the discussion illustrates dramatically the dependence of canonical studies on textual studies; hence the headnote to *H6* offers a somewhat fuller summary of earlier scholarship, with emphasis on the contributions of Malone and Alexander. *H8* presents an unusually interesting case. Since 1850 large portions of this late play have been widely accepted as Fletcher's on purely internal evidence, and the long discussion of its special characteristics provides a kind of microcosm of canonical studies since the days of Roderick and Johnson. Here, therefore, the entries reach back to the 18th C. *TNK* presents a parallel case: Shak.'s share has frequently been denied despite the Q title-page attribution to him and Fletcher, so that those who believe that the play belongs in the canon have had to develop internal evidence for Shak.'s partial authorship. Moreover, early discussions of Shak.-Fletcher collaboration in *TNK* played an important and at present largely forgotten part in alerting critics to the possibilities of a similar collaboration in *H8*. Hence the bibliography provides an account of the pre-1850 debate concerning *TNK*, a non-Folio play that many scholars would today admit to the canon along with *Per*.

Since the field of Shak. criticism is so ample, this bibliography can include books and chapters of books only if they deal separately with problems of attribution. To include incidental discussion of such problems in works of general Shak.'n criticism would swell the entries beyond manageable proportions. Reasons of space also compel one to exclude scholarly reviews of books and editions that deal with canonicity—regrettably, since a reviewer may make a valuable contribution to an inquiry. Reviews of Shak.'n studies to 1958 may be traced readily in the excellent bibliographies by Ebisch and Schücking (1931, 1937) and Gordon Ross Smith (1963), after 1958 in the annual bibliographies of *SP* and *SQ*.

The entries that follow sometimes deal with problems of textual transmission, chronology, and theatrical history, for these matters may be closely related to questions of authorship. Textual studies are sufficiently important to receive separate mention below. As to chronology, Shak.'s style, from which canonical arguments are frequently derived, naturally changed in the course of time; furthermore, questions arise concerning the priority of one of two closely similar treatments of a story (cf. *Per.* and Wilkins' *Painfull Adventures*). As to theatrical history, the title pages of Q's of plays that may be dated between 1589 and 1594 sometimes mention the companies which presented the plays, so scholars have had to examine the tangled story of the dramatic companies, and of Shak.'s possible connections with them, during those years.

Some preliminary remarks on the external evidence for the Shak. canon are in order. Of contemporary allusions to Shak.'s dramatic authorship, the fullest is by Francis Meres in *Palladis Tamia* (1598). With symmetrical neatness, Meres praises Shak. for six comedies ("his *Gentlemen of Verona,* his *Errors,* his *Love labors lost,* his *Love labours wonne* [an unsolved riddle], his *Midsummers night dreame,* & his *Merchant of Venice*") and for six tragedies—actually four histories and two tragedies ("his *Richard the 2. Richard* the *3. Henry the 4. King John, Titus Andronicus* and his *Romeo and Juliet*"). But as Chambers says (p. 205), the canon "rests primarily on the authority of title-pages." Shak.'s fellows Heminges and Condell collected 36 of his plays in the Folio. "Quartos, good and bad, of fifteen of these also bear his name; it is not on those of *Titus, Romeo,* or *H5.* Quartos also ascribe to him *Per.* and a share in *TNK*" (Chambers).

Proponents of Shak.'s sole authorship of all the Folio plays have tended to maintain that this external evidence is too strong to be overthrown. Heminges and Condell, they point out, were in a unique position to determine which works were Shak.'s and which were not, and they excluded from the Folio the collaborative plays *Per.* and *TNK.* They would likewise have excluded other plays now in the Folio, the argument continues, if the authorship of these were as divided as some believe. To the proponents of divided authorship, however, such arguments do not seem conclusive. Without suggesting that Shak.'s fellows were disingenuous or ill-informed witnesses (an extreme and generally rejected position), these scholars nevertheless state that the testimony of the Folio must not be interpreted so narrowly as to exclude the possibility of collaboration or interpolation. Heminges and Condell are, to be sure, responsible and impressive witnesses, but they must be judged in their own terms; they did not treat their texts with the minute precision of modern scholars establishing a definitive critical edition. "All that we can legitimately assume," in Sir Walter W. Greg's words about the pre-1594 plays (*The Shak. First Folio* [Oxford, 1955], p. 76), is that the works Heminges and Condell admitted "passed in the company as [Shak.'s]," not that they were known in all cases "to be his unaided production." And so, even conservative scholars, addressing themselves to internal evidence, have kept controversy alive by questioning the degree of Shak.'s responsibility for the ten plays discussed below. Since the debate about the testimony of the Folio tends to be repetitive, it is not reproduced in the following entries.

Textual Studies

The transmission of Shak.'s text is one of the significant areas of evidence relevant to problems of authenticity, and is often examined by scholars investigating the authorship of individual plays. For valuable general background and particular discussion, the student should consult the following volumes.

The Library, 1889 to date.
The leading British journal devoted to problems of text and bibliography; it has published classic articles by Greg, McKerrow, and others.

Papers of the Bibliographical Society of America, 1904 to date.
The American counterpart of *The Library.*

Studies in Bibliography, ed. Fredson Bowers, 1948 to date.
This journal has important articles on editing Shak., the printing of the Q's and the Folio, and the roles of scribes and compositors in transmitting the text, as well as annual checklists of bibliographical scholarship. It may be said to represent "the new wave" of post-McKerrow and post-Greg bibliography. Bibliographers through Greg were mainly concerned with the nature of the copy from which the plays were printed. Bowers, Alice Walker, and Charlton Hinman have emphasized another important concern—the kinds and amount of changes introduced into the copy in the printing house.

Walker, Alice. *Textual Problems of the First Folio: R3, Lear, Troil., 2H4, Oth.* (Cambridge, Eng., 1953).
Though not concerned with plays of disputed authorship, an important work of the newer bibliography.

Greg, W. W. *The Shak. First Folio: Its Bibliographical and Textual History* (Oxford, 1955).
An outstanding figure in 20th-C. bibliography and textual criticism gives comprehensive summaries of data and theories concerning the texts behind the Folio plays.

Kirschbaum, Leo. *Shak. and the Stationers* (Columbus, Ohio, 1955).
Kirschbaum differs radically from Pollard as to whether entrance in the S.R. had any necessary relation to the quality of a text and from Greg as to whether entrance was necessary for copyright. The publishers of the bad Q's were not disreputable. He reviews the histories of the bad Q's and the relations of Shak.'s company with the stationers to the publication of the Folio in 1623.

Bowers, Fredson. *On Editing Shak. and the Eliz. Dramatists* (Philadelphia, 1955).
The editor and founder of *Studies in Bibliography* surveys the field in three lectures delivered when he was the A. S. W. Rosenbach Fellow in Bibliography. He gives detailed discussions of varieties of copy behind the printed texts. New techniques suggest that "traditional estimates [of Shak.'n printer's copy] need the most scrupulous re-evaluation." (A valuable supplement is Bowers' *Textual and Literary Criticism* [Cambridge, Eng. 1959].)

Hinman, Charlton. *The Printing and Proof-reading of the First Folio of Shak.* (2 vols.; Oxford, 1963).
This monumental study indicates by meticulous analysis the marks left by printing house procedures on the texts in the Folio. Among the topics discussed in Vol. ɪ are edition size and speed of production, types and their distribution as evidence of setting by formes, differentiation of compositors by spelling and type-cases (there were five compositors, including E, a "prentice hand" who introduced much corruption into good copy), and the kind and extent of proofreading (the printed sheets were *not* proofread against copy). The Folio contains an indeterminable amount of error. Vol. ɪɪ offers a detailed account of the printing of each quire of the Folio.

General Studies

Armstrong, Edward A. *Shak.'s Imagination* (London, 1946), "Appendix: The Study of Image Clusters as an Aid to the Authentication of Shak.'s Work," 184–188.
Certain image clusters are peculiar to Shak. and are not likely to have been duplicated by an early imitator. The absence of all such clusters in a

work of disputed authorship suggests that it has a weak claim to inclusion in the canon, whereas the presence of even a single complex cluster may authenticate a passage as Shak.'n. "Typically Shak.'n clusters" occur in the *H6* plays, *Timon*, and the Porter's soliloquy in *Mac.*, but an examination of clusters in *H8* and *TNK* suggests that Shak. had little to do with those works. (For Armstrong's later opinion [1963], see the last entry under *TNK*, below.)

For cluster criticism, see also Kenneth Muir, *Shak. as Collaborator* (London, 1960), and for similar analysis Caroline Spurgeon, *Shak.'s Imagery* (Cambridge, Eng., 1935). For objections to imagery criticism, see R. A. Foakes (1952) and Moody Prior (1955), below.

Price, Hereward T. *Construction in Shak.* (Univ. of Michigan Contributions in Modern Philology No. 17; Ann Arbor, 1951).

In this compact and influential monograph, the author emphasizes Shak.'s command, from the earliest stages of his career, of intricate and coherent design. "Design," the "organization of parts with relation to an idea," is a more comprehensive term than "plot," the ordering of incidents in a sequence which will "pyramid such emotional effects as fear, hope, or suspense." Unity of design, rather than unity of plot, is the foundation of all romantic art, Shak.'s no less than Spenser's, and unity of design may require a wide range of styles within a work. "Times are changing, and scholars no longer distribute a Shak.'n play among as many authors as it has varieties of style."

For particular comments on *1H6* and *Titus*, see below.

Foakes, R. A. "Suggestions for a New Approach to Shak.'s Imagery," *ShS*, v (1952), 81–92.

This study is not concerned with authorship, but should be consulted by those who evaluate essays in attribution that depend on imagery-analysis. It criticizes Spurgeon's focus on the subject-matter of imagery rather than on its object-matter, and warns against the danger of determining importance of imagery by statistical counts. Disease-imagery in *Ham.* and blood-imagery in *Mac.* are very important thematically, though not preponderant numerically.

Feuillerat, Albert. *The Composition of Shak.'s Plays: Authorship, Chronology* (New Haven, 1953).

The usual Eliz. play was collaborative and moreover underwent revision when revived (cf. Henslowe's records). The "bad quarto" theory of modern bibliography has shunted aside valid earlier views that various Shak. quartos are source plays by some other dramatist partially revised by Shak., whose final revisions of these plays were ultimately printed in the Folio. Shak.'s poems provide the only secure evidence for determining his style, the development of which may be inferred from analysis of ten probably early and ten probably late sonnets. Percentages of feminine endings offer an important means of dating Shak.'s work and of separating his work from that of others. One can distinguish four levels of composition: (1) passages of the old source play retained verbatim, (2) passages slightly changed by Shak., (3) passages more radically changed by Shak., (4) passages rewritten or added by Shak.

These methods are applied to *2,3H6, Titus, R2, R3,* and *Romeo.*

Nosworthy, J. M. "The Integrity of Shak.: Illustrated from *Cymbeline,*" *ShS,* VIII (1955), 52–56.

Because there are so many different styles in *Cym.,* Furness, Granville-Barker, and others have believed that various passages are not Shak.'n. But parallels of idea, word, and metaphor link these passages to Shak.'n plays, early and late. Parallels to *Lucr., Ven.,* and *Titus* show Shak. returning to his works of the early 1590's for "pastoral, and decorative, and even conventional" effects. "In the last analysis, all the styles [in *Cym.*] are Shak.'s, and what applies to this play must surely hold for others more closely integrated." One should look throughout the canon for parallels to Shak. instead of "following Greene, Peele, Chapman, Wilkins, Middleton, or Fletcher into the shadows."

Prior, Moody E. "Imagery as a Test of Authorship," *SQ,* VI (1955), 381–386.

The author of *The Language of Tragedy* (New York, 1947), a work that analyzes the dramatic function of imagery, commends K. Wentersdorf (see under *Shrew* [1954], below) for his explicit discussion of method, but points out that his propositions, instead of being self-evident axioms, are debatable assumptions. The additions to Kyd's *Spanish Tragedy* show that the reviser (Ben Jonson) did use images of hell and night similar to Kyd's for similar purposes. The Shak. canon reveals a predilection for intricately developed musical metaphors (*Shrew, Ham., Gent., Troil., Romeo*) but Heywood's *A Woman Killed with Kindness* has similar musical metaphors: if the play were anonymous, on Wentersdorf's principle of method, one would be inclined to assign the passage to Shak. Nor is purposive iterative imagery limited to Shak.; it occurs in Marlowe and Kyd. "The hazards [of the method] are great and . . . the principles as at present stated cannot be relied upon."

Baldwin, T. W. *On the Literary Genetics of Shak.'s Plays: 1592–1594* (Urbana, Ill., 1959).

Baldwin uses casting patterns and minor and major structural parallels to determine authorship. See below under *H6.*

Henry VI

For reviews of evidence and controversy, see Chambers, 277–293; Munro, III, 1–10, 105–112, 222–234, 235–242, 355–358; and Andrew S.

Cairncross, introductions and appendices to the New Arden *2H6* (1957), *1H6* (1962), and *3H6* (1964).

The three parts of *H6* were printed in the *Histories* section of the Folio, and the epilogue to *H5* (about 1599) refers to the reign of Henry VI, "which oft our stage has shown." Important references occur in 1592. On March 3, Philip Henslowe's diary records receipts for a performance by Lord Strange's company of "Harey the vi," here marked "ne" (possibly for "new"); the diary further records 14 additional performances of this play, the last on June 19, shortly before the closing of the London theaters on account of the plague. In *Pierce Penilesse his Supplication to the Divell* (entered in S.R. Aug. 8), Thomas Nashe mentions the triumph on the stage of Talbot (a leading character in *1H6*), who bleeds to death to "the teares of ten thousand spectators at least, (at severall times)." Robert Greene, who died in early September, wrote on his deathbed *Greenes Groats-worth of witte, bought with a million of Repentance* (1592). This pamphlet contains an attack on Shak. (the first known allusion to his theatrical activities in London), in the course of which Greene parodies a line from *3H6* (I.iv.137), substituting "player's" for "woman's": "there is an upstart Crow, beautified with our feathers, that with his *Tygers hart wrapt in a Players hyde,* supposes he is as well able to bombaste out a blanke verse as the best of you [Greene's fellow playwrights]: and beeing an absolute *Johannes fac totum,* is in his owne conceit the onely Shake-scene in a countrey." No *H6* plays are mentioned by Meres, and the Q versions of *2,3H6* (there is no Q of *1H6*) are unattributed: *The First part of the Contention betwixt the two famous Houses of Yorke and Lancaster,* 1594 (hereafter *Contention* or *Cont.*) and *The true Tragedie of Richard Duke of Yorke, and the death of good King Henrie the Sixt,* 1595, actually in octavo (hereafter *True Tragedy* or *Trag.*). The title page of *Trag.* claims to reproduce the play "as it was sundrie times acted by the Right Honourable the Earle of Pembrooke his servants," a company with an apparently brief and certainly obscure history, which toured the provinces in 1593, returned impoverished that summer, and shortly afterwards disbanded. Q2 of *Cont.* and Q2 of *Trag.* (1600) are reprints of the editions of 1594–1595, and all of these were printed for Thomas Millington. In 1602 the S.R. enters a transfer of copyright in "The firste and Second parte of Henry the vi^t" (i.e., *Cont.* and *Trag.*) from Millington to Thomas Pavier. *Cont.* and *Trag.* are respectively about 1,050 and 800 lines shorter than *1* and *2H6*. Many of the longer Folio speeches are abridged; the blank verse is often defective or hypermetrical; verse is printed as prose and prose as verse; the language is generally commonplace, with frequent errors in sense; Folio lines are anticipated and then repeated in their proper places; there are frequent borrowings and echoes from other plays, including *1H6, Titus,* Marlowe's *Edward II,* and Kyd's *Spanish Tragedy;* yet the sequence of the action generally and at times the words themselves (including the famous "O tiger's heart wrapped in a woman's hide!") are those of the Folio, and several full stage directions are virtually identical. Q3, undated but printed in London in 1619 for Thomas Pavier, gathered *Cont.* and *Trag.* into a single volume, labeling *Cont.* as *The first Part of the Contention* and *Trag.* as *The Second Part.* Pavier's texts follow the earlier Q's, but sometimes agree neither with them nor with Folio *2,3H6.* "The thirde parte of Henry the sixt" is one of 16 previously unprinted Shak.'n plays named in a S.R. entry of Nov. 8, 1623, assigning to the Folio publishers such "Copies as are not formerly entered to other men." This title is usually taken to mean *1H6,* the second and third parts having been entered (in the form of *Cont.* and *Trag.*) to Pavier in 1602 and at that time called "the first and second parts."

In the 18th C., Theobald was moved by the obsolete diction and the "mean and prosaical" poetry of *H6* to suggest that Shak. contributed no more than "several master-strokes" and "some finishing beauties" to the trilogy. Farmer rejected *1H6* altogether, perhaps, Steevens hinted, because its classical allusions did not agree well with Farmer's thesis that Shak. was ignorant of the classics. Warburton also rejected *1H6.* Johnson defended Shak.'s authorship, stating that arguments from literary inferiority were invalid, since "in the productions of wit there will be inequality," and that the play was Shak.'s in style and versification. Anticipating modern bibliographical views, Johnson denied that *Cont.* and *Trag.* were Shak.'s early drafts; they were mutilated versions compiled by an auditor in the course of several performances. Steevens and others supported this theory, pointing out that Heywood complained of his plays' being very inaccurately "copied by the ear" and "by stenography" and that the Q's omitted or badly garbled the Latin verses in the Folio. Tyrwhitt called attention to the passage in Greene's *Groats-worth,* which in his opinion indicated Shak.'s authorship of *H6.*

Edmond Malone at first accepted the views of Johnson and Tyrwhitt (1778) but changed his mind in a work that became the fountainhead of disintegrationist theories, *A Dissertation on [1,2,3H6] tending to shew that those plays were not written originally by Shak.* (1787; reproduced in Malone's ed. of 1790 and in the Malone-Boswell "Third Variorum" of 1821, vol. xviii); *2,3H6,* he argued, were Shak.'s revisions of *Cont.* and *Trag.,* which Malone ascribed to Peele and Greene. Shak.'s style and borrowings from his own works were present only in Folio *2,3H6,* and not in *Cont.* or *Trag.* As for *1H6,* that was entirely the work of an older dramatist, for it is unlike Shak. in its diction, in its heavy classical allusions (resembling those in Greene, Peele, Lodge), in its excessively high proportion of end-stopped lines, and in the paucity of rhymes and double endings characteristic of Shak.'s early work. (This seems to be the first use of metrical tests of authorship.) *Proditor* and *immanity* (*1H6* I.iii.31 and V.i.13) are found nowhere else in Shak. Furthermore, the historical facts assumed in *1H6* (e.g., H6's age when H5 died) are inconsistent with those in *2,3H6*, in *R3*, and in *Cont.* and *Trag*. Greene's dying attack in *Groats-worth of Witte* could now be seen as a charge of plagiarism against Shak., pointed up by the parody of "O tiger's heart," which, since it was already in *Trag.*, must have been Greene's. Later, Malone thought that Marlowe was the author of *Cont.* or *Trag.* or both. In printing *2,3H6*, Malone indicated presumed layers of composition typographically. He put quotation marks around the lines "retouched and greatly improved" by Shak., and asterisks before those which "were his own original production." Lines normally printed were presumably taken over bodily from the Q's.

Malone was the first Shak.'n scholar to undertake a systematic examination of almost all the major areas from which arguments about canonicity could be drawn. Among other things, he evaluated external evidence, diction, style, prosody, bibliography (the Q's, he showed, could not have been produced by shorthand), and use of sources (he mistakenly believed that Holinshed was Shak.'s only source and that *Cont.* and *Trag.*, containing facts from Halle, must therefore be independent of *2,3H6*). His *Dissertation* is a fundamental document in the history of dramatic attribution.

In one form or another, theories of multiple authorship dominated discussion of *H6* from 1790 to 1929, when Peter Alexander's *Shak.'s "H6" and "R3"* brought about a reversal of scholarly opinion. Before Alexander, German critics including Ulrici and Elze (who regarded *Cont.* and *Trag.* as pirated, shorthand reports) argued for Shak.'s sole authorship. And a few English-speaking critics also defended Shak.'s right to *H6*. W. J. Courthope, for instance (*History of English Poetry*, IV [1903], 462–463), maintained that the entire trilogy and the earlier Q's were Shak.'n in structure and characterization, the Q's being drafts of *2,3H6*. But apart from these few, the trend was the other way. Shak. was usually deprived of much of the trilogy, Fleay going so far as to say that he did not write any of *2,3H6* (*Shak. Manual* [1878], 43, 58). This is of course an extreme view by a capricious writer, but even so responsible a scholar as Tucker Brooke held that Shak. "merely elaborated . . . scenes and speeches" in a play written by Marlowe (ed. of *2H6*, 1923, p. 142). In *1H6*, the Temple Garden scene (II.iv) was frequently allowed to Shak., but he was held to be incapable of the denigration of Joan of Arc. ("I confess I want Peele so bitterly in *1H6*," wrote Alfred W. Pollard in Alexander, *Shak.'s "H6*," 24–25, "to shoulder the Joan of Arc libels . . . that I am loth to give him up.") When the disintegrationists disagreed, it was mainly as to which playwrights were responsible for the non-Shak.'n portions. Peele, Marlowe, and Greene were favorites, but Lodge, Kyd, and Nashe were also contenders. The external evidence offered included Malone's interpretation of Greene's gibe at the "upstart Crow, beautified with our feathers," and certain circumstances of performance and printing: Tucker Brooke pointed out that the Earl of Pembroke's company put on Marlowe's *Edward II* as well as *Trag.*, and that Millington held the copyright to Marlowe's *Jew of Malta* as well as to *Cont.* and *Trag.* Brooke also made use of metrical percentages. But the evidence most frequently brought forward consisted of parallels between *Cont.*, *Trag.*, and *H6* on the one hand and the plays of Marlowe, Greene, Peele, *et al.* on the other.

It remained for Alexander to develop a counterthesis (first announced by him in *TLS*, Oct. 9 and Nov. 13, 1924) based, as no previous argument about *H6* had been, on the findings of the new bibliography associated with the names of Pollard, Greg, Wilson, and McKerrow. These scholars had shown that the Shak. quartos, to which most previous writers had indiscriminately applied Heminges and Condell's Folio phrase "diverse stolne, and surreptitious copies, maimed, and deformed," fell into two classes. Some, such as *Ham.* Q1 and the Q's of *H5* and *Wives*, were "bad quartos," piratical in origin, to which Heminges and Condell's censure fully applied; others, such as *Ham.* Q2 and *1H4* Q1 were "good quartos," which provided accurate, authentic texts derived more or less closely from the "True Originall Copies" mentioned on the Folio title page. Several scholars clarified the process of "memorial reconstruction" which produced the copy for certain bad Q's of works by Shak. and by other dramatists. Greg (*The Library*, 3rd ser., x, Oct., 1919; *Two Eliz. Stage Abridgments*, London, 1923) indicated that actors touring the provinces were sometimes compelled to put together their own inferior versions of popular London plays. R. Crompton Rhodes, a student of both Shak. and Sheridan, then showed (1925) how provincial actors, according to their own account, had constructed from memory and invention scripts purporting to represent Sheridan's *The Duenna* and *The School for Scandal*. (In commenting on *H6*, Steevens had mentioned but not developed this fact.)

It was therefore no longer necessary to argue, in the face of Malone's counterevidence, that *Cont.* and *Trag.* were products of a piratical publisher who sent his agents into the theater to write down the plays. *Cont.* and *Trag.*, Alexander declared, were memorial reconstructions by the Pembroke's men, who, when they were hard pressed for money, turned over their inferior versions of *2,3H6* to a printer. The accuracy of various passages suggested to Alexander that one of the reporters played Warwick and the other Suffolk and Clifford, and furthermore that these reporters "had in their possession certain manuscripts or portions of them." Since Q's of *Titus* and *Shrew* also stated that the plays were performed by Pembroke's company, Shak. was probably a Pembroke man before he joined the Lord Strange's–Lord Chamberlain's Men (by late 1594). And *1H6*, of which there are echoes in the Q's, must also have been written for Pembroke's company and the "Harey the vi," recorded by Henslowe in 1592 as a Strange's play cannot be Shak.'s: there are many instances of two Eliz. plays on the same subject, written by different authors. The echoes of Marlowe's *E2* in *Cont.* and *Trag.* can be explained as actor's recollections of another play in the Pembroke repertory (the Q of *E2*, 1594, states that the play was performed in London by Pembroke's servants). Indeed, it looks as if Shak. and Marlowe were for a time associates in the same company, and since *E2* is structurally different from Marlowe's other plays and similar to *H6*, Shak. probably influenced Marlowe rather than the other way around.

Alexander's arguments thus pointed to an important re-evaluation of Shak.'s early career. According to his view, Shak. the dramatist came forward not as a reviser of other men's work, but as an original, highly competent, and popular playwright. This, and not Shak.'s alleged plagiarism, was what aroused Greene's jealousy. He had earlier complained (*Never Too Late*, 1590) that actors, though dependent on playwrights for the very words they spoke, were "proud with *Esops* Crow, being pranct with the glorie of others feathers." Now, to Greene's dismay, here was one of those detested actors, an "upstart Crow, beautified with our feathers" who insolently aspired to the playwright's role and regarded himself as "the onely Shake-scene in a countrey."

Nor was the abundance of classical allusions in *1H6* a reason for denying the play to Shak. Shak. would have received a sound classical education in the Stratford Grammar School; there is also a reliable tradition that he was for a time a schoolmaster: the conception of him as an unlearned country boy was a myth, supported in the 18th C. by prejudice and conjecture masquerading as scholarship. Indeed, the earliest works of Shak. reveal his knowledge of the classics. His first comedy, *Err.*, is modeled on Plautus; his first tragedy, *Titus*, on Seneca; and his first poems, *Ven.* and *Lucr.*, on Ovid.

Alexander's theses were not unique. He was in several important respects following up the leads of his teacher John S. Smart (see *Shak., Truth and Tradition*, posthumously published in 1928). At about the same time, Hereward T. Price (*Beiblatt zur Anglia* [1928]) and Madeleine Doran (*H6* [Univ. of Iowa Studies, 1928]) were arriving independently at similar conclusions. And some years after his book was printed, Alexander learned that Thomas Kenny in the virtually forgotten *Life and Genius of Shak.* (1864) had anticipated his theses about *Cont.* and *Trag.* But the cogency and thoroughness of Alexander's presentation made it a turning point in the study of the Shak. canon. The view that the Q's are memorial reconstructions of Shak.'s *2,3H6* has won near-unanimous consent, including the powerful approval of Pollard, Chambers, Greg, McKerrow, and Kittredge. The chief disagreements have been about the identifications of the reporters, the explanation for certain verbal identities between the Q's and the Folio, and, more important, the authorship and early theatrical history of *1H6*—a play that Chambers in 1930 and others afterwards regarded as heterogeneous, only in small part Shak.'s, and composed after *2,3H6*. Tillyard, on the other hand, wrote in 1944, "I am fully in accord with a growing trend of belief that Shak. wrote this play." He believed, further, that *1H6* was written before *2* and *3H6* and that it displays remarkable powers of organization and design (*Shak.'s History Plays*, 161–173).

As the following entries indicate, the debate is still a lively one but moving, despite Wilson's, Feuillerat's, and Prouty's recent revival of older views, in Smart's and Alexander's direction rather than in Malone's and Fleay's.

Jordan, John E. "The Reporter of *2H6*," *PMLA*, LXIV (1949), 1089–1113.

Leo Kirschbaum, *PMLA*, LX (1945), suggests that identities of form, in certain passages, between bad Q's and authoritative texts must be due to pirating by visual rather than auditory means by someone with access to theatrical MSS. Jordan believes that correct identification of a pirate-actor may indicate who had such access. "The present study, therefore, seeks to measure quantitatively and qualitatively the amount of memorial corruption in each role by assaying the lines and classifying the variants as accurately and objectively as possible." The evidence suggests that the reporter was "the bit player who portrayed Armourer-Spirit-Mayor-Vaux-Scales . . . who would have had access to several parts and doubtless the opportunity to examine the prompt copy."

Wilson, J. Dover. "Malone and the Upstart Crow," *ShS*, IV (1951), 56–68 (first read as a lecture at Oxford, Oct. 14, 1949).

Malone was wrong in regarding *Cont.* and *Trag.* as texts revised by Shak., and Alexander was right in labeling them bad Q's. But this does not mean that Malone was wrong in holding that the *H6* plays were interspersed with the work of earlier poets, for the manifest inequalities of the trilogy *are*, as he emphasized, "of quite a different complexion from the inferior parts of our author's undoubted performances." Malone's interpretation of Greene's "upstart crow" gibe is valid, despite Alexander's criticism. The crow decked in others' colored feathers was used by Horace as a metaphor for plagiarism (Malone in fact quoted from the Horatian passage), and Horace's crow was widely identified during the Renaissance with the crow in Aesop. Greene himself openly associated Aesop's crow with plagiarism (in the dedication of his *Mirror of Modesty*, 1584). Shak. doubtless felt that this familiar metaphor for plagiarism in *Groats-worth of Witte* was damaging to his reputation, and he therefore took steps to secure from Chettle a retraction pointedly emphasizing Shak.'s "uprightnes of dealing, which argues his honesty." (The apology for Greene's attack on Shak. occurs in Henry Chettle's *Kind-Harts Dreame*, registered Dec. 8, 1592, less than three months after the registration of *Groats-worth*.)

Price, Hereward T. *Construction in Shak.* (Univ. of Michigan Contributions in Modern Philology No. 17; Ann Arbor, 1951).

In answer to scholars who regard *1H6* "as something artless, chaotic, or merely discursive," Price argues that its "design or pattern is . . . severely controlled" by "an idea that constructs the play." *1H6* is at the same time highly effective theatrically. Every event in the drama leads up to the Talbot disaster and emphasizes the loss of English power and glory through dissension and weak leadership. The Margaret-Suffolk scenes are part of this theme and tie in with events in Part II. *1H6* is "essential Shak." and achieves "what was for modern times a completely new form."

See also Price, under "Shak., General Studies," above.

Kirschbaum, Leo. "The Authorship of *1H6,*" *PMLA,* lxvii (1952), 809–822.

Although E. K. Chambers moved from disintegrationism to conservatism between 1923 (*Eliz. Stage*) and 1930 (*Shak.*), he still disintegrated *1H6, Shrew, Titus,* and *H8.* But such judgments, though they are put forward by distinguished scholars, are found, upon analysis, to proceed from subjective notions of what is and is not "Shak.'n." Greene's "upstart crow" gibe implies imitation, not appropriation [see Wilson, above]. There is no lack of consistency in the characterization of Joan or in the Talbot scenes of *1H6.* Both French and English refer to Joan cynically and deprecatingly in the several parts of the play. The Talbots die because of dissension between York and Somerset which begins in the Temple Garden scene; disintegrators accept this scene as Shak.'n but fail to see its connection with the later Talbot scenes; *1H6* is "solely Shak.'n, written by him as the first of a trilogy, and written by him at one time."

Wilson, J. Dover, ed. *1,2,3H6* (Cambridge, 1952) (in three separate volumes, referred to below as i, ii, iii).

This avowed disintegrationist approach to the trilogy starts from several assumptions, among them (1) a "simple faith . . . that Shak. was a born poet" and that any poetic inadequacies "are to me certain indications of foreign matter when they occur in the plays of the canon" (iii, xiv–xv); (2) a belief that Greene's phrase "upstart crow," interpreted in Malone's sense (see 1951, above), meant that Shak. refurbished the work of Greene and his fellow "University Wits."

Wilson's procedures are in some ways bolder than Malone's. Malone distinguishes layers of composition by comparing *2,3H6* with the Q's. Wilson, accepting the view that the Q's are memorial reconstructions, distinguishes layers of composition by analysis of the Folio texts themselves. He apportions authorship for all the scenes in the trilogy, and he does not hesitate to divide very precisely, sometimes assigning a dozen lines, or even a couplet, to one of several presumed hands (cf. ii, 119–120, 149). Shak. is present in all three plays, but others provided the groundwork; *1H6,* "one of the worst plays in the canon," was written precipitately after *2,3H6* were already on the boards; hence the inconsistencies in the character of Humphrey, Duke of Gloucester (a brawler in *1H6*, the good Protector in *2H6*) and in the age of H6 when his father dies. Greene furnished the plot of *1H6;* Nashe wrote the first act; Greene is responsible for most of the remaining four acts, though there are traces of Nashe and Peele; Shak. revised much of II–V and added II.iv (Temple Garden) and IV.v (a Talbot battle scene). Wilson disarmingly records (i, xliv ff.) his changes of opinion about the authorship of IV.v: Peele, then Greene, perhaps Nashe "aping both Peele and Greene," and, finally, Shak.

Wilson also changed his mind about the original versions of *2,3H6:* he first thought Peele might be the author, then decided on Greene aided by Nashe, the latter being responsible for the Cade scenes (*2H6* IV.ii–x). Shak. later introduced various revisions in both parts.

Stylistic inferiority is Wilson's usual reason for postulating non-Shak.'n authorship. He then supports the theory of an alien presence by verbal parallels, "syntactical peculiarities, little mannerisms and tricks of style, proverbial phrases (sometimes used incorrectly or with a special twist), classical or other allusions, and clichés of various types" (ii, xxvii–xxviii). He also offers evidence from use of sources (i, xxxii–xxxviii) and from inconsistencies of facts, names, titles, relationships of characters, and characterization (ii, xliv–l). In addition, Wilson finds a contrast between classical erudition in non-Shak.'n parts of *H6* and ignorance in Shak.'n passages of the *Aeneid*, I–II, "either in the original or translation" (ii, lii)—an argument that carries us back to "the unlearned author" (Wilson's phrase, ii, liii) of Farmer's essay of 1767. Finally, the editor sketches a conjectural history of the dramatic companies in the early 1590's that would account for his intricate history of dramatic composition (i, xlviii–l; ii, vii–xiv).

Richardson, Arleigh D., III. "An Edition of *The first part of the contention*" (unpub. Yale diss., 1953).

According to C. T. Prouty (1954, below), Richardson's examination of sources for *Cont.* and *2H6* rules out "any possibility of Q being a text derived from" the Folio.

Prouty, Charles T. *"The Contention" and Shak.'s "2H6"* (New Haven, 1954).

Cont. is not a memorial reconstruction but an original play, of which *2H6* is a revision [cf. Feuillerat, 1953, under "General Studies," above]. The argument depends on differences between the two texts in staging, style, characterization and structure, use of sources, and essential details. On sources, Prouty refers to Richardson (1953, above). Comparison with revisions in *The Spanish Tragedy* and *Sir TM* (the illustrations here are from Hand C rather than Hand D) suggests that *2H6* stands in a similar revisory relationship to *Cont.*

Ch. 5 criticizes the views of Alexander, Miss Doran, Chambers, and Alfred Hart (*Stolne and Surreptitious Copies,* 1943). The confusions by *Cont.* of the genealogy in *2H6* II.ii, of which Alexander makes much, are due to insertions in the printer's copy and to a careless compositor's mix-up of facts from Grafton's chronicle. The use of Grafton by *Cont.* is proved in part by the mention of Alice as one of the daughters of Roger, Earl of March—a detail missing in the Folio's source, Holinshed. [Wilson, 1952, however, finds frequent recourse to Grafton in *2H6,* and Alice *is* mentioned by Holinshed in his chronicle of the reign of R2.] Some features that Miss Doran points to in *Cont.* as characteristic of a reported text occur also in the Folio, where they are signs of revision.

Kernan, Alvin B. "A Comparison of the Imagery in *3H6* and *Trag.,*" *SP*, LI (1954), 431–442.

In *3H6,* Shak. makes complex use of a "comprehensive symbol . . . a sea-wind-tide figure in which the sea is now forced toward the land by the tide and now blown back by the wind." The absence of this complex pattern in *Trag.* may be readily accounted for by Malone's theory that the Folio is a revision of Q, but it raises difficulties for (though it does not invalidate) the theory that Q is a memorial reconstruction of *3H6.*

Austin, Warren B. "A Supposed Contemporary Allusion to Shak. as a Plagiarist," *SQ*, VI (1955), 373–380.

> "*Greene,* gave the ground, to all that wrote upon him.
> Nay more the men, that so Eclipst his fame:
> Purloynde his Plumes, can they deny the same?"
> —R. B., *Greenes Funeralls* (1594) [hereafter *GF*].

Since Dyce cited these lines in his edition of Greene's *Dramatic Works* (1831), they have been taken by both friend and foe of the Malone hypothesis to refer to the attack on Shak. in Greene's *Groats-worth.* But this assumption is erroneous. Since *GF* refers to Thomas Watson as a surviving friend of Greene's, it must have been written between Greene's death on Sept. 3 and Watson's burial on Sept. 26 of 1592. But *Groats-worth* was not registered until Sept. 20, and so R. B. had probably not read the passage on the "upstart Crow, beautified with our feathers." *GF* is marked above all "by a succession of bitter references to Gabriel Harvey and the pamphlets in which he had maligned Greene [and all his writings] within days of the playwright's death." Harvey had just referred contemptuously to Greene's "borrowed & filched plumes," and R. B. in the lines cited is trying to retort that Harvey's very phrase is filched from Greene's attack in *Never Too Late* (1590) on actors "pranct with the glorie of others feathers." R. B. is indignant that the men who darkened Greene's reputation ("Eclipst his fame") not only derived their subject matter from Greene himself, capitalizing "on the great popularity of the man and his writings" ("*Greene,* gave the ground, to all that wrote upon him"), but also stole from him their very language, "Purloynde his Plumes." "Purloynde" refers back ironically to Harvey's "filched & borrowed," and "Plumes" is Harvey's very noun, as against Greene's and Nashe's "feathers."

Williams, Philip, Jr. "New Approaches to Textual Problems in Shak.," *SB*, VIII (1956), 7–9.

"The copy for *1H6* was almost certainly heterogeneous." This is shown by sudden changes in Act III, set, like Acts I and II, by Compositor A, who followed copy faithfully. There are no scene divisions in I and II, but III has four scenes. In I and II, Burgundy always has a *d*; in III, the spelling is *Burgonie*. In I, Joan of Arc is *Puzel* (18 times); in III, the spelling is *Pucell* (26 times).

McManaway, James G. "*The Contention* and *2H6*," in *Studies in English Language and Literature Presented to Karl Brunner, WBEP*, LXV (1957), 143–154.

Invariability of speech headings rules out authorial foul papers as copy for *Cont.*; indefiniteness as to numbers of actors required rules out a promptbook. Both kinds of copy are likewise ruled out by long narrative stage directions, poor meter, unintentional malapropism, crude verbatim repetitions, sheer nonsense, anticipations, recollections, and hiatuses. All these phenomena, however, are compatible with the hypothesis of a memorial report of an acted version. Analysis of cuts during Restoration performances of *Hamlet* and of Beaumont and Fletcher plays indicates slashing of "the literary passages, especially those of an introspective or moralistic nature," and replacement of imagery by simpler language. Similar cutting in the acting version behind *Cont.* can account for paucity of imagery in that text as compared with *2H6*. McManaway criticizes the arguments of Feuillerat and Prouty.

Cairncross, Andrew S., ed. *2H6* (Arden ed.; London and Cambridge, Mass., 1958).

Cont. is a bad Q of an abridged version of *2H6*, but Q3 (1619) was used in printing about one-fourth of the Folio version. Hence the transcriptional links between the texts. There was also rewriting, possibly because of censorship, "of about three hundred lines of the original text, after the performance reflected in Q." Thus there are elements of truth in both the "mutilation" (bad Q) and "revision" theories. As to sources, "Shak., in all three parts of *H6*, drew on *both* Hall and Holinshed," especially on Hall. Grafton may be ruled out. In any case, "variation in the chronicle sources is not a decisive test of single or multiple authorship." Cairncross disagrees with Wilson's interpretation of Greene's and Chettle's references to Shak. And one could prove by parallels of Wilson's sort that Edmund Spenser had a hand in *2H6*. "Shak. wrote the play as part of a carefully planned tetralogy, probably in 1590, for Pembroke's Men, or their predecessors."

McNeal, Thomas H. "Margaret of Anjou: Romantic Princess and Troubled Queen," *SQ*, ıx (1958), 1–10.

The author deliberately avoids "any discussion of multiple authorship," but his article shares with such discussions the view that *1H6* was written so as to link up with the already completed *2,3H6*, "conceived from the start as twin plays," and *R3*. The scenes that serve specifically for linkage are the Temple Garden, the Suffolk-Margaret, and Suffolk-Henry scenes. There is a discrepancy between the romantic Margaret of *1H6* and the villainess of *2H6*.

Pruvost, René. "Robert Greene a-t-il Accusé Shak. de Plagiat?" *EA*, xıı (1959), 198–204.

In this comprehensive survey of the question posed in his title, Pruvost disagrees with J. Dover Wilson, concurs with Warren B. Austin (see above), and returns a verdict of "not proven."

Baldwin, T. W. *On the Literary Genetics of Shak.'s Plays: 1592–1594* (Urbana, Ill., 1959).

Baldwin doubts that bibliographers can distinguish good and bad Q's, and proposes new means of establishing authorship and chronology. He believes that analysis can determine relative chronology of parallel passages and of whole plays (e.g., *Romeo* must precede *R3*, since it supplies the basic structural element of warring houses, later represented in *R3* by Richard and Margaret). Changing "casting patterns" of the various dramatic companies are also clues to chronology. Thus the *Shrew* has the casting pattern of plays after the reorganization of companies in 1594. Baldwin believes that Shak. was with Lord Strange's company before the closing of the theaters in 1592.

Chapters on Greene's "Shake-scene" reference (p. 55), on the chronology of Greene's, Marlowe's, Peele's, and Kyd's works, and on the casting patterns of the Queen's, Admiral's, and Strange's players take up more than half of this long book. Texts such as *Cont.* and *Trag.* are not bad Q's, but the products of abridgment by theatrical officials who whittled down and took liberties with the original scripts submitted by dramatists; *2,3H6* are "in some sense Shak.'s"; *1H6* belongs to 1591–1592. The Folio texts represent the earliest forms of those plays which, however, were preceded by *LLL*, *Err.*, *Gent.*, and *Romeo*.

Mincoff, Marco. "*3H6* and *The True Tragedy*," *ES*, xlıı (1961), 273–288.

Both Prouty and Feuillerat (above) overlook the evidence that *Cont.* and *Trag.* are bad quartos. Feuillerat forgets that "metrical statistics simply do not have room to work themselves out" in passages of from 7 to 50 lines, and both he and Tucker Brooke forget that such statistics cannot in any case include data from a corrupt text. Analysis of equivalent passages supports the view that *Trag.* is a memorial reconstruction of a deliberately abridged acting version of *3H6*. The images that Kernan believes were "added" by *3H6* to *Trag.* could simply have been cut in the version behind *Trag.* Some of the mislineations in *Trag.* were probably the work of a "not very intelligent printer." Since *3H6* is purposively linked to *R3*, those who argue that Shak. merely revised *3H6* should logically conclude that he also merely revised *R3*.

Bradbrook, Muriel C. "Beasts and Gods: Greene's *Groats-worth* and the Social Purpose of *Venus and Adonis*," *ShS*, xv (1962), 62–72.

This study emphasizes the insulting theatrical implications of "Anticks" ("grotesque characters with animal heads and bombast figures") in Greene's thrust at "those Anticks garnisht in our colours." Since the whole of *Groats-worth* is organized so as to concentrate its invective on the churlishness and inward beastliness of the "upstart Crow," Miss Bradbrook favors Alexander's rather than Dover Wilson's interpretation of the famous passage. In response to the insult, Shak. first extracted an apology from Henry Chettle (Dec. 1592) and then "went on to safeguard his reputation" with *Ven.* (registered April 18, 1593), a "sumptuous and splendidly assured" work "designed not to answer Greene, but to obliterate the impression he had tried to make."

Cairncross, Andrew S., ed. *1H6* (Arden ed.; London and Cambridge, Mass., 1962).

Chiefly indebted, for critical approach, to Alexander and to Price's *Construction in Shak.* (1951, above). "In the course of editing, I have become increasingly convinced on every side of the integrity of the play." Inconsistencies noted by Wilson, Williams, and others are due partly to theatrical, scribal, and compositorial intervention and partly to Shak.'s use of different sources and his forgetfulness (detailed examination of these postulated causes). Opposing views are summarized and rebutted. Shak. wrote the whole play, before and not after *2,3H6*, probably in 1590. Margaret-Suffolk scenes were not added afterwards but are part of the structure and movement of the whole play. And *1H6* has an admirable design, both in relation to the tetralogy *H6-R3* and in itself. It is a coherent, powerful, and highly original fusion of event, pageantry, rhetoric, and imagery. "Greene spoke more truly than he knew when he called Shak. 'the onely Shake-scene in a countrey.'" (For a brief discussion, see also Cairncross's ed. of *3H6* [1964], xli–xliii.)

Titus Andronicus

For comprehensive reviews of the authorship controversy to 1960, see the Arden ed. of *Titus* by J. C. Maxwell (1953, 1961) and Horst Oppel's monograph of 1961, below. Cf. also Chambers, 312–322, and Munro, v, 1–8.

Titus is attributed to Shak. by Meres and printed with the tragedies in the Folio. The Q's, 1594, 1600, 1611, are anonymous. Q1 is a good text, printed, it would seem, from author's foul papers. Q2 was printed from Q1, Q3 from Q2, and the Folio text from Q3, with additions from a theatrical manuscript (the most important addition is III.ii, missing in the Q's). Q1 states that *Titus* was played by the companies of the Earls of Derby, Pembroke, and Sussex; Q2 adds the Lord Chamberlain's Men (Shak.'s company from late 1594); Q3 mentions only the King's company (the name assumed by the Chamberlain's Men in 1603). On Jan. 24, 1594, Henslowe recorded receipts for a performance by Sussex's Men of "Titus & Ondronicous," marked "ne."

Edward Ravenscroft claims, in his adaptation of *Titus* (1687): "I have been told by some anciently conversant with the Stage, that [*Titus*] was not Originally [Shak.'s], but brought by a private Authour to be Acted, and he only gave some Master-touches to one or two of the Principal Parts or Characters; this I am apt to believe, because 'tis the most incorrect and indigested piece in all his Works; It seems rather a heap of Rubbish then a Structure." According to Chambers (p. 316), the first part of Ravenscroft's statement "is the only bit of external evidence against the authenticity of any play" in the Folio. Kittredge (*Works of Shak.* [Boston, 1936], 971) characterizes the witness as "irresponsible" and his testimony as "idle gossip which he reports (or invents)." The testimony is in any case too weak to sustain an argument for divided authorship, and those who have denied the canonicity of *Titus* have tended rather to amplify the second half of Ravenscroft's comment. In their eyes, the work is so tastelessly horrifying, crude in style, and ill-constructed that it cannot be Shak.'s. This has been the view of the vast majority of scholars and critics since the early 18th C. As late as 1927, T. S. Eliot called *Titus* "one of the stupidest and most uninspired plays ever written, a play in which it is incredible that Shak. had any hand at all."

In recent decades, however, there has been an increasing tendency to vindicate Shak.'s authorship. An early tragedy of blood and revenge, it has been argued, is not to be judged by the same standards as *Lear* and *Ant.* *Titus* was highly popular in its time, and with good reason, such critics maintain. Kittredge speaks of its "skilful construction . . . its dramatic power, and . . . the magnificence of many poetical passages. With all its faults, it is far beyond the abilities of either Peele or Greene." The late H. T. Price, who devoted many years to editing the forthcoming Variorum Edition of *Titus*, insisted on the excellence of the play in its own terms and on its Shak.'n integrity.

The entries below reflect this trend. Even Dover Wilson limits Peele's share very largely to Act I. The chief points of recent contention have been: (1) Do parallels between Peele and Shak. indicate Peele's hand in *Titus*, or imitation of one author by the other? (2) If *Titus* is all Shak.'s, how can one reconcile what would be very early style with the supposed date of appearance, 1593–1594 (Henslowe, Q1)? (3) How is one to explain the performance of the play by the companies of Derby, Pembroke, Sussex, and the Lord Chamberlain-King James? (4) Is praise such as Kittredge's and Price's overstated, and are not the defects of *Titus* in fact sufficient to raise questions about Shak.'s sole authorship?

Wilson, J. Dover, ed. *Titus* (New Cambridge ed.; Cambridge, Eng., 1948).

Titus is crude, "less homogeneous in style and more ramshackle in structure" than most tragedies of blood, "while its incidents are often merely absurd." But those who, like J. M. Robertson and T. M. Parrott, deny Shak.'s authorship most strenuously depend too much on unconvincing metrical tests and fail to give the "overwhelming" parallels between *Titus* and *Lucr.* their due. (Wilson approves of Miss Byrne's warnings about parallels; see under "Eliz. Drama, General Studies," 1932, above.) Since *Lucr.* was entered in the S. R. May 9, 1594, "i.e. more than three months later than the earliest recorded performances of *Titus*," the parallels can be due only to common authorship. There are also many parallels to Shak.'s early plays.

But the frequent emptiness, monotony, repetitiveness, and triteness of the verse, especially apparent in Act I, demonstrate the presence of Peele, as do many parallels to his known work. Robertson's parallels to Greene, Marlowe, Kyd, and Lodge, on the other hand, "amount to very little indeed," and though Kyd may have helped Peele with the mad scenes (III.ii, IV.i, IV.iii, V.ii), "it was not beyond [Shak.'s] power to play the sedulous ape to Kyd as he did to Marlowe." [This concession would seem to undermine Wilson's argument about Peele, as does his observation that Shak. and the early dramatists shared a common diction.] Peele is "solely responsible for the basic play," the last four acts of which were extensively revised (and at times parodied) by Shak. Wilson indicates Peele's and Shak.'s shares in his first note to each scene (for a minute discrimination, see p. 143). His attempts "to fix the dates both of the writing [spring and summer of 1593] and the revision [by mid-Jan., 1594] with an exactitude unusual in Eliz. stage-history" involve him in considerable conjecture about relations among dramatic companies and between Shak. and Peele.

Maxwell, J. C. "Peele and Shak.: A Stylometric Test," *JEGP*, XLIX (1950), 557–561.

The test proposed is the use of a possessive adjective or pronoun as antecedent of a relative clause, as in *Titus* I.i.5–6: "I am his first-born son that was the last/That ware the imperial diadem of Rome." The construction is six times more common in Peele's nondramatic works than in Shak.'s *Ven.* and *Lucr.* It is also fairly common in Kyd and Marlowe, rare in Shak., Greene, and Lodge. In *Titus,* the construction occurs 6 or 7 times in the 500 lines of Act I, but only 4 times in the remaining 2,000 lines. This provides independent support for Dover Wilson's assignment of Act I to Peele. [It would be interesting to hear from a statistician whether Maxwell's sample is large enough to support his conclusion.]

Price, Hereward T. *Construction in Shak.* (Univ. of Michigan Contributions in Modern Philology No. 17; Ann Arbor, 1951), 37–40.

Price criticizes Wilson for giving Act I of *Titus* to Peele. "[Wilson] will not allow that Shak. imitates Peele. As a matter of fact Shak. puts *Titus* together by shamelessly pillaging every contemporary." More importantly, Wilson neglects the Shak.'n structure of Act I; Peele was incapable of such control and dramatic relevance.

Maxwell, J. C., ed. *Titus* (Arden ed.; London, 1953; 3rd ed., 1961).

Nothing in the obscure external evidence "flatly contradicts a date of about 1589–90" for *Titus.* The Shak.'n structure of the whole play (Maxwell commends the discussion by H. T. Price, *JEGP,* 1943) argues against Peele as the original author; stylistic and syntactic evidence (see 1950, above) suggests Peele's presence in Act I and in the first 25 lines of the next scene (II.i). But this view involves the unsatisfactory assumption that Peele in 1589–1590 was willing to subordinate himself to a younger and less experienced playwright.

In a 1961 addition, Maxwell agrees with Hill (1957, below) that "to contend for sole Shak.'n authorship of *Titus* and composition in 1593–4 is nonsense." He feels that his 1953 account failed to allow for structural weaknesses pointed out by Hill, though Maxwell "would still hold (and Hill does not deny) that [the structure of *Titus*] is beyond the ascertained power of any contemporary dramatist except Kyd."

Hill, R. F. "The Composition of *Titus,*" *ShS,* x (1957), 60–70.

Studies have shown the unreliability of verbal parallels, supposedly "characteristic" words and phrases, metrical and imagery tests as evidence for authorship in Eliz. drama. Recourse to the structure of *Titus* also yields uncertain results, since some features seem beyond the reach of Shak.'s contemporaries, others within the compass of Kyd, still others seriously weak. In general, our tests have been insufficiently comprehensive and thoroughgoing, and "internal evidence cannot satisfactorily assign small patches, or even whole scenes or acts, to particular writers." Hill's method, admittedly subject to the stated limitations, is to analyze the style of *Titus,* in comparison with the styles of 11 early plays by Shak., according to 130 rhetorical figures based on Puttenham's scheme in *The Arte of English Poesie* (1589). The forms and frequencies in *Titus* of alliteration, simple and continued metaphors, iterative wordplay, tautology, methods of amplification, and peculiarities of style, such as epizeuxis with a vocative set between repeated words, suggest either (1) Hill's "interim conclusion" that the play, if it is entirely Shak.'n, was written before *H6* (1590–1591), or (2) that it is collaborative.

Oppel, Horst. *"Titus": Studien zur dramengeschichtlichen Stellung von Shak.'s früher Tragödie* (Schriftenreihe der deutschen Shak.-Gesellschaft, IX; Heidelberg, 1961).

Titus is all Shak.'s and was written about 1590. If one dates it in 1593, it becomes difficult, Oppel believes, to insist on Shak.'s sole authorship. The author derives his arguments from the structure of *Titus*, from the absence of similar characteristics in the plays of other candidates, and from the close relation of the play to the rest of Shak.'s work (see ch. 7, "Die Stellung von *Titus* in Shak.'s Gesamtwerk").

The Taming of the Shrew

For surveys of evidence and arguments, see Chambers, 322–328; Munro, I, 65–69; Greg, *The Shak. First Folio* (1955), 210–216.

The division according to Chambers (p. 324) is as follows:

A ("Shak.'n"): *Ind.* I, II; I.ii.1–116 (in part); II.i.1–38, 115–326; III.ii.1–129, 151–254; IV, i,iii,v; V.ii.1–181.

B ("non-Shak.'n"): The rest of the play.

The Taming of the Shrew (hereafter *The Shrew*) was printed with the comedies in the Folio. It is not mentioned by Meres, unless it is the mysterious *Love labours wonne*. A great problem is posed by the relation of the Folio play to earlier printed Q's (1594, 1596, 1607), *A Pleasant Conceited Historie, called The taming of a Shrew* (hereafter *A Shrew*), "as it was sundry times acted by the . . . Earle of Pembrook his servants." Henslowe records a performance of "the tamynge of A shrowe" at the Newington Butts theater on June 11, 1594, a time when the new companies, the Admiral's servants and the Chamberlain's (Shak.'s company) were both playing there; the play to which he refers may thus be Shak.'s. (In regard to the two versions, Henslowe and other Elizabethans do not observe a precise distinction between "a" and "the.") Although both *The Shrew* and *A Shrew* have similar, but not identical, main plots and subplots (these diverge more than do the main plots), they are quite different texts. *A Shrew* is much shorter (about 1,550 lines as against about 2,750), gives different names to its characters, has very little verbal coincidence with *The Shrew*, frequently echoes Marlowe and sometimes quotes several of his lines, and carries through, as *The Shrew* does not, the framework of the drunkard Sly's being deceived into thinking he is a lord. *The Shrew* has a full, two-scene induction concerning Sly and then drops him completely with a few lines at the end of I.i; in contrast, *A Shrew* follows the induction with four brief Sly interludes and a somewhat longer epilogue in which Sly is awakened "out of the best dreame that ever I had in my life," resolving to apply to his own spouse the play's lesson of "how to tame a shrew." It has generally been assumed that *The Shrew* at one time had a Sly epilogue which was lost through cuts or inadvertence; but see Hosley (1961), below.

Three major explanations have been offered to account for the resemblances and differences between *A Shrew* and *The Shrew*. (1) *A Shrew* is the source play for *The Shrew* and was greatly revised in the course of adaptation (Boas, Chambers). (2) *A Shrew* is a memorial reconstruction which bears roughly the same relation to *The Shrew* that *Cont.* and *Trag.* bear to *2,3H6* (Hickson, Creizenach, Alexander, Dover Wilson, Greg). (3) *A Shrew* and *The Shrew* are independent versions of a lost play (Ten Brink, who suggests that the lost play was by Shak.; Raymond Houk; G. I. Duthie, who believes that *A Shrew* is a bad Q of the lost play). This view has won favor since it was revived in the early 1940's.

Obviously, one's view of the relationship between the two versions will affect one's theories of chronology and authorship. As to authorship, scholars have variously held that Shak. wrote neither *A Shrew* nor *The Shrew*, that he is the ultimate author of *A Shrew* and the immediate sole author of *The Shrew*, and that he is the author of the induction and the main plot of *The Shrew*, but not of the stylistically distinct subplot concerning Bianca and her suitors. Chambers is a notable proponent of the last-cited theory. The close integration of plot and subplot has won the praise of critics; on the consistency of Petruchio's character in both plots, Chambers remarks, "The collaborators may well have agreed upon a common conception of Petruchio." A variant of this argument could of course be applied to defences of unitary authorship on the grounds of integrated imagery.

A selection of post-1950 essays relevant to authorship follows. For interesting recent developments, see especially the 1961 entries by Brunvand and Hosley.

Bergin, Thomas, ed. *The Shrew* (New Haven, 1954).
   Though generally inferior, *A Shrew* "is in certain respects a more finished product than *The Shrew*": Sly is not "ignored after the introductory scenes . . . and at the end he goes off content with the moral of wife-beating" (see Hosley [1961], below). Also, "Katerina is provided with a second sister who pairs off with Hortensio." But "the similarities . . . are much more noteworthy than the differences" and are open to various explanations (reference to the views of Alexander, Dover Wilson, and others).

Wentersdorf, K. "The Authenticity of *The Shrew*," SQ, v (1954), 11–32.
   Disparities of style within an early Shak.'n play are probably characteristic of the youthful dramatist rather than indicative of multiple authorship. Imagery is a better criterion, since one would not expect integrated,

specific, and elaborate imagery patterns in the various parts of a rough-and-ready dramatic collaboration. Ten "cluster-images" occurring in both A and B of *The Shrew* suggest single authorship (though Wentersdorf admits they are not all "equally convincing and only a few can be regarded as peculiarly Shak.'n"): so do ten less immediately "Shak.'n" images. There are also "sparse traces" of a running image derived from "the idea of taming a hawk." (For a reply, see Prior [1955], under "Shak., General Studies.")

Schroeder, John W. "*A Shrew* and *The Shrew*: A Case Reopened," *JEGP*, LVII (1958), 424–443.

"The modern and orthodox view [revived in the 1940's, that both plays derive independently from a lost common original, possibly by Shak.] rests on bases less solid than is presently supposed . . . and there is still something to be said for the old-fashioned notion that *A Shrew* is simply a text, admittedly imperfect, of an old play which Shak. used as one of the sources for his own comedy." Since 1950, the Hickson-Alexander view that *A Shrew* is a pirated and mangled version of *The Shrew* has been rejected, but the parallels they used in support of their thesis are still used for the post-Houk claims of a common source. The parallels are not very parallel, however, and the supposedly derived terms in *A Shrew* are used ably and independently. The author also criticizes Houk's arguments from presumed chronological difficulties and misplacing of scenes in *A Shrew*, and suggests, finally, that the probable sequence of Marlovian echoes in *A Shrew* and *The Shrew* supports "the old-fashioned view."

Schroeder, John W. "A New Analogue and Possible Source for *A Shrew*," *SQ*, x (1959), 251–255.

Details about "mewing up" a wife found in *A Shrew* and in Caxton's translation of *The Book of the Knight of La Tour Landry* (1484), but not in Shak.'s *The Shrew*, suggest *A Shrew's* independent use of Caxton as a source.

Waldo, Tommy Ruth and T. W. Herbert. "Musical Terms in *The Shrew*: Evidence of Single Authorship," *SQ*, x (1959), 185–199.

As indicated in the title, the authors find that Shak. is sole author. They believe that quantity and complexity of musical references can differentiate one poet from another. Shak.'s references are considerably more numerous (statistics are cited) and more complex in their allusiveness than are those of suggested collaborators. Here, as in other comedies of Shak., "the musical allusions . . . taken as a whole form a pattern" (from discord to harmony), and there is no differentiation suggesting divided authorship between the "Shak.'n" and "non-Shak.'n" parts of *The Shrew*.

Brunvand, Jan H. "The Taming of the Shrew: A Comparative Study of Oral and Literary Versions," *Dissertation Abstracts*, XXII (1961), 1570–1571.

A study of 418 versions of the folk tale (Aarne-Thompson Type 901) indicates that Shak. "could not have derived his plot" from either *El Conde Lucanor* (a 14th-C. Spanish analogue) or *A Shrew*. Shak. "must have known the tale as it was developed in oral tradition." His play "is closer to oral tradition than is the plot of *A Shrew*."

Hosley, Richard. "Was There a 'Dramatic Epilogue' to *The Shrew*?" *SEL*, ɪ (1961), 17–34.

Theories as to whether Shak. originally did or did not write for *The Shrew* a dramatic epilogue involving Christopher Sly (as in *A Shrew*) depend upon a priori aesthetic judgments that the Folio play would or would not be better with such an epilogue. But 26 out of 45 Eliz. plays with an induction lack an epilogue. Since 20 of the 26 without an epilogue, but only 7 of the 19 with one, are dated in or after 1600, the dramatic epilogue would seem to have been an old-fashioned device which was falling into disuse at about that time. Doubling of parts in Eliz. companies often made it difficult for actors to change costume for an epilogue (the last scene of *The Shrew* requires 12 or 13 parts, not counting servants). Furthermore, the epilogue in *The Shrew* and in other plays would be anticlimactic and inartistic.

Henry VIII

For reviews of scholarship, see Chambers, 495–498; Munro, VI, 1143–1150; R. A. Foakes in New Arden *H8* (1957); and J. C. Maxwell in New Cambridge *H8* (1962).

Shak.'s and Fletcher's presumed shares in *H8* have usually been assigned as follows:

A (Shak.): I.i,ii; II.iii, iv; III.ii.1–203 (to exit of the king); V.i.
B (Fletcher): Pro.; I.iii, iv; II.i,ii: III.i,ii.203 (from exit of the king) —458; IV.i.ii; V.ii–v; Epi.

The case for a non-Shak.'n hand in *H8* depends entirely on internal evidence. The play was included as Shak.'s in the Folio, and there is no contemporary attribution to any other writer. Yet today a majority of scholars accept the theory of Fletcher's partial authorship, though a sturdy minority deny it. A wide range of methods has been applied to the solution of this problem of authorship: broad literary tests of structure, characterization, and style; parallels in phraseology; and perhaps most notably, various statistical tests. Indeed, the controversy over *H8* has played a leading role in the introduction of metrical and linguistic tests of authorship. Among students of Eliz. drama, there is a direct line of descent from the perceptive comments of Richard Roderick and Charles Lamb to the metrical tests of Henry Weber, James Spedding, Robert Boyle, Frederick G. Fleay, and John K. Ingram, and from these again to the tables of linguistic preferences by Ashley Thorndike, Willard Farnham, Cyrus Hoy, and others. A review of *H8* scholarship to date is therefore, in the Eliz. phrase, a "mirror" for canonical scholars.

1733.

In the 18th C., hypotheses of interpolation contributed to the theory that a second hand was responsible for parts of *H8*. Theobald (*Works of Shak.* [1733], v, 99–100, note to *H8* V.v.39–55) is the first to suggest interpolation: he regards Cranmer's prophecy concerning King James as a later insertion by Shak. himself into a speech originally written while Queen Elizabeth was still alive. Johnson (*Works of Shak.* [1765], v, 490) initiates the policy of putting square brackets around the presumed "interpolation."

1758.

Richard Roderick, in Thomas Edwards, *Canons of Criticism*, 225–228, points out that *H8* contains more "redundant syllables" (i.e., more verses with double or feminine endings) than any other play by Shak.; that the caesura comes very frequently after the seventh syllable in the line; and that the emphasis required by the sense of the line often clashes with that required by the metrical pattern. Roderick assumes that these features were deliberately put into the play by Shak. and says nothing about the possibility of another author.

1765.

Samuel Johnson (*Works of Shak.*, v, 492–493) does not question Shak.'s authorship of the play proper, but voices the suspicion that the prologue and epilogue are not by the poet (*"non vultus, non color"*). They were supplied either "by the friendship or officiousness" of Ben Jonson while Shak. was still active in the theater, or by some writer, "whoever he was," after Shak.'s "departure from the stage, upon some accidental revisal [*sic;* apparently an error for "revival"] of the play." But Johnson ends on a characteristic note of caution: "All this, however, must be received as very dubious, since we cannot know the exact date of this or the other plays, and cannot tell how our authour might have changed his practice or opinions."

1773.

Richard Farmer seems to be the first to suggest (in his appendix of glosses on *The Plays of Shak.*, ed. Johnson and Steevens, x, sig. Qq^v) that portions of the play proper are non-Shak.'n: Ben Jonson not only wrote the prologue and epilogue, but also "drew up the directions for the parade at the christening, &c." (V.v), and one could "now and then perceive his hand in the dialogue."

1773–1803.

George Steevens, beginning with a note on the epilogue of *H8* (in the Johnson-Steevens *Shak.*, vii [1773], 288; vii [1778], 325) and increasingly on other portions of the play in subsequent editions up to Reed's "First Variorum" of 1803, cites parallel passages in support of the theory of partial Jonsonian authorship. He also argues (ɪ [1778], 317) that the prosodic features noted by Roderick were due either to Shak.'s negligence (rather than to his design) or were interpolations by Jonson, as Farmer had suggested.

1778.

In a path-breaking essay (Johnson-Steevens *Shak.*, I) Edmond Malone attempts to remedy ignorance concerning the chronology of Shak.'s works and thereby encourages scholars to write more confidently about the "interpolations" in *H8*. The first version of that play, according to Malone, was written in 1601. The panegyric of Elizabeth in V.v, he argues, was plainly intended for her ear, and he valiantly tries to explain away two embarrassing facts: first, the passage mentions the old age and death of the Virgin Queen, and secondly, Sir Henry Wotton's letter of 1613 referred to *H8*, under the title of *All is True*, as "a *new* play." The play as we have it, Malone insists, was merely revived and retitled in 1613. "The pecularities which [Roderick] has animadverted upon (if such there be)," Malone observes (ɪ, 317), "add probability to the conjecture that this piece underwent some alterations after it passed out of the hands of Shak."

1790.

In his edition of Shak., Malone adds to Steevens' citations of parallels from Jonson, and here and there implies that the second author might have been someone other than Jonson. In a note on the epilogue, he observes, "This play was revived in 1613, at which time, without doubt, the prologue and epilogue were added by Ben Jonson, or some other person." He attributes the stage directions describing Katharine's vision (IV.ii) "to the too busy reviver of this play" (vɪɪ, 106). And in an even more important note, he suggests that the second author was responsible for a change in the whole texture of the style; the lines about King James, Malone suggests (vɪɪ, 139), "were added in 1613, after Shak. had quitted the stage, by that hand which tampered with the other parts of the play so much, as to have rendered the versification of it of a different colour from all the other plays of Shak."

1793.

Steevens (*Plays of Shak.*) somewhat changes his position of 1778 in order to demur from Malone's remarks on the versification of *H8*. "Such indeed were the sentiments of Mr. Roderick, though the examples adduced by him in support of them are, in my judgment, undecisive . . . . But were the fact as he had stated it, we know not how far our poet might have intentionally deviated from his usual practice of versification.

"If the reviver of this play (or tamperer with it, as he is styled by Mr.

Malone,) had so much influence over its numbers as to have entirely changed their texture, he must be supposed to have new woven the substance of the whole piece; a fact almost incredible."

Accordingly, Steevens contents himself (1793 *et seq.*) with illustrating possible interpolations here and there by Jonson.

1816.

William Gifford, in his edition of Jonson's works (I, cclxix–cclxxiv), vigorously denies that Ben had anything to do with the prologue or epilogue of *H8*.

1821.

The reprinting of the various 18th-C. conjectures and discussions, in edition after edition up to the Malone-Boswell "Third Variorum" of 1821, doubtless had something to do with the attribution to Fletcher three decades later. And Boswell himself seems to have facilitated the Fletcherian hypothesis. He accepts Gifford's 1816 arguments against Jonson's partial authorship, and though he does not say that Fletcher had a hand in *H8*, he points out, in some remarks on Shak.'s versification (I, 560–561) that the "licence" whereby "two words of equal quantity occur at the close of a line, and a trochee is formed of them by an artificial accent laid upon the first," as in *H8* III.ii.441–442,

> "By that sin fell the angels; how can *man then,*
> The image of his Maker, hope to *win by't,*"

"is perpetually to be met with in Fletcher." And in the same discussion Boswell calls attention to a note on *Cym.* V.v.138–139 in which he comments further (XIII, 212), "There is scarcely a page in Fletcher's plays where this sort of versification ['an hypermetrical line of eleven syllables'] is not to be found." Readers of the 1821 Variorum could thus find laid out before them the theory that someone other than Shak. was responsible for various parts of *H8*, that this writer (perhaps Jonson, but probably someone else) had "rendered the versification [of the play] of a different colour from all the other plays of Shak.," and that certain features of the versification in *H8* were to be found virtually everywhere in Fletcher.

To 1833.

Meanwhile, a prolonged discussion of *TNK* which began in the mid-18th C. (see below, especially the comments of Charles Lamb, Henry Weber, S. T. Coleridge, and William Spalding) steadily developed the view that Shak. had collaborated with Fletcher in the composition of that play and was therefore bound to encourage the view that he had also done so in *H8*. In the penultimate paragraph of his essay on *TNK* (1833), Spalding suggested: "Perhaps there is none of [Shak.'s] works with which [*TNK*] could be so fairly compared as *H8*. In the tone of sentiment and imagination as well as in other particulars, I perceive many circumstances of likeness."

1843.

The anonymous editor of Shak.'s *Works* (London: Robert Tyas) asserts (III, 441) "that Shak. wrote a portion only of [*H8*]." Explicitly, he regards two of the famous scenes—Wolsey's long farewell to all his greatness, followed by his pathetic remarks to Cromwell (III.ii.350 ff.), and "the double character of Wolsey, drawn by Queen Katherine and her attendant" (IV.ii.29–80)—as fine in their own right but without the living reality that Shak. alone could have breathed into them. "The easy, but somewhat lax and familiar, although not inharmonious numbers" of the non-Shak.'n portions were added, the editor suggests, by "a reverent disciple" after Shak.'s death, for "what man . . . would dare to tamper [as Malone had put it] with [Shak.'s] text" while he "was yet living."

1846–1850.

A few years later, in a lecture on Shak. afterwards incorporated in *Representative Men* (1850), Ralph Waldo Emerson offered a diametrical theory of dual authorship: in *H8*, Shak. is the younger dramatist who has imposed his material on an older play. (Emerson cites Malone's argument that the same thing happened in *H6*.) "I think I see plainly," Emerson states, "the cropping out of the original rock on which [Shak.'s] own finer stratum was laid. The first play was written by a superior thoughtful man, with a vicious ear. I can mark his lines and know well their cadence. See Wolsey's soliloquy, and the following scene with Cromwell, where—instead of the metre of Shak., whose secret is, that the thought constructs the tune, so that reading for the sense will bring out the rhythm,—here the lines are constructed on a given tune, and the verse has even a trace of pulpit eloquence. But the play contains, through all its length, unmistakable traits of Shak.'s hand, and some passages, as the account of the coronation, are like autographs. What is odd, the compliment to Queen Elizabeth [V.v] is in the bad rhythm."

This oracular pronouncement is astute, if curiously uneven. In particular, Emerson leaves one uncertain of his grasp of the history of Eliz. dramatic prosody. What older poet before Shak. did he hold capable of the languid strains of the "non-Shak.'n" portions? Nevertheless, Emerson's contribution was significant: during his tour of England and Scotland (Nov. 1847–Feb. 1848), he told large audiences in Manchester, Liverpool, Derby, Nottingham, Leicester, Leeds, Sheffield, Newcastle, and Edinburgh that there were distinct and divided stylistic realms in *H8*. And in 1850 alone, his remarks were printed in at least three separate English editions of *Representative Men*.

1850.

In "Who Wrote Shak.'s *H8*," *The Gentleman's Magazine*, n.s., xxxiv (1850), 115–123 J[ames] S[pedding] sets forth a full and consecutive argument for Fletcher's coauthorship. He states that he was stimulated by Tennyson's casual remark, some years earlier, "that many passages in *H8* were very much in the manner of Fletcher." He also acknowledges his indebtedness to the arguments of Samuel Hickson in 1847 on *TNK* (see below), a play "the condition and supposed history of which," Spedding points out, "is in many respects analogous" to that of *H8*. But if the ground had been prepared for Spedding's theory, he nevertheless deserves full credit for his important contribution. He was the first to announce openly and to marshal arguments in favor of the Fletcherian thesis.

To the divided authorship Spedding attributes what he regards as the structural and emotional incoherence of the play, its failure to carry "the moral sympathy of the spectator . . . along with the main current of the action to the end." By a generic critical analysis similar to Lamb's, Spalding's, and Hickson's of *TNK*, Spedding distinguishes in *H8* two or perhaps three essentially different modes of language and prosody. He then supports his arguments by a thoroughgoing statistical analysis of the double endings in *H8*, which tends to confirm his division of authorship on what he himself considers the "higher grounds" of total literary response by an experienced reader. In the "Shak.'n" scenes the proportion of feminine endings, ranging from one in 2.5 to one in 3.5, is similar to the proportions in *Cym.* and *Wint.*, whereas the proportion in the "Fletcherian" scenes, ranging from one in 1.5 to one in 2, corresponds with those in Fletcher's known work. Spedding suggests what has since become the traditional division of shares between Shak. and Fletcher (see A and B in the head-note to the *H8* entries, above), except that he argues for a third hand, possibly Beaumont's, as chiefly responsible for Act IV. Although this last hypothesis has not won general acceptance, Spedding was at any rate singling out an act about which later proponents of dual authorship have disagreed.

1850–1851.

As soon as Spedding's article appeared, Samuel Hickson (*N&Q*, ii [1850], 198) announced a virtually identical allocation of authorship at which he had arrived independently three or four years earlier. In a later note (*ibid.* 401–403), Hickson mentioned other writers, including the editor of the 1843 Shak. and Emerson, who had seen two hands in *H8*. Shortly afterwards (*N&Q*, iii [1851], 33–34), he suggested that certain locutions —e.g., the use of "one" as a substantive, of "thousand" without the indefinite article, of "else" at the end of a phrase—appear both in *H8* B and in Fletcher's unaided work. A similar, expanded list is provided by Charles K. Pooler in the Old Arden ed. of *H8* (1915).

1851–1874.

In the two decades following the Spedding-Hickson articles, the Fletcherian hypothesis was received with reservations by leading scholars. Alexander Dyce (*Works of Shak.* I [1857], clxxvi) mentioned it noncommittally. J. O. Halliwell (*Works of Shak.* XII [1864], 10) warned that "it is worse than hazardous" to make peculiarities of diction, dramatic construction, or versification "the grounds of an argument tending to deprive Shak. of the authorship" of *H8*. Henry N. Hudson (*Shak.: His Life, Art, and Characters* [1872], II, 174–177) was willing to admit Fletcher's presence in I.iii,iv, and IV.i, but thought that the Fletcherian argument seemed "to kill itself by proving too much" and cautioned that Shak.'s later versification is characterized by many double endings.

1874.

But Spedding's argument, especially the statistical portion, proved nevertheless to be the wave of the future. In an age when scientific studies were achieving spectacular successes in many fields (the years between 1851 and 1874 saw the appearance of important works by Boole, Darwin, Galton, Huxley, Lyell, Marx, Maxwell, Spencer, Tyndall, and others), the statistical method promised to elevate literary studies to something like a science. When F. J. Furnivall formed the New Shak. Society (1873), he put metrical tests at the top of its agenda. "In this Victorian time," he wrote in his Founder's Prospectus (back of vol. I of *NSS Trans.* [1874], 7), "when our geniuses of Science are so wresting her secrets from Nature as to make our days memorable for ever, the faithful student of Shak. need not fear that he will be unable to pierce through the crowds of forms that exhibit Shak.'s mind, to the mind itself." The first papers read before the Society were F. G. Fleay's on metrical tests, and both Fleay and Furnivall hailed Spedding's paper on *H8* as a model for future research (*ibid.*, I, 2 and 242). They differed in their emphasis, to be sure. Fleay, to whose apportionment of authorship in the Shak. and the Beaumont and Fletcher canons the whole first part of *NSS Trans.*, I, was devoted, gave enthusiastic priority to Spedding's tabulation of double endings: "This . . . is the great step we have to take; our analysis, which has hitherto been qualitative, must become quantitative; we must cease to be empirical and become scientific" (p. 2). Furnivall, like other members of the NSS, found fault with Fleay's heavy reliance on metrical statistics, and he followed Spedding in giving "taste or critical power" priority over figures and tabulations: "a Tennyson, a Spedding has no need of [such] aids" (p. 242). But both Fleay and Furnivall nevertheless praised Spedding as a pioneer, and in an appendix to the first volume of *NSS Trans.*, Furnivall reprinted Spedding's essay, along with Hickson's first *N&Q* article of 1850, his essay on *TNK* of 1847, and Roderick's observations of about a century before on the versification of *H8*.

In the same volume, John K. Ingram observes that a study of light and weak endings in *H8* "strikingly confirms" Spedding's conclusions. There are few such endings in Fletcher's known work, whereas they occur with increasing frequency in Shak.'s plays from *Mac.* onwards. In A, Ingram finds 45 light and 37 weak endings, as against only 7 and 1 in B. "And these weak endings occur in every Shak.'n scene," but the single weak ending in B occurs in the uncertainly assigned IV.i.

1875.

In Edward Dowden (*Shak.: A Critical Study of His Mind and Art*, 414), the NSS found an important early convert. Dowden stated that the Spedding-Hickson division was confirmed by the tests of Fleay and Ingram.

1876.

But then an even more distinguished opponent entered the lists. In *The Examiner* of April, Algernon Swinburne published his shrewd parody, "Report of the Proceedings on the First Anniversary Session of the Newest Shak. Society" (reprinted in *A Study of Shak.* [1880], 276–309). Swinburne chose as his special targets the excesses of the wilder members of the statistical school and their already alarming tendency to disintegrate the Shak. canon. The parody presents as having been delivered before the Newest SS, papers such as that by Mr. F. "on the date of *Oth.*, and on the various parts of that play respectively assignable to Samuel Rowley, to George Wilkins, and to Robert Daborne. It was evident that the story of Othello and Desdemona was originally quite distinct from that part of the play in which Iago was a leading figure. This [Mr. F.] was prepared to show at some length by means of the weak-ending test, the light-ending test, the double-ending test, the triple-ending test, the heavy-monosyllabic-eleventh-syllable-of-the-double-ending test and the central-pause test." At the end of the anniversary session, the Chairman congratulates the members of the Society and himself for having established "an entirely new kind of criticism, working by entirely new means towards an entirely new kind of Shak. . . . The first step towards this end must of course be the demolition of the old [Shak.]; and he would venture to say they had already made a good beginning in that direction. They had deprived or would deprive the claim of Shak. to the sole authorship of *Mac.*, *Caes.*, *Lear*, *Ham.*, and *Oth.*; they had established or they would establish the fact of his partnership in *Locrine, Mucedorus, The Birth of Merlin, Dr. Dodipoll*, and *Sir Giles Goose-cap.*"

In the same year, John Jeremiah published anonymously a very similar but less skillful satire, in rough and ready heroic couplets: *Furnivallos Furioso! and The Newest Shak. Society . . . By the Ghost of Guido Fawkes.*

To these outrageous thrusts Furnivall, dubbing his opponents "Pigsbrook & Co.," replied in a series of counterattacks (1879–1881) more notable for their fury than their finesse. See Furnivall's ed. of *Ham.* Q2 (1880) and the Brit. Mus. Catalogue, LXXXI (1961), cols. 684, 690–692.

1880.

Swinburne said nothing about *H8* in his parody of the NSS, but in *A Study of Shak.* he devoted some eloquent pages to the defense of Shak.'s sole authorship. His is the most complete and strategic statement of the Shak.'n case before Peter Alexander's essay of 1930. As might be expected, Swinburne relies on literary analysis. His concessions to the other side are effective. He pays tribute to Spedding's "fine and subtle criticism"; he agrees that the play is "wanting in unity, consistency, and coherence of interest" and that often its meter and language very much resemble Fletcher's and are very different from Shak.'s. But he vigorously denies that Fletcher is capable of the restraint and elevation of Buckingham's and Cromwell's last speeches, though they seem Fletcherian in their "smooth and fluent declamation," their "prolonged and persistent melody." Neither can he "bring [himself] to believe" that Fletcher could have written "the crowning glory of the whole poem, the death-scene of Katherine." (Samuel Johnson stated that the vision of the dying Katharine is tender and pathetic "above any other part of Shak.'s tragedies, and perhaps above any scene of any other poet." Later critics who argue that the great passages of B soar above the artistry shown in Fletcher's known works include Alexander, G. Wilson Knight, and R. A. Foakes.) There is not nearly as much distance, Swinburne maintains, between such allegedly Fletcherian scenes and the Shak.'n ones as there is between the Fletcherian and Shak.'n scenes of *TNK*, "undoubtedly a joint work of these poets," where, in contrast to *H8*, the respective shares can be differentiated "with absolute certainty."

Though Swinburne does not think much of metrical arguments, he points out that *H8* lacks "the perpetual predominance of those triple terminations so peculiarly and notably dear" to Fletcher. "And if the proof by mere metrical similitude," in itself an isolated and very inadequate criterion, "is thus imperfect, there is here assuredly no other kind of test which may help to fortify the argument." The "exceptional quality" of the play "might perhaps be explicable as a tentative essay in a new line by one who tried so many styles before settling into his latest. . . . Without far stronger, clearer, and completer proof than has yet been *or can ever be* advanced, the question is not solved but merely evaded by the assumption of double authorship" (italics added). Some may think that the italicized phrase is in itself an evasion which attempts to preclude all future argument on the subject.

1881–1887.

In the seven editions of *Outlines of the Life of Shak.*, J. O. Halliwell-Phillipps, to whom Swinburne's *Study* of 1880 is dedicated, expressed great skepticism about the Fletcherian hypothesis. He argued that Shak. was following fashion in using a large number of hypermetric syllables and that opinions as to the extent of alien work in a play that "the players or their confederates" had probably tampered with "rest too frequently upon the treacherous foundation of a belief in the powers of assigning a definite limit to the writer's mutations in style and excellence" (1886 ed., II, 295).

1885.

At this time actuality moved uncomfortably close to Swinburne's parody of 1876. In a paper addressed to the NSS, Robert Boyle proposed to deprive Shak. of any share in *H8* (*NSS Trans.*, 1880–1886, 443–487). He believed it improbable that Shak., who had been a collaborator or reviser at the outset of his career, should have degraded his art by collaboration after he had become a master of the drama. (Yet Boyle at the same time argues that the late plays *Troil.*, *Tim.*, and *Per.* are only partly Shak.'s.) Moreover, and Boyle places very great emphasis on this point, none of *H8* rises to the superb poetry and characterization that Shak. had achieved in *Mac.*, *Temp.*, and other late plays. The play about Henry VIII produced when the Globe Theater burned down in 1613 was not necessarily the play printed in the Folio. The latter is rather the work of Fletcher and Massinger, to whom Boyle assigns all of A, plus I.iv.1–24, 64–108; II.i.1–53, 137–169; IV.i; V.iii.1–113. The rest of *H8* is Fletcher's. Fletcher and Massinger worked together closely, Boyle believes, sometimes writing alternately in the same scene.

Boyle uses metrical evidence (double, weak, and light endings), parallels in phrasing with plays attributed to Massinger (sometimes on uncertain grounds), and historical allusions appropriate to the years 1616 and 1617. Boyle admits that some of the allusions can be found in Halle's account of the reign of Henry VIII, but he contends (p. 461), "These topics were put into the play on account of their like later parallels." As for parallels in phrasing to Shak.'s acknowledged work, these are Massinger's weak echoes of the master.

Richard Garnett, W. A. Harrison, and others offered sharp criticism of the flaws in Boyle's arguments (*NSS Trans.*, 1880–1886, *118–*126), but to balance this, support came from no less a figure than Robert Browning. For about fifty years, the poet states, he had believed that Shak. had but a scanty share in *H8;* and he then flatly asserts that "Mr Boyle's judgment is right altogether" and that "the versification [of the play] is nowhere Shak.'s." Others who subsequently deprived Shak. of most or all of *H8* were Furnivall (happy, he now declared, to discard the Shak.'n portion of Spedding's argument), Fleay, W. Aldis Wright, W. J. Craig, Sir Sidney Lee, A. H. Bullen, H. Dugdale Sykes, and E. C. Oliphant. (Oliphant changed his assignments somewhat in each of three reviews of the evidence; see his *The Plays of Beaumont and Fletcher* [New Haven, 1927], 306–316.)

1885–1942.

Despite the support for Boyle's extreme views, Spedding's division between Shak. and Fletcher rapidly became the acknowledged "orthodox view." It won the approval of many editors of *H8*, including Edward Dowden in *The International Shak.* (1892), the Renaissance Shak. (1910), and in the Oxford U. P. volume of Shak.'s *Histories,* ed. W. J. Craig (1911); C. H. Herford in the Eversley Shak., VII (1899); E. K. Chambers in the Red Letter Shak. (1908): Charles K. Pooler in the Old Arden Shak. (1915, 1936); M. R. Ridley in the New Temple Shak. (1935); and G. L. Kittredge (1936) and W. A. Neilson and C. J. Hill (1942) in their editions of Shak.'s complete works. A frequent practice in separate 20th-C. editions of *H8* (and of *TNK*) is to give scholars' various assignments of authorship in the first note to each scene.

This growing majority in favor of a hypothesis unsupported by external evidence is probably to be explained by the steady accumulation of internal evidence, set forth below. Yet the debate continues, down to the two most recent editions of *H8* (1957 and 1962).

1901–1912.

In *The Influence of Beaumont and Fletcher on Shak.* (1901), Ashley H. Thorndike offered (pp. 24–28, 37–45) "a new test" of slight linguistic preferences. He pointed out that in their unaided plays, Fletcher uses *'em* about fifteen times more often than *them,* whereas Shak. uses *'em* infrequently and Massinger never. (In an errata slip, Thorndike stated that he was wrong about Massinger, having discovered too late that Gifford, whose edition he had used, normalizes all of Massinger's *'em*'s to *them*'s. Copies without the errata slip have misled some later investigators: cf. *PMLA,* XXXVII [1922], 487). Thorndike applied the test in the first instance to *H8* and *TNK* and found that it corroborated "the usual verse-tests in separating [Shak.'s and Fletcher's] work distinctly" (there are 5 *'em*'s to 17 *them*'s in *H8* A, but 57 *'em*'s to 4 *them*'s in B). He believed, moreover, that the *'em-them* test could "serve to call attention to interpolations or additions by a second author, which verse-tests alone would not indicate" (p. 28). His tables indicate that "the Shak. and Fletcher parts are distinct, free from interpolations and revisions" (p. 42), and Thorndike therefore concluded that in both *H8* and *TNK* "the method of composition seems to have been collaboration, pure and simple."

Although Robert Boyle, of whose views Thorndike was critical, in his turn poured scorn upon the *'em-them* test (*Englische Studien,* XXXI [1902], 420–421), Thorndike was here the originator of one of the more fruitful 20th-C. methods of determining Eliz. dramatic authorship. The method was soon extended by R. B. McKerrow, who noticed that the choice of *ye* over *you* seems an effective test for separating the work of Fletcher and Massinger in *The Spanish Curate,* and W. W. Greg, who applied the same test to *The Elder Brother,* with the warning that one must avoid texts normalized by modern editors (see the Variorum Beaumont and Fletcher, II [1905], 4, 104). Paul Elmer More then came upon the *ye-you* test independently in an article in *The Nation* in 1912 (see *Shelburne Essays,* 10th ser. [1919], 37–40), finding that Fletcher's practice differs markedly from those of Shak., Beaumont, Jonson, Massinger, Middleton, Field, and Rowley. He applied the test to a dozen plays in the Beaumont and Fletcher canon and to *H8* and *TNK,* confirming Fletcher's presence in *H8* I.iv; II.iii; III.i, iib; IV.i, ii; and V.iii, iv, v. More suggested that more refined conclusions might be obtained by those willing to push the test further.

1916.

Willard E. Farnham's "Colloquial Contractions in Beaumont, Fletcher, Massinger, and Shak. as a Test of Authorship," *PMLA,* XXXI, 326–358, seems to have been the first work to apply a battery of linguistic preferences on a large scale to the solution of problems in Eliz. dramatic attribution. It is also a kind of culmination of the efforts instituted in 1874 by the NSS. Farnham announces his indebtedness to Fleay's "epoch-making paper" on metrical tests and to Boyle's work for "the fundamental idea of this paper." The acknowledgment has its unintentional ironies, since the tendency of Farnham's tables is to disprove Boyle's and Fleay's theories that the non-Fletcherian portions of *H8* and *TNK* should be assigned to Massinger.

Farnham selects three broad groups of colloquial contractions: *t*-contractions such as *in't, on't, pour't; the*-contractions such as *i'th', o'th';* and *s*-contractions ("the most uncommon of all") such as *on's* (for *on us* or *on his*) and *make's* (for *make us* or *make his*). In some cases the opposition of preferences is striking: Shak. in his later plays uses *s*-contractions frequently, Fletcher sparingly, Massinger before 1622 never. Altogether, "Shak. and Massinger are . . . almost at opposite extremes in their use of contractions." A tally of contractions in *H8* and *TNK* thus tends not only to bear out the traditional assignments to Fletcher but also to prove that Shak., rather than Massinger or Beaumont, is the author of the non-Fletcherian scenes.

Farnham indicates that the use of colloquial contractions is a matter of the author's literary taste and that it cannot be attributed to the printers. Although he has recourse to early printed editions of the plays, he does not consider the possible leveling out of linguistic preferences by the interference of scribes.

Farnham's important work was neglected by a surprising number of later studies.

1918.

In "*H8:* Fletcher's Werk überarbeitet von Shak.," *Englische Studien,* LII, 204 ff., H. Conrad, while maintaining the thesis of his title, indicated that there are many more parallels to Shak.'s diction in A than in B.

1919.

H. Dugdale Sykes (*Sidelights on Shak.*, 18–47) agreed with Boyle that *H8* A is really by Massinger; Massinger and Fletcher are both present in I.iii, III.i, IV.ii, which Boyle gave to Fletcher alone. Boyle used metrical tests, but since Massinger's meter "is so like Shak.'s," Sykes believed that firmer evidence could be found in an array of verbal parallels between *H8* and Massinger's works. Sykes frequently cites as parallels such phrases as "Let reason rule your passion," "I am a suitor," "Would I were [etc.]."

1922.

In "The Authorship of *H8*" (*PMLA*, xxxvii, 484–302), Marjorie Nicolson aimed to clarify the nature of Shak.'s contribution by examining structure and characterization. The shares of Fletcher and Shak., she maintained, cannot be differentiated by their equally heavy use of sources, though if Shak. wrote A, "he showed himself less original than usual in his versifying of the chronicles." Nevertheless, *H8* "*is* Shak.'s in part, and . . . is less an anticlimax than a fitting climax to his dramas." *H8* A constitutes "the framework of a play" which would have been less a companion for *H5* than for *Tim.* or *Lear,* a play that was "to deal . . . with the strange revolutions of fortune which now exalt one, now another." The first half of the play was to show the increasing power of a cunning Wolsey over a weak king, the second half Wolsey's fall and the rise of Cranmer. Buckingham and Katharine would not have been sentimentalized, as they are in B. Fletcher's change of Shak.'s characterization and emphasis suggests that Shak. simply handed over his six scenes for the younger dramatist to use as he wished. Properly speaking, then, there was no collaboration between the two.

1923.

In "Fletcher and *H8*" (*Manly Anniversary Studies,* 104–112), Baldwin Maxwell points out that Spedding failed to show that the so-called Fletcherian characteristics were peculiar to that poet, "nor did he suggest to what extent they appear in Fletcher's undoubted work." Apart from *TNK*, there is little reliable evidence of Flecher's collaboration with Shak., and in *TNK* the Fletcherian parts lack the proportion of general truths and the economy of expression of *H8* B. Other stylistic traits which occur in smaller proportions in B than in Fletcher's known work are insertions of "parenthetical matter in the center of a clause" and repetitions such as "O, very mad, exceeding mad, in love too" (*H8* I.iv.28). Moreover, Fletcher does not elsewhere follow historical sources verbatim, as Miss Nicholson indicates he does in *H8*. If Fletcher is present in *H8*, "either he was revising another's work, or the peculiarities of his style and method were modified by a collaborator."

1926.

A few years later, Baldwin Maxwell (*MP*, xxiii, 365 ff.) criticized H. Dugdale Sykes's use of parallels, approved by A. H. Bullen and Dover

Wilson. Sykes's field of investigation is so narrow, Maxwell argued, that one cannot properly interpret his data. It is not enough to find Massinger parallels to *H8*. One ought to look for parallels in the other plays (there are more Massinger parallels to *Ham.* and *Oth.* than to *H8*, and the parallels increase after the publication of Shak.'s Folio), and in the work of all possible claimants, including Shak. himself. Frequency does not necessarily indicate priority: though Massinger uses "star-cross'd" four times, Shak. uses it first in *Romeo* and does not use it again. Parallels can be due to self-repetition, to imitation or influence, to chance, and to the idiom of the day.

1930.

In reply to the Massingerians, E. K. Chambers stated (*Shak.*, I, 495–498) that "it is easier to make out a case against Fletcher than against Shak." As Maxwell observed, *H8* is not "very characteristic Fletcher," nor for that matter is it "very characteristic Shak. either." Shak. may have been tired, and Fletcher may have been writing under Shak.'s influence; collaboration seems more likely than revision. On balance, Chambers saw "no reason to dissent" from Spedding's division.

In "Conjectural History, or Shak.'s *H8*" (*Essays and Studies*, xvi, 85–120), Peter Alexander, fresh from the triumphs of his book on *H6* (see above), made an analogous, closely reasoned attack on the Fletcherian hypothesis. "What is now the orthodox story concerning *H8*," he maintained, "begins and ends in conjecture." He associated the hypothesis with arbitrary 18th-C. practices (e.g., Pope's treatment of Shak.'s text and versification) encouraged by unhistorical assumptions about Shak.'s prosody, his learning, and the descent of his texts. Theories of divided authorship presumably supported by metrical and other statistics are no less arbitrary, Alexander declared, and their logical conclusion is the thorough disintegration proposed by J. M. Robertson in his series on *The Shak. Canon* (1922–1932). In some cases, the alleged facts are erroneous: though Hickson, Abbott, and Boyle claim as a peculiarly Fletcherian trait the double ending with a heavy final monosyllable, such endings occur frequently in *Wint.* and *Temp.* But the more important issue is one of principle: what is in question is not the existence of the tabulated facts, but rather the validity of the theories attached to them. Spedding, Alexander stated, fails to satisfy elementary mathematical and logical requirements. He "has not isolated the essentials of the problem, for the vital question of how modifications arise in the development of Shak.'s verse is never seriously considered by him. He merely assumes, contrary to evidence, that such a modification as is found in *H8* could not arise. Nor has he considered the question of variation within the individual plays."

Alexander offered analyses of Shak.'s varying practices in versification. Even in earlier plays, Shak. sometimes uses double endings in one speech but none in another. Why not assume that he adopts the same method in different scenes of *H8*? True, there are more double endings in *H8* than in earlier plays. But such dramatic differences can also be found between admittedly canonical plays. In *2H4*, 16% of the endings are double; in *1H4* only 5%. In *Ant.*, Ingram counts 71 light and 28 weak endings, but gives "no earlier play . . . more than two weak endings, and *Mac.* comes closest in number of light endings with twenty-one." And in *Ant.*, as in *H8*, there is great variation from scene to scene in the proportion of such features. Shak. uses double endings increasingly in his last plays, and "the rhythm which Emerson found so vicious is clearly in process of development in parts of *Wint.* and *Temp.*" In fact, *H8* "has as it stands the compassionate outlook so characteristic of the Fourth Period." The different parts of the play are harmonious, and the birth of Elizabeth, so glorified in the supposedly Fletcherian speech of Cranmer, is foreshadowed in two scenes usually assigned to Shak. (II.iii.75–79 and III.ii.49–52).

Alexander does not discuss the linguistic evidence set forth by Thorndike, More, and Farnham. He reiterated his arguments in an unpublished paper delivered at Stratford-on-Avon Aug. 16, 1948, and in *Shak.* (Oxford, 1964), 199–203; on these pages, he criticizes the interpretations of metrical statistics by Ants Oras and J. C. Maxwell but does not mention the linguistic arguments of A. C. Partridge and Cyrus Hoy. (The essays of these scholars are summarized below.)

1934–1943.
In an article on the vocabulary of *TNK* in *RES* in 1934 (see below), Alfred Hart drew attention to the "remarkable fact" that in *Shrew*, *Per.*, *Tim.*, *H8*, *E3*, and *TNK* "all the 'new' words [i.e. words not previously recorded by the *OED*] beginning in *un-* are in the portions usually assigned to Shak." (p. 285). In "Vocabularies of Shak.'s Plays," *RES*, xix (1943), 134, Hart observed that in *H8* the vocabulary in A is proportionately much larger than in B.

1935.
Since Caroline Spurgeon found that images of bodily movement are present in both *H8* A and B (*Shak.'s Imagery*, 253–258), the pattern, she concluded, "distinctly goes to prove" that in addition to A, III.2b and V.iii are also Shak.'s, "and that he at least gave some touches to II.ii."

1936–1948.
In an argument expanded from that in the *Criterion* of 1936, G. Wilson Knight affirmed (*The Crown of Life*, 1947, 1948) that *H8* is the grand climax of Shak.'s histories. The play is wholly Shak.'n, and the stylistic differences between A and B are to be explained by deliberate changes in rhythm as Shak. moves his characters from ambitious and aspiring states

(here the style is "packed, metaphoric, allusive, complex"), to isolation amid enemies (here the style becomes expostulatory, with weak endings, run-on effects, and mid-line pauses), and finally to utter worldly defeat (here the lines are "simple, falling units with a delicate but reiterated stress on personal pronouns in collaboration with feminine endings"). All of these traits can be illustrated from Shak.'s later plays, and there is thus no need to assume the presence of Fletcher, whose looseness of rhythm and mechanical use of double endings do not appear in *H8*. "Indeed, how do we know that Fletcher" in his own plays was "not copying Shak.?" (1948 ed., p. 268). Knight warns also that one must not apply imagery tests rigidly, since a change in the experience represented "will tend to dictate some variation . . . in choice, and amount, of imagery," as well as in rhythm (p. 271).

1948.

In *An Interpretation of Shak.*, Hardin Craig independently used arguments similar to Wilson Knight's about the change of prosody to suit the characters' moods. In double endings *H8* (47%) exceeds *Temp.* (35%) "but little more than that play exceeds Mac." (26%). Logically, one should transfer those parts of *H8* A with a large number of double endings to Fletcher. But in fact, the proportion of double endings in B falls below Fletcher's usual frequencies, and the partition of such scenes as III.ii between Shak. and Fletcher "would seem to be based on a low estimate of Shak.'s versatility and a failure to recognize the features of his later style" (p. 370). This "consistently planned and well integrated" drama, faithfully "following the same sources throughout," looks "like the work of one man."

After commenting on the peculiar claims of intuition about authorship ("no amount of internal evidence could prove it right, and no amount will prove it wrong"), Frank Kermode pointed out that *H8* may be unified whether or not there is more than one author ("What is Shak.'s *H8* About?" *Durham Univ. Journal*, n.s. IX, 48–55). Kermode himself believes that it is unified and that it has two authors. Alexander's examples of "Fletcherian" lines in Shak. are not all good, and as for Wilson Knight's claims, the transition from one manner to another in *H8* is more abrupt than in Shak.'s unaided plays. Moreover, none of the "Fletcherian" passages in Shak. is as long as those in *H8* and none of them "really achieves the studied valedictory cadences of Buckingham and Wolsey."

1949.

A. C. Partridge's *The Problem of "H8" Reopened* returned to the analysis of linguistic preferences, neglected for many years. *Do* is used as an expletive 40 times in A, Partridge finds, but only 5 times in B; the ratio of *hath* to *has* in A is 22/14, in B, 2/33; of *them* to *'em* in A, 23/5 in B,

7/59: there are 5 instances of *ye* or *y'* in A, 81 in B. These figures agree closely with the linguistic preferences in Shak.'s and Fletcher's known work. Partridge also discusses the difficult syntax in A, e.g., the tendency "to lose track of . . . relative clauses, especially in continuative function and in proximity to participial phrases, or adverbial clauses, of time."

The divisions on a linguistic basis "substantiate broadly" the Spedding-Hickson division. But Shak. may originally have written more than A, for it seems probable that Fletcher had "final oversight of the play" and overlaid Shak.'s share with his characteristics. This may have happened in I.i.1–2, II.ii, III.iib, and V.iii (cf. Hoy [1962], below). It seems more likely to Partridge that Fletcher completed an unfinished work by Shak. than that they collaborated simultaneously.

1952.

Examining *The Pattern of Tragicomedy in Beaumont and Fletcher,* Eugene M. Waith found (pp. 118–124) that B in *H8* displays Fletcher's traits in quintessential form, presenting "in the declamatory style the figure of the hero, larger than life, and clothed in a ready-made nobility." Thus both Buckingham and Wolsey, otherwise quite different from each other, give voice to similar valedictories, for each "appears as the pitiable victim of forces largely exterior to him."

1953.

In " 'Extra Monosyllables' in *H8* and the Problem of Authorship," *JEGP,* LII, 198–213, Ants Oras provided a thorough and judicious analysis of a single prosodic feature—the double ending with a final monosyllable. Alexander showed that Abbott was wrong in claiming that such extra monosyllables (hereafter "e.m.'s") do not occur in Shak. But the question, Oras points out, is really one of the relative frequency of this trait in Shak. and Fletcher and in A and B. A total count shows that 14.2% (54 out of 380) of the feminine endings in A have e.m.'s as against 29% (254 out of 878) in B. Differences in frequencies of e.m.'s in the unaided plays of Shak. and Fletcher are closely comparable. (On the other hand, the relatively slight difference in frequency of e.m.'s between *H8* III.iia, 23.8%, and III.iib, 28.9%, may suggest close collaboration.)

The qualitative differences in the e.m.'s are also revealing. Shak.'s, and those in A, are light and unemphatic; Fletcher's, and those in B, are frequently heavy, tending to be accompanied by sonal devices such as assonance and alliteration ("him*self else*," *H8* II.ii.23; "*graves* of *great* men," II.i.67) and causing a conflict between normal sentence stress and metrical stress, with a consequent dictation of rhythm by meter rather than by meaning. Fletcher and B frequently conclude successive lines with the same e.m.; Shak. and A seldom do so. Fletcher's excesses are somewhat toned down in *H8*, however, perhaps owing to Shak.'s influence.

1956.

Philip Williams, Jr. ("New Approaches to Textual Problems in Shak.," *SB*, vⅢ, 3–14) pointed to bibliographical evidence that no previous investigator of *H8* had taken into account. Of the two compositors who set the pages of *H8*, Compositor B tends to change *ye* in his copy to *you*, and *'em* to *them*. The ratio of *ye* to *you* on Compositor B's pages is 1 to 8, on the pages of the other compositor (identified by Williams, Foakes, and others as A, but more recently by Charlton Hinman as X) 1 to 4. On Compositor B's pages, there are only 11 *'em*'s, on X's 55. Unless one takes Compositor B's practices into account, the linguistic tests can be "dangerously misleading."

1957.

M. M. Mahood observed (*Shak.'s Wordplay*, pp. 26–27): "Once we have grown accustomed to Shak.'s verbal habits, the absence of any of them from a play casts doubt upon his authorship. The parts of *H8* held to be non-Shak.'n contain remarkably few puns, except for some *double-entendres* which do not recur among the Folio plays."

Robert Adger Law ("Holinshed and *H8*," *Texas St. in Eng.*, xxvi, 5–11) found that the handling of sources by A and B supports Spedding's division of authorship. A is imaginative and original in departing from the words of the chronicle, whereas B displays "greater dependence on Holinshed and less exercise of the fancy."

Irving Ribner (*The English History Play in the Age of Shak.*, 288–291), felt, on the other hand, that despite the efforts of Partridge and others, the Fletcherian hypothesis, "although certainly possible, has yet to be definitely established." The "diversity of point of view" in the sources followed may be used as an argument, but that too is insufficient. The play's inconsistencies and its lack of integration are not the result of divided authorship; rather do they illustrate "the decline of the history play as a dramatic genre."

In the New Arden edition of *H8*, R. A. Foakes reversed the position of the Old Arden editor (1915, 1936) and argued in favor of Shak.'s sole authorship. The evidence for dual authorship from Spedding onwards was inadequate, Foakes felt. "The weight [Oras] lays on many extra syllables," for instance, "is surely all his own." Of particular interest are Foakes's observations on linguistic evidence. Farnham's evidence he regards as "so narrow [in range] as to establish little more than that both authors were inconsistent in their usage." Partridge's argument is "the fullest and most compelling yet put forward in Fletcher's behalf," yet the usages of *ye* and *'em* in *H8* B are "not Fletcherian enough": in *Bonduca*, there are 349 *ye*'s, very few *you*'s, and nothing parallel to *H8* IV.i with 12 *you*'s as against 3 *ye*'s, "and these three concentrated into four lines of farewell." Scribes and compositors may have altered the frequency of linguistic preferences, as in Compositor B's changes of *ye* to *you* in *Troil.* (Alice Walker, *Textual Problems of the First Folio*, [1953], 87). To be sure, the work of the compositors of *H8* cuts across the usual assignments of authorship, but "we do not know how far, or in what differing degrees these compositors altered their copy for this particular play" (cf. Williams [1956], above, and Hoy, [1962], below). Nor do we "know enough about Shak.'s practice": the distribution of *the*-contractions in *Cor.* permits one to arrive at a division similar to Farnham's in *H8*.

In addition to previous arguments in favor of Shak.'n authorship, Foakes points out that irregular speech headings which cannot be attributed to compositors suggest a single author (see 1958, below), as does the use of sources in A and B (e.g., the bringing together in a single scene of "widely-scattered extracts"). The cluster of *ye*'s and *'em*'s within a few lines in certain scenes (II.i; IV.ii; V.iii) makes it "possible to argue . . . that *H8* is a text touched up here and there, sometimes for a whole scene, by Fletcher." Apart from such revising, Fletcher "perhaps contributed one or two scenes." But such allegedly "Fletcherian" scenes as II.ii, IV.ii, and V.iii are Shak.'n in their powers of characterization and language. In any case, "considerations of authorship do not affect the intrinsic worth" of this integrated and felicitous play.

1958.

R. A. Foakes ("On the First Folio Text of *H8*," *SB*, xi, 55–60) stated that a study of variant compositorial spellings and of speech headings supports Greg's view that *H8* was printed from "carefully edited" fair copy and suggests further that the copy was in a single hand and derived from the foul papers of a single author.

1959.

Robert A. Law responded to recent attacks on the Fletcherian case by a defense ("The Double Authorship of *H8*," *SP*, LVI, 471–486) which offered, among other arguments, a new test—the percentages of feminine lines ending with a verb followed by an unstressed pronoun. The figures are as follows: (1) *H8* A, 2.1%; *Cym.*, 3.1%, *Wint.*, 3.1%; *Temp.*, 3.6%. (2) *H8* B, 8.1%; *Bonduca*, 9%; *Valentinian*, 10%; *Wild Goose Chase*, 11.2%.

Law agrees with Miss Nicolson (1922, above) that the characterization of *H8* is inconsistent, and the parts of the play poorly joined. The Fletcher scenes II.i, III.iib, and IV.i,ii, he feels, are weak and loose as compared with Shak.'s scenes. (Cf. Partridge and Foakes, above, and Hoy, below.)

1961.

In "*H8* and Fletcher," *SQ*, XII, 239–260, Marco Mincoff strongly emphasized the cumulative force of the evidence. He argued that "ten objectively measurable and essentially independent indicators" (metrical, lexical, and grammatical) plus three not easily quantified (sentence structure, Fletcherian phrasing, and Fletcherian "alliterative humor") all point to a division of *H8* between Shak. and Fletcher. "Each new test," Mincoff urged, "no matter how little decisive by itself, increases the probabilities in a steady geometrical progression, resulting very soon in almost astronomical figures."

Mincoff rebuts the various objections of Maxwell, Alexander, Knight, and Foakes. To the argument "not Fletcherian enough" he replies that in Fletcher's collaborations with Beaumont, his peculiar characteristics are likewise diminished and modified—and to a greater extent than in *H8* and *TNK*. If Shak. is imitating Fletcher's prosody, as some maintain, why should the imitation be confined to certain scenes? Contentions that various Fletcherian traits can also be found in Shak. overlook the high frequency of the traits in Fletcher and *H8* B, and their conjunction with certain rhetorical and stylistic effects that change the total quality of the writing. Mincoff regards as "merely frivolous" Foakes's attempt to minimize the argument from linguistic preferences by referring to scribal and compositorial intervention. Such intervention might explain the reduction of Fletcher's characteristic frequencies; it cannot explain away the concentration of Fletcherian preferences that are nevertheless evident in B. The running images to which Foakes points are very commonplace and occur frequently in Fletcher. In any case, "unity of theme is no argument against double authorship"; the anticipations of Elizabeth's birth in two passages of A, e.g., can be explained by the collaborators' coordinating their efforts. The toning down of Fletcherian traits suggests that Shak. was the dominant partner.

E. M. W. Tillyard, in "Why Did Shak. Write *H8*?" *Crit. Quart.*, III, 22–27, gave it as his opinion that the play is the work of a tired and aging Shak., "the product of a perfected technique yet so little animated by his individual fire as to approximate the current manner of the time." The prologue too is probably Shak.'s.

1962.

In "The Shares of Fletcher and His Collaborators in the Beaumont and Fletcher Canon (VII)," *SB*, XV, 71–90, Cyrus Hoy stated that linguistic criteria have only a limited validity in determining Shak.'s presence in a play of doubtful authorship, but that they may nevertheless be helpful. (See Hoy, under *TNK*, 1962, below.) After a comparison of Fletcher's and Shak.'s linguistic usages, Hoy finds that the most striking differences are in Shak.'s general avoidance of *ye* as against Fletcher's addiction to it, and in Shak.'s preference for *hath* and *doth* as against Fletcher's for *has* and *does*. Foakes's attempts to explain away such differences by alluding to possible scribal or compositorial interference are misleading: Philip Williams (see above) demonstrated that in *H8* Compositor B's interference acted to *diminish* rather than increase the Fletchian preferences *ye* and *'em*.

In three of Shak.'s problem plays and six of his last plays, Hoy points out, there is a total of 64 uses of *ye* or *y'* as against a total of 84 in *H8* alone, only five of these being in *H8* A. Nevertheless, Hoy does not believe that all of B should be assigned to Fletcher. The clustering of a small number of *ye*'s (already noted by Foakes) in II.i,ii; III.iib; and IV.i,ii, indicates, even when one allows for Compositor B's interference, that Fletcher is merely touching up and making minor interpolations in Shak.'n passages. This hypothesis seems to be corroborated by the absence in these scenes of "convincing traces of Fletcher's syntactic or rhetorical practices," which are, on the contrary, vividly present in the scenes that are solely his. If this view is correct, then Wolsey's farewell and Katharine's vision are saved for Shak., though Cranmer's prophecy is still assigned to Fletcher.

In his New Cambridge edition of *H8*, J. C. Maxwell affirmed that "the case for joint authorship is as fully established as such a case ever can be on fully internal evidence." His ample review of the controversy emphasizes that though Spedding sought confirmation for his hypothesis in metrical statistics, his argument owed its origin to his feeling of sharp contrast between the poetry of passion and nature in scenes such as I.i and the conventional stage-language of scenes such as I.iii. So far as quantifiable evidence is concerned, Maxwell feels that Partridge's statistics of linguistic preferences "establish the case for Fletcher beyond any reasonable doubt." Oras's work on extra monosyllables furnishes strong independent corroboration. Maxwell finds *H8* "one of the least interesting plays in the canon": Shak. seems bored in much of his share, and Fletcher's inferiority is especially evident in scenes such as II.i, IV.i, and IV.ii.

MacD. P. Jackson introduced a new pair of linguistic discriminators ("Affirmative Particles in *H8*," *N&Q*, n.s., IX, 372–374). In the 36 plays of the Folio, Jackson finds, the average preference of *ay* over *yes* is 18 to 4. This predominance holds throughout, except for *2H4*, *Ado* (3 and 6 *yes*'s respectively) and *H8* (*ay*, 6; *yes*, 18). After 1600, *yes* began to replace *ay* in general usage, but not in Shak.'s plays (*Cym. ay*, 16; *yes*, 6; *Wint.* 16/2; *Temp.* 14/3). But in Fletcher's unaided plays of that period, the *ay/yes* proportions are reversed (*Bonduca*, 3/16; *Valentinian*, 2/28; *Monsieur Thomas*, 6/15). In *H8* A, the proportions are 3/3; in B, 3/15; all instances of *yea* (very seldom used by Fletcher) occur in A. Jackson analyzes further refinements in the use of *ay, yes,* and *yea* by Shak. and Fletcher. "The overall picture seems certainly more consistent with the theory of collaboration than with that of single authorship."

Thus far had the long and frequently heated debate progressed when this bibliographical essay was completed, at the beginning of 1963. In retrospect, one can only echo and extend the final comment of MacD. P. Jackson. When one takes into account all the metrical, rhetorical, and linguistic discriminators that have been brought forward in more than a century of controversy about *H8,* "the overall picture seems certainly more consistent with the theory of collaboration than with that of single authorship." That the result has been achieved almost entirely by the use of internal evidence, both literary and statistical, should give heart to those who wish to support their intuitions about authorship by patient and responsible argument. When the battle is still dubious, critics on both sides are fighting the good fight if they are thoughtful and cogent. For intelligent challenge provokes intelligent response, and skeptics like Alexander are thus in some significant measure the architects of a victory they could not have foreseen. As for those who are tempted to be impatient, irresponsible, or overswayed by the authority of poet or pundit, let them remember the proceedings of 1885 and grow wise. Then if ever in canonical studies, the Comic Muse must have looked down, and, as she took in the twists, turns, and contradictions of Boyle, the bray of approval by Browning, and the cheerful, mindless reversals of Furnivall and Fleay, must have greeted the spectacle with her famous volleys of silvery laughter.

Edward III

For a review of the authorship problem, see Chambers, 515–518, to be supplemented by G. C. Moore Smith's preface to his ed. of 1897. *E3* has recently been reprinted, with a brief discussion of authorship, in *Three Eliz. Plays,* ed. James Winny (London, 1959).

A ("Shak.'n"): I.ii.94–II.ii.211
B ("non-Shak.'n"): The rest of the play.

E3 was registered anonymously to Cuthbert Burbie (see under "Spenser," above) on Dec. 1, 1595; Burbie's Q1 (1596) and Q2 (1599) are also anonymous. As Chambers says, "There is no external evidence for ascribing any part of *E3* to Shak., since we can hardly account as such its inclusion with *Edward II* and *Edward IV* as his in Rogers and Ley's play-list of 1656." The line "Lilies that fester smell far worse than weeds" appears both in *E3* II.i.451 and Shak.'s Sonnet 94.14, the phrase "scarlet ornaments" both in *E3* II.i.10 and Sonnet 142.6. Less specific parallels have been found with *Meas.* and other plays in the canon. Attribution to Shak. has been due largely to the parallels and the fine, vigorous poetry. But to some readers the construction and the frequently undramatic dialogue have seemed below the level of Shak.'s early plays. Others will perhaps wonder whether the arguments from parallels are sufficiently comprehensive and rigorous. If chronology did not rule out Marvell as an author, someone would doubtless propose that the lines (*E3* II.i.63–64), "Since green our thoughts, green be the conventicle [the summer arbour]/Where we will ease us by disburdening them," were distinctively Marvellian (cf. "A green thought in a green shade"). The parallel is closer than many cited on behalf of Shak.'s candidacy.

For the most part, the debate about *E3* has been over Shak.'s possible presence in A; Marlowe, Greene, Peele, and Kyd have been proposed as authors of B. The paucity of studies in the last fifty years may indicate that the Shak.'n claim is too weak to win wide attention. Of the studies below, Hart introduces new vocabulary tests and Muir and Wentersdorf depend largely on image clusters. (On "cluster criticism," see under *TNK*, below.)

Hart, Alfred. "The Vocabulary of *E3*," *Shak. and the Homilies* (Melbourne, 1934), 219–241.

Hart draws inferences from detailed word counts (7 tables). "Shak. commenced dramatist," he concludes, "with a much larger and more varied stock of words than [did] any of his contemporaries." *E3* is very close to Shak. in this respect; multiple authorship is therefore unlikely, since two or more authors with smaller vocabularies would not attain such a total. Tests of percentages of shared vocabularies are almost useless because of "the extraordinary similarity of the language used in the tragedies and histories" of 1587–1594. But choice of specific word formations yields significant differences. The number of words in *E3* beginning with 17 selected prefixes differs greatly from the average number in three plays by Marlowe but is extremely close to Shak.'s practice in *H6*, *R2*, and *John*. Similar results obtain for adjectival, nominal, and adverbial suffixes and for adjectival compounds; these favor Shak. rather than Marlowe, Greene, or Peele as author of *E3*. The compound-tests indicate that the same author wrote *E3* A and B. "Accordingly, if we must father B upon some author known to us we are forced to suggest Shak. The other possibility is to accept the facts, confess our ignorance, and permit the play to remain authorless." Hart points out that the same facts and arguments support Shak.'s authorship of *H6* much more strongly than they do his authorship of *E3*.

Crundell, H. W. "Drayton and *E3*," *N&Q*, CLXXVI (1939), 258–260.

Drayton is suggested as the author of *E3* because of "the general likeness (in both parts) to Drayton's work" and particular resemblances, including the flight of crows that strikes fear into French hearts (*E3* IV.iii, v, vi, and

Drayton, "The Battaile of Agincourt," 1627)—an incident not mentioned in the chronicles. In reply (*ibid.*, pp. 318–319), Kathleen Tillotson doubts that "the parallels in themselves prove more than that Drayton knew the anonymous play." Using parallels, one could claim that Drayton was the author of Marlowe's *E2* and Shak.'s *H6*. Crundell (*ibid.*, pp. 356–357) thinks one should indeed consider Drayton's presence in the Margaret-Suffolk scenes of *1H6* and warns against theories referring to unknown yet quite talented playwrights.

Muir, Kenneth. "A Reconsideration of *E3*," *ShS*, vi (1953), 39–48.

Though some of Hart's tests (above) seem inconclusive, the greater frequency in A, as compared with B, of compound participial adjectives, words not previously used by Shak., and various iterative images (classified by subject matter) suggests Shak.'s authorship. The presence of certain image clusters "is one of the strongest arguments for Shak.'s authorship, and most of these are in" A. Muir cites various verbal and metaphoric parallels, with special emphasis on those between *E3* and *Meas.*: "If Shak. was not the author, he was at least intimately acquainted with, and deeply influenced by *E3*."

Wentersdorf, Karl Paul. "The Authorship of *E3*," *Dissertation Abstracts*, xxi (1960), 905–906.

Depends upon imagery analysis, with chief emphasis on image-subjects and on "image-clusters" in Shak. ("groupings of ideas and images in unusual and evidently idiosyncratic chains of association"). Homogeneity of images in *E3* suggests single authorship, and their similarity in kind, relation, vocabulary, and tone to Shak.'s indicates that he is the author. Examination rules out echoing of Shak. by an unknown plagiarist or borrowing by Shak. from an unknown author of *E3*.

Sir Thomas More

For an admirable review of research down to 1949, see essay No. 10, above. Since that time, *Sir TM* has been printed in whole or in part in editions of Shak. by Peter Alexander, C. J. Sisson, and John Munro. In the entries below, questions of chronology and paleography continue to play an important part.

Nosworthy, J. M. "Shak. and *Sir TM*," *RES*, n.s., vi (1955), 12–25.

Examines interrelations of date and authorship. Mundy's, Chettle's and Dekker's hands have been clearly identified. After writing *The Two Italian Gentlemen* ca. 1584, Mundy "does not reappear as a dramatist until the mid-nineties with *John-a-Kent*" [but see Shapiro, below.] Henslowe's diary suggests that the odds are in favor of 1600–1601 as a likely year for a Mundy-Chettle-Dekker collaboration. Examination of words and themes common to the Shak. canon and to Addition III (Hand D) and Addition II

(Hand C—but detailed evidence is offered in support of Bald's and Chambers's view that Shak. is the author) shows that they are mainly associated with the plays of 1598–1602, and above all with *Troil.* (1601–1602). Shak.'s intent in making additions was not semipolitical but, as with the other additions, theatrical—"to give shape and dramatic urgency" to a frequently pedestrian piece.

Shapiro, I. A. "The Significance of a Date," *ShS*, VIII (1955), 100–105.

Experts agree that Mundy's writing in *Sir TM* (much of it in his hand) should be placed between the date of his holograph play *John-a-Kent and John-a-Cumber* and his translation of a religious work *The Heaven of the Mynde* (dated by him Dec. 22, 1602), but much nearer to *John-a-Kent.* The date (not in Mundy's hand) on that play has been read as December 1595 or, more frequently, 1596. Careful examination shows, however, that the last figure is a zero and the date therefore 1590. This redating is supported by a punning allusion to Mundy and *John-a-Kent* in a Marprelate tract printed "about mid-September 1589." It follows that Mundy must have written *Sir TM* by 1593, possibly by 1591, and the revision of *More*, in which Shak. may have had a hand (Shapiro regards the case from style and content as "not proven") may have occurred about 1593, "when Lord Strange's men, who then included Shak., were temporarily associated with the Admiral's company." Various possible inferences from the evidence emphasize how uncertain "are our assumptions about the development of Eliz. drama in the 1580's" (a point with obvious implications for studies of dramatic authorship).

Nosworthy, J. M. "Hand B in *Sir TM*," *Library*, 5th ser., XI (1956), 47–50.

The differences in letter formation, capitalization, and spelling between Hand B and Thomas Heywood in *The Captives* (recently edited by Arthur Brown for the Malone Society) are "quite serious" and tend to invalidate Samuel Tannenbaum's claim that Hand B is Heywood's.

Wilson, J. Dover. "The New Way With Shak.'s Texts. . . . III: In Sight of Shak.'s Manuscripts," *ShS*, IX (1956), 69–80.

A colorful personal account of the identification of Hand D as Shak.'s and of the implications of such a finding. Though the discovery has "unique value," the pages in *Sir TM* "clearly cannot be regarded as a typical piece of copy."

Huber, R. A. "On Looking over Shak.'s 'Secretarie,' " in *Stratford Papers on Shak., 1960* (Toronto, 1961), 52–70.

Sisson, C. J. "Postscript," in *ibid.*, 70–77.

After studying Eliz. handwriting intensively for two months, Sergeant Huber applied to photoduplicates of Shak.'s six genuine signatures and to Hand D the skills he had acquired as Examiner of Questioned Documents for the Royal Canadian Mounted Police. Huber finds that the similarities between the two hands justify placing Shak. among the small number of dramatists who might have written the pages in question, but that the differences are such as to prevent positive identification of Shak. In an appendix on the Shak. signature in the Folger copy of Lambarde's *Archaionomia* (see Giles Dawson, under "Eliz. Drama: General Studies," above), Huber concludes: "Certainly there is less justification within the writing to consider the Folger signature as genuine than to attribute Hand D to Shak."

In his "Postscript" Sisson observes that the first examination of the Hand D problem by a scientific expert bears out "on the whole the general view of recent scholar-paleographers that a convincing case for identification cannot rest upon handwriting alone, but depends [in addition] on the cumulative effect of other evidence. . . ." Sisson notes, among other things, that during "some forty years of continuous reading of a wide variety of contemporary manuscripts," he has found no instances, apart from Shak. and Hand D, of the "spurred *a*" and the spelling "scilens." As to the Folger signature, "Sergeant Huber's report seems to support [Sisson's] suggestion that it may be an unskilful attempt to copy the Mortgage Deed signature."

Pericles

The authorship controversy is reviewed to 1955 in the New Cambridge ed. of *Per.* by J. C. Maxwell (1956) and to 1961 in the New Arden ed. by F. D. Hoeniger (1963). Cf. also Chambers, 518–528, and Munro, II, 1068–1074.

A ("Shak.'n"): Acts III–V.
B ("non-Shak.'n"): Acts I–II.
PA: George Wilkins, *The Painfull Adventures of Pericles Prince of Tyre* (1608).

Per. is the one non-Folio play which, since 1790, has been generally admitted to the canon. On May 20, 1608, two books called "Pericles" and "Anthony and Cleopatra" (probably, though not necessarily, Shak.'s plays) were entered anonymously to Edward Blount, but for reasons unknown Blount failed to print either play. The phrasing of the entry, "A booke called. The booke of Pericles prynce of Tyre," suggests that the copy submitted (and approved by Sir George Buc, Deputy Master of the Revels) was a promptbook. But this surely was not the copy for Q1, published by Henry Gosson in 1609, the sole substantive text (Q2–Q6, 1609–1635, and the reprint in the second issue of the Third Folio, 1664, are all derivative). Q1, *The Late, And much admired Play, Called Pericles, Prince of Tyre . . . As it hath been diuers and sundry times acted by his Maiesties Seruants, at the Globe on the Banck-side. By William Shak.*, is seriously corrupt and has an unusual amount of verse-prose confusion. Its most remarkable feature, however, is the extraordinary qualitative gap between A and B. From its opening speech in III.i, A (though at times badly reported) is Shak.'n in its power and originality, whereas B is stylistically inferior to anything else in the Shak. canon. Dryden's attempt to account for the inferiority by calling *Per.* the first child of Shak.'s muse was therefore unconvincing, quite apart from its being contradicted by the external evidence. Since 1738, when George Lillo wrote, "We dare not charge the whole unequal play/Of Pericles on [Shak.]," critics have agreed that multiple authorship is the best explanation of the artistic gap. Those who recall the seamy realism of *Troil., All's Well, Meas.,* and of much else in the canon, will not be disposed, as some Victorians were, to deny to Shak. the brothel scenes in *Per.* (IV.ii, v, vi). The archaic and perhaps deliberately naïve rhymed couplets by Gower are a separate, and minor, problem, which need not be considered here. A more serious problem is presented by *PA:* the title page describes it as "The true History of the Play of *Pericles,* as it was lately presented by the worthy and ancient Poet *John Gower,*" and the Argument, again referring to Gower, states that "this Historie" was "by the kings Majesties Players excellently presented." Now much of *PA* is based on Laurence Twine's *The Patterne of Paynfull Adventures,* registered in 1576 and reprinted in 1607. But it also contains some verbatim passages from both A and B of *Per.* (see Chambers, 524–526), embodies much blank verse in its prose, and shares with the play the names "Pericles" and "Marina," present in no other versions of the story.

These facts give rise to a series of questions:

1. What is the nature of the text of *Per.?* Most scholars agree that it is a reported text and they go along with Pollard's classification of it as a "bad" Q (though they sometimes point out that there is no good text with which its badness may be compared). Since Philip Edwards' article of 1952, discussion has focused on whether one or two reporters produced the copy for Q1. Despite Edwards' contribution to the bibliographic analysis of Q1, most critics have not accepted his theory of dual reporting.

2. Is the play behind Q1 the source for the common passages in *PA* or is *PA* the source for the play behind Q1? Or do Q1 and *PA* both draw upon an earlier play, an *Ur-Pericles?* Current opinion holds with the first of these possibilities.

3. Assuming that the qualitative gap between A and B is due to multiple authorship, did Shak. revise an older play or did he collaborate with a much inferior playwright? Of the most recent editors, J. C. Maxwell favors the hypothesis of revision, and F. D. Hoeniger, though he uses "collaborator" freely (pp. lxvi–lxii), elsewhere suggests that revision seems the "more attractive" theory (p. liii).

4. In any case, who is the other author? Wilkins, Rowley, Heywood,

and most recently Day have been suggested, but there is nothing like a critical consensus. That is natural, given the textual problem, for in a reported text, such discriminators as authorial spelling and punctuation do not appear, and the style of the original is frequently leveled out. Since the style of *Per.* B is very flat indeed, it would seem that a convincing identification of the non-Shak.'n hand(s) in *Per.* must await the discovery of new external evidence or (what seems rather unlikely) of an independent witness to the text of the original.

Parrott, Thomas M. "*Per.:* The Play and the Novel," *Shak. Ass'n Bull.*, xxiii (1948), 105–113.

Disputes John Munro's thesis (*TLS*, Oct. 11, 1947) that W. first wrote his novel, then submitted to the King's Men a play on the theme which they handed over to Shak. for revision, and later published *PA* in protest against the changes. Heywood has a better claim than Wilkins to the *Ur-Per.* (this was possibly the play entered to Blount); Heywood's classical scholarship is sufficient (as Wilkins' is not) to account for the play's many changes in nomenclature. Taken at their face value, the statements on the title page and in the Argument of *PA* "certainly affirm the priority of the play," and this conclusion is supported by the internal evidence.

Craig, Hardin. "*Per.* and *PA*," *SP*, xlv (1948), 600–605.

Comparison of the brothel scenes in *Per.* and *PA* indicates that "the play was revised after Wilkins rewrote it as a novel." Important revision begins with IV.i. *Per.* is not a bad Q, but a good Q of a much revised play. "Considerable parts" of the Q may have been printed "from Shak.'s own manuscript." (For the general approach of which this essay is an example, see Craig's heterodox *A New Look at Shak.'s Quartos* [Stanford, 1963].)

Muir, Kenneth. "The Problem of *Per.*," *ES*, xxx (1949), 65–83.

Although he recognizes that most of Dugdale Sykes's parallels (*Sidelights on Shak.*, 1919) between Wilkins' works and *Per.* are "not very convincing," Muir accepts Sykes's theory that an *Ur-Per.* was by Wilkins but rejects his view that this hypothetical play came after *PA*. The novel has speeches inappropriate in a narrative but acceptable in a play. The large number of blank-verse lines in *PA* but not in *Per.* are best explained not as inadvertent omissions by the reporter of Q1 (why should he have reproduced the brothel scenes less accurately than the reunion in V.i?), but as survivals from an *Ur-Per.* And the many parallels between *Per.* and *PA* "can mostly be explained on the assumption that Shak. himself retained parts of the *Ur-Per.*, virtually unchanged." *PA* has been "contaminated" by two or three passages from Shak.'s *Per.*, and the copy for Q1 may in turn have been corrected by reference to *PA*. (The assumptions seem excessively complex, as when Muir argues that in *Per.* III.i.8–10 Shak. is echoing Wilkins' echo of Shak.'s own line in *Oth.* II.i.188.)

Muir denies Munro's thesis (cited in Parrott, above).

Edwards, Philip. "An Approach to the Problem of *Per.*," *ShS,* v (1952), 25–49.

Per. is a bad Q "of a very strange kind," the product of two reporters: one patched up a text of Acts I–II as best he could in his own poor verse; the other reproduced the rest of the play "very much more faithfully," but made little effort to distinguish the verse lineation. The hypothesis is supported, Edwards believes, by bibliographic and aesthetic analysis and by a comparison of the confusions in *Per.* with parts of the text of Wilkins' *PA* which probably report the play. If this theory is correct, then an entirely Shak.'n play may lie behind the bad Q. Edwards rejects the views of Craig (1948) and Muir (1949); Muir's evidence points "equally clearly to the fact that [Wilkins] based [*PA*] on the original of the Q."

Tompkins, J. M. S. "Why Pericles?" *RES,* n.s., III (1952), 315–324.

Not primarily on authorship, but at one point (pp. 321–322) suggests a new reason for regarding *PA* as derived in part from *Per.* In contradistinction to other versions, Shak.'s emphasizes the hero's great patience in adversity. Wilkins' insistence on the "gentle" and "courteous" bearing of the hero, though "the epithets do not rise immediately from the context," suggest Wilkins' conscious effort to evoke Burbage's playing of the part.

Muir, Kenneth, ed. *"PA" by George Wilkins* (Liverpool, 1953).

The introduction to this useful reprint repeats concisely the main points of Muir's earlier essay. Muir rejects the views of Craig and Edwards; he believes that mixed authorship affords a more reasonable explanation for the state of the text than does dual reporting and concludes that both Wilkins and Heywood may have collaborated in *Per.*

Maxwell, J. C., ed. *Per.* (Cambridge, Eng., 1956).

Maxwell rejects, in detail, the arguments of Edwards (1952) that the inequalities in *Per.* are due to two reporters, and finds, instead, that *Per.* is a bad Q in which B probably derives from non-Shak.'n and A from Shak.'n material. But Maxwell agrees with Edwards and Spiker (*SP,* xxx [1933], 551–570), against Craig and Muir, that *PA* is derived from Q and not in part from an *Ur-Per.* The dramatist behind B must remain anonymous; he is not Wilkins. Shak.'s company may have obtained an old play, of which he rewrote only the last three acts "while leaving the first two more or less as they stood."

Hoeniger, F. D. "How Significant Are Textual Parallels? A New Author for *Per.*?" *SQ* XI (1960), 27–37.

Evidence from parallels has been widely discredited, but they can be used if one is cautious, as Sykes and J. M. Robertson were not. The many parallels between the works of John Day and *Per.* II.i,iii (including the "remarkable" parallel with II.i.30–46) suggest Day's presence in those two scenes. It seems probable that an unknown writer is responsible for other scenes, especially in Acts I and II. [The "remarkable" parallel can be explained in several ways, and the remaining parallels are commonplace.]

Hoeniger, F. D., ed. *Per.* (Arden ed.; London and Cambridge, Mass., 1963).

Hoeniger's informative introduction deals very fully with problems of text and authorship. He agrees that Q1 is bad, but not so bad as Edwards says it is, and he rejects the theory of two different reporters, as well as Craig's and Sisson's theory that author's foul papers furnished the copy for Q1. The compositors contributed their share to the corruption of the text. Reviewing candidates for authorship, Hoeniger gives short shrift to Rowley and eliminates Heywood after more detailed consideration. The internal evidence for Wilkins' presence is "just about as considerable as . . . [it] can be," but why, in writing *PA*, did Wilkins not follow his own presumed scenes more extensively? His dependence on Twine (much greater than Muir indicates) suggests very poor memory of the play (the *Per.* behind Q1 rather than an *Ur-Per.*). Also against Wilkins' candidacy is the evidence (here relegated to App. B) of Day's presence in II.i,iii.

The Two Noble Kinsmen

Harold Littledale gives a full account of the debate about authorship to 1880 in Part II of his edition of *TNK* (NSS 1876–1885) pp. 70*–81*. Part II also contains detailed discussion of external and internal evidence, including metrical tables, a scene-by-scene analysis of authorship, and a useful concordance to the play. Chambers, 528–532, evaluates the evidence and scholarship to 1927. The entries below summarize the discussion after that date.

    A ("Shak.'n"): I.i–iv; II.i; III.i,ii; IV.iii; V.i,iii,iv.
    B ("non-Shak.'n"): The rest of the play.

Among Shak.'n scholars, a growing consensus would include *TNK* in the canon (though Kittredge is as yet the only 20th-C. editor to print the play with Shak.'s works).

TNK is but one of three probable Shak.-Fletcher collaborations, but it is in some ways the crucial one. For the collaboration *Cardenio,* we have only external evidence, none too satisfactory—an S.R. entry (Sept. 9, 1653) of "The History of Cardennio, by Mr. Fletcher & Shak." to Humphrey Moseley, who at the same time makes several impossible ascriptions to Shak.; a record of court performances of a *Cardenno* or a *Cardenna* by Shak.'s company in 1612–1613; and an alleged palimpsest—*Double-Falsehood; Or, the Distrest Lovers,* "Written Originally by W. Shak.; And now Revised and Adapted to the Stage" by Lewis Theobald (1728)—in which one cannot detect with any assurance passages that might once have been Shak.'s. For another Shak.-Fletcher collaboration, *H8*, we have only internal evidence, and though that now seems pretty good, one may doubt whether Fletcher in 1850 would have been proposed so confidently as coauthor had it not been for the example of *TNK*—the only Shak.-Fletcher collaboration attested by good external and internal evidence. For that reason among others, it is worth examining the development to about 1850 of the internal evidence for Shak.'s authorship of *TNK* A.

On April 8, 1634 "a Tragi Comedy called the two noble kinsmen by John ffletcher and William Shak." was entered in the S.R. to John Waterson. In that year Waterson brought out a Q of *TNK* which announced that the play was written by both Fletcher and Shak. *TNK* was printed again in the Beaumont and Fletcher folio of 1679, this time without the ascription to Shak. In the 18th C. there was considerable debate, not always very evidential or consecutive, as to whether that ascription was to be trusted. (No one denied that Fletcher was at least part-author.) In 1780 Steevens reviewed the opinions of his predecessors and offered several pages of parallels between the language of *TNK* and of Shak.'s indubitable works (in Malone's *Supplement*, ii, 168–175), but nevertheless took the position that the play was entirely the work of Fletcher, who was writing "in silent *imitation* of [Shak.'s] manner." Steevens asserted indeed "that the general current of the style [of *TNK*] was even throughout the whole, and bore no marks of a divided hand."

That the play had distinct styles was too apparent, however, to be very long denied, and a sensitive critic joined issue with Steevens. In his *Specimens of English Dramatic Poets* (1808), 403–404, 419, Charles Lamb made some acute impressionistic distinctions between the structure and style of Fletcher's dramas and Shak.'s. Lamb held that Shak. was responsible for I.i of *TNK*, I.iii, "the death of Arcite, and some other passages." These portions, he pointed out, "have a luxuriance in them which strongly resembles Shak.'s manner. . . . That Fletcher should have copied Shak.'s manner through so many entire scenes (which is the theory of Mr. Steevens) is not very probable, that he could have done it with such facility is to me not certain. His ideas moved slow; his versification, though sweet, is tedious, it stops every moment; he lays line upon line, making up one after the other, adding image to image so deliberately that we see where they join: Shak. mingles every thing, he runs line into line, embarrasses sentences and metaphors; before one idea has burst its shell, another is hatched and clamorous for disclosure. If Fletcher wrote some scenes in imitation, why did he stop? or shall we say that Shak. wrote the other scenes in imitation of Fletcher? that he gave Shak. a curb and a bridle, and that Shak. gave him a pair of spurs: as Blackmore and Lucan are brought in exchanging gifts in the Battle of the Books?"

Henry Weber, editor of *The Works of Beaumont and Fletcher* (1812), agreed heartily with Lamb that there were two markedly different styles in *TNK*, and that the authorship of the play was accordingly to be divided between Shak. and Fletcher (XIII, 166ff). Weber little deserves to be neglected by students of *TNK*, *H8*, and Eliz. drama generally, for apart from his sensible comments on the styles of *TNK*, he introduced into the discussion the novel evidence of metrical statistics. Of Act II, Weber observed that "the number of double terminations of the verses is greater here, as well as in the plays of Fletcher, than in the metre of any contemporary dramatist," and he supported his claim by the following footnote (XIII, 166): "Taking an equal number of lines in the different parts which are attributed to Shak. and to Fletcher, the number of female, or double terminations in the former, is less than one to four; on the contrary, in the scenes attributed to Fletcher the number of double and triple terminations is nearly three times that of the single ones." He also observed that Shak. was "peculiarly fond" of hemistiches and that in *TNK* almost all of these occur in the scenes in Shak.'s style. To Shak., Weber assigned all of *TNK* A except II.i; the rest of the play was presumably Fletcher's.

William Hazlitt, in some remarks (*Lectures on Eliz. Dramatic Lit* [1820], 156–165) notable for their generality and inaccuracy (he attributes to unnamed critics—he surely could not have meant Lamb and Weber!— the view that the last four acts of *TNK* "are confessedly Fletcher's"), took a position similar to Steevens': the play was a "monument of Fletcher's genius" and "the first part of it" (Act I, presumably) was merely "written in imitation of Shak.'s manner." Hazlitt made no effort to confront Lamb's objections to this theory. Samuel Taylor Coleridge, despite some wavering, was convinced that Shak. had a hand in the play and that the first act was certainly his (see *Shak'n Criticism*, ed. Raysor [1930] II, 32–33, *Misc. Criticism* [1936], 92–93, and *Table-Talk* [1835], II, 119). In the 1821 Shak. Variorum (XXI, 233–241), Boswell reproduced the views of the question from Pope through Steevens, but unfortunately omitted later opinions.

Lamb's and Weber's arguments were carried a significant step further by William Spalding's widely admired 113-page discussion of *TNK* (1833; reprinted by NSS, 1876). Spalding spelled out in detail the distinctions between Shak.'s and Fletcher's prosody and style already noted by Lamb and Weber. He emphasized the "oracular brevity" of Shak.'s highly original diction and figurative language—compressed, inclined to metaphor rather than simile, given to personifications "of mental powers, passions, and relations," rapid, energetic, abrupt, surcharged with intellectual content, and frequently difficult. By contrast, Fletcher's style is delicate, deliberate, inclined to simile rather than metaphor, amplified step by step, thin in personifications, and generally "diffuse both in his leading thoughts and in his illustrations." Because of this striking opposition of intricate combinations of qualities, it was easier to differentiate between Shak. and Fletcher, Spalding believed, than between Shak. and almost any other contemporary. In Spalding's opinion, the best means of differentiation was the intuitive judgment of a cultivated reader, and he proceeded to parcel out *TNK* scene by scene. He agreed with Weber's division, except that he denied IV.iii to Shak., to whom, however, he assigned the responsibility for choice of subject, management of the main plot, and conception of character and motivation. *H8* was mentioned only once in the entire essay, but that reference (see *H8*, above, under "To 1833") was a crucial one.

The controversy about *TNK* was continued in England (German controversy is here omitted) by Henry Hallam, who paid his respects to Spalding's essay (*Introduction to the Literature of Europe* [1839], III, 597–599) but inclined to the view that Fletcher was imitating the master in the "Shak.'n" portions; by George Darley, who paid his respects to the theory of imitation (*Works of Beaumont and Fletcher* [1840], I, l–li) but concluded that the "enormous" conception and style of the speeches in V.i,ii,iii made Shak.'s coauthorship "quite possible"; by Charles Knight, who was the first to reprint *TNK* in an edition of Shak. (Pictorial ed. [1839–1841] V, 123, 169–187) and who justified his course by citing the views of Lamb and Coleridge, but who nevertheless argued that the "Shak.'n" portions were written by George Chapman; by Alexander Dyce, who summarized all the views from Lamb to Knight (*Works of Beaumont and Fletcher* [1843], I, lxxx–lxxxvii) and agreed "that Shak. undoubtedly wrote all those portions of [*TNK*] which are assigned to him by Mr. Spalding," though he believed "that in some places they have suffered by alterations and interpolations from the pen of Fletcher"; and by William Spalding, who in several articles in the 1840's modified his confident assertions of 1833 (cf. *Edin. Rev.*, July 1840, p. 468, and July 1847, pp. 57ff).

Of direct influence on Spedding's *H8* article was a long essay by Samuel Hickson reviewing Spalding's *TNK* study of 1833 and the treatments of the play by Knight and Dyce (*Westminster Rev.*, XLVII [April 1847], 59–88). Hickson found that one writer in *TNK* (Shak. of course) had far more dramatic power than the other (Fletcher), that one "was a delineator of character, and the other not so," that the metaphors of Shak. were extremely bold and that he was given "to philosophical reflections, suggested by the situations and circumstances of the drama." Hickson's other observations on style and prosody in *TNK* were similar to those of Spalding, Dyce, *et al.*, but he differed from his predecessors in assigning to Shak. the structure and the key scenes of the subplot in addition to the lion's share of the main plot. Shak., he was convinced, was chiefly responsible for both "the framework of the play" and "the groundwork of every character"; Fletcher followed up Shak.'s leads, but so inorganically and inconsequentially that his contribution must have been a product of his youth. (Hickson did not

fix the date of composition.) Hickson's differentiation of authorship depends for the most part on informed literary analysis. He is unconvincing
when he tries to parcel out consecutive speeches of Arcite and Palamon
(II.ii) now to Fletcher, now to Shak. But his taste is generally sound, and
his assignment of scenes corresponds closely to those of later critics.

The effect of the *TNK* controversy, spilling over as it did into journals of
general circulation, was to spread ideas of Shak.'s collaboration with
Fletcher to a broad public. Such ideas and the idea of divided authorship
in *H8* were both very much in the air in the second half of the 1840's
when Tennyson made his casual remark to Spedding about the Fletcher-
like passages in the last of Shak.'s history plays.

After 1850, the course of discussion concerning *TNK* closely parallels
that concerning *H8*. Hickson's essay of 1847 is reprinted by the NSS in
1874 and freshly "confirmed" by the metrical tests of Fleay and Furnivall.
Then doubts set in: Furnivall (1876) retreats from his 1874 position at
the promptings of "the cleverest and most poetic-natured girl-friend" (NSS
reprint of Spalding, p. vii); Delius (1878) proposes to substitute an anonymous playwright for Shak. as the author of *TNK* A; Boyle (1882) speaks
up for his own favorite, Massinger; C. H. Herford (*TNK*, The Temple
Dramatists, 1897) quotes Boyle's views with approval (mistakenly attributing them to "Rolfe"); Sykes again seconds Boyle (1919). Meanwhile, the defenders of Shak.'s authorship are also active. Swinburne
(1880) feels that, with a few minor exceptions, there can be "no room for
doubt or perplexity on any detail" of the Spalding-Dyce division. Littledale
amasses abundant evidence to show that Shak. is responsible for A (1876–
1885). Thorndike and Farnham use linguistic preferences to confirm Shak.'s
presence and to disprove Massinger's (see *H8*, 1901, 1916). By the time
Chambers reviews the evidence (pp. 531–532) he unhesitatingly casts his
vote for Shak.: the "great invocations" of Act V "are quite outside the
imaginative range of Massinger, whom Boyle and Sykes, regardless of the
title-page would substitute for Shak." on the "poor evidence" of parallels.

Among the interesting developments since 1927 are Hart's vocabulary
test (1934), Kittredge's inclusion of *TNK* in his edition of Shak. (1936),
and Hoy's indication of the limits of linguistic counts in determining Shak.'s
presence (1962). The method of cluster-criticism, as applied below, seems
insufficiently rigorous and generally unconvincing.

Bradley, A. C. "Scene-Endings in Shak. and in *TNK*," *A Miscellany* (London, 1929), 218–224.

In a paper "not recently composed and . . . not . . . revised," the
author notes that, of blank verse scenes in the Globe text of *Mac.*, *A&C*,
Cor., *Cymb.*, *Temp.*, and *WT*, 59.6% (62 out of 104) end with incomplete
lines. This compares with about 3.7% (3 out of 83 scenes in five plays by

Fletcher, and less than 5% (2 out of 42 scenes) in six plays by Massinger. In *TNK*, there is only one possible part-line ending in B, but 6 or 7 such endings in 9 blank-verse scenes of A (66% or 77%). The proportion in A agrees closely with Shak.'s practice and disagrees considerably with Massinger's. Bradley ends with examples of Shak.'n vocabulary in A.

Hart, Alfred. "Shak. and the Vocabulary of *TNK*," *RES*, x (1934), 274–287.

Hart proposes to determine Shak.'s presence by a novel procedure, which differs from the methods of the parallelist school in that it looks for *differences* in vocabulary and for the *absence* "of identical phrases and parallel passages." Shak. is an outstanding linguistic innovator and in every undisputed play in the canon uses many words not found in his other plays, some of which are not previously recorded in English literature. *TNK* A has on the average one word not found elsewhere in Shak. every 10 lines, B every 22 lines; A one word not previously recorded by the *O.E.D.* every 17 lines, B every 47 lines. Examination of "parasynthetic combinations" (e.g., "bride-habited"), of nouns and adjectives used as verbs, and of other departures from ordinary diction reveal a similar concentration of original vocabulary in A as against B. Chapman, who has been called a great neologist, invents far fewer new words per play than Shak. or *TNK* A. The evidence strongly supports the play's claim for admission to the Shak. canon. (See also Hart's essay under *E3*, above.)

Kittredge, George Lyman, ed. *The Complete Works of Shak.* (Boston, 1936), 1409–1449.

TNK is included, with brief discussion of canonicity: Q's ascription to Fletcher and Shak. "is undoubtedly correct." *TNK* A is "certainly Shak.'s," with the exception of II.i and IV.iii, which are "perhaps Shak.'s"; I.iv is "probably Shak.'s." Some "of the Shak.'n scenes may have been touched up by Fletcher, and possibly Fletcher's work includes a bit of Shak. here and there. Exact details are beyond the scope of sane criticism." The prologue and epilogue "are surely not Shak.'s, and they may not be Fletcher's either."

Spencer, Theodore. "*TNK*," *MP*, xxxvi (1939), 255–276.

Alfred Hart's "remarkably able and interesting" *RES* article of 1934 clinches the attribution of *TNK* A to Shak. Analysis indicates that Shak.'s share is less effective dramatically but in poetic and human terms far more interesting than Fletcher's glibly romantic contribution. Shak. "seems no longer to be interested in process or in change and hence is no longer interested in the development of character." Shak.'s part displays grandeur, remoteness, and stasis, the style and imagery of old age. III.i begins in Shak.'s style, and changes over to Fletcher's at about l.72.

Mincoff, Marco. "The Authorship of *TNK*," *ES*, xxxiii, (1952), 97–115.

Though caution customarily seconds bardolatry in rejecting non-Folio plays from the canon, *TNK* has as good a right to admission as *Per.* and *H8*. The cumulative evidence of a Shak.-Fletcher collaboration in *H8* and the lost *Cardenio* greatly strengthens the external evidence of such a collaboration in *TNK*. The internal evidence is likewise strong. The style of B is lucid and correct, that of A original, abstruse, and richly metaphysical, uniquely Shak.'n and far beyond the pedestrian Massinger or other claimants. The imagery that Caroline Spurgeon describes as Shak.'n abounds in A, as do orotund circumlocutions, bold personifications, and equally bold word coinages. (Mincoff does not mention Hart's *TNK* article of 1934, though he cites his more general *RES* article of 1943.) There is a marked concentration of these in I.i, which also contains a running image of "pressing or stamping a seal or coin."

Muir, Kenneth. "The Kite-Cluster in *TNK*," *N&Q*, cxcix (1954), 52–53.

Edward A. Armstrong denied *TNK* to Shak. because of a lack of characteristic image clusters (*Shak.'s Imagination* [1946], 188). But I.i contains within about 25 lines what Armstrong did note as a Shak.'n cluster—the association of *kite* with "bed (or sleep), death, spirits, other birds, and food." The last item "could be represented by a pun on the word pie in the list of birds" in the song at the beginning of the scene. ["Spirits" are likewise represented by "angels" in the song, and "bed" is related to Theseus's marriage, not to the birds. The "association" would thus seem to be contiguity within a given number of lines rather than linkage by development of idea or image.]

Muir, Kenneth. "Shak.'s Hand in *TNK*," *ShS*, xi (1958), 50–59.

Image clusters may offer "some new and quite unanswerable evidence" that Shak. wrote at least I.i,iii and V.i. Important clusters include the association of "wind-fanned snow" with "white," of "kite" with previously specified features (see under *TNK* 1954, above), and of a hind (V.i) with "dirt, smell, lust, disease, crime and death." [Here again there is contiguity rather than intrinsic linkage, and to bring in "disease," one must go back about 30 lines to a speech by another character.] This evidence supports arguments from metrical and linguistic traits (Littledale, Bradley, Hart, Mincoff, and others) for Shak.'s authorship of A.

Waller, Frederick O. "Printer's Copy for *TNK*," *SB*, xi (1958), 61–84.

The copy for *TNK* derived ultimately from two authors' foul papers annotated by Edward Knight rather than from prompt copy, as Tucker Brooke, E. K. Chambers, and W. W. Greg believe. Shak.'s part of the copy seems to have been rougher than Fletcher's. "Inconsistency in character-names" and "irregularity in the articulation" of II.i and II.ii are a result of the two authors' writing "their shares simultaneously but without close consultation." The diminished number of *ye*'s in Fletcher's scenes suggests an intermediate literal transcript of the foul papers, made by some-one other than Knight. Archaic and eccentric spellings in A point to Shak.'s hand. Fletcher gave the text a final reworking and made some minor additions, e.g., V.iv.22–38. (For comment, see Hoy [1962], below.)

Bertram, Paul. "The Date of *TNK*," *SQ*, xii (1961), 21–32.

"My own view is that the play was written wholly by Shak., although my presentation of the reasons and evidence for this opinion is at present accessible only in my doctoral dissertation, "Shak. and '*TNK*' (Harvard University, 1960)—a study of *H8* and *Cardenio* as well as *TNK*" (p. 32 n. 26).

Hoy, Cyrus. "The Shares of Fletcher and His Collaborators in the Beaumont and Fletcher Canon (vii)," *SB*, xvi (1962), 71–90.

Hoy finds that Shak. is author of *TNK* I; II.i; III.i, ii; V.ib (from exit of Palamon and Knights to end), iii, iv. The case for Shak.'s presence, "based solely on stylistic grounds, is a strong one," but it cannot be proved on linguistic grounds alone. "Shak. uses no language forms which, either in themselves or by virtue of their rate of occurrence, can serve to point immediately and unmistakably to his presence in a play of doubtful authorship." Linguistic forms can positively determine Fletcher's presence, however (see Hoy's other articles in the Beaumont and Fletcher series), and one can say in addition that "the linguistic pattern displayed in the non-Fletcherian scenes" of *TNK* is not inconsistent with the patterns in the plays of Shak.'s last period. Moreover, the contrasts between Shak.'s and Fletcher's linguistic usages (for these contrasts, see Hoy under *H8*, 1962, above) may provide some help in distinguishing their shares in a collaborative play. Thus, "all of the Q's 37 *ye*'s [in *TNK*] are Fletcher's; none occur in scenes that do not otherwise bear the signs of his stylistic manner."

The linguistic evidence in the Q of *TNK* militates against F. O. Waller's suggestions (see under *TNK*, 1958, above) that annotated foul papers served in part as printer's copy and that Fletcher gave "the text a final reworking." If so, Hoy asks, why the rather low incidence of Fletcherian *ye*'s? Waller's alternative suggestion of "an intermediate scribal transcript of the sort posited by Fredson Bowers" meets "the linguistic facts of the case more satisfactorily than any other theory."

Armstrong, Edward A. "Shak.'n Imagery in *TNK*," sec. B of Appendix to Part II in the 2nd ed. of *Shak.'s Imagination* (Lincoln, Neb., 1963).

In looking for image-clusters, Kenneth Muir (see above), casts his nets too widely: the kite-bed cluster in *TNK* I.i is dispersed over 54 lines, the osprey-sovereignty-death cluster in *Cor.* over 47 lines. "Obviously the wider the search the greater the chance of bringing a given image within a cluster and the weaker the evidence. . . ." Armstrong's own analysis of clusters in *TNK* "demonstrates" that "at least most of two scenes and probably parts of others are from Shak.'s pen" (p. 213), but there is a falling off because the poet's " 'unconscious cerebration' was flagging" (p. 215); Shak., "feeling he had run his course, was letting his imagination dwell on his youth. . . . in Leontes we have the countryman recalling his boyhood, in Prospero the dramatist surveying his achievement" (p. 217).

JAMES SHIRLEY

Harbage, Alfred. "The Authorship of the Dramatic *Arcadia*," *MP*, xxxv (1938), 233–237.

External evidence shows the attribution to Shirley to have been a bookseller's ruse; internal evidence, slightly touched upon, confirms the conclusion that the play was not Shirley's. Possible authors that might be investigated are Henry Shirley, John Kirke, and Thomas Heywood—for "anyone wishing to apply verbal and metrical tests."

English Literature 1660 to 1789

ADDISON

Bateson, F. W. "The *Errata* in *The Tatler*," *RES*, v (1929), 155–166.

Bateson deduces that Addison, not Steele, was author of the *Tatler* errata lists concerned with stylistic emendations. With this clue, he tries several internal tests on six *Tatler* essays and attributes them to Addison.

ARBUTHNOT

Mayo, Thomas F. "The Authorship of *The History of John Bull*," *PMLA*, xlv (1930), 274–283.

Mayo reaffirms traditional attribution to John Arbuthnot, disputed by Teerink (see below, under "Swift"), on complex grounds, with internal evidence for good measure. More convincing "than any number of parallel passages are the salty native flavor of the Sister Peg passages (cited by Sir Walter Scott as decisive evidence for Arbuthnot); the strong medical preoccupation of the writer . . . ; and above all the racy, kindly personality which can be felt through the style."

BRADSHAW

McBurney, William H. See under "Marana."

BURKE

Copeland, Thomas W. "A Body of Anonymous Writing," ch. 4 in *Our Eminent Friend Edmund Burke: Six Essays* (Yale, 1959), 118–145.

An extended examination of evidence for Burke's authorship of contributions to the *Annual Register;* adds several pieces to the canon.

England, Martha Winburn. "Edmund Burke's Part in the Jubilee Oration," in *Garrick and Stratford* (New York, 1962), 59–66; reprinted from *BNYPL*, lxvi (1962).

Attributes to Burke, on circumstantial and stylistic grounds, the philosophical center of the oration read (but never claimed) by David Garrick at the Stratford Jubilee of 1769.

BURNS

Ferguson, DeLancey. "Burns and *The Merry Muses*," *MLN*, lxvi (1951), 471–473.

Few songs in this collection have been attributed to Burns, because of the assertion: "a very few of them are my own." But this proves to be apocryphal; so a closer look at internal evidence is called for.

Werkmeister, Lucyle. "Robert Burns and the London Newspapers," *BNYPL*, LXV (1961), 483–504.

The journalistic context of certain verses attributed to Burns shows them to have been spurious concoctions; on the other hand the context removes doubts about a genuine, but parodistic, ode.

CONGREVE

Barnard, John. "Did Congreve Write *A Satyr against Love?*" *BNYPL*, LXVIII (1964), 308–322.

A poem hitherto known in a MS of 47 lines and circumstantially attributed to Congreve has been discovered in a 300-line version: the alleged internal evidence is found to be infirm and the circumstances to produce a case against the attribution.

DEFOE

Moore, John Robert. *Defoe in the Pillory and Other Studies* (Indiana University Publications, Humanities Series No. 1; Bloomington, 1939).

Several works are attributed to Defoe, chiefly on internal evidence. Method is discussed in ch. 5, "Some Remarks on the Assignment of Authorship to Defoe."

Baine, Rodney M. "Defoe and Mrs. Bargrave's Story," *PQ*, XXXIII (1954), 388–395.

The very slight evidence for Defoe's authorship of *A True Relation of the Apparition of Mrs. Veal* is deemed sufficient—because it indicates that Defoe *edited* the story, and that Mrs. Bargrave invented it.

Moore, John Robert. "The Canon of Defoe's Writings," *The Library*, 5th ser., XI (1956), 155–169.

"It was . . . Defoe's common practice to conceal his authorship. It is the task of the student of Defoe to discover it."

Scouten, A. H. "At That Moment of Time: Defoe and the Early Accounts of the Apparition of Mistress Veal," *Ball State Teachers College Forum*, II, No. 2 (1961–1962), 44–51.

Scouten does not directly discuss the authorship of the account assumed to be Defoe's but affirms it indirectly. He correlates findings about early sources, arguing all alternatives of transmission of the tale to Defoe, and demonstrates Defoe's artful rearrangement of the story, a stylistic achievement greater than supposed.

Watt, Ian. See under "Hammond."

FIELDING

Woods, Charles B. "Fielding and the Authorship of *Shamela*," *PQ* XXV (1946), 248–272.

Woods confirms the attribution to Fielding with "a rather detailed treatment of certain features of the internal evidence . . . to convince any remaining skeptics." The strongest evidence is in parallels in idea and expression, especially in attitude toward the clergy, and in the analysis of the characterization of Parson Williams in *Shamela* as closely related to the characterization of Parson Adams in *Joseph Andrews*.

Greason, A. LeRoy, Jr. "Fielding's *An Address to the Electors of Great Britain*," *PQ*, xxxiii (1954), 347–352.

Adduces some internal evidence for attribution to Fielding. See criticism by Coley, next entry.

Coley, William B. "The Authorship of *An Address to the Electors of Great Britain* (1740)," *PQ*, xxxvi (1957), 488–495.

Criticizes as weak the internal evidence noted by Greason (see above). Cites some evidence for attribution to James Ralph, but finds the evidence inconclusive either for Ralph or for Fielding.

Baker, Sheridan. "Henry Fielding's *The Female Husband*: Fact and Fiction," *PMLA*, lxxiv (1959), 213–224.

An obscure pamphlet, hitherto taken as factual, is found to be largely fictional. This should dispel skepticism about Fielding's authorship. The previous external evidence is supplemented by internal analysis, chiefly of "parallels from his known fiction" (including *Shamela*).

Sherbo, Arthur. See under "Smart."

GILDON

Wells, Staring B. "An Eighteenth-Century Attribution," *JEGP*, xxxviii (1939), 233–246.

Wells exposes the ambiguity of parallel passages. *A Comparison between the Two Stages* (1702) was ascribed to Charles Gildon in the 18th C., largely on the evidence of parallels. Scrutiny of their exact nature and of their context makes the ascription seem improbable.

Scheurweghs, G. "Brightland's or Steele's Grammar," *English Studies* (Amsterdam), xl (1959), 136–141.

The Grammar was actually written by Charles Gildon. The evidence is chiefly bibliographical, a matter of assembling all editions and references.

GOLDSMITH

Tupper, Caroline F., "Essays Erroneously Attributed to Goldsmith," *PMLA*, xxxix (1924), 325–342.

R. S. Crane (see below) accepts Miss Tupper's demonstration that Goldsmith could not have written the "Belles-Lettres" papers, but notes that the suggestion of Smollett as author "is hardly more than a plausible guess."

Crane, R. S. *New Essays by Oliver Goldsmith* (Chicago, 1927), Intro., xi–xxxv.
Ground rules for Goldsmith attribution. See also Crane, essay No. 20.

Stein, Harold. "Goldsmith's Translation of the *Roman Comique*," *MLN*, LXIX (1934), 171–178.
A convincing demonstration that Goldsmith was the translator.

Friedman, Arthur. "Goldsmith and the *Weekly Magazine*," *MP*, XXXII (1935), 281–299.

Friedman, Arthur. "Goldsmith's Contributions to the *Critical Review*," *MP*, LXIV (1946), 23–52.

Friedman, Arthur. "Goldsmith's 'Essay on Friendship': Its First Publication and the Problem of Authorship," *PQ*, xxxv (1956), 346–349.
An ascription hitherto based on weak internal evidence is strengthened by external evidence.

Golden, Morris. "Goldsmith and the *Universal Museum and Complete Magazine*," *N&Q*, CCII (1957), 339–348.
Five articles are attributed as probably by Goldsmith, two as possibly his, mainly on internal evidence.

Golden, Morris. "Two Essays Erroneously Attributed to Goldsmith," *MLN*, LXXIV (1959), 13–16.
"Since the external evidence is not only questionable but contradicted . . . and since the internal evidence ranges from the ambiguous to nonexistent, the two essays should be rejected from the Goldsmith canon."

HAMMOND

Watt, Ian. "*Considerations upon Corrupt Elections of Members to Serve in Parliament*, 1701: by Anthony Hammond, not Defoe," *PQ*, xxxi (1952), 45–53.
"The evidence for Hammond's authorship is . . . strong, although not conclusive. The evidence against Defoe's is decisive."

HOOKE

Keynes, Geoffrey. See essay No. 18.

JOHNSON

Wimsatt, W. K., Jr. *The Prose Style of Samuel Johnson* (Yale Studies in English 94; New Haven, 1941).
Wimsatt does not deal with attribution, but his discussion is frequently relevant, esp. concerning qualities of style and the subordinate place of statistical data—esp. p. 24 and all of ch. 5 on the consistency of Johnson's style.

McAdam, Edward L., Jr. "New Essays by Dr. Johnson," *RES*, xviii (1942), 197–207.

Attributes a series of three essays in the 1760 *Public Ledger* to Johnson on the basis of external and internal evidence. (See further the third study by S. Krishnamurti, below.)

McAdam, Edward L., Jr. "Pseudo-Johnsoniana," *MP*, xli (1944), 183–187.

Dismisses seven attributions as false, often from negative stylistic evidence and usually from lack of positive or presence of negative external evidence.

Greene, D. J. "The Johnsonian Canon: A Neglected Attribution," *PMLA*, lxv (1950), 427–434.

"The ascription of these 'Observations' to Johnson by the editor of 'Volume xiv' was no doubt based only on 'internal evidence'—but then so were all but seven of Boswell's thirty-two ascriptions to Johnson of pieces in the *Literary Magazine*." The strength of the ascription depends somewhat on who that editor was; Greene suggests Chalmers.

Krishnamurti, S. "Frequency-Distribution of Nouns in Dr. Johnson's Prose Works," *Jour. of Univ. of Bombay*, xx, Part 2 (Sept. 1951), 1–16.

Krishnamurti, S. "Vocabulary Tests Applied to (Dr. Johnson's) Authorship of the 'Misargyrus' Papers in *The Adventurer*," *ibid.*, xxi, Part 2 (Sept. 1952), 47–62.

Krishnamurti, S. "Vocabulary Tests: Applied to the Authorship of the 'New Essays' Attributed to Dr. Johnson," *ibid.*, xxii, Part 2 (Sept. 1953), 1–5.

In these articles, G. Udny Yule's statistical methods are applied to, and found to confirm (though with admittedly smaller samples than Yule's stipulated minimum), some recent tentative Johnson attributions. In the first the vocabularies of Macaulay, Bunyan, and Johnson are tabulated and discussed. In the second and third the measurable components of the vocabularies of the new attributions are found to fall "within the range" of Johnson's.

Greene, D. J. "Was Johnson Theatrical Critic of the *Gentleman's Magazine?*" *RES*, n.s., iii (1952), 158–161.

Greene suggests six brief reviews for consideration, but cautions against reliance on "almost purely subjective" evidence; "it is sobering to recall what a large proportion of the journalistic writing that most readers now accept without question as Johnson's was originally ascribed to him on no more solid grounds."

Greene, D. J. "Johnson's Contributions to the *Literary Magazine*," *RES*, n.s. vii (1956), 367–392.

Leed, Jacob. "Two New Pieces by Johnson in the *Gentleman's Magazine*," *MP*, liv (1957), 221–229.

Leed, Jacob. "Samuel Johnson and the *Gentleman's Magazine,* an Adjustment of the Canon," *N&Q,* n.s. IV (1957), 210–213.

Kolb, Gwin J. "Dr. Johnson and the *Public Ledger:* A Small Addition to the Canon," *SB,* XI (1958), 252–255.
"I believe I detect in each of the sentences the genuine Johnsonian hallmark."

Greene, D. J. "Some Notes on Johnson and the *Gentleman's Magazine,*" *PMLA,* LXXIV (1959), 75–84.
Twelve notes on problems of attribution.

Moser, Edwin. "A Critical Examination of the Canon of the Prose Writings of Samuel Johnson" (diss., New York Univ., 1959) see *Dissertation Abstracts,* XX (1960), 3283–3284.
Suggests twenty criteria of internal evidence, including characteristic use of tonality, *cursus,* periodicity, repetition, inversion, and other syntactic and rhythmic components of style. Applies the Johnsonian criteria to attributions made by Boswell and finds him "almost entirely correct." Lists "all other ascriptions" to the Johnson canon.

Gibbs, F. W. "Dr. Johnson's First Published Work?" *Ambix,* VIII, No. 1 (Feb. 1960), 24–33.
On circumstantial and stylistic evidence, Johnson is assigned the authorship of a translation of Boerhaave's *Elementa Chemicae* in 1732.

Kolb, Gwin J. "More Attributions to Dr. Johnson," *SEL,* I (1961), 77–95.
Kolb adds five prose works or parts of works, four in the *Gentleman's Magazine,* as probably Johnson's on the basis of style, parallels, and subject; he notes one worth further study, and another, "The Mask," as not convincing despite much apparent evidence.

[Clifford, James L.] "The Canon of Johnson's Works," *JNL,* XXI, No. 1 (March 1961), 1–3.
Discusses some recent highly speculative attributions and the work in progress and remaining to be done in this field.

Sherbo, Arthur. "Samuel Johnson and the *Gentleman's Magazine,*" in *Johnsonian Studies,* ed. Magdi Wahba (Cairo and London, 1962), 133–159.
Sherbo discusses several Johnson attributions in the course of noting many long and short things in the *Gentleman's Magazine* for 1750–1755 which "smack of Johnson." Although largely a series of impressionistic assertions with almost no attempt at demonstration beyond an occasional quotation, the impressions add up to an "inevitable" conclusion that Johnson, contrary to previous assumptions, contributed largely to the *Gentleman's Magazine* in these years. Sherbo begins, however, by offering "to be considered a raiser of questions" if no more.

Sherbo, Arthur. "The Electronic Computer and I," *Univ. Coll. Quarterly* VII, No. 3 (1962), 8–11.

Sherbo explains his hope to find help in attributions of Johnsonian prose from statistics of "nouns, verbs, adjectives, monosyllables, words per sentence, and different words per passage" in Johnson and a close imitator, John Hawkesworth.

See also Sherbo, Arthur, essay No. 1, Fogel, Ephim G., No. 4, and Keast, William R., No. 22.

JUNIUS

See Ellegård, Alvar, under "Statistical Studies and Computer Applications."

Maclean, James N. M. *Reward Is Secondary: The Life of a Political Adventurer and an Inquiry into the Mystery of "Junius"* (London, 1963).

This study attributes the Junius letters to Lauchline Macleane [*sic*] on the basis of coincidences between a fictionalized reconstruction of the career of "Junius" and a similarly hypothetical biography of Macleane. The analysis is fantastic, but elaborately "documented" in ways that may prove useful if plaguy to subsequent scholars of the problem.

For comment on Macleane as a shaky candidate, see the index of Alvar Ellegård's *Who Was Junius?* and Ellegård's letter in *TLS*, Dec. 19, 1963, 1054.

MRS. MANLEY

McBurney, William H. See under "Marana."

MARANA

McBurney, William H. "The Authorship of *The Turkish Spy*," *PMLA*, LXXII (1957), 915–935.

Certain MSS have disappeared, and "until they are found, the authorship of *The Turkish Spy* [1684–1686] must remain a partial mystery, but upon various indications, external and internal, Giovanni Paolo Marana, the Genoese exile in Paris, can be credited with the entire work as well as with the original idea" (p. 935).

This comes under English literature, because the last 500 *Turkish Spy* letters appeared only in English and were attributed to or claimed by several English writers: Robert Midgley, William Bradshaw, and Mrs. Mary De la Riviere Manley.

MIDGLEY

McBurney, William H. See under "Marana."

Annotated Bibliography

MONTAGU

Halsband, Robert. "Pope, Lady Mary, and the *Court Poems* (1716),"
PMLA, LXVIII (1953), 237–250.

MURPHY

Sherbo, Arthur. *New Essays by Arthur Murphy* (East Lansing, 1963).
Attributes thirty-six anonymous essays to Arthur Murphy, primarily on
the basis of internal evidence.

Miller, Henry Knight. "Internal Evidence: Professor Sherbo and the Case
of Arthur Murphy," *BNYPL*, LXIX (1965), 459–470.
Criticizes Sherbo's methods and conclusions.

Sherbo, Arthur. "Imitation or Concealment: Who Wrote the *Entertainer*
Essays?" *BNYPL*, LXIX (1965), 481–486.
A rebuttal of Miller's arguments.

POPE

Dearing, Vinton A. "Pope, Theobald, and Wycherley's Posthumous Works,"
PMLA, LXVIII (1953), 223–236.

Fabian, Bernhard. "Popes Konzeption der 'Ruling Passion,'" *Archiv für das
Studium der neueren Sprachen*, CXCV (1959), 290–301.
Attribution of *Spectator* Essay 408 to Pope is rejected, despite many
parallels, on grounds that the theory of the "ruling passion" in the essay
differs from Pope's.

Halsband, Robert. See under "Montagu."

RALPH

Coley, William B. See under "Fielding."

ROCHESTER

Vieth, David. See essay No. 19, and Vieth's book on Rochester, there cited.

SADLER

Benham, Allen R. "*The Perfect Politician* and Its Author," *MLQ*, XIX
(1958), 21–27.
Clues are the author's initials; evidence is found in parallels between
the author's experience and John Sadler's experience, some of it fairly
unusual.

SHERIDAN

Williams, George Woods. "A New Source of Evidence for Sheridan's Authorship of *The Camp* and *The Wonders of Derbyshire*," SP, LXVII (1950), 619–628.

Williams finds evidence in patterns of theatrical bookkeeping, and also in style.

SMALLWOOD

Horn, Robert D. "The Authorship of the First Blenheim Panegyric," *HLQ*, XXIV (1961), 297–310.

A combination of external and internal evidence establishes James Smallwood as the author of a 1704 poetic tribute to Marlborough.

SMART

Sherbo, Arthur. "Fielding and Chaucer—and Smart," *N&Q*, n.s., V (1958), 441–442.

Sherbo takes internal evidence to indicate that Smart rather than Fielding wrote the "Plesaunt Balade" in imitation of Chaucer in No. 50 of Fielding's *Covent-Garden Journal*.

Sherbo, Arthur. "Survival in Grub-Street: Another Essay in Attribution," *BNYPL*, LXIV (1960), 147–158.

Four of John Newbery's "collections" are attributed to Smart, on circumstantial and internal evidence of various kinds.

See also Sherbo, essays Nos. 1, 6, and 21, and Fogel, Ephim G., No. 4.

SMOLLETT

Tupper, Caroline F. See under "Goldsmith."

STEELE

Bateson, F. W. See under "Addison."

Scheurweghs, G. See under "Gildon."

SWIFT

Teerink, H. *The History of John Bull . . . Re-issued from the Original Pamphlets, 1712, together with an Investigation into Its Composition, Publication and Authorship* (Amsterdam, 1925).

Ch. 7, "Internal Evidence" (pp. 82–131), consists chiefly of tables of parallels of subject, expression, and style. Concludes that the evidence is overwhelmingly in favor of Swift. But see Thomas F. Mayo, above under "Arbuthnot."

Annotated Bibliography

Fussell, Paul, Jr. "Speaker and Style in *A Letter of Advice to a Young Poet* (1721), and the Problem of Attribution," *RES*, n.s., x (1959), 63–67.

Fussell supports the attribution to Swift, on a 1721 title page, of *A Letter* signed "E.F." in its first, 1720, edition. What seemed negative stylistic evidence is to be interpreted as the ironic, Swiftian use of a "ventriloquial mask." Herbert Davis should not have rejected *A Letter* from the Swift canon.

Jarrell, Mackie L. "A New Swift Attribution: The Preface to Sheridan's Sermon on St. Cecilia's Day," *PMLA*, LXXVIII (1963), 511–515.

English Literature since 1789

ARNOLD

Neiman, Fraser. "Some Newly Attributed Contributions of Matthew Arnold to the *Pall Mall Gazette*," *MP*, LV (1957), 84–92.

Using MS material from Arnold notebooks, correlating entries of payment with other evidence, Neiman identifies a number of unsigned book reviews, miscellaneous articles, and pseudonymous letters—some only tentatively.

In Neiman's edition of *Essays, Letters, and Reviews by Matthew Arnold* (Cambridge, Mass., 1960) he withdraws one of the attributions (381 n.). See also the next entry.

Super, R. H. "Arnold's Notebooks and Arnold Bibliography," *MP*, LVI (1959), 268–269.

Discusses Fraser Neiman's attributions; makes two more.

Neiman, Fraser. "Matthew Arnold's Review of the *Lettres et opuscules inédits* by Joseph de Maistre," *MLN*, LXXIV (1959), 492–494.

Simultaneously makes one of the attributions noted in Super's article (above).

Brooks, Roger L. "Matthew Arnold and the *London Review*," *PMLA*, LXXVI (1961), 622–623.

Adds two attributions, by internal evidence, and suggests how to look for more.

AUSTEN

Southam, B. C. "Interpolations to Jane Austen's 'Volume the Third,'" *N&Q*, n.s., IX (1962), 185–187.

In a MS notebook 11 pages are judged to be in a hand not that of Jane Austen, an impression clinched above all by comparison of the style of the additions with that of the novelist.

BAGEHOT

Tener, Robert H. "Bagehot, Jeffrey and Renan," *TLS*, Aug. 11, 1961, 515.

Attributes two anonymous reviews, of 1852 and 1863, to Walter Bagehot, the second on evidence "chiefly internal."

BLACKWOOD'S MAGAZINE

Wardle, Ralph M. "Who Was Morgan Odoherty?" *PMLA*, LVIII (1943), 716–727.

Sorts out several "Odoherty" pieces in *Blackwood's* and assigns many. See Eugene Nolte, below.

Wardle, Ralph M. "The Authorship of the *Noctes Ambrosianae*," *MP*, XLI (1944), 9–17.

Some "fragmentary conclusions" as to the contributions of Lockhart, Maginn, and Wilson to this *Blackwood's* series.

Nolte, Eugene. "David Macbeth Moir as Morgan Odoherty," *PMLA*, LXXII (1957), 803–806.

From MS evidence, corrects Ralph M. Wardle (above).

Strout, Alan Lang. *A Bibliography of Articles in Blackwood's Magazine 1817–1825* (Lubbock, Tex., 1959).

Letters and a "Contributor's Book" resolve many earlier conjectures. Strout mistrusts the evidence of style or even handwriting for assigning the individual contributions of a team of writers; he emphasizes "the difficulty of being absolutely certain that a given sentence, a given paragraph, or even a given page is by a particular author and not the work of a collaborator" (p. 11). But he does assign some pieces "to Lockhart and Wilson on the basis of style."

COLERIDGE

Greever, Garland, ed. *A Wiltshire Parson and His Friends . . . with Four Hitherto Unidentified Reviews by Coleridge* (London, 1926), 165–167, 168–200.

Considers Coleridge's letter as unequivocal evidence for his authorship of reviews of *Udolpho, The Italian, Hubert,* and *The Monk* in the *Critical Review;* gives texts, with slight inaccuracies.

Griggs, Earl Leslie. "Notes Concerning Certain Poems by Samuel Taylor Coleridge," *MLN*, LXIX (1954), 27–31.

Rejects from the canon the Stanhope sonnet in the *Morning Chronicle.*

Erdman, David V. "Immoral Acts of a Library Cormorant: The Extent of Coleridge's Contributions to the *Critical Review*," *BNYPL*, LXIII (1959), 433–454, 515–530, 575–587.

In a methodical survey of the *Critical Review* of 1794–1800, the attributions proposed by Garland Greever (see entry above) are confirmed and reviews of *Musae Etonenses, A Sketch from the Landscape,* and *The Negro Slaves* are attributed to Coleridge, while reviews of *Augusta Fitzherbert* (a novel), *Institutes of Hindu Law,* and *The Castle Spectre* are assigned to Coleridge conjecturally. The texts are given in full. The reviewing style of Robert Southey is briefly distinguished (pp. 441, 587).

Parrish, Stephen M., and David V. Erdman. "Who Wrote *The Mad Monk?* A Debate," *BNYPL*, LXIV (1960), 209–237.

Parrish concludes for Wordsworth, Erdman for Coleridge, both relying heavily on internal evidence and somewhat on word frequencies. "It is agreed that the poem contains significant Wordsworthian elements. The question is how they got there."

Roper, Derek. "Coleridge and the 'Critical Review,' " *MLR*, LV (1960), 11–16.

Dismisses the review of *Udolpho* in 1794, on indirect external evidence alone.

Woof, R. W. "Wordsworth's Poetry and Stuart's Newspapers: 1797–1803," *SB*, xv (1962), 149–189.

Woof confirms attribution of "The Mad Monk" to Coleridge (pp. 174–176) and considers "The Old Man of the Alps" basically his, though with possible Wordsworth origin. He rejects "Written in a Grotto" from the Wordsworth canon; adds a new translation from the Italian (pp. 183–186); and gives thorough textual collation, with discrimination of Wordsworthian and Coleridgean elements in collaborative works when possible.

Braekman, W., and A. Devolder. "Three Hitherto Unpublished Letters of S. T. Coleridge to J. J. Morgan," *Studia Germanica Gandensia*, IV (1962), 203–223.

Evidence in these new letters reopens the question of Morgan's share of responsibility for the critique of Maturin's *Bertram*, which Coleridge published in his *Biographia Literaria*.

Beaty, Frederick L. "Mrs. Radcliffe's Fading Gleam," *PQ*, XLII (1963), 126–129.

Beaty suggests *Udolpho* as the source of the fading gleam idea in "The Mad Monk" (assumed to be Coleridge's) and in Wordsworth's *Ode*, perhaps meaning to imply that the poems are independent of each other.

See Erdman, David V., essays Nos. 3, 24, and 27; Fogel, Ephim G., No. 4; Colmer, John A., No. 25; and Johnson, S. F., No. 26. See also the articles cited in the footnotes of these essays.

DICKENS

Houtchens, Carolyn W. and Lawrence H. "Three Early Works Attributed to Dickens," *PMLA*, LIX (1944), 226–235.

All three are signed "by Boz"; the conclusion is "necessarily tentative, since all the evidence is internal."

Carlton, William J. "Mr. and Mrs. Dickens: The Thomson-Stark Letter," *N&Q*, n.s., VII (1960), 145–147.

Carlton accounts for all puzzling details—of address, date, etc.—and thus strengthens case for the authenticity of a letter, not for its textual accuracy.

Annotated Bibliography

HAZLITT

Carver, P. L. "Hazlitt's Contributions to *The Edinburgh Review*," *RES*, IV (1928), 385–393.

Sikes, Herschel M. "Hazlitt, the *London Magazine*, and the 'Anonymous Reviewer,'" *BNYPL*, LXV (1961), 159–174.
Attributes to Hazlitt, and reprints, an 1822 review of Cunningham's *Sir Marmaduke Maxwell*. Hazlitt's editor P. P. Howe had faltered between attribution to Hazlitt and to Reynolds.

Marshall, William H. "An Addition to the Hazlitt Canon: Arguments from External and Internal Evidence," *PBSA*, LV (1961), 347–370.
Attributes "Pulpit Oratory, No. IV." in *The Yellow Dwarf* of 1818 to Hazlitt, rather than his imitator Reynolds, on external evidence that is against Reynolds and on internal evidence of parallels in ideas, in proper references, and in literary quotations—significantly to *later* work in the Hazlitt canon.

Review of Christabel

Schneider, Elisabeth. "The Unknown Reviewer of *Christabel*: Jeffrey, Hazlitt, Tom Moore," *PMLA*, LXX (1955), 417–432.
Internal and external evidence points to Moore as the culprit.

Jordan, Hoover H. (1956). See essay No. 28.

Schneider, Elisabeth. "Tom Moore and the *Edinburgh* Review of *Christabel*," *PMLA*, LXXVII (1962), 71–76.
New evidence has appeared in passages of two letters in which Moore implies that he did not write the review yet discloses "what had not previously been known except by inference, that he had in fact intended to write it and that, if he had written it, it would have been what it is, a scornful one." Miss Schneider now thinks "quite certainly" the review "could have been written only by Moore."

Dowden, Wilfred S. "Thomas Moore and the Review of *Christabel*," *MP*, LX (1962), 47–50.
Comes to an opposite conclusion about the new Moore letters, which are quoted in full.

Baker, Herschel. *William Hazlitt* (Cambridge, Mass., 1962), 356, 356n.
Seems divided on the question: in his text Baker states that "it is probable that Hazlitt had no hand in it at all," but in his note he states that "Howe's conclusion on this moot question (*Life*, 398ff.) seems to me to be substantially correct." But Howe's conclusion was that the review contained "something of Hazlitt and a good deal of Jeffrey." "What appears to be plain," Howe added, "is that Coleridge *believed* this review to be

Hazlitt's and that the review as printed is not in its entirety, or even substantially, his."

[Perhaps the present debate has strengthened the case *against* Hazlitt as author as well as the case *against* Moore as author, though critics arguing *against* one author incline to make a positive case *for* the other.]

JEFFREY

See "Review of *Christabel*" under "Hazlitt."

KEATS

Brooks, Elmer L. " 'The Poet' an Error in the Keats Canon?" *MLN,* lxvii (1952), 540–546.

There are many reasons to doubt Keats's authorship of this sonnet, signed "S." Brooks tentatively suggests Charles Strong as author. See next entry.

Steele, Mabel A. E. "The Authorship of 'The Poet' and Other Sonnets," *K-SJ,* v (1956), 69–80.

Accepts MS evidence ascribing "The Poet" not to Keats but to John Taylor, and agrees with "Mr. Brook's suggestion that the sonnet 'is a poetical picture *of* Keats. . . .' " See above.

See also Jones, Leonidas M., essay No. 29.

LANDOR

Super, R. H. "The Authorship of *Guy's Porridge Pot* and *The Dun Cow*," *The Library,* 5th ser., v (1950), 55–58.

Complicated evidence leads to the conclusion that of two satiric poems of 1808, the first named was the work of Robert Eyres Landor; the second "was not the work of his elder brother."

Paden, W. D. "Twenty New Poems Attributed to Tennyson, Praed, and Landor: Part Two," *Victorian Studies,* iv (1961), 291–314.

Paden argues, with the aid of metrical tables, that the metrical practice of "The Descent of the Naiad," printed in the *Literary Chronicle* of July 12, 1828, is compatible with Walter Savage Landor's; furthermore, "the Naiad as a lovely and open-hearted girl, unaware or incredulous of impending evil" is a central image in this poem and in Landor's work. In the same issue, the Landor scholar R. H. Super finds that the poem "is far inferior stylistically to Landor's verse and well within the range of skill of any number of versifiers who contributed to English literary journals in the same decade" (p. 409).

JOHN STUART MILL

Rees, J. C. *Mill and His Early Critics* (Leicester, 1956), 38–54.

The essay "On Social Freedom," wrongly attributed to Mill, is not in his hand or that of his amanuensis and is probably by E. R. Edger, to whom Mill wrote a letter of acknowledgment of his receipt of a MS entitled "Social Freedom" in 1862.

Scanlan, James P. "J. S. Mill and the Definition of Freedom," *Ethics,* LXVII (1958), 194–206.
Scanlan takes as evidence against Mill's authorship of "On Social Freedom" (see Rees, above) the deductive demonstration that it contains what Mill could not have said, though, ironically, he ought to have done so to strengthen his system of social thought at a crucial joint.

MOIR

Nolte, Eugene. See under *"Blackwood's Magazine."*

MOORE

See "Review of *Christabel*" under "Hazlitt."

W. M. PRAED

Paden, W. D. "Twenty New Poems Attributed to Tennyson, Praed, and Landor: Part Two," *Victorian Studies,* IV (1961), 291–314.
Attributes eight periodical poems to Praed.

REYNOLDS

See Sikes, Herschel M., and Marshall, William H., under "Hazlitt."

SMITH

Halpern, Sheldon. "Sydney Smith in the *Edinburgh Review:* A New List," *BNYPL,* LXVI (1962), 589–602.
Uses internal and external evidence to assign to Smith 85 articles from 1802 to 1828.

SOUTHEY

See Erdman, David V., under "Coleridge."

CHARLES STRONG

Brooks, Elmer L. See under "Keats."

JOHN TAYLOR

Steele, Mabel. See under "Keats."

TENNYSON

Paden, E. D. "Twenty New Poems Attributed to Tennyson, Praed, and Landor: Part One," *Victorian Studies*, IV (1961), 195–218.

Part One attributes to Tennyson eleven poems which appeared in the *Athenaeum* of 1829, but defends the attribution of only four of these by citing "similarities of thought, technique, and imagery" between them "and Tennyson's known work." R. H. Super (*VS*, V [June 1961], 409–410) finds that this failure to defend the other seven attributions raises "a serious question of scholarly practice. . . . An affirmation once published is almost ineradicable, even if proved wrong, and is a trap for the most careful of us." As for the four poems, the attribution is based "chiefly on commonplaces of imagery that [Paden] finds also in *In Memoriam*, but not in the poetry Tennyson was actually writing in 1829."

WORDSWORTH

Parrish, Stephen M., and Erdman, David V. See under "Coleridge."

Woof, R. W. See under "Coleridge."

American Literature

Gaines, Pierce Welch. *Political Works of Concealed Authorship during the Administrations of Washington, Adams and Jefferson, 1789–1809: With Attributions* (New Haven, 1959).

A checklist, indicating sources of attributions and which attributions have been disputed or presented as doubtful.

HENRY ADAMS

See several entries under *"Diary of a Public Man."*

ETHAN ALLEN

Anderson, George Pomeroy. "Who Wrote 'Ethan Allen's Bible'?" *NEQ*, x (1937), 685–696.

BIERCE

Monaghan, Frank. "Ambrose Bierce and the Authorship of *The Monk and the Hangman's Daughter*," *AL*, II (1931), 337–349.

Monaghan reduces to irrelevance the claims of Bierce and his "collaborator" to have written what proves to have been an essentially straight translation of a German original.

DIARY OF A PUBLIC MAN

The Diary of a Public Man, and a Page of Political Correspondence, Stanton to Buchanan, with Foreword by Carl Sandburg and Prefatory Notes by F. Lauriston Bullard (New Brunswick, N.J., 1946).

Authorship of the *Diary* is not attributed. Here reprinted is the text of the diary (dated Dec. 28, 1860–Mar. 15, 1861) from its unique extant source, the *North American Review*, CXXIX (1879), 125–140, 259–273, 376–388, 483–496.

Anderson, Frank Maloy. *The Mystery of "A Public Man": A Historical Detective Story* (Minneapolis, 1948).

Anderson reprints the text of the anonymous diary of 1860–1861 (see above). After exhausting the attempt to find the author on the assumption that the diary is authentic, Anderson tests the assumption that the diary as printed is fictional, though based on an actual diary, and attributes the printed diary to Samuel Ward (1814–1884). Unfortunately, there are fatal flaws in Anderson's procedure: he fails to consider Ward in the early chapters, when he would have had to eliminate this candidate along with the others, and he forgets to reconsider as possible authors of a fictional diary those whom he *has* eliminated as authors of an authentic one. Later scholars have failed to analyze the grave weaknesses in the logic of this glaring example of (doubtless unconscious) special pleading.

Page, Evelyn. "The Diary and the Public Man," *NEQ*, xxii (1949), 147–172.
Attributes the unsigned diary to Henry Adams, chiefly on basis of style and circumstances.

Bullard, F. Lauriston. "Communications," *NEQ*, xxiii (1950), 404.
Makes some points against the attribution to Henry Adams.

Hume, Robert A. *Runaway Star: An Appreciation of Henry Adams* (Ithaca, N.Y., 1951), 47–51.
Discusses and to some extent supports the attribution to Adams, but awaits "solid evidence, pointing one way or another."

Lokken, Roy N. "Has the Mystery of 'A Public Man' Been Solved?" *Miss. Valley Hist. Rev.*, xl (1953), 419–440.
Lokken argues, at length, that there is insufficient evidence to conclude that the diary is semifictional and not at all enough to name Sam Ward as the diarist. He believes that the authenticity and the author will remain unknown until "numerous lacunae in the history of the secession winter of 1860–1861" have been filled. He merely mentions the attribution to Adams. (Rejoinder by Frank Maloy Anderson, *MVHR*, xlii [1955], 101–107; reply by Lokken, 107–109.)

Price, Benjamin M. "That Baffling Diary," *SAQ*, liv (1955), 56–74.
A recapitulation of Miss Page's arguments for attribution to Adams, with a few additions.

DWIGHT

Leary, Lewis. "The Author of *The Triumph of Infidelity*," *NEQ*, xx (1947), 377–385.
The internal evidence for authorship of *The Triumph* is meager, yet the external evidence is considered too formidable to be broken by the mere statement that Timothy Dwight, accused of authorship, did "not acknowledge" the production.

THE *FEDERALIST* PAPERS

Adair, Douglass. "The Authorship of the Disputed Federalist Papers," *Wm. & Mary Q*, 3rd ser., i (1944), 97–122, 235–264.
Whether Alexander Hamilton or James Madison wrote certain of the numbers of *The Federalist*, which they coauthored, has been "an American *cause célèbre;* a mystery quite as intriguing as the authorship of Junius; and one far more worthy of scholarly attention." In his first section Adair

surveys the arguments and polemics of the dispute; in the second he assembles cumulative evidence to confirm "Madison's right to the twelve disputed papers."

Cooke, Jacob E., ed. *The Federalist* (Middletown, Conn., 1961).

The introduction discusses external evidence for authorship of the disputed papers, pp. xix–xxvii, and internal evidence, pp. xxvii–xxx.

See also Mosteller and Wallace, under "Statistical Studies and Computer Applications."

FRANKLIN

Crane, Verner W., ed. *Benjamin Franklin's Letters to the Press 1758–1775* (Chapel Hill, N.C., 1950), lvii–lviii.

Discovery of MS evidence was "heartening because it confirmed the validity of arguments from internal evidence which had already convinced [Verner] that [a newspaper letter] was a Franklin extract."

Aldridge, Alfred Owen. "Franklin's Deistical Indians," *Am. Phil. Soc. Proc.,* xciv (1950), 398–410.

Through a French reprinting, a *London Chronicle* article of 1768 is traced to Franklin, who later drew upon it for a work he published in 1784. From the internal evidence, "either Franklin wrote the *Captivity of William Henry* or he was guilty of copying from another author. Everything we know of Franklin points against the latter possibility."

"The *Captivity* is another hoax by Franklin similar to his *Dogood Papers* and his *Speech of Polly Baker*." (See below.)

Echeverria, Durand. " 'The Sale of the Hessians': Was Benjamin Franklin the Author?" *Am. Phil. Soc. Proc.,* xcviii (1954), 427–431.

The traditional attribution of "The Sale," on the basis of wit and style, does not stand up well under bibliographical scrutiny.

Labaree, Leonard W., *et al.,* eds. *The Papers of Benjamin Franklin,* i, ii (New Haven, 1959, 1960).

Problems of attribution are mentioned or exemplified in the following pages, chiefly in headnotes: i, xxiv, 46, 52–53, 112, 114, 164, 170, 176, 177, 182, 318, 325, 328, 333; ii, 21, 65, 126, 128, 129, 145, 146, 149, 150, 173, 184, 302, 352–353, 383.

Smeall, J. F. S. " 'Miss Polly Baker's Speech': An American Text," *North Dakota Q,* xxvii, No. 3 (Summer 1959), 78–80; continued as "The Readership of the Polly-Baker Texts," xxviii, No. 1 (Winter 1960), 20–29.

Smeall questions the anecdotal attribution to Franklin, noting the effect of assumptions about readership on assumptions about authorship. He makes plausible deductions from limited data. (For implications in a larger context, see Hall, below.)

Hall, Max. *Benjamin Franklin and Polly Baker: The History of a Literary Deception* (Chapel Hill, N.C., 1960).

Hall traces "The Speech of Miss Polly Baker" from its first printing (*General Advertiser*, London, 1747) through a maze of indirect and finally direct evidence to Franklin, using a dragnet approach, with much instructive detective work on provenance. Hall treats internal-external evidence in ch. 8. He notes ten other Franklin hoaxes and considers possible authors of embellished versions.

This study gives a useful demonstration of the continual alteration in the shape of a problem as more and more data accumulate. See the briefer, independent work of Smeall, above.

HAMILTON

Marsh, Philip. "Hamilton's Neglected Essays, 1791–1793," *New-York Hist. Soc. Q*, xxxii (1948), 280–300.

Hamilton's characteristic style is defined pp. 286–287, as in next entry.

Marsh, Philip. "Further Attributions to Hamilton's Pen," *New-York Hist. Soc. Q*, xl (1956), 351–360.

"No other political writer of his time used a style closely resembling his—and so the problem of recognition is greatly simplified. Thus though there is no positive proof, the unsigned essays of the time and place, and those bearing new signatures, carrying his style and ideas, may justifiably be entertained as his. Herewith have been presented six distinctly Hamiltonian essays and three examples of quite possibly . . . Hamiltonian political verse—all of which may well be ascribed to him, at least 'conditionally.'"

See also "The *Federalist* Papers," above.

HEARN

Mordell, Albert. Introduction to *An American Miscellany* by Lafcadio Hearn; Articles and Stories Now First Collected (New York, 1924), i, v–lxxix.

Discovers and identifies contributions to the Cincinnati *Enquirer* and *Commercial* in 1874–1877, some by external evidence, some mainly by style and content.

Mordell, Albert. "A Discovery of Early Hearn Essays," *Today's Japan*, iv, No. 1 (Jan. 1959), 41–54.

Identifies five articles in the Boston *Investigator*, Sept. 1870–March 1871, signed "Fiat Lux" as Hearn's. Hearn had said he "used to contribute"; evidence is found in parallels of idea and style.

See also Mordell, essay No. 31, and *Discoveries* (Tokyo, 1964).

MADISON

See "The *Federalist* Papers."

MELVILLE

Thorp, Willard. "Did Melville Review *The Scarlet Letter?*" AL, xiv (1942), 302–305.
No; but the legend is traced. Evidence of style is found highly negative.

PAINE

Aldridge, Alfred Owen. "Some Writings of Thomas Paine in Pennsylvania Newspapers," *AHR*, lvi (1951), 832–838.
Aldridge adds several items "to the Paine canon"—some by fiat, some because they are signed "Common Sense" and are possibly extra numbers in Paine's series, two because they are apologia.

Gimbel, Richard. "New Political Writings by Thomas Paine," *Yale Univ. Lib. Gaz.*, xxx (1956), 94–107.
One is attributed on internal evidence (p. 106).

Aldridge, Alfred Owen. "Thomas Paine and Comus," *Penn. Mag. of Hist. and Biog.*, lxxxv (1961), 70–75.
Paine used the pseudonym "Comus" in 1804; a "Comus" satire of 1779 is attributed to him on this and other grounds.
"In addition to the Comus pieces, there are scores of Paine's newspaper essays which have never been collected or identified in print." The field is wide.

POE

Lloyd, J. A. T. "Who Wrote 'English Notes'?" *Colophon*, n.s., i (1935), 107–118.
Poe, obviously—but "questions of authorship die hard. Whether Lucian wrote *Lucius or the Ass* still perplexes people who have given up asking if Shak. wrote the plays of Shak. The authorship of *Wuthering Heights*, against so much external and internal evidence, is still a matter of dispute. But perhaps the famous reply to Charles Dickens' *American Notes* is as good an example as any of the obstinate incredulity attached to cases of this kind." (See the next item.)

Webb, Howard W. Jr. "A Further Note on the Dickens-Poe Relationship," *Nineteenth C. Fiction*, xv (1960), 80–82.
A letter from Poe's associate C. J. Peterson to J. Tomlin furnishes additional evidence that Poe did not write *English Notes* or the *Blackwood's* review of *American Notes* and that there was no enmity between Poe and Dickens in 1842.

MARK TWAIN

Brinegar, Claude S. See under "Statistical Studies and Computer Applications."

SAM WARD

Anderson, Frank M. See under "Diary of a Public Man."

WHITMAN

Bergman, Herbert. " 'Chicago,' an Uncollected Poem, Possibly by Whitman," *MLN*, LXV (1950), 478–481.

A poem in the Toronto *World* signed with Whitman's name; possibly his or a parody.

Shephard, Esther. "Walt Whitman's Whereabouts in the Winter of 1842–1843," *AL*, XXIX (1957), 289–296.

Whitman may have written some articles in the *Daily Plebeian*, on which he was editorial assistant.

Golden, Arthur. "An Uncollected Whitman Article," *BNYPL*, LXIV (1960), 353–360.

An obituary in the Brooklyn *Daily Eagle* is traced to Whitman through a MS note and parallel passages.

Detections of Forgery

See Middleton, Arthur P. and Adair, Douglass, essay No. 30, and Mordell, Albert, essay No. 31.

Altick, Richard D. *The Scholar Adventurers* (New York, 1950).
See the survey of studies of literary forgeries, ch. 6, and the bibliographical note, pp. 324–325.

Morrissette, Bruce. *The Great Rimbaud Forgery: The Affair of "La Chasse spirituelle"* (Saint Louis, 1956).
An illuminating, detailed account of a modern forgery (1949) and its reception. See esp. ch. 5, with a variety of tests of style. The imitation was almost perfect, and most "exposées" (published after the forgery was admitted) rested on mistaken grounds. What the forgers ignored was the problem of *development* in an author's thought and style; they failed to "intercalate" the forgery convincingly into the chronological pattern of Rimbaud's works (p. 164).

Harrison, Wilson R. *Suspect Documents: Their Scientific Examination* (London, 1958).
Extensive section on handwriting evidence.

Statistical Studies
and Computer Applications

The entries below (except for Titherly's, included as a curiosity) summarize studies which use statistical techniques that go beyond raw counts of certain verbal and metrical traits, supplemented on occasion by simple percentages. Such elementary statistics have been used in attribution studies for well over a hundred years (see *Henry VIII* and *The Two Noble Kinsmen*, above). But it is a question whether they will be able to compete with studies such as Ellegård's and Mosteller and Wallace's, which attempt to express in precise terms the odds in favor of a given attribution. For a useful review and critique of this new wave of statistical studies, see Rebecca Posner, "The Use and Abuse of Stylistic Statistics," *Archivum Linguisticum*, xv (1963), 111–139; see also Stephen Ullman, *Language and Style* (Oxford, 1964).

Attribution studies have recently found a powerful servant in the electronic computer, already used by Mosteller and Wallace and others for literary data processing. For an account of computer applications in the humanities, with comments on the possible value of the machine in canonical studies, see Stephen M. Parrish, "Problems in the Making of Computer Concordances," *SB*, xv (1962), 1–14, and Ephim G. Fogel, "Electronic Computers and Eliz. Texts," *ibid.*, 15–31. Other essays on computer concordances may be found in later volumes of *Studies in Bibliography*. In addition, twenty papers were recently presented at an international conference, the first of its kind, devoted entirely to literary data processing. The conference, sponsored by the IBM corporation, was held at Yorktown Heights, N.Y., Sept. 9–11, 1964, and the proceedings, multilithed by IBM and edited by Harry F. Arader, Jess B. Bessinger, Jr., and Stephen M. Parrish, were available, as this volume went to press, from the Materials Center of the Modern Language Association, 4 Washington Place, New York, N.Y., 10003. Two of the papers—Ephim G. Fogel's "The Humanist and the Computer" and Alan Markman's "Litterae Ex Machina"—may also be found in *The Journal of Higher Education*, xxxvi (1965), 61–68, 69–79. Two books on the use of computers in literary scholarship are to be published in 1966: Jacob Leed, ed., *The Computer and Literary Style: Introductory Essays and Studies* (Kent, Ohio: Kent Univ. Press), with essays on the disputed *Federalist* papers by Ivor S. Francis and on *"The O'Ruddy, a Novel by Stephen Crane and Robert Barr,"* by Bernard O'Donnell; and a comprehensive introduction to computer programming for literary scholars by Vinton A. Dearing of the University of California at Los Angeles.

Annotated Bibliography

Although computers can relieve canonical scholars of much mechanical drudgery by providing accurate information about a variety of discriminators (vocabulary, linguistic preferences, prosodic and stylistic traits) in a wide range of texts, these data processing machines also have limitations. The results they help to produce are no better than the logic and scholarship of the men who use them. "Will a special pleader in a hurry," it has been asked (*SB*, xv [1962], 30), "pause to reflect merely because aids to reflection are more abundant? . . . Computers will not do away with the Idols of the Tribe; to guard against such illusions is the province of education in the spirit of scholarly and scientific argument." Recent developments suggest that such warnings, though obvious, are far from superfluous. In 1963, Rev. Andrew Q. Morton of the Church of Scotland announced that his computer analysis of sentence length and function words such as *and, in, but,* and *the* proved statistically that nine of fourteen New Testament epistles attributed to St. Paul had been written by at least five non-Pauline authors (The New York *Times*, Nov. 7, pp. 1, 17). But in 1965 Rev. John W. Ellison of Winchester, Mass., charged Morton with "an abuse of both computers and scholarship" (N.Y. *Times*, Jan. 23, p. 17). By applying Morton's methods, Ellison was able to "prove" that Morton's own papers on the Biblical epistles must have been written by five authors, that five authors must have written Joyce's *Ulysses*, and that yet a sixth had written *A Portrait of the Artist as a Young Man*. Morton's arguments were also subjected to searching criticism on the Third Programme of the BBC (March 16 and 23, 1965) by the British linguist David Crystal, whose talk was entitled "Computing St. Paul: A Cautionary Essay in Stylistics." Statistics and computers are enormously useful servants, but they will not necessarily save their masters from folly.

Yule, G. Udny. *The Statistical Study of Literary Vocabulary* (Cambridge, Eng., 1944).

Yule began with a study of "a particular vocabulary in a case of disputed authorship"; put it aside to investigate the general assumptions and problems of measuring word distributions; derived a statistical expression of the repetitiveness of an author's vocabulary which he calls "the characteristic"; tested it with Bunyan and Macaulay; and returned (ch. 9) to the disputed authorship of *De Imitatione Christi*. The tests "almost exclude" one candidate, Gerson; "are entirely consistent with the authorship of Thomas à Kempis; but "one cannot . . . say that the authorship . . . is proved, for statistical data can only balance the claims of one author against those of another." (See also p. 499, above; Herdan and Bennett, below.)

Herdan, G. "Stylostatistics," Part I of *Language as Choice and Chance* (Groningen, Holland, 1956), 12–63.

Presents "stylostatistics" as a branch of quantitative linguistics. See sections 2.3 (richness of vocabulary), 3.5 (a new statistical parameter—the characteristic), 3.7 (Yule's experiment), 4.6 (correlation and disputed authorship), and the Bibliography (pp. 62–63).

Section 2.5.1 (special and total vocabulary) treats of the percentages of Romance vocabulary in Chaucer and in "The Equatorie of the Planetis" (see Derek J. Price under "Chaucer, *Equatorie*," above).

Bennett, Paul E. "The Statistical Measurement of a Stylistic Trait in *Julius Caesar* and *As You Like It*," *SQ*, viii (1957), 33–50.

G. Udny Yule's "characteristic" provides an objective measurement useful for purposes of attribution. A count of the frequencies of nouns in *Caes.* and *AYL*, with repetitive "characteristics" of 49.2 and 40.5, indicates that Shak.'s practice is consistent with itself in two rather different plays of the same period of his career. Thus, the characteristics of a play by Marlowe or Jonson might turn out to be similar, and so Yule's test alone would not in itself solve problems of attribution. But authorship might "confidently be ascribed when two or three or four" separate objective measurements "were in substantial agreement." (Bennett incidentally finds that Bartlett's concordance frequently omits occurrences of nouns.)

Titherley, A. W. *Shak.: New Side Lights (Overt and Covert)* (Winchester, Eng., 1961).

The author, Fellow of the Royal Institute of Chemistry and formerly Dean of the Faculty of Science, Univ. of Liverpool, holds that "Shak." was the pen name adopted by William Stanley, 6th Earl of Derby. He has submitted the question to the "search-light of scientific (inductive) criticism, which not only involved scrutiny of relevant documents but the evaluation of fundamental literary frequencies in various manuscripts and printed texts. These frequencies, handled mathematically, introduced a new element of precision into a sadly vague problem that bristled with interpretative ambiguities. Definite quantitative criteria characteristic of Shak. permitted both date-calculation and the detection of his hand in anonymous noncanonical poems and plays. Comparison of these multiple numerical data with those of Derby's script, as well as his handwriting, proved beyond doubt that he was indistinguishable from Shak."

Ellegård, Alvar. *Who Was Junius?* (Stockholm, 1962).

Ellegård, Alvar. *A Statistical Method for Determining Authorship: The Junius Letters, 1769–1772* (Gothenburg Studies in English No. 13; Gothenburg, 1962).

The first volume surveys and analyzes the history of attempts to identify the author of the Junius letters. The second details the methods used and makes a strong case short of certainty for Philip Francis.

Having found Yule's tests insufficiently sensitive, Ellegård devised statistical tests of his own, arriving at ratios between the frequencies of "typical" words and expressions in Junius (157,100 words) and in a general contemporary sample of over a million words, then testing these ratios against those for Francis' writings (231,300 words). Another test, of preferred "alternatives" of phrase or vocabulary, still further narrowed the field. Francis proves to be one of perhaps only three writers who could have been Junius, statistically speaking.

An extensive discussion of handwriting is in the first book, the bibliography of which (pp. 149–154) contains a critique of previous bibliographies.

See review in *TLS*, Jan. 25, 1963, p. 67, and letter by Ellegård, *ibid.*, Mar. 1, 1963, p. 153, clarifying the use of tables in the second book.

Murray, Peter B. (1962). See under "Middleton," above.

Mosteller, Frederick, and David L. Wallace. "Notes on an Authorship Problem," *Annals of the Computation Laboratory of Harvard Univ.* xxxi (1962), 163–197.

Summarizes the *Federalist* problem, early work on it, and a recent "pilot study." Presents an application of the ideas of Bayesian inference, a section on assumptions behind statistical analysis, and a useful list of references.

Mosteller, Frederick, and David Wallace, "Inference in an Authorship Problem," *Jour. of the American Statistical Assoc.*, lviii (1963), 275–309.

[Two sentences of the author's abstract are here excerpted—Eds.]

"This study has four purposes: to provide a comparison of discrimination methods; to explore the problems presented by techniques based strongly on Bayes' theorem when they are used in a data analysis of large scale; to solve the authorship question of the *Federalist* papers; and to propose routine methods for solving other authorship problems. . . . The conclusions about the authorship problem are that Madison rather than Hamilton wrote all 12 of the disputed papers."

[The following "remarks on authorship problems" are here reprinted from p. 306 of the essay—Eds.]

"(1) The function words of the language appear to be a fertile source of discriminators, and luckily the high-frequency words are the strongest. Use of our rate table (not presented here) for high-frequency words may help an investigator quickly form a pattern of rates for a new author.

scale; to solve the authorship question of the *Federalist* papers; and to have a variety of sources of material, to allow 'between writings' variability to emerge and to give a basis for the elimination of words that show substantial heterogeneity.

"(3) Pronouns and auxiliary verbs appear to be dangerously contextual; other function words are not entirely safe, and should not be taken for granted, but should be investigated for contextuality.

"(4) Paired authorship problems should not ordinarily be as difficult as this one, but there is plenty of room for original ideas on the problem of selecting one from among many authors, or of factoring a collection of essays into component groups of similar authors."

Brinegar, Claude S. "Mark Twain and the Quintus Curtius Snodgrass Letters: A Statistical Test of Authorship," *Jour. of the American Statistical Assoc.*, LVIII (1963), 85–96. [The author's abstract is here reprinted—Eds.]

"Mark Twain is widely credited with the authorship of 10 letters published in 1861 in the *New Orleans Daily Crescent*. The adventures described in these letters, which were signed "Quintus Curtius Snodgrass," provide the historical basis of a main part of Twain's presumed role in the Civil War. This study applies an old, though little used statistical test of authorship—a word-length frequency test—to show that Twain almost certainly did not write these 10 letters. The statistical analysis includes a visual comparison of several word-length frequency distributions and applications of the x^2 and two-sample t tests."

After he completed his research, Brinegar asked Henry Nash Smith, the literary editor of the Mark Twain Papers, for his opinion about the Q. C. Snodgrass letters. On the basis of the internal evidence of style and the external evidence of Twain's movements, Smith was certain that Twain did not write the letters.

Mosteller, Frederick, and David L. Wallace. *Inference and Disputed Authorship: "The Federalist"* (Reading, Mass., 1964).

A full-scale development of arguments first presented in the papers of 1962 and 1963 (above). "A reader who wants to know quickly our main results," the authors suggest, "could read Chapters 1 ["*The Federalist* papers as a case study"], 2 ["Words and their distributions"], 3 ["The main study"], 8 ["Other studies"], and 9 ["Summary of results and conclusions"].

LIST OF CONTRIBUTORS
AND INDEXES

List of Contributors

DOUGLASS ADAIR, Professor of History at the Claremont Graduate School, is a student of early American history and has written on the authorship of the disputed *Federalist* papers.

R. C. BALD (1901–1965), late Professor of English at the University of Chicago, author of *Donne and the Drurys* (1959), wrote widely on Shakespeare, Middleton, and other Elizabethan dramatists; at the time of his death, he was bringing to completion a definitive life of Donne.

GERALD EADES BENTLEY, Murray Professor of English, Princeton University, has now completed the sixth and seventh volumes of his *The Jacobean and Caroline Stage* (Vols. I–V, 1942–1956), and is also the author of books on Shakespeare and Jonson.

FREDSON BOWERS, Alumni Professor and Chairman of the Department of English at the University of Virginia, textual editor of *The Dramatic Works of Thomas Dekker* (4 vols., 1953–1958), has recently added *Bibliography and Textual Criticism* (1964) to his own bibliography.

R. W. CHAMBERS (1874–1942), Quain Professor of English at University College London (1922–1941), was author of *Sir Thomas More* (1935), studies in Old, Middle, and Renaissance English literature, and many essays on *Piers Plowman*.

JOHN COLMER, Professor of English at the University of Adelaide, Australia, is the author of *Coleridge: Critic of Society* (1959).

R. S. CRANE, Emeritus Distinguished Service Professor, University of Chicago, and editor of *Modern Philology*, 1930–1952, is author of *New Essays by Oliver Goldsmith* (1927) and *The Languages of Criticism and the Structure of Poetry* (1953).

ROBERT H. ELIAS, Professor of English, formerly Ernest I. White Professor of American Studies, Cornell University, has written *Theodore Dreiser: Apostle of Nature* (1949) and has edited Dreiser's letters (3 vols., 1959).

Contributors

DAVID V. ERDMAN, Editor of Publications at The New York Public Library, and author of *Blake: Prophet against Empire* (1954), is now editing two volumes of Coleridge's *Essays on His Own Times.*

EPHIM G. FOGEL, Professor and Chairman, Department of English, Cornell University, has made a study of Sir Philip Sidney's *Arcadia* and *Astrophil and Stella* and is compiling a collection of Cornell essays on Shakespeare.

CYRUS HOY, Professor of English, University of Rochester, is preparing the commentary volume for the Cambridge University Press *Dramatic Works of Dekker* and has edited *Hamlet* and two Beaumont and Fletcher plays.

S. F. JOHNSON, Associate Professor of English, Columbia University, has written on Elizabethan drama and has edited the Pelican edition of Shakespeare's *Julius Caesar.*

LEONIDAS M. JONES, Associate Professor of English at the University of Vermont, has published articles on Keats and John Hamilton Reynolds.

HOOVER H. JORDAN, Chairman of the Department of English, Eastern Michigan University, contributed the chapters on Thomas Moore and Thomas Campbell to the M. L. A. volume *The English Romantic Poets and Essayists* (1957).

WILLIAM R. KEAST, President of Wayne State University, is the author of studies of Samuel Johnson and Edward Gibbon and is preparing an edition of Johnson's critical essays.

SIR GEOFFREY KEYNES, Chairman of The William Blake Trust, has recently published his *Bibliotheca Bibliographici* and a bibliography of Sir Thomas Browne.

GEORGE DE FOREST LORD, Associate Professor of English and Master of Trumbull College, Yale University, has written on Homer and George Chapman and is editing *Poems on Affairs of State* (Vol. I, 1963).

BALDWIN MAXWELL, Emeritus Professor of English, the State University of Iowa, editor of *Philological Quarterly*, 1938–1953, is the author of *Studies in Beaumont, Fletcher, and Massinger* (1939) and *Studies in the Shakespeare Apocrypha* (1956).

Contributors

ARTHUR PIERCE MIDDLETON, Rector of St. James' Episcopal Church, Great Barrington, Massachusetts was the first Research Associate of the Institute of Early American History and Culture and served in the Research Department of Colonial Williamsburg for fourteen years, six of them as Director.

ALBERT MORDELL, lawyer, has written on Henry James, John Greenleaf Whittier, and other authors; his latest book is *Discoveries: Essays on Lafcadio Hearn* (1964).

WILLIAM A. RINGLER, JR., Professor of English, University of Chicago, author of a study of Stephen Gosson (1942) and editor of the *Poems of Sir Philip Sidney* (1962), is preparing a study of early Tudor poetry.

S. SCHOENBAUM, Professor of English, Northwestern University, author of *Middleton's Tragedies* (1955) and reviser of Alfred Harbage's *Annals of English Drama* (1940; revised edition, 1964), has written on *Internal Evidence and Elizabethan Dramatic Authorship* (1966) and is collaborating on the Yale edition of Middleton's plays.

ARTHUR SHERBO, Professor of English at Michigan State University, author of *English Sentimental Drama* (1957) and *New Essays by Arthur Murphy* (1963), is editor of Samuel Johnson's essays on Shakespeare for the Yale edition of Johnson's works.

DAVID M. VIETH, Professor of English at Southern Illinois University, is the author of *Attribution in Restoration Poetry: A Study of Rochester's "Poems" of 1680* (1963).

Index of Names and Titles

Index of Names and Titles

Athenaeum, The, 511
Attempt for the Explication, 254
Atwood, J., 13
Aubrey, John, 27
Augusta Fitzherbert, review of, 506
Austen, Jane, 505
Austin, Warren B., 447–448, 449
Axiochus, 424–427

Bacon, Francis, 56, 147, 251, 253–255, 432
Baconians, 147, 180, 432–433
Bagehot, Walter, 505
Baine, Rodney M., 496
Bakeless, John, 163
Baker, Herschel, 508–509
Baker, Sheridan, 497
Bald, R. C., 71, 84, 134, 207, 215, 217, 397, 429, 430, 481; essay, 146–175
Baldwin, T. W., 438, 449
Baldwin, William, 86
Bale, John, 411
Bancroft, George, 315
Bang, W., 201
Banks, Theodore, 27
Barbour, John, 399
Bargrave, Mrs. Mary, 496
Barish, Jonas, 192, 202
Barker, E. H., 21
Barker, Richard Hindry, 190, 191
Barnam, Benedict, 424, 426
Barnard, John, 496
Barnavelt, The Tragedy of Sir John van Olden, 208, 209
Barr, Robert, 519
Bartlett's *Concordance to Shakespeare*, 521
Bashful Lover, The, 220, 221
Basset, Sir Arthur, 238, 245
Bateson, F. W., 51, 495
Baudelaire, Charles, 391
Baugh, Albert C., 408
Baxter, Nathaniel, 229
Bayes' theorem, 522
Bazire, Joyce, 406
Beaty, Frederick L., 507
Beaumont, Francis, 99–100, 180, 182, 183, 185, 186, 190, 192, 195, 204–223, 430, 463, 468, 476
Beaurline, L. A., 427
Beauty of Buttermere, The, 47–50
Bee, The, 277, 278, 280
Beggar's Opera, The, 371
Behn, Aphra, 258, 265, 270
Believe as You List, 185, 196, 220, 221, 227

Belle Dame Sans Mercy, La, (Sir Richard Ros), 400, 401
Beloe, William, 21
"Benedicite Paraphrased, The," 87–88, 119, 292–293
Benham, Allen R., 502
Bennett, Paul E., 51, 521
Bentley, Gerald Eades, 71, 134, 135, 190, 191, 193, 199, 201, 428; essay, 179–187
Bentley, Richard, 18
"Beppo," 369
Berdan, John M., 421
Bergen, Henry, 408
Bergin, Thomas, 455
Berkeley, Thomas, Lord, 413
Berman, Herbert, 517
Bernard, F. V., 115
Bertram, Paul, 493
Bertram, review of, 507
Bessinger, Jess B., Jr., 519
Bethurum, Dorothy, 420
Bew, John, 311
Bianca, 455
Bible, The, 12, 16, 41, 141, 142, 143, 412
Bierce, Ambrose, 512
Biographia Dramatica, 14
Biographia Literaria, 59–60, 61, 340, 507
Birth of Merlin, The, 433, 464
Bisland, Elizabeth, 388
Blackwell, Thomas, 20, 21
Blackwood's Magazine, 62, 505–506, 516
Blenheim Panegyric, 503
Bloody Banquet, The, 186, 190
Bloomfield, M. W., 409
Blount, Edward, 482, 484
Blurt, Master Constable, 200
Boas, Frederick, 455
Boerhaave, Hermann, 500
Boethius, 141, 403
Boileau-Despreaux, Nicolas, 366
Boleyn, Anne, 366
Bonaparte, *see* Napoleon
Bond, R. W., 85–86, 232
Bondman, The, 219, 220
Bonduca, 207, 215, 216, 217, 218, 219, 220, 430, 475, 477
Bonner, Francis W., 400
Book of the Duchess, The, 414
Book of the Knight of La Tour Landry, The, 456
Booke of Sir Thomas More, The, 71, 84, 98, 134, 146–177, 427, 433, 446, 405–406, 480–482

Index of Names and Titles

Index of Names and Titles

Index of Names and Titles

Index of Names and Titles

Price, George R., 431
Price, Hereward T., 85, 437, 443, 445, 450, 451, 453
Prick of Conscience, 141
Prideaux, Col. W. F., 357
Prince Charles's Company, 182
Prior, Moody E., 192, 199, 437, 438, 456
Propertius, 23
Prophetess, The, 208, 209
"Proposal for an English Academy in 1660, A," 253
"Proposals for Printing . . . Shakespeare," 21
Prothero, *see* Ernle
Prouty, Charles T., 446–449
Proverbs, 141
Pruvost, René, 449
Psalter, 141–142
Public Ledger, The, 279, 282, 499, 500
"Pulpit Oratory, No. IV," 508
Puritan, The, 197, 433
Puttenham, George, 86, 88, 453
Pyramus, 65

Queen, The, 201, 202
Queen's company, 182, 449
Quintilian, 70

Radcliffe, Alexander, 259, 265, 271
Radcliffe, Mrs. Ann, 507
Ralegh, Walter, 421
Ralph, James, 497
Rambler, The, 8, 14, 15, 115, 304
Raoul de Houdan, 411
Rape of the Lock, The, 286
Raphael, 280
Ravenscroft, Edward, 451
Raysor, Thomas Middleton, 488
Reed, Isaac, 459
Rees, J. C., 509–510
Religious Musings, 326, 354
Remaines of a Greater Work, 245
Renan, Ernest, 505
Renegado, The, 220–221
Repentance, 177
"Reported Changes, The," 57
Representative Men, 461
Revenge for Honor, 191
Revengers' Tragedy, The, 179, 190, 193, 198, 203, 431–432
Reynolds, John Hamilton, 310, 370–374, 508
Reynolds, Sir Joshua, 6, 314
Rhodes, R. Crompton, 442
Ribner, Irving, 474

Richard, Duke of York, review of, 370–374
Richard II, 84, 136, 160, 170, 434, 438
Richard III, 434, 438, 449
Richard the Redeless, 142
Richardson, Arleigh D., III, 446
Richardson, Charles F., 123
Ridley, M. R., 467
Rimbaud, Jean Arthur, 378, 518
Ringler, William A., Jr., 71, 98, 135, 243, 247, 423; essay, 229–242
Ritchie, William, 5
Robb, Dewar M., 198
Robert Earl of Huntington, 429
Robertson, J. M., 185, 432, 452, 470, 485
Robinson, F. N., 400, 402, 403, 405, 406
Robinson, Humphrey, 184, 185
Robinson, Mrs. Mary, 351
Robson, M. B., 66–67
Roche Guilhem, Mlle. de la, 229
Rochester, John Wilmot, Earl of, 256–272
Rock, Dr., 78, 117–118, 290
Rodd, Thomas or Horatio, 248
Roderick, Richard, 433, 457–459, 463
Rogers, Richard, 429, 478
Rogers, Samuel, 367
Rokayle, Peter de la, 138
Rokayle, Stacy de, 138, 411, 416–418
Rollins, Hyder E., 201, 232
Rollo, Duke of Normandy, 218
Rolt, Richard, 287
Roman Actor, The, 220, 221
Roman Comique, 498
Romaunt of the Rose, The, 401, 402, 405
Romeo and Juliet, 167, 434, 438, 449, 470
Roper, Derek, 507
Rosenbaum, S. P., 99
Rosoman, Thomas, 118, 287
Rowe, Nicholas, 12, 24
Rowley, Samuel, 464
Rowley, William, 183, 185, 190, 191, 196, 198, 202, 204, 468, 483
Rule a Wife and Have a Wife, 207, 208, 214, 217–220
Rupert, Prince, 31, 39, 41, 110
Russell, G. H., 410, 413
Ruteboeuf, 411

Sabin, Joseph, 311
Sadler, John, 502

Index of Subjects

[Proper nouns will be found in the "Index of Names and Titles," but a few names and titles are included here under a limited number of headings, particularly "External and internal-external evidence, specific authors or works." Citations under this heading are limited to authors who are the chief subjects of discussion in essays Nos. 1–31 or who are represented by two or more entries in the Annotated Bibliography.]

Abbreviations (Elizabethan Drama), 427
Absurdity, argument from, 58
Actors, 155, 158
Advice to a Painter, convention of, *see* "Painter" convention
Alliteration: obvious and inferior, 235; combined with metrical peculiarities, 473; humorous, 476
Allusions, classical: 39–41, 94, 107, 422, 440, 443; commonplace, 90–91, 114
Allusions, contemporary: 27–37, 77–83, 159–162, 287–290, 466; conditions for analysis of, 78; tone of, 79–81, 113, 121; misinterpretations of, 78–81; commonplace, 81–83
Allusions, literary and artistic, 95, 278, 280–281, 365–366, 370–372
Anachronism: of topical allusion, 241; linguistic, 401
Annotations in printed books, 429
Apologia, 516
Argument from silence: employed, 159, 285–286, 482; defended, 119; criticized, 75–76, 181–182, 417
Assumption, economy of, 76, 399, 484
Attitudes: literary, 14–17, 19–20, 275–281, 361–369; toward language and thought, 342–343
Attitudes, political: 27–37, 108–110, 412–413, 420; toward other nations, 321–322, 325–327; agreement of author's with fictional character's, 312–320; not probative if unsupported by stylistic evidence, 54–55; commonplace, 37, 54, 82–83, 114
Attitudes, religious and moral: 404, 409–410, 413–414, 431, 497, 502, 510; change in, 410–411; commonplace, 410, 414
Attribution: essential problem of defined, 77, 188, 190; difficulties of,

129, in dealing with drama, 188–189; degrees of certainty required, 293; criteria for, graded, 423; percentage of accuracy of a. as test, 235–236; textual criticism as a form of a., 252; hypothetical, 287–288; studies in a. tend to concentrate on older canons, 309, 397; need for caution in, 423; value of studies in a. questioned, 432; influence of science on, 463; readiness to affirm a. criticized, 511
Attribution, erroneous or false: 26–27, 61–62, 119, 229–242, 350, 352; for commercial reasons, 71, 180, 191, 229–230; entry of into standard editions, 230
Author: characteristic workings of mind of, 52–56; congruity of work with character of, 367–368; nationality of, 414
Authorities: credence to be given to, 9; judgments by, 54–56, 63–64, 68, 102–103, 283–284, 290, 392, 408, 422, 443, 478, 500; *see also* Judgment, oracular *and* Intuition

Bad faith, charge of to explain away external evidence, 74–75
"Bad" quartos, 436–437, 439–440, 445–450, 455, 482–485; reporters of, 442–444; publishers of not disreputable, 436; *see also* Bibliographical evidence
Bibliographical evidence: 149–155, 195–197, 224–228, 237, 256–272, 294–305, 425, 429–432, 435–436, 440–444, 448, 474–477, 485, 492–493, 497, 514; hypothetical, 409; use in dating, 411; validity of questioned, 437, 449; *see also* "Bad" quartos, Compositors, Contents,

Index of Subjects

Bibliographical evidence: (*cont.*)
order of, Copy, printer's, *and*
"Good" quartos

Biographical evidence: 402, 409, 412,
421, 425–427, 497, 502, 516; naïve
use of, 415; and esoteric reader, 419;
medical preoccupations, 495; agreement of author's biography with
fictional character's, 312–320; presumptive or hypothetical biography,
409, 412, 501; *see also* Plagiarism,
Shakespeare and

Bits of evidence, value of, 3, 5, 10,
121; *see also* Cumulative effect

Borrowing, *see* Plagiarism

Brief passages, difficulty of identifying,
50

Canon, relation of work to entire, 170,
378, 454, 518

Casting, indications of in theatrical
copy, 155; casting patterns, 438, 449

Caveats, general: 69–101; comments on
these caveats, 102–114, 115–120; rebuttal, 121–127, 128–129; seven principles of canonical procedure,
191–197; five rules to improve parallel hunting, 200

Caveats, specific: cautionary instances,
85–88; on deriving evidence from
certainly authentic works, 73–74,
103–104, 108–110, 119–120, 195–196,
200, 205–209; on the presence of external or internal-external evidence,
70–72; on the relation between weak
external and strong internal evidence,
74–76; on equivocal, misleading, or
false external evidence, 70–71,
181–185, 189, 191–192, 229–242; on
the nonsignificance of isolated parallels, 76–77, 97, 192–193, 202; on the
argument from silence, 75–76,
181–182, 417; on accuracy and correct interpretation of contemporary
allusions, 78–81, 121; on commonplace allusions, 81–83; on oracular
judgments, 83, 196, 284; on the
larger features of literary art, 84–85,
170; on the influence of genre and
on commonplaces of thought and
style, 85–87, 192–193; on reminiscence, plagiarism, imitation, parody,
or independent similarities, 87–88; on
variations of style, 88; on the importance, in stylistic analysis, of large
contexts and total patterns, 88–95,
170; on the prerequisites for valid

statistical analysis, 96–100, 122–127;
on "rare" or "uncommon" usages,
99; on scribal or compositorial alteration of linguistic preferences, 99–100,
196–197; on attempts to disintegrate
a dramatic canon, 179, 185–186, 204;
on attempts at dramatic attribution,
185–186; on special pleading, 89,
100–101, 186–187; on the use of stylistic criteria, 192–193; on the need
for textual analysis, 193–195,
196–197, 433, 439–450, 467–468,
474–477; on inference from hypothetical attributions, 73–74, 103,
108–109, 119–120, 200, 287–288; on
admitting one's inability to solve a
problem, 187, 202–203, 479; on statistical studies, 520, 522; *see also*
Literary history, conjectural

Censorship, effect of on texts, 216–217,
430

Character of author, 401–402

Characterization: modes of, 469, 473,
491, 497; consistency of, 445–446,
449, 455, 469, 475

Chronology, 419–421, 434, 437,
449–454, 458–459, 480–481, 483–
485, 518; of association with dramatic
companies or theatrical entrepreneur,
158–159; of versification, 160; of
political events affecting censorship,
160–162; effect of on style, 88, 404;
see also Dictionaries

Circumstantial evidence, *see* Internal-
external evidence.

Clusters, image, *see* Imagery, image
clusters

Coincidence, 3, 10–11, 53, 428

Collaboration, 455–478, 482–494,
506–507; incomplete, 469; modification of one's style by, 469, 473, 476;
see also Revision *and* essays Nos.
10, 14, 15

Companies, dramatic: 434, 452; conjectural history of, 446; Admiral's men,
158–159, 161, 449, 481; Pembroke's
men, 439, 442, 449, 451–452, 454;
Queen's men, 449; Strange's-
Derby's-Chamberlain's-King's men,
158–159, 161, 192, 430, 439, 449,
451–452, 481; Sussex's men, 451–452

Composition, methods of, 233–234

Compositors: intervention of,
295–302, 435, 474–477; and spellings
or speech-prefixes, 168, 448; and linguistic preferences, 213–215, 224,

Index of Subjects

Compositors: and linguistic preferences (*cont.*)
468, 474–477; differentiation of, 436, 474

Compounds, hyphenated, 225–226

Computers, 51, 96, 99, 202, 501, 519–520

Concordance tests, 309–310, 345–347, 348–354, 422; defined and discussed, 348–349; limitations of, 349

Concordances, 9–10, 19, 51, 61–62, 99, 169, 202–203, 486

Confusions, factual, 447

Construction, 38–39, 85, 90, 93–94, 107–108, 437, 445–446, 449, 451–454, 462–463, 465, 469, 471–472, 474–475, 479, 489, 491, 496; looseness of in "Advices" and "Last Instructions," 105–107; dramatic c., 432; structural parallels, 438; linking of plays, 450; unity of c. no argument against dual authorship, 472, 476

Contents, order of, 256–272

Contributors to journals, *see* Zone of conjecture

Convention, literary, alleged ignorance of, 117–118, 121; *see also* Dreamer-narrator *and* Signature

Copy, printer's, 430, 435–436; holograph, 448, 484, 486, 492–493; intermediate transcript, 492–493; promptbook, 155, 492; *see also* Holograph, extant or postulated

Cornell Concordances, 99, 203

Cover, of manuscript, 148, 158

Cumulative effect, 4, 26, 96–97, 115–116, 168, 201–202, 422, 426, 428, 476, 482, 492, 514, 521; *see also* Bits of evidence *and* Parallels

Data processing, literary, 519

Date, *see* Chronology

Decorum, literary, 91–92, 112

Design, *see* Construction

Dialect, authorial vs. scribal, 133–134, 144–145, 402–403, 405–406

Dialogue, 479

Diary: Henslowe's, 454; American Civil War d., possibly fictional, 512–513

Diction, *see* Vocabulary

Dictionaries, and dating of usage, 377, 382

Disintegrators, 433, 437–438, 440–441, 444–446, 464, 466, 469–471, 490, 520; of Elizabethan drama criticized, 98, 179, 185–186, 190, 437–438

Drama, *see* Elizabethan drama

Dramatic effects, 431

Dreamer-narrator, convention of, and poet, 137–138, 409–414, 418–419

Editorials and brief notices, 323

Elimination of known competitors, 171, 245–247

Elizabethan drama (includes Jacobean and Caroline): 146–175, 179–187, 188–203, 204–223, 224–228, 427–494; attribution in, 134; anonymous plays, 179; on eliminating attempts at attribution of, 179–180; mistakenly analogized with epic and lyric forms, 180–181; *see also* Actors, Casting, Companies, dramatic, Copy, printer's, Disintegrators, *and* Theatrical entrepreneurs

Emendation, textual, 300

Epilogue, *see* Framework, completion of

Errata lists, 495

Errors acknowledged, 61–63, 98, 128, 191, 324, 331, 408, 422–423; errors and real contributions, 147

Evidence, kinds to be considered, 72–73; *see also* Bibliographical evidence, Biographical evidence, Internal evidence, Internal-external evidence, Statistical evidence, Stylistic evidence, *and* Vocabulary

External evidence: Coleridge's definition of, 45; scope of, 284; direct and indirect, 45–46, 50, 53; relation of to internal ev., 71–72; importance or decisiveness of, questioned, 7, 283–284, affirmed, 70–72, 190–192, 231, 411, 415–416, 419, 513; confirmation of prior attribution by, 67–68, 72, 86, 248, 399; weak or contradictory, 74–76, 498–499, 504, 508; equivocal, misleading, or false, 26–27, 61–62, 70–71, 181–185, 189, 191–192, 229–242, 256–272 (esp. 258), 264–265, 370, 399–403, 405, 411, 417–418, 421–422, 429–430, 494–496; autograph notes, 67–68; use of initials, 344, 349–350; Latin title-page mottoes, 429; exclusion from collected works, 347; scribal practice, 407; *see also* Attribution, erroneous or false, Bad faith, Biographical evidence, Bibliographical evidence, Caveats, specific, Chronology, Companies, dramatic, Internal-external evidence, Paleographical evidence, Play lists, Surnames, Title-pages, *and* Zone of conjecture